Palm OS® Bible

Palm OS® Bible

Glenn Brown

IDG Books Worldwide, Inc.
An International Data Group Company

Foster City, CA ✦ Chicago, IL ✦ Indianapolis, IN ✦ New York, NY

Palm OS® Bible

Published by
IDG Books Worldwide, Inc.
An International Data Group Company
919 E. Hillsdale Blvd., Suite 400
Foster City, CA 94404
www.idgbooks.com (IDG Books Worldwide Web site)

Library of Congress Card Number: 00-101539

ISBN: 0-7645-3408-4

Printed in the United States of America

10 9 8 7 6 5 4 3 2

1B/TQ/QV/QQ/FC

Distributed in the United States by IDG Books Worldwide, Inc.

Distributed by CDG Books Canada Inc. for Canada; by Transworld Publishers Limited in the United Kingdom; by IDG Norge Books for Norway; by IDG Sweden Books for Sweden; by IDG Books Australia Publishing Corporation Pty. Ltd. for Australia and New Zealand; by TransQuest Publishers Pte Ltd. for Singapore, Malaysia, Thailand, Indonesia, and Hong Kong; by Gotop Information Inc. for Taiwan; by ICG Muse, Inc. for Japan; by Intersoft for South Africa; by Eyrolles for France; by International Thomson Publishing for Germany, Austria, and Switzerland; by Distribuidora Cuspide for Argentina; by LR International for Brazil; by Galileo Libros for Chile; by Ediciones ZETA S.C.R. Ltda. for Peru; by WS Computer Publishing Corporation, Inc., for the Philippines; by Contemporanea de Ediciones for Venezuela; by Express Computer Distributors for the Caribbean and West Indies; by Micronesia Media Distributor, Inc. for Micronesia; by Chips Computadoras S.A. de C.V. for Mexico; by Editorial Norma de Panama S.A. for Panama; by American Bookshops for Finland.

For general information on IDG Books Worldwide's books in the U.S., please call our Consumer Customer Service department at 800-762-2974. For reseller information, including discounts and premium sales, please call our Reseller Customer Service department at 800-434-3422.

For information on where to purchase IDG Books Worldwide's books outside the U.S., please contact our International Sales department at 317-596-5530 or fax 317-572-4002.

For consumer information on foreign language translations, please contact our Customer Service department at 800-434-3422, fax 317-572-4002, or e-mail rights@idgbooks.com.

For information on licensing foreign or domestic rights, please phone +1-650-653-7098.

For sales inquiries and special prices for bulk quantities, please contact our Order Services department at 800-434-3422 or write to the address above.

For information on using IDG Books Worldwide's books in the classroom or for ordering examination copies, please contact our Educational Sales department at 800-434-2086 or fax 317-572-4005.

For press review copies, author interviews, or other publicity information, please contact our Public Relations department at 650-653-7000 or fax 650-653-7500.

For authorization to photocopy items for corporate, personal, or educational use, please contact Copyright Clearance Center, 222 Rosewood Drive, Danvers, MA 01923, or fax 978-750-4470.

ABOUT IDG BOOKS WORLDWIDE

Welcome to the world of IDG Books Worldwide.

IDG Books Worldwide, Inc., is a subsidiary of International Data Group, the world's largest publisher of computer-related information and the leading global provider of information services on information technology. IDG was founded more than 30 years ago by Patrick J. McGovern and now employs more than 9,000 people worldwide. IDG publishes more than 290 computer publications in over 75 countries. More than 90 million people read one or more IDG publications each month.

Launched in 1990, IDG Books Worldwide is today the #1 publisher of best-selling computer books in the United States. We are proud to have received eight awards from the Computer Press Association in recognition of editorial excellence and three from Computer Currents' First Annual Readers' Choice Awards. Our best-selling *...For Dummies®* series has more than 50 million copies in print with translations in 31 languages. IDG Books Worldwide, through a joint venture with IDG's Hi-Tech Beijing, became the first U.S. publisher to publish a computer book in the People's Republic of China. In record time, IDG Books Worldwide has become the first choice for millions of readers around the world who want to learn how to better manage their businesses.

Our mission is simple: Every one of our books is designed to bring extra value and skill-building instructions to the reader. Our books are written by experts who understand and care about our readers. The knowledge base of our editorial staff comes from years of experience in publishing, education, and journalism — experience we use to produce books to carry us into the new millennium. In short, we care about books, so we attract the best people. We devote special attention to details such as audience, interior design, use of icons, and illustrations. And because we use an efficient process of authoring, editing, and desktop publishing our books electronically, we can spend more time ensuring superior content and less time on the technicalities of making books.

You can count on our commitment to deliver high-quality books at competitive prices on topics you want to read about. At IDG Books Worldwide, we continue in the IDG tradition of delivering quality for more than 30 years. You'll find no better book on a subject than one from IDG Books Worldwide.

John Kilcullen
Chairman and CEO
IDG Books Worldwide, Inc.

Eighth Annual
Computer Press
Awards ≥1992

Ninth Annual
Computer Press
Awards ≥1993

Tenth Annual
Computer Press
Awards ≥1994

Eleventh Annual
Computer Press
Awards ≥1995

IDG is the world's leading IT media, research and exposition company. Founded in 1964, IDG had 1997 revenues of $2.05 billion and has more than 9,000 employees worldwide. IDG offers the widest range of media options that reach IT buyers in 75 countries representing 95% of worldwide IT spending. IDG's diverse product and services portfolio spans six key areas including print publishing, online publishing, expositions and conferences, market research, education and training, and global marketing services. More than 90 million people read one or more of IDG's 290 magazines and newspapers, including IDG's leading global brands — Computerworld, PC World, Network World, Macworld and the Channel World family of publications. IDG Books Worldwide is one of the fastest-growing computer book publishers in the world, with more than 700 titles in 36 languages. The "...For Dummies®" series alone has more than 50 million copies in print. IDG offers online users the largest network of technology-specific Web sites around the world through IDG.net (http://www.idg.net), which comprises more than 225 targeted Web sites in 55 countries worldwide. International Data Corporation (IDC) is the world's largest provider of information technology data, analysis and consulting, with research centers in over 41 countries and more than 400 research analysts worldwide. IDG World Expo is a leading producer of more than 168 globally branded conferences and expositions in 35 countries including E3 (Electronic Entertainment Expo), Macworld Expo, ComNet, Windows World Expo, ICE (Internet Commerce Expo), Agenda, DEMO, and Spotlight. IDG's training subsidiary, ExecuTrain, is the world's largest computer training company, with more than 230 locations worldwide and 785 training courses. IDG Marketing Services helps industry-leading IT companies build international brand recognition by developing global integrated marketing programs via IDG's print, online and exposition products worldwide. Further information about the company can be found at www.idg.com.

1/26/00

Credits

Acquisitions Editor
Michael Roney

Project Editors
Sara Salzmann
Michael Christopher
Chris Johnson
Julie M. Smith

Technical Editor
Michael Lunsford

Copy Editors
Michael D. Welch
Richard H. Adin

Media Development Specialist
Joe Kiempisty

Permissions Editor
Jessica Montgomery

Media Development Manager
Stephen Noetzel

Project Coordinators
Linda Marousek
Danette Nurse
Marcos Vergara

Production Supervisor
Chris Pimentel

Graphics and Production Specialists
Robert Bihlmayer
Jude Levinson
Michael Lewis
Dina F Quan
Ramses Ramirez
Victor Pérez-Varela

Book Designer
Drew R. Moore

Illustrators
Mary Jo Richards
Clint Lahnen
Brent Savage
Karl Brandt
Glenn Brown

Proofreading and Indexing
Patsy Owens
York Production Services

Cover Illustration
Andreas F. Schueller

About the Author

Glenn Brown is the author of a number of books, including *Macintosh Crash Course* (APP, 1995) and the *PalmPilot Resource Kit* (IDG Books Worldwide, 1998). He spends his days working for Canada Customs, and evenings playing with computers, guitars, and magic.

For Mom and Dad

Foreword

In the two years that have passed since I wrote the introduction to Glenn's previous book (the *PalmPilot Resource Kit*), handheld computing has come a long way, and yet here we are at another beginning.

Handhelds are entering an age where they are no longer seen as "Personal Digital Assistants" or simple business productivity tools. With the breadth of uses they now bring to all types of people in all kinds of environments, they are poised to become a more integral and meaningful part of the daily lives of people all over the world.

As computing becomes more Internet-centric and communications-focused, handhelds will play an even larger role. People will one day be accessing all types of content wirelessly from the Internet from a small handheld device that fits in their pocket, and we are only now seeing the first steps to making this type of information exchange simple and valuable for the mass market.

As is evident from the CD-ROM that accompanies this book, the Palm developer community that provides the fuel for making these steps is flourishing. Applications are rich and plentiful, from games and utilities to vertical applications that have led people to rethink their perception of a handheld. And now with the Springboard expansion platform we're starting to see more and more interesting and useful handheld hardware add-ons.

One thing that has not changed in the past two years is the overwhelming support and acceptance the Palm platform and now the Springboard expansion platform have received from both developers and users. For that I am truly grateful.

Jeff Hawkins
Cofounder and Chairman
Handspring

Preface

I bought Apple's Newton at a Macworld conference the second day the product was available. It was, unfortunately, not ready for prime time — size, recognition issues, and bad press killed it. Palm's handheld device has had none of these issues: with the perfect "form factor" (all Palm Organizers fit in a shirt pocket), Graffiti, and nothing but good press, it was destined to succeed where the Newton failed. I've used almost all of Palm's products, and I can no longer live without my Palm Organizer.

Whether you've just bought your first Palm handheld or your tenth, the *Palm OS Bible* offers you a comprehensive guide to practically all aspects of using a Palm device. I include lots of inside tips and real-world examples and cover topics as diverse as Graffiti and Date Book basics, software enhancements for e-mail, financial management, OS performance, and more. With a CD-ROM produced by PalmGear that contains more than 2,000 Palm applications, the *Palm OS Bible* is your one-stop shop for practically everything you need to know to get the most out of your Palm Organizer.

Is This Book for You?

This book is intended for Palm users of all levels:

+ **Just bought your first Palm Organizer?** The *Palm OS Bible* leads you through all of the basics of handheld computing: HotSyncing, the built-in applications, and the applications installed on your computer.

+ **Just upgraded to a new Palm Organizer?** The *Palm OS Bible* leads you through the upgrade process, highlighting the new or added features in your new handheld.

+ **Are you a Palm poweruser?** The *Palm OS Bible* covers Palm Organizers from the original Pilot to the latest Palm IIIc, with extensive coverage of third-party software, and technical details not found elsewhere.

How This Book Is Organized

This book follows a simple formula: Each chapter covers an aspect of using the Palm Organizer, starting with a detailed explanation of how to use the tools that Palm has provided, and then moving on to third-party applications — both how to use them and why you would want to. Wherever practical, I have included detailed illustrations, so you can see exactly what the various products look like and what they offer. When I cover third-party products, I provide the name of the product and developer, along with the price and the "footprint" (the amount of memory the software takes when installed on your Palm Organizer). You'll find a complete list of developer contact information in Appendix F.

More specifically, I've organized the book into four main parts, as follows:

✦ **Part I, "Getting to Know Your Palm Handheld,"** starts with a brief history of the Palm platform, and then moves into detailed coverage of the built-in applications, the HotSync process, and two recent additions to the platform: the wireless Palm VII and the Handspring Visor.

✦ **Part II, "Using the Desktop Software,"** looks at Palm's desktop applications for both Windows and Macintosh users, and includes detailed coverage of third-party software.

✦ **Part III, "Enhancing Your Palm Lifestyle,"** takes a good look at some of the great third-party software available for the Palm platform, including financial packages, document readers, travel and telecommunications utilities, multimedia applications, and even games. Where possible, these chapters also include coverage of the applications and functionality that came with your Palm Organizer.

✦ **Part IV, "Making Your Palm Even Better,"** is intended for more advanced users, with coverage of applications that can replace or supplement your handheld's built-in applications, utility software, and using HackMaster and HackMaster Hacks to extend the Palm OS, and concludes with a chapter on troubleshooting the problems that may occur on your Palm Organizer.

Finally, the **Appendixes** cover a wide range of topics, from the hidden features (Easter eggs) buried within the Palm OS, the programmers' dot commands for those who have to know them, guest-written articles on error messages and batteries, how to create forms using Pendragon Forms (excerpted from *The Official Pendragon Forms for Palm OS Starter Kit* by Debra Sancho and Ivan Phillips, published by IDG Books Worldwide), a contact listing for the developers covered in this book, and a brief listing of the products that those of us who wrote this book have installed on our Palm Organizers. The *Palm OS Bible* also features a glossary explaining the technical terms used throughout the book.

How to Navigate Through This Book

Each of this book's chapters begins with an overview of its information, and ends with a quick summary. In addition, various icons appear throughout the *Palm OS Bible* and assist you by identifying especially helpful or important items. Here's a list of the icons and their functions:

 Caution These notes are ones you should definitely read; they point out pitfalls that you should avoid in order to keep you Palm Organizer running smoothly.

 Cross-Reference Cross-references direct you to other parts of the book that may relate to what you're reading at the time.

 New Feature As of this writing, the Palm OS is up to version 3.5; these notes point out some of the features added by the newer versions.

 Note Notes provide background information that may not be essential, but should still be worthwhile.

 Tip Tips provide tips and tricks that will help turn you into a poweruser of your Palm Organizer.

About the CD-ROM

One of this book's most outstanding features is its accompanying CD-ROM. Produced by the leading Palm Web site, PalmGear (www.palmgear.com), the disc is jam-packed with shareware, freeware, and demo versions of commercial software to try on your Palm Organizer. See Appendix H for more information about the CD-ROM.

Further Information

You'll be able to find more information about me and this book on my Web site (www.magimac.com). If you have any questions or comments on the *Palm OS Bible*, you can reach me at glenn.brown@home.com. I'll do my best to reply to your messages.

Production Notes

This book would not have been possible without some amazing hardware from Palm and other companies, along with computer hardware and software that enabled me to put it all together. Here I summarize my equipment and applications to give you an idea of how this book came to be.

Hardware

I have two home systems, both PC and Macintosh. The PC is a Hewlett-Packard Pavillion 8370, a 350mHz Pentium II with 128MB of RAM running Windows 98 on a 17-inch LG monitor. It has a few toys that make it a better games machine: an internal DVD, a 16MB 3Dfx 2000 video card, and a SoundBlaster Live card with FPS2000 speakers.

I use a Macintosh G3/266 with 256MB of RAM running Mac OS 9.0 as my main machine. It has 11GBs of hard drive space, an internal Zip drive, a 16MB ATI XClaim VR/128, a 19-inch Samsung monitor, and a Keyspan USB/PCI card, to which I have attached a Microsoft IntelliMouse and Handspring's Visor cradle. Attached to the Mac are an APS 230 MicroOptical drive, an APS 6x4x16 CD-RW drive, an ATI Xclaim TV box (so I can watch Letterman while working), a Visioneer Paperport vx scanner, and a Wacom drawing tablet. I use a five-port Kingston Ethernet hub to attach a Laserwriter IIg printer and to enable both computers to share a 2.2 mbps ADSL connection to the Internet. Both computers share the use of an Epson 740 color printer. At the office, I use a 300mHz Digital Pentium II running Windows NT 4.0.

I have a number of Palm Organizers: a Palm Vx, which I used as my main Organizer throughout the writing of the book; a Handspring Visor Deluxe with 16MB (8MB internal, and 8MB on a Springboard Flash module); and a TRGpro with 30MB (8MB internal, 2MB Flash, with a 20MB Compact Flash card). I've just started playing with Palm's new IIIc.

All three of my computers have various cradles attached to enable me to HotSync various configurations. After reading all this, I suspect I have too many toys.

Software

I use Internet Explorer to browse the Internet and Outlook Express as my e-mail client. I have built a custom FileMaker Pro 4.0 database, which I use to track software version and release information. I used Microsoft Word 98's mail merge feature to prepare correspondence from the database, which was then sent using Outlook Express. I used a combination of tools to create the Palm OS screen shots in this book—where possible, I used POSE, a program that Palm makes available to developers for emulating the Palm OS on the Macintosh. I used Andreas Linke's excellent shareware, ScreenShot Hack, to capture those screens that could not be done in POSE.

I used SnagIt to capture Windows screen shots, and Ambrosia Software's Snapz Pro 2.0 to capture Macintosh screens. All images were converted to TIF format and edited using Adobe Photoshop 5.5. All of the custom graphics and callouts were done using Macromedia Freehand 8.0. I did the writing and editing using Microsoft Word 98. I did printouts for IDG Books Worldwide's production department using QuarkXPress 4.0. Final production and layout was done by IDG Books using Macintosh versions of QuarkXPress and Macromedia Freehand.

Two outstanding utilities kept my Mac running throughout production: Casady & Greene's Conflict Catcher 8 and Alsoft's Disk Warrior.

Acknowledgments

I have an amazing number of people to thank for their help with this book; all have been generous to a fault with their time and ideas.

First, I'd like to thank the folks at IDG Books Worldwide, especially Mike Roney, Sara Salzmann, Michael Christopher, and Chris Johnson for their guidance and assistance through what was for me a major project. Their editing and other skills have resulted in the book you hold in your hands. There are many others to thank at IDG Books, most of whom are listed in the Credits, but I would like to add a special thanks to Lenora Chin Sell, Michael Welch, Stephen Noetzel, Julie Smith, and Linda Marousek for effort above and beyond on this book's behalf.

This book would not have been possible without the creative genius of Jeff Hawkins and those who started Palm. I received help and assistance from many at Palm, including John Cook, Michael Mace, Alan Urban, Paul Osborne, Chris Weasler, and Douglas Wirnouski. Thanks to May Tsoi of the Palm VII Group for writing the chapter about the Palm VII. I'd particularly like to single out Michael Lunsford, who is the manager for the Palm V organizers. Michael acted as technical editor for this book and went far beyond the call of duty, truly adding his stamp to the book.

Thanks to Jeff Hawkins at Handspring Computing, both for writing the foreword to this book and for creating the handheld we all can't live without. I'd also like to thank Rob Haitani and Allen Bush at Handspring.

Thanks to Alan Pinstein and Peter Strobel for providing technical appendixes that help us all understand two critical aspects of the Palm Organizer: error messages and batteries.

Thanks to those who helped me with the telecommunications issues in Chapter 16: Sean Costello, Karl Joseph, Angela Power, John Powers, Alan Urban, and Lorraine Wheeler.

Special thanks to Kenny West, J. D. Crouch, and all the staff of PalmGear for producing the great CD-ROM that is included with this book. Special thanks have to go to Rodney Capron, who is responsible for producing the CD, including the cool FileMaker interface.

Beyond all that, this book — and, indeed, the success of the Palm Organizer itself — would not have been possible without the support of an incredible developer community. I'd like to single out a few who were especially helpful: Phil Purpura at Chapura Software, Ivan Phillips of Pendragon Software, Mike Walter at TRG, Alan Pinstein of Synergy Software, and Paul Schiller of PDA Panache. I'd also like to thank Don Adams, Gary Amstutz, Michael Arena, Dave Arnold, Jeff Arrigotti,

Andrew Ball, Bozidar Benc, John Bothwell, Lori Burzinzki, Frank Colin, Gail Delano, Art Deleon, Steuart Dewar, James Einolf, Jean-Paul Ferguson, Frank Feyes, Dave Flanagan, Elia Freedman, Bob Fullerton, George Gerwe, Rick Goetter, Brian Hall, Jerry Halls, Rick Huebner, Jean Ichbiah, Blake Johnson, Tom Kambouris, Cassidy Lackey, Ken Landau, Vince Lee, Steve Mann, Ed Martin, Dave Melamed, Gary Mayhek, Julie Moe, Kathleen McAneany, Jake Murakami, Jeff Musa, Steve Patt, Shannon Pekary, Angela Power, Jake Rivas, Randy Rorden, Jonathan Rowe, Craig Schmidt, Michael Shawver, Mike Sullivan, Lisa VanZant, Russell Webb, Tom Weishaar, Lorraine Wheeler, Lyn Wong, George Woods, and Andrew Zosk.

I've saved the best for last: thanks have to go to Roelof Mulder, a good friend who helped research many of the tips in this book, and also wrote Chapter 12, and to the love of my life, Bonnie Blair.

Contents at a Glance

Foreword ix
Preface. xi
Acknowledgments xv

Part I: Getting to Know Your Palm Handheld 1
Chapter 1: Introducing the Palm Handheld 3
Chapter 2: First Flight 23
Chapter 3: Using Graffiti 43
Chapter 4: Using the Built-In Applications 67
Chapter 5: Examining the Palm Utility Suite 101
Chapter 6: HotSyncing Your Palm 121
Chapter 7: What Is the Palm VII Handheld? 155
Chapter 8: Introducing the Handspring Visor 173

Part II: Using the Desktop Software 191
Chapter 9: Using the Palm Desktop for Windows 193
Chapter 10: Using the Palm Desktop for Macintosh 219

Part III: Enhancing Your Palm Lifestyle 255
Chapter 11: Installing and Using PalmWare 257
Chapter 12: Tracking Projects 281
Chapter 13: Managing Finances with PalmCalc 299
Chapter 14: Reading with PalmBook 353
Chapter 15: Traveling with Your Palm Handheld 379
Chapter 16: Communicating via Your Palm OS Handheld 405
Chapter 17: Drawing and Listening with Your Palm 441
Chapter 18: Adding Toys to Your Palm 461
Chapter 19: Downloading and Accessing Applications 493

Part IV: Making Your Palm Even Better 513
Chapter 20: Maintaining and Enhancing Your Palm 515
Chapter 21: Customizing Your Palm with Utilities 547
Chapter 22: Extending Functionality with HackMaster 583
Chapter 23: Accessorizing Your Palm 599
Chapter 24: Troubleshooting Your Palm 639

Appendix A: Easter Eggs 667
Appendix B: Dot Commands 671
Appendix C: Palm Errors 673
Appendix D: Palm Batteries 679
Appendix E: Using Pendragon Forms 687
Appendix F: Contacts 713
Appendix G: On Our Palms 729
Appendix H: What's on the CD-ROM 735
Glossary 739
Index 751
End-User License Agreement 775
CD-ROM Installation Instructions 782

Contents

Foreword ix

Preface. xi

Acknowledgments xv

Part I: Getting to Know Your Palm Handheld   1

Chapter 1: Introducing the Palm Handheld 3

Palm History 3
    Jeff Hawkins 4
    Four original goals 5
    Palm, Inc. 5
    Pilot 7
    PalmPilot 7
    Palm III 7
    Palm IIIx/IIIe 7
    Palm IIIc/IIIxe 8
    Palm V/Vx 9
    Palm VII 10
Licensees 10
    IBM 11
    Franklin-Covey 12
    Symbol 12
    Qualcomm 13
    Handspring 15
    Technology Resource Group 16
Palm Products Overview 16
A View of the Future 19
    My predictions 19

Chapter 2: First Flight 23

First Steps 23
Post-Palm III Handhelds 24
    Palm III 28
First Synchronization 29
A Quick Walk Around 32
    Front 32
    Back 35

Anatomy of the Palm OS Interface 38
  Pick lists 38
  Dotted boxes 38
  Buttons 39
  Black triangles 39
  Boxed text 39
  Checkboxes 40
  The text cursor 40
  Scrolling windows 40

Chapter 3: Using Graffiti **43**
  The Basic Alphabet 46
    Numbers 48
    Essential punctuation 48
  Advanced Strokes 49
    Movement 49
    Shift strokes 50
    ShortCuts 51
    Punctuation Shift 53
    Extended Shift 53
  Graffiti Enhancements 56
    Help 56
    Feedback 57
    Characters 59
  Graffiti Alternatives 63
    Fitaly 63
    Jot 64
    TapPad 64
    T9 64

Chapter 4: Using the Built-In Applications **67**
  Interactive Scheduling with the Date Book 67
    Accessing the Date Book 68
    Entering data into the Date Book 69
    Day View 73
    Month View 76
    Agenda View 76
    Date Book menus 77
  Maintaining Contacts with the Address Book 83
    Opening the Address Book 83
    Adding a contact 84
    Finding a contact 85
    Editing contacts 86
    Assigning contact categories 87
    First import 88
    Menus 90

Staying Organized with the To Do List 91
    Opening the To Do List 92
    Adding To Do items 92
    Editing To Do items 93
    Assigning categories To Do items 94
    Menus 94
Using the Memo Pad 95
    Opening the Memo Pad 96
    Entering a memo 96
    Editing memos 97
    Assigning Memo categories 97
    Menus 97
Learning High-Efficiency Command Strokes 98

Chapter 5: Examining the Palm Utility Suite **101**
Managing Your Palm Handhelds with Utilities 101
    Graffiti Tips 101
    Launcher 102
    Calculator 106
    Find 107
    HotSync 107
    Preferences 107
    Security 113
Tracking Your Money with Expense 114
    Accessing expenses 114
    Moving expenses to your PC 115
Mail 116
    Setting up Mail 117
    Mail setup confirmation using Mail 117
    Mail menus 118

Chapter 6: HotSyncing Your Palm **121**
Accessing HotSync Manager 122
Configuring Conduits 125
    Macintosh Conduit Settings 127
    Configuring PocketMirror 128
File Linking 131
Connections 132
    Modem HotSync 133
    Network HotSync 136
    IR HotSync 137
Inside HotSync 138
    HotSync Log 139

Think Sync 141
    Third-Party Sync Products 141
    More sync products 144
    Macintosh conduits 146
    Sync utilities 148
Multiple Devices 151
    One device, two computers 152
    Multiple handhelds 152
    Usernames 152

Chapter 7: What Is the Palm VII Handheld? 155

What is the Palm VII handheld? 155
    Antenna 156
    Batteries and internal transmitter 157
    Other hardware features 157
    Software 158
    Palm.Net wireless communication service 159
Setting Up Your Palm VII 160
Using Web Clipping Applications 161
    Launching Web clipping applications 161
    Working with Web clipping applications 161
Exploring the Basic iMessenger Features 166
    Creating messages 167
    Outbox and draft messages 167
    Editing unsent messages 168
    Check and send messages 168
    Reading messages 168
    Filing and deleting messages 169
Using the Advanced iMessenger Options 169
    Preferences 169
    Your iMessenger mailbox features on www.palm.net 170
Using the Palm.Net Resources 171
    Coverage maps 171
    My Account 171
    Support information 171
    Download more Web clipping applications 172
    Other Web resources 172

Chapter 8: Introducing the Handspring Visor 173

Background 173
The Visor 174
    Models 174
    First impressions 175
Springboard 178

Software 179
    Date Book+ 179
    Advanced calculator 180
    CityTime 182
    Springboard cards 184
    Other enhancements 187

Part II: Using the Desktop Software   191

Chapter 9: Using the Palm Desktop for Windows 193

    Accessing the Palm Desktop 194
    Mirror Applications 194
        Date Book 194
        Address book 199
        To Do list 201
        Memo Pad 204
    Menus 206
        File 207
        Edit 208
        View 208
        Tools 209
        HotSync 209
        Help 213
    User-Named Folders 213
    Microsoft Outlook 215

Chapter 10: Using the Palm Desktop for Macintosh 219

    Palm Desktop for Macintosh 219
        New in Palm Desktop 2.5 219
        How is Palm Desktop different from the Windows version? 220
        How is Palm Desktop different from the handheld version? 221
        Interface 222
        Calendar 227
        Contacts 228
        Tasks 231
        Notes 233
        Menus 235
        Help 244
        Instant Palm Desktop 244
        Macintosh conduits 246
    Chronos Consultant 249
        What is it? 249
        What features does it add? 251
        How is it different? 252
        How do I convert my data to Consultant? 253

Part III: Enhancing Your Palm Lifestyle   255

Chapter 11: Installing and Using PalmWare 257

What is Shareware? 257
   Loading programs on your Palm Handheld 258
   Running new applications 262
   Deleting files 265
A Few Essential Shareware Applications 267
   Action Names 267
   DateBk3 268
   Cesium 268
   Clock III 269
   HackMaster 269
   ListMaker 274
   OmniRemote 275
   PocketQuicken 275
   TealDoc 276
   Vehicle Log 276
   UnDupe 277
   FlashPro 277
   BackupBuddy 278

Chapter 12: Tracking Projects 281

Creating High-Powered Lists 281
   CheckList 282
   JShopper 283
   ListMaker 284
   ShopList 285
   ToDo PLUS 286
Recording Activities with Logs 286
   Athlete's Diary 287
   DietLog 287
Using Outliners to Stay Organized 288
   Arranger 289
   BrainForest 290
   Hi-Note 292
   ListMaker 294
   ThoughtMill 294
Microsoft Project on Your Palm Handheld 296
   Project@Hand 296
   PalmProject 297

Chapter 13: Managing Finances with PalmCalc **299**

    Calculators 299
        Built-in 300
        Shareware 301
    Spreadsheets 309
        TinySheet 311
        MiniCalc 311
        Quicksheet 313
    Expense Managers 314
        Built-in (PALM OS) Expense 317
        AllMoney 321
        Money Minder 322
        PocketMoney 322
        Informed Palm Expense Creator 322
        QuikBudget 324
        QMate 325
        PocketQuicken 332
        UltraSoft Money Pocket Edition 333
        MAM Pro (Report Pro) 333
        ExpensePlus 336
        ExpenzPro 338
        TimeReporter 2000 343
    My Choices 349

Chapter 14: Reading with PalmBook **353**

    Reading Documents 353
        Opening documents 354
        Navigating documents 354
        Bookmarks 354
        Find 354
        Display 355
        AutoScroll 355
    Document Tools 355
        AportisDoc Reader 355
        AportisDoc Mobile Edition 356
        SmartDoc 358
        TealDoc 360
        CSpotRun 361
        RichReader 362
        OnTap 363
        iSilo 364
        Documents To Go 366
        Feature Comparisons 368

Making Your Own Documents 369
    Preparing a document for conversion 369
    Conversion utilities 372
Finding and Loading Docs 376
    On the Internet 376

Chapter 15: Traveling with Your Palm Handheld 379

Using What You Have 379
    TravelWare 380
Conversions 380
    Advanced Traveler 381
    CurrCalc 381
    Currency 382
    CurrencyX 383
    Foreign 384
Time Travel 384
    Big Clock 385
    CClock 385
    Cesium 386
    Clock III 386
    ClockPro 387
    FPS Clock 387
    multiClock 388
    TimeZone 389
Finding your way 390
    HandMap 390
    StreetSigns 390
Travelogue 391
    AirMiles 391
    Vehicle logs 392
    Travel data 396
    Travel tools 400

Chapter 16: Communicating via Your Palm OS Handheld 405

Built-in E-mail 406
    Setup 406
    Using e-mail 407
    Settings 409
Telecommunications 410
    E-mail 411
    Browsing 415
    Faxing 418
    Paging 419
    Other tools 421
    Setup 422
    Connection settings 424
    Mail setup 427

How to Connect 432
  Devices 432
  Wireless connections 435

Chapter 17: Drawing and Listening with Your Palm 441

Graphics 441
  Art in your Palm 441
  Graphics viewers 445
  Converting images 448
  Graphics utilities 449
Music 452
  Palm instruments 452
  Musical tools 455

Chapter 18: Adding Toys to Your Palm 461

Palm's Games 461
  Hardball 462
  Mine Hunt 462
  Puzzle 463
  SubHunt 463
Adventure Games 464
  Dark Haven 464
  Dragon Bane 464
  Dungeoneers 464
  Kyle's Quest 465
Arcade Games 466
  Anakin 466
  Bubblet 466
  Cue*pert 467
  Dakota 468
  Froggy 468
  Galax 469
  Impactor 469
  PAC 470
  Mulg II 470
  Reptoids 471
  Tetrin 471
Board Games 472
  BattleShip 472
  Blackout 472
  Chinese Checkers 472
  Desdemona 473
  JStones 474
  Mind Master 474
  Overload 474
  PalmJongg 475
  Pegged! 475

Perplex 476
PilotSenso 476
Sokoban 476
yahtChallenge 477
Card Games 478
4Corners Solitaire 478
BlackJack Simulator 478
BlackJack Solitaire 479
Crazy 8's 479
Cribbage 479
Golf Solitaire 480
Hearts 480
Klondike 481
Pyramid Solitaire 481
Rally 1000 481
Rummy 482
Texas Hold'Em 482
Diversions 483
Biorhythms 483
Buzzword Generator 483
PilotCE 484
TrekSounds 484
Tricorder II 485
Word Games 486
Jookerie! 486
Scramblet 486
Wordlet 487
XWord 487
Game Utilities 488
DicePro 488
Gamer's Die Roller 488
GolfTrac 489
IntelliGolf 489
Pilot-Frotz 490
What's the Score? 490

Chapter 19: Downloading and Accessing Applications 493

Downloading Software 493
Filename extensions 494
File organization 495
Shareware 495
Accessing Company Sites 496
3Com/Palm 496
IBM WorkPad 496
Concept Kitchen 496
DovCom 496
Landware 497
TealPoint 498

Accessing Author Sites 498
   Daggerware 498
   PalmGlyph Software 499
   Peter's Pilot Pages 499
   pilotBASIC 499
   Ron's Palm Information Page 499
   Tap This! 499
   Uberchix 499
Accessing Software Collections 501
   Eurocool 501
   The PilotZone 501
Accessing Online Stores 502
   Computer Concepts 502
   Handago 503
   PalmGear HQ 503
   PDA Mart 504
Palm Hardware Sites 504
   20-20Consumer 504
   Bike Brain 504
   efigV8 504
   MidWest PCB Designs 505
   Option International 505
   PageMart 505
   PalmColors 505
   Palm Keyboards 505
   PDA Panache 505
   Revolv Design 506
   Rhinoskin 506
   Steve's Pilot Tech Page 506
   TaleLight 506
   Technology Resources Group 506
Finding News and Information 506
   Calvin's PalmPilot FAQ 507
   Canada's Premiere Palm User Group 507
   The Gadgeteer 507
   Interactive fiction 507
   John's Palm Organizer page 507
   MemoWare.com 507
   The PalmGuru 508
   PalmOS.com 508
   PalmPilot World 508
   PalmPower Magazine 509
   PalmStation 509
   The Palm Tree 509
   Pen Computing Magazine 509
   Pilot Tips 'n Tricks 509
   Pilot Internet File Converter 509
   The Starfleet Pilot 510
   Tap Magazine 510

Finding More 511
    Calvin's Web Links 511
    MagiMac Publishing 511
    New England Palm Users Group 511
    Palm Organizer Web Ring 511
    PalmStock 511

Part IV: Making Your Palm Even Better   513

Chapter 20: Maintaining and Enhancing Your Palm 515

Core Application Replacements 515
    DateBook replacements 516
    Address Book replacements 522
    To Do List replacements 526
    Memo Pad replacements 527
    Application launchers 528
Application Helpers 534
    DateBook helpers 534
    Startup displays 536
    Logging tools 538
    More essentials 542
Supercharging Your Palm Handheld 543
    Mapping the buttons 544
    Utilities 544

Chapter 21: Customizing Your Palm with Utilities 547

Backup 547
    Palm Resets 547
    Restoring your data 548
Batteries 550
    Extending battery life 550
    BatteryInfo 551
    Battery Monitor 552
    Voltage Control 552
    Voltage Display 553
Beaming 553
    Built-in applications 553
    IR applications 555
    Remote controls 558
Memory 561
    Recovering space 562
    Memory fragmentation 562
    FlashPro 562
Security 565
    Third-party security applications 566

Speedups 573
  EcoHack 574
  Afterburner][. . . . 575
  CruiseControl 576
  Tornado V 576
System Tools 577
  ATool! 577
  Pilot Explorer 577
  FPS Utility Pro 578
More Tools 580
  dbScan 580
  TrapWeaver 580
  UnDupe 581

Chapter 22: Extending Functionality with HackMaster **583**

What Is HackMaster? 583
  Care and feeding 584
Daggerware Hacks 585
  AppHack 585
  MenuHack 586
Third-Party Hacks 586
  AltCtrlHack Pro 586
  CatHack 587
  ClockHack 587
  Contrast Button Hack 588
  Daylight Savings Hack 589
  EVEdit 589
  FlashHack 589
  GadgetHack 590
  Glowhack 590
  HushHack 590
  LeftHack 591
  LightHack 591
  PhoneLookUp Hack 592
  StreakHack 592
  SpellCheck 593
  SymbolHack 593
  TealMagnify 594
  TrekSounds 594
Registered Hacks 594
  FindHack 595
  HotTime 595
  MagicText 596
  ScreenShot Hack 596
  Snoozer 597
  SwitchHack 597

Chapter 23: Accessorizing Your Palm 599

    Cases 599
        Bumper case 600
        BurroPak 600
        Deluxe leather carrying case 600
        Dooney & Bourke cases 602
        FlipCase 602
        Hardshell case 604
        Leather belt clip case 604
        PalmGlove 604
        RhinoPak 1000 Sport Case 606
        RhinoPak 2000 Sport Ute case 606
        Rhinoskin Palm V molded hardcase 607
        Rhinoskin ShockSuits 610
        Slim leather carrying case 610
        Slipper 611
        SportSuit 612
        Targus case 612
        Titanium hardcase/TI Slider 613
        Visionary 2000 case 615
    Styli 615
        Concept Kitchen 616
        iPoint 5 617
        PalmPoint Dual Action stylus 617
        PDA Panache 618
    Keyboards 618
        FreeKey 618
        GoType Pro 619
        KeySync 620
        Palm Portable Keyboard 620
    Memory Upgrades 622
        SuperPilot, Xtra Xtra Pro 622
        eFig V8 upgrade 624
    Assorted Goodies 624
        Brain Wash 625
        BikeBrain 625
        CardScan 626
        goVox digital voice recorder 627
        GSM upgrade kit 628
        ImagiProbe 629
        Karma Cloth 630
        PalmConnect USB kit 630
        Palm Navigator 631
        TaleLight, TaleVibes 632
        Travel kit 632
        UniMount 633
        WriteRight 634

Springboard Cards 634
    InfoMitt 634
    MiniJam 636
    6Pack 636

Chapter 24: Troubleshooting Your Palm **639**
    General Troubleshooting Tips 639
        Backup loaded files 639
        A bulletproof Palm Organizer 640
        CD-ROM software 640
        Deinstalling third-party launchers on a Palm III 640
        Graffiti notes 641
        Memory 641
        Resetting your Palm 643
    Hardware 645
        Handheld 645
        Batteries 645
        Rechargeable batteries 646
        Loose memory board 646
        Repairs 650
        Screen issues 651
        Palm VII Diagnostics application 653
    HotSync Problems 654
        HotSync Log 654
        Overwritten data 654
        Rebound data 655
        Windows 655
        Registry Problems 656
        HotSync problems with Windows 3.11 658
        Mac HotSync problems 659
    Software 661
        Handheld 661
        Computer 663
        Corrupted Palm Desktop Preferences 664
    Telecommunications 664
        Long-distance calling cards 664
    More Help 665

Appendix A: Easter Eggs **667**

Appendix B: Dot Commands **671**

Appendix C: Palm Errors **673**

Appendix D: Palm Batteries **679**

Appendix E: Using Pendragon Forms **687**

Appendix F: Contacts **713**

Appendix G: On Our Palms **729**

Appendix H: What's on the CD-ROM **735**

Glossary **739**

Index 751

End-User License Agreement 775

CD-ROM Installation Instructions 782

Getting to Know Your Palm Handheld

P A R T

1

◆ ◆ ◆ ◆

In This Part

Chapter 1
Introducing the
Palm Handheld

Chapter 2
Taking Your First
Flight

Chapter 3
Using Graffiti

Chapter 4
Using the Built-In
Applications

Chapter 5
Examining the
Palm Utility Suite

Chapter 6
HotSyncing
Your Palm

Chapter 7
Using the Palm VII
Handheld

Chapter 8
Introducing the
HandSpring Visor

◆ ◆ ◆ ◆

Introducing the Palm Handheld

In This Chapter

Palm history

Licensed products

Working at Palm

Palm's future

I was lucky enough to interview three people for this chapter: Jeff Hawkins, Palm's founder; Michael Mace, Palm's chief competitive officer; and Michael Lunsford, the product manager for the Palm V series. Through the writing of this book, I've talked to Michael Lunsford on a regular basis — he also served as the technical editor for the *Palm OS Bible*.

I originally interviewed Jeff Hawkins for the *PalmPilot Resource Kit*; this chapter includes some of his background on the history of Palm. I talked to Michael Lunsford at length on what it has been like to work at Palm and to Michael Mace about the future of the Palm platform.

Palm History

There can be no doubt: with the Pilot, Palm struck and mined gold that others missed or ignored. One million Pilots were sold in the first 18 months, making it the fastest-adopted new technology in recent history — beating out successes such as the CD-ROM and Sony's Walkman. While others went after the personal digital assistant (PDA) market, Palm created a market of its own: the electronic connected organizer. Whatever you call it, Palm now owns the market, with two-thirds of all handheld electronic organizers in use. Apple abandoned the market some say it created with the Newton, and Microsoft agreed to stop using the Palm name on their Windows CE devices.

Figure 1-1 illustrates the early time line, with the Palm III in front of its predecessors: an IBM WorkPad, a 3Com PalmPilot Professional, a US Robotics PalmPilot Personal, and an original Pilot.

Figure 1-1: Palm history *(photograph © 2000 2 Black Dogs)*

Jeff Hawkins

Palm's founder has many accomplishments: he has a degree in electrical engineering from Cornell, and he's worked for four companies since graduation: Intel, Grid Systems (where he was responsible for the world's first pen-based computer: the GRiDPad), Palm, and Handspring. Jeff left his position as vice president of research at Grid Systems in January 1992 to start Palm , where he was vice president of advanced developments. In 1998, Jeff and Donna Dubinski left Palm to form Handspring, where they now manufacture the Visor.

Palm developed software for others before the Pilot. Jeff invented Graffiti, which was marketed for various handheld devices, and gave the GEOS Zoomer its name. In early 1994, Palm started work on what was to become its greatest success to date: the Pilot.

Jeff has always liked playing with product concepts; the story of how he carried around a pocket-sized block of wood as a Pilot prototype has been told many times. He told me that he practiced Graffiti before it existed, writing characters in the same place on a sheet—creating a doodle that few would recognize.

Four original goals

Jeff attributes much of the Pilot's success to the company's goals for it:

✦ It had to be small enough to fit in a shirt pocket.

✦ It had to communicate seamlessly with your computer.

✦ It had to be easy to use — fast and simple. Rather than looking at existing handheld products, they viewed paper as their competitor.

✦ It had to be inexpensive — $299 or less.

If there was a fifth goal, it was that the device be programmable and upgradable. At the time, these goals seemed to be unattainable; in retrospect, they have met and exceeded all of their goals. Palm's continued focus on its founder's original goals enables it to dominate the handheld marketplace.

Another key to the Pilot's success is the incredible developer community. There, too, Palm has made good moves, including giving out the source code to all of its applications in its Software Development Kit (SDK).

Palm, Inc.

Throughout the development stages and initial sales of the Pilot, Palm had a stable group of 28 employees. The company today has approximately 300 employees, excluding technical support and manufacturing. Half of its manufacturing is done in its factory in Salt Lake City; the other half is done for Palm in Malaysia.

Table 1-1 outlines the company's major milestones.

Table 1-1 **Palm Time Line**		
Date	*Milestone*	*Device (Version/RAM)*
January 1992	Palm founded	
October 1993		GEOS Zoomer
September 1994	Graffiti introduced	
August 1995	USR buys Palm	
January 1996	Pilot announced	

Continued

Table 1-1
Palm Time Line

Date	Milestone	Device (Version/RAM)
March 1996	Pilots ship	Pilot 1000 (1.0; 128K) Pilot 5000 (1.0; 512K)
December 1996	*350,000 Pilots ship by the end of the first year*	
February 1997	3Com/USR merger announced	
April 1997	PalmPilots introduced	PalmPilot Personal (2.0; 512K) PalmPilot Professional (2.0; 1MB)
June 1997	3Com/USR merger completed	
September 1997	*1,000,000th Pilot shipped*	
September 1997	IBM WorkPad shipped	IBM WorkPad (2.0; 1MB)
April 1998	Palm III shipped	Palm III (3.0; 2MB)
May 1998	Motorola PageCard shipped	Motorola PageCard (3.0; 2MB)
November 1998	*2,000,000th Palm shipped*	
February 1999	Palms shipped	Palm IIIx (3.1; 4MB) Palm V (3.1; 2MB)
March 1999	*3,000,000th Palm shipped*	
June 1999	Palm VII New York Pilot	Palm VII (3.2; 2MB)
August 1999	*4,000,000th Palm shipped*	
September 1999	Qualcomm ships pdQ	pdQ (3.1; 2MB)
October 1999	Palms shipped	Palm IIIe (3.1; 2MB) Palm Vx (3.3; 8MB) Palm VII (3.2; 2MB)
November 1999	Handspring releases Visor	Visor (3.1; 2MB) Visor Deluxe (3.1; 8MB)
November 1999	*5,000,000th Palm shipped*	
November 1999	Supra Real Estate device announced	
December 1999	TRGpro ships	TRGpro (3.1; 8MB)
February 2000	Palms shipped First color Palm device	Palm IIIxe (3.5; 8MB) Palm IIIc (3.5; 8MB)

Pilot

The original Pilot was announced in January 1996. From the beginning, Palm described it as an electronic connected organizer, rather than a personal digital assistant. They always intended the Pilot to be a data-viewing device — one that lets users access data they have stored elsewhere: on their computer, their LAN/WAN, or the Internet.

PalmPilot

In April 1997, the second generation was introduced: the PalmPilot, available in two flavors, Personal and Professional. New features included a backlit screen, an updated operating system, and more memory (512K in the Personal and 1MB in the Professional). New applications provided expense tracking and e-mail capabilities (Professional only), and new synchronization products supported a variety of third-party PIM (personal information manager) products.

Along with the new PalmPilot, US Robotics (USR) shipped two new synchronization options: a modem and a Network HotSync kit. For those who use VIM (Lotus) or MAPI (Microsoft) e-mail systems, the Professional model offered a portable version of the desktop e-mail client.

Palm III

The third-generation Palm III added infrared connectivity, a sleek new case and cradle, more memory, and an updated version 3.0 of the Palm Connected OS. Full backward compatibility was part of the package, along with countless improvements, including:

- ✦ Improved desktop software
- ✦ Redesigned stylus that unscrews to reveal a reset tool
- ✦ Removable hard-plastic cover for the screen
- ✦ Flash-upgradable operating system
- ✦ Bundled Network HotSync software

At the same time as the release of the Palm III, Motorola offered a 2MB PalmPilot upgrade with an important twist — an integrated paging card.

Palm IIIx/IIIe

The Palm IIIx has been the poweruser's choice since it was introduced. With 4MB of RAM, 2MB of flash memory, and a greatly improved screen, this device is a big step forward from the Palm III that it replaced. The Palm IIIe was designed as a price leader, offering 2MB of RAM and the improved screen. A clear-cased special edition version of the Palm IIIe (see Figure 1-2) is also available.

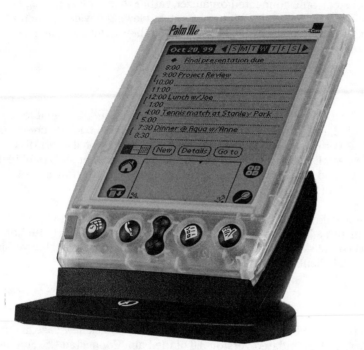

Figure 1-2: Palm IIIe Special Edition

Palm IIIc/IIIxe

The most recent additions to the Palm family are the new Palm IIIxe and the Palm IIIc. These devices share the Palm III case, with the Palm IIIc adding seven millimeters to the size of the device. Both devices share a new darker gray casing, along with the latest version of the Palm OS, 3.5. With 8MB of RAM, the Palm IIIxe is a budget poweruser's dream. As the first color device, the Palm IIIc has grabbed most of the spotlight. The screen features 256 colors, and is so bright that backlighting is no longer necessary. Another welcome addition is a lithium-ion battery that recharges in the HotSync cradle. Palm's engineers have designed the IIIc to work in a standard HotSync cradle, and a standard III will work in a IIIc cradle — neither setup involves charging, but the compatibility shows some great thinking. The Palm IIIc shares Motorola's new 20MHz DragonBall EZ processor with the Palm Vx.

Tip   The Palm IIIc no longer sports a contrast wheel; but hold down the power button for an extra second and a brightness dialog box opens. You can use either your stylus or the scroll button to adjust the level to your liking.

Palm V/Vx

Originally code-named "Razor," these devices (see Figures 1-3 and 1-4) represent a high point for Palm. A superthin brushed aluminum case surrounds a Palm Organizer with the best screen available on a Palm device: a doublescan version of the Palm IIIx screen. In addition to the sexy case, the Palm V series shares another unique enhancement: a lithium-ion battery that charges when in the HotSync cradle. The newer Palm Vx bumps the memory to 8MB with the new 20MHz version of Motorola's DragonBall EZ processor.

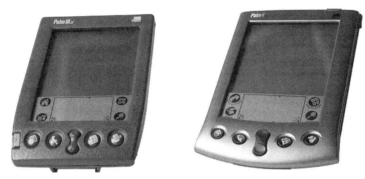

Figure 1-3: The Palm IIIx and the Palm V

Figure 1-4: The Palm Vx in front of a Visor Deluxe, a TRGpro, and Synapse Pager-equipped PalmPilot Professional

Palm VII

The Palm VII (see Figure 1-5) is the truly connected Organizer. The casing is similar to the Palm III series, with a half-inch extension at the top to house new batteries, and an antenna. Raising the antenna means you're connected (at least in the 260 regions of the United States with coverage), giving you access to e-mail, the Internet, and more. See Chapter 7 for in-depth coverage of the Palm VII.

Figure 1-5: The Palm VII.

Licensees

A secret of Palm's success is its careful management of licensees that were carefully selected to maintain the quality of the Palm line. Too many licensees too early in the process would have meant each would have a small piece of a small pie. With over five million Palm devices shipped to date, it is evident that Palm has done a lot of things right.

IBM

Palm went looking for the company that would be the best fit to give them enterprise sales skills. IBM was the logical choice, and it was receptive to the idea when approached. Essentially, the WorkPad and the WorkPad c3 (see Figure 1-6) are IBM - labeled versions of the Palm IIIx and Palm V, in black. Interestingly, Palm pays IBM a royalty for all WorkPad and C3 sales.

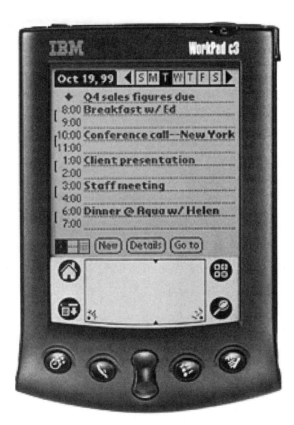

Figure 1-6: The IBM WorkPad c3

The IBM WorkPad offers a number of advantages to corporate customers, including:

✦ IBM offers 24-hour global support for the WorkPad PC companion during its warranty period.

✦ The WorkPad is available on a worldwide basis, and is the only Palm device sold in Japan.

✦ The WorkPad's infrared capability supports cradle-less synchronization between the WorkPad PC companion and your IBM PC or ThinkPad notebook.

✦ The WorkPad includes EasySync for Lotus Notes software, which provides a conduit for accessing your Lotus Notes calendar, e-mail, and address book.

Franklin-Covey

Franklin-Covey markets the Palm III and Palm V series, and the Palm VII, with its sophisticated time- and life-management software integrated into the Palm Operating System. Franklin-Covey also markets this software separately, enabling users of Palm Organizers to HotSync with either Franklin Planner or Microsoft Outlook.

Tip   Once you start using Franklin-Covey's software, you'll be using its Task List instead of Palm's To Do List. To make your life easier, use Preferences ⇨ Buttons to remap the To Do button to open the Task List.

Symbol

It is quite natural that Symbol, one of the world's leading manufacturers of bar code scanners, would make a Palm OS device that integrates a bar code scanner. Symbol makes Palm OS-based devices that are truly for vertical markets: the SPT 1500 series is based on the Palm III series, with an integrated bar code reader. The 1700 series (see Figure 1-7) is a new, more robust design that is based on the Palm IIIx and is able to withstand a four-foot drop to a concrete floor. The SPT 1740 also offers a wireless LAN capability. All of these devices are available in different memory configurations.

Figure 1-7: The Symbol 1700

Qualcomm

The Qualcomm pdQ (see Figure 1-8) is an impressive device that combines a number of technologies. On the surface, it is the marriage of a cellular telephone and a Palm Organizer. A key feature of the device is that it uses a wireless technology that Qualcomm pioneered, CDMA, which enables the device to serve as a means of data access. The Qualcomm pdQ acts as a pager, and enables you to send and receive e-mail, as well as browse the Internet. What makes it even more impressive is the level of integration with the Palm OS that Qualcomm has built into the pdQ. Want to phone someone? Flip open the phone and the Palm Organizer is activated; look up a number, and the pdQ dials it for you. Want to take notes at the same time? Simply plug in the earphone. Call-tracking software enables you to keep a record of calls; there is even integration with the built-in Expense application to bill calls.

Figure 1-8: The Qualcomm pdQ smartphone

The hidden strength of the pdQ smartphone is the software integration between the voice (cell phone), data (paging, browsing, e-mail), and Palm aspects of the device. The pdQ uses more grayscale than most Palm applications, which enabled Qualcomm to create some sophisticated software for its handheld:

✦ **Call History:** This application keeps track of all calls on your pdQ—incoming, outgoing, and missed—and enables you to return calls and to track data from calls that can be exported to the Expense application.

✦ **Dialer:** As soon as you open the pdQ, the Dialer screen displays (see Figure 1-9). You can make calls using the onscreen keypad, the built-in Address Book, or Speed Dial.

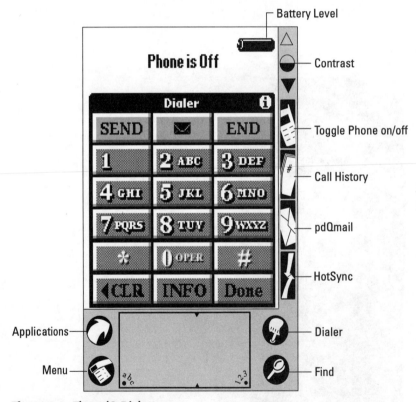

Figure 1-9: The pdQ Dialer

✦ **pdQalert:** This feature lets you know if you have received text or pager messages and whether your voice mailbox contains any messages.

✦ **pdQbrowser:** You can access the Internet with this text-only browser.

✦ **pdQmail:** Send and receive e-mail directly on your smartphone.

This device is definitely first-generation, bleeding-edge technology. The pdQ strikes some as a "shoe phone" because of its size, but it is much smaller and better integrated than the combination of a Palm Organizer, modem, and cellular telephone. The only drawback is the screen technology: the pdQ uses a 240 × 160–pixel version of the Palm III's screen. I'm confident that the next generation of this device will feature a screen like that used in the newer Palm IIIx and Palm V Organizers, in an even smaller device. The pdQ does have one big advantage over the Palm III series organizers (other than the new Palm IIIc) — it has a cradle-rechargeable battery.

Handspring

Jeff Hawkins and Donna Dubinsky left Palm to found Handspring in July 1998. The company recently released its first product, the Visor (see Figure 1-10), which is an overwhelming marketplace success. See Chapter 8 for in-depth coverage on the Handspring Visor.

Figure 1-10: The Handspring Visor

Technology Resource Group

The wizards at Technology Resource Group (TRG), the guys behind the SuperPilot, the Xtra Xtra, and FlashPro, among other accomplishments, have finally put their name on a Palm device: the TRGpro. The TRGpro is basically a Palm IIIx on steroids: 8MB of RAM, 2MB of Flash memory, an improved speaker, and a Compact Flash Slot. All of this power is housed in a case barely one-sixteenth of an inch thicker than a Palm IIIx! Upgraded software with support for Compact Flash rounds out the package. An advantage of Compact Flash is that it is already a standard — you can buy inexpensive memory cards, modems, even a 340MB hard drive that will fit into the slot. The first thing I did with my first prototype was to buy a 20MB Flash Card (for less than $80) to give me bragging rights to a 30MB Palm Organizer!

The TRGpro is designed for vertical markets, where its expansion capabilities are needed to run large corporate databases and other applications. I suspect that it will also become popular with Palm powerusers, who always seem to need to find more room on their handhelds. See Chapters 20 and 23 for more on TRG's products.

Palm Products Overview

The Palm product line is much more diverse than ever before. Table 1-2 is a quick overview of the relative prices and features of some of the licensed Palm OS handhelds.

Table 1-2
Current Palm Devices

Manufacturer	Device	SRP	MB	Flash	Expansion	Highlight
Qualcomm	PDQ	$799	2		None	Integrates cell phone
Symbol	SPT 1500	$685	4	2	None	Integrates bar code reader
Symbol	SPT 1500	$535	2	2	None	Integrates bar code reader
Palm	Palm VII	$449	2		None	Wireless
Palm	Palm IIIc	$449	8	2	None	Color, 20MHz processor, rechargeable
Palm	Palm Vx	$399	8	2	None	20MHz processor
IBM	C3	$369	2	2	None	Black case

Manufacturer	Device	SRP	MB	Flash	Expansion	Highlight
Palm	Palm V	$329	2	2	None	Razor-thin design, rechargeable
TRG	TRGpro	$329	8	2	Compact Flash	Improved audio
Palm	Palm IIIxe	$249	8	2	None	OS 3.5
Handspring	Visor Deluxe	$249	8		Springboard card	Loaded
Palm	Palm IIIx	$229	4	2	Internal memory	The standard
Handspring	Visor	$179	2		Springboard card	USB cradle
Palm	Palm IIIe	$149	2		None	Clear case
Handspring	Visor Solo	$149	2		Springboard card	No cradle

Note   A quick search on the Internet yielded much lower prices for some devices — for example, $249 for the Palm V and $189 for the Palm IIIx. I suspect that some of these prices will drop before this book is published.

Working at Palm

In 1986, Michael Lunsford founded and was the president of Macropac International. He sold the product line to become vice president of individual software, and then an author (with 13 computer books published), consultant, and lecturer. After a stint as multimedia producer for Etak System (a Sony Company that makes a Car Navigation system), Michael joined Palm as the manager of the Palm V device. One of his first suggestions for the then-new design was to make the application buttons concave, so that they could be stylus-tappable. Palm has since been granted a patent on this design feature.

Michael is also the technical editor for the *Palm OS Bible*, and has been intimately involved in the book from the beginning. What follows is a portion of an interview with Michael.

Corporate culture
What is your role at Palm ?

I am senior product manager for the Palm V series.

Continued

Continued

How long have you been at Palm? What is it like to work there?

I started work for Palm in 1997; it is the best job I've ever had. It is great to work for such a successful company, one that has been able to bring to market a revolutionary new product like the Palm Organizers. I give Jeff Hawkins a lot of the credit, he made sure that Palm was staffed by smart and creative people, and that has made Palm a great place to work. Palm has its own set of buildings across a bridge from 3Com, and that characterizes the autonomous relationship between the two companies. Dress is business casual — I don't wear a tie.

A lot of teamwork and consensus building goes on at Palm — decisions are made by the group. Choices are made based on what can be called the *Zen of Palm*: simplicity, ease of use, giving the customers what they need without burdening them with nice-to-haves that can adversely affect things like size, price, and battery life. Pragmatic innovation; Graffiti is an example that turned around the problem of workable handwriting recognition. Bleeding-edge technology isn't used just because it is cool; proven technologies that work are often chosen. Palm is a very market-driven company.

How have things changed when USR and 3Com acquired Palm and since Palm's founders left?

In the beginning, Palm was a software company, writing applications for the Newton. Graffiti was one of the best-selling add-ons for the Newton. Prolific people created software for the Zoomer. Rob Haitani (original product manager for the PalmPilot and now product manager for the Handspring Visor) referred to the Zoomer software as "intuitive once you figure it out." After the failure of the Zoomer, Jeff Hawkins used a clean slate approach to rethink the product and came up with what became the Palm OS. Neither USR nor 3Com attempted to control Palm, leaving Palm quite autonomous. The strong hiring practices institutionalized by Palm's founders (Ed Culligan referred to this as "staying away from the bozo factor") have meant that Palm has remained a great place to work.

Hardware

The new Palm Vx is great. Other than 8MB of memory, OS 3.3, and AvantGO, are there other changes?

The Palm Vx uses the new 20MHz version of the Motorola DragonBall EZ processor; Windows users get faster HotSyncing at 115K (Mac users have had this since the release of MacPac 2.1), support for the new Euro character, improved IR support, and better security.

What is the timeframe that Palm is looking at to expand Palm VII coverage to other markets such as Canada, Europe, and Asia?

The Palm VII uses CDPD coverage in the United States provided by Bell South; Palm is looking at rearchitecting Web clipping to work with other technologies, which may provide coverage in other areas.

A View of the Future

I talked to Michael Mace, Palm's chief competitive officer, about the future of the Palm platform. He explained that Palm's goal is to provide all mobile information access and management, with fast access to information. Palm wants to cover the complete range, from the convergence of voice-related devices (such as the Qualcomm pdQ and products that may come from Palm's recent agreement with Nokia) to entertainment devices that can serve as media players or game devices.

The evolution of Palm as a company had to be carefully managed so as to permit enough growth and business to make it worthwhile for all involved. The company has reached a point where it can allow multiple licensees such as Handspring and TRG.

Palm is now in the process of dividing the company into several units that may end up with different names — these units will be able to act independently, without need to rely on the other units. In general terms, the three units are:

 ✦ The **Platform Business Unit**, whose goal is to make the Palm platform the standard for handheld devices

 ✦ The **Devices Team**, whose goal is to produce the best Palm-based hardware systems

 ✦ **Palm.net**, whose goal is to provide the best wireless and online information services

Palm's recent agreement with Nokia is a partnering to develop a smart phone platform. Just as Nokia has licensed the use of the Palm OS, it is quite possible that Palm may license from Nokia the results of this enterprise. I asked whether Palm might ever consider licensing technologies such as Handspring's Springboard; Mace responded that Palm is not averse to licensing back technologies. He went on to explain that Palm wants to encourage innovation, and that we can expect to see a lot of work done with various expansion options. He also mentioned that systems will generally become smaller.

In the long term, everyone will expect to have access to key information using some type of information device. Information devices will let users do whatever they want, whenever they want. Michael believes that access to information will become ubiquitous — Palm wants a chance at being involved in setting the new standards for information access.

My predictions

Palm's successes leave its fans counting on it for the next great thing. I suspect that the Palm 2000 will include some or all of the following features. I should add that these are *my* speculations, not Palm's. Having said that, I want one of these when it comes out!

✦ **Faster processor:** Motorola has recently announced faster versions of the DragonBall EZ processor used in Palm Organizers: 20 and 33MHz versions. The 20MHz version is already used in the new Palm Vx; I expect to see a new model with the 33MHz chip.

✦ **Color:** The new Motorola processors support color; now that the Palm IIIc is out, I expect to see a Palm Vc. The release of faster devices with color support will also bring with it games and other entertainment software.

✦ **Rechargeable Batteries:** The Palm V series' rechargeable lithium-ion battery is too convenient to believe that Palm will not extend this technology to other models, as they recently have with their new Palm IIIc.

✦ **8MB Standard RAM with Expansion Options:** The Palm OS is compact enough that it is unlikely that standard RAM will need to be larger than the current 8MB; but I expect that other technologies — either proprietary, such as Handspring's Springboard module, or standard, such as TRG's Compact Flash — will allow for expansion.

✦ **Wireless/Cellular Integration:** The release of the Qualcomm pdQ and the recent deal that Palm signed with Nokia also foretell another area in which we will see development: the convergence of cellular telephone, data, and hand-held devices. I also expect to see an expansion of Palm's Web clipping technology, to enable its use with other wireless technologies and other Palm devices.

✦ **More Vertical Applications:** Devices such as the Symbol 1500/1700 and the TRGpro make larger databases practical — the Palm VII and the Qualcomm pdQ make wireless communication effortless. These and other upcoming developments will continue to make the Palm OS the premiere handheld OS, and, as these developments are implemented, we can expect to see huge growth in the number of vertical applications.

Summary

✦ Palm's Organizers have come a long way since the original Pilot — with improvements in screen, memory, size, connectivity, and more.

✦ Palm has worked with a number of companies to offer different solutions: IBM in the corporate world; Franklin-Covey for use with the Franklin Planner; the bar code-reading Symbol devices for commercial, industrial, medical, and other vertical applications; and the Qualcomm pdQ to enable voice and other data to converge. I expect to see some interesting announcements from these companies, along with Sony and Nokia, over the course of the next year.

✦ The recent introduction of the Handspring Visor and TRG's TRGpro bring expansion and other options to the Palm marketplace — they also are the first true clone devices, offering functionality that will in some cases compete with Palm. I presume both companies are working on color devices as I write this.

✦ The legacy left at Palm by Jeff Hawkins and Donna Dubinsky is a company staffed by some of the very best and brightest — which makes it a great place for creative people to work.

✦ The future looks great for Palm, with the next year offering new technologies and devices, along with further convergence of voice, Internet, and handheld data.

✦ I predict that the Palm IX will be released in the year 2000. It will have a 33MHz processor, a color screen, rechargeable batteries, 16MB of RAM along with an expansion slot, and wireless capabilities. I want one!

✦   ✦   ✦

First Flight

This chapter is for those of you who have just bought a new Palm Organizer and who would like some help getting started. We look at the first things that you need to do after opening your new toy, walk through your first HotSync operation (after learning what that is!), and quickly look at some of the basic features.

✦ ✦ ✦ ✦

In This Chapter

First steps

First synchronization

A quick walk around

Anatomy of the
Palm OS interface

✦ ✦ ✦ ✦

First Steps

If you have a Palm Organizer with replaceable batteries, you probably won't have the patience to install the desktop software and connect the synchronizing cradle (as the "Getting Started" card suggests) before opening and playing with your new toy. If you're lucky enough to have a Palm V or Vx organizer, then you don't have much choice; you need to charge its internal battery for four hours before you can start playing.

Tip　The "Getting Started" cards and the Users' Manuals that Palm, Inc. provides with its organizers are excellent—don't forget to read them; you're sure to pick up some new tricks.

Here's how to get started with the Palm Organizer:

1. Unwrap your new Palm Organizer and remove the plastic sheet that covers the screen. If you like the idea of a clear protective sheet for the screen, there are third-party products available (see Chapter 23). Unfortunately, the plastic static sheet that covers your Palm Organizer in shipping is not meant for this.

2. Install the batteries, or, if you own a Palm V or Vx organizer, set up the cradle/charger assembly and start your organizer's initial four-hour charge.

Occasionally, you'll find that the battery cover door on Palm Organizers with replaceable batteries (the III, IIIx, IIIe, and VII) doesn't close cleanly. This may be due to a misaligned door. I have found that if the batteries are not put in carefully, the spring that holds them in can bow out just enough to impede the door. The fix is simple—remove and carefully reinstall the batteries.

3. Press the green button (gray if you have a WorkPad) to turn on your Palm Organizer. Press it for two seconds if you want backlighting.

You may find that the text on your Palm Organizer sometimes looks blurry. This usually is a sign that you've inadvertently activated the backlighting by pressing the power button for too long a time; the cure is to power off and on.

Post-Palm III Handhelds

Unless you have the original Palm III organizer, the "Palm Computing Platform" splash screen (Figure 2-1) will appear. The Welcome application will then take over and help you set up your Palm.

Figure 2-1: The Palm splash screen

The operating system (numbered 3.1) in Palm Organizers shipped after the Palm III, has a few subtle differences from that used in the Palm III (3.0) and PalmPilot (2.0). The first and most obvious of these is a new Welcome application that leads you through the initial setup of your Palm Organizer. Palm III owners can skip ahead to read how to do their setup.

The first page of the Setup application (Figure 2-2) introduces you to the most basic element of the Palm Interface: tapping on the screen with the stylus. For more information on this topic, see the end of this chapter ("Anatomy of an Interface: The Palm OS").

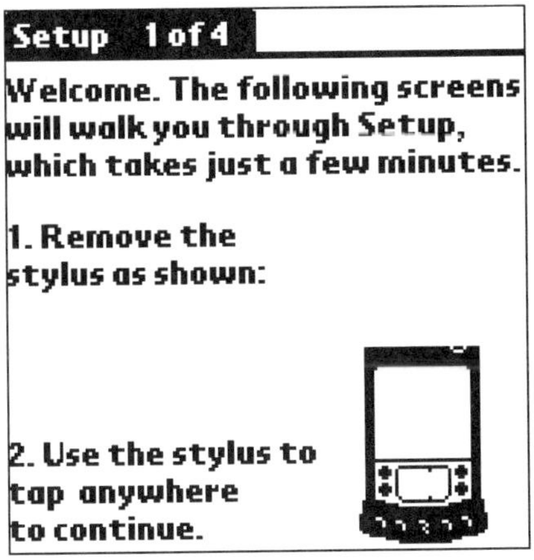

Setup   1 of 4

Welcome. The following screens
will walk you through Setup,
which takes just a few minutes.

1. Remove the
stylus as shown:

2. Use the stylus to
tap anywhere
to continue.

Figure 2-2: Welcome to Palm is the
first setup step.

Tip   The Palm V and Vx organizers ship with two styli, one in each side rail. These are
grooves cut into the sides of the device, which are designed to enable you to put
the cover on either side. Try the pen and cover on both sides, and then use
whichever feels best for you.

The next step is what Palm refers to as "aligning the Digitizer," as shown in Figure 2-3.
Tap on three onscreen targets in sequence to setup pen recognition.

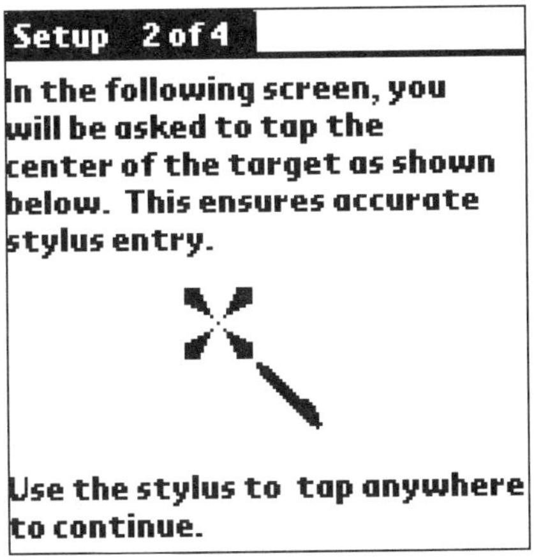

Setup   2 of 4

In the following screen, you
will be asked to tap the
center of the target as shown
below. This ensures accurate
stylus entry.

Use the stylus to tap anywhere
to continue.

Figure 2-3: Aligning the Digitizer is the
second setup step.

Tip   If you later find that your Palm Organizer is reading taps above or below where you think they should be, it's probably a good idea to open the Preferences application and select Digitizer from the pull-down menu in the upper-right corner to redo this step.

The third step in the setup process is to tell your Palm Organizer where you are and what time it is. Figure 2-4 shows these basic settings for your Palm Organizer. Tap the choice to the right of Country, and a list of countries will pop-up for you to select from. Tap a country from the list to select it.

Tap the time (to the right of Set Time) to make adjustments. Click the hours or minutes, and then adjust up or down by tapping the triangles in middle of the dialog box (as shown in Figure 2-5). Once you're satisfied, tap OK to close the dialog box.

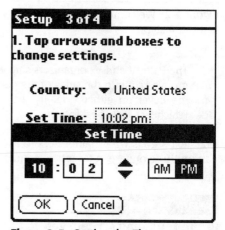

Figure 2-4: Setting the Country, Date, and Time is the third setup step.

Figure 2-5: Setting the Time

Click the date (shown to the right of Set Date) to get the Set Date calendar shown in Figure 2-6. Use the triangles to the left and right of the year to adjust, and tap the month and day to select the current date.

Note   Your Palm Organizer will display what it thinks is the current date in parentheses.

At this point, setup is complete (Figure 2-7), so you can tap Done. The first time through, however, you may want to view a few of the built-in tips by tapping Next.

Figure 2-6: Setting the Date

Figure 2-7: The setup of your Palm is complete.

The first tip screen (Figure 2-8) shows three basic ways to enter data on your Palm Organizer; you'll know many more ways to enter data by the time you finish reading this book! Clicking Next takes you to a series of screens (Figure 2-9) that help you learn Graffiti, Palm's handwriting recognition system. You can move from screen to screen by tapping Next, or you can jump directly to another screen by using the pick list to the right of the triangle in the upper-right corner of the screen ("Where do I write?").

Figure 2-8: Tips for entering data on your Palm

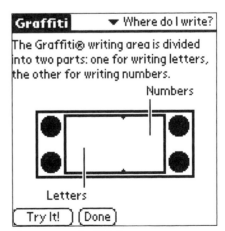

Figure 2-9: Graffiti tips

Cross-Reference You'll find more coverage of Graffiti in Chapter 3.

Once you've finished with the Graffiti tips screens, tap Done to go to your Palm Organizer's application launcher. There you'll find some of your Palm Organizer's many applications (Figure 2-10).

Figure 2-10: Palm applications

Palm III

After tapping the Welcome application, the "Welcome to Palm III" (Figure 2-11) displays. Palm Organizer owners see "Welcome to Palm Organizer" and WorkPad owners see "Welcome to the IBM WorkPad." Palm III owners don't have the Welcome application discussed above, but the Palm III setup process is very similar.

Figure 2-11: Welcome to Palm III.

Tip   If you don't see the Welcome screen, try adjusting the contrast wheel on the left-hand side of your Pilot.

Take the stylus out from the slot in the back right-hand corner of your Palm Organizer — you'll have to tap on three targets to align the digitizer. This tells your Palm Organizer where you tap, and enables it to adjust for angle and position.

After you finish, your Palm Organizer will bring you to the Preferences screen, so you can set the time and date. Much of what you will see on your Palm Organizer's screen is live (there is rarely the need to "save" anything) — you can tap on it with the stylus to do something. As with Palm Organizers shipped after the Palm III, all you need do is tap on Time or Date to adjust them.

First Synchronization

Before you start entering data into your Palm Organizer, set up the cradle so that you can do your first HotSync operation. This is the process your Palm Organizer uses to synchronize data between it and the data on your computer. Unless you tell it to do otherwise, a HotSync operation makes both versions the same, providing you with two identical copies. Figure 2-12 shows a Palm III in the HotSync cradle.

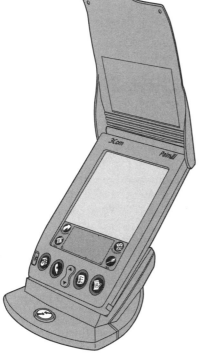

Figure 2-12: A Palm III in the HotSync cradle

New Feature The Palm V and Vx cradle assemblies come in two pieces: the docking cradle itself, which has a serial plug for the back of your computer, and the power adapter, which plugs into a wall socket at one end and into the back of the serial plug at the other. You don't need to plug it into a computer to start charging just as long as these two are connected correctly. Slide your Palm V or Vx organizer into the cradle, and a green light comes on, which indicates that the cradle is receiving power and that your organizer is well-seated in the cradle. The "light" is actually a handy desktop holder for your stylus.

Tip You may want to secure your cradle to your desk so that it cannot easily be knocked off (with your Palm Organizer in it). Palm V and Vx owners may not feel the need to do this; their cradles are heavier and less likely to have this problem.

Put the Palm Organizer CD in your computer's CD-ROM drive and it should start the setup application automatically (if not, Windows 98 or NT users should choose Run from the Start menu, and then type **D:\SETUP** where D is your CD-ROM).

If you do not have a CD-ROM drive, you can easily download Palm Desktop organizer software from www.palm.com for free; or, if you prefer, you can order 3.5" diskettes for a nominal price.

Macintosh users need to download PalmConnect, Palm's new desktop software for the Macintosh, also available for free at www.palm.com. Alternatively, you can go to www.palm.com and order the complete PalmConnect kit for the Macintosh, which consists of Palm Desktop organizer software, HotSync software, a Getting Started Guide, and a small serial or USB connector (your choice). The USB connector is especially important for iMac users, because the iMac has no standard serial port.

While Mac users will have to reboot their computers once more in order to load the Palm Organizer HotSync software, Windows 98 users will discover that HotSync is operational immediately after installation (a new HotSync icon will show in the process tray).

New Feature Microsoft Outlook users with Palm IIIx, V, Vx, or VII organizers will be asked during installation if they wish to link their data to the Palm Desktop or to Outlook. Choosing Outlook will install Chapura's PocketMirror to do the synchronization process. If you have the Palm IIIe and use Microsoft Outlook as your PIM, you might want to visit www.chapura.com to order Chapura's PocketMirror synchronization software.

The Palm HotSync software loads itself when you boot up your computer and stays in the background until you need it. Windows 98 or NT4 users will see the HotSync icon in the process tray; Mac users can access it from the Apple Menu as a Control Panel.

Here's one of the best things about the Palm Organizer: put it in the cradle, press the cradle's synchronizing button, and the synchronization work is done for you (see Figure 2-13).

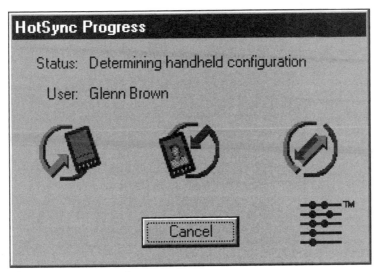

Figure 2-13: HotSync in progress

For those who want the grand tour, here's what happens:

1. Your Palm Organizer displays three syncing icons (similar to the desktop icons shown in Figure 2-13); the right two icons are grayed out. Above the icons it says "Connecting with the desktop."

2. Within ten seconds, your Palm Organizer will give a distinctive "up" chime, the middle icon will no longer be grayed out, and the message changes to "Identifying user." In a few more seconds, your desktop software will show a dialog box similar to that shown in Figure 2-13.

 See Chapter 6 if you are having problems HotSyncing.

3. The first time you synchronize your Palm Organizer, it asks you to select a user. Select the username you entered when you installed the Palm Desktop software, and then click OK. Your name is now highlighted; click OK or press Enter to continue.

4. The HotSync operation synchronizes the data in your Palm Organizer with that on the desktop. When it is finished, a distinctive "down" chime plays and "HotSync complete" displays at the top of your organizer's screen.

 You can turn off your Palm Organizer's system sounds using Preferences, but one of the disadvantages of doing so is that you lose the audible cues to synchronization progress.

Synchronizing your Palm Organizer, including synchronization with third-party personal information managers (PIMs), is discussed in greater detail in Chapter 6.

A Quick Walk Around

Let's take a quick walk around your new Palm Organizer to discover its many useful features.

Front

By now you've probably found and used the stylus and are ready to explore other features on the front of your Palm Organizer. Figure 2-14 displays the front of a Palm V organizer. Counterclockwise, from the bottom left, are the Date Book, Address Book, Scroll Button, To Do List, and Memo Pad.

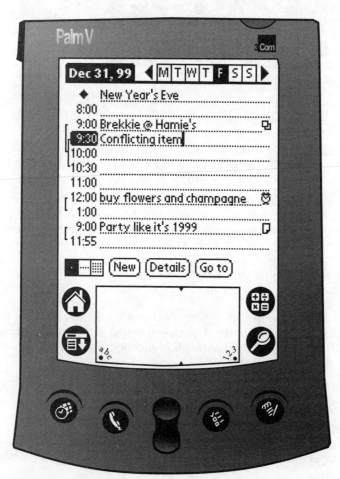

Figure 2-14: The front of the Palm V organizer

Tip   All of the main buttons across the front of your Palm Organizer also double as power on buttons—press the Calendar button and your Palm Organizer turns on displaying the calendar; press the Address Book button and your Palm Organizer turns on using the Address Book . . . (you get the idea).

Date Book

The Date Book is your Palm Organizer's calendar. The first time you press the Date Book button, the day view for today's date displays. Subsequent presses display the week and month views. (Version 2.0 of the Palm Organizer operating system added a month view; Pilot owners using OS 1.0 get only the day and week views.)

Address Book

The Address Book is your Palm Organizer's contacts listing. The first time you press the button, all your contacts display. Subsequent presses display lists in each of the categories you created (more on that in Chapter 4).

Tip   If you press and hold the Address Book button, your organizer will use its infrared to "beam" your business card to another Palm Organizer (see Chapter 20).

Scroll Button

The Scroll Button in the middle of your Palm Organizer enables you to scroll up and down in lists, or to page up and down in memos, to do's, e-mails, and address views. You can also use it to jump from day to day in the Date Book's day view.

Note   Pilot and PalmPilot owners have two scroll buttons that serve the same purpose.

To Do List

The To Do application is your Palm Organizer's listing of things to do. The first time you press the button, your to do items display. Subsequent presses display lists in each of the categories you created.

Memo Pad

The Memo Pad is your Palm Organizer's notes collection tool that you can use as a simple word processor. As before, the first time you press the button displays all your to do items. Subsequent presses display lists in each of the categories you created.

Power

The green power button (gray if you have a WorkPad) doubles as a light switch. Press it for two seconds to activate backlighting. (Pilot 1000 and 5000 users do not have backlighting).

New
Feature
The Palm V design has the Power button at the top right to make it easier to press each time you remove and replace the stylus. All other Palm designs have it in the lower left-hand corner.

Infrared Port

The infrared port at the top of your Palm Organizer enables you to "beam" information to another Palm Organizer user.

Note
The Infrared Port was added with the Palm III, and Palm includes one in its memory upgrade kit for earlier devices.

Contrast Button

The Palm V organizer has one unique control: The Contrast Button just to the left of the Infrared Port calls up a dialog box that enables you to adjust the contrast either with your stylus or by repeated pressing of the scroll button. Users of earlier devices have a Contrast Dial on the left-hand side of the Palm Organizer.

Note
One of the big advantages of the Palm Organizer is that there is no such thing as "saving a file" — if you make changes to a memo or a to do item, and then switch off the power, it will be there when you turn it on again.

Silk screen

The silk-screened area at the bottom of your Palm Organizer's screen (Figure 2-15) is where you do most of your data entry:

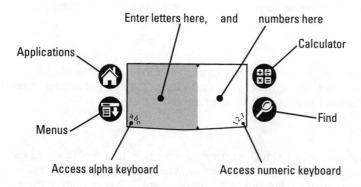

Figure 2-15: The silk-screen area is where data is entered.

The first thing you need to recognize is that the screen is divided into halves — the left for text entry and the right for numbers. Until you get comfortable with Graffiti (your Palm Organizer's text-recognition system), you can "cheat" by accessing the alpha and numeric keyboards from the lower-left and right-hand corners of the Graffiti area by tapping the "abc" or "123" buttons. The icons in the corners to the left and right of the silk-screened area are:

Applications

This calls up a window of the applications installed on your Palm Organizer. It starts out looking like the one shown in Figure 2-10. By the time you finish this book, your applications list should look much different!

Menus

The lower-left icon drops down menus in the application you're running (if it has any). See MenuHack in Chapter 20 for a more elegant way of accessing menus.

Calculator

The Calculator gives you the functionality of a handheld pocket calculator (albeit an expensive one). One nice thing about the built-in calculator is that the buttons are big enough to use with your fingers.

Find

The lower right-hand icon enables you to find text in records in all of the applications stored on your Palm Organizer.

 Tip To easily find a contact by first name, switch to the Address Book, tap Find in the lower-right corner of the Graffiti area, enter the first name you want to find, and tap OK. Shortly, a handy listing of both the full name and telephone number of each person in your Address Book with that first name displays.

Back

Before we start using the Palm Organizer, let's have a quick look under the hood, as shown in Figure 2-16.

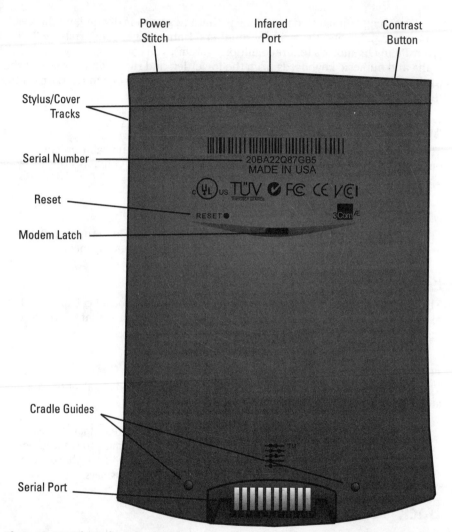

Figure 2-16: The Palm V backside

There are a few important things to note about the backside of your Palm V:

✦ The **Serial Number** is right under the bar code on the label in the center of your Palm Organizer—I recommend that you take a moment and write it down now. Create a new memo called Palm Organizer S/N, and enter your serial number— the next time you HotSync it will be stored on your computer.

Note Palm III owners will find the reset button above and to the right of the serial number (see Figure 2-17).

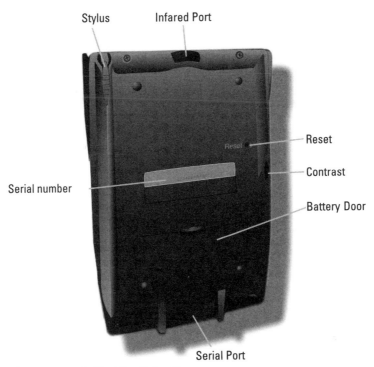

Figure 2-17: Behind the Palm III

✦ The **Reset button** is a tiny hole under the serial number, conveniently labeled Reset. If your Palm Organizer locks up or has problems, the first thing to try (after Power off/on) is to stick a paper clip in this hole. Palm calls this a *soft reset*. If it works, the Welcome screen displays and things should return to normal. If it doesn't work, try doing what Palm calls a *hard reset*. Press the Power button while doing a soft reset and when the Welcome screen appears, release the Power button.

New Feature The styli that Palm has shipped since the Palm III work like a three-piece pool cue: unscrewing the top exposes a hidden reset pin.

✦ The **Serial Port** is where your cradle makes the connection between your Palm Organizer and your desktop computer.

✦ The miniscule **pins** on either side of the Serial Port fit into tracks in the Palm V's cradle, providing a secure fit. For those who are curious, the rectangular hole under the serial number is used to help secure the Palm V modem.

The backs of the Palm III and IIIx are a little different:

Devices before the Palm III also had a memory compartment, which few owners ever need to open, although Pilot 1000/5000 and Palm Personal owners need to if they upgrade their memory. Palm III owners don't have a memory door, so, to insert a memory expansion card, they need to unscrew the four #0 screws at each corner and pry the case open (see Chapter 23 for details).

Anatomy of the Palm OS Interface

Now that you've set up your new Palm Organizer, let's step back and have a look at some of the elements of the Palm interface. If you're already comfortable with computers, you will already be familiar with most of this; substitute the stylus for a mouse, and you've got the basics. Here are the components that we've just used, and a few more that you'll soon discover. Don't worry if you're not familiar with these applications yet; they are discussed in detail in Chapter 4.

Pick lists

Any time you see text to the right of a small downward-pointing triangle (remember the Country field in Figure 2-4?), tapping it drops down a pick list. Just tap your selection, or tap anywhere outside of the list to close the list without changing the selection.

In many of the standard applications on your Palm Organizer, there is a categories pick list in the upper right-hand corner. This list starts with All. Tap Edit Categories at the end of the list to add, rename, or delete categories — just remember that you are limited to 15 categories per application.

Dotted boxes

Dotted boxes on your screen indicate that tapping them opens other screens where you can make changes to information. (For an example of this, look back to the time and date dotted boxes in Figure 2-4.)

Buttons

Tapping a button typically does what the button's label says — the Previous and Next buttons In the Setup screens move you forward or backward by a screen. Buttons with an ellipses (for example the Details button in the To Do List screen) opens a dialog box to enable you to make or confirm changes.

Black triangles

Left- and right-facing triangles move your view forward and backward, as shown in the Date Book view in Figure 2-18. Clicking these triangles moves your view forward and backward one week at a time.

```
Dec 31, 99  ◀ S M T W T F S ▶
 8:00 ............................................
 9:00 ............................................
10:00 ............................................
11:00 ............................................
12:00 ............................................
 1:00 ............................................
 2:00 ............................................
 3:00 ............................................
 4:00 ............................................
 5:00 ............................................
 6:00 ............................................
 ▪ ⋯ ▦ (New) (Details) (Go to)
```

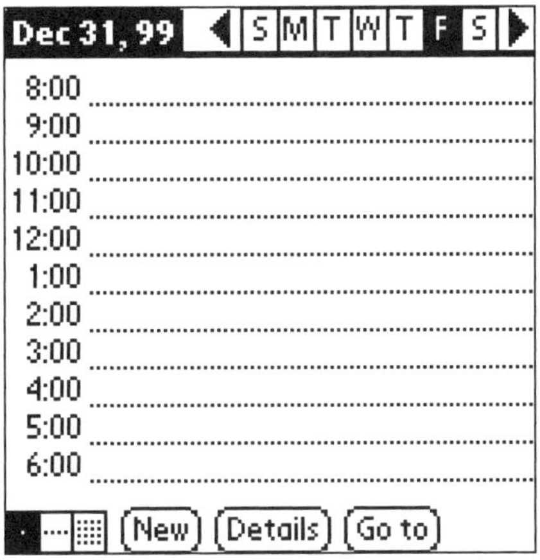

Figure 2-18: The triangles in Date Book move your view forward and backward one week at a time.

Boxed text

If you want to move to another day within the week, just tap the day that you want to view and it is highlighted. These types of boxes act like radio buttons on your computer — only one can be active at a time.

Checkboxes

Open boxes enable you to make selections; tap once to add a checkmark, tap again to remove it. Tapping a circle with an "i" in the upper right-hand corner of a window (as shown in Figure 2-19), opens a tips screen (shown later in Figure 2-22).

The text cursor

The text cursor is a vertical bar that indicates where text will be entered (the bar after Look Up in Figure 2-20 is an example). There is one key difference between this and the cursor on your computer—you enter the text in the Graffiti area (not at the cursor), and the text displays at the cursor.

Figure 2-19: To Do Preferences

Figure 2-20: Address List

Scrolling windows

The Palm interface uses three different graphics to indicate that your view of a window can be scrolled up or down. A scroll bar (Figure 2-21) is used in some applications such as the Application Launcher, Memo List, and Expense.

Up and down facing triangles (Figure 2-22) are used in some applications and dialog boxes such as the Address List and To Do List.

Up and down arrows (Figure 2-23) are used in most Pick Lists, such as categories, expense types, and country lists. These elements are all on-demand: they only appear when there is more data to display. The diamonds gray out if there is no more information to be shown in one direction. The arrows only appear if there is data in that direction.

Figure 2-21: Application Launcher uses the scroll bar to move up or down in a window.

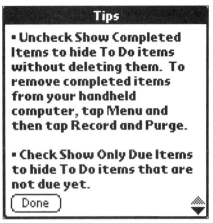

Figure 2-22: The To Do Tips screen uses up- and down-facing triangles to move between window screens.

Figure 2-23: Use up and down arrows to move through Address List categories.

Tip   If you find it difficult to find the exact spot to tap to scroll up or down, use the scroll button located on the bottom of your Palm Organizer.

Summary

✦ The initial setup for the Palm Organizer is simple: add batteries or — in the case of the Palm V or Vx organizer — charge up your unit, create a few settings, and you're off. The first HotSync operation, which synchronizes information between your Palm Organizer and your computer, is one of the best features of the Palm Organizer — one button does it all.

✦ A quick tour of the Palm Organizer shows the basic controls and applications. Buttons across the bottom open the main applications: Date Book, Address Book, To Do List, and Memo Pad.

✦ The Palm Interface is simple and easy to learn and use, much like that on your personal computer — buttons can open dialog boxes, tapping checkboxes toggles their status on and off, and triangles open pick lists.

✦ The logical next step is to learn a bit about Graffiti. The best place to start is to take the Graffiti reference card (or this book) in hand and run through your Palm Organizer's Graffiti tutorial until you're comfortable entering basic text. Just tap the silk-screened Applications button, and then tap the Graffiti icon to start. When you're ready for more detail, move ahead to Chapter 3 to learn about Graffiti.

✦   ✦   ✦

Using Graffiti

The Graffiti handwriting recognition system is one of the features that distinguishes the Palm Organizer from the pretenders. Unlike Apple's now-deceased Newton handwriting system, which learned your handwriting, Graffiti forces *you* to learn *it*. Fortunately, Graffiti is easy to learn. Can you write block capital letters? Then you already know 85 percent of what you need to know. This chapter helps you visualize Graffiti strokes, while teaching you everything you ever wanted to know about your Palm Organizer's handwriting-recognition capabilities.

First, you need to write your characters in a specific place (the letters are written on top of each other). The Palm Organizer makes this easy, with a silk-screened Graffiti area at the bottom of the screen. What could be simpler? You write in the boxed area at the bottom of the screen (see Figure 3-1).

Two marks divide the screen; the larger left side is for letters and the smaller right side is for numbers. If you're in a rush, or you can't remember a character you need, you can always access the pop-up keyboard (see Figure 3-2) from the "abc" and "123" symbols in the lower left and right corners of the Graffiti area.

◆ ◆ ◆ ◆

In This Chapter

The basic alphabet

Advanced strokes

Graffiti enhancements

Graffiti alternatives

◆ ◆ ◆ ◆

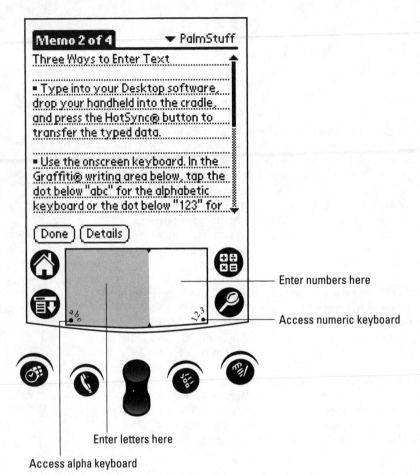

Enter numbers here

Access numeric keyboard

Enter letters here

Access alpha keyboard

Figure 3-1: The silk-screened Graffiti area

Tap Done when you're finished

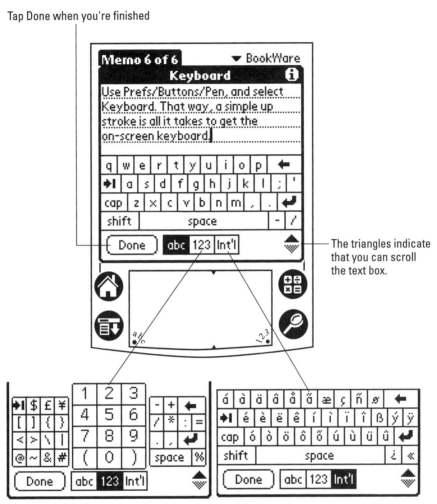

The triangles indicate that you can scroll the text box.

Figure 3-2: Pop-up keyboards

The Basic Alphabet

The basic Graffiti alphabet, as shown in Figures 3-3 and 3-4, is easy to learn — most of the characters are based on block capital letters.

To help you get started, here are a few notes about the Graffiti alphabet:

✦ Form fairly large characters — the larger the better.

✦ Make sure you enter Graffiti characters straight up and down. Even a small slant can reduce Graffiti's capability to recognize your handwriting.

✦ The exceptions to the block-letter rule are the H (based on a lowercase letter), and Y (based on a handwritten letter).

✦ The A, F, K, and T strokes are *partials* of the letters (meaning that, if you were writing, you'd need to add a line to complete the character). Once you've visualized them, they are easy to remember.

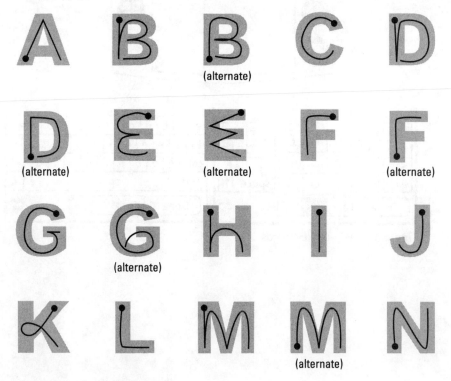

Figure 3-3: The Graffiti alphabet

✦ In my interview with Jeff Hawkins (Palm's founder; see Appendix A), the first tip he mentioned when we discussed Graffiti was that some of the alternate strokes may be less intuitive, but they are often more reliable. This is especially true for the V and Y strokes.

✦ With the exception of the regular X, all of the strokes are done without lifting your stylus.

Tip You can call up a Graffiti "hint-sheet" on the screen at any time while you're in text entry or text edit mode. Simply drag your stylus from the bottom of the Graffiti area to the top of the screen. Also, included with your Palm Organizer is a self-adhesive sheet with two tear-off hint sheets. One shows the Graffiti alphabet, the other shows more advanced characters. Figure out where these would be most useful to you; they can go almost anywhere — on the back of your Palm Organizer, inside the cover, or inside the case. My favorite place to put it is on the back of a business card that is kept in the case with the Palm Organizer — that way, if you lose it, you have a better chance that someone might return it to you.

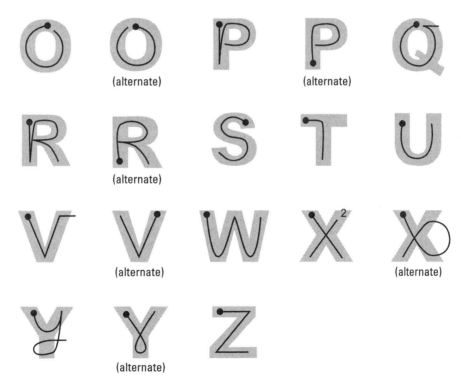

Figure 3-4: More Graffiti alphabet

Numbers

Graffiti numbers (see Figure 3-5) are easy to learn; just remember to form them on the right-hand side of your Palm Organizer's silk-screen area. You can form all of the numbers except the 4 by drawing the number. The 4 is formed without the down stroke—once you've visualized it, you've got it.

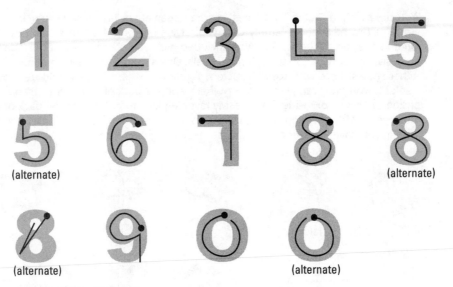

Figure 3-5: Graffiti numbers

Essential punctuation

A few more strokes to learn, and you'll know 90 percent of what you'll ever use on your Palm Organizer. Like the rest of Graffiti, these punctuation strokes are pretty intuitive (see Figure 3-6). Space and backspace are two you'll use a lot. The period, shift, and caps lock strokes introduce extended characters.

Figure 3-6: Basic punctuation

✦ An upstroke puts you in shift mode. A solid arrow appears above the silk-screened calculator, and the next character that you type is capitalized. The Address Book and some other applications automatically capitalize the first letter in some fields.

✦ Two upstrokes put your Palm Organizer in caps lock mode, which is signified by a broken arrow just above the silk-screened Calculator icon. All characters are capitalized until you turn caps lock off with another upstroke.

✦ Tap in the Graffiti area (either side), and a dot appears above the silk-screened Calculator icon. This indicates the punctuation mode, which enables you to enter a follow-up Graffiti stroke to create any of a number of punctuation marks. For example, tapping again enters a period. See the Advanced Strokes section of this chapter for more punctuation information.

Tip   To erase a block of text, tap and drag on the text to highlight it, and then backspace.

If you are learning about Graffiti for the first time as you work through this chapter, I recommend that you stop now. If you haven't already done so, run through the Graffiti tutorial (Palm IIIx and up only). Load the Giraffe game from the CD-ROM, and play a game or two—you'll be surprised how quickly you learn.

Advanced Strokes

The advanced capabilities of Graffiti are pretty amazing; learn all of these and you'll never need the pop-up keyboard again. Just as with your computer's operating system, if you find yourself using or needing any of these characters, the effort to learn the ShortCut (on your computer) or Graffiti equivalent (on your Palm Organizer) will pay off.

Movement

You've already seen the basic Graffiti movements, so now you're ready for some advanced strokes. Learning the strokes shown in Figure 3-7 may make your life even easier. I particularly like the cursor left and right strokes (which I learned while writing this chapter). It is often difficult to get the cursor exactly where you want it using the stylus. The last three are movement strokes that only work when you're in the Address Book.

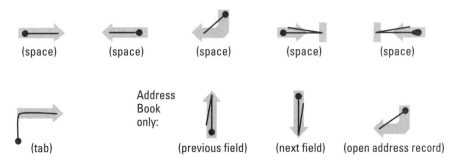

Figure 3-7: Graffiti movement strokes

Shift strokes

Warning: The material you are about to read may make you a Graffiti geek. One thing that makes you a Palm poweruser is the use of the extended character sets in Graffiti. These characters are formed with two strokes: the first stroke changes the mode and the second stroke executes the character. If you've made a period, you've already used an extended character. Figure 3-8 is mock-up of a screen I made using Adobe PhotoShop and Macromedia Freehand, displaying all of them at once.

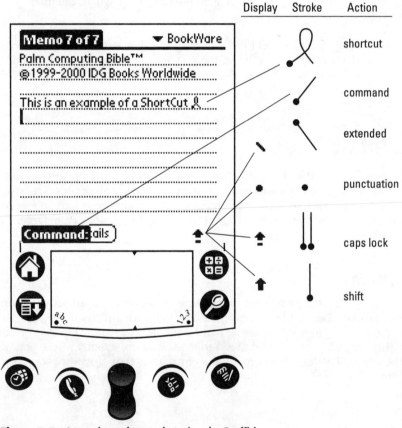

Figure 3-8: Accessing advanced strokes in Graffiti

Here are the strokes I've illustrated:

✦ **ShortCut** is written like a fat, lowercase, longhand, letter L, and accesses preestablished ShortCuts (see Figure 3-9 in the next section). Your cursor is replaced by a symbol (that looks just like the stroke) until you complete the ShortCut.

✦ **Command** is a forward slash — a diagonal stroke from lower left to upper right (/). The word Command appears above the silk-screened Applications button, and you have about two seconds to complete the command. Those using Palm OS 3.5 or better will have a command bar displayed at the bottom of the screen for a few seconds after making this stroke (see Chapter 4 for more on the new command bar in Palm OS 3.5).

Cross-Reference

See Chapter 2 for a list of the command strokes in your Palm Organizer's basic applications.

✦ **Extended Shift** is a diagonal stroke from upper left to lower right (\); a similar onscreen backslash displays to let you know you are in Extended Shift mode.

✦ **Punctuation Shift** is a single tap; a bullet displays onscreen to let you know you are in Punctuation Shift mode.

✦ **Caps Lock** is activated by two vertical bottom-to-top strokes; a broken arrow indicates you are in Caps Lock mode.

✦ **Caps Shift** is activated by a single up stroke; a solid arrow indicates you are in Caps Shift mode.

ShortCuts

ShortCuts are like glossary entries on your computer — a longer word or phrase that you can access with a few simple strokes. Making the ShortCut stroke shown previously in Figure 3-8 replaces your cursor with a symbol (it looks just like the stroke) until you complete the ShortCut.

Those who want a more elegant means of entering abbreviated text might want to try either QuickText, part of Landware's QuickPac collection, or Rick Bram's Pop! You can find these and other useful third-party applications on the Palm OS Bible companion CD-ROM.

To create the time and date shown in Figure 3-9, I made the ShortCut stroke followed by the letters d, t, and s — my Palm Organizer replaced the ShortCut with the date and time.

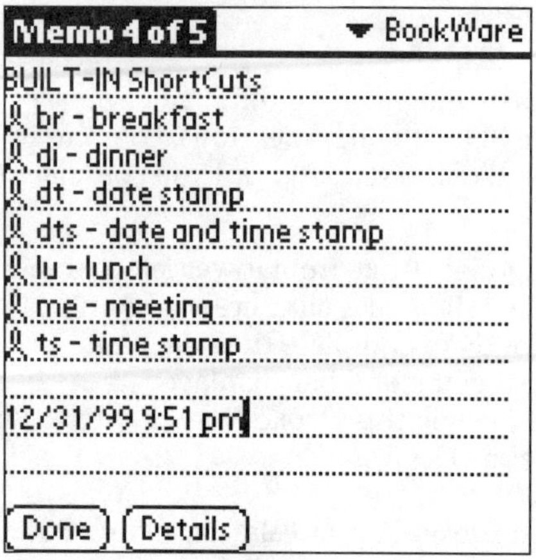

```
┌──────────────────────────────────┐
│ Memo 4 of 5            ▼ BookWare │
├──────────────────────────────────┤
│ BUILT-IN ShortCuts               │
│ 𝄞 br - breakfast                  │
│ 𝄞 di - dinner                     │
│ 𝄞 dt - date stamp                 │
│ 𝄞 dts - date and time stamp       │
│ 𝄞 lu - lunch                      │
│ 𝄞 me - meeting                    │
│ 𝄞 ts - time stamp                 │
│                                  │
│ 12/31/99 9:51 pm|                 │
│                                  │
│ ┌──────┐ ┌─────────┐             │
│ │ Done │ │ Details │             │
│ └──────┘ └─────────┘             │
└──────────────────────────────────┘
```

Figure 3-9: Time/Date by ShortCut

The following ShortCuts are built in your Palm Organizer:

✦ br — breakfast

✦ di — dinner

✦ dt — date stamp

✦ dts — date and time stamp

✦ lu — lunch

✦ me — meeting

✦ ts — time stamp

Creating your own ShortCut entries

What makes the ShortCut feature so powerful is the capability to create your own ShortCuts. Want to be able to add "left a message with . . ." with three taps? Here's how to do it:

1. Tap the silk-screened Application icon to the left of the Graffiti area and tap the Preferences icon.

2. Select ShortCuts from the drop-down menu in the upper right-hand corner. You'll get a screen similar to that shown in Figure 3-10.

3. Tap New to get the ShortCut Entry dialog box shown in Figure 3-11, and then enter the abbreviation that you want to use, followed by the text that you want inserted by the ShortCut. Be sure to leave a blank space after the last word in your entry if you want your ShortCut to be inserted in a sentence.

Figure 3-10: Adding a ShortCut    **Figure 3-11:** ShortCut entry

Tip When creating a ShortCut, don't use capitals to create your abbreviation. ShortCuts require more steps to activate if capitals are used.

Tip Want to make the ShortCut illustrated in Figure 3-11 truly useful? Why not have you Palm Organizer automatically time and date stamp your entry. Here's the trick: Enter @ **Left a message DTS** as the ShortCut Text. This way, if I'm trying to reach someone, I can quickly document the process by using this ShortCut; the end result is "Left a message @ 05/13/00 10:04 pm."

Punctuation Shift

The Punctuation Shift characters are far more useful than a first glance might indicate. I've memorized about half of them so far. All of these are two-stroke characters — first a tap, and then the strokes shown in Figures 3-12 and 3-13.

Tip Punctuation can be entered on either side of the Graffiti entry area.

Extended Shift

Most users have little reason to learn all of these Extended Shift strokes (I know I haven't). These are also two-stroke characters — first a diagonal stroke (\ ) from upper left to lower right, and then the strokes shown in Figure 3-14. Like Punctuation Shift, Extended Shift characters can be entered on either side of the Graffiti entry area.

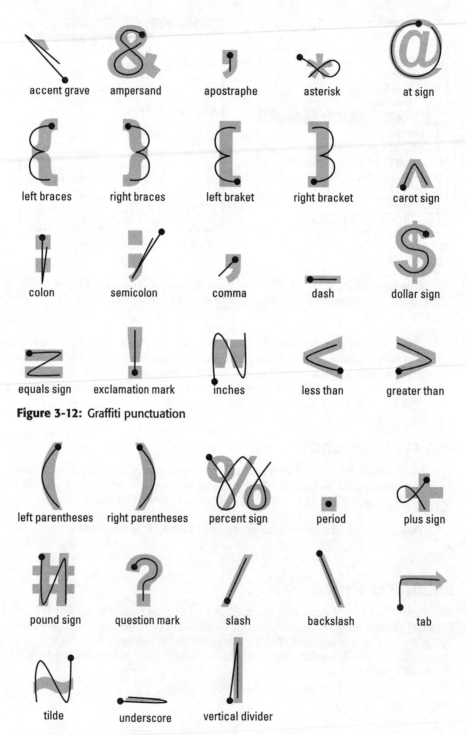

Figure 3-12: Graffiti punctuation

Figure 3-13: More Graffiti punctuation

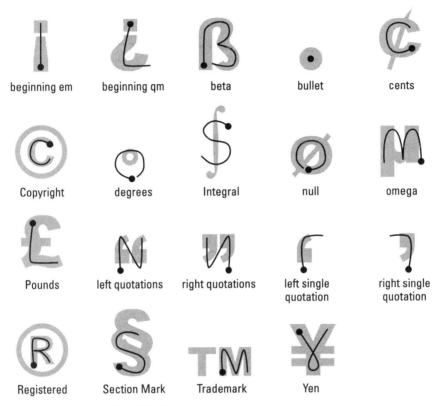

Figure 3-14: Extended Shift characters

Graffiti math

Here's something that may surprise you: You can control your Palm Organizer's calculator with Graffiti. Enter numbers with Graffiti, and use the Extended Shift symbols in Figure 3-15 to perform basic calculations. As with Symbol Shift characters, most users will use the pop-up keyboard rather than memorize these. The memory functions also work — use a Graffiti M for MC (memory clear), R for MR (memory recall), P for M+ (memory add), E for CE (clear entry), and C for C (clear).

Figure 3-15: Extended Shift math characters

Foreign characters

The Palm Organizer is used worldwide; Graffiti's support of foreign characters makes it easier to correctly enter accented and other foreign-language characters. Just enter the character followed by the accent as shown in Figure 3-16. Your Palm Organizer will place the accent on the character already entered. Those who regularly use their handheld to capture Web addresses may want to memorize the stroke for tilde (~), which is often used in URLs (Web addresses).

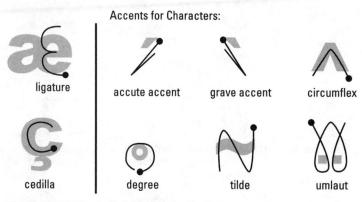

Figure 3-16: Foreign characters in Graffiti

Graffiti Enhancements

Graffiti enhancements include a number of useful tools to help you learn Graffiti, see the graffiti you've entered, and even ways to help you enter Graffiti more quickly.

Help

Palm provides you with lots of tools to help you learn Graffiti — the upstroke, the stickers, a wallet card, and an excellent online tutorial for those with OS 3.1 or better. You'll also find help in some of the shareware products on the CD-ROM. Look for Chris Crawford's Grafaid, Bill Kirby's Graffiti Help, and David Haupert's WPM (which measures how fast you can enter Graffiti characters). My favorite learning tool is still Palm's Giraffe game (see Figure 3-17) — thirty minutes playing this game, and you'll have mastered Graffiti's basics.

Cross-Reference   If you load Palm's Giraffe game, make sure you check out the Easter Eggs in Appendix A — many of them can be found in this game!

Figure 3-17: Giraffe opening screen

Giraffe

Developer: Palm, Inc.
Cost: Freeware
Footprint: 1K

3Com shipped this arcade game with OS 2. It's a simple clone of the classic Atari arcade game Space Invaders — the twist is that you have to perform the Graffiti stroke for each of the characters coming down the screen in order to clear them.

Feedback

One of the techniques that can speed learning and improve your technique is onscreen feedback. The following three products help you visualize how your Palm Organizer is interpreting your Graffiti strokes.

EVEdit

Developer: Evsoft
Cost: $16.00
Footprint: 76K

This HackMaster Hack provides a number of enhancements to your Palm Organizer, including an onscreen display of the Graffiti area that shows the characters you are writing (see Figure 3-18).

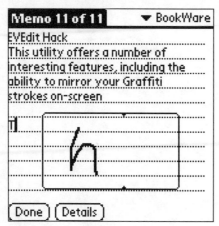

Figure 3-18: EVEdit

Cross-Reference   For more on HackMaster and other Hacks, see Chapter 22.

ScreenWrite

Developer: Jeremy Radlow
Cost: $5.00
Footprint: 16K

This HackMaster Hack enables you to write onscreen, and can be set to automati-cally capitalize characters drawn on the border between the text and numeric areas (see Figure 3-19).

TealEcho

Developer: TealPoint Software
Cost: $11.95
Footprint: 3K

TealEcho (see Figure 3-20) is the original of this group. It mirrors what you've writ-ten in the Graffiti area at the bottom of your Palm Organizer's screen.

Figure 3-19: ScreenWrite options

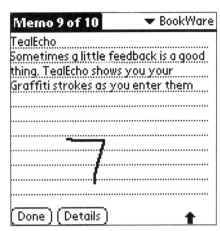

Figure 3-20: TealEcho

Characters

One feature that programmers have created to make entering capitalized characters faster is to further divide the Graffiti area, so that capitals are drawn automatically if you draw in the center area. Graspeedy and MiddleCaps (along with ScreenWrite in Figure 3-19) use this method. CaseToggle helps with text manipulation. CharHack and SymbolHack help you enter symbols and other extended characters.

Graspeedy

Developer: Daniel McCarty
Cost: $4.95
Footprint: 6K

As shown in Figure 3-21, Graspeedy is a HackMaster Hack that lets you configure exactly which part of the screen should be used for capitals. With this utility enabled, Graffiti capitalizes strokes made in the middle of the screen. It also helps with some of the characters that you may find yourself mixing up: B/D, C/E, G/O, and U/V.

MiddleCaps

Developer: Rui Oliveira
Cost: Freeware
Footprint: 7K

This HackMaster Hack (see Figure 3-22) takes a slightly different approach: you can specify that caps should be made if you start on or cross the text/numeric line.

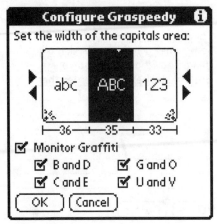

Figure 3-21: Graspeedy configuration

Figure 3-22: MiddleCaps Preferences

CaseToggle

Developer: Rui Oliveira
Cost: Freeware
Footprint: 4K

This elegant little freeware Hack (see Figure 3-23) enables you to change the case of selected text, and to tap to select words or sentences. If you like the idea of tap selecting, and want drag and drop, check out Synergy Solutions' Magic Text, which is covered in the Chapter 21.

CharHack

Developer: Harry Ohlsen
Cost: Freeware
Footprint: 3K (+5K for CharPanel)

Even after you finish reading this book, you may find it difficult to remember the correct Graffiti strokes for all of the extended symbols. CharHack (see Figure 3-24) includes CharPanel, which enables you to configure your most frequently used characters, and is designed to work in concert with SymbolHack, the next Hack described.

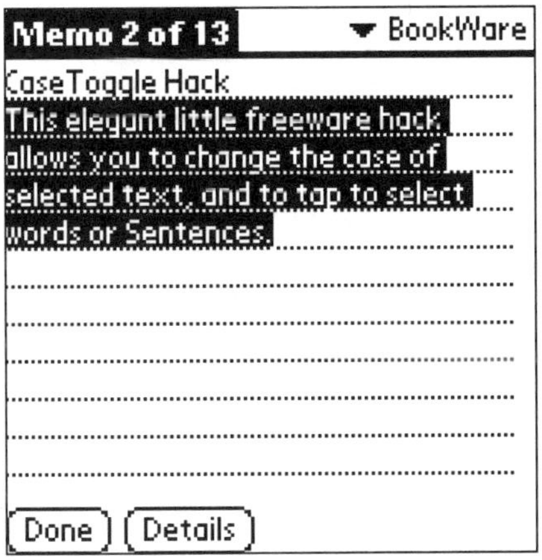

Figure 3-23: CaseToggle opening screen

Figure 3-24: CharHack

SymbolHack

Developer: Florent Pillet
Cost: $6.00
Footprint: 8K

No excuses if you can't find a symbol with SymbolHack (see Figure 3-25). This little Hack gives you access to all of Graffiti's extended characters.

TealScript

Developer: TealPoint Software
Cost: $16.95
Footprint: 86K (+11K for e-manual)

Have you found that you can't get Graffiti to recognize how you do a G or a V (or any other character you have trouble with)? Wish you could make it recognize the way you wrote? You can — TealScript is a powerful Hack that lets you reconfigure Graffiti by adding or changing strokes to make it recognize your style of writing. It does take some work — you need to train it to recognize your writing (see Figure 3-26), but the result can pay off.

Figure 3-25: SymbolHack

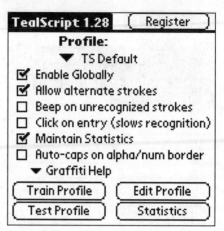

Figure 3-26: TealScript profile

FastPhrase

Developer: Asycs
Cost: $19.95
Footprint: 26K

FastPhrase (see Figure 3-27) takes a different approach — it watches the words you use, building a dictionary of commonly used words. After a few minutes use, it dramatically speeds your Graffiti entry by completing words for you.

Figure 3-27: FastPhrase

Graffiti Alternatives

If you find Graffiti lacking, or you wish you could enter text faster on your Palm Organizer, you may want to try one of these products, each of which supplants Graffiti with its own improvements. All of them still provide easy access to standard Graffiti to ease the transition. I recommend that you check out the demo versions and chose the one that suits your style. Those who still want to type should check out the keyboards covered in Chapter 23.

Fitaly

Developer: Textware Solutions
Cost: $25.00
Footprint: 78K

The pop-up keyboard used in your Palm Organizer is based on the QWERTY keyboard that was designed in the late 1800s. Textware Solutions designed a keyboard layout optimized for use with a stylus. The pop-up keyboard is the only floating dialog box I know of for the Palm Organizer (it moves up and down, depending on where you are entering text). Even better, you don't lose your regular keyboard — tap in the left-hand corner of the Graffiti area to open the Fitaly Keyboard (see Figure 3-28), and the right-hand corner to open the standard keyboard. The Fitaly keyboard can be loaded either as a standard application or as a HackMaster Hack.

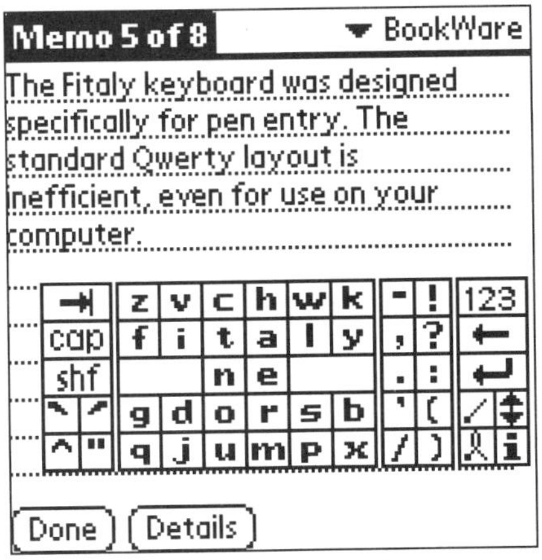

Figure 3-28: Fitaly keyboard

Jot

Developer: Communications Intelligence Corp.
Cost: $39.00
Footprint: 118K

Frustrated by learning Graffiti, which requires that you learn the exact stroke? Wish you could use the whole screen, and see what you are doing? Jot enables you to do all that, and more. This powerful application gives you as many as five alternates for each stroke, and most are more intuitive than Graffiti strokes. Use the built-in tutorial to learn, although you're not likely to need it more than once. At the top of the screen in Figure 3-29 is a down-facing triangle that divides the screen into areas for text and numeric characters. You enter characters on the border to create capitals and all your strokes are mirrored onscreen.

TapPad

Developer: Brochu Software
Cost: $19.95
Footprint: 41.7K

This wonderful little application has the distinction of being the last one added to the book; after trying the demo, I had to have it. The concept is simple: a clear plastic overlay gives you a new Graffiti area, with protection and a numeric keypad. There is a lot of additional functionality: copy, paste, undo, delete, pop-up menus, even the capability to recognize numeric Graffiti strokes. For $19.95 you get six overlay sheets (they attach using a temporary glue somewhat like that on a 3M PostIt Note) and a HackMaster Hack that does all the magic. This tool is good enough to be Graffiti version 2.0.

T9

Developer: Tegic Communications, Inc.
Cost: $29.95
Footprint: 179K

When I saw the first advertisements for this one, I couldn't imagine using a telephone keypad to type the alphabet. I though it would mean one tap for A, two taps for B, three taps for C, and so on. Was I wrong! This is one powerful application—Tegic has combined an extensive dictionary with an interface that is simplicity itself. As you enter characters, it compares them against its dictionary, forming the words you are typing (see Figure 3-30). It really is amazing! I found it difficult to fool because it provides choices that invariably include the word that you intended.

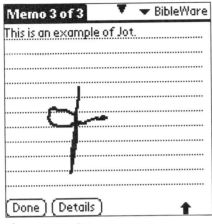

Figure 3-29: Jot

Figure 3-30: T9

Summary

The basic Graffiti alphabet is easy to learn: create large capital characters and learn a few simple exceptions, and you're done.

✦ Graffiti provides for more control than most people will ever learn. The Command and ShortCut strokes are worth learning because both will speed data entry. The Punctuation Shift and Extended Shift characters enable you access to almost any character you'd care to make.

✦ The CD-ROM includes some great enhancements to Graffiti, such as products that help you learn and improve on Graffiti. Other products on the CD-ROM offer onscreen mirroring, automatic capitals, instant access to extended characters, and a trainable Graffiti.

✦ The CD-ROM also includes demo versions of Graffiti replacements, each taking a different approach: keyboard, touchpad, and new alphabet.

✦   ✦   ✦

Using the Built-In Applications

In This Chapter

Interactive scheduling with the Date Book

Maintaining contacts with the Address Book

Staying organized with the To Do List

Using the Memo Pad

Learning high-efficiency command strokes

The simplicity of the Palm operating system is one of the things that makes it great. While other people use huge paper planners that require writing, erasing, and redoing of their work, you can have it all in your pocket, in your Palm Organizer. Many users will never need more than the basic applications that Palm, Inc. ships built in its organizers. This chapter is for those users.

Across the bottom of your Palm Organizer, as shown in Figure 4-1, are four round buttons. Pressing each turns it on and opens one of the primary applications—Date Book, Address Book, To Do List, or Memo Pad. This chapter takes a closer look at these applications and how to use these applications, along with some practical tips and tricks for using them more efficiently.

Figure 4-1: Primary Palm applications

Interactive Scheduling with the Date Book

Your Palm Organizer's Date Book is an interactive, electronic version of a desktop calendar. You can use it to make timed and untimed appointments, to set alarms and reminders to keep yourself aware of appointments and events, and to view your calendar in one of three views: by day, week, or month. The calendar is much more powerful than a first glance would lead you to believe—many users run their lives with it.

Accessing the Date Book

The easiest way to access the Date Book is to press the Date Book button. If your Palm Organizer is already running, you can also tap the Applications icon (see Figure 4-2), and then tap the Date Book icon.

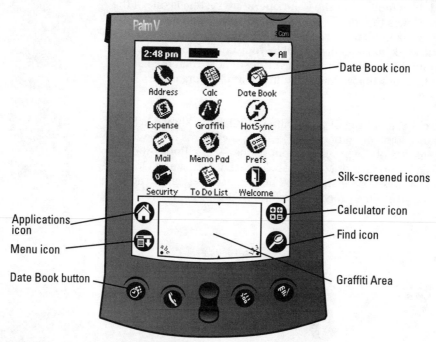

Figure 4-2: Opening the Date Book

Tip The four primary buttons across the bottom of your Palm Organizer serve multiple purposes. They all double as power on (but not power off) buttons; press one and your Palm Organizer turns on, displaying the chosen application. These buttons also cycle you through various displays in each of the applications. For example, pressing the Date Book button repeatedly cycles you through the day, week, and month views of your calendar.

Entering data into the Date Book

For your first appointment, tap to the right of one of the hours on the left-hand side of the Day View screen, and then use Graffiti (see Chapter 3) to write in the details. To set an appointment (see Figure 4-3) with a different start time or duration (the default is one hour), tap the New icon on the Day View screen to set the starting time.

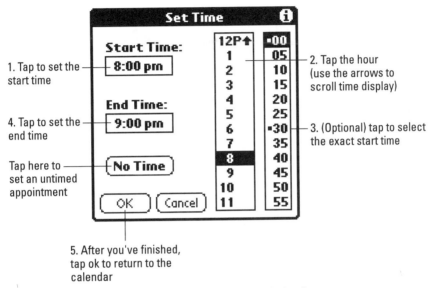

Figure 4-3: Set an event time using the Set Time dialog box.

Setting an appointment time

After tapping New in the Day View, you can create an untimed event (with no Start Time or End Time) by simply tapping OK in the Set Time dialog box. You will be returned to the Day View, with a blinking cursor shown next to a black-diamond (untimed) event indicator.

Alternatively, you can tap New and set the Start and End time in the Set Time dialog box by following four simple steps:

1. Tap any hour in the column to the right of the Start Time. If you can't see the hour you want, use the arrows at the top and bottom to scroll the time up and down.

2. If you want to be more exact, tap one of the five-minute intervals in the column to the far right.

3. If your appointment is longer or shorter than the one hour default, then tap in the End Time box and repeat Steps 1 and 2.

4. Once you've finished, tap OK to return to the Day View.

Tip

If you want to set your appointments to the minute, check out Pimlico Software's DateBk3. This great shareware program makes big demands in terms of RAM (it takes over 260K), but it delivers impressive new Date Book functionality, including a multiweek view.

If you tap the "i" in the upper right-hand corner of the Set Time dialog box, it will tell you the three other ways to access it:

1. **Tap the time next to an event.** If the time for your new appointment is among the hours displayed on the left side of the Day View screen, tapping directly on the hour simultaneously kicks off a new appointment, presets the Start Time for you, and leaves you in the Set Time dialog box where you can accept or change the default End Time displayed.

2. **Tap the time in the Event Details dialog box.** From the Day View, you can select an event, tap on Details, and tap in the Time box to call up the Set Time dialog box where you can edit the Start and End times for that event. You might take this route if you also have other things to change about the event, such as setting or removing an alarm.

3. **Enter the time using Graffiti.** When you're in the Day View, write a number in the Graffiti numbers area and it will open, defaulting to a one-hour appointment at the time you wrote it (this only works if an event isn't already selected). For example, to start a new appointment at 11:50, just write 115 and you'll be in the Set Time dialog box with 11:50 a.m. already entered as the Start Time. To start a new appointment at 1:15, write 0115.

Editing appointments

So, how do you change an appointment, such as that shown in Figure 4-4? First, use your stylus to tap an entry in your calendar; the hour will display in reverse text, and the cursor (a vertical line) will show in the entry.

31 Dec 00 ◀ M T W T F S S ▶

```
8:00
9:00
10:00
11:00
12:00
1:00
2:00 Sample Palm Computing Bible
     entry
3:00
4:00
5:00
```
⊞ (New) (Details) (Go to)

Figure 4-4: Editing an appointment

New Feature Those who are observant will see a fourth view (the icons in the lower-left hand corner of the screen). This new Agenda view was added with Palm OS 3.5, and shows both To Do and Date Book items in one convenient display.

Tap Details at the bottom of the screen to open the Event Details dialog box (Figure 4-5).

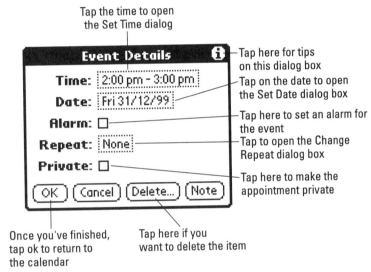

Figure 4-5: Event Details dialog box

You'll see this dialog box a lot; this is where you can change most of the settings for your appointments — change the time or date, add an alarm, make the event a recurring one, attach a note, or even delete the whole thing and start again. Let's have a look from top to bottom:

✦ Tapping in the Time box takes you to the Set Time dialog box (see Figure 4-3 earlier) where you can adjust the time of your appointment or change it to an untimed event, such as a birthday or anniversary.

✦ Tapping in the Date box takes you to the Set Date dialog box (see Figure 4-6). The month and day of the appointment display in reverse type; the current day has parentheses around it. Tap the day to which you'd like to move the appointment, or Today, and your appointment is rescheduled.

|| **Set Date** ||

Figure 4-6: Using the Set Date dialog box to schedule an appointment

✦ If you tap the Alarm box, you can set an alarm. The default alarm is five minutes; if you want to change it, highlight the number by dragging through it, and use Graffiti to change the duration to your choice. A pop-up list enables you to select minutes, hours, or days. Once you've set an alarm for an item, the item displays in the Day View with an alarm icon to the right of the event.

Tip Use Date Book's Preferences (tap on the Menu icon, then select Preferences from the Options Menu), then tap on the box to the left of Alarm Preset to have Date Book automatically set alarms for your new appointments, and select how far in advance of the appointment you would like to set the default alarm.

New Feature Palm OS 3.5, which shipped with the Palm IIIc and Palm IIIxe models, finally makes menus work as they should: You can tap the menu to access it (the menu icon still works, for those who have upgraded from an earlier OS).

✦ Tapping None to the right of Repeat opens the Change Repeat dialog box (see Figure 4-7). Here you can set daily, weekly, monthly, or yearly repeating events, and how long the events should last. Like alarmed items, repeating items display with a special icon in the Day View of your calendar.

✦ Tapping the Private box enables you to make an item private (see "Security" in Chapter 5 for more on private items).

✦ Tapping Note enables you to add notes or background information for your appointment.

Tip From the Day View, you can go straight to creation of a new note by simply tapping in the blank area where the Note icon will appear after the note is created.

Figure 4-7: Scheduling a recurring appointment

✦ Tap Delete to delete appointments (you will be offered the opportunity to save an archival copy on your computer).

✦ Use Cancel if you'd rather not make your editing changes; otherwise, tap OK to proceed.

Tip

If you want to set a recurring alarm as a reminder, but you don't want to see it in your Date Book, tap Private to make the record private, and then use the Security preferences to hide private records. The reminder won't display, but the alarm will still go off.

Day View

Now that we've looked at basics, let's delve a little deeper. The Date Book normally opens in the Day View. You can get back from the Week or Month view by tapping on the box with the single dot just above the silk-screened Applications icon. The Day View is where you'll spend most of your time (pun intended); it is the only screen from which you can enter or edit your appointments. Figure 4-8 shows some of the functionality Palm provides.

Figure 4-8 illustrates some of the functionality in the calendar's Day View. Starting from the lower left:

✦ Tapping New brings you to the Set Time dialog box (refer to Figure 4-3).

✦ You can either press the Date Book button or tap the icons above the Applications launcher to switch between day, week, and month views.

New Feature

Palm's OS 2 (which shipped with the PalmPilot) introduced the month view, which Pilot 1000/5000 owners did not have.

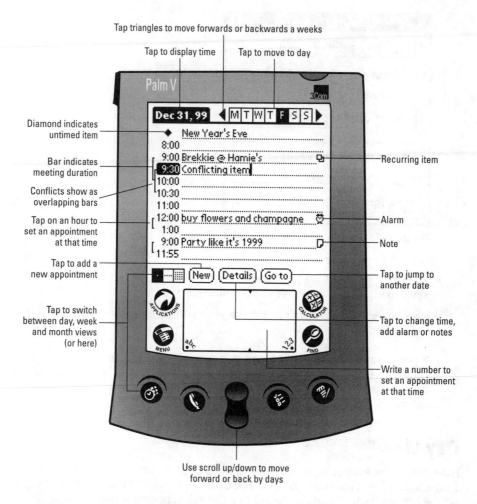

Figure 4-8: Date Book Day View

✦ Bars to the left of the time indicate the duration of your appointments; overlapping bars graphically illustrate conflicts.

✦ Untimed items are indicated with a diamond instead of time—these are great to remind you of birthdays, anniversaries, and other major events.

Tip   Untimed events actually have a time: 12:00 a.m. on the date of the event. If you want to be reminded the day before an untimed event, just set an alarm for 12 hours earlier and it will go off at noon.

✦ Tap the date in the upper left-hand corner to have your Palm Organizer display the time for a brief second.

✦ With the cursor (the edit bar |) in an appointment, tap the Details button to open the Event Details dialog box (refer to Figure 4-5).

✦ Tap the Go to button to jump to another date using the Go to Date dialog box (refer to Figure 4-6).

Onscreen icons give you instant access to your appointments' details, as shown in Table 4-1.

	Table 4-1 Calendar Day View Icons	
Icon	**Name**	**Description**
	Recurring Event	This icon indicates that this is a recurring event; tap on it to open the Event Details dialog box (see Figure 4-6) to review or change the settings.
	Alarm Set	This icon indicates that there is an alarm set for this appointment; tap it to open the Event Details dialog box (see Figure 4-6) to review or change the settings.
	Note Attached	This icon indicates that there is a note attached to an appointment; tap it to read or edit.

Now that you've gotten comfortable with the basics of the Day View, let's take a quick look at the week and month views.

From the day or month view, tap the second icon (with a row of 4 dots) above the silk-screened Applications icon to open the Week View. This view gives you a quick overview of your schedule, and, as you can see in Figure 4-9, a quick tap is all it takes to get details on any of your appointments.

Tip   You can get details about any event in the Week View by tapping the shaded area representing that event. If you want to jump to the Day View on a particular day, just tap on that day in any area *without* an appointment or tap the day letter or date number at the top. To move an appointment, just tap and hold (a bold highlight appears as in Figure 4-9), and then drag to another day or time in the week.

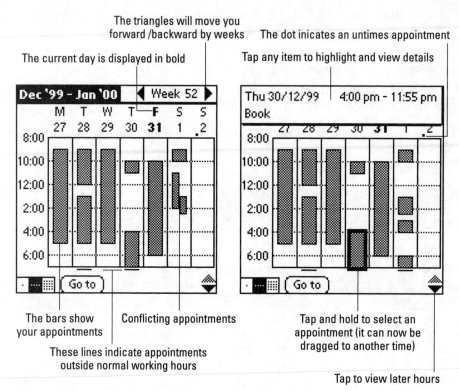

The current day is displayed in bold

The triangles will move you forward /backward by weeks

The dot inicates an untimes appointment

Tap any item to highlight and view details

The bars show your appointments

Conflicting appointments

Tap and hold to select an appointment (it can now be dragged to another time)

These lines indicate appointments outside normal working hours

Tap to view later hours

Figure 4-9: Showing details in the Week View

Month View

From the day or week view, tap the third icon (filled with 16 dots) above the silk-screened Applications icon to open the Month View. This view gives you a thumbnail overview of your month, with small dots showing you where your calendar is filled. Tapping a day opens the Day View for that date.

Tip

Just as you can move forward or backward a day at a time by pressing Scroll Up and Scroll Down in the Day View, you can also use the Scroll button to move forward or backward by weeks in the Week View or by months in the Month View.

Agenda View

Palm's new OS 3.5, which shipped with the Palm IIIc and IIIxe models, added another new Date Book View. Tapping on the fourth view icon (see Figure 4-4) gives you an Agenda view that combines To Do and Date Book Items on one screen, as shown in Figure 4-10.

Figure 4-10: The Agenda View in OS 3.5

Date Book menus

Tapping the Menu icon in the lower left-hand corner of the screen drops down the menus in any Palm Organizer application. Many of the Data Book's menu commands mirror functionality available by other means, but there are some commands here that you won't find elsewhere.

Record menu

The Record menu enables you to add or delete items or notes on your calendar, and to purge events gone by.

✦ **New Event** is the same as tapping the New button — it creates a new appointment.

✦ **Delete Event** deletes a selected appointment, without having to go through the Event Details dialog box.

✦ **Attach Note** enables you to attach a note to a selected appointment without opening the Event Details dialog box (see preceding tip).

✦ **Delete Note** enables you to delete notes attached to a selected appointment.

✦ **Purge** brings up a dialog box enabling you to purge records older than one week to one month. You can elect to archive deleted appointments on your computer.

✦ **Beam Event** is a new menu item that enables Palm III and higher users to beam appointments to each other.

Edit menu

The Edit menu uses cut, copy, and paste, which will look familiar to most Windows or Macintosh users. Just tap and drag to select a block of text, and then use these menu commands:

- **Undo** enables you to undo your last action.

- **Cut** enables you to cut a block of highlighted text, which can be pasted elsewhere.

- **Copy** enables you to copy a block of highlighted text for pasting elsewhere.

- **Paste** enables you to paste text previously copied.

- **Select all** selects all of the text in the selected record (the one your cursor is in at the time).

- **Keyboard** displays the keyboard (provided you have a record selected) for those symbols you can't quite remember.

- **Graffiti Help** displays Graffiti help screens (provided you have a record selected) so you'll know the stroke the next time.

Tip

Do you know how much faster you work when you use the keyboard equivalents for cut, copy, and paste on your computer? Well, the same is true for your Palm Organizer—learn the command strokes for these basics to save yourself a lot of time. Table 4-2, found at the end of this chapter, has a complete list of the command strokes used in the basic Palm Organizer applications.

Options menu

The Options menu in the Date Book, and in most other Palm Organizer applications, is where you'll find settings for the application, a cool tool (Phone Lookup), and information about the application and it's authors.

Font

This menu item enables those using Palm OS 3 to change the display size of their Date Book entries.

New Feature

Palm OS 3 first shipped with the Palm III, and later with a 2MB memory upgrade for the PalmPilot, and with Synapse's pager card. All the features of OS 3 are available in subsequent releases of Palm Organizers. PalmPilot users with OS 2 have multiple sizes in their Memo Pad, but are otherwise restricted to one font size.

New Features in Date Book Preferences

With the release of the Palm III in early 1998, Palm added three new features to this dialog box: Alarm Sound, Remind Me, and Play Every.

✦ **Alarm Sound** enables you to change the sound of the default alarm to Alert, Bird, Concerto, Phone, Sci-fi, or Wake up. If you find that you're having trouble hearing the default alarm, call up this dialog box and change it to something longer and more distinctive — such as the Concerto sound.

✦ **Remind Me** lets you change the number of times the alarm sounds in addition to the alarm that goes off at the scheduled time of the event.

✦ **Play Every** lets you set how many minutes pass between alarms.

Preferences

The preferences for the Date Book (shown in Figure 4-11) are pretty simple: you can set your normal working hours, and you can have your alarms default to your favorite settings. (For example, you might want to add a check mark to Alarm Preset so it always adds an alarm automatically when you create a new event.)

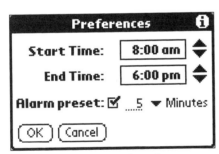

Figure 4-11: Date Book Preferences

If you set the Start Time and End Time so that a default day is longer than can be seen on one screen, then you have to scroll up and down to see it all. Remember that even if you change your default preferences in this dialog box, you can still set appointments outside your working day, or change alarm settings for individual events by selecting the event and tapping Details.

Display Options

The Date Book Display Options dialog box (shown in Figure 4-12) enables you to make settings for your day views.

Figure 4-12: Date Book Display Options

Show Time Bars enables you to turn on and off the time duration bars that show to the left of your appointments. Compress Day View automatically removes some times to show the complete day. Unchecked, it shows all blank and scheduled times, beginning with your start time. This one is easier to see than explain, so I used a little PhotoShop magic to create the screen shot in Figure 4-13—the left side is uncompressed, and the right is the same day compressed.

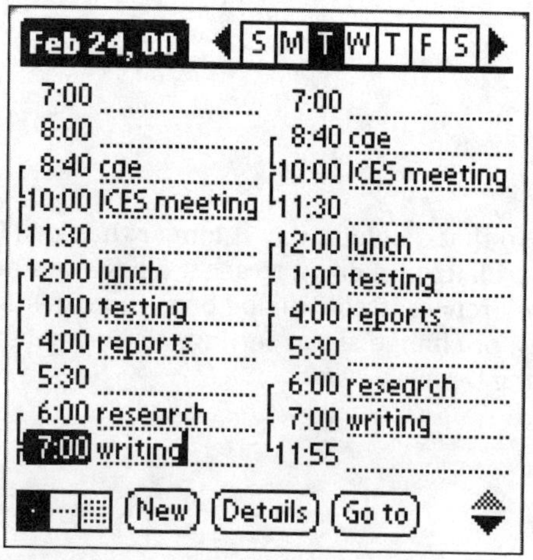

Figure 4-13: A day with and without compression

The Date Book Display Options, as follows, also enable you to make settings for Month Views (see Figure 4-14):

✦ **Show Timed Events** enables you to display or hide timed events in the Month View.

✦ **Show Untimed Events** enables you to display or hide untimed events in the Month View.

✦ **Show Daily Repeating Events** enables you to display or hide daily repeating events in the Month View.

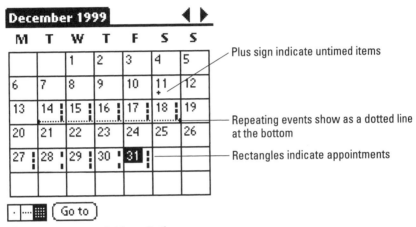

Figure 4-14: Month View Options

Phone Lookup

Remember the cool tool I mentioned? Well this is it: you can use this menu item to jump from the Date Book or the To Do List to the Address Book, look up a number, and have it pasted in your appointment or to do item. Just start your item ("Meet with . . ." or "Call . . ."), select this menu item to jump to your Address Book where you can look up the person you want, and then tap Add to have the name and number automatically added to your item. You'll end up with an entry similar to "Call Palm Accessories 800-881-7256 W" (the "W" indicates that this is a work number).

Tip   If the name of the person you're meeting is already entered in the item and you'd like simply to add the phone number to that entry, tap anywhere in the name before you use the Phone Lookup command. Then, when you use Phone Lookup, the phone number appears like magic at the end of the entry — that is, provided there's only one Address Book contact that matches. If the entered name has more than one match, you'll be switched to the Address Book view with the first matching contact highlighted. Pick the appropriate name (or accept the highlighted name) and tap Add.

Learn the Graffiti command stroke as a great timesaver. A simple diagonal stroke from lower left to upper right activates the command mode (see Figure 4-15). You then have a few seconds to do the second stroke (in this case an "L"). Don't forget to check out the table of basic command strokes at the end of this chapter.

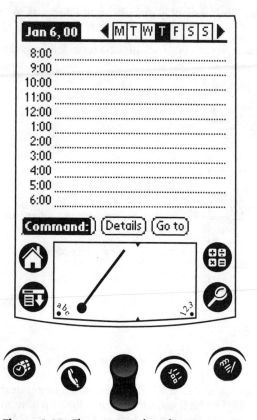

Figure 4-15: The command stroke

New Feature

Another new feature added with Palm's OS 3.5 is the command bar, which pops up when you execute the command stroke shown in Figure 4-15. This bar (see Figure 4-16) is context-sensitive, changing depending upon where you access it, and offers quick-access icons for commands such as copy, beam, and delete.

Figure 4-16: The command bar in OS 3.5

Maintaining Contacts with the Address Book

The Address Book is the main reason many of us bought a Palm Organizer — for pocket-sized access to all of our contacts. In many ways, the Palm Organizer is the perfect update to the "little black book" — it is fast, easy to use, and smaller than most books, including this one! The Address Book enables you to store and retrieve an incredible number of contacts — up to 2,500 on the PalmPilot Personal, up to 4,000 on the Professional, up to 6,000 on the Palm III, IIIe, V, and VII, and up to 10,000 on the Palm IIIx and Palm Vx. You can maintain your address list, complete with up to five phone numbers or e-mail addresses per contact, as well as notes on each individual, and categories (work, home, or whatever works for you) that enable you to filter out those you don't need at any given moment.

Note As of this writing both the Palm Desktop Organizer software and Chapura's PocketMirror (the conduit to Microsoft Outlook) have artificial limits of 10,000 contacts; so larger contact lists are not practical. Both Palm and Chapura will be resolving this issue, but most users will find that contact lists of that size are not practical on the Palm Organizer because of the length of time they take to HotSync.

Opening the Address Book

The easiest way to access the Address Book is to press its button (the one with a telephone icon). If your Palm Organizer is already running, you can also tap the Applications icon, and then tap the Address Book icon. Certainly, the most innovative way to open the Address Book is to use the Phone Lookup feature from within one of the other basic applications (see Phone Lookup in the previous section).

Adding a contact

The Address Book itself is easy to use—a quick look here, and you'll be on your way. To start, tap New from the Address List screen to get a new blank contact record. Last Name is displayed in reverse text, with the cursor ready for you to add your first contact. The shift indicator is on, which shows that the first letter you enter will be capitalized. Use Graffiti to enter a name, and tap the other fields to complete the screen (see Figure 4-17). The phone number fields are all selectable— tap the triangle to change any of them to one of eight categories:

✦ Work	✦ E-Mail
✦ Home	✦ Main
✦ Fax	✦ Pager
✦ Other	✦ Mobile

Figure 4-17: Contact screen top

Tip

There is no reason that you can't have multiples—so if, for example, you have two e-mail addresses for a contact, simply tap the down triangle for one of the other field names (Main, for example) and change it to display a second E-Mail field name.

Once you've finished with the first Address Edit screen, tap the lower of the two triangles just above the silk-screened Calculator to display the second screen of contact information (Figure 4-18). You can also use the scroll up and down buttons at the bottom center of your Palm Organizer to flip between these two screens.

Figure 4-18: Contact screen bottom

Tip

The Address Card icon to the right of Address Edit at the top of Figure 4-16 indicates that this is my personal contact information, and I have selected it to be the one that will beam to another Palm user when I tap on Beam Business Card. To do this yourself, tap on the Menu icon, and then select Select Business Card from the Record menu. If you're like me, you may want to use your Palm Organizer to store all sorts of personal information about yourself; if that is the case, create a simpler (and less private) version of your contact information that you use for beaming purposes.

Using the same technique as before, complete the address information and, if you like, select a category for the contact from the pop-up list in the upper right-hand corner of the screen. At this point, you can attach a Note, adjust Details, or tap Done to complete the contact. For now, just tap Done—we'll get to the Details screen in a minute.

Don't be concerned that it takes forever to enter each record because, if you're like most people, most of your Address Book records will be added on your computer and loaded on your Palm Organizer with a HotSync operation. See First Import later in this chapter for more on moving your information from your computer to the Palm.

New Feature

Palm OS 3.5 added the ability to duplicate contacts, which can be handy when you need to add contact information for more than one person from the same company.

Finding a contact

To find a contact, enter the last name of the contact whose information you need on the Address List screen (the one you get when you press the Address Book button). Each letter that you enter in the Graffiti area will display to the right of Look Up. This list will scroll up or down, refining the search as you enter letters. You'll probably need only to enter a few letters before the information you need appears onscreen.

Tip If you can't find the contact you just added, try entering the first few letters of the first name — just in case you've entered the contact backwards, reversing the positions of the first and last names.

After you've looked up one name, chances are you'll need to find another. Instead of selecting the "find" text, and then deleting it so that you can again use the search feature, try using the scroll button, which instantly clears the field. This is also an easy way to start over if you've entered the wrong characters in the Look Up field.

If you can't remember someone's name, you can always tap Find to search using whatever information you do remember. To speed up your search, make sure you're already in the Address Book before you tap Find. That way, instead of searching through all of the information on your Palm Organizer, you'll get matching entries from the Address Book first.

Cross-Reference For another way to search only the Address Book, check out FindHack, described in Chapter 22.

Editing contacts

After you've added a few contacts, you'll probably want to adjust their settings. This process is less intuitive than most on the Palm Organizer, because the Address List view is not editable (otherwise, you could accidentally change or delete information while looking for it). Figure 4-19 shows an Address List with some sample entries. Tap an entry in the listing to get the larger Address View screen, and from there you can tap Edit (or almost anywhere on the display) to call up the Address Edit screen.

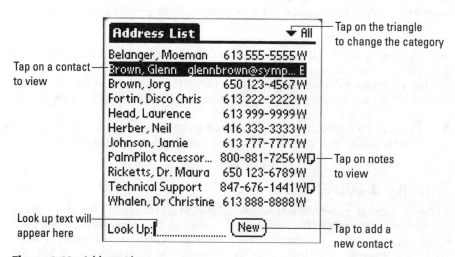

Figure 4-19: Address List

From the Address Edit screen, you can set the details for the entry or add a note (see Figure 4-20). Details are simple: Determine which telephone number you want shown in the main list, and which category you want assigned to the contact. You can also change the Category by tapping on it in the Edit screen.

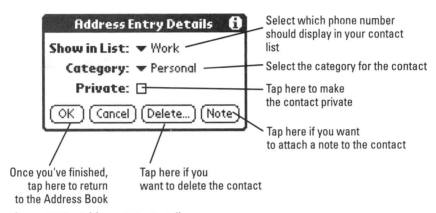

Select which phone number should display in your contact list

Select the category for the contact

Tap here to make the contact private

Tap here if you want to attach a note to the contact

Once you've finished, tap here to return to the Address Book

Tap here if you want to delete the contact

Figure 4-20: Address Entry Details

Tip

If you find that the telephone number you expect to see in the Address List view is superceded by another telephone number (Home number instead of Work, for example), check the Details dialog box to make sure that the Show in List designation for that record is correct.

Assigning contact categories

You can tag any or all of your contacts with up to 15 categories such as home, office, friend, family, or whatever you choose. Categories enable you to filter information, enabling you to quickly find what you need at the time. This functionality is also available in the To Do List and Memo Pad, although the categories are not shared. The lack of categories in the Date Book is one of the few shortcomings of the Palm OS.

If you tap the triangle next to All in the upper right-hand corner, the Categories menu pops down (see Figure 4-21). Selecting a category filters out other records, showing only the record that you've selected.

If you select Edit Categories at the bottom of the drop-down list, the dialog box shown in Figure 4-22 appears, where you can add, rename, or delete categories (the maximum number of categories is 15).

Figure 4-21: Categories list

Figure 4-22: Editing Categories

You can use the Address Book button to cycle through your categories — each tap changes the list, displaying a different category. The scroll up and down buttons at the bottom center of your Palm Organizer move the view of your list up and down.

 Tip   If you use one category more than another, then use the Preferences (under the Options menu) and tap Remember Last Category. That way, your Address Book will reopen in the same category you used the last time.

First import

One thing that many new users want to do is import their existing (computer-based) contact list into the Palm Organizer. Follow these steps to complete this relatively painless process:

1. Open your computer-based contact software, switch to the contact view or list, select Export from the File menu, and then select Export as tab-delimited. You may need to consult your software's manual for details.

2. Switch to the Address Book in the desktop (computer) version of your Palm Organizer software.

3. Select Import from the File menu, and choose the file you exported in Step 1. Change Files of type to Tab Separated values (*.tab, *tsv, or *.txt).

4. The next screen displayed is Specify Import Fields (see Figure 4-23); start by dragging the left-hand Palm Organizer fields up and down until they match as closely as possible your data fields on the right. Use the triangles to the left and right of Scan Records to move through your contact data. Remember that if you don't have information for one of the Palm Organizer fields, you can turn it off by unchecking it.

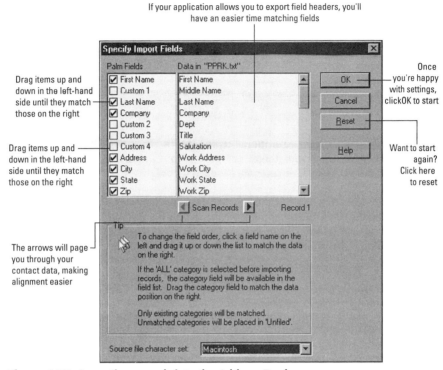

If your application allows you to export field headers, you'll have an easier time matching fields

Drag items up and down in the left-hand side until they match those on the right

Drag items up and down in the left-hand side until they match those on the right

Once you're happy with settings, click OK to start

Want to start again? Click here to reset

The arrows will page you through your contact data, making alignment easier

Figure 4-23: Importing records into the Address Book

5. Click OK when you're ready to import your contact data into your Palm Organizer Desktop.

6. Now that you have your address information in the computer application, there's only one step left — perform a HotSync operation to copy your contact list into your Palm Organizer (see Chapter 6 for more on HotSyncing).

If you're not happy with your first import, don't worry — you can start over. Just select the first record in your Palm Desktop Address Book, press Shift, scroll down, and select the last record. This selects all records; all you need to do is press Delete to blank your address book and start again. If you do this, pay careful attention to the Palm Organizer address fields when you configure the export from your old software. The default order (on your Palm Organizer) is:

✦ Last Name	✦ Work
✦ First Name	✦ Home
✦ Title	✦ Fax
✦ Company	✦ Other

✦ E-Mail   ✦ Custom 1

✦ Address   ✦ Custom 2

✦ City   ✦ Custom 3

✦ State   ✦ Custom 4

✦ Zip   ✦ Note

✦ Country   ✦ Private

Tip

If you later want to import records into a particular category, use the Category Filter to select your target category before importing; otherwise, you'll have to manually assign the category for each record.

Cross-Reference

See Chapters 9 (Windows) and 10 (Macintosh) for more on your Palm Organizer's Desktop applications, and Chapter 6 information on products that enable you to synchronize your Palm Organizer with third-party PIMs (personal information managers).

Menus

There are three menus available in the Address Book—a Record menu for Palm III users, an Edit menu identical to that in the Date Book, and the Options menu.

New Feature

The Palm III was the first Palm Organizer to ship with an infrared port. For owners of earlier devices, Palm also sold a 2MB upgrade kit that included an infrared port and software to enable infrared beaming of data.

Record menu

This menu has two items: Beam Category and Beam Business Card. These options enable users to beam an Address Book category (for example, their office phone numbers) or their business card to another user. To select your information as the business card to beam:

✦ Open your address information by tapping it in the Address Book list (or tap New if you need to create one).

✦ Tap the menu icon, and then tap Select Business Card.

✦ Select Yes in the dialog box to confirm your choice. You'll see a card icon at the top of the screen which indicates this is the record selected as your business card (see Figures 4-17 and 4-18).

Options menu

The Options menu enables you to customize the Address Book by setting your Preferences and adding your own Custom Fields.

Font

This new menu item enables those using Palm OS 3 or greater to change the display size of their Date Book entries.

Preferences

Preferences in the Address Book are somewhat spartan: you can select whether or not your Address Book should reopen in the last category you used, and you can have it sort by Last Name, First Name or Company, Last Name.

Rename Custom Fields

This menu option (see Figure 4-24) enables you to rename four of the fields, and can be truly useful. I've shown a few simple examples, but I know that you'll come up with ones more meaningful to you.

Figure 4-24: Rename Custom Fields

Staying Organized with the To Do List

This application is my personal favorite. I think keeping lists is hereditary—I get my tendency to write lists from my Mom—not that that's a bad thing. The To Do List enables you to do just about everything you can think of with your to dos: create, categorize, prioritize, sort, assign due dates, even procrastinate! Maintenance is easy, too—you can check off items and have them disappear from the screen, reassign an item until another day, change its category, or even delete it.

Opening the To Do List

The easiest way to access the To Do List is to press its button (the button with a checklist icon). If your Palm Organizer is already running, you can also tap the Applications icon, and then tap the To Do List icon.

Adding To Do items

There's a lot under the hood on this screen—almost everything can be tapped, changed or modified to the way you'd like it. To enter a new to do item, just tap New. As Figure 4-25 shows, a blank item with the cursor (|) at the beginning of the item and the caps indicator on (the first letter you write will be capitalized) appears. Use Graffiti or the pop-up keyboard to write your item, and you're done!

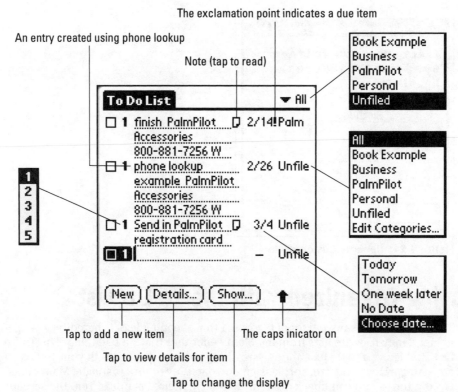

Figure 4-25: Adding a To Do item

If you want to create a new To Do item quickly, with the same settings as an existing item, just tap that item to select it, and then tap New to create a new item with the same priority, due date, and category.

Tip If you tap New and then decide that you don't really want to add a new To Do item, just tap elsewhere on the screen, and the Palm OS erases the blank item for you.

Editing To Do items

If you want to make changes, it's pretty easy — tap the number to the left of the item to change it's priority, and tap the date or category to open change pop-up lists. Tap a record to select it, and then tap Details to open the To Do Item Details dialog box (Figure 4-26), where you can delete an item, make it private, or attach a note. This dialog box also brings together some of the screen functionality, enabling you to change an item's priority by selecting the number, and to change its category or due date by making a selection from the lists that pop down from the triangles next to each item.

Figure 4-26: To Do Items Details

Tip You must have a record selected before you tap either Details or Show on the To Do List screen; otherwise, the message "You must have a record selected . . ." appears. You can tell when you have a record selected, it's priority number is displayed in reverse (black on white) colors, and the cursor (the |) is somewhere in the record.

The Show button is one you may find yourself using a lot. It shows the Preferences for the To Do screen. Figure 4-27 illustrates how I usually have my To Do Preferences configured — I leave the bottom three on because I want the detail, I leave completed items hidden, and I normally only display due items. This lets me focus on what I need to do at the time, confident that my Palm Organizer will later remind me of the tasks I have assigned myself. Lastly, I prefer to have due items sorted by priority.

Tip This is how I set my preferences. However, with these settings, if you accidentally check off an item as done, or if you change the date of an item by mistake, you'll need to revert the top two settings in Figure 4-24 in order to find them.

Figure 4-27: To Do Preferences

One of the great things about an electronic to do list is the ability to automatically procrastinate. If you find yourself moving items forward because you haven't completed them, take a look at Brad Goodman's shareware utility Plonk!, which can automatically move uncompleted to do items forward.

Assigning categories To Do items

As with the Address Book, you can tag any or all of your to do items with a category. These don't necessarily have to be the same as those you've assigned in your Address Book or Memo Pad, although you'll find it less confusing if most of your categories are common. Categories enable you to filter information, helping you quickly find what you need at the time.

Tip   You can use the To Do button to cycle through the categories that have active to do items; use the scroll up and down buttons to look up and down your list.

Tip   If you run out of categories (the limit is 15), and want to combine two, the quickest way is to rename one of the categories the same as the second, your Palm Organizer will do the rest of the work.

Menus

The menus in the To Do list are very similar to those in the Date Book:

✦ **Record** menu enables you to delete an item, attach or delete notes, or purge old items. OS 3 users will also find Beam Item and Beam Category here. One surprising omission is the lack of a new item; you need to use the New button. (Palm explains this by noting it's analogous to keeping your stapler on the desk and your staple remover in a desk drawer.)

Tip

If your Show preference is set to hide completed items, they can stack up over time without your realizing it. It's therefore a good idea to purge your completed items from time to time to free up memory. If you're concerned about losing important information, tap Save archive copy on PC, and a copy of the purged information will be saved for you on your computer.

✦ **Edit** menu is identical to that in the Date Book, with cut/copy/paste, along with access to the Keyboard and Graffiti Help.

✦ **Options** menu, for unexplained reasons, does not include Preferences (tap Show to get these), but it does include Phone Lookup, which is even handier here than it is in the Date Book, and Font.

Using the Memo Pad

Not much here, right? Wrong! Your Palm Organizer's easy synchronization with the desktop makes the Memo Pad a powerful tool for carrying important information in your pocket. Here are a few of the many notes I have on my Palm Organizer *now*:

✦ A few jokes that I particularly like

✦ A couple of great recipes

✦ A number of household sizes (room dimensions and so on) that I use when shopping (how many times have you looked at something, and then wondered if it would fit?)

✦ Coming soon (things I'm expecting in the mail)

✦ I store passwords in a memo, categorized as "Private," which I then hide using Palm's security feature (see Chapter 5). I use the same category to store credit card and other vital information.

✦ Meeting notes from a conference we had at the office (I was able to synchronize and then e-mail copies to participants five minutes after the meeting)

✦ My daily exercise routine

✦ Notes to explain how to use Toast to master a CD-ROM (which I used to create the CD-ROM with the book)

✦ Price comparisons (this is one I use all the time when shopping; what's the best price/features, and so on at one place versus another)

✦ Serial numbers (This is handy: Keep your computer programs' serial numbers on your Palm Organizer — if you only keep them on your computer, how will you access them if you need to re-register? I now do the same for my Palm applications, so the serial numbers are available when I reinstall them.)

✦ Some common Spanish phrases (dos cervezas por favor; eso es el mejor de los libros de PalmPilot)

✦ The bus schedule from downtown to home for the hours between five and seven

✦ The rules for Contract Rummy

Tip There are unlimited possibilities with your Palm Organizer's Memo Pad. Want to read a memo on the ride home? Copy it from your computer's word processor, and paste it in the Palm Organizer desktop application's Memo Pad. The memo will appear on your Palm Organizer with the next sync!

Opening the Memo Pad

The easiest way to access the Memo Pad is to press its button (it has a pencil and pad icon). If your Palm Organizer is already running, you can also tap the Applications icon and then tap the Memo Pad icon.

Entering a memo

Adding a new memo item is easy. From the Memo Pad screen, tap New to get a new memo (Figure 4-28). A few simple controls here: as with the other basic apps, you can set and view by categories, and you can change the font size of the display (OS 3 users change the font size using the Options menu; OS 1 and 2 users should tap the Font size selector between the Done and Details buttons). Tapping Details opens the Memo Details dialog box, where you can also set the category, make an item private, or delete it.

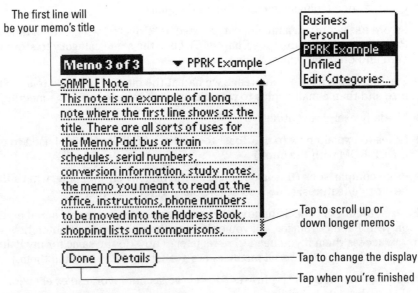

Figure 4-28: Creating a new memo

Tip The first line of your memo becomes its title in the Memo Pad list.

Editing memos

Editing a memo item is simplicity itself — just tap an item in the Memo List, and you'll get the memo. If you want to delete a block of text, tap and drag to select it, and then do a Graffiti backspace to delete it. To add information, tap to place the cursor where you want text entered and write away. You can use the up and down scroll buttons on your Palm Organizer (as well as the onscreen scroll arrows) to view memos larger than a single screen.

One of the best places to edit menus is on your PC — copy memos or other information you want as a memo on your Palm Organizer from your word processor on your computer, and paste them in Palm's Desktop software. Once you've HotSynced, the information will be in both places! Palm 3 and higher users can also use the new File Linking command to have this type of information automatically update. See Chapter 5 for more on Palm's Desktop Software.

Assigning Memo categories

As with the Address Book and To Do list, you can tag any or all of your memos with a category. Categories enable you to filter information, which helps you quickly find what you need at the time.

 Tip In the Memo list view, you can use Memo Pad button to cycle through the categories that have active memos; the scroll buttons will scroll any category lists that exceed the size of your Palm Organizer's screen.

Menus

There are actually two sets of menus for the Memo Pad. The first is accessible from the Memo list view, and enables you to beam a category, change the font, read the About Memo Pad screen, and change between manual and alphabetic sort of your memo list.

 Tip In Memo Preferences, if you change the memo list Sort from Alphabetic to Manual, you get a new, often overlooked feature: you can drag-and-drop individual memo titles from one location in the list to another.

Opening a memo enables many more choices in the Menu options. The Record and Edit menus are similar to those you already know. The Options menu gives commands to change the font, jump to the bottom or top of a large memo, display the About Memo Pad screen, and run the Phone Lookup feature.

Learning High-Efficiency Command Strokes

The command stroke gives you access to shortcuts that can be seen as the equivalent of keyboard shortcuts on a PC. Begin with a diagonal stroke from lower left to upper right (you may want to look again at Figure 4-15); the word Command will appear above the silk-screened Applications button and you have about two seconds to complete the command. Table 4-2 shows the command strokes for the basic applications covered in this chapter. Once learned, these commands can dramatically speed your use of the Palm Organizer, especially when you realize how many are standard from application to application.

Table 4-2 Basic Application Command Keys						
Menu	**Key**	**DB**	**AB**	**TD**	**MP**	**Action**
Record	N	✓			✓	New Event ⇨ Memo
	D	✓		✓	✓	Delete Event ⇨ Item
	A	✓		✓		Attach Note
	T		✓			Duplicate Address (3.5)
	O	✓		✓		Delete Note
	E	✓		✓		Purge
	B	✓		✓	✓	Beam Event ⇨ Item ⇨ Memo
			✓	✓	✓	Beam Category
			✓			Beam Business Card
			✓			Select Business Card
Edit	U	✓	✓	✓	✓	Undo
	X	✓	✓	✓	✓	Cut
	C	✓	✓	✓	✓	Copy
	P	✓	✓	✓	✓	Paste
	S	✓	✓	✓	✓	Select All
	K	✓	✓	✓	✓	Keyboard
	G	✓	✓	✓	✓	Graffiti Help
Options	F	✓	✓	✓	✓	Font
	R	✓	✓		✓	Preferences
	Y	✓	✓			Display Options
	L	✓		✓	✓	Phone Lookup
	F		✓			Rename Custom Fields
					✓	Go to Top of Page
					✓	Go to Bottom of Page
		✓	✓	✓	✓	About

A few notes: AB (Address Book), DB (Date Book), TD (To Do List), and MP (Memo Pad) are the columns. Palm OS 1 and 2 users do not have beaming or fonts. Palm OS 3.5 added the ability to duplicate Address Book entries.

Summary

You can take advantage of your Palm Organizer's Date Book, Address Book, To Do List, and Memo Pad to keep your life meticulously organized.

✦ You can start up your Palm Organizer in one of the four basic applications — Date Book, Address Book, To Do List, or Memo Pad — by pressing the appropriate button at the bottom of your Palm Organizer; pressing the button again cycles you through different views of your data.

✦ You can speed up your use of the Palm Organizer by learning and using the command strokes, in the same fashion as you learn the command keys equivalents in applications on your computer.

✦   ✦   ✦

Examining the Palm Utility Suite

In This Chapter

Managing your Palm Organizer with utilities

Tracking your money with Expense

You've got e-mail

Now we're ready to look at the balance of your Palm Organizer's software: utilities. This chapter teaches you to use the Application Launcher and the Calculator and to customize your Palm Organizer with Preference and Security settings so that it works the way you want it to. We also look at the Expense Application and Mail.

Managing Your Palm Handheld with Utilities

What kind of toy would the Palm handheld be without utilities? You will find utilities to load and manage applications, a Find capability, and settings for the Palm and Security. Windows users with Palm OS 2.0 or greater also get Expense and Mail capabilities; Macintosh users can add these capabilities with third-party products (see Chapters 13 and 16).

Graffiti Tips

 If you read Chapter 3, then you are probably already a Graffiti expert. If you want a quick review, try the Graffiti Tips application (shown in Figure 5-1) as a quick refresher.

New Feature Welcome and Giraffe are two new applications that Palm added to OS 3.1 for Palm IIIx and Palm V users. Tapping Welcome reruns the startup procedure discussed in Chapter 2. Tapping Giraffe opens a series of tips to help you get started using Palm's handwriting system.

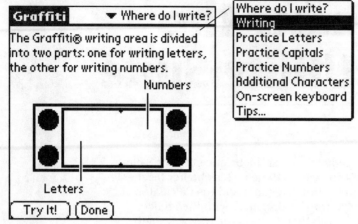

Figure 5-1: The Graffiti Tips application

Launcher

The Application Launcher (see Figure 5-2) and the silk-screened area below it are the basis for moving from application to application on your Palm Organizer. Tap the Applications icon in the silk-screened area on the bottom of your Palm Organizer's screen to access the Application Launcher from any application, and then tap an icon to access that application. If there are more applications than fit on the screen, a scroll bar appears so that you can move your view up and down.

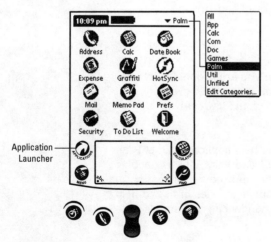

Figure 5-2: The Application Launcher

New Feature Palm Organizers that use OS 2 have a simplified Application Launcher; it doesn't have the pop-up categories list. Palm integrated the capability to delete applications in Launcher with OS 3; users of earlier Palm Organizers used a Memory Application.

Tip Want quick access to the time? Just tap the Application Launcher; the time displays in the upper left corner (OS 2 users will find it at the bottom of their screens). In the Date Book, tap the date in the same location and it changes to display the time.

The new Application Launcher makes it easier to get at all the applications that you load on your Palm Organizer. Tap the Menu icon in the Launcher, and we'll look at the new features by taking a quick tour of the menus.

App menu

The App menu adds some utility features to the Launcher, such as deleting, beaming, categorizing, or getting information on any of the applications installed on your Palm Organizer.

Delete

Deleting an application is simple — select Delete from the App Menu to get a list of installed applications, tap the one you want to delete, tap Yes in the confirmation dialog box, and you're done. For those using Palm OS 2.0, the process is similar using the Memory Application.

Beam

Want to send a shareware application to a friend with a Palm Organizer? It's easy, just select Beam from the App Menu to get a list of installed applications, tap the application to send, and tap Beam (see Figure 5-3). As long as you are within range, (between 4 and 36 inches), your friend will be asked to confirm, and infrared transfer will begin. Wait until you see the file transfer complete dialog box, and you're finished.

```
┌─────────────────────────────┐
│        Beam            (i)   │
├─────────────────────────────┤
│ Act Names        ☻142K  ▲   │
│ Address          ☻  2K      │
│ ATool!              16K      │
│ BrainForest         73K      │
│ Bubblet             21K      │
│ Clock               31K      │
│ Date Book        ☻  1K      │
│ Datebk3            262K      │
│ Expense          ☻  1K      │
│ finCALC             52K  ▼   │
│ ┌──────┐ ┌──────┐           │
│ │ Done │ │ Beam │           │
│ └──────┘ └──────┘           │
└─────────────────────────────┘
```

Figure 5-3: Beaming an application

Note The lock icons in Figure 5-3 indicate that you cannot beam those applications. As you can see, some (but not all) third-party applications are locked to prevent you from beaming them. Remember that you cannot legitimately beam or copy a commercial or registered shareware application to a friend.

Category

The Category feature added in Palm OS 3.0 mimics that found in third-party applications such as Launch'Em, PAL, and QuickLaunch (see Chapter 20), enabling you to create categories of applications. Select Edit Categories from the Categories pop-up list to tailor the Categories to your liking (see Figure 5-4), and then select Categories from the App Menu. You can assign each of your applications to your new categories. These are the categories I use: Applications, Calculators, Communications, Documents, Games, Palm, and Utilities. I find that flipping to another screen with applications of the type that I am looking for is easier than scrolling up and down a long list. I also prefer to keep the standard applications shipped by Palm on a self-named screen.

Figure 5-4: Edit Categories dialog box

Tip Want a quick way to call an application icon into view when your category is set to All? Simply write the Graffiti letter that corresponds to the first letter of the application's title. Instantly, all the icons whose titles start with that letter are displayed.

Cross-Reference If you want more features in an Application Launcher, especially if you are using OS 1.0 or 2.0, be sure to check out the Application Launchers in Chapter 20.

Tip As with the main application buttons, tapping the Application icon will cycle through your application categories.

Info

The Info screen is surprisingly handy. Want to know how many address book entries you have or how much precious RAM that new game is taking up in your Palm Organizer? The Info screen (see Figure 5-5) displays the size in kilobytes of each of your installed applications. Tap Version to see the version number for each installed application, and then tap Records to see how many records are stored for each application.

Figure 5-5: Application Version view

 New Feature Palm OS 3 added version information. Users of OS 2 need to use their Memory application (see Figure 5-6) to view the size and number of records they have installedz in their Palm Organizers.

Figure 5-6: OS 2's Memory application

Options menu

You won't find much that's new here. Preferences enables you to have Applications automatically open to the last category you used (otherwise, it opens All), and you can view your applications in a more compact list view. The list view (see Figure 5-7) can be handy if you want to squeeze all of your most-used applications onto one screen.

Figure 5-7: The Application List view

Calculator

The Calculator is pretty basic, but a few gems hide in the menus. The Edit menu reveals support for cut and paste, and the Options menu enables you to display Recent Calculations (see Figure 5-8), giving you the electronic equivalent of the tape in an adding machine.

Recent Calculations	
23.	=
124.	=
124.	/
-89.	+/-
-89.	=
-1.3932584	=
-1.3932584	*
5.	=
-6.9662921	=

OK

Figure 5-8: Recent Calculations

Find

The Find icon in the lower-left corner of the screen will search all of the databases in your Palm Organizer for whatever you'd like to find. This is handy when you remember someone's first, but not last, name. The power of the Find command is also its downfall: Because it searches all databases, it can find corrupted records that may crash your Palm Organizer. The cure is usually to reset your Palm Organizer. For more on Troubleshooting, see Chapter 24.

 Cross-Reference FindHack is a great utility. It enables wildcard searching and has the capability to limit which databases are searched. You'll find more information on FindHack in Chapter 22.

HotSync

For the most part HotSyncing is automatic. Unfortunately, this is where most reported problems occur (see Chapter 24 for help). The HotSync application on your Palm Organizer enables you to view the log of your last HotSync and enter a telephone number for HotSyncing with a modem. The HotSync Options Menu is where you specify which components should be synced, and where you set up your modem for remote HotSyncing. OS 3.1 (or greater) users also use these settings for Network HotSyncing.

It only takes a second for HotSync to determine that a third-party application on your Palm Organizer and that same application on your desktop are already in sync and don't need to be resynchronized.

Preferences

Tapping Preferences brings you to General Preferences, where you can tweak the performance of your Palm Organizer to your liking. The pop-up list in the upper right corner of the screen takes you to one of eight areas: Buttons, Digitizer, Formats, General, Modem, Network, Owner, or ShortCuts.

Buttons

Here's a useful feature—you can reassign all of your Palm Organizer's Buttons, including the HotSync button (see Figure 5-9). Tapping any one of the icons on this (and the HotSync screen) will give you a pop-up list of all of the applications on your Palm Organizer. Select the button that you want to reconfigure, select the new application, and you're done. One obvious use for this feature is to reassign the calculator button when using a third-party product (see Chapter 13), but you can invent lots of other uses, too (who needs the Memo Pad button when it can launch a game instead?).

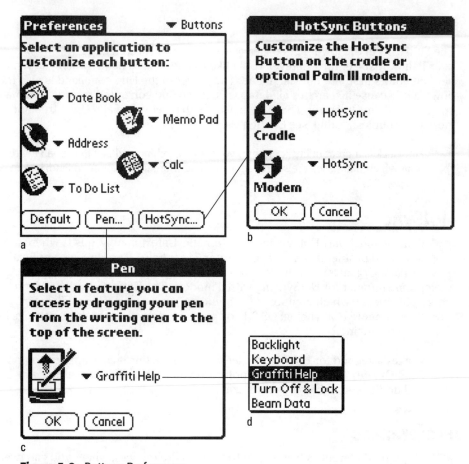

Figure 5-9: Buttons Preferences

I've made a few changes on my Palm Vx. I've reassigned the Date Book button to call up Pocket Journal, and the To Do button to open Action Names. I've also changed the silk-screened icons (using the applications themselves) so that the Applications button calls Launch'Em, the Calculator button calls SynCalc, and the Find button uses FindHack. I've even used Contrast Button Hack to remap the Contrast Button to open Cesium. You can learn more about these applications in Chapters 13, 21, and 22.

Tip   If you reassign your buttons, you can still launch the original applications — just use the Applications Launcher.

Tapping Pen enables you to configure a special stroke (a drag from the Graffiti area to the top of your screen) to:

- ✦ Turn on the backlight
- ✦ Display Graffiti help
- ✦ Beam data (OS 3.0 or greater users only)
- ✦ Display the Graffiti keyboard
- ✦ Turn off and lock your Palm Organizer

Digitizer

The Digitizer realigns the software that keeps track of where your stylus is onscreen. If you find yourself tapping without result, it may be time to redigitize your Palm Organizer (this process is covered in greater detail in Chapter 24).

Formats

Here's a screen you'll set once and then forget. Format Preferences (Figure 5-10) enables you to specify your country and your choice of formats for time, date, and numbers. This is also where you tell your Palm Organizer whether you want your calendar week to start on Sunday or Monday.

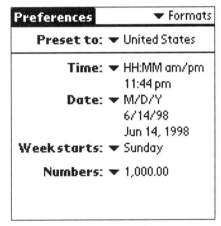

Figure 5-10: Formats Preferences

General

Here's another screen you're not likely to change often. As discussed in Chapter 2, the General Preferences screen (see Figure 5-11) is where you set your Palm Organizer's time and date, how long it stays on before auto-shutoff, levels for system, alarm, and game sounds, and whether you want to be able to receive beams from another user. Palm V users also get to select whether they want their Palm V to stay on while it's recharging in the cradle.

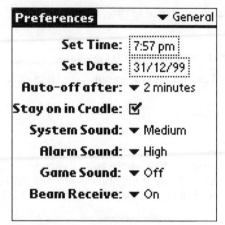

Figure 5-11: General Preferences

Tip

My auto-off is set to one minute to preserve my batteries, and my sound settings are system low, alarms high, and games off. Without system sounds, you don't hear the "up" chime that signifies that start of a HotSync—which makes at least a low setting essential for me. Some Palm Organizer games use system sounds, so turning their sound off here may have no affect.

Modem

If you have a modem for your Palm Organizer, you first need to set the Modem Preferences. As always, the triangles indicate pop-up lists, as shown in Figure 5-12.

The default settings for the 3Com Palm Organizer modem are as follows:

✦ **Modem:** Palm Organizer US/Canada (U.K. users should select the MegaHertz modem). If you have a Palm V, the default setting is Palm V Modem.

✦ **Speed:** 57,600 bps

✦ **Speaker:** Low

✦ **Flow Control:** Automatic

✦ **Country (Palm V only):** United States

✦ **String:** AT&FX4

Check your manual for the appropriate settings for your modem.

Tip

To get to the Modem Preferences screen you can select Modem from the Preferences pop-up list, or you can open it from the HotSync screen—OS 2.0 users tap the Modem Setup button and OS 3.0 users use Modem Setup in the HotSync Options menu.

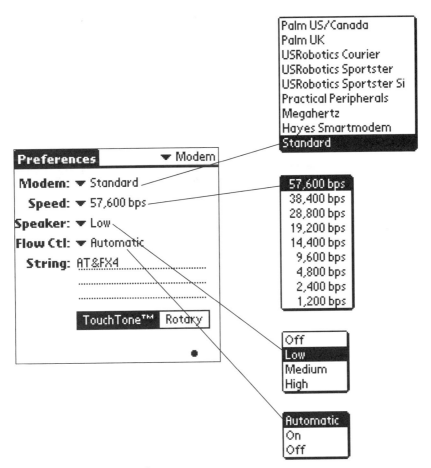

Figure 5-12: Modem Preferences

Network

If you plan to use your Palm Organizer to get e-mail, do a remote HotSync, or browse the Internet, you first have to set up your Network Preferences (see Figure 5-13), which is fairly easy to do:

✦ Select your Network from the Service pop-up list.

✦ Enter your User Name on the service.

✦ Tap -Prompt- to enter your password.

✦ Tap the phone area to enter the service number, to specify a dial prefix (such as 8 or 9 to get out of an exchange), to disable call waiting (I use *70), and to specify your calling card number.

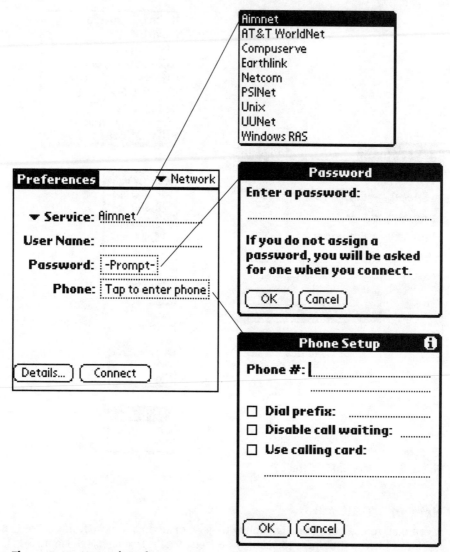

Figure 5-13: Network Preferences

Tapping Details enables you to set your connection type, idle timeout, DNS Query, and Automatic IP addressing. Script makes it easy to set up your login script.

Owner

If you haven't entered your name and address in Owner Preferences yet, put this book down and do so now — it may mean you get your Palm Organizer back if you lose it. I include my name, address, phone number, and e-mail address, along with the message "A REWARD IS OFFERED FOR THE RETURN OF THIS DEVICE."

Shortcuts

The ShortCut Graffiti stroke is best described as a lowercase cursive letter
"l." Try this:

✦ Open a new To Do item.

✦ Make the shortcut key (it shows onscreen if you do it right).

✦ Enter the letters **d**, **t**, and **s**.

✦ As soon as you finish the **s**, the current date and time replace your text!

Date/Time Stamp, or "dts," is just one of the built-in shortcuts. See the Preferences
screen for other built-in shortcuts.

ShortCuts Preferences (see Figure 5-14) enable you to create your own abbrevia-
tions — simple ideas include rc (return call from), gtb (groceries to buy), and your
initials (your name and address). See Chapter 3 for more on ShortCuts.

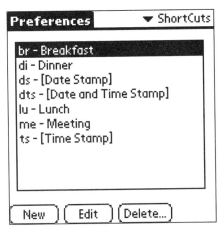

Figure 5-14: ShortCuts Preferences

Tip   Want to impress your Palm Organizer friends with your Graffiti skills? Make a "qbf"
ShortCut that expands to "The quick brown fox . . . ," and then offer to show off
your speed!

Security

If you're worried about someone being able to read private or personal
information on your Palm Organizer, you can make any Calendar, Address
Book, To Do, or Memo item private using each application's Details button.
Once you've assigned a password, you can use the Security Preferences
screen (see Figure 5-15) to show or hide private records, to change your
password, or to turn off and lock your Pilot.

Figure 5-15: Security Preferences

 If you forget your password, you can use the Forgotten Password button, but it will erase your private records.

Tracking Your Money with Expense

The Expense Application is a simple utility for expense tracking. One of its biggest limitations is that it doesn't add or subtotal your expenses — you need to move your data into Excel to do any calculations. For more sophisticated expense tracking options, see Chapter 12.

Accessing expenses

To open Expenses, tap the Expense icon from the Applications Launcher; a blank screen displays. Tap New to create your first entry. You'll see a line entered with the current date, "-Expense Type," and a blank dollar amount. Enter an amount using the right-hand side of the Graffiti area, and then tap Details to get the screen in Figure 5-16.

Here you select the Category (this is editable in the same fashion as the basic applications), Type, Payment method, Currency, Vendor, and City. If you're recording a business lunch, tap Attendees to enter those present. You can also attach a note, giving more details. Once you've finished, tap OK to complete the transaction. When you return to the Expense listing, your new transaction will show, and the data is editable using pop-up lists or Graffiti. The next time you enter a transaction, you'll find that the Vendor and City fields have become "smart" — type or Graffiti-write the first letter of a Vendor or City already entered, and your Palm Organizer completes the entry for you. After you've entered a few transactions, you may have to enter a few letters in order for your Palm Organizer to find a unique entry.

Figure 5-16: Expense details

Tip   Avoid the temptation to use the pop-up lists before you go to the Details screen; I've found that most times, this causes me to lose the transaction and to have to start again. If you don't have an expense selected, you can write in the first letter or two of an expense type and the expense will be created — all you have to do is fill in the amount.

The Menus in the Expense application are pretty simple: the Record menu gives you the capability to delete or purge items, and the Edit menu is the same as found in the basic applications. The Options menu enables you to set Preferences — you can turn on or off automatic data filling and select the default currency, and Custom Currencies enables you to create up to four currencies.

Moving expenses to your PC

Now that we've entered a few expense records, let's look at moving your data into Excel (5.0 or greater) so that you can prepare a report. After you've done a HotSync operation, your newly entered expenses are copied to your organizer, ready to use.

Click the Expense icon from the Desktop software. The application asks whether you want to disable macros — don't — and then the Expense Report Open dialog box displays. Select the categories and, if you want, the date range for the data you want to import. If you've used multiple currencies, the first time you open the spreadsheet you also see the Expense Exchange dialog box; if you want to set rates, you can. Clicking Options enables you to enter personal information and to select which of the five supplied templates to use. After you've finished, your data is in Excel (see Figure 5-17).

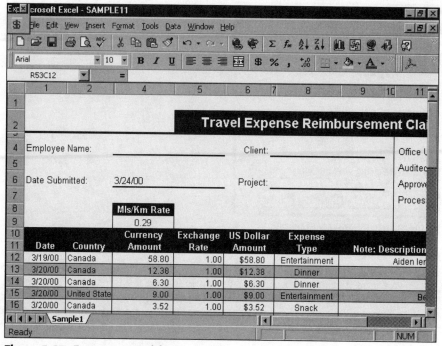

Figure 5-17: Expense spreadsheet

Advanced Excel users will want to create their own template and map their data to it — details are in your Palm Organizer manual. I've found it just as easy to copy the data into a spreadsheet that I build on the fly.

Macintosh users can also bring Expense data into Excel by opening the Expense.txt file within the User folder (itself in the Palm folder) using Excel.

In the past, the Expense feature is one that Macintosh users have had to do without. Shana Corporation now offers two versions of its Informed Expense Creator: the freeware basic version and a commercial advanced version. WalletWare also sells a conduit that offers HotSyncing of Expense data to Excel for Macintosh users. For more information, see Chapter 12.

Mail

Another capability that Palm Organizer users have had since the PalmPilot Professional is the capability to review and deal with e-mail directly on their Palm Organizers. This feature is not direct access to your e-mail on your Palm Organizer (see Chapter 15 if that is what you want to do). Instead, it is the capability to copy e-mail to your Palm Organizer during a HotSync operation. This procedure requires a MAPI (Microsoft) or VIM (Lotus) e-mail application — consult your manual for details. If you are not sure what you have, ask your LAN administrator. After you've set this up, you can transfer e-mail to your Palm Organizer during a HotSync operation, deal with it on your Palm Organizer, and send your responses back to your desktop computer with the following HotSync operation.

Setting up Mail

I was amazed at how easy it was to get set up to read my office mail on my Palm Organizer. A few simple steps and you're done:

✦ Select Custom from the HotSync menu of the Desktop application.

✦ Highlight Mail and click Change.

✦ If you haven't yet set up your mail, the Desktop software runs a setup program. All you need to do is select the mail program to synchronize. OS 2.0 users also need to add a user name and password at this point.

✦ You can change your configuration at any time by changing the Mail HotSync Action (Figure 5-18).

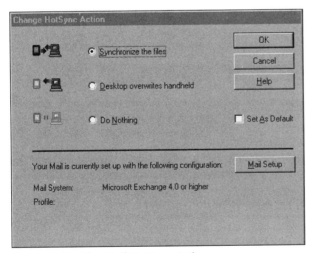

Figure 5-18: The Mail HotSync Action

Mail setup confirmation using Mail

After you've done the Desktop setup, the next HotSync will load mail from your computer's inbox. Tap the Mail icon in the Applications Launcher to see a screen similar to that shown in Figure 5-19. Tap each item to read it.

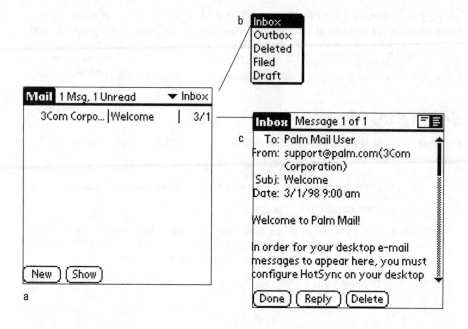

Figure 5-19: Reading your mail

To create a new message, tap New on the main mail screen to get the New Message screen; tapping Details enables you to set your message's priority and other details.

Mail menus

The Message menu offers two choices in the Mail List view: New and Purge Deleted, both of which are self-explanatory. When viewing a specific e-mail, you will see that the Message menu offers a third choice: File. This feature enables you to move or copy an e-mail message to the Filed folder.

The Options menu offers a few more choices:

 ✦ OS 3.0 users can change the display font.

 ✦ Preferences enable you to set your signature block and specify whether you want to confirm deleted messages.

A separate screen of HotSync Preferences for Mail is where can specify settings for both local and remote HotSyncing:

 ✦ **All** syncs all messages between your Palm Organizer and your mail system.

 ✦ **Send Only** sends messages from your Palm Organizer but does not retrieve them from your mail system.

✦ **Unread** retrieves copies of only unread mail from your mail system, leaving the originals untouched.

✦ **Filter** enables you to retrieve or ignore messages based on your criteria. Clicking the truncate button enables you to shorten long messages so that they don't overflow your Palm Organizer's memory.

Summary

Your Palm Organizer's built-in utilities enable you to do a lot of customizing and tweaking:

✦ You can use the application launcher to show the time at any moment.

✦ You can use the built-in Expense and Mail tools to help you stay organized when you're traveling on business.

✦ Take the time to discover your Palm Organizer's treasures — a little exploration reveals a lot of power.

✦ ✦ ✦

HotSyncing Your Palm

◆ ◆ ◆ ◆

In This Chapter

Accessing HotSync Manager

Configuring conduits

Connections

HotSync log

Third-party products

Macintosh conduits

Multiple devices

◆ ◆ ◆ ◆

The HotSync operation is one of the best features of the Palm OS; its simplicity and elegance have contributed in no small part to the incredible success of the platform. Simply put, your Palm Organizer examines the records on your computer and in your handheld and *synchronizes* both to the current version. All of this magic occurs by simply placing your Palm Organizer in its cradle and pressing HotSync. Figure 6-1 shows the Windows version of HotSync, and Figure 6-2 shows the Macintosh version. Palm, Inc. recently received the six millionth United States patent for the HotSync process.

Tip   A three-note ascending chime accompanies the connection to your computer; a three-note descending chime signals a complete HotSync. This is one of the best reasons for leaving the System Sound in Preferences turned on to at least a low level.

Four components work in harmony to perform a HotSync: your Palm Organizer, your computer, the physical connection, and software called *conduits*, which perform the transaction. This chapter takes an in-depth look at the HotSync process — how to set it up and what to do if things go wrong. It also looks at some third-party software for synchronizing your Palm Organizer with the PIM (Personal Information Manager) on your computer and at synchronization utilities.

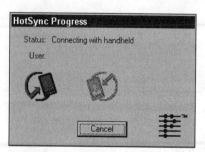

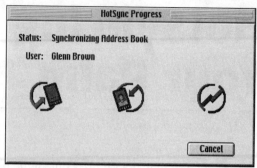

Figure 6-1: Windows HotSync   **Figure 6-2:** Mac HotSync

Accessing HotSync Manager

If you've installed the Palm Desktop, the odds are good that it is already configured and ready to go. Let's have a quick look at the Setup dialog box, just to see what's there. Windows users will see the HotSync icon in the Process Tray in the bottom right corner of the screen (see 1 in Figure 6-3). Right-click it to open the Palm Utility menu. From there, select Setup (2 in Figure 6-3) to open the Setup dialog box. Tabs in this dialog box enable you to change the HotSync settings for Local and Modem; those using OS 3.1 or greater also have a Network tab.

The Setup tab enables you to specify one of these three settings:

✦ **Always available** enables you to HotSync at any time.

✦ **Available only when the Palm Desktop is running** requires that the Desktop application be running.

✦ **Manual** requires that you turn on the HotSync Manager (Start ➪ Programs ➪ Palm Desktop ➪ HotSync Manager) before HotSyncing.

My recommendation is to use the default unless you have conflicts that prevent you from doing so.

Tip   If you're having difficulties making a connection between your handheld and your computer, try turning off HotSync, and then turning it on again. For some reason, this often kick-starts HotSync on both Windows and Macintosh computers.

The Local choice enables you to set the preferences for your HotSync cradle. The Installer will identify the port that your computer uses (most likely COM1 or COM2) to talk to your Palm Organizer. The speed setting defaults to As Fast As Possible — if you have problems syncing, I suggest that you drop this to 9600 baud, and then gradually move the speed up to the highest connection speed that works.

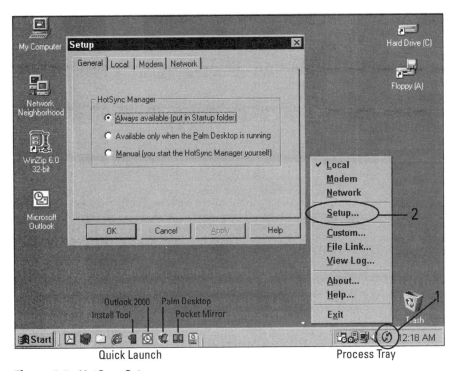

Figure 6-3: HotSync Setup

Tip

If you want direct, instant access to the Palm Desktop or the Install Tool, why not place a shortcut in the Quick Launch area of the Task Bar? Just right-click and drag the program icon to the Quick Launch area, and then select Make Shortcut. If the Quick Launch area is not active on your computer, right-click the Task Bar and select Toolbars ➪ Quick Launch.

New Feature

A new feature in Palm OS 3.3 is the capability of the HotSync Manager to recognize all available serial ports—earlier versions were limited to COM1 through COM4, regardless of which ports were actually available.

Note

If you have a Palm Vx, the highest cradle HotSync speed is a baud rate of 115,200. While this doesn't cut the HotSync speed exactly in half (due to some behind-the-scenes processing), Palm Vx users are still able to perform their HotSync operations 30 to 40 percent faster.

Macintosh users can access their version of this dialog box by clicking the Instant Palm Desktop icon (see 1in Figure 6-4), and selecting Setup (2 in Figure 6-4) from the HotSync submenu.

HotSync Alias in Apple Menu

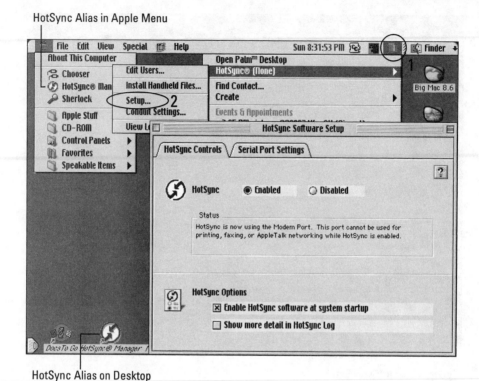

HotSync Alias on Desktop

Figure 6-4: Accessing the Mac HotSync Setup

The HotSync Controls tab has two settings: on or off. Those who wish to use the serial port (whichever the cradle is connected to — modem or printer) for another device may need to leave HotSync off. Most other users will prefer to leave it turned on. If you do not enable HotSync at startup, you will have to manually turn it on using this screen before you can HotSync.

The "Show more detail in HotSync Log" is basically for geeks. It adds sync type, conduit versions, database names, and application details to the report that each HotSync generates.

My advice on Serial Port Settings (see Figure 6-5) is to leave the speed set to As Fast As Possible, unless problems dictate a slower speed.

Tip   Mac users will want quick access to the HotSync Manager — it is a tool you'll load frequently. I suggest making an alias of the HotSync Manager file (it should be in the Palm folder) and dragging it to the desktop or to the Apple Menu Items folder (in the System folder). My personal solution is to place an alias in the QuickLaunch area of Action GoMac.

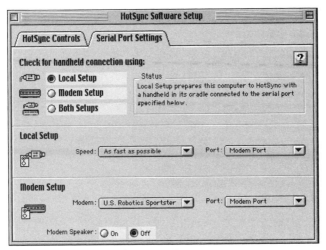

Figure 6-5: Mac Serial Port Settings

Configuring Conduits

Conduits transfer information between the applications on your Palm Organizer and those on your computer. The device ships with conduits to install new applications, to synchronize your To Do List, Memo Pad, Date Book, and Address Book, and to back up the program data. Windows users also have conduits for Expenses and Mail. In addition to the default conduits, a number of applications include their own custom conduits to enable a connection between the application on your Palm Organizer and the mirror or partner application on your computer.

New Feature Starting with Palm OS 3.3, the backup conduit not only syncs program preferences and data, it also backs up your applications. This is a real timesaver in the case of a (fortunately rare) system crash: reinstalling is simply a matter of HotSyncing.

Tip If you like the idea of backing up your applications, but are using an older version of the Palm OS, check out Alexander Hind's shareware program BackupBuddy. It does a great job, has support for applications loaded in Flash memory using TRG's FlashPro, and is available for Windows and Macintosh users.

Windows users can access the settings for their conduits by right-clicking the HotSync icon in the Windows Process tray and selecting Custom from the pop-up menu (see Figure 6-3). You'll see a dialog box similar to that shown in Figure 6-6. This screen shot shows that I am syncing with Microsoft Outlook, Pocket Quicken, and BackupBuddy.

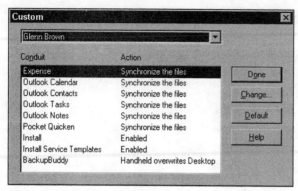

Figure 6-6: Custom conduits

To change the settings for a conduit, double-click it (or select it and click Change), to display a dialog box, similar to that in Figure 6-7, showing the options for the conduit.

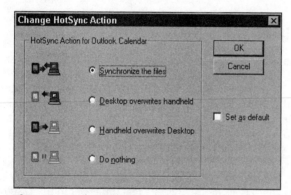

Figure 6-7: Change HotSync Action

Macintosh users access their conduit settings (see Figure 6-8) by opening the HotSync Manager and then selecting Conduit Settings from the HotSync Menu. Those who prefer more direct access can select Conduit Settings from the HotSync submenu of the Instant Palm Desktop menu. Double-click a conduit to open its setting, or select the conduit you want to change and then click the Conduit Settings button. This screen looks similar to the Windows' settings shown in Figure 6-7, except it says Macintosh instead of desktop.

Let's have a look at the Macintosh Conduit Settings and what they mean to you. Changes you make to settings only apply for the next HotSync, unless you click the Set as default checkbox (refer to Figure 6-7).

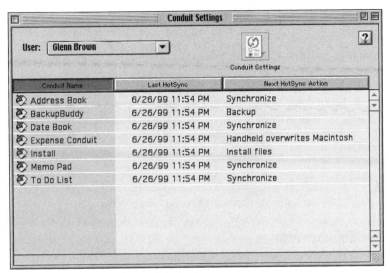

Figure 6-8: Macintosh Conduit Settings

Macintosh Conduit Settings

The following settings control the Macintosh conduit.

Synchronize the files

This setting is the normal default for conduits; it compares the versions of each record on your handheld and your computer. Any changes that you've made to the handheld appear on your computer, and any changes made to the computer appear on your handheld.

Tip

In the rare case in which you make different changes to the same record (for example, you might have added a home phone number to a contact on the handheld and changed that person's title on the Desktop), two separate records are created. At this point, all you need to do is manually copy-and-paste the changes in one record to the other, and then delete the first.

Desktop overwrites handheld

This choice completely replaces the data in your handheld with that in your computer. This option should be used with caution because once you have overwritten the data in your handheld, there is no way to recover any unique data you might have entered on the handheld since your last HotSync operation.

Handheld overwrites desktop

This option replaces the data on your computer with that in your handheld. The same caution applies as above, although you can make a backup of your user folder as a safeguard if you are unsure of the end result.

What if you've overwritten all of the data on your computer, and you haven't made a backup? There is still hope. First, back up your user folder for security, and then open your User folder. Inside you will find a number of folders, including folders for your four main applications. Each folder has at least two files; for example, Address.dat and Address.bak. Macintosh users using the original version of MacPac will find the same. Those using MacPac 2.0 or greater will find two files: User Data and User Data Archive. In all cases, the principle is the same: first, make a backup copy for insurance, and then rename the backup file to match the main one. Perform another HotSync, and your files will have recovered to their status as of the previous HotSync!

Do nothing

The Do nothing option disables the specific conduit selected.

Changing the default settings

The default for all of your conduits is to synchronize the files. There are times, however, when you may want to change the settings:

✦ If you have data on your Desktop that you want to transfer to your handheld without also sending data from your handheld to your Desktop, you should select Desktop overwrites Handheld.

✦ If you are syncing with two machines, and the version on your computer desktop is outdated, you may want to select Handheld overwrites Desktop.

✦ If you're in a rush, and you've already done a HotSync, you may want to turn off synchronization of some components by selecting Do Nothing.

Changes made in the Custom dialog box affect only the next HotSync, unless you click Set as Default in the Change HotSync Action dialog box. You should be careful with the settings in this dialog box, because it is easy to overwrite your data.

Configuring PocketMirror

Windows users with OS 3.1 or greater (Palm IIIx, V, Vx, or VII) can choose whether to synchronize with the Palm Desktop or with Microsoft Outlook. This choice changes the tool that your computer will use to HotSync. If you choose to synchronize with Outlook, then Chapura's PocketMirror synchronization utility is installed on your computer. (Palm IIIe users do not have the option for automatic links to Microsoft Outlook, but they can purchase Chapura's PocketMirror by visiting www.chapura.com.)

It is obvious to me that the designers of PocketMirror have listened to their customers — their latest version offers tweaks and settings that make it easy to configure the HotSync process (see Figure 6-9).

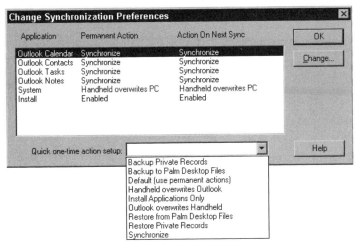

Figure 6-9: PocketMirror quick settings

Note The version of PocketMirror that shipped with the Palm IIIx and Palm V between February and July 1999 is limited in some ways. One is that you cannot specify that other applications take over an individual conduit. I discovered this while trying to help a friend configure a Palm V to sync using PocketMirror, with Maximizer Link handling the contacts portion. The cure is to phone Chapura's technical support to obtain an updated version.

Caution If you are using Microsoft Outlook 2000, you should download version 2.04a (or newer) from Chapura's Web site (www.chapura.com) for full compatibility (as of this writing, the current version is 2.04b).

Each of the PocketMirror conduits offers settings for both permanent and one-time synchronization. If you want to speed up synchronization, you can set individual conduits to sync only once a day. Some of the settings are worth noting. Figure 6-10 shows the Calendar settings.

Contacts Category mapping (see Figure 6-11) enables you to specify whether you want to use Outlook's categories or the 15 categories that you can specify on your Palm Organizer. If you have a lot of categories in Outlook, then use the first setting; if you can limit yourself to the 15 categories allowed on the Palm Organizer, then choose the second setting.

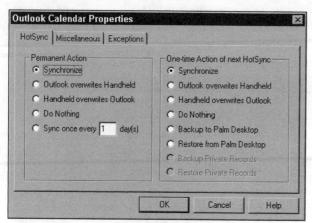

Figure 6-10: PocketMirror Calendar settings

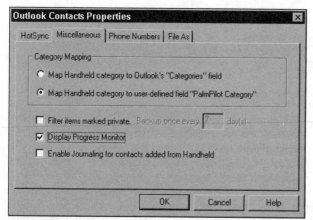

Figure 6-11: PocketMirror Contacts Properties

 Note

> Add a check mark to Enable Journaling for contacts added from Handheld if you are using the Journaling feature in Outlook—doing so ensures that contacts added on your Palm Organizer are correctly journaled in Outlook on your computer. If you want complete support for journaling, check out Pocket Journal later in this chapter.

Microsoft Outlook has many more options and possibilities than does your Palm Organizer—which is not surprising, given the differences between your computer and your handheld. An example is the due date for to do items—Outlook has both a start date and a due date, whereas your Palm's To Do List has only the due date. If you're like me, you'll want to map the Outlook Task Start Date to your Palm Organizer's Due Date (see Figure 6-12).

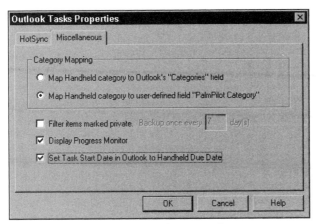

Figure 6-12: PocketMirror Tasks Properties

File Linking

File Linking is a powerhouse feature which Windows users have had since Version 3.0 of the Palm OS. It enables you to specify a link between an Address Book or Memo Pad file and one on your computer. If the file on your computer is updated, the one on your Palm Organizer is automatically updated with your next HotSync. This enables you to synchronize documents, lists, even the company telephone book, and always have the current version on your handheld.

Here's how to set up a file link:

1. Select File Link from the HotSync menu; a dialog box asks which user you want to set up the link for (that would be you) and whether you want to create a new link or modify an existing one.

2. Next you see the dialog box shown in Figure 6-13. Here you have to answer three simple questions:

    • To which application do you want to link (Address Book or Memo Pad)?

    • To which file on your computer do you want to link? Memo Pad supports CSV, Memo Archive, or text; the Address Book supports CSV or Address Archive file formats.

    • What would you like to name the new category that will be used to store the data you are linking?

After you've made your selections, the next dialog box confirms your settings, and enables you to set the frequency of updates (whenever the file is updated or daily, weekly, or monthly).

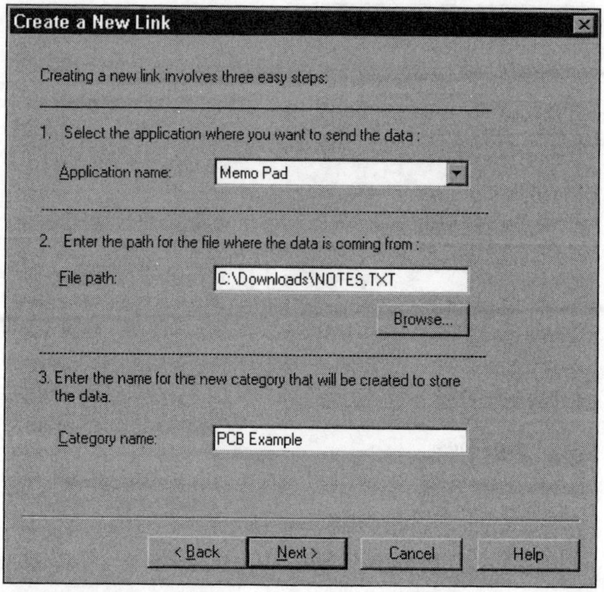

Figure 6-13: Setting up a file link

Connections

The cradle is the device that is used most often to HotSync your Palm Organizer. The Palm cradle comes in three versions.

PalmPilot

The original Pilot through the PalmPilot Professional all used the same square-shaped cradle. The Palm III models can also be HotSynced using this cradle, although the fit isn't perfect.

Palm III

This cradle is a more rounded, swoopy design, with the HotSync button moved to bottom center. This cradle works for the Palm III, IIIe, IIIx, IIIxe, and VII models; older devices do not fit. Palm used clever design for the Palm IIIc: it can HotSync in the older Palm III cradle, although it obviously cannot recharge in that cradle. Conversely, the older devices can use the Palm IIIc's cradle, and are unaffected by the cradle's power.

Palm V

The newest cradle is unique: it is a weighted design that is attached to A/C and recharges the Palm V's batteries whenever the Palm V (or Palm Vx) is in the cradle. For those who travel, Palm also sells a travel kit that enables you to recharge or HotSync your Palm V anywhere in the world.

All cradles connect to a serial port on your computer; Macintosh users need to use a connector that is included as part of the MacPac kit for Mac users. This connector can be connected to either the modem or printer port. The modem port is a better choice if you use a PostScript printer—HotSync requires that you turn off AppleTalk. Those with an iMac or a blue and white G3 will want to look at Keyspan's USB to serial connector or Palm's PalmConnect USB kit. (Also see the section on IR HotSync later in this chapter.)

Tip

If you have both Windows and Macintosh computers that you want to HotSync to, you will probably want to invest in a second cradle. Make sure you buy the Mac version of the cradle—it adds the connector you need to the standard cradle at no extra cost. The MacPac software is freely available from Palm's Web site at www.palm.com, which enables you to save the retail cost of the kit.

The Bridge

Developer: Midwest PCB Designs, Inc.
Cost: $14.95

So, what do you do for cradles when you have multiple Palm Organizers? There is a more elegant solution than multiple cradles: The Bridge. This device is a small connector that fits in the HotSync cradle, and enables you to sync a Palm III in a PalmPilot cradle. A new version synchronizes with Palm V users.

Modem HotSync

The more you travel, the more likely it is that you'll want to set up and configure for a modem HotSync. A modem HotSync requires two modems: one attached to your computer and one attached to your Palm Organizer. Some configuration is also required in order to make it all work.

Note

Those with a fast cable modem or DSL connection to the Internet at home aren't necessarily out of luck. Most computers now ship with an internal modem, which you would need to configure and connect to a telephone line before using it for a modem HotSync.

Computer setup

Leave your computer running and make sure that nothing (for example, an online service or fax modem) is left running that can interfere with the process. Let's open HotSync Manager and set things up on your computer.

The Modem settings in your HotSync Manager's Setup dialog box (see Figure 6-14) are fairly straightforward.

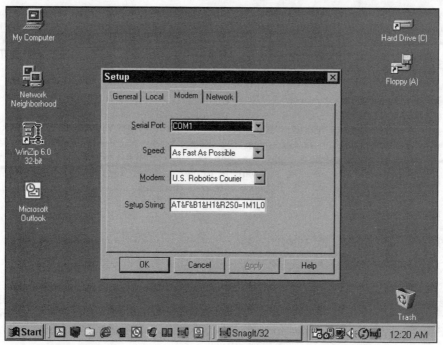

Figure 6-14: Modem setup

Serial port

This is the COM port for your computer's modem (see Control Panels ⇨ Modem Properties).

Speed

Speed is the transfer rate. As with a direct HotSync, start with As Fast As Possible, and adjust if necessary.

Modem

This is the type of modem that is attached to your computer. If yours isn't listed, select Hayes Basic.

Setup String

Check your modem's manual to see whether you should enter a setup string here.

After you finish, click OK. Make sure that you leave HotSync Manager running and your computer turned on (the monitor can be turned off).

Handheld setup

You'll need to tell your handheld what number to call when you select a modem HotSync. Just open the HotSync application (see Figure 6-15) on your Palm Organizer and tap Enter phone # to enter the telephone number of the line that your computer's modem is attached to. Figure 6-16 shows the OS 3.3 version of the HotSync screen.

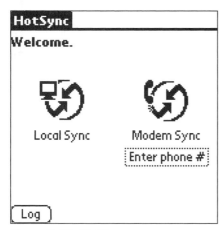

Figure 6-15: HotSync

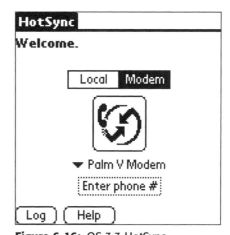

Figure 6-16: OS 3.3 HotSync

Tip

If you have a Palm V, it might appear that you have only one modem choice: Palm V. However, if you change the String field, a new choice magically appears in the Modem field: Custom. This is especially useful if you want to use a cable to connect to a GSM cellular phone, so you can use the phone's built-in modem. Just enter the string for the GSM modem and you're all set to perform a remote, wireless HotSync operation.

Phone Setup

The Phone Setup dialog box (see Figure 6-17) enables you to configure how your Palm Organizer dials out. Here is where you can add prefixes for dialing out (usually 8 or 9), disabling call waiting (1170 in my area code), and entering your calling card number. Once entered, all of these settings can be toggled off and on as needed.

Conduit Setup

Typically, a modem HotSync is what you'll do while on the road to get your latest e-mail, to make sure that you have a backup, and maybe to update your handheld if someone else is adding information to your home base computer. You certainly don't need to synchronize everything, just the essentials. Just open the HotSync app on your Palm Organizer, tap the menu icon, and select Conduit Setup to get the dialog box shown in Figure 6-18. Here you can specify exactly which databases should be backed up when you do a modem HotSync.

Figure 6-17: Phone Setup   **Figure 6-18:** Modem Conduit Setup

Initiating a modem HotSync

Now that the setup is complete on your computer and your handheld, let's try it. With your handheld modem connected to a telephone line, open the HotSync application and tap Modem Sync.

Network HotSync

Prior to the release of OS 3.1 with the Palm IIIx and Palm V, Network HotSync was a separate commercial product. This option enables you to HotSync your Palm Organizer via your office network.

Requirements

As with the modem HotSync, your Palm Organizer needs an attached modem. You should talk to your LAN administrator to make sure that:

✦ Your office network, the remote access server, and your computer all support TCP/IP.

✦ You have a remote access account to your office LAN or WAN.

Computer setup

Follow a few simple steps on your computer for a Network HotSync:

✦ From the HotSync Manager menu, choose Network (this action causes it to be checked in the pop-up menu).

✦ Reopen the same menu and choose Setup, and then click the Network tab — your name should have a check mark next to it.

✦ Put your handheld in its cradle and push the HotSync button — this sets up your Palm Organizer to remember the IP address, so that it can find your computer later over the network (see Figure 6-19).

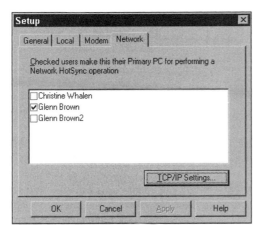

Figure 6-19: Network Setup

Handheld Setup

This setup is easier than you think: open the HotSync application, tap the menu icon, select Modem Sync Prefs, and tap Network. You'll see a new button in the HotSync screen, called What do I do?, that tells you how to dial into a network modem from your handheld modem.

If you want to be able to synchronize your Palm Organizer from a cradle anywhere on your company LAN, there's one more step: In the main HotSync screen, tap the menu icon, select LANSync Prefs, and tap LANSync. This feature enables you to synchronize your handheld via the LAN back to *your* computer — assuming you've left your computer on and connected to the network.

Tip   If your HotSync configuration includes e-mail, you can also use Network HotSync to get your company e-mail remotely — either through a remote cradle on the LAN or via a modem attached to your organizer.

IR HotSync

The OS 3.3 upgrade brought with it a major upgrade to the infrared capabilities of your Palm Organizer. Those with an IR port and the upgrade now have a handheld that supports the IrCOMM implementation of standards for infrared communication established by the Infrared Data Association (IrDA). What does this mean to you? You may be able to beam data to your cellular phone, providing it has an IR port and is data enabled. More importantly, you can now use the IR port to do a wireless HotSync.

Requirements

Your computer must support the IrCOMM implementation of the IrDA standards, and you must have an enabled infrared port built into or attached to your computer. If you use Windows 98, or have a Macintosh G3, the infrared communications software is built into your operating system. Check with the OS 3.3 documentation if you're not sure whether your computer supports infrared communication.

Computer Setup

The IR HotSync computer setup is fairly simple. Just follow these steps:

1. Open the HotSync Manager and make sure Local is checked.

2. Choose Setup and select the Local tab.

3. Select the same COM port as is assigned to your Infrared Monitor and click OK.

You'll need to switch the settings back when you want to use the cradle again, because this process prevents a normal cradle HotSync from occurring.

Initiating an IR HotSync on your handheld

This process is a piece of cake: open the HotSync application, tap Local, select IR to a PC/Handheld from the pop-up menu below the HotSync icon, hold your handheld with its IR port within a few inches of the computer's, and tap HotSync.

Inside HotSync

Every record in your Palm Organizer—every address, contact, to do item, recipe, *everything*—has an invisible flag assigned to it. This flag can have one of four statuses: new, changed, deleted, or synced. When you perform a HotSync, these records in your Palm Organizer and on your computer are compared, and then the flag is updated to synced.

Want to speed up the HotSync process? The less data you have to sync, the less time it takes, so why not purge old data from your Palm Organizer? Just open the Date Book and To Do applications and select Purge from the menu. I recommend that you check Save archive copy on PC. That way, you can still find old data.

HotSync performs in one of three ways: slow, fast, and recovery. I'm referring to the way the software synchronizes records, not the transfer rate. The first time you synchronize your Palm Organizer, it will perform a slow sync, checking every record; after that, it will transfer only updated records (a fast sync). If you HotSync on two computers, every time you switch, the first sync will be slow—subsequent syncs are normally fast. Recovery syncs are initiated when the conduit finds data missing on one side or the other, usually after a hard reset.

Tip

Macintosh users who want to force a slow sync, so as to ensure that all records are updated, can do so by holding down Shift on their computer throughout the entire HotSync.

Another Mac-only tip: There may come a time when you feel that your computer and your handheld are not exchanging data properly. If this is the case, hold down the Command and Option keys throughout a HotSync to force a slow sync that will reset the sync status of all records.

New Feature

Starting with Version 3.3 of the Palm OS, a recovery sync automatically initiated after a hard reset recovers your data as well as the third-party applications that you installed on your Palm Organizer.

HotSync Log

The HotSync Log is a transcript of what happened during your last several HotSyncs. This can be a powerful tool when you try to decipher what may have gone wrong with a HotSync. As you can see in Figure 6-20, HotSync Log provides a minimum of information if things are going fine, but it warns you if it runs into anything out of the ordinary.

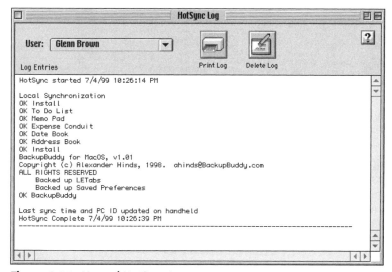

Figure 6-20: Normal HotSync Log

Note

Here's an interesting piece of trivia: The HotSync Log on Windows displays the most recent sync at the top. You scroll down to view earlier syncs. The reverse is true on the Macintosh: Syncs are appended to the log, so you scroll up to view previous log information.

Verbose logging

HotSync logs information in two ways: regular and verbose (geek). Mac users can turn on verbose logging by selecting Show more detail in HotSync Log; Windows users will find it easiest to use BackupBuddy's option to select Verbose output to HotSync Log file. Figure 6-21 shows the start of a verbose HotSync Log — details include the speed at which you connect, whether or not each conduit was run fast or slow, and to which database each connected, as well as tons of information on each of the files in your Palm Organizer.

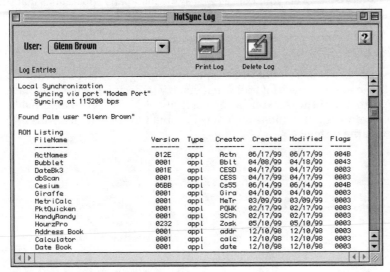

Figure 6-21: Verbose HotSync Log

Deciphering messages

Always make sure to read the HotSync Log if it reports an error; doing so is bound to make your life easier in the end. A typical message tells you something that the program has done that may be out of the ordinary. As an example, if you change or delete a record on your Palm Organizer, and you change the same record on your computer before HotSyncing, it should detect this and tell you so with a message similar to this:

```
The following task was modified on both platforms: "buy book ",
Due: Jan 1, 2000, Priority: 1
The handheld changes have replaced the Palm Desktop changes,
and the handheld task has been replaced with the next instance
of the repeating task.
```

In most cases, when you modify a record on both your Palm Organizer and on your computer, HotSync will duplicate the records on both, and ask you to choose which record to delete. Remember that you should make the correction on only one platform (handheld or computer), and then perform a HotSync operation to make the correction universal.

Note   PocketMirror records abnormal HotSyncs with these codes: SS indicates a slow sync, RS indicates a recovery sync, PH indicates that you've chosen the option for your Palm Organizer to overwrite the Handheld, and HP indicates that you've chosen the option for your Handheld to overwrite your PC.

Think Sync

HotSyncing your Palm Organizer with your computer is straightforward if you use the provided desktop software. Things get a bit more complex when you want to sync with your favorite tool: Microsoft Outlook, Lotus Organizer, Symantec Act!, Maximizer, or whatever else you're fond of using. Fortunately, help is available.

Third-Party Sync Products

Let's start with a look at three products that enable you to synchronize your Palm Organizer with versions of Microsoft Outlook.

PocketMirror

Developer: Chapura
Cost: $39.95

PocketMirror's claim to fame is simplicity — as discussed earlier, it does a great job at synchronizing your Palm Organizer and Microsoft Outlook. A quick and easy installation, a push of a button, and you're done. Features include Quick Sync Setup that enables you to change conduit settings, support for your Palm Organizer's categories, and more. If you're looking for a quick, easy fix, this is it.

PocketJournal

Developer: Chapura
Cost: $39.95 (included in the Palm III, IIIx, V, Vx, and VII box for free)
Footprint: 57K

Microsoft Outlook has a powerful journaling function that enables you to automatically track what you do with your contacts. It can track phone calls, conversations, e-mail, basically anything you can enter into Outlook. PocketJournal (see Figure 6-22) is the only solution available that enables you to enter and track this information on your Palm Organizer and synchronize it with Outlook.

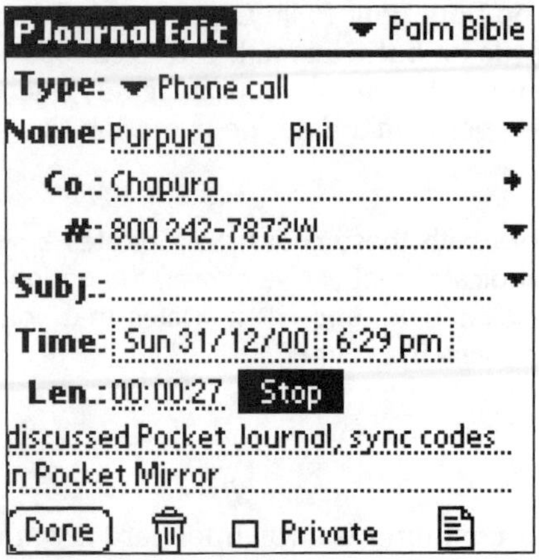

Figure 6-22: PocketJournal

Desktop To Go

Developer: DataViz
Cost: $49.00

Where PocketMirror is exclusively an Outlook synchronization product, Data Viz's Desktop To Go (see Figure 6-23) adds support for Schedule +, which can be especially useful if your office is still running an older version of Windows (Outlook requires Windows 95 or better).

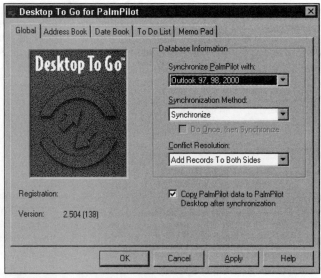

Figure 6-23: Desktop To Go's settings

Desktop To Go has power and flexibility, too: features include a Setup Wizard to get you started, user-customizable field mapping, and field-level synchronization for contacts, appointments, tasks, and memos. I particularly like the option to save completed items only on my computer (see Figure 6-24).

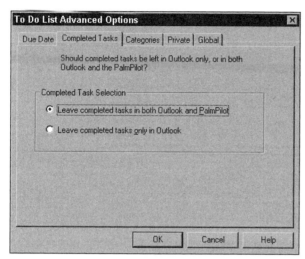

Figure 6-24: Desktop To Go's Advanced To Do Options

IntelliSync

Developer: Puma Technologies
Cost: $69.95

Puma's IntelliSync (see Figure 6-25) is truly a jack-of-all-trades, with support for Microsoft Outlook and Schedule, ACT!, LotusOrganizer, GoldMine, Sidekick and Internet Sidekick, ECCO, InterOffice, MeetingMaker (for activities only), and Day-Timer Organizer. You can map all of your Palm Organizer's fields to multiple PIMs, if you care to. All this power is wrapped up in an interface that is one-button simple. I particularly like the way it handles conflicts by offering to flexibly resolve things when changes are made to both my handheld and Outlook. Version 3.1 added e-mail support for Lotus Notes, Version 3.5 added Lotus Organizer 5.0 (more recent versions were already supported) and Microsoft Outlook 2000, and Version 3.6, which is due by the time this book is printed, adds e-mail support for Novell GroupWise.

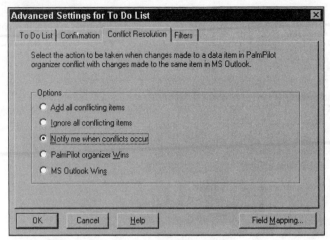

Figure 6-25: IntelliSync Conflict Resolution

IntelliSync Anywhere
Developer: Puma Technologies
Cost: $99.95 (per user, based on 100 users)

Those who work in a corporate environment may also want to look at Puma's
IntelliSync Anywhere, a server-based product that enables secure dial-in and
LAN access to Microsoft Exchange and Lotus Domino servers.

More sync products

In addition to the five programs above, there are a wide variety of third-party
products available to synchronize your Palm Organizer. The chances are good that
there is a specific tool designed to help with your favorite PIM. Here are some of
the additional PIM conduit products available for Windows users.

ACT Palm Organizer Link
Developer: Symantec Corporation
Price: Freeware (ACT is $69.95)

This freeware product is available from Symantec's Web Site (www.symantec.com).

ChaosSync for Palm Organizers
Developer: Isbister International
Cost: $24.95

This product enables you to synchronize with Time & Chaos32.

Companion Link

Developer: Tele-Support Software
Price: $39.95

Tele-Support Software make versions of their Companion Link software that enable you to synchronize with ACT!, Goldmine, and Telemagic.

Day-Timer Organizer for Windows

Company: Day-Timers, Inc.
Day-Timer for Windows includes Palm synchronization software.

Desktop Set

Developer: Okna Corporation
Cost: $25.00 (shareware)

Desktop Set includes Palm Organizer synchronization software.

Easy Sync

Developer: Lotus Development Corporation
Cost: $49.00

Easy Sync enables you to synchronize your Palm Organizer with Lotus Notes.

Franklin Ascend

Developer: Franklin Covey
Cost: $99.00

Franklin Ascend includes Palm synchronization software.

Lotus Organizer

Developer: Lotus Development Corporation
Cost: $79.00

Lotus Organizer includes Palm synchronization software.

Maximizer Link

Developer: Maximizer Technologies
Cost: $49.00

Maximizer Link enables you to synchronize with Maximizer.

Macintosh conduits

The release of MacPac 2.0 brought with it a new desktop based on new conduits and what was originally Claris Organizer. The new structure has enabled more developers than ever to support synchronization of their applications. This section lists a few examples. Windows users need not feel left out — all but two of these conduits (Consultant and FMSync) are available for both platforms.

Consultant

Developer: Chronos LC
Cost: $39.95

Macintosh users who want a choice of PIMs should check out the discussion of Chronos Consultant in Chapter 8.

Caution

I find that the Consultant conduit does not always work correctly if it is used in conjunction with the standard Palm conduits. The problem is that Palm's conduits perform a sync on a conduit (for example the Address conduit), and then set the conduit's flag to synced. When the Consultant conduit sees the data, it presumes that it is synced, so it may ignore it, leaving you with incomplete records in the desktop application. The cure is to create a folder inside your Palm folder called Conduits Off, and drag the four main Palm conduits (Address, Date Book, Memo, and To Do) to the folder (leaving the Consultant conduit in the Conduits folder). You should then do your next HotSync while pressing the Command and Option keys to force a slow sync that will reset the sync status of all records. If that doesn't work, just create a new user in Consultant, and repeat that process. After that, things should work fine.

Athlete's Diary

Developer: Stevens Creek Software
Cost: $39.95 ($19.95 with the purchase of the desktop version)

If you're serious about fitness training, you owe it to yourself to check out the products offered by Stevens Creek Software. Athlete's Diary, shown in Figure 6-26, enables you to track training and performance data, and synchronize it with the desktop version of the application.

BrainForest Professional

Developer: Aportis
Cost: $39.95

Who doesn't need an outliner? The category that started with ThinkTank is brought to our favorite handheld with Aportis BrainForest, and now there are Windows and Macintosh versions that you can HotSync your data to. See Chapter 11 for more on BrainForest.

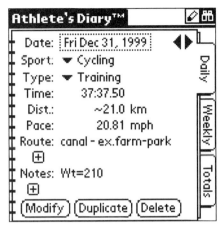

Figure 6-26: Athlete's Diary

Documents to Go

Developer: DataViz
Cost: $39.95

Documents to Go offers a quick an easy method of reading your computer's documents, including spreadsheets and word-processing documents, on your Palm Organizer. See Chapter 13 for more on Documents to Go.

Expense Manager

Developer: Shana Corporation
Cost: Freeware (the Advanced version is $39.95)

A major shortcoming of the PalmConnect software is the lack of a conduit to transfer expense data to your Macintosh. No longer; both this application and Walletware's ExpensePlus Reporter (covered next) enable you to transfer expense data to your Macintosh. See Chapter 12 for more on both applications.

ExpensePlus

Developer: Walletware
Cost: $39.95

Walletware offers two solutions for Mac users: ExpensePlus Reporter, a $19.95 application that gives you the capability to HotSync your Palm Organizer's Expense data, and ExpensePlus, a full-blown expense manager with a Macintosh conduit. See Chapter 12 for more on ExpensePlus.

FMSync

Developer: Rob Tsuk
Cost: $38.00

On the Windows side, those who want to do forms-based development have tools such as Pendragon Forms (for the more advanced) and Satellite Forms (an easier-to-use but less powerful form builder) available. FMSync enables Macintosh users to JFile databases with FileMaker Pro. See Chapter 22 for more on FMSync.

Meeting Maker

Developer: ON Technology
Cost: $900.00 (starter kit with server and 20 users)

ON Technology offers a Macintosh conduit for its enterprise-level scheduling and calendaring application, Meeting Maker.

MultiMail Pro

Developer: Actual Software Corporation
Cost: $29.95

Mac users who envy the ability of Windows users to HotSync their e-mail no longer need to be jealous: MultiMail Pro is available for both Windows and Macintosh users and offers complete synchronization of your e-mail, included as part of a superior e-mail package for your Palm Organizer. See Chapter 16 for more on MultiMail Pro.

Pocket Quicken

Developer: Landware
Cost: $39.95

Pocket Quicken is one of those products that, just to take advantage of it, users will buy a Palm Organizer. Available for both Windows and Macintosh users, this package enables you to maintain pocket control over your finances. See Chapter 13 for more on Pocket Quicken.

Sync utilities

You didn't think shareware authors would ignore a function as vital as HotSyncing, did you? These stellar applications add priceless functionality.

BackupBuddy

Developer: Andrew Hinds
Cost: $19.95 (shareware)

One major limitation to versions of the Palm OS prior to 3.3 is that the backup conduit backs up your data, but it doesn't back up all of your applications. This means that after a hard reset or crash, you are faced with finding all of your applications and reinstalling them. Install BackupBuddy, and it will replace Palm's backup conduit with a more powerful one that automatically backs up all of your applications and data. It even supports TRG's FlashPro, and can back up files stored in flash memory.

Two versions are available: an install-and-go Macintosh version and a Windows version that enables you to completely configure your backup (see Figure 6-27). Two settings are worth noting here: Archive files deleted on handheld will maintain backup copies of the applications you delete from your Palm Organizer, and Verbose output to HotSync log file turns on verbose logging, as described earlier.

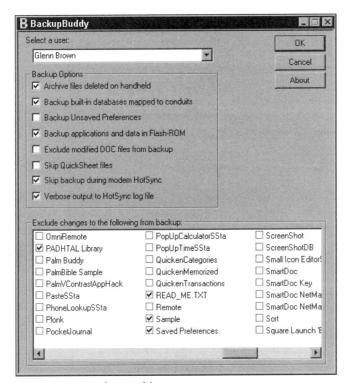

Figure 6-27: BackupBuddy

Tip

One way to manually duplicate the functionality of BackupBuddy is to maintain a folder of installed applications, with updates and deletes as you update or delete applications on your Palm Organizer. That way, reinstalling is as simple as dragging those apps to the Install Tool. To be honest, it is a pain to maintain such a folder; which makes BackupBuddy worth every penny of the shareware fee.

Palm Buddy

Developer: Florent Pillet
Cost: $20.00 (shareware)
Footprint: 14K

Florent takes a different approach to backup and install with his Macintosh application Palm Buddy—turn off HotSyncing, and Palm Buddy creates a direct link to your Palm Organizer. The window shown in Figure 6-28 is *live*: drag a file in, and it is installed; drag a file out, and it is deleted. I use Palm Buddy to make weekly, dated backups of the contents of my Palm V. Backups take a few simple steps: I click Yukinari Suzuki's freeware HotSync CSM (control strip module) to turn off HotSyncing, load the Palm Buddy app on my handheld, load the Palm Buddy application on my Macintosh, and then click Backup.

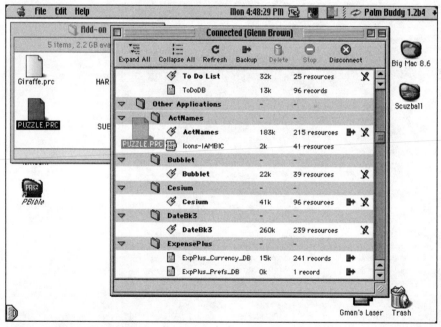

Figure 6-28: Palm Buddy

HotSync CSM

Developer: Yukinari Suzuki
Cost: Freeware

Mac users will want to use this control strip module (see Figure 6-29) because it enables you to toggle HotSync Monitoring on and off with a single click.

Figure 6-29: HotSync CSM (control strip module)

Undupe

Developer: Stevens Creek Software
Cost: $4.95 (shareware
Footprint: 10K

One of the sad realities of the HotSync process is that it is not perfect. One problem is duplicate entries. One or two are easy to deal with — check and delete the extra copy. What do you do when an errant HotSync creates hundreds of duplicates? Undupe (see Figure 6-30) does this one thing very well; searching your Palm Organizer for duplicates, and deleting them. The shareware version will identify the scope of your problem by telling you how many duplicates you have; if you want the automatic deleting of dupes, you'll need to pay the shareware fee. This is one utility that pays for itself the first time you use it.

Figure 6-30: Undupe

Multiple Devices

I understand that one of the best-selling Palm accessories is the cradle. More and more Palm users synchronize to more than one machine. The same can be said for multiple users backing up to a single computer. In my case, I synchronize to the Palm Desktop (or Chronos Consultant) on my Mac, to Outlook 2000 on my Windows 98 PC, and to Outlook 97 on the Windows NT4 machine in my office. To make it even more confusing, three different Palm Organizers sync to the Windows 98 box. The reality is that most users end up with their *life* in the Palm Organizer, so losing even a few records can be a disaster.

One device, two computers

One device and two computers works fine as long as you take some care. If one machine is at home and the other at the office and you HotSync on each regularly, things should go fine. If you go on vacation for a few weeks, things can get a bit out of kilter. The problem is that there will be appointments or tasks on the office machine that are probably done, recorded, and synced at home, but your office machine doesn't know it. The cure is to do your first HotSync after an extended absence as Handheld overwrites computer — that way, the outdated tasks in your desktop machine are flushed as it is brought up to date.

Another circumstance in which you should take some care is after a hard reset. If you're using OS 3.3 or greater or BackupBuddy, all of your data will be recovered on your first HotSync; if not, you will need to reinstall all of your third-party applications. Once you've HotSynced on one of your computers, the next HotSync on your *other* computer should be to ensure that all three devices are back in sync.

Caution   The one problem with HotSyncing to multiple computers is that it can give you a false sense of security when overwriting data. Technical support people tell me that these users are more likely to lose data than those HotSyncing to one computer. The lesson here is to take great care when you change your conduit settings.

Multiple handhelds

No problem here; you can create and HotSync as many users as you'd like on one computer. You will need to use some caution when you change conduit settings — the first thing you have to confirm is that you have selected the correct user, otherwise you may fry the data in someone else's handheld.

If you use PocketMirror, open your Folder List, select the PocketMirror directory, and add a note with the new usernames. Remember that you should not delete these notes; they are the means that PocketMirror uses to track multiple users.

Usernames

The username you select will be coded in the HotSync process, and folders are created to store your data on the computer. The usernames must be unique, as the Palm OS can get confused when you have multiple devices with the same name.

Note Prefs ⇨ Owner does not set the username on your handheld. Under normal circumstances, the username can only be changed by using Tools ⇨ Users ⇨ Rename in the Windows desktop application or by using Edit Users in the Macintosh HotSync menu.

Caution A relatively safe way to have more than one unit with the same username is to hard reset the second unit before you do a HotSync. The PC will think it's the first unit, just reset. Of course, you'd only want to make changes in the unit that you don't hard reset. If you upgrade to a new device (a Palm VII, for example), all you have to do is make sure the new device is hard reset before you do that first HotSync. But afterwards, don't make changes to the data on both units.

So, what should you do when you upgrade to a spanking new Palm XI? Simple: create another name (I use Glenn Brown2, and so on), and drag-copy the data from your old user directories to the new ones. You may find that some of your registered shareware applications no longer work because the serial number is based on your username — all developers that I know of are happy to support their registered users by generating a new serial number.

Summary

✦ Windows and Mac users who want easy access should make a shortcut or alias to HotSync Manager and place it in Quick Launch or Apple Menu Items.

✦ Take care when changing the settings for your conduits; the capability to overwrite can be unforgiving.

✦ A second cradle is a great investment for those who HotSync to more than one computer. Just remember that syncing to two machines can create headaches if you're not careful.

✦ Windows users should try File Linking for data on their computers that is subject to change; this procedure results in the latest version of the file on your Palm Organizer after a HotSync.

✦ The HotSync Log can be a powerful tool to help you discover what may have gone wrong in a HotSync.

✦ If you're not using Palm OS 3.3 or greater, consider BackupBuddy for painless restoration of your Palm Organizer after a hard reset.

✦ Remember that it is possible, but not advisable, to have more than one handheld with the same username.

✦   ✦   ✦

What Is the Palm VII Handheld?

◆ ◆ ◆ ◆

In This Chapter

What is the Palm VII?

Setting up your
Palm VII

Discovering Web-
clipping applications

Introducing
iMessenger

Exploring Palm.Net

◆ ◆ ◆ ◆

The Palm VII handheld comes with a built-in antenna that enables you to query the Internet wirelessly through the new feature Web clipping. Web clipping applications enable you to request specific information from different Web sites for which the applications are designed. For example, the E*Trade application enables you to download stock quotes directly from the E*Trade Web site. iMessenger, which also is a new application, lets you send and receive messages wirelessly. Palm.Net wireless communication service provides the wireless connectivity for the Palm VII.

What is the Palm VII handheld?

The Palm VII handheld, which is shown in Figure 7-1, comes with all the Palm III hardware features, but also includes hardware components that enable wireless connectivity. The major hardware differences are the internal transmitter and the integrated antenna. It's an impressive piece of engineering work. Although it is only slightly larger and heavier than a Palm III (the Palm VII is 6.7 ounces including the batteries), it has almost triple the number of hardware components inside.

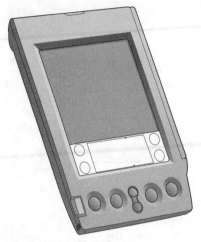

Figure 7-1: The Palm VII

Antenna

The Palm VII handheld looks very much like a stretched version of the Palm III, with a flip-up antenna positioned along its right side (see Figure 7-2). The antenna might seem a bit flimsy at first, but this is deliberate. It is made from a flexible material that bends easily in case you bump it against something hard or accidentally drop the unit. If you do manage to break or damage the antenna, you don't have to worry; its design makes removal and replacement a snap.

Figure 7-2: The Palm VII
antenna

Using the Antenna to Launch Applications

You can use the antenna to turn on your Palm VII handheld by raising it. If you want to get even more out of your antenna, however, you can also program it to launch applications on your Palm VII handheld.

1. Tap the Prefs icon from the Applications Launcher.

2. Tap the pick list next to the antenna icon.

3. Select the application that you want to launch by raising the antenna.

4. Tap the Applications Launcher to exit the Preferences screen.

5. The next time you raise the antenna, the application you selected will launch.

You can raise the antenna to three different angles: 90, 135, or 180 degrees. If the organizer is on a flat surface, raise the antenna to 90 degrees (first click) for the best reception. If you hold the organizer in your hand, the best position is at 135 degrees (second click).

Batteries and internal transmitter

Like the Palm III series handheld, the Palm VII uses two AAA batteries. Depending on your use, these should last two to three weeks. The internal transmitter, which handles the wireless transmission functions, also powers the organizer. The AAA batteries charge the internal transmitter; the initial charge takes about 70 minutes. After the initial charge, the Palm VII handheld detects your usage pattern and charges the internal transmitter through the AAA batteries at a preset time when you're unlikely to be using the organizer. When your batteries are low in power, a message prompts you to change them. The battery indicator on the Application Launcher screen is an indicator of the combined power level of the AAA batteries and the internal transmitter.

Other hardware features

The Palm VII handheld features the same great screen as the Palm IIIx and IIIe models. It comes with 2 Megabytes of flash memory, which means the software can be upgraded when new enhancements become available. The Palm VII handheld is compatible with the all the Palm III series hardware peripherals — the HotSync cradle, HotSync cable, snap-on modem, and stylus. This form factor compatibility extends to everything but leather covers, which are slightly larger for the taller Palm VII height.

Software

The Palm VII handheld comes with the same core applications as the Palm III and Palm V series handhelds. This section provides an overview of the wireless software features Web clipping and iMessenger.

Web clipping applications

Web clipping is a fast and simple way to "clip" specific information from the Internet. The process is simple; you send a query and receive a real-time response in seconds.

This approach is innovative because your Web clipping applications reside on your device, so you can call them up in an instant without having to go through the World Wide Wait that you might have experienced on your PC.

Unlike Web browsing, Web clipping technology gets you the Internet information you need, when you need it, without the elaborate, graphics-laden Web pages that are inappropriate for the screen size of your organizer.

As of this writing, 23 different Web clipping applications are included in the Palm VII box, and over 200 more applications are available through www.palm.net. These applications enable you to query some of the best-known providers of information on the Web, giving you instant access to the latest traffic conditions, directions, weather, stock quotes, business and general news, sports scores, and much more. See "Using Web Clipping Applications" later in this chapter for more information on using the applications.

iMessenger application

The second new wireless feature that the Palm VII offers, the iMessenger application, lets you send and receive text messages to and from any Internet e-mail address. When you activate the wireless communication service on your Palm VII, you acquire an address on the wireless network (for example, FredSmith@palm.net). So long as you are within the wireless network coverage, you can communicate with anyone else who has an Internet e-mail address.

The iMessenger feature wasn't originally intended to be a replacement for your daily e-mail messages, although some users treat it this way. Palm, Inc. always expected that customers would use it the way one uses a pager or cell phone — as an auxiliary method for receiving short (and often more important) messages. For this reason, many Palm VII users only give their Palm.Net addresses to their most critical contacts (such as a boss, spouse, business partner, or important client).

Whether you broadcast your Palm.Net address to a wide group or not, the iMessenger feature is enormously useful. Imagine that you're in a taxi on the way to your hotel, and you want to arrange a dinner meeting. The Palm VII handheld makes it easy. You can also use a Web clipping application to query the Internet for a restaurant, directions, and a traffic report, and you should receive a response within 10 to 30 seconds. After that, you can send a message to your invitees informing them of the time and place, and they can reply directly to your @palm.net address.

Palm.Net wireless communication service

Palm.Net is the name of the wireless communication service that wirelessly connects the Palm VII handheld to the Internet. The network is based on the BellSouth Wireless Data Network, which provides wireless coverage in over 260 metropolitan areas in the U.S.

As of this writing, Palm.Net offers three service plans: Basic, Expanded, and Unlimited. Users are charged by the amount of data sent and received using the Palm VII handheld, not by air time. Each plan includes a different amount of usage, an overage fee for additional data transferred, and a one-time set up fee, as listed in Table 7-1.

Table 7-1 Palm VII Service Costs			
	Costs	**Kilobytes**	**Screens**
Basic	$9.99/month	50	150
Expanded	$24.99/month	150	450
Unlimited	$44.99/month	Unlimited	Unlimited
Overage	$0.20/kb	n/a	n/a
Set-up Fee	$9.99	n/a	n/a

Note The set-up fee is a one-time cost. The number of screens is an approximation; your mileage may vary—each kilobyte equals about three screens of information.

Palm.Net application

A special Palm.Net Web clipping application comes preloaded on the Palm VII handheld. This application enables the user to check monthly usage of the wireless service and submit questions or comments to customer support.

Secured transmission

The Palm VII handheld is equipped with built-in encryption software from Certicom. This encryption technology is used to secure your credit card or purchase order (P.O.) number when you activate the wireless service, and while you send sensitive information, such as passwords. Information is secured both when sent from your organizer over the network and when received on your organizer from the Internet.

Setting Up Your Palm VII

The Palm VII handheld comes with everything you need to get connected to the Internet, including:

✦ Palm VII handheld

✦ HotSync cradle

✦ Palm Desktop handheld software

✦ Getting Started Guide

✦ Palm.Net Service Plan card

✦ User manual

✦ DB9-25 serial adapter

✦ Protective carrying case

✦ 2 AAA batteries

Here are the quick steps for setting up the Palm VII handheld:

1. Remove the plastic film on the screen of the organizer.

2. Insert the two AAA batteries.

Note   Note the correct orientation of the batteries. As soon as you insert the AAA batteries, the internal transmitter will start charging and will continue to charge for about 70 minutes. Once the internal transmitter is charged, you can activate the Palm.Net wireless service.

3. Follow the Setup screen instructions to set the digitizer, date, and time, and to learn about Graffiti writing.

4. While you are waiting for the organizer to charge, connect the HotSync cradle to a serial port on your computer.

5. Install the Palm Desktop handheld software by inserting the CD-ROM in the CD-ROM drive, and follow the onscreen instructions. One screen lets you install additional Web clipping applications to your Palm VII handheld.

6. Synchronize your Palm VII with the Palm Desktop software. You will see the additional Web clipping applications on your organizer.

7. When the transmitter is charged, raise the antenna and you will see the first screen of the Activation application. To activate, you need a credit card number or a corporate account number.

8. Fill in the information (name, company, service plan, and so forth) as requested by the Activation application and record the username and password you are assigned. Your username is your address for sending and receiving messages.

Tip The username for the iMessenger application is also stored in Preferences application in the Wireless panel.

Using Web Clipping Applications

Web clipping is a fast and simple way to "clip" specific information from the Internet. A Web clipping application can also be called a "query form." The response received from the Internet is called a "clipping." Filling out a query form to get a clipping is simplicity itself.

Launching Web clipping applications

You launch Web clipping applications in the same way that you launch the basic applications. All the Web clipping applications are grouped by default under the Palm.Net category in the Launcher. Raising the antenna automatically takes you to the Palm.Net Launcher screen (see Figure 7-3), unless you've changed the Preferences option to have it call up a specific Web clipping application. Note that the titles of the applications are cut off in the figure.

Figure 7-3: Raising the antenna takes you to Palm.Net's Launcher screen.

Working with Web clipping applications

There are three basic steps for getting information from the Internet using the Palm VII handheld:

1. Select the Web clipping application for the type of information you want by tapping the application from the Launcher screen. A query form instantly appears (see Figure 7-4).

Note Because the query form resides on the organizer and is not downloaded over the air, calling it up and filling out its field(s) does not incur cost.

Figure 7-4: MapQuest query form

2. Specify the information you want from the Internet by filling out the query form for the application. Figure 7-5 shows a completed query form.

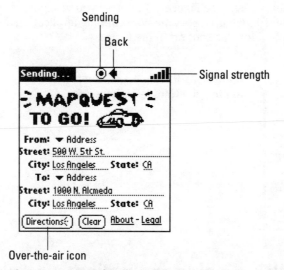

Figure 7-5: Completed query form

3. Raise the antenna and submit the query by tapping the icon with the "over the air" symbol. The clipping from that Web site returns in seconds (see Figure 7-6).

While the query is being sent, the sending and receiving status is displayed at the upper left-hand corner of the query form. You can tap the round, blinking Stop icon to stop the transaction at any time. Tap the back arrow to go back to a previously viewed page on the Web clipping application.

Tap for size

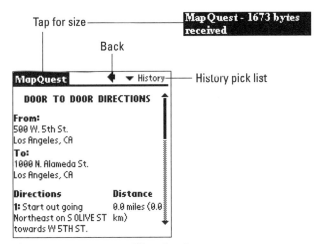

Back

History pick list

Figure 7-6: Response (directions)

The signal strength bars at the upper right-hand corner indicate the wireless signal strength. You can move the organizer around to improve the signal strength, which, in turn, improves the transmission speed.

Caution Tapping a command button or other object that displays the over-the-air icon initiates a wireless transaction and incurs a cost. Each query and response uses some kilobytes included in your monthly plan. If you exceed the included usage, you pay an overage fee.

Calling up and filling out a query form, viewing the contents of a clipping, and navigating through different clipping screens do not incur a cost because they take place locally on the organizer.

Size of clippings

To see the size of a clipping from the Internet, tap the title area, which expands to show the number of bytes received.

New Feature Those using OS 3.5 will find that they can no longer tap the title bar to get the size of a clipping. Instead, tap the Menu icon, select Options, and then Info (or use Command I as a shortcut).

History list

Each Web clipping application stores a list of clippings pertaining to that application, so that you can view contents downloaded previously. You do not incur a cost when you view contents from the History list. The History feature is especially useful for viewing static information, such as ATM locations or street directions, that you might have downloaded during an earlier session. If you think you might have queried for some static information already, check the History list to avoid paying twice for downloading the same information.

Preloaded Web clipping applications

The Palm VII comes with a number of Web clipping applications preloaded on the device itself. Here is a list of the applications included on the Palm VII with a brief description of each (as of the time of writing):

✦ **ABCNEWS.com.** Get up-to-the-minute U.S. and international news, business updates, technology reports, and the latest on health and living.

✦ **ESPN.com.** Get up-to-the-minute sports news, scores, schedules, and standings for all of the sports covered at ESPN.com.

✦ **Fidelity Investments.** Obtain delayed market information. Fidelity Brokerage customers can receive real-time market information, access to their account information, as well as certain order-entry capability.

✦ **MapQuest To Go.** Provides easy access to driving directions. Enter a starting point and destination and receive instant detailed driving directions for your trip.

✦ **The Weather Channel.** Check weather conditions for more than 40,000 locations worldwide through Weather.com. Receive current conditions and extended forecasts.

✦ **Travelocity.com.** Receive flight schedules for more than 700 airlines worldwide. Get up-to-the-minute flight arrival and departure information. Access existing itineraries and a flight paging service.

✦ **US WEST Dex.** Get quick, easy access to business listings throughout the United States. Search by category or business name to receive listings with phone numbers and addresses.

✦ **WSJ.com.** Get the latest headlines and summaries from some of the most popular areas of the *Wall Street Journal*'s Web site to keep you informed throughout the day. Receive information from areas such as Top News, Technology, and Markets.

✦ **Yahoo! People Search.** Search over 100 million telephone numbers and the world's largest e-mail directory to help you find the people you want.

Web clipping applications on the Palm Desktop CD-ROM

You can find more Web clipping applications on the Palm Desktop CD-ROM included in the Palm VII box. You can use the Install tool in your Palm Desktop handheld software to install these Web clipping applications to your Palm VII handheld. The process is the same as installing other add-on applications such as games or shareware.

As of this writing, the Palm Desktop CD-ROM includes these financial Web clipping applications:

✦ **Bank of America.** Use this application for quick and easy home banking needs.

✦ **E*Trade.** Retrieve instant stock quotes over the air.

✦ **MasterCard.** Locate the nearest ATM without having to tell your Palm VII handheld where you are (it already knows).

✦ **TheStreet.com.** Download all the latest financial news and analysis.

✦ **Visa.** Do you have Visa instead of MasterCard? This is the ATM locator application for you.

The Palm Desktop CD-ROM's current travel and entertainment Web clipping applications include:

✦ **Etak.** Stuck in traffic? Late for an appointment and worried you won't get there on time? Check out Etak's real-time traffic information.

✦ **Fodor's.** This is one of two applications that you can use to find the nearest recommended restaurant, hotel, museum, tourist information center, and so on.

✦ **Frommer's.** This is the other travel and tourist information guide.

✦ **Moviefone.com.** Use this application to find out what movie is playing, what time it's playing, and what people are saying about it. You can even purchase a movie ticket from here.

✦ **OAG.** If you've ever held an Official Airline Guide in your hands, you know how big it is. This application gives you all the same information in a much smaller (and faster) package.

✦ **Ticketmaster.** Just like the Ticketmaster you can call on the phone, this application lets you reserve your seat and pay for your ticket wirelessly.

The Palm Desktop CD-ROM's reference Web clipping applications include:

✦ **Merriam-Webster.** Looking for a definition, correct spelling, or an alternative word to use? Rely on the Merriam-Webster solution.

✦ **UPS.** Use this application for wireless package tracking or to find the nearest UPS drop-off location.

The Palm Desktop CD-ROM also includes USA Today.com as a Web clipping application for general, nationwide news.

Web clipping applications at www.palm.net

You can find more Web clipping applications at the Palm.Net Web site at `www.palm.net`. More than 200 Web clipping applications have been posted to this site. As with the applications found on the Palm Desktop CD-ROM, you can use the Install tool in your Palm Desktop handheld software to install additional Web clipping applications that you download from www.palm.net.

Developing a Web clipping application

If you are interested in developing a Web clipping application for the Palm VII, you can find the development tools and guidelines at www.palm.com/devzone/tools. You can also submit your application to www.palm.net for review and posting on the Palm.Net Web site.

Exploring the Basic iMessenger Features

The Palm VII also offers iMessenger, wireless Internet messaging. When you activate the Palm.Net wireless service, you acquire an address on the Palm.Net network for sending and receiving messages. Through the iMessenger application, you can do the following directly from your organizer:

✦ Download messages waiting in your Palm.Net Inbox.

✦ Read, delete, reply to, and reroute incoming messages.

✦ Draft messages.

✦ Send messages to any Internet e-mail address.

To open the iMessenger application, raise the antenna, and tap the iMessenger icon (see Figure 7-7).

 Figure 7-7: The iMessenger icon

The list view of your Inbox messages appears as shown in Figure 7-8.

Folder list

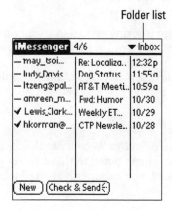 **Figure 7-8:** iMessenger e-mail list

The iMessenger application provides folders for categorizing your messages. To select a folder, tap the pick list in the upper-right corner to open the list of folders:

✦ **Inbox** contains messages downloaded from your Palm.Net Inbox.

✦ **Outbox** contains messages you created and saved in the Outbox.

✦ **Deleted** contains messages you deleted.

✦ **Filed** contains messages you want to file and store on the organizer.

✦ **Draft** contains messages you created but are not yet ready to send.

Creating messages

To create a message, tap New. A New message screen appears (see Figure 7-9). Next to the To field, enter the e-mail addresses to which you want to send the message. Separate the addresses with commas or spaces, or enter each address on its own line.

Figure 7-9: iMessenger's new message screen

Tip   To look up an address from the Address book, tap the To field to expand that field. Tap Lookup. Enter the first few letters of the first or last name of the person whose address you want to find. Select the desired name, tap Add, and then tap Done.

Enter the subject in the Subj field and the message in the Body field. To send the message immediately, raise the antenna (if not raised already), and tap Check & Send. A Transaction Progress dialog box appears and confirms the transaction. To cancel the transaction, tap Cancel.

Outbox and draft messages

You can save new messages in the Outbox folder by tapping the Outbox button on the New message page. Messages saved in the Outbox are sent the next time you tap Check & Send.

You can also save new messages in the Draft folder. To do that, tap Cancel on the New message page. A Save Draft dialog box appears. Tap Yes to save the message in the Draft folder.

Editing unsent messages

You can edit messages saved in the Outbox or Draft folders at any time. From the List view, tap the pick list at the upper-right corner and select the folder you want. Tap the message you want to edit and tap Edit.

Check and send messages

Tapping Check & Send creates two actions: it downloads messages waiting in your Palm.Net Inbox and it sends out messages stored in the iMessenger Outbox folder.

Reading messages

The iMessenger application downloads ten messages at a time. Each downloaded message is compressed. When you open the message, it is uncompressed and converted to a readable form. The first 500 characters are downloaded initially. A message at the end of the download tells you if more characters still need to be retrieved. You can download the rest of the message or ignore what is left (see Figure 7-10).

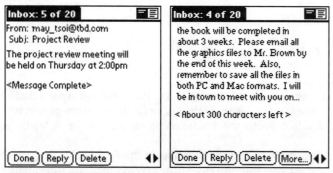

Figure 7-10: The message on the left is complete, but the rest of the message on the right must be downloaded.

Note   The iMessenger application does not support attachments, with the exception of a simple ASCII text file. It appends the text of the ASCII text file to the end of the message.

Filing and deleting messages

There are two ways to file a message: from within the message or from the List view of the Inbox, Outbox, Deleted, or Draft folders.

From within the message, tap the Menu icon and select File under the Message menu. The message is filed under the Filed folder.

From the List view, tap the dash, check, or diamond icon in the left-most column. A list appears with options to file, edit, delete/undelete, or move to Draft (see Figure 7-11). The options vary depending on which folder you are viewing.

Figure 7-11: File or delete messages.

Using the Advanced iMessenger Options

The more advanced iMessenger options enable you to set your preferences.

Preferences

The iMessenger application provides several preference settings (see Figure 7-12):

✦ Sort list view by date, sender, or subject

✦ Confirm deleted message

✦ Reroute replies to another e-mail address

✦ Add a signature to your message

Tap the Sort by pick list and select to sort by date, sender, or subject. The Sort by Date option sorts the most recent items first in the list view. Sort by Sender or Sort by Subject arranges the list view in alphabetical order by sender or by subject respectively.

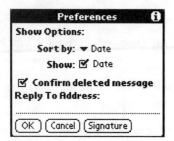

Figure 7-12: Preferences screen

By default, the Date column option is set to display in the list view. You can turn off this option by unchecking the Show by Date option. This increases the amount of screen space available for the From and Subject fields.

If you want to see a confirmation dialog box before a message is deleted, check the Confirm deleted message option.

If you want recipients of your messages to reply to a different address than your Palm.Net address, enter an e-mail address in the Reply to Address field.

Tap the Signature button to enter text that can be appended to a message as your signature. Signatures must be added individually to each message, so you can minimize the amount of data sent in each message.

Your iMessenger mailbox features on www.palm.net

Your iMessenger mailbox resides on the Palm.Net network, not on your Palm VII. It has a storage capacity of up to 2MB. When your mailbox is full, incoming messages are returned to the sender as undeliverable. You can make room in your mailbox by deleting messages from your mailbox.

Deleting messages from your mailbox

You can delete blocks of messages directly from your Palm.Net mailbox. Go to the My Account area of the Palm.Net Web site and follow the onscreen instructions. You can delete messages older than two weeks, older than four weeks, or all messages in the mailbox. Messages you downloaded (either complete or partial) remain in the Inbox for 30 days. After 30 days, they are deleted automatically. A message that you have not downloaded remains in the Inbox for 60 days. After 60 days, it is deleted automatically.

Carbon copy of messages you send

In the www.palm.net Web site My Account area, you can specify an address to which a blind carbon copy of your messages will be sent.

Backing up messages

Unlike the other basic applications, such as Address Book, on your organizer, when you synchronize the iMessenger application with your Palm Desktop handheld software, you will not see the content of the messages on your computer. Instead, your iMessenger application preferences and a record of downloaded messages on your organizer are stored on your computer.

If you do a hard reset of your organizer, which erases all data including messages in the iMessenger application, synchronize immediately after the hard reset to restore the record of messages on your organizer. Then, the next time you check messages in your Palm.Net mailbox, only messages that you have not downloaded are downloaded from the network.

To synchronize the iMessenger application with a Macintosh computer, you need the iMessenger conduit for the Macintosh. Visit www.palm.net for information about this software.

Using the Palm.Net Resources

The Palm.Net Web site at www.palm.com has useful information about the wireless features of the Palm VII and the Palm.Net wireless service. The following information is available at the Web site:

Coverage maps

Check indoor and outdoor coverage of the Palm.Net wireless service. Click a city or enter a zip code to see whether an area is within Palm.Net's wireless service coverage area. You can also report weak or no coverage problems on this site. As of the publication date of this book, the Palm.Net wireless service provides coverage in more than 260 metropolitan areas in the United States. The Palm VII product currently works in the U.S. only.

My Account

My Account is the place to check your billing and account status. You can get an account summary of your monthly usage and a detailed report on your daily usage.

In addition, you may change your account information (name, address, e-mail), your credit card information, and your service plan. My Account serves current Palm.Net customers and a valid username and password is required to access it.

Support information

Get technical support information about the Palm VII handheld and the Palm.Net wireless service. Submit questions to customer support.

Download more Web clipping applications

The Palm.Net Web site features all Web clipping applications developed and submitted by third-party developers. You can find the week's newest Web clipping applications or the ten most-downloaded applications. Search for applications by name or by categories (news, financial, entertainment, travel and more). Each application is posted with a description and rating.

Other Web resources

The Palm Web site at `www.palm.com` links you to different sources of information about the Palm VII, other Palm, products, and third-party products. You can also sign up for InSync Online to get the latest news, Web clipping applications, and tips via e-mail.

Summary

The Palm VII comes with all the core applications that the other Palm products offer, plus wireless capabilities. The main features that Palm VII has and the other Palm products lack are:

✦ Wireless access to the Internet via Web clipping applications

✦ Wireless Internet messaging via the iMessenger application

✦ Access to the Palm.Net wireless service

✦ Dedicated customer care service

✦ Dedicated Palm.Net Web site

✦   ✦   ✦

Introducing the Handspring Visor

✦ ✦ ✦ ✦

In This Chapter

From the PalmPilot to the Visor

Introducing the Visor

Using the Springboard cards and software

✦ ✦ ✦ ✦

This chapter discusses the latest from the founders of Palm, Inc.: the Handspring Visor. In many ways, this device is identical to the Palm Organizer — it uses the same operating system, runs the same applications, and looks very similar. I focus on those features that make the Visor unique — the rest of the *Palm OS Bible* covers common functionality.

Background

In 1994, Jeff Hawkins invented the Graffiti text entry method, which made handwriting recognition practical for handheld devices. Jeff also came up with a simple set of design goals for what would become the original PalmPilot device. According to the design goals, in addition to Graffiti, the new device should:

- ✦ Fit in a shirt pocket
- ✦ Be designed for desktop synchronization
- ✦ Deliver instant performance
- ✦ Be easily affordable

Within a year, Palm was seeking financing to bring their vision to market. In September 1995, that goal was achieved by the purchase of Palm by US Robotics. 3Com Corporation subsequently purchased US Robotics in 1997. The PalmPilot became the most successful handheld device ever made, capturing over 70 percent of its market, with over 4 million devices shipped to date.

In July 1998, Jeff Hawkins, Donna Dubinsky, and Ed Colligan left Palm, the company they founded, to form Handspring, Inc. The product they left to create was cloaked in secrecy until recently — everyone knew it would be based on the Palm OS, but the details were unknown until the Visor was ready.

 Note I'd like to thank Rob Haitani, Visor Product Manager at Handspring, for his help with this chapter. Rob was the original product manager for the Pilot at Palm — see the Easter Eggs in Appendix A for details on how to find his picture in the operating system.

The Visor

The Handspring Visor is a handheld personal digital assistant (PDA) that is similar to the Palm IIIx. It runs a licensed version of the Palm OS that is based on Palm OS version 3.1. The Handspring OS incorporates most, if not all of the improvements made in Palm OS 3.3, including support for the Euro currency symbol and USB HotSyncing (USB HotSyncing is available from Palm as the PalmConnect Kit).

 Caution One feature of OS 3.3 that is not included in Handspring's version is the automatic backup of all installed applications. See Chapter 22 for an explanation of how to manually make backups, or read about the great shareware alternative BackupBuddy.

The Handspring OS resides in a nonflashable ROM chip, as opposed to the flash memory used in Palm's handheld devices. This means that operating system changes will be made with patches, whereas a new operating system can be copied to a Palm device's flash memory. The Visor ships with either 2 or 8MB of memory, depending on the model.

 Note With the exception of the Palm IIIe, all Palm devices since the Palm III have incorporated flash memory.

Handspring has tweaked the Palm OS to wring out even more performance from the Motorola DragonBall EZ processor that it shares with the Palm IIIx and Palm V. It is hard to quantify the performance improvement, because benchmarking tools for the Palm OS are dependant on your software configuration. I estimate that it is 20 to 25 percent faster than the Palm IIIx — there is no question that this device offers snappier performance than all but the latest from Palm (the Palm Vx uses the 20MHz DragonBall EZ processor).

Models

There are three models of the Visor available as of this writing: the Visor Solo, the Visor, and the Visor Deluxe. The Solo model is designed for those who have no need for the HotSync cradle, either because they don't have access to a personal computer, or because they already have a Visor cradle. The basic Visor adds a USB

HotSync cradle to the 2MB Solo device, making it functionally similar to Palm's IIIe model, and the Visor Deluxe bumps the memory to 8MB, along with the USB cradle and a leather slipcase. All Visor models ship with an infrared port, backlight, and built-in microphone.

Note An optional serial cradle is available for those who do not have a USB connection.

Table 8-1 compares the prices and features of the three Visor models.

Table 8-1 Visor Models					
Model	Price	Memory	Cradle	Colors	Case
Visor Solo	$149.00	2MB	No	Graphite	No
Visor	$179.00	2MB	Yes	Graphite	No
Visor Deluxe	$249.00	8MB	Yes	5 Available	Yes

First impressions

The first thing you notice with Visor is that it is slightly narrower than the Palm III series. The size is otherwise virtually identical to the Palm III series, although the narrow shape and side ribbing give it a distinctively different feel in your hand. At 5.4 ounces, the Visor is also slightly lighter (by a half an ounce) than the Palm IIIx.

Following Apple's lead with the iMac, the Visor Deluxe is available in five colors: a standard graphite color (a dark gray close to black), and four translucent colors: Ice (clear), Blue, Green, and Orange. The screen, which is identical to the wonderful 160×160 screen used in the Palm IIIx, is offset slightly to the right. The asymmetrical design lets Handspring make the Visor slightly narrower than the Palm III series; it also adds to the strength of the device — it feels more solid than the Palm III. A slick, hard-shell cover that fits neatly on the back of the Visor caps it all off. The HotSync cradle is another improvement on Palm's design: a small tab in the back of the Visor helps prevent accidentally knocking the Visor from the cradle. A significant addition for Macintosh users is out-of-the-box compatibility, without the need to buy additional connectors or software.

As you can see in Figure 8-1, Handspring has updated the button and silk-screened graphics that you use to access the Visor's applications. In the lower left-hand corner of the silk-screened icons, is a half-filled circle, which is used to access the screen contrast controls for the Visor. Those who pay attention to detail will notice a small hole in the casing beneath the Date Book button — this houses a microphone to be used by future Springboard devices.

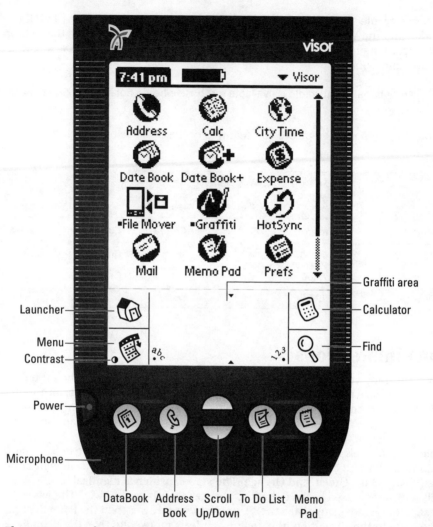

Figure 8-1: Handspring's Visor

A look behind the Visor (see Figure 8-2) reveals some of the interesting changes that Handspring has made for its handheld device. First and foremost is the Springboard card slot, which is perhaps the most exciting innovation of this new device. The Springboard slot's open-ended design, which allows for some creative expansion, also necessitated the side placement of the infrared port. The port at the bottom of the Visor may look similar to Palm's serial port, but it is another of Handspring's innovations: a USB port with a corresponding USB cradle for faster HotSyncing.

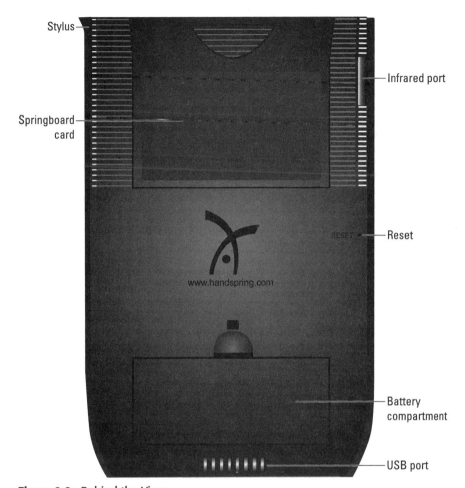

Figure 8-2: Behind the Visor

Note My experience so far is that the Visor's USB cradle is faster than Palm's serial cradle, although not ten times faster as the specifications may suggest. (USB transfers can be as fast as 1.5 megabits per second, whereas the maximum transfer rate for Palm's serial connection is 115 kilobits per second.)This is because the HotSync process itself carries a heavy overhead, which means that a faster connection is not the only factor in your syncing speed.

Even the stylus offers improvements, with a distinct pen-on-paper feel. One feature I do miss is Palm's integrated reset pin. You need to carry a paperclip for emergency resets, because Palm's reset pin does not work on the Visor.

Springboard

The Springboard card is at the heart of the innovation in the new Visor. This little card is truly plug and play — any required drivers are found on the Springboard module; they are loaded when the card is inserted, and unloaded when the card is removed. The process is magical: with the Visor running, adding a card instantly gives you that card's functionality. This is a refreshing change from ordinary computer standards, which are closer to plug-and-pray for add-on devices. The other significant feature of the Springboard design is that it is an open-faced card slot — cards can extend out the back, have attachments or buttons, and even use their own batteries or processor.

There were four cards available when the Visor shipped: an 8MB quick backup module, an 8MB Flash memory module, a Tiger Woods PGA Tour Golf module (a palm-sized golf game), and a 33.6-baud modem card. I've been playing with the 8MB module; there is nothing quite like a 16MB Visor! Table 8-2 describes the modules in greater detail.

Table 8-2
Springboard Modules

Developer	Module	Expected Availability
Concept Kitchen	Lonely Planet CitySync PDA Travel Guides	Now available
Datastick Systems	MyCorder Analog Data Acquisitions System	Now available
Electronic Arts	EA Sports Tiger Woods PGA Golf Tour	Now available
Franklin Covey	Covey Reference Library	Now available
Glenayre	Wireless Communications Solutions	2000
Handspring, Inc.	Modem	Now available
Handspring, Inc.	8MB Flash	Now available
Handspring, Inc.	Quick Backup	Now available
Imagiworks	Sensor Science	Now available
Imagiworks	Personal TechCoach	Now available
Innogear	MP3 Player	Q2 2000
Innogear	Voice Recorder	Q2 2000
JP Systems	One-Touch Messaging	Q2 2000
Landware	Merriam Webster Dictionary	Q2 2000
MarcoSoft	Streetrak Integrated GPS & Street-Level Mapping	Q2 2000

Developer	Module	Expected Availability
Navicom	GPS Radio	Q2 2000
Pacific Neo-Tek	OmniRemote Universal Remote Control	Now available
Peanut Press	Electronic Books	Now available
RioPort	Digital Audio Player	Winter 2000
Sycom	Sycom Recorder Digital Recorder and Playback	Now available
Widcomm Inc.	Bluetooth Communications	Fall 2000

Other products coming as Springboard modules include:

✦ Bar code readers

✦ Cellular phones

✦ Digital cameras

✦ Pagers — one-way and two-way

✦ Smart Card readers

✦ Video games

✦ Video out modules

✦ Wireless modems for Internet access

Software

In addition to the OS speedups, Handspring has added its own touches to the built-in applications, offering additional functionality that will be particularly interesting to the power user. Three new applications, based on shareware programs, add considerable functionality and value (other Palm users who register these three products will pay $47.95 in shareware fees).

Date Book+

The Visor includes both Palm's standard Date Book application and Date Book+, which is based on Pimlico Software's excellent shareware application DateBk3. The differences between the shareware and the Visor version are subtle; Date Book+'s are designed to make the product easier to use. In addition to a cleanup of the DateBk3's interface, the major changes involve the removal of support for icons, time zones, and categories within Date Book+. The result is a cleaner-looking application that is easier to use (see Figure 8-3) and includes most of the functionality of this great shareware application (see Chapter 21 for more on DateBk3). For new users, the major improvements over the standard Date Book are the integration of

To Do items, which can now display on your calendar, and additional views, which offer a better overview of your schedule.

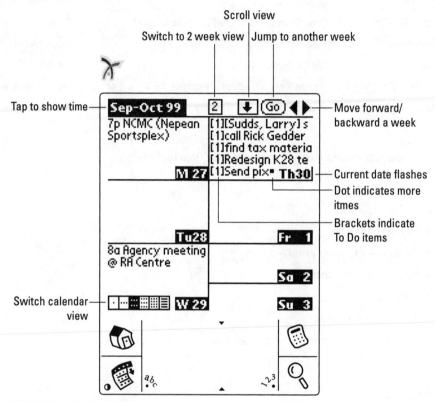

Figure 8-3: Date Book+

New users will be happy with the standard Palm application, whereas power users will prefer the advanced features of the alternate application. Changing your default Date Book is easy: just select Default Date Book from the Options menu to get the dialog box shown in Figure 8-4, and tap the version you prefer. This will change the version displayed when you press Visor's Date Book button.

Advanced calculator

Palm's built-in calculator is the weakest of the built-in applications, opening the door for improvements by creative shareware authors. One of the best improvements is Rick Huebner's Parens, which is used as Visor's Advanced Calculator. (A limited shareware version, Parens Lite, is included with every Palm device.) As you can see from Figure 8-5, this powerhouse offers math, trigonometry, finance, logic, and statistical functions, along with conversions for weight, temperature, length, area, and volume.

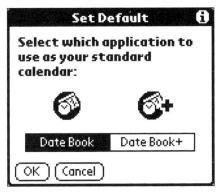

Figure 8-4: Changing the Visor's Date Book

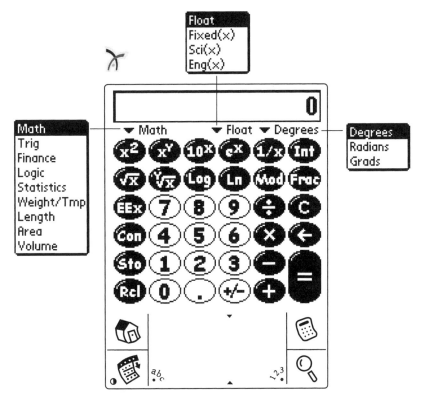

Figure 8-5: Parens

Changing your default Calculator is easy: just select Change Mode from the Options menu to get the dialog box shown in Figure 8-6, and tap the version that you prefer. This will change the version displayed when you tap the calculator icon.

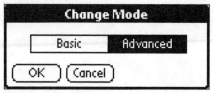

Figure 8-6: Changing the Visor's calculator

CityTime

CityTime is a world clock based on Code City's shareware program of the same name. A unique display (see Figure 8-7) shows the time in your home time zone, plus four other cities, along with a world map showing the current areas in daylight.

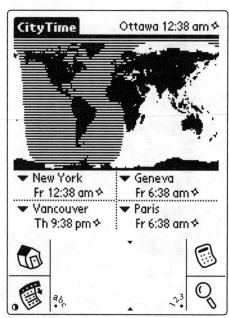

Figure 8-7: CityTime

Adding your city

To add your home town to the list, if it isn't already there, follow these steps:

1. Select Edit Cities from the Options menu and select the nearest city in your time zone.

2. Note the +/– GMT number, along with the Daylight savings rules, and then tap OK.

3. Tap New to get the dialog box shown in Figure 8-8.

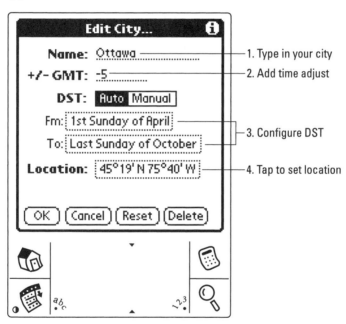

Figure 8-8: Adding a new city

4. Enter your city name, along with the GMT adjustment number and Daylight savings rules you noted above.

5. Tap Location to get the dialog box shown in Figure 8-9, and drag the coordinates to your city's location on the world map. If you want to be accurate, tap Coordinates and enter your longitude and latitude.

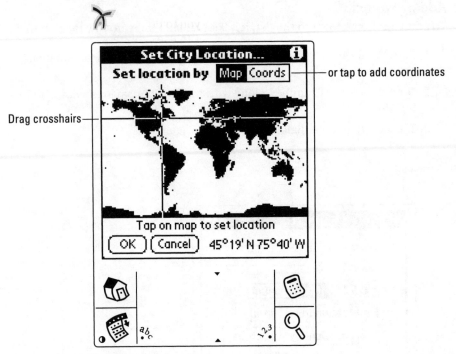

Drag crosshairs — [map showing "Set City Location...", "Set location by Map Coords"] — or tap to add coordinates

Figure 8-9: Setting your city's location

Tip

If you don't know your city's longitude and latitude, you can look them up on the Internet at www.bcca.org/misc/qiblih/latlong.html. **Time offset values can be found at** www.timeanddate.com/worldclock/full.html.

Once you've added your city to the list, use Select Home City from the Options menu so that the correct time is displayed at the top of the CityTime screen.

Springboard cards

As of this writing, very few of the Springboard cards are available; most of the listing earlier in this chapter should be out by the time you read this. The applications covered here automatically appear in your Launcher when you insert the card, and disappear when you remove it. This seamless integration provides one of the best demonstrations of Visor's capabilities.

Backup

The 8MB Springboard backup card enables you to do a quick backup or restore of any Visor model. The card couldn't be easier to use — inserting the card automatically starts the backup application shown in Figure 8-10, giving two simple choices: backup or restore.

Figure 8-10: Backing up with the Springboard card

FileMover

The 8MB Springboard flash module is what has impressed me the most with Visor — if the instant plug and play and elegant integration with the OS are indicative of anything, we're in for a treat with these modules. As Figure 8-11 shows, applications that are loaded on the Flash card are marked with a bullet. The Launcher also includes support for applications loaded on a Springboard card; selecting Info from the App menu gives a display that can be toggled between those files that are loaded in your Visor and those that are loaded on the card.

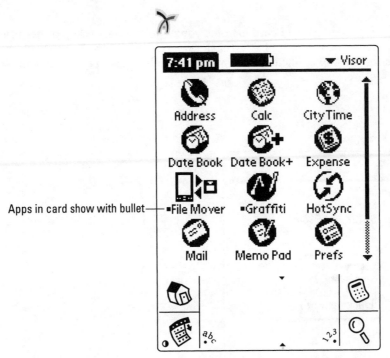

Apps in card show with bullet

Figure 8-11: A bullet indicates that an application, such as FileMover, is loaded on the Flash card.

Moving files into Flash memory is simple — open the File Mover application (see Figure 8-12) and select the applications that you want to copy, move, or delete. While moving applications to the card may be easy, it is a good idea be cautious, because not all applications work well running out of Flash memory. This is because some programmers have written their programs so that the software expects to find the application and its data in the same location, which will not always be the case when an application is moved to the Flash card. Programs such as HackMaster and TrapWeaver, along with read/write databases, should not be loaded in Flash memory. When things go wrong, it is usually a matter of moving the errant application back to regular memory. I have run into instances where a hard reset is necessary — see Chapter 24 details on how to hard reset and restore your Visor.

Tip　If you're not sure whether an application will run on Handspring's Flash module, check out the Flash compatibility listing at `www.asynccomputing.com/cgi-bin/displayTRGCompatListing.pl`. This listing, which is intended to cover compatibility with TRG's Flash memory, provides a good idea of what will and won't work in the card.

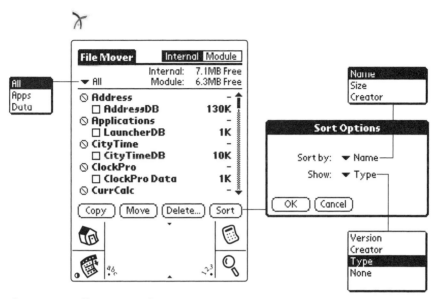

Figure 8-12: FileMover settings

Tiger Woods PGA Tour golf module

When Electronic Arts released Tiger Woods Golf, it was the first commercial arcade game for the Palm OS, complete with grayscale support, electronic opponents, and 18 holes of game play (see Figure 8-13). The only real limitation was the file size: at 500K, this application used a significant amount of your precious RAM. The Springboard version fixes that limitation: there are no memory requirements — just plug it in and play!

Other enhancements

There are other subtle enhancements to the Palm OS. I particularly like the clever way that the Visor integrates the Palm V's contrast control, without needing a new button. Macintosh users have a new USB setting in their HotSync setup (see Figure 8-14); MacPac is otherwise identical.

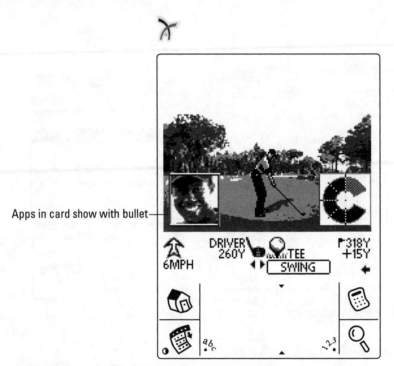

Apps in card show with bullet

Figure 8-13: Tiger Woods golf module

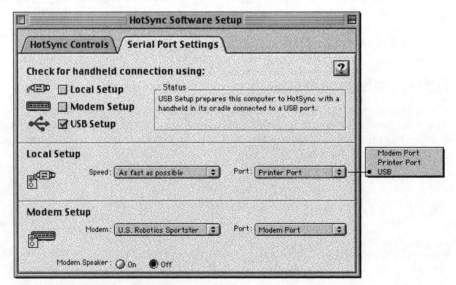

Figure 8-14: MacPac USB settings

Summary

The Visor is the new handheld device from the founders of Palm. The Visor offers a different look, with five colors, but the biggest improvement is the new Springboard card, which enables the addition of new functionality.

The Visor offers a number of subtle enhancements to the Palm OS, including advanced versions of the built-in Date Book and Calculator, along with CityTime, a multicity time display.

Users of the 8MB Springboard card should slowly add applications to their new device to ensure compatibility between the card and the applications.

The Visor is designed for users at all levels — the price, colors, and ease of use will appeal to the novice; the additional memory, advanced applications, and Springboard capabilities will entice the power user.

✦   ✦   ✦

Using the Desktop Software

P A R T

II

♦ ♦ ♦ ♦

In This Part

Chapter 9
Using the Palm
Desktop for Windows

Chapter 10
Using the Palm
Desktop for
Macintosh

♦ ♦ ♦ ♦

Using the Palm Desktop for Windows

◆ ◆ ◆ ◆

In This Chapter

Accessing the Palm Desktop

Mirror applications

Menus

User-named folders

Microsoft Outlook

◆ ◆ ◆ ◆

Your Palm Organizer's Desktop software is a powerful set of tools that mirrors the functionality of the four basic applications on your Palm Organizer: Date Book, Address Book, To Do List, and Memo Pad. Jeff Hawkin's original concept for the Pilot was as a viewer of data created elsewhere — and the Desktop software provides an elegant means to that end. Many users spend most of their time using the Desktop application. In this chapter, I take a closer look at the functionality available to Windows Palm users (Macintosh users need not feel left out; MacPac is discussed in Chapter 8). This chapter focuses on version 3.01 of the Palm Desktop software, which is available for download at www.palm.com/custsupp/downloads. This software is currently available for Windows 95, 98, and NT 4.0, and works with all of Palm's products from the original Pilot on. I highly recommend that all Windows users upgrade to this version.

Caution   Palm, Inc. warns that if you upgrade to Version 3.0 of the Palm Desktop software, third party conduit applications that you installed to synchronize with other PIMs (personal information managers) may no longer work. If the conduit relies on earlier versions of HotSync Manager, you need to contact the manufacturer of the conduit software to obtain an upgrade. This does not affect you if you synchronize only with the Palm Desktop application.

The version may change by the time you read this. For the latest versions of Palm Desktop software for your computer, check out the Palm Web site at the above URL. The latest version of the Palm OS (which runs on your handheld) is 3.5 as of this writing.

Note   In the past, no cross-platform PIMs (personal information managers) that I know of could share a common data file. This meant that users with Windows and Macintosh computers were forced to choose a platform for their PIMs. The Palm Desktop software has changed that—users can HotSync to multiple machines, regardless of platform! When I get to the office, I HotSync my Palm V organizer to my desktop machine (PII/300 running Windows NT 4.0), and use the Desktop applications until I leave the office. When I get home, I do the same with my Macintosh (G3/266 running Mac OS 8.6) and my PC (PII/350 running Windows 98).

Accessing the Palm Desktop

Windows 95, 98, or NT 4.0 users should use the Start menu to navigate to Programs ➪ Palm Desktop ➪ Palm Desktop.

Here's a time-saver for new users: create a desktop shortcut for the Palm Desktop application. Open your C drive (or the drive that you installed to), and find the Palm Desktop application (the default is C:\Palm\Palm.exe). Right-click the icon and drag it to the desktop to create a desktop shortcut that you can use to launch the application.

Mirror Applications

The Desktop is one of the strengths of the Palm Organizer. Other products charge for synchronization; 3Com includes HotSyncing (Chapter 6) *and* applications for your computer. I use the Palm Desktop software to run my life.

Date Book

The first thing displayed when you open the Palm Desktop is an expanded version of your handheld's Date Book application. As you can see from Figure 9-1, much of the screen is "live"; clicking, right-clicking, or dragging brings up the expected menus. The icons on the left-hand side of the screen let you change the application to Address, To Do, or Memo view.

If you installed the Expense Application when you installed the Palm Desktop (you need Microsoft Excel 95 or better installed on your computer), you will see an Expense icon below the applications icons. Clicking this icon opens Microsoft Excel and the expense data that has been HotSynced from your handheld. See Chapter 12 for more on the Expense Application.

The Install icon was added with version 3.0 of the Palm Desktop; it lets you install multiple files at once. If you prefer, you can call up the Windows File Manager and double-click any .prc program file to open the Install Tool and have it installed at the next HotSync.

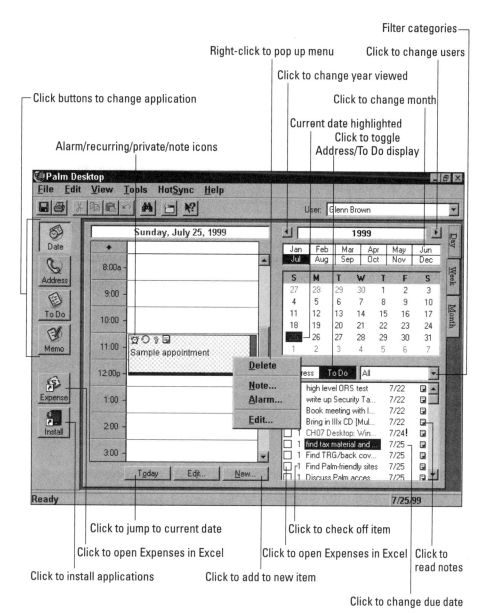

Figure 9-1: The Palm Desktop opening screen

Cross-Reference

See Chapter 11 for a complete rundown on loading applications on your Palm Organizer.

The tabs on the right side of the screen enable you to switch between a day, week, or month view of your calendar. The latter two views will take over most of the application window, but the day view manages to cram in a monthly calendar overview, along with a small portion of either your Address Book or To Do List. This may make it the best choice as your opening view.

Tip   While you can use the Tools ➪ Options dialog box to change the view displayed when you first open the Palm Desktop, the main view (Date Book ➪ Day) does the best job of incorporating all PIM elements on one screen.

Viewing your calendar for another day is simple; you can jump to another day or month by clicking directly on the calendar. Clicking the arrows to the left and right of the year change the year shown. To get back to the current date, just click Today from any calendar view.

The menu bar at the top of the screen (see Figure 9-2) provides quick access to basic Windows functions. If you have multiple users synchronizing their Palm Organizers to your computer, clicking the pop-up list at the right of the menu bar enables you to switch the view to another user. A key icon displays to the left of your username if your private records are hidden.

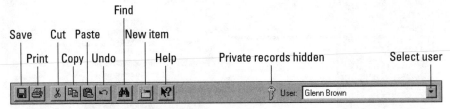

Figure 9-2: Palm Desktop menu bar

Adding a new appointment

There are all sorts of ways to add a new appointment to your calendar. Here are some possibilities:

✦ Click the New button to open the Edit Event dialog box (see Figure 9-3); from there you can set the time and date of your appointment, attach a note, set recurring appointments, set an alarm to remind you of your appointment, and make the appointment private.

Note   Alarms set in the Desktop application will only show up on your handheld; they do not remind you while you are using your computer.

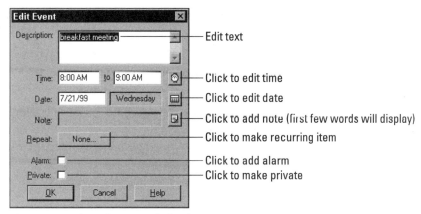

Figure 9-3: The Edit Event dialog box

✦ Select New Event from the Edit menu.

✦ Press either Alt+N or Ctrl+N from the Date Book window.

✦ Click your calendar and a box will appear; start typing to add your appointment.

✦ Drag an Address to your calendar to create an appointment with that person.

✦ Drag a To Do item to your calendar to block out a time to complete the task.

✦ Right-click your calendar in the month view and select New Event.

Editing appointments

Editing an existing appointment is easy — you've already seen how easy it can be to change the time by dragging, but that's not your only choice:

✦ Double-click an item to edit the appointment's description (the appointment changes from the yellow highlight color to white, and the edit cursor appears).

✦ Click an appointment to select it; a black bar appears at the bottom of the item. After it is selected, you can click the Edit button, or press Delete, if that is your choice. You can also drag it to another day on the calendar or, if you are in the week view, to another time on another day in the week.

✦ Double-click in the right side border of any item to open the Edit dialog box.

✦ Right-click any appointment to get a pop-up menu that enables you to delete, edit, add a note, or include an alarm.

The Changing Cursor

As you drag things around your calendar, the cursor changes to indicate what mode you are in:

✦ Click the bottom border of an appointment and it changes to an up and down arrow, indicating that you can drag the finish time up or down.

✦ Click the right border of an appointment and a four-sided arrow appears under your cursor, indicating that you can drag your appointment. This enables you to move the time earlier or later in the day — you can even drop the appointment on another day in your calendar.

✦ Dragging an Address or a To Do item to your calendar changes the cursor to indicate that you are dragging information.

Drag an appointment to another day to reschedule

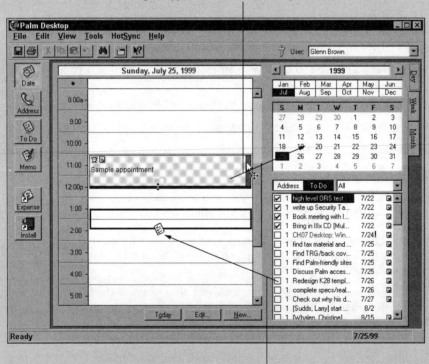

Drag a contact or to do item onto your calendar to make an appointment

Calendar cursors

Address book

Can you imagine entering your entire address book using Graffiti? I certainly cannot. The Desktop version of the Address Book enables you to enter contact information using your computer (see Figure 9-4). Chapter 4 discussed how to import your existing computer-based list; this chapter looks at how to add new records.

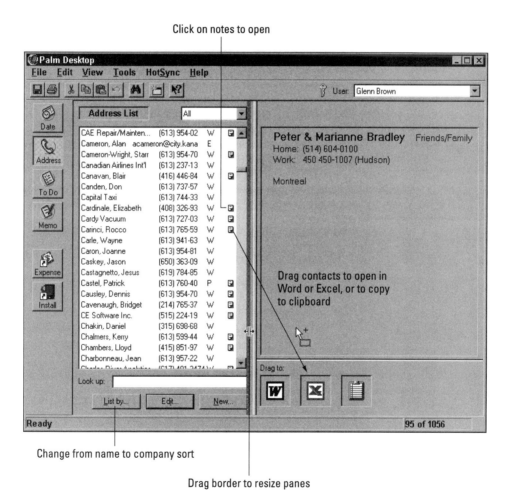

Figure 9-4: Address Book

Tip If you click the gray area between the contacts listing and the Details pane, your cursor changes to one indicating column adjustment, and you can change the relative sizes of the two panes.

Adding a contact

As with the Date Book, there are several ways to add a new contact to your Address Book:

✦ Click the New button

✦ Select New Address from the Edit menu

✦ Press either Alt+N or Ctrl+N from the Address Book window

Each method brings you to the Edit Address dialog box shown in Figure 9-5. Here you have three tabbed panes that enable you to enter name and address information, along with notes, for each of your contacts. To the left of the phone number listing is a radio button. Whichever of these is selected will be the phone number displayed in your Address listing, both on your computer and on your Palm Organizer. There are four fields at the bottom of the address pane that you can customize using the Tools ➪ Custom Fields Labels. I use Birthday, Spouse, Children, and Key; you can set these to whatever you'd like to help you remember important information about your contacts.

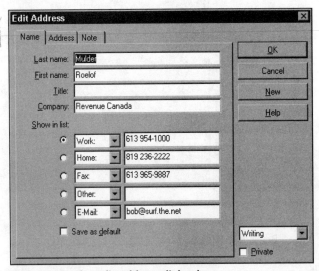

Figure 9-5: The Edit Address dialog box

Tip After you've entered several contacts, you'll probably want to set the numbers you use most as the default numbers in your Address Book. To do this, use the adjacent pop-up lists to order the appearance of the numbers in the list, click the radio button next to the number to select which ones should show in the default list, and then click Save **as** Default check box. From then on, all new records will start with that configuration, which you can use or change as you please. Unfortunately, category settings aren't saved this way.

Tip If you travel a lot, you probably have stacks of business cards you've received from people you've met. Don't you wish there were an easy way to get them into your handheld? There is: check out the Corex CardScan, which is described in Chapter 22.

Copying contact information

If you want to quickly copy a contact's information, right-click the entry and select Copy from the pop-up menu; the information will now be in your computer's clipboard. Alt+Tab to another application and then select Paste from the Edit menu. You can also drag a contact to the icons at the bottom right of the screen. Dragging to the Word icon opens Word and opens a dialog box that enables you to choose:

✦ Formatted Addresses (a new letter)

✦ Form Letters (sets up a new letter for mail merge)

✦ Mailing Labels (creates mailing labels)

✦ Envelopes (sets up to print envelopes)

✦ Leave Data as a Table (formatted in a Word table)

Dragging contacts to the Excel icon opens the program with your information laid out in a spreadsheet; dragging to the Clipboard icon is the same as selecting Copy as described above. Selecting multiple entries works the same way as in Program Manager: click an item, hold down Shift, and then click a second item to select a group of items; Ctrl+Click to make individual selections from the list at different points.

To Do list

I can't live without a To Do list; I need one to effectively procrastinate. The Palm Organizer's To Do list, and its Desktop mirror aren't perfect, but they're close.

Adding a new To Do item

Adding a new item to the list is easy. From the To Do list view just:

✦ Click the New button, or

✦ Select New To Do from the Edit menu, or

✦ Press Crtl+N

You'll see a new, blank To Do item, similar to that shown in Figure 9-6. Add your text and, if you want, set the item's priority, due date, and category. You can also add a note or make the item private. Once you've finished, click the Apply button and the text of your item should show in the left pane. Otherwise, your To Do item will be applied (whether you want it to be or not) as soon as you switch to another screen or application.

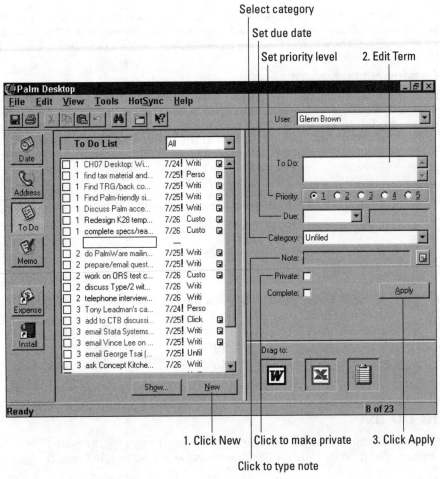

Figure 9-6: Adding a To Do item

Note Overdue To Do items display in your list in red with an exclamation point next to the date.

Show Options

Depending upon your display items, your item may or may not show on your current To Do list. Click the Show button, and I'll show you what I mean. The dialog box shown in Figure 9-7 lets you filter your To Do items.

Figure 9-7: Show Options

My preference is to mirror the settings I use on my Palm Organizer. Once items are complete, I don't want to see them, so I check the second option. If an item is due in the future, I'd rather focus on my current tasks, so I uncheck the second option. I do like to keep track of when items are completed, and I find the balance of the displays useful, so I leave them all checked. I sort by priority, and then due date.

Editing a To Do item

This screen rivals the Day view for live items — both the left-hand listing and the right-hand Details pane are completely editable. As you can see in Figure 9-8 (created with a bit of magic in Adobe Photoshop), the two panes provide almost identical functionality.

Table 9-1 explains the To Do editing actions in greater detail.

Table 9-1 Editing To Do Items		
Action	**List Pane**	**Details Pane**
Change an item's due date	Click the date	Click the triangle to the right of Due:
Change an item's priority	Click the number	Click a radio button
Change the category of an item	Click the category to select from the pop-up list	Click the triangle to the right of Category:
Delete an item	Highlight the item by clicking it, and then hit Delete (or right-click and select Delete; or select Delete from the Edit menu)	n/a
Edit a note attached to an item	Click the note icon	Click the note icon
Edit the text	n/a	Type in the To Do box
Mark an item as complete	Click the checkbox	Click complete

Copying a To Do list item

As with the Address Listing, there are multiple ways to copy To Do items:

✦ Highlight the item by clicking it, and then select Copy from the Edit menu.

✦ Highlight an item, and then click the Copy icon on the menu bar.

✦ Right-click an item, and then select Copy from the pop-up menu.

✦ Drag an item to the icons at the lower right-hand corner of the window to open in Microsoft Word or Excel or to copy to the clipboard. Selecting multiple entries is easy: click an item, hold down Shift, and then click a second item to select a group of items; Ctrl+Click if you want to make individual selections from the list at different points.

Memo Pad

The Memo Pad is where the Palm Desktop application really shines. Many Palm users overlook the potential of this application. Although you can easily add a new memo, the real key is to use the Memo Pad as a means to view data that you have on your computer. Product numbers, schedules, serial numbers — you name it — cut and paste means any text on your computer can be a HotSync away from your PalmPilot. This feature is shown in Figure 9-9.

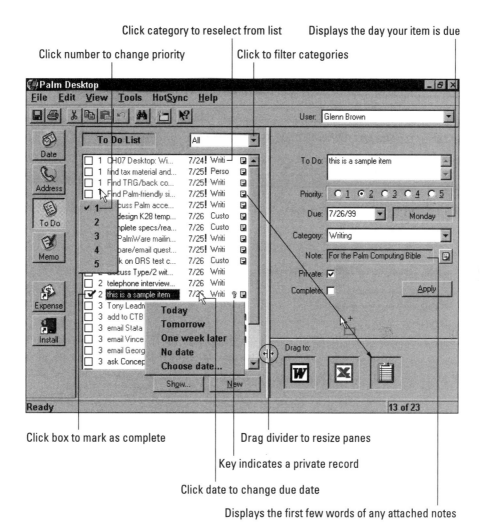

Click category to reselect from list | Displays the day your item is due
Click number to change priority | Click to filter categories

Click box to mark as complete | Drag divider to resize panes

Key indicates a private record

Click date to change due date

Displays the first few words of any attached notes

Figure 9-8: Editing a To Do item

1. Highlight the text you want to copy in your word processor.

2. Select Copy from the File menu (even better, use Ctrl+C).

3. Switch to the Palm Desktop Memo Pad.

4. Click the New button (or Edit ➪ New Record, or Ctrl+N).

5. Select Paste from the File menu (or use Ctrl+V).

The key indicates a private note

Right-click a note to pop-up menu

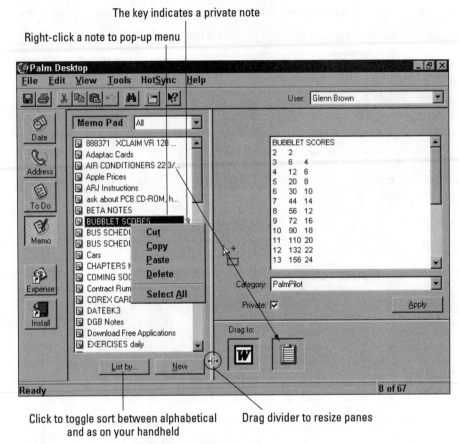

Click to toggle sort between alphabetical
and as on your handheld

Drag divider to resize panes

Figure 9-9: Editing a Memo Pad item

Tip The List By button enables you to change the sort order of your memos from the way they are displayed on your Palm Organizer to an alphabetical sort. The problem is that a HotSync won't force the same on your handheld. You can select an alphabetical sort from the Options ➪ Preferences menu on your Palm Organizer, but new memos will still be added to the end of the list. I use Jeremy Laurenson's freeware utility Memo Sort, which I've mapped to the Memo Pad button, to force a new sort each time I open my memos.

Menus

Some of the essential utility functionality of the Palm Desktop application is only available through the menus. Most of the menus are static as you switch views, but there are some subtle changes. Let's have a quick look at the menus.

File

The File menu, shown in Figure 9-10, is where you'd expect to find printing and saving. This menu also enables you to Open Archives (files that you've purged from your Palm Organizer, and marked as Save Archive on PC). When you're in the Address Book, items enabling you to import or export contact records are added.

Figure 9-10: Desktop File menu

When you load an archive file to recover information that you didn't mean to delete from your Palm Organizer, you will find that you have switched views to one that includes only the limited data that is covered in the archive. If you go back to the File menu, you'll see a new item: Open Current, which you need to use to switch back to your data.

Printing

The print functionality in the Palm Desktop is rather basic. As you switch from application to application, different settings appear in the print dialog box that enable you to do some customization — just don't look for a fancy printout on custom paper. Here are your options:

✦ **Date Book** — Today, Dates in list format, Months (you tell it which ones) in month format

✦ **Address Book** — Viewed category (which can include all) or the highlighted selection, with or without notes. A simple list of names and numbers can also be printed.

✦ **To Do List** — Viewed category or the highlighted selection, with or without notes.

✦ **Memo Pad** — Viewed category or the highlighted selection. You can also specify Memos within a numeric range, such as 1 to 5.

Edit

As usual, the Edit menu, which is shown in Figure 9-11, includes Undo, along with Cut, Copy, and Paste. The New items in a particular Edit menu change with the application—New Event, Address, To Do, and Memo—depending on your view.

Figure 9-11: Desktop Edit menu

Tip

If you copy an item (Address Record, To Do item, Memo) in the list view, the Palm Desktop selects the entire record for pasting in another application.

View

The View menu (see Figure 9-12) gives you command keys for switching between views. It also lets you hide or reveal records that you have marked as private. List By changes to Show when viewing To Do items, enabling you to change your view preferences.

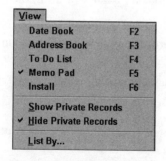

Figure 9-12: Desktop View menu

Private Records

If you want to keep prying eyes from some of the records in your Palm Organizer, you can mark your records—Date Book, Address Book, To Do, and Memo Pad—as private. Selecting Hide Private Records hides them; to view them, you need the password that you assigned in the Security icon on your handheld.

Caution If you forget your password, you can use the Forgotten Password feature in the Security application on your handheld to assign a new one, but all of your private records will be deleted. Don't forget your password.

Tools

The Tools menu enables you to edit categories (Date Book does not yet support categories), and select the user (you can also select from the pop-up user list in the upper right-hand corner of the screen). Figure 9-13 is a sample Desktop tools menu. Purge Completed To Do's is replaced by Purge Events when viewing the Date Book. In the Address Book, Purge Completed To Do's is replaced by Custom Field Names, a choice that enables you to change any or all of the Custom Fields in the Address Book. Finally, Options gives you access to basic settings — including which module you start with, security, and how you want your day and week displayed.

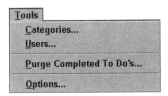

Figure 9-13: Desktop Tools menu

Profiles

If you have a number of Palm Organizers to deploy, and you want to preload them with standard applications (maybe including the company telephone book), Profiles does the trick. You can load a configuration and preinstall it on as many devices as you want.

 Note If you install a number of applications using the Profiles feature, you'll need to manually move them out of the Install folder after you've finished. The Installer has no way of knowing when you're finished, so it can't automatically delete applications after installing.

HotSync

The HotSync menu (see Figure 9-14) enables you to change the settings for local and modem synchronizing, and to view the HotSync log, if there were messages recorded about your last connection. See Chapter 6 for more on HotSyncing your Palm Organizer.

Custom

The Custom setting (see Figure 9-15) enables you to selectively turn off or change the settings for components that you may not need to synchronize.

Figure 9-14: Desktop HotSync menu

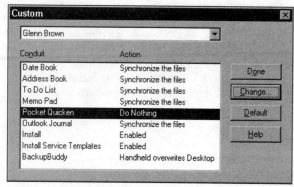

Figure 9-15: Custom HotSync

To change an item, highlight it and then click Change to display the HotSync action dialog box (see Figure 9-16). Using this dialog box, you can force the Desktop version to overwrite your handheld, or vice versa, or you can have it do nothing in any specific application where there are no changes to make.

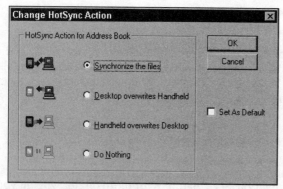

Figure 9-16: HotSync settings

Let's have a look at each setting and what it does:

✦ **Synchronize the files** — The files are synchronized. If you made changes to multiple records on both your handheld and on your computer, HotSync implements the changes in both places. If you've made changes to the *same* record on both your handheld and on your computer, HotSync duplicates the record on both platforms, and HotSync Log includes a message telling you to delete the record that you don't want. Just make sure to delete the record on only one platform (handheld or PC) before you HotSync.

✦ **Desktop overwrites Handheld** — The files in your computer completely overwrite those in your Palm Organizer. You might use this feature when, for example, all the changes, additions, or deletions you've made in a specific handheld application since the last HotSync operation turn out to be a mistake that you want to undo. It is a good idea to be extra sure before using this setting; you can overwrite a complete database with a single record, with no chance of recovering the database.

✦ **Handheld overwrites Desktop** — The files in your Palm Organizer completely overwrite those on your computer. You might use this feature when, for example, you've accidentally deleted or otherwise corrupted data in a Desktop application that you want to recover from your handheld. As above, it's a good idea to be sure before using this setting, even though there is a chance of recovery (see User Folders later in this chapter).

✦ **Do nothing** — Just what it says. This can be useful when you want to do a quick HotSync to install a file or move a particular record, without waiting for all of your data to be synchronized.

Caution

Be careful: HotSync settings give you the ability to overwrite your hard work with a blank version. In almost all circumstances, the default (Synchronize the files) is the best choice.

Cross-Reference

See Chapter 6 for more details on HotSync settings.

File Link

File linking is a powerhouse feature that was added with Version 3.0; it enables you to specify a link between unique files stored on your computer and a set of Address Book entries or specific Memo Pad records on your handheld. If the file on your computer is subsequently updated, the one on your Palm Organizer can be automatically updated with your next HotSync. This enables you to synchronize changing documents, lists, even the company telephone book, and you'll always have the current version on your handheld. Here's how to set up a File Link:

✦ Select File Link from the HotSync menu; a dialog box asks which user you want to set up the link for (that would be you . . .), and whether you want to create a new link or modify an existing one.

✦ Next, the dialog box shown in Figure 9-17 displays.

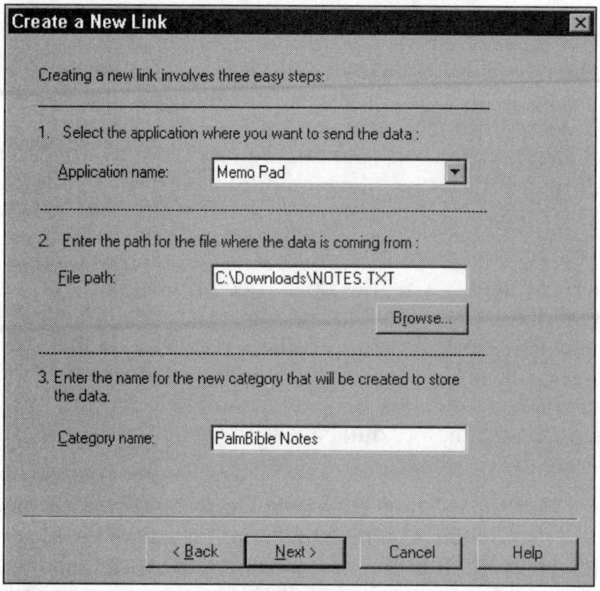

Figure 9-17: Creating a File Link

You have to answer the three simple questions in the Create a New Link screen:

1. Which application do you want to link to (Address Book or Memo Pad)?

2. Which file on your computer do you want to link to? Memo Pad supports CSV (*.csv), Memo Archive (*.mpa), or text (*.txt); the Address Book supports CSV or Address Archive (*.aba) file formats.

3. What would you like to name the new category that will be used to store the data you are linking?

   After you've made your selections, the next dialog box confirms your settings, and enables you to set the frequency of updates (whenever the file is updated, or daily/weekly/monthly).

Setup

This menu item enables you to configure how HotSync should run. Refer to Chapter 6 if you need more information about the HotSync menu.

Help

Need more help? Want a multimedia tutorial on your new Palm Organizer? Figure 9-18 shows you where to find it.

Figure 9-18: Desktop Help menu

User-Named Folders

Each user who HotSyncs to your computer has a user-named folder on your hard drive. To have a better understanding of user-named folders, let's dissect mine, which is named BrownG (see Figure 9-19).

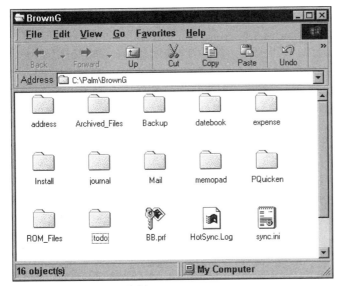

Figure 9-19: My user folder

Table 9-2 identifies the details of my user folder.

Table 9-2
Details of My User Folder

Folder	Files	Notes
Address	address.dat, address.bak, PMSettings.dat	My Address Book and a backup; my PocketMirror settings.
Archived_Files	Various.prc	These are files that have been deleted from my Palm V and that have been archived by BackupBuddy.
Backup	Various .prc and .pdb files	These are backups of the data and application files on my Palm V. Starting with OS 3.3, all installed applications are backed up here.
Datebook	datebook.dat, datebook.bak, PMSettings.dat, various.dba	My Date Book and a backup; my PocketMirror settings. DBAs are archived Date Book records.
Expense	expense.db, expense.bak, expense.txt	My Expense data and a backup, plus a tab-delimited text version.
Install	Various .prc and .pdb files	Any files scheduled for loading on your handheld at the next HotSync are temporarily stored here.
Journal	journal.dat, PMSettings.dat	A copy of my PocketJournal data, along with PocketMirror settings.
Mail	mail.dat., mail.bak	The mail from my handheld, along with a backup.
Memopad	memopad.dat, memopad.bak, PMSettings	My Memos and a backup along with PocketMirror settings.
PQuicken	Normally empty	A placeholder created by Pocket Quicken
ROM_Files	various .prc files	A backup, made by BackupBuddy, of all files stored in FlashPro.

Folder	Files	Notes
Todo	todo.dat, todo.bak, various.tda, PMSettings.dat	My To Do list and a backup, along with PocketMirror settings. TDA files are To Do list archives.
	BB.prf	The preferences file for BackupBuddy.
	HotSync.log	The data file for my HotSync Log.
	sync.ini	The .ini file for HotSync.

Note Pocket Quicken, BackupBuddy, and FlashPro The shaded folders and files in Table 9-2 are created by third-party software, which you may or may not have installed on your Palm Organizer. For more on Pocket Quicken, see Chapter 12; for more on BackupBuddy and FlashPro, see Chapter 20.

Tip Here's the *real* undo for your Palm Organizer: if you accidentally overwrite your data files by selecting Handheld overwrites Desktop, and you need to recover those files, you can rename the newly written .dat files, and then change the extension of the backup files to .dat.

Microsoft Outlook

Starting with version 3.1 of the OS (the Palm IIIx and Palm V Organizers), Palm included Chapura's PocketMirror, which enables you to synchronize with Microsoft Outlook instead of the Palm Desktop (see Figure 9-20). All of your Palm Organizer's PIM functionality is retained; in fact, Outlook offers far more ways to view, sort, and categorize your information. I particularly like the integration of e-mail—this raises the program's functionality to another level. One feature you give up when using Microsoft Outlook is File Linking, which is available only from within the Palm Desktop.

Caution If you're using Outlook 2000, you need to contact Chapura (www.chapura.com) to obtain version 2.04 or better of PocketMirror.

Another key feature of Outlook is its capability to automatically create journal entries for you—any aspect of projects, people, or activities that you need to track can be recorded. I started using Outlook's journaling feature after trying Chapura's PocketJournal, which enables you to synchronize and create journal entries on your Palm Organizer.

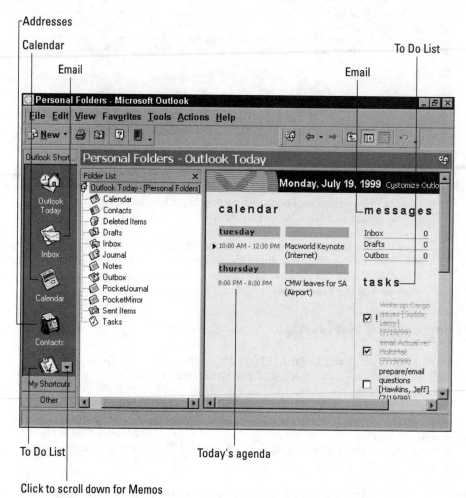

Figure 9-20: Microsoft Outlook 2000

Summary

✦ Most of the Palm Desktop's Date Book Day view is live — almost everything can be clicked or dragged to do something.

✦ The Date Book Day view enables you to drag Address or To Do items to your calendar; the other applications let you drag information that will open in Microsoft Word or Excel, or be copied to your clipboard.

✦ Use the function keys (F2 to F7) to instantly switch between applications, or open the Expense or Install applications.

✦ Editing items can be done through the menus, or by right-clicking your data.

✦ Use Window's copy and paste capabilities to move information to your Memo Pad; if the data regularly changes, use the File Linking feature to keep the data current.

✦ Use the HotSync Settings with caution; it is easy to accidentally overwrite your data if you're not careful.

✦ The User-Named Folder has backups of your data, in case of disaster.

✦　　✦　　✦

Using the Palm Desktop for Macintosh

✦ ✦ ✦ ✦

In This Chapter

Palm Desktop for
Macintosh 2.5

Macintosh conduits

Chronos Consultant

✦ ✦ ✦ ✦

This chapter focuses on Palm Desktop for Macintosh 2.5, a few of the new conduits for the Mac, and Chronos Consultant, a great alternative to the Palm Desktop.

Palm Desktop for Macintosh

The first release of the Macintosh desktop suffered in comparison to the Windows counterpart—it was slower, offered less functionality, and was difficult for third-party developers to create conduits so that their products could HotSync with the Macintosh. This all changed when Palm, Inc. released MacPac 2.1, a program based on what was originally Apple's Claris Organizer. All of a sudden, Mac users had a faster product (Windows users have since caught up with the release of Palm OS 3.3) with a true Mac interface. There are still shortcomings, but they are more than made up for by expanded functionality.

MacPac was recently upgraded to version 2.5 and rechristened as Palm Desktop for Macintosh. It is available for free from Palm's Web site at www.palm.com; the download includes a comprehensive manual in Adobe PDF format. This section provides a brief overview of the program, a few tips and tricks, and a look at the new features in Version 2.5.

New in Palm Desktop 2.5

Probably the biggest change for most users is that Palm Desktop 2.5 supports USB HotSyncing with the new PalmConnect USB connection kit available from Palm. Some of the other changes in this upgrade are discussed here.

Multiple users

Palm Desktop now supports multiple users HotSyncing to the same computer, with user selection made either through the new HotSync menu in the Palm Desktop or via a Users pop-up list on the right side of the icon bar.

HotSync menu

The new HotSync menu is available in the Palm Desktop Application, as well as through a submenu in the Instant Palm Desktop. This menu enables you to change users or profiles, install files, set up the HotSync process, change conduit settings, or view the HotSync log.

Alarms

A global setting now enables you to turn alarms on or off for all users, without requiring a restart.

New extensions

The new version of Palm Desktop includes HotSync Manager along with two new extensions: HotSyncLibPPC (non-PPC users have a file called HotSyncLib), which enables conduits to run, and Instant Palm Desktop, which sets up the Instant Palm Desktop menu.

Installation

The installation process has also changed somewhat, including the addition of the components needed to support Palm's new USB connection; the renaming of the Install Items folder to Add-on, making it consistent with the Windows version; and the installation of updated ROM and tour files. The new installer also offers the opportunity to register your handheld online.

How is Palm Desktop different from the Windows version?

Even though the two products share similar functionality, they are very different under the hood. The Windows version includes unique features such as File Linking and remote synchronization via a LAN or WAN network; the Macintosh version offers customizable lists, the Instant Palm Desktop menu, and support for AppleScript. Aside from the obvious interface differences, the biggest visible difference between the two is how they handle notes: the Mac version handles notes as attachments, the Windows version integrates them in a fashion that more closely mirrors the functionality of your handheld.

How is Palm Desktop different from the handheld version?

Palm Desktop for Macintosh was based on Claris Organizer, which offered the capability to capture far more information than could be stored on your handheld. Rather than remove this functionality, Palm wisely decided to retain this information in Palm Desktop. There is a caveat: This information is not HotSynced with your Palm Organizer because the fields do not exist to display the information. Table 10-1 lists these additional Palm Desktop fields.

Table 10-1 Additional Palm Desktop Fields	
Component	*Field*
Calendar	Category (neither)
Contacts	Second Category Prefix Suffix Nickname Division Second Address Custom Fields 5–9
Tasks	Second Category
Notes	Second Category Date Time

Other differences

There are a few differences between the Palm Desktop and the handheld version that affect notes, multi-day banners, alarms on To Do items, and the treatment of overdue items.

Notes

The biggest single difference between the Palm Desktop and the handheld version is that notes attached to items (Appointments, Contacts, To Do Items) all end up as notes in Palm Desktop. Although they are attached, I prefer the method used by MacPac version 1, where a notes field was part of each item.

Another difference is the file size supported by the Palm OS — Memo Pad entries are limited to 4K, whereas Palm Desktop allows notes approximately 16 times larger.

Caution   You'll find that notes that exceed the 4K limit will be truncated when you HotSync them to your handheld. The problem is that the shorter truncated version will overwrite the original with the next HotSync. A safer approach is to create a standalone text file and attach it to the Note in Palm Desktop.

Multi-day banners

The Palm OS does not support banners, so these are converted to a series of one-day untimed events. Fortunately, these remain as banners on your Mac, and daily repeating events created on your Palm Organizer are converted to banners when HotSynced to your Mac.

Alarms on To Do items

The Palm OS does not support alarms for To Do items. While you can create alarms for your Task items on your Mac, they won't make it to your handheld. Although there are third-party products that enable you to attach alarms to To Do items (see Action Names and DateBk3 in Chapter 21), these products rely on Palm's Date Book conduit to transfer information, so To Do alarms remain unsynchronizable.

Overdue items

The setting to Carry Over After Due has no affect on a Task HotSynced to your handheld; the Palm OS automatically carries all overdue items to the next day, displaying them with an exclamation point to let you know that they are overdue.

Interface

The first thing you'll notice when you open Palm Desktop (see Figure 10-1) is that this is truly a Mac application with AppleScript, elegant drag-and-drop support, and the customization options we all expect. Windows users wish they had it so good!

Multiple views

The icon bar at the top of Palm Desktop (see Figure 10-2) offers the most immediate means of changing the view of your data; these bars are mirrored in the View menu and with command key equivalents. After you've selected yourself from the Users list, you can view the information of your choice: Contacts, Tasks, Notes, or Calendar. The Palm Desktop is always open to your last view.

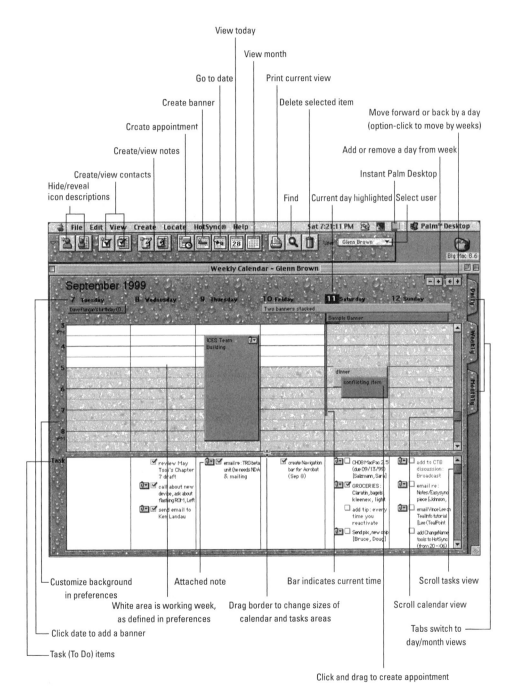

Figure 10-1: Palm Desktop 2.5

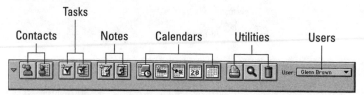

Figure 10-2: Palm Desktop icon bar

Attached notes

I can't decide whether the way Palm Desktop for Macintosh handles notes is its best or worst feature. On the one hand, the Windows version mirrors the functionality of your Palm Organizer, with notes attached to items in each of the built-in categories or standalone as memos. The Mac version treats notes separately, which enables you to attach notes in whatever manner you choose.

You'll see a paperclip icon (see Figure 10-3) everyplace there is an attached note. Click the paperclip icon and a pop-up menu will enable you to read it, attach a copy to a new or existing item, or detach the item, which turns it back into a standalone memo. Attaching an existing item is easy. After the dialog box shown on the right in Figure 10-3 appears, open your target item, and then drag the gray bar to it to create the link. Although it can be confusing when you first use it, this power and flexibility simply isn't available in the Windows version.

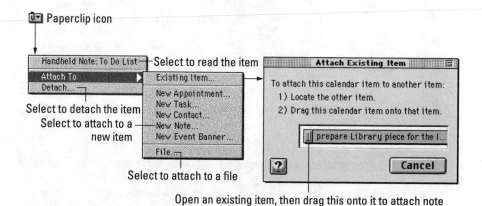

Figure 10-3: Options for notes in Palm Desktop

Dividers

The Calendar/Task displays and the columns in the Contacts, Tasks, and Notes lists can all be resized. If you click in the border area, your cursor will change as shown in Figure 10-4; just drag to change to the size you want.

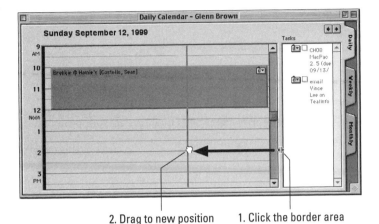

2. Drag to new position   1. Click the border area

Figure 10-4: Resizing the daily tasks area

Sorting

Palm Desktop's filtering and sorting capabilities enable you to create almost any view that you want. In Figure 10-5, I've created a PalmBIBLE Example view with my Notes, which I use to illustrate some of Palm Desktop's capabilities.

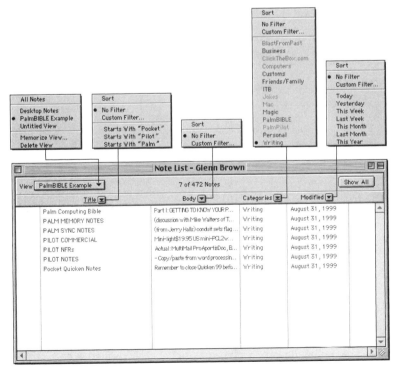

Figure 10-5: Sorting Notes in Palm Desktop

Here's how to create this custom Notes view:

1. View the Note List (click the icon, select the menu item, or press Shift+ Command+N).

2. Select Columns from the View menu and then make sure Title, Body, Categories, and Modified are checked.

3. Select a filter (in my example, Writing) from the Categories pop-up list.

4. Select Custom Filter from the Title pop-up list, select Starts With, and then type in **Palm**, as shown in Figure 10-6.

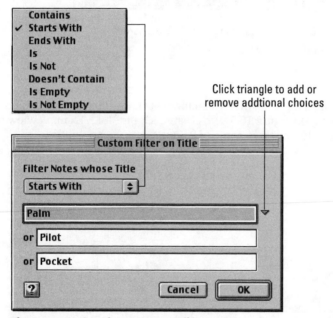

Figure 10-6: Creating a Custom Filter

5. Click the triangle to the right of the Custom Filter dialog box to expand it, type in **Pilot** and **Pocket**, and then click OK.

6. Click the View pop-up list and select Memorize View to save the view as PalmBIBLE Example.

Tip

If you want to create primary and secondary sorts for your view, click the first field header that you want to sort by to display it with a solid underline, which indicates that it is the primary sort. Shift+click the next field (which displays with a dotted underline) to create your secondary sort. This enables you to do multilevel sorts, such as sort notes by category, with each entry alphabetically sorted in each category, or sort contact names by company, with names alphabetically sorted in each company.

As you can see, the sorting capabilities open up all kinds of opportunities for customization, enabling you to make Palm Desktop work the way you want it to. Now let's look at the core functionality of the application.

Calendar

The weekly calendar is where I do most of my work; the combination of appointments and tasks gives me a snapshot of the week to come.

Navigating

The calendar is a breeze to get around. Tabs on the right give you access to Daily, Weekly, and Monthly views. Command keys abound; you can open any of these views directly, or switch between them using Command+Shift+D (for Daily), Command+Shift+W (for Weekly), and Command+Shift+M (for Monthly). If you want to change the number of days shown in the weekly view, use the plus and minus icons at the top right to add or subtract days (you can display from one to seven days in your week). The arrows enable you to move your view one day at a time; holding down Option jumps your view one week at a time. Using Command and the arrow keys gives you the same functionality from the keyboard. Command+↑ (up arrow) and Command+↓ (down arrow) scroll the view of your Daily or Weekly calendar up and down. If you want to quickly get back to your starting date, just double-click the date in the upper left-hand corner to open a dialog box that will take you back. The current date is the default.

Navigating monthly

The Monthly view works in a similar way — pressing Command with an arrow key moves your view one month at a time; however, neither Option nor clicking the date has any effect. Double-clicking the shaded number bar at the top of any day jumps you to that day displayed in the daily view. If you click a day with more appointments than can be displayed in the window, a scroll bar appears, so you can view all of your tasks and appointments. Double-clicking an empty spot on your monthly calendar will open a dialog box asking whether you want to add an appointment, task, or banner.

Adding an appointment

You have all sorts of ways to create a new appointment. Here are a few:

✦ The easiest and most obvious: click+drag out the time you want for an appointment directly on your calendar.

✦ Double-click a used space on the calendar.

✦ Select Appointment from the Create menu.

✦ Press Command+Shift+Option+A.

✦ Drag a task to your calendar; an appointment starting with "Work on . . . (your task)" is created at that time.

✦ Open your Contacts list and drag a contact to your calendar to create an appointment at that time with that person.

✦ Open your Notes list and drag a note to your calendar; an appointment is created at that time with the first line of your note as the title, and the balance as an attached note.

✦ For any item that already has an attachment, click the Paperclip icon and select Attach to New Appointment (this attaches the two items).

As you type in your new appointment, Palm Desktop checks whether you've used a name from your Contact list. If it finds a possible match or matches, it offers you the opportunity to attach Contacts to your appointment. This works two ways: not only do you have a note attached to your Calendar entry, but your Contact also displays appointments as attachments. This setting can be turned off in Preferences.

Contacts

Start using the contacts manager in Palm Desktop, and you'll be surprised by the elegance of this application. There are still a few rough edges left over from previous versions, but this component is a powerful one.

Adding a contact

Let's add a new contact, so we can take a look at a few of the features here. We'll start by selecting Contact from the Create menu — those who prefer the keyboard can use Command+Option+C. The contact window expands each of five sections as you complete a new entry. Figure 10-7 shows all five areas expanded (assisted by the magic of Adobe PhotoShop); Figure 10-8 shows the completed contact.

As you start entering the name information, you'll notice that Palm Desktop can auto-capitalize, and even auto-complete, most fields. You can also customize the pick lists, adding items that you'd like to use. When you complete the Name area, you can either tab to or click in the Phone area — Names will return to its original size and Phones will expand. You can enter what each phone number should be (home, business, cell, and so on), and the number auto-formats as configured in your Preferences. If you want a number to be available from the Instant Palm Desktop menu, click in the box to the right. Work and Home addresses aren't necessarily fixed — you can configure them to be what you want. One remnant of Claris Organizer is the button that enables you to open a preformatted document in ClarisWorks or MacWrite Pro, neither of which has been available for years. The Notes area offers even more customization capabilities: you can specify whether you want five, seven, or nine customizable fields.

Name
Most fields will autocapitalize and autocomplete

Work address
Editable pick lists make data entry easy

Comments
This area has 5, 7, or 9 customizable fields

Click to send e-mail
Click to open URL

Phone numbers
Click to add number to Instant Palm Desktop

Home address
Click to open a document template in AppleWorks or MacWrite Pro

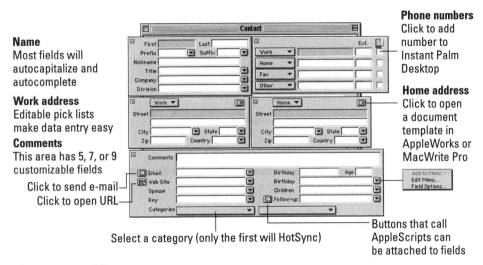

Select a category (only the first will HotSync)

Buttons that call AppleScripts can be attached to fields

Figure 10-7: Adding a new contact

Click to view attached items

Indicates the number of attached items

Drag this tab to another item to attach

Click to move to another contact

Number formatting set in preferences

The addresses are valid (but I will have moved before this sees print . . .)

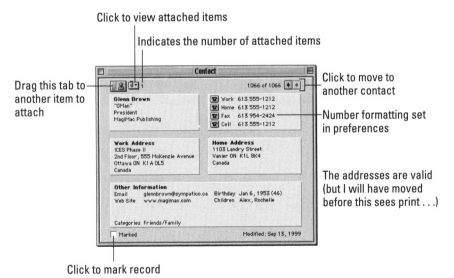

Click to mark record

Figure 10-8: A new contact

Field events

Clicking the triangle button to the right of each of your custom fields gives you the pick list previously shown in Figure 10-7. Selecting Field Options and Palm Desktop opens the dialog box shown in Figure 10-9. First, name your custom field, and then select the auto-capitalization options new entries. Things get interesting with the next options. Selecting the first option adds new entries to the pop-up list (so you only need to type them once). The next option enables you to create a link or call an AppleScript. The last option enables you to add a button to call that link or AppleScript. I'd like to see this updated (because none of the listed products are still sold); it has great potential.

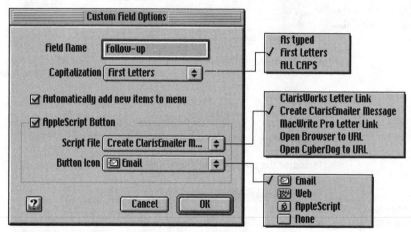

Figure 10-9: Custom Field Options

Viewing contacts

Viewing your Contact List is simple. Just do one of the following:

✦ Click the Contact List icon (second from the left).

✦ Select Contact List from the View menu.

✦ Press Shift+Command+C.

Like most views in Palm Desktop, the Contacts List (see Figure 10-10) is completely customizable (see the "Dividers" and "Sorting" sections for more details). Marked records are unique to the Contact List; using them enables you to create a contacts group that spans your categories.

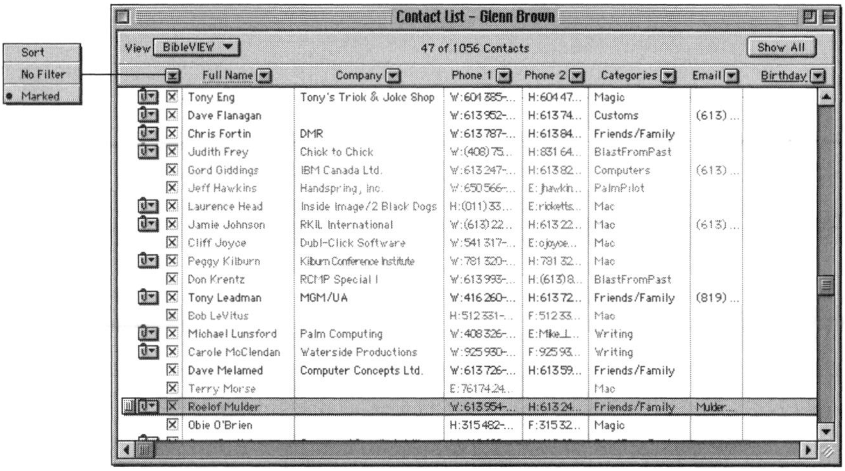

Figure 10-10: The Contacts List

Finding contacts

If you have the Contacts List open and you start typing the name of the person you are looking for, Palm Desktop will scroll to that part of your list. You'll probably prefer the Find command, which is found in the Locate menu. Find will auto-complete entries for you, which can be quite handy when you're searching for someone's information.

Tasks

What PIM would be complete without a To Do list? The Task List in the Palm Desktop mirrors your handheld's To Do List. To open it, do one of the following:

✦ Click the Task List icon (fourth from the left).

✦ Select Task List from the View menu.

✦ Press Shift+Command+T.

As you can see in Figure 10-11, the Task List view comes with preset views for uncompleted tasks, and you can quickly create those views that you need (see "Sorting" earlier in this chapter).

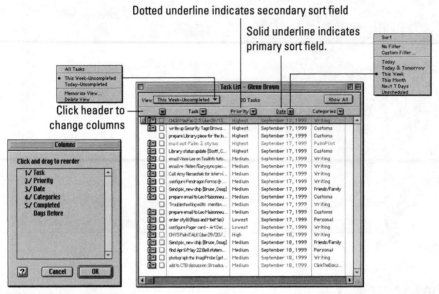

Figure 10-11: Task List

Adding a task

A new task can be added in any of these ways:

- ✦ Double-click an unused space on the Task List.

- ✦ Double-click the Task area in any of the calendar views to create a task due on that day.

- ✦ Select Task from the Create menu.

- ✦ Press Option+Command+T.

- ✦ Open your Contacts list and drag a contact to your Task List; Palm Desktop creates a Task that reads Call Contact Name.

- ✦ Open your Notes list and drag a note to your calendar; an appointment is created at that time with the first line of your note as the title and the balance as an attached note.

- ✦ For any item that already has an attachment, click the Paperclip icon and select Attach to New Task (this attaches the two items).

Once you've opened the new task dialog box (see Figure 10-12) the process can be as simple as describing the task.

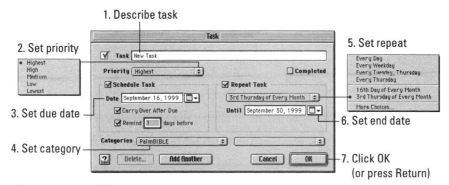

Figure 10-12: Adding a task

You can also add a new task by performing these steps:

1. Describe the task — if you need more space, you'll need to create a Note (see below) and attach the Note to your new task.

2. The priority for your new task is default as set in Preferences; change it if you need to.

3. Your new task is, by default, due on the date you enter it; tap the calendar icon to the right of the date to select a new due date. You can also select whether you want uncompleted items to carry over after their due date, and tell Palm Desktop to remind you before the task is due.

4. The category is the default as set in Preferences; change it if necessary.

5. Set a repeat for recurring tasks.

6. Set the date that repeats should end.

7. Click OK (or press Return) to close the Task dialog box, or click Add Another if you want to add another task.

Notes

Notes are the Palm Desktop equivalent of Memo Pad items on your handheld. There is, however, a significant difference in the way Palm Desktop handles notes: Each note, including notes attached to Appointments, Contacts, or To Do items, is treated as a separate Note when it is HotSynced to your Macintosh. This can be confusing at first, but it enables Palm Desktop to link items in a fashion that is not possible with the Windows version of the Palm OS.

Adding a Note

As with the other Palm Desktop components, it is easy to create a Note:

1. Select Note from the Create menu.

2. Press Option+Command+N.

3. For any item that already has an attachment, click the Paperclip icon and select Attach to New Note (this attaches the two items).

4. Scroll to the bottom of your Notes list and double-click the used space at the bottom.

5. Dragging a contact to the blank space at the end of your Notes List creates a Note that begins "Conversation with . . ."

6. Dragging a Task to the blank space at the end of your Notes List creates a Note that begins "Note regarding . . ."

Palm Desktop's Notes (see Figure 10-13) include Date and Time fields that are auto-filled when you first create the Note. The only problem with these is that the fields are not HotSynced to your handheld. However, clicking the clock icon to the left of the Categories pop-up list will insert the current date and time (mirroring the DTS ShortCut on your Palm Organizer). Using this method the time stamp does make it to your handheld.

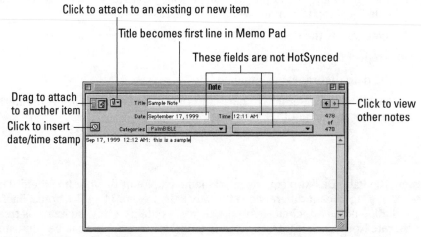

Figure 10-13: A new Note

Viewing Notes

Viewing your Note List is simple; just do one of the following:

✦ Click the Note List icon (sixth from the left).

✦ Select Note List from the View menu.

✦ Press Shift+Command+N.

The first time you open your Note List in Palm Desktop, a long list of entries displays that reads "Handheld Note: Address Book," "Handheld Note: To Do List," and so on. These items are the notes fields from the Address Book, Calendar, and To Do List entries on your Palm Organizer. The first thing to do is to select Desktop Notes from the View pop-up list (the upper left-hand corner of Figure 10-14); this filters out those entries, leaving just your Memo Pad entries listed.

Menus

In addition to mirroring the commands we've already covered, there are a number of utility functions that are only available through Palm Desktop's menu commands.

File

The file menu (see Figure 10-15) enables you to back up or create a new desktop data file, to merge records with another file, and to import, export, or print records; all of which are covered in great detail in Palm's user manual.

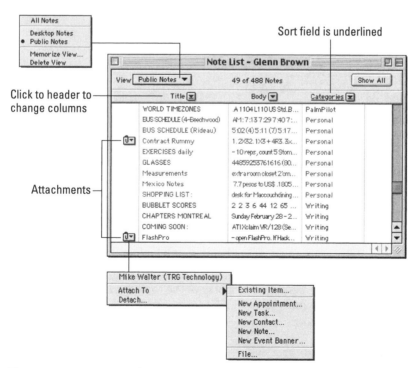

Figure 10-14: My Note List

Figure 10-15: Palm Desktop file menu

Edit

In addition to the standard undo, cut, copy, and paste commands, this menu includes commands to edit, duplicate, delete, mark, and unmark items, depending on your view. If you happen to be looking at your Contacts List, there will also be a Copy Special command, as shown in Figure 10-16, which enables you to select which parts of your contact information should be copied for pasting in another application. The Edit menu also enables you to change the category for the selected item, or edit the categories themselves.

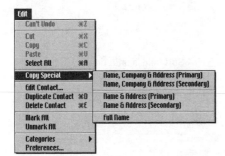

Figure 10-16: Palm Desktop Edit menu

Preferences

There are seven screens of Preferences, starting with Decor (see Figure 10-17). The only preference missing is the capability to turn off the display of completed items in your calendar views.

✦ **Decor** enables you to change the background look of Palm Desktop.

✦ **General** settings include the display of the Instant Palm Desktop menu, warnings, color printing, sound, the display of the toolbar, date format, and how you want auto-attachments to work.

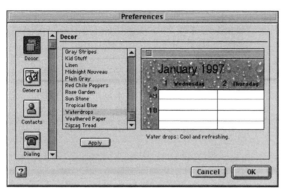

Figure 10-17: Decor selections in Preferences

✦ **Contacts** enables you to configure how your contacts should be entered, whether or not you want the auto-capitalization or auto-completion features to be active, phone number formats, and labels. The international address formats will restructure your city, state, and zip entries, but they don't account for countries (such as Canada) with different addresses (Canada, for example, has provinces and postal codes).

✦ **Dialing** enables you to set up dialing using either a modem or through your computer's speaker (by generating tones that your phone will use to dial for you).

✦ **Calendars** lets you set up your working hours (these display as white on y our daily or weekly calendars), whether or not you want the week to start on Sunday or Monday, week numbering, and how appointments should be displayed.

✦ **Alarms** is a new preference screen that was added with Palm Desktop 2.5. It enables you to specify whether a default alarm should be set for all new appointments, and whether alarm dialog boxes should be displayed.

New Feature

Alarms is a feature new to Palm Desktop 2.5.

✦ **Fonts** enables you to specify the display fonts for Palm Desktop's components.

View

The View menu (see Figure 10-18) enables you to quickly jump to any of the views of your data, pre-configured or custom. All of your saved views display in this menu, which means that it's better if you choose unique names for each view, such as Office-Contacts, Office-Notes, and so on; otherwise, there may be duplicate entries in this menu. These duplicates do no harm, they just make it difficult to determine which view belongs to which menu item.

Figure 10-18: Palm Desktop's View menu

Create

The Create menu (see Figure 10-19) enables you to create new items—Appointments, Tasks, Contacts, Notes, Banners, or Templates. If you have an item selected, it enables you to attach the item to a new or existing item or a file on your computer. Instant Attach enables you to quickly connect Appointments or Tasks to contacts when the contact name is part of the item itself.

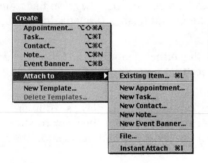

Figure 10-19: Palm Desktop's Create menu

Locate

The Locate menu lets you jump to a calendar view, either today or a selected date, and to view your 20 most recently viewed items (see Figure 10-20).

Figure 10-20: Palm Desktop's Locate menu

The true power, however, is in the Find command (see Figure 10-21). Finding anything in Palm Desktop is quick, easy, and painless—just start typing and Palm Desktop will start searching for matches. If you're looking for a contact, it doesn't matter if you start typing the contact's first, last, or nickname, company, or even the contact's dog's name—if it is there, Palm Desktop will find it. After you've found an entry, you can add it to the Locate menu for easy access. If you want to build more complex searches, click More Choices to get a powerful, context-sensitive query tool. Need to know if there are birthdays coming up in the next month? Easy—just configure a query similar to that shown in Figure 10-21.

HotSync

HotSync (see Figure 10-22) is probably the most important utility menu in Palm Desktop. It enables you to change or add users, install files on your handheld, change the settings for local and modem synchronizing, and view the HotSync log if there were messages recorded about your last connection. See Chapter 6 for more on HotSyncing your Palm Organizer.

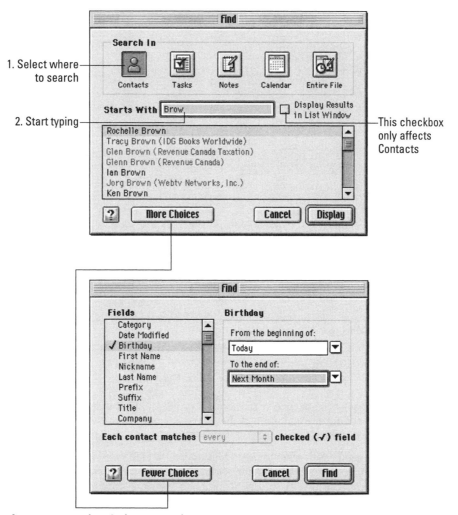

Figure 10-21: The Find command

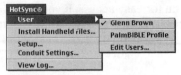

Figure 10-22: Palm Desktop's HotSync menu

User

Selecting User enables you to select which users' data should be viewed or to edit users, as shown in Figure 10-23. The Profiles feature enables those who need to configure a number of Palm devices to create a preset setup with standard applications and data loaded on a number of handhelds.

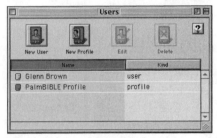

Figure 10-23: Users dialog box

> **Caution**   Both the Windows and Macintosh versions of the Palm desktop software do strange things to your data when you try to HotSync more than one device with the same username. Symptoms include duplicate or missing data and other problems. If you need to duplicate the data from your standard applications, it is far better (and easier) to copy the files in your user-named folder and duplicate them in the user-named folder for a new device.

Install handheld files

Installing files is a simple matter of clicking the Add to List button, and selecting the files you want to load at your next HotSync (see Figure 10-24). You can also drag files into the dialog box to have them added to the list.

> **Tip**   If you've navigated to where you think your file is, but it doesn't display, change the Show setting at the bottom of the dialog box from Handheld Files to All Files — not all Palm files show correctly at the default setting.
>
> There are even easier ways to install files on your handheld — you can make a desktop alias of the Files to Install folder (within your user-named folder) and drop files there, or you can use Masatoshi Yoshizawa's freeware product SimpleInst, which gives you drag-and-drop installs.

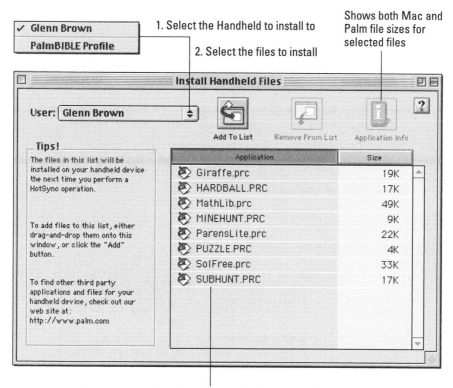

1. Select the Handheld to install to

2. Select the files to install

Shows both Mac and Palm file sizes for selected files

3. Listed files will be installed during the next HotSync

Figure 10-24: Installing files on your handheld

New Feature   Version 2.5 of Palm Desktop opens to a folder called Add-On inside your Palm folder (this is the same file path as used by the Windows version of the Palm OS); in it are a few goodies that Palm has left there for you.

Setup

Normally you won't need to adjust the settings of the HotSync Software Setup dialog box (Figures 10-25 and 10-26), although I find it handy when I want to fix connection problems with HotSync. The local setting should be set to As Fast as Possible unless you are having problems maintaining a connection — in which case you may want to trade a lower speed for a more reliable connection.

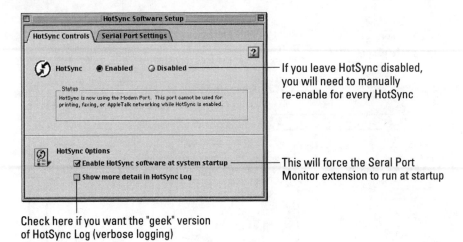

If you leave HotSync disabled, you will need to manually re-enable for every HotSync

This will force the Seral Port Monitor extension to run at startup

Check here if you want the "geek" version of HotSync Log (verbose logging)

Figure 10-25: HotSync Software Setup

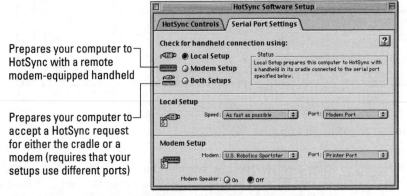

Prepares your computer to HotSync with a remote modem-equipped handheld

Prepares your computer to accept a HotSync request for either the cradle or a modem (requires that your setups use different ports)

Figure 10-26: Serial Port Settings in HotSync Software Setup

Conduit Settings

Conduits Settings (see Figure 10-27) enables you to selectively turn off or change the settings for components that you may not need to synchronize.

To change the settings for an item, double-click it to open its Settings dialog box (see Figure 10-28). If you prefer, you can open the dialog box by highlighting the conduit you want to change, and then clicking the Conduit Settings button. These settings enable your Macintosh version to overwrite your handheld — or vice versa — or you can have it do nothing when there are no changes to make.

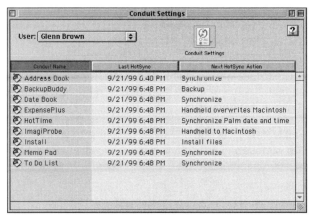

Figure 10-27: Conduit Settings

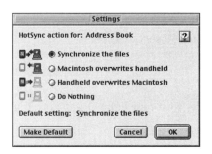

Figure 10-28: Changing the settings for the Address Book conduit

Let's have a look at each setting and what it does:

✦ **Synchronize the files.** The files will be synchronized, and if you made changes to multiple records on both your handheld and on your computer, HotSync will select the most current. If you've made changes to the *same* record on both your handheld and on your computer, HotSync will duplicate the record on both platforms, and HotSync Log will include a message telling you to delete the record that you don't want. Just make sure to delete the record on only one platform (handheld or Mac), and then HotSync.

✦ **Macintosh overwrites handheld.** The files in your computer will completely overwrite those in your Palm Organizer. It is a good idea to be extra sure before using this setting; you can overwrite a complete database with a single record, and have no chance of recovering the database.

✦ **Handheld overwrites Macintosh.** The files in your Palm Organizer will completely overwrite those on your Mac. As above, it's a good idea to be sure with this one, even though there is a chance of recovery (see "User-Named Folders" in Chapter 9).

✦ **Do nothing.** Like it says, it does nothing. This can be of use when you want to do a quick HotSync to install a file or move a particular record, without waiting for all of your data to be synchronized.

 Be careful: This powerful feature gives you the ability to overwrite your hard work with a blank version. In almost all circumstances, the default (Synchronize the files) is the best choice. See Chapter 6 for more details on HotSync settings.

View Log

This menu choice opens the HotSync Log so that you can view what happened during your last HotSync. The Mac version has some subtle differences from the Windows version: The log appends new entries to the end of the list, so you scroll up to read previous entries (the opposite of the Windows version). Also, if the log has something for you to read, the dialog box will stay open until you dismiss it (the Windows version closes automatically after 60 seconds).

Help

Need more help? Want a multimedia tutorial on your new Palm Organizer? Try the Desktop Help menu, shown in Figure 10-29.

 Figure 10-29: Desktop Help menu

 The first time you use Palm Desktop, turn on Balloon Help—you'll be surprised at how helpful it can be.

Instant Palm Desktop

I've saved one of the best features of Palm Desktop for last—the Instant Palm Desktop gives you quick access to important data without your having to open the full Palm Desktop application.

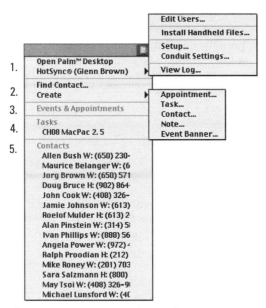

Figure 10-30: Instant Palm Desktop

As you can see in Figure 10-30, the menu is divided into five sections.

1. This section enables you to open the Palm Desktop, or to switch to it if it is already open. It also includes a complete duplicate of the HotSync menu from the application.

2. Here you can find (but not modify) a contact using a spartan version of the application's Find tool, and you can create new items.

3. Events and Appointments will display any appointments that you have scheduled for the day.

4. Tasks shows any uncompleted tasks that you have due for the day.

5. Contacts displays those contacts that you have identified by checking the box under the menu icon in the contact screen.

Tip

With version 2.1 of MacPac and version 2.5 of Palm Desktop, when some applications are in the foreground, Instant Palm Desktop's menus display incorrectly. The cure is simple — (temporarily) hide the foreground application and the menus work correctly.

Macintosh conduits

MacPac 2.1 (now Palm Desktop 2.5) brought incredible new functionality to Macintosh/Palm users — the new conduit capability has enabled third party developers to add desktop synchronization to their products. The following are a few of the conduits that are now available for Mac users:

Athlete's Diary

Developer: Stevens Creek Software
Cost: $39.95
Footprint: 48K

If you are involved in any kind of exercise or endurance training, you owe it to yourself to check out Stevens Creek Software's sports-related Palm products. Athlete's Diary enables you to HotSync training information captured on your handheld with your Mac.

BackupBuddy

Developer: Alexander Hinds
Cost: $19.95 (shareware)

This essential utility backs up all of the data in your Palm Organizer, including programs and data loaded into Flash memory, so that recovery from a hard reset is as easy as a HotSync. The Macintosh version offers little of the options and flexibility of the Windows version, but there is something to be said for the "set it and forget it" version.

Note   The backup functionality of BackupBuddy is included in the Palm OS with Version 3.3, but BackupBuddy is still an essential utility for those who use TRG's FlashPro (because it backs up data saved to Flash memory).

BrainForest

Developer: Aportis Technologies
Cost: $39.95 (commercial)
Footprint: 111K

BrainForest is an outline processor that enables you to create hierarchical lists on your Palm Organizer. The Professional version includes a Macintosh version and a conduit to synchronize data between the two.

Documents to Go

Developer: DataViz
Price: $39.95 (commercial)
Footprint: 101K

This great utility enables you to read word-processing documents or spreadsheets from your computer, with drag-and-drop conversion of Microsoft Word and Excel documents into Palm-readable format. The only limitation is that the documents are read-only on your Palm Organizer — all changes must be done on your Macintosh.

ExpensePlus

Developer: WalletWare
Cost: $69.95 (commercial)
Footprint: 294K

ExpensePlus offers a comprehensive means of means of capturing expense data, which can be HotSynced to your Mac. WalletWare also offer a less expensive ($19.95) conduit that mirrors a Windows user's ability to HotSync data from the built-in Expense application with Microsoft Excel.

FMSync

Developer: Ron Tsuk
Cost: $38.00 (commercial)

This program acts as a conduit between a JFile on your handheld and a FileMaker database on your Macintosh.

HotTime

Developer: AVStor
Cost: $5.00 (shareware)
Footprint: 6K

This little utility HotSyncs the time between your Mac and your Palm Organizer, so that you'll always be on time (okay, so you'll have one less excuse . . .).

ImagiProbe

Developer: ImagiWorks, Inc.
Cost: $399.00
Footprint: 262K (plus 3K for Sensors)

ImagiProbe is a data acquisition product that enables high school students (or anyone else, for that matter) to conduct scientific experiments, gathering data using different probes that can be attached to the Palm Organizer, and then transfer the data gathered to their Macintosh or Windows computers. See Chapter 23 for more on ImagiProbe.

Informed Expense Creator

Developer: Shana Corporation
Cost: Freeware (the Advanced version is $39.95)

One of the inequities between the Windows and Macintosh versions of the Palm Desktop software is that Windows users have the ability to HotSync their expense data. This shortcoming is overcome with the freeware version of Shana's Informed Expense Creator, which gives Macintosh users similar functionality.

Meeting Maker

Developer: ON Technology
Cost: $499.00 (six users)

ON Technology's Meeting Maker 6, a group scheduling and calendaring product, ships with conduits to enable both Windows and Macintosh users to HotSync Meeting Maker data to their Palm Organizers.

MultiMail Pro

Developer: Actual Software
Cost: $39.95
Footprint: 198K

Actual Software's MultiMail Pro addresses another inequity for Mac owners by providing the capability to HotSync e-mail with Palm Organizers.

Now Contact/Up To Date

Developer: Power On Software
Cost: To be determined (currently in late beta testing)

Now Contact and Up To Date offered the first conduit for Macintosh users, but the product itself stagnated somewhat after Now Software closed. The product was recently bought by Power On Software (the makers of Action Utilities), which has updated the product for OS 9, including a conduit for complete synchronization with the Palm Organizer.

Outlook Express

Developer: Microsoft
Cost: Freeware

Version 5.0 of Microsoft's Outlook Express is a great e-mail client for the Macintosh. The supplied conduit enables you to synchronize your e-mail address book with that in your Palm Organizer. To be honest, I don't find the conduit particularly useful—my e-mail address book includes a number of e-mail addresses for people for whom I have no other information, and my Palm Vx's Address Book includes a number of contacts for whom I have no e-mail address. Merging the two provides little value, and dramatically slows the HotSync process, so I leave the conduit disabled. That being said, I've upgraded from Claris Emailer (which is no longer supported) to Outlook Express as my e-mail package.

Pocket Quicken

Developer: Landware
Cost: $39.95
Footprint: 70K

Pocket Quicken enables you to keep your personal finances in order by HotSyncing data between your handheld and Intuit's Quicken (both the 98 and 2000 versions are supported).

TealPoint Software

TealPoint (`www.tealpoint.com`) makes or distributes a number of products to help Macintosh users with their products, including TealDoc (see Chapter 15), TealInfo (see Chapter 24), TealMeal (see Chapter 16), and TealPaint (see Chapter 18).

Chronos Consultant

Developer: Chronos LC
Cost: $49.95 (including Palm conduit)

What is it?

Chronos Consultant is an inexpensive shareware alternative to Palm Desktop that is arguably the best PIM available for the Macintosh. I registered the shareware version within an hour of downloading it.

Consultant also has the distinction of beating even Palm to the punch when it came to implementing a new conduit for the Macintosh — Chronos had its Palm conduit out before the release of MacPac 2.1.

Consultant consists of four main components:

✦ **Consultant**, the main application (see Figure 10-31 for the monthly view).

✦ **MiniConsultant**, shown in Figure 10-32, is a mini-view that gives you quick access to your data.

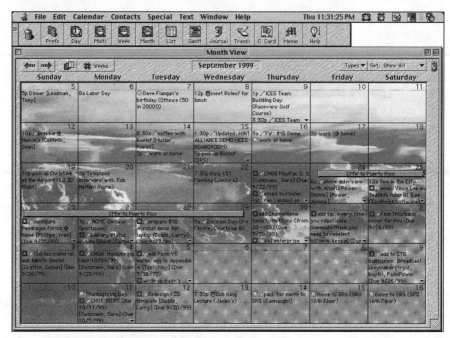

Figure 10-31: Consultant monthly view

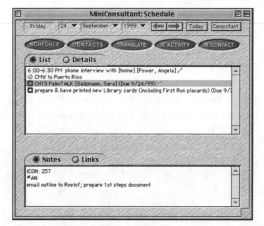

Figure 10-32: MiniConsultant

✦ **Activities and Contacts**, two extensions that give you instant desktop access to your data (Figure 10-33 shows the Activities menu).

✦ **The Palm conduit**, which enables you to HotSync your data with your Palm Organizer.

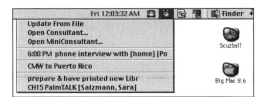

Figure 10-33: Activities menu

What features does it add?

Consultant includes almost all of the functionality offered by Palm Desktop — linking, colorized categories, smart text entry, and more — and adds a number of significant features, which are described as follows.

Flexible views

Consultant offers more views, including month views that extend beyond a single month, Gantt charting, and the capability to show multiple views at the same time, with complete support for drag and drop.

Integrated text editor

Consultant includes a powerful, integrated text editor that is used to create and view notes, Journal entries, even help. Comprehensive templates offer everything from Memo Pad functionality to mail-merge creation of custom reports based on your data. The program also includes two floating toolbars: Chronograph Tools, which enables you to either insert date and time information or to time an activity, and Text Tools, which gives you formatting and editing capabilities throughout the application.

Journal

The Journal is a version of the text editor that enables you to maintain a journal of events.

Sets

Sets enable you to create groups of categories that you can then use to filter your views. You may have multiple personal categories (such as Family, Hobbies, Shopping) that you can combine into a Personal set.

To Do items

Consultant offers much more control over your To Do items. The pop-up menu shown in Figure 10-34 enables you to forward, assign, or set and track goals for your tasks.

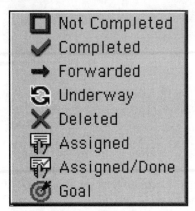

Figure 10-34: To Do choices

Themes

Consultant includes editable background Themes, which can include a photograph as a background to your calendar views.

Translate

Translate is a feature that does smart conversion of English phrases — type in "Meeting with Bob Smith at 2:00 pm tomorrow" and Consultant will correctly schedule your appointment, complete with a link to your contact.

How is it different?

Even though they mirror the same information from your Palm Organizer, Chronos Consultant and Palm Desktop have a number of significant differences in addition to their feature sets. Some of these differences are described as follows.

Notes

This is one of the most requested additions to Palm Desktop: Consultant integrates notes. If you have a note attached to a contact, task, or appointment, you do not need to open a link or attachment to find it, because it's already there.

HotSyncing

Consultant is much faster than Palm Desktop at HotSyncing your data.

Completed items in calendar views

Consultant can hide completed items in calendar views, a feat that neither MacPac nor Palm Desktop can duplicate (yet).

Consultant 3.0

Version 3.0 of Consultant is now available for a modest upgrade fee ($19.95). Features of the new release include:

✦ The capability to HotSync both public and private information

✦ A new Palm setup wizard that automates the setup process

✦ Categories synchronization: the setup wizard will analyze your categories, both on your handheld and on your Mac, and offer you alternate means of dealing with them

To Do items

Consultant handles To Do items in a significantly different manner than your Palm Organizer. Consultant lets you assign To Do items to specific dates, and the Palm OS lets you assign due dates to your tasks. Consultant handles this difference by adding the due date to the To Do item's title when it is brought over from your Palm Organizer; it reverses the process when you HotSync the information back to your handheld. I view this as one of the few shortcomings of Consultant — it is very disconcerting to see all of your To Do items show up on the current day, and this is what happens after every HotSync.

Sorting

Consultant offers sorts on up to four fields at once; Palm Desktop is limited to two sort fields.

How do I convert my data to Consultant?

I suspect that most people reading this who want to try Consultant will already have their data in either MacPac 2.1 or Palm Desktop 2.5 — in either case, the conversion is easy, provided you follow these simple steps to get your data to HotSync correctly:

1. Create a Conduits Off folder in your Palm directory, and drag Palm's primary conduits (Address, Date Book, Memo, and To Do) to the folder.

2. Drag the Consultant Conduit file to the Conduits folder (in your Palm folder).

3. Open Consultant and create a new user file.

4. Select Palm Sync Setup from the File menu.

5. *Setup Step 1:* Uncheck Enable Palm Synchronization.

6. *Setup Step 2:* This should read "No user selected/YOURFILE"; click Choose User and select User from the list (it will now read "User/YOURFILE").

7. *Setup Step 3:* Uncheck all four boxes to synchronize all of the (Palm) data in your handheld.

8. Hold down the Command and Option keys, and then press the HotSync button on your cradle. This will force a slow HotSync, which should ensure that all of your records make it to your Mac. You'll need to hold the keys down for the entire HotSync for this to work, but you should only have to do it for your first HotSync.

If you have a lot of records to HotSync, you may want to increase the memory allocation for the Conduit Manager. The default is 2248K; I increased mine by 8MB.

You will probably also want to disable Palm's Instant Palm Desktop extension after you have Consultant installed, because the data will quickly become outdated as you HotSync with Consultant. If you use Extensions Manager or Conflict Catcher, just make sure that the extension is not checked; otherwise, just drag the file out of your System folder.

Summary

Palm Desktop 2.5 (the successor to MacPac 2.1) offers a number of improvements, including support for USB and improved utility access.

✦ Palm Desktop's means of attaching notes to items takes some getting used to, but it offers amazing power and flexibility once you learn how to use it.

✦ Remember that if you HotSync multiple handhelds on your Macintosh, each must have a unique username.

✦ Be careful when changing your conduits' settings because this is the easiest way to lose precious data.

✦ Chronos Consultant is a great alternative to Palm Desktop for those who want greater power and flexibility. A 30-day trial demo version is on the CD-ROM, so you can try it yourself.

✦   ✦   ✦

Enhancing Your Palm Lifestyle

◆ ◆ ◆ ◆

In This Part

Chapter 11
Installing and Using
PalmWare

Chapter 12
Tracking Projects

Chapter 13
Managing Finances
with PalmCalc

Chapter 14
Reading with
PalmBook

Chapter 15
Traveling with Your
Palm Handheld

Chapter 16
Communicating via
Your Palm

Chapter 17
Drawing and
Listening with
Your Palm

Chapter 18
Adding Toys to
Your Palm

Chapter 19
Downloading
and Accessing
Applications

◆ ◆ ◆ ◆

Installing and Using PalmWare

♦   ♦   ♦   ♦

In This Chapter

What is shareware?

Loading programs on
your Palm Organizer

Running new
applications

Deleting files from
your Palm Organizer

The essential
applications

♦   ♦   ♦   ♦

The huge success that 3Com has had with the Palm Organizer is in no small part due to an incredible developer community. There are thousands of applications available for the Palm Organizer — everything from utilities and developers' tools to games and diversions. There are hundreds of examples waiting for you to try on the CD-ROM accompanying this book. This chapter tells you how to load software on your Palm Organizer and highlights some of the very best available.

What is Shareware?

Shareware is a "try before you buy" means of distributing software, which enables you to use the software before buying it. Sometimes, the software is limited by a reduced feature set or a time limit; but just as often the programmer relies on the goodwill and honesty of users. If you find yourself using a shareware application — either from the CD-ROM or downloaded from the Internet — you are obligated to pay the author. Many shareware applications offer better value than competing commercial applications because they don't have the overhead of boxes or retail distribution. Other benefits include the upgrades and support you often receive by registering. Try it — you'll like it!

Paying shareware fees has never been easier. Services such as Kagi (http://order.kagi.com) offer shareware registration, and both PalmGear HQ (www.palmgear.com) and Handango (http://www.handango.com) enable you to register many titles online.

Wares

There are several variations on the soft*ware* theme:

✦ **Freeware** is software that the author makes freely available, but to which the author retains all rights.

✦ **Postcardware** is basically freeware, but the author asks for a postcard if you use the software.

✦ **Public Domain Software** is software that an author makes freely available, usually with source code, so that others can use and modify it as they like.

✦ **Commercial Demos** are time or otherwise limited versions of software that enable you to assess whether or not the software fits your needs.

Note   The shareware fees, Web, and e-mail addresses listed may have changed since this book's publication.

Loading programs on your Palm Handheld

Palm supplies you with all the software you need to load applications on your Palm. The first step, which most of us overlook, should be to read the documentation that comes with the application—here you may find tips, tricks, or warnings that you should know before you proceed. The documentation will usually be a text Readme file, but you may also find documentation in HTML format (to be read with your Web browser) or PDF format (to be read with Adobe Acrobat Reader). From there, the processes are virtually identical for Windows and Macintosh users, but there are a few subtle differences. Let's have a look.

Windows users

There are two basic types of files you can load on your Palm Organizer using Palm's Install Tool: Application files (.prc) and data files (.pdb). The easiest way to open the Install Tool in Windows is to double-click the file that you want to load. The Install Tool will open with that file listed (see Figure 11-1). From there you can click Add to locate and load more files, or click Done to indicate that you're finished. If you want to remove a file from the list, select it and click Remove. After you've finished, a HotSync is all it takes to load the files on your Palm Organizer.

Note   There are several other ways to open the Install Tool. You can click the Start menu, and select Programs ⇨ Palm ⇨ Install Tool, or you can open the Palm Desktop PIM and click the Install button on the left side of the screen.

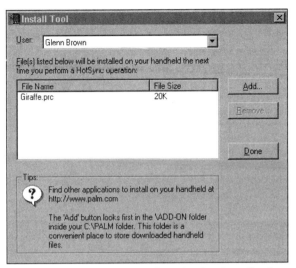

Figure 11-1: Using the Install Tool to load applications

Tip The first place the Install Tool looks for files to load is C:\Palm\Add-Ons; this makes it a convenient place to put downloaded or other files you plan to load on your Palm Organizer.

If you install many applications, it might be handy to put a shortcut on your Windows Desktop or in the QuickLaunch tray. To do so, follow these steps:

1. Navigate to INSTAPP.EXE (the default installation puts it in C:\Palm).

2. Right-click and drag the icon to either the Desktop or the QuickLaunch Tray.

3. When you release the mouse button, select Create Shortcut Here, and you're done.

4. You can then drag .prc/.pdb files directly to either location to load.

My Little Buddy
Developer: Precise Solutions
Cost: $20.00 (shareware)

My Little Buddy has a somewhat deceptive name; its capabilities are anything but little. Once installed, you can open it from the Start menu (Programs ➪ Precise Solutions ➪ My Little Buddy), and it will remain minimized in your Process tray until you need it. Double-click to open it, and you'll get an icon bar. Double-click the second icon to get the My Little Buddy Installer, shown in Figure 11-2. The capabilities of this utility go far beyond that of a simple installer: features include support for drag and drop, multiple users and file installs, file type association for .prc and .pdb files, an organizer for your favorite Palm-related Web sites, support for BackupBuddy, and more. There is a 30-day demo on the CD-ROM, so check it out for yourself.

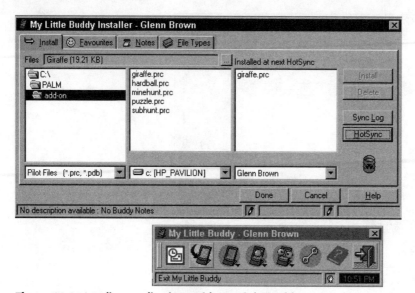

Figure 11-2: Loading applications with My Little Buddy

Macintosh users

Macintosh users have an additional step, but the process is no more difficult than under Windows. As shown in Figure 11-3, select the HotSync Manager from the Palm Desktop menu, select Install from the HotSync menu, and drag applications into the window to load them. You can drag additional .prc/.pdb files to the window or click the Add To List button to open a dialog box that will enable you to locate the file you want to load. Highlighting a file and clicking the Remove From List button will do just that. Clicking Application Info displays file information, including files sizes, both on your Mac and on your Palm Organizer.

All of the Macintosh loading processes and features covered in the *Palm OS Bible* relate to MacPac 2. This is a significant upgrade for Macintosh users, featuring an updated Palm Desktop (based on Claris Organizer) and improved conduit support.

Tip

If you want easy access to the HotSync Manager, place an alias where you find it most convenient. To do so, just select the file (by default, the installer places it in a folder named Palm), and press Command+M. Drag the alias to where you want it, and you're done. In Figure 11-3, you'll see aliases on the Desktop, in the Apple menu (just put the alias in the Apple Menu Items folder, which you'll find in your System folder), and in Action GoMac's QuickLaunch area.

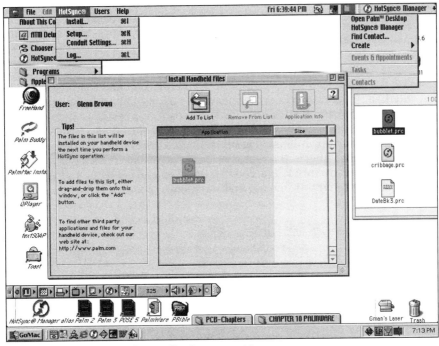

Figure 11-3: Loading Palm applications on a Mac

PalmMac
Developer: Precise Solutions
Cost: Freeware

How would you like the Windows users' capability of double-clicking a .prc/.pdb file to open the Install Tool? Alan Pinstein of Synergy Solutions has written an AppleScript droplet to help you — drop your .prc/.pdb files on it, and it will change their type and creator (to Gld0/Gld1). The icon for your files will change, and from then on, double-clicking any of those files opens the Install Tool. The Bubblet and Cribbage icons in Figure 11-3 have been changed; the DateBk3 icon still displays the generic icon.

HotSyncCSM
Developer: Yukinari Suzuki
Cost: Freeware

This freeware Control Strip Module enables you to open the HotSync Manager directly, and to start or stop Monitoring. To configure for your setup, you'll first need to Command+click the module in the Control Strip. Yukinari also wrote SimpleInst, which gives users of the original MacPac (now called the Palm Connect Kit) drag-and-drop installation.

Palm Buddy

Developer: Florent Pillet
Cost: $20.00 (shareware)
Footprint: 13K

This one is a poweruser's dream. To run it, you turn off Palm's serial port monitoring, and then run the Palm Buddy application on your Palm Organizer and its companion application on your Macintosh. As a result, you get a live hierarchical view of your Palm Organizer's contents (see Figure 11-4), with drag-and-drop backup and install at up to 115,200 bps! Palm Buddy also ships with an AportisDoc plug-in that automatically converts text files dropped onto the handheld window into Palm-readable Doc files and sends them to your Palm Organizer. I registered this one the first day I saw it.

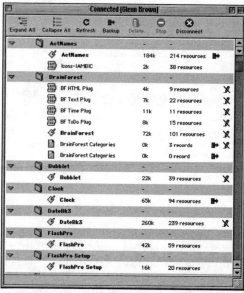

Figure 11-4: Palm Buddy

Running new applications

Now that you've finished with the Install Tool, the only thing left to perform is a HotSync, which will load your new applications on your Palm Organizer. Once the HotSync is complete, just tap the Application Launcher (see Figure 11-5). You'll find your new applications in the Unfiled category.

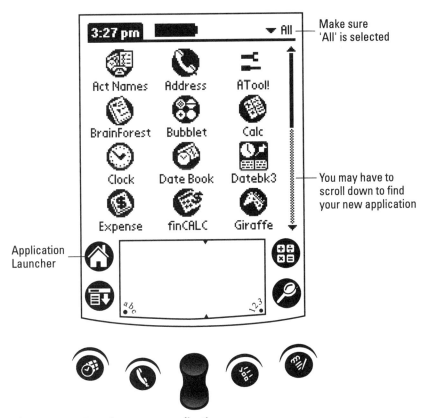

Figure 11-5: Running a new application

Tip Don't forget that you can use the hardware buttons when you want to scroll your view of applications up or down. Even better, you can use Graffiti (discussed in Chapter 3): just enter the first letter of the application you want to find (such as H for HackMaster), and the screen scrolls automatically, with the items starting with that letter at the top of the display.

The Palm IIIx, IIIe, VII, and most organizers in the Palm V family have updated silk-screened icons to make them easier to decipher. For example, the inscrutable arrow originally used for the Application Launcher has been replaced with a picture of a house, to indicate that this is the icon to tap to return to the Launcher's "home" position.

Note If you have a pre-3.x version of the Palm OS installed, you won't have the new categories display, and up/down triangles will display at the bottom right-hand corner of the screen to indicate scrolling direction.

HackMaster

If you have loaded a HackMaster Hack, you will need to open the HackMaster application and make sure that it is checked in HackMaster's list (see Figure 11-6).

Figure 11-6: Enabling Hacks in HackMaster

Cross-Reference For more on HackMaster, see Chapter 21.

Loading documents

If you loaded a document file, you need to have loaded a document viewing utility, such as AportisDoc or TealDoc, in order to read the file on your Palm Organizer.

Cross-Reference For more coverage of using document files on your Palm Organizer, see Chapter 13.

Run-time files

Occasionally, you run into files that require that an interpreter (such as cBaspad or PocketC) be loaded on your Palm Organizer. The documentation for these files will invariably tell you the loading requirements and procedure.

More applications

The most obvious place to start is the CD-ROM that accompanies this book—see Appendix B for a complete listing of its contents. For updates, start exploring the Internet. You'll find a lot of good Web sites covered in Chapter 18.

Tip   Still confused? There is a complete, interactive walkthrough of the application-loading process on Synergy Solutions Web site at `www.synsolutions.com/support/install`.

Deleting files

Running out of space? Need to delete a few files so that there is room for a new game? Nothing could be easier: just tap the Applications button, and then tap the silk-screened Menu icon directly below the Applications button. A drop-down menu displays; just tap Delete to get the screen shown in Figure 11-7. Scroll up or down until you see the file that you want to delete, tap it to highlight it, and then tap the Delete button. A dialog box asks you to confirm that this is what you want to do; just tap Yes, and the file will disappear.

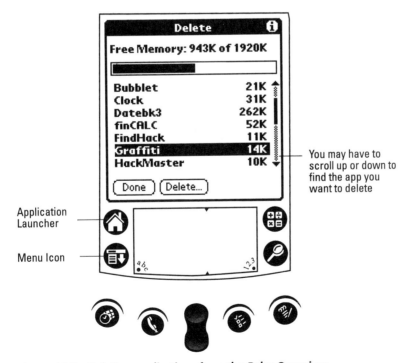

Figure 11-7: Deleting applications from the Palm Organizer

Tip

If you are using Launch'Em or any of the third-party application launchers discussed in Chapter 19, you will discover you have a new Application icon (see Figure 11-8). You need to launch this application if you want to access the Palm Application Launcher's menu items, including delete.

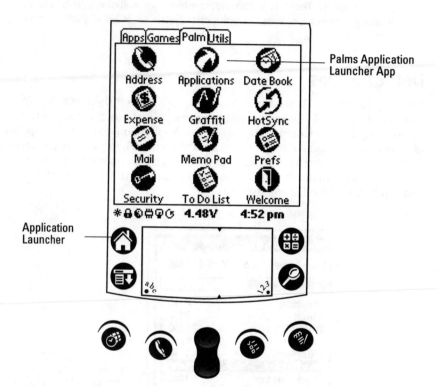

Palms Application Launcher App

Application Launcher

Figure 11-8: Palm's Application Launcher application

Caution

If you want to delete any HackMaster hacks, they must be disabled in the HackMaster application first. If you want to delete all of your HackMaster hacks, open the HackMaster application and tap the 'Uninstall All' button before calling up the Delete choice in the Application Launcher window.

Note

Those using Palm OS 1.x or 2.x need to use the Memory Application to delete files.

A Few Essential Shareware Applications

You may not ever load an application on your Palm Organizer—maybe Palm's built-in applications are enough for you. I suspect, however, that if you are reading the *Palm OS Bible*, you will load and try more than a few third-party applications. This chapter closes with a few applications that I have purchased and can no longer live without. Each of these programs offers value beyond their price—I recommend them all highly. I start off with a couple of tough choices: Action Names or DateBk3 (I use both), and Cesium or Clock III, and I end with three easy ones: UnDupe, FlashPro, and BackupBuddy. I should add that these are *my* essentials—you can try the demos on the CD-ROM and decide for yourself what you need on your Palm Organizer.

Action Names

Author: Iambic Software
Cost: $19.95
Footprint: 187K

This pumped-up application started as a combination of the Date Book and Address Book with multiple views; the company has followed up with a series of impressive updates. Action Names offers four views: Agenda (Figure 11-9), Single or Double Week (Single Week view shown in Figure 11-10), Month, and Quarter. For more on Action Names, see Chapter 20.

Figure 11-9: Action Names daily agenda

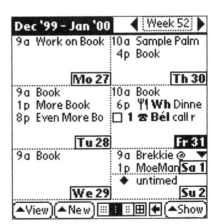

Figure 11-10: Action Names full week view

One thing Action Names does not support is beaming of contact or appointment information – if you need to beam information, you'll need to use the appropriate Palm application.

DateBk3

Author: C. E. Steuart Dewar
Cost: $20.00 (shareware)
Footprint: 262K

DateBk3 is an application that completely replaces your Palm Organizer's Calendar application with a new, improved one. The simplest description is a combination of Palm's Date Book and To Do List applications on steroids. The look is virtually identical, until you scratch the surface. Look in the lower left-hand corner of Figure 11-11, and you'll see extra views added.

The pop-up menu shown in Figure 11-12 gives a hint of DateBk's capabilities: integrated Phone Lookup, To Do items on your calendar, Journal entries, and more. For more on DateBk3, see Chapter 20

Figure 11-11: DateBk3 adds extra views

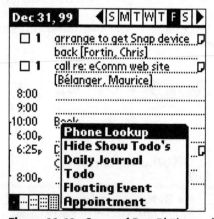

Figure 11-12: Some of DateBk3's capabilities

Cesium

Author: Andrew Ball
Cost: $7.00
Footprint: 36K

Cesium (Figure 11-13) turns your Palm Organizer into a sophisticated clock/timing device, with support for multiple time zones, alarms, a timer, and a stopwatch. I particularly like the way the stopwatch is done—almost the entire screen becomes the start/stop button.

Clock III

Author: Little Wing Software
Cost: $24.95
Footprint: 31K

Like Cesium, Clock III (Figure 11-14) is a combination clock/timer, with support for multiple time zones, alarms, a timer, and a stopwatch. The support for multiple time zones is better implemented in Clock III, but the biggest difference is Clock III's use of the hardware keys when used as a timer.

Figure 11-13: Cesium

Figure 11-14: Clock III is a combination clock/timer.

As Figure 11-15 shows, your Palm Organizer's buttons are remapped, turning it into a very expensive stopwatch.

HackMaster

Author: Edward Keyes
Company: DaggerWare
Cost: $5.00 (or what you think it is worth)
Footprint: 10k

HackMaster (Figure 11-16) is software that enables programmers to write hacks. Hacks are little programs that are loaded with the operating system, much like Terminate and Stay Resident (TSR) applications under Windows or Control Panels on the Macintosh.

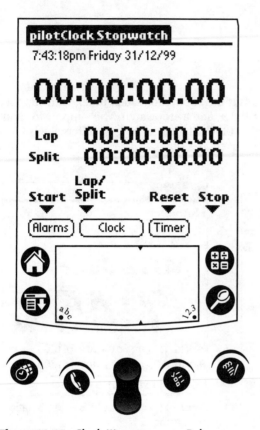

Figure 11-15: Clock III remaps your Palm
Organizer's buttons.

Figure 11-16: HackMaster settings

Contrast Button Hack

Author: Synergy Solutions
Cost: Freeware
Footprint: 3K

There's an extra button on the Palm V, the contrast button, that enables you to adjust the screen brightness. Alan Pinstein of Synergy Solutions wrote this great little freeware hack (Figure 11-17) that enables you to open the application of your choice with the Palm V's contrast button. Don't worry, you still have access to contrast — all it takes is a second tap on the button to open the control panel.

Figure 11-17: Contrast Button Hack

FindHack

Author: Florent Pillet
Cost: $6.00
Footprint: 11K

One of the problems with the built-in Find command is that it searches all of the databases in your Palm Organizer; if it runs into corrupted data, it crashes. Florent has removed all of the limitations of the Palm Organizer's built-in find command with this little powerhouse (see Figure 11-18). You can limit the databases searched, do wildcard searches, and even preconfigure your own favorites.

MagicText Hack

Author: Synergy Software
Cost: $17.95
Footprint: 44K

Do you miss the capabilities of your word processor when you're using your Palm Organizer? Try MagicText — it may be the cure. Double-tap a word to select it, and then drag it around the screen

Use your pen to stroke up from the silk-screened Menu button to the Applications button (see Figure 11-19) to pop up a contextual menu of actions you can perform.

Figure 11-18: FindHack lets you select what to search.

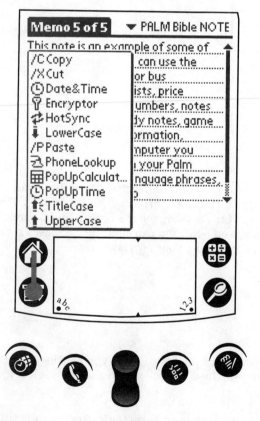

Figure 11-19: MagicText pops up a contextual menu of performable actions.

MenuHack

Author: Edward Keyes
Cost: Freeware
Footprint: 2K

Don't you wish that the menus on your Palm Organizer worked the same as they do on your computer? With MenuHack enabled, they do — just tap the menu bar to tap down the menu.

Launch'Em

Author: Synergy Solutions
Cost: $39.95 (as part of Hi-Five)
Footprint: 47K

One of the limitations of the early PalmPilots was the launching utility: it really didn't support a lot of apps. This left room for developers to write utilities to replace that functionality. The one I use is Launch'Em. I find the tabbed metaphor much easier to navigate with, and the extra features are a bonus. Version 2 of this great utility (see Figure 11-20) has made it the undisputed powerusers' choice.

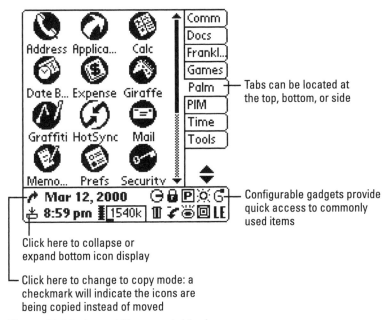

Tabs can be located at the top, bottom, or side

Configurable gadgets provide quick access to commonly used items

Click here to collapse or expand bottom icon display

Click here to change to copy mode: a checkmark will indicate the icons are being copied instead of moved

Figure 11-20: Launch'Em uses tabbed menus.

One handy addition is the recent applications list, which you can pop up by stroking up from the silk-screened Applications button (see Figure 11-21).

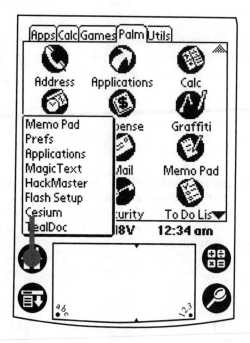

Figure 11-21: Launch'Em's recent applications list

 See Chapter 19 for more third-party launching utilities.

ListMaker

Author: Synergy Solutions
Distribution: $39.95 (as part of Hi-Five)

The first two applications I bought for my Palm Organizer were ListMaker (as part of Hi-Five) and QuickSheet. ListMaker enables you to create lists that you can reuse. You can create a reusable list of common items (like the grocery list shown in Figure 11-22); clicking Update generates a new checklist. This one represents another tough decision: I also like and use Aportis BrainForest.

See Chapter 12 for more on listmaking and outlining utilities.

OmniRemote

Author: Pacific Neo-Tek
Cost: $20.00
Footprint: 48K

People can't believe OmniRemote when they see it; it enables the Palm Organizer to function as a remote control (see Figure 11-23). I have mine set to control my TVs and surround-sound system. My wife and I no longer fight over who gets the remote, and I haven't lost my Palm Organizer yet. See Chapter 19 for more on OmniRemote.

Figure 11-22: ListMaker creates reusable lists.

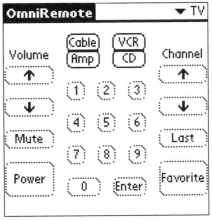

Figure 11-23: OmniRemote turns the Palm Organizer into a remote control.

Pocket Quicken

Author: Landware
Cost: $39.95
Footprint: 69K (depends on data stored; mine is now 118K)

For me, this one was a total no-brainer. I wanted to get a handle on my finances; now I know exactly how little I have and how much I owe, just by checking my Palm Organizer. Pocket Quicken (see Figure 11-24) is a great companion to Intuit's Quicken software. It enables you to carry a miniature version of Quicken with you for transaction entry and account balances.

TealDoc

Author: TealPoint Software
Cost: $16.95
Footprint: 44K

Want to read documents on your Palm Organizer? There are all sorts of documents you could load on your Palm Organizer, including most of this book. The first thing you need is a document reader. TealDoc (Figure 11-25) supports graphics and text. See Chapter 14 for more on TealDoc and other document tools for your Palm Organizer.

Figure 11-24: Pocket Quicken is a portable, miniature version of Quicken.

Figure 11-25: TealDoc supports graphics and text.

Vehicle Log

Author: Little Wing Software
Cost: $19.95
Footprint: 34K

If you keep a little logbook in your car to record gas mileage, this one is for you. Vehicle Log (Figure 11-26) tracks gas, trips, maintenance, and more for up to seven vehicles. See Chapter 11 more on Vehicle Log and other expense-tracking utilities.

UnDupe

Author: Stevens Creek Software
Cost: $4.95 (shareware)
Footprint: 10K

This chapter ends with three essential tools; the first is UnDupe (See Figure 11-27). Occasionally when HotSyncing, especially if you do so on two different computers, you'll get duplicate entries. Sometimes you get one or two duplicate entries; sometimes you get hundreds. HotSync again in this condition and you usually double what you have; pretty soon you're out of room and out of luck. Run into this once (and you will), and you'll need UnDupe. The shareware version on the CD-ROM will identify duplicates for you. Send in the registration fee, and you'll get the version that deletes duplicates — well worth the five bucks! See Chapter 20 for more utilities for your Palm Organizer.

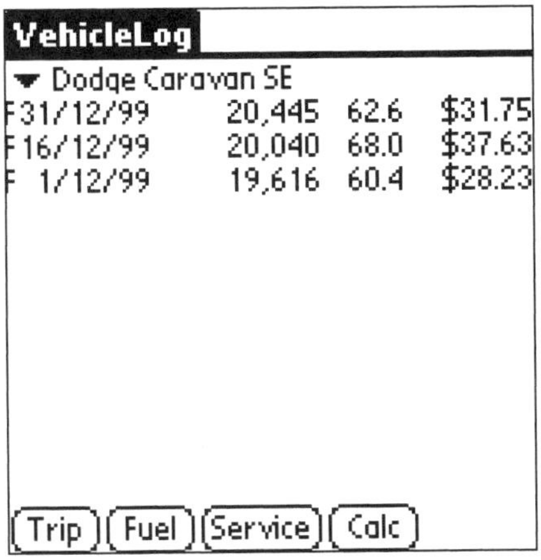

Figure 11-26: Vehicle Log tracks the costs for up to seven vehicles.

Figure 11-27: UnDupe deletes duplicate entries.

FlashPro

Author: Technology Resource Group
Cost: $29.95
Footprint: 60K (includes 17K setup)

If you have a Palm III or better and you load software, you need FlashPro (Figure 11-28). Palm ships its Palm III, V, and VII organizers with 2MB of RAM and the operating system with 2MB of Flash ROM. The Palm IIIx has 4MB of RAM and 2MB of Flash ROM. The trick is that the operating system only takes about 1.2MB of the

Flash ROM, leaving another 800K that you can load with this great little utility. Even better, it is nonvolatile, so it can survive a hard crash. You can even configure it to store backups of your essential data in flash, so that you can recover from a crash without having to HotSync. See Chapter 20 for more utilities for your Palm Organizer.

FlashPro	▼ All
Name	▼ Size
1 FlashPro	39.5K
2 FPSUtil3	34.5K
3 Giraffe	19.4K
4 HackMaster	9.5K
5 HardBall	18.1K
6 JFile	58.3K
7 MineHunt	9.3K
8 Puzzle	4.9K
9 Reptoids	34.7K
1723K 671K	0.0K
RAM Flash	(Move)(Delete)

Figure 11-28: FlashPro gives access to the unused Flash ROM.

Note FlashPro is not compatible with the Palm IIIe or Palm Organizers prior to the Palm III (they didn't have flash memory). It also does not work with the PageMart Synapse pager card. Palm, Inc. does not support or recommend this application because it writes in the same ROM space where Palm's projected system upgrades are intended to go. (Unfortunately, there's that pesky law of physics that tells us two things can't occupy the same space at the same time.)

BackupBuddy

Author: Alexander Hinds
Cost: $19.95

Can you imagine running your computer without being able to make backups? If you have a Palm operating system that predates release 3.3, the HotSync process (see Chapter 6) will backup all of your data, but not all of your programs. This wonderful utility (see Figure 11-29) does just that: it backs up all of your applications and data, even if it is stored using FlashPro (listed previously).

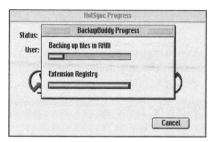

Figure 11-29: BackupBuddy at work

There are versions for both Windows and Macintosh users. The Windows version (see Figure 11-30) can be fine-tuned to specify exactly what should be backed up. See Chapter 20 for more utilities for your Palm Organizer.

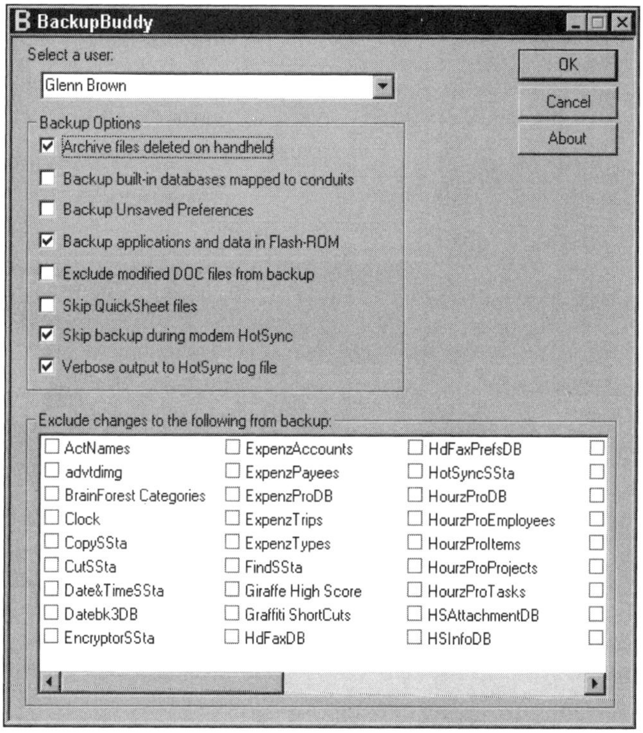

Figure 11-30: BackupBuddy settings for Windows

Summary

This chapter should just give you a taste of the literally thousands of great applications available for your Palm Organizer. Start with those you like from the CD-ROM, and then start exploring the Internet for more applications.

✦ Shareware enables you to "try before you buy" software; just remember that you are honor-bound to pay the author for software that you use.

✦ Loading applications on your Palm Organizer couldn't be easier — just drag the .prc/.pdb files to the Install Tool window, do a HotSync, and you're done!

✦ Once you start loading applications on your Palm Organizer, you'll appreciate the value of FlashPro (for more space) and BackupBuddy (for backups).

✦   ✦   ✦

Tracking Projects

In This Chapter

Creating high-powered lists

Recording activities with logs

Using Outliners to stay organized

Integrating your Palm Organizer with Microsoft Project

The Palm Organizer is the ideal device for managing lists. The built-in To Do List and Memo Pad applications both have uses that certainly go beyond those originally envisioned by their designers. Still, there is always room for improvement and innovation. This chapter covers a few of the third-party applications that you can use to keep lists and logs. It also compares outliners that take lists to a new level and includes coverage of Palm-based software that enables you to monitor your Microsoft Project files.

Creating High-Powered Lists

Soon after purchasing a new Palm Organizer, many people begin making lists — to do lists, shopping, groceries, gifts, or any other imaginable list. Let's take a quick look at some of the third-party list-making utilities, to see how they stack up to Palm's built-in tools. Palm makes the source code to its built-in applications available to developers, which makes it fairly simple for developers to create modified versions.

Table 12-1 compares some of the better list-making applications that are available for your Palm Organizer. Remember that the interface rating is subjective. Import/export capabilities are important because it is much easier to type in your master grocery list on your computer than it is to tap it in on your handheld! The real key to these applications is whether they add the functionality that *you* need. The best way to find out is try them.

Table 12-1						
List Applications						
Application	Price	Size	Interface Rating	Import/ Export	Graphics	Adds
Palm To Do	n/a	n/a	B	No	No	—
CheckList	Freeware	37K	B	Yes	No	Reusable lists
JShopper	$10.00	28K	B	Export only	No	Multiple stores, prices
ListMaker	$17.95	143K	A	Yes	No	Hierarchical display, common items
ShopList	Freeware	29K	B	No	No	Multiple stores
ToDo PLUS	$19.95	85K	B	No	Yes	Graphics, memo templates

CheckList

Developer: AHo Interactive Software
Cost: Freeware
Footprint: 37K

CheckList adds the capability to import and export lists using Memo Pad as well as the capability to manually change the sort order (see Figure 12-1). To my mind, this utility is best as a *reusable* checklist, enabling you to create lists that you use frequently.

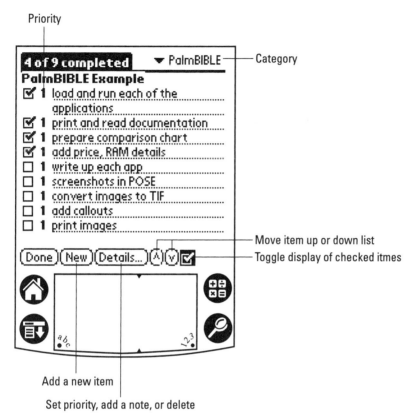

Priority

Category

Move item up or down list

Toggle display of checked itmes

Add a new item

Set priority, add a note, or delete

Figure 12-1: CheckList

JShopper

Developer: Land-J Technologies
Cost: $10.00
Footprint: 28K

JShopper is specifically designed for shopping. It enables you to enter details for up to 15 stores, and then create reusable shopping lists that can track prices, quantities, coupons, and even the aisle that products are found in! The program operates in two modes: All and Need. First, you create lists of what you need in the All mode. These lists are reusable; just check off the items and select the quantities that you need. After you arrive at the store, switch to the Need mode (see Figure 12-2). In this mode, items disappear from the screen after you check them off.

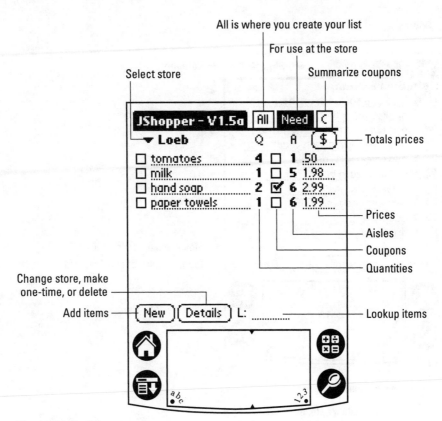

Figure 12-2: JShopper

ListMaker

Developer: Synergy Solutions
Cost: $17.95
Footprint: 143K

ListMaker is one of the first applications I bought for my original PalmPilot. It not only includes the capability of creating reusable lists, but it also adds the capability of creating hierarchical items, which are nested items that can be expanded or revealed as you choose. Once you select an item in an outline, you can drag it up or down or underneath another item. ListMaker has quickly accessible and reusable common lists. It ships with editable grocery and packing lists, but you will soon begin adding your own. To quickly create a new grocery list, tap Common, then tap the items that you need, and then tap Update. ListMaker then generates your shopping list (see Figure 12-3). Because this program blurs the distinction between list applications and outliners, I have included it in both tables in this chapter.

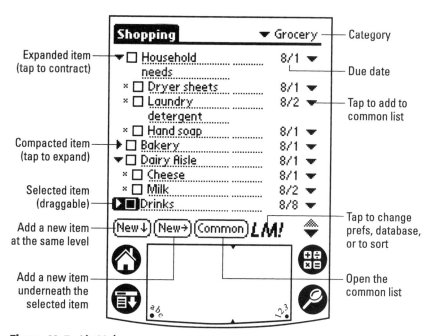

Figure 12-3: ListMaker

ShopList

Developer: Gregg Geschke
Cost: Freeware
Footprint: 29K

ShopList enables you to create multiple reusable lists for multiple stores (see Figure 12-4). I particularly like the ability to assign items to more than one store, because I occasionally shop at different stores for the same things (such as groceries).

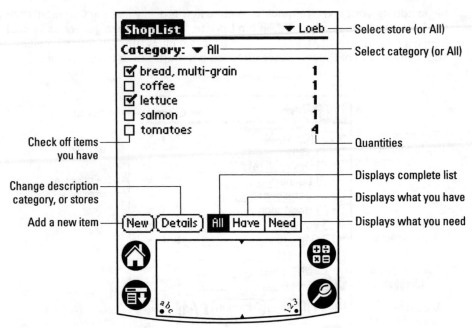

Figure 12-4: ShopList

ToDo PLUS

Developer: Hands High Software
Cost: $19.95
Footprint: 85K

ToDo PLUS, from Hands High Software, enables you to add drawings or alarms to your To Do items and to create repeating tasks. This comes in handy if, for example, you want a recurring reminder to pay a bill on the 15th of the month or to submit a report to your boss every Thursday. The viewing options also let you span categories to see what you need to do now.

Recording Activities with Logs

Logging, the act of recording activities, is well suited to the Palm Organizer — especially because most users carry their handhelds with them most of the time. There are literally hundreds of specialized logging applications available for the Palm OS, including programs to help aviators, divers, collectors, and others. Here I discuss a couple of exemplary applications to inspire you to find (or even write) your own.

Cross-Reference Look to Chapter 13 for products that help you log time and expenses, and Chapter 15 for travel-related logging products, including those that track your car's gas mileage.

Athlete's Diary

Developer: Stevens Creek Software
Cost: $39.95
Footprint: 48K

Stevens Creek Software specializes in utility applications, particularly those to help athletes track training and performance. The Athlete's Diary (see Figure 12-5) is a product designed to help those involved in endurance sports such as running, cycling, and swimming. AutoFill features make it easy to enter data, and you can HotSync to companion products that are available for both Windows and Macintosh users. Other sports-related products from Stevens Creek Software include Athlete's Calculator, PocketTimer, Race Announcer, Race Base, SplitTimer, and SwimCoach.

Figure 12-5: Keeping a training log with Athlete's Diary

DietLog

Developer: Softcare Clinical Informatics
Cost: $59.00
Footprint: 333K

One of the biggest challenges of a diet is recording your food intake, and then calculating the fat, calories, and cholesterol, plus anything else you've decided to track. DietLog (see Figure 12-6) is a sophisticated program that does the work for you—all you need is the willpower. The program includes a built-in database of nutritional information, recipes, and menus. You can edit the existing recipes and menus, or create your own. Softcare Clinical Informatics specializes in health-related Palm Organizer products, including ExerLog and GlucoLog.

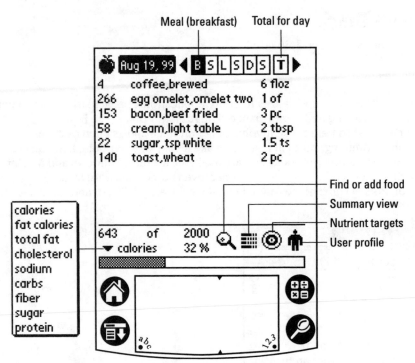

Figure 12-6: Recording breakfast with DietLog

Using Outliners to Stay Organized

Outliners help you capture and organize ideas and thoughts. The hierarchical structure makes it easy to nest concepts and projects in an overall plan.

I've been a big fan of outline software since I purchased my first copy of Living Videotext's ThinkTank. Since then, the concept has come full circle. Almost every type of computer software integrates outlining features, while the stand-alone products seem to have disappeared. Recently, Dave Winer of Userland Software, Inc. was able to convince Symantec to enable him to re-release some of his classic outlining software — ThinkTank, Ready, and MORE — as freeware (see www.outliners.com). If you're interested in more of the history, be sure to read Dave's article at http://davewiner.userland.com/outlinersProgramming.

Outline applications are a natural for the Palm OS, because the software's capability to focus on detail or zoom out to see the larger picture really shines. Table 12-2 compares outliners currently available for the Palm OS. As before, the interface rating is strictly my opinion — be sure to try the product for yourself. The interface for these outliners is particularly important and must enable you to add, expand, and move items easily. Similarly, the capability to move your outlines to your computer is beneficial, so they can become part of larger projects. Graphics may not be an essential element, but they do help to clarify concepts.

Table 12-2
Outliners for the Palm OS

Application	Price	Size	Interface Rating	Import/ Export	Desktop	Graphics
Arranger	$19.00	46K	A+	Yes	No	No
BrainForest	$39.95	126K	B	Yes	Yes	No
Hi-Note	$20.00	37K	B	Yes	Third party	Yes
ListMaker	$17.95	143K	A	Yes	No	No
ThoughtMill	$17.95	55K	A+	Yes	No	No

All of these applications are worth investigating; you owe it to yourself to see what these programs can do for you if you haven't already done so.

Arranger

Developer: Olive Branch Software
Cost: $19.00
Footprint: 46K

Arranger is a unique outliner. Items in the outline can either be notes up to 32K, or they can be links to items in your Palm Organizer's built-in Date Book, Address Book, To Do List, Memo Pad, or Expense applications. Adding a new item is simple: just tap New or select one of the application choices from the Edit Menu to create a link. Plus marks are used to represent collapsed outlines; simply tap on the plus to expand and reveal the contents.

As Figure 12-7 shows, the drag-and-drop implementation is especially well done. After you drag an item, an arrow appears to show where you can place it. Dragging to the left of the outline displays a right-facing triangle and places your item between two items. Dragging to the right displays a left-facing triangle and places your item beneath the item above it.

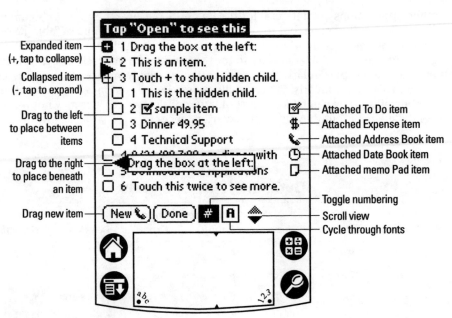

Figure 12-7: Drag and drop in Arranger

Those interested in programs that link to Palm's primary applications should also look at Vision 7 Software's TrackFast in Chapter 20.

BrainForest

Developer: Aportis Technologies
Cost: $39.95
Footprint: 111K

BrainForest by Aportis Technologies started out as Florent Pillet's Outliner. Two versions are now available: BrainForest Mobile Edition, a $30.00 version for your Palm Organizer, and BrainForest Professional, which adds a desktop version for your computer. The program uses a tree metaphor to describe its operation; files are trees, subjects are branches, and subtopics are leaves. New items are added in a pop-up window (see Figure 12-8), and can be set as To Do items with checkboxes or Project items with completion percentages. Simply drag-and-drop to move items up and down the structure. Note that items cannot be moved under one another — you need to create a new leaf instead. BrainForest Mobile Edition also includes plug-ins that enable you to import and export data to and from your Palm Organizer's built-in To Do and Memo Pad applications.

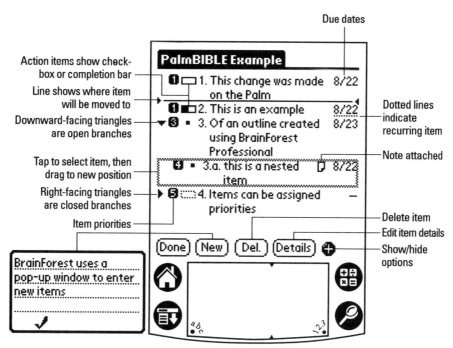

Figure 12-8: BrainForest Mobile Edition

BrainForest Professional adds companion software for both Macintosh and Windows users. The desktop software offers a nice clean interface, without any of the dragging limitations of the Palm OS version. It does not, however, include a true conduit to transfer data. You can move outlines to your computer from your handheld and back, but the software does not synchronize, so you need to keep track of the current version. Figure 12-9 shows the Macintosh version, which has one idiosyncrasy: you can only display priorities *or* action status (checkbox or percent complete), but not both at the same time. The Windows version overcomes this limitation, but its implementation of drag-and-drop is not as smooth as that of the Mac version.

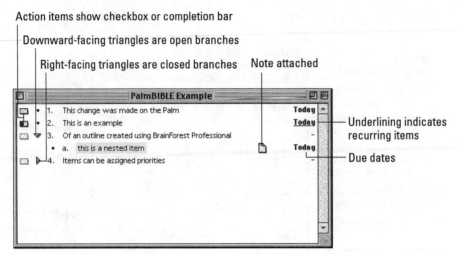

Figure 12-9: BrainForest Professional on a Macintosh

Hi-Note

Developer: Cyclos
Cost: $20.00   (shareware)
Footprint: 37K

Cyclos' Hi-Note is from Bill Goodman, the author of Compact Pro, a popular Macintosh file compression utility. Hi-Note is the only outliner for the Palm OS that supports both text and graphic items (see Figure 12-10).

Rearranging outlines is easy: drag an item up or down. If you drop one item on top of another, it becomes a subnote (see Figure 12-11). If you drag between items, a line appears to show you the new location. Hi-Note enables you to import or export items through the Memo Pad, although you must import an entire category (exporting enables you to select a single note).

Some third-party products enable you to move Hi-Note data to and from your computer. PCHi-Note by SoftEssence (see Figure 12-12) is a $20 shareware product that mirrors Hi-Note's functionality for Windows users. HiView is a $5 shareware product by Bell*2 Lab that enables viewing of Hi-Note outlines and graphics on the Macintosh.

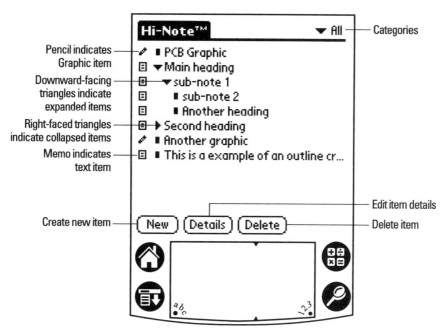

Figure 12-10: Hi-Note

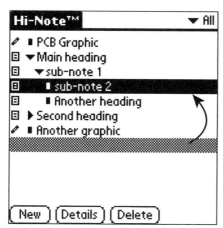

Figure 12-11: Drag an item on top of another to convert it to a subnote.

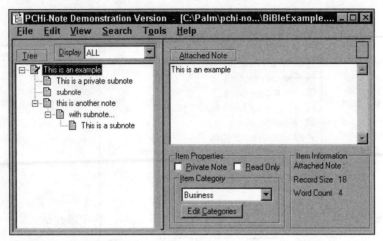

Figure 12-12: PC Hi-Note

ListMaker

Synergy Solutions' ListMaker is discussed earlier in the section "Creating High-Powered Lists."

ThoughtMill

Developer: Hands High Software
Cost: $17.95
Footprint: 55K

Of the outliners discussed in this section, I think Hands High Software's ThoughtMill has the most elegant interface (see Figure 12-13). The drag and drop is particularly well done and, at under $18, it's a great buy.

To move an item, simply tap and hold the bullet to the left of the item, and drag it to the desired position. As shown in Figure 12-14, a hollow version of the icon follows your stylus, and crosshairs make it easy to move your item precisely. ThoughtMill can display lists as checkbox items and import and export to your handheld's Memo Pad by category.

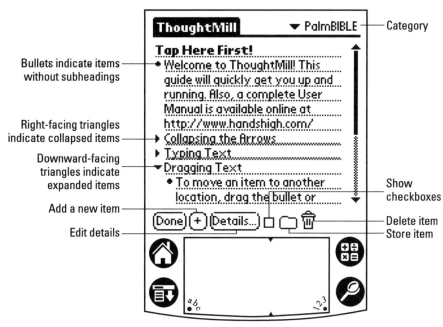

Figure 12-13: ThoughtMill

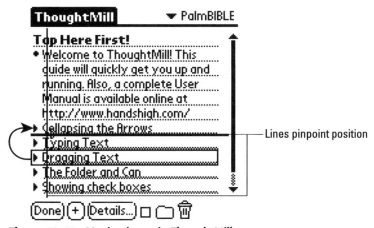

Figure 12-14: Moving items in ThoughtMill

Microsoft Project on Your Palm Handheld

Until the advent of third-party solutions, you couldn't carry a Microsoft Project plan with you on your Palm. Fortunately, that has changed with new products for the Palm OS. Thanks to Roelof Mulder for writing this section.

Project@Hand

Developer: Natara Software
Cost: $49.95
Footprint: 46K

Project@Hand (see Figure 12-15) is a fantastic program that mirrors Microsoft Project 98 (or 2000) and enables you to modify or add projects. Just like any other linked application (PC to Palm), the initial data is taken from the desktop through a HotSync conduit.

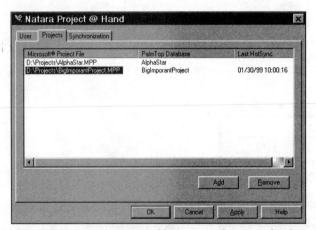

Figure 12-15: Project@Hand helps you choose a database.

In addition to displaying the entire project as a Gantt chart or similar visualization, Project@Hand gives you the data in appropriate screens related to project-management principles. Starting the application (after you have HotSynced at least one Microsoft Project data file into your organizer) presents a project database screen. Figure 12-16 shows the main task screen of a project database. If you choose a database from this screen, you see a list of the high-level tasks contained in the project database. At this point, you can add a new task or view the related resources tied to the project.

If you touch a task description, the details for that task appear, as shown in Figure 12-17. You see the type of task, duration in days (or other time element, depending on the setup of the database from the desktop), percentage completed, and a short bar graph that provides you with a graphic display and the start and finish time elements, as applicable. At this point, you can add Resources (either human or financial), add a note, and identify predecessors of the task. You can also page through the subsequent tasks by using the scroll arrows at the top of the screen.

Figure 12-16: Main task screen   **Figure 12-17:** Task information

When you add Resources, you can choose from a list of all the identified project resources. Navigate through a project by using the drop-down menus or scroll arrows.

Project@Hand is a practical application to have—particularly if your field of business is project oriented. You can travel to meetings and have your project data with you, available for reference or change.

Tip   If you change project information on your Palm Organizer, don't forget to copy the information from the HotSynced data file back to the original desktop project file.

PalmProject

Developer: PDAWare
Cost: $19.95
Footprint: 18K

Palm Project Scheduler offers an interesting approach to shareware. Its current version (1.2 as of this writing) is available as a commercial product for $19.95, and an earlier release (numbered 1.1) is available as shareware. The shareware version does little other than capture and maintain tasks, associated resources, percentage completion, and start and end dates. It also provides for a means to link to Microsoft Project via an exported .csv file, which is stored in the directory identified through the setup routine for PalmProject.

The conduit requires Windows 95 or better and processes the data from your organizer in a format that has a special header or "map" that Microsoft Project can read. When you import a project file into PalmProject, rename the subject file **import.csv** and place it into the directory as identified in the setup. The conduit imports the file to your Palm Organizer on the next HotSync. When you create the file for import, you must be sure to follow Microsoft Project's instructions to save your project as a .csv file and create a "map." The conduit parses the file appropriately for importing to your organizer.

The updated commercial version includes some minor bug fixes, and removes a number of limitations of the shareware version, including the capability to work on more than one project.

Summary

The list-making programs available for the Palm OS all offer functionality beyond Palm's built-in tools. If reusable lists, import and export capabilities, support for prices, or graphics are important to you, try one of the demo versions on the CD-ROM.

You can find logging tools of almost every kind for the Palm Organizer.

Outlining utilities are almost perfect for the Palm OS — the form factor is ideal. My personal preference is for those that enable drag-and-drop editing, so that rearranging an outline is easy. Try those on the CD-ROM and choose for yourself.

✦   ✦   ✦

Managing Finances with PalmCalc

✦ ✦ ✦ ✦

In This Chapter

Managing finances on your Palm Organizer

Calculators

Spreadsheets

Expense/finance managers

My choices

✦ ✦ ✦ ✦

This chapter provides several solutions for managing your finances and expenses — from financial calculators to spreadsheets and from expense trackers to full-fledged financial management software. Versions of some of these applications are built in; more are available as freeware, shareware, or as commercial products. Some are standalone and others include a desktop component that automatically synchronizes with your handheld during HotSync operations.

Here are the questions you might ask:

✦ What financial software is included with my Palm Organizer?

✦ How and what use can I make of these programs?

✦ What third-party software is available if the built-in does not meet my needs?

The answers to these questions are a bit more involved than simple, one-line responses. To provide you with everything you need to know to use the built-in applications, as well as giving you the best alternatives for your needs, let's just step through the process.

Calculators

Remember when a handheld calculator cost $500? It wasn't that long ago that the functionality built into the Palm Organizer was expensive, so you did most calculations in your head. But not anymore!

Built-in

The built-in calculator found in Palm's own software can be used for day-to-day base functions, such as addition, subtraction, multiplication, and division, and has a memory function for often-used figures. Its interface is rather cheesy, with large rounded buttons, as shown in Figure 13-1. Its functionality *appears* to be limited to what you see on the interface. At first glance one could say, "So, what is this?"

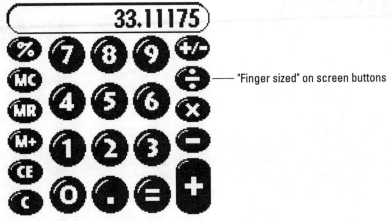

"Finger sized" on screen buttons

Figure 13-1: The Palm calculator

Yet, there are a number of surprising benefits to the application. You can use your finger to tap the numbers right on the screen, similar to a full-blown standalone calculator. If you have small stubby fingers like me, you may need the eraser-end of a pencil to tap the screen accurately enough so that you don't make too many errors.

You can use Graffiti for all functions from data to function entry, including everything that you see on the screen, but none of the calculator functions require Graffiti (see Chapter 3 for the Graffiti strokes for the built-in calculator).

You can use the Options ⇨ Recent Calculations menu to view all of your latest entries (see Figure 13-2), just as if it were a data tape. When you're finished with the calculator, you can transfer your results to the Memo Pad or any other text-entry program by highlighting the result and using the Copy and Paste menu options. This lets you save your results as well as your backup notes to your desktop computer during your next HotSync operation. You did remember to note your calculation results didn't you?

Why would you need anything else in a calculator? As a business entrepreneur, you may be into real estate, stocks and bonds, or other areas of high finance. For that matter, you may be a student who needs advanced math functions or a programmer who needs a calculator featuring reverse Polish notation (RPN) and a stack function. The built in just does not make the grade for advanced needs; that is, unless you can remember all of your high school and college math formulas by heart. I don't think I fall into that category, so I need all the help I can get.

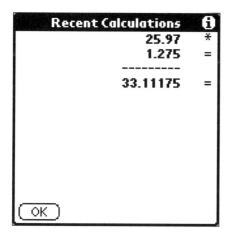

Figure 13-2: Recent Calculations

Shareware

In the shareware arena, there are calculators for any function, including metric conversions, scientific calculations, finance formulas, and so on. A few of the more notable ones are listed in this section. Many of these calculators have a specific audience in mind and address solutions for that audience.

The real estate salesperson, accountant, or college student may want to perform fast calculations related to present value, future value, mortgage payments, or to some of the more esoteric functions related to logarithms, square roots, or powers. You may also want to be able to cut and paste your responses to a note or other text document so that you have a documented trail of what you told your prospective customer or teacher. You might even want to cut and paste the answer/formula to another Palm application. For greater efficiency, you might also want to store these values so as to be able to make repeated complex calculations. As a final requirement, you might like to have all these formulas as stored functions within the calculator application so that you do not have to remember them yourself. Have I described you here? Let's look at a few superb shareware products that may meet your needs.

Rather than listing and commenting on each of the calculator features, Table 13-1 itemizes the most common attributes of calculators. Simply identify your personal needs and then match those needs to the chart to find the appropriate calculator. Each product is listed after the chart with any salient facts that do not naturally fall within the chart format.

Table 13-1
Calculators — Application Comparison

Product	Maker	Memory Footprint	Cost	Drag/Drop	Algebraic Notation	Data Tape	Plug-ins	Hex/Octal/Binary	Logics	Memory Storage	RPN	Shortcuts	Copy/Paste	Graphing	On-Line Help	Graffiti Capable	Programmable Buttons	Extensive Functions	Metric conversion	Notes
Calc (build-in)	Palm	n/a	n/a			×	×	×	×	×	×	×	×	×	×	×	×	×	×	×
finCalc	Landware	51	$29.95	×		×				×			×		×					
MetriCalc	unknown	13.7	free		×					×										
SynCalc	Synergy Solutions	71.4	$17.95	×	×	×	×	×	×	×		×	×				×	×		
FCPlus (Prof)	Infinity Softworks	131.6	$39.99		×	×			×	×	×		×		×	×	×	×	×	×
RPN	Russell Y. Webb	37.8	$20.00		×			×	×	×	×		×							

SynCalc

Developer: Synergy Solutions Inc
Cost: $17.95
Footprint: 71.4K

SynCalc is a full algebraic calculator. Features include algebraic parsing of expressions, 12 text-memory locations, and 26 numeric variables. You can develop your own plug-ins with the freely available SDK (software development kit). SynCalc's manual is designed for reading from your favorite Web browser, running you through the basic functions of the calculator and displaying the calculator's power and utility.

The usual Preferences choice (see Figure 13-3) is available from the drop-down menu and covers the clearing of expressions on launch, the display options for answers, font size, display type (normal, fixed, scientific, or hexadecimal), and the thousands separator (on/off).

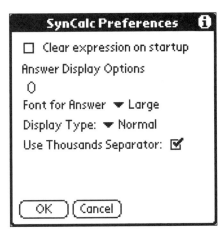

Figure 13-3: SynCalc Preferences screen

The power of this program is that plug-ins can be loaded into the application to extend its features. Such extensions can be metric conversion-specific calculator functions related to financial needs of real estate or banking, and so on. This is a program that is extensible and, therefore, will be useful far longer than a program that has no such facility. Naturally, it requires that users or the company continue to develop plug-ins.

> **Note**   As the *Palm OS Bible* is being written, Synergy is developing version 2.0 of SynCalc. This upgrade will include three major new features: a solver, improved scripting, and a graphing capability, along with an updated interface.

FCPlus Professional

Developer: Infinity Softworks
Cost: $39.99
Footprint: 131.6K

In addition to the features covered in the chart, FCPlus (Figures 13-4 and 13-5) has mathematical functions including power, square root, reciprocal, natural log, square, exponential, and factorial. In RPN Input Mode, the program allows for advanced stack manipulation: duplicate, move, swap, or drop from anywhere within the 20-item stack; also rotate clockwise and counterclockwise (great for programmers).

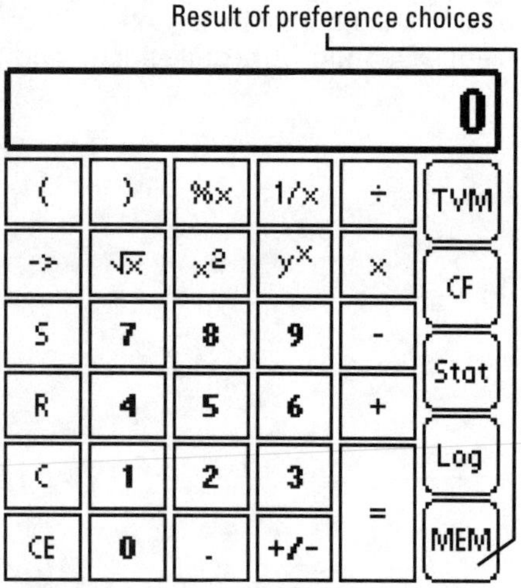

Figure 13-4: FCPlus Professional

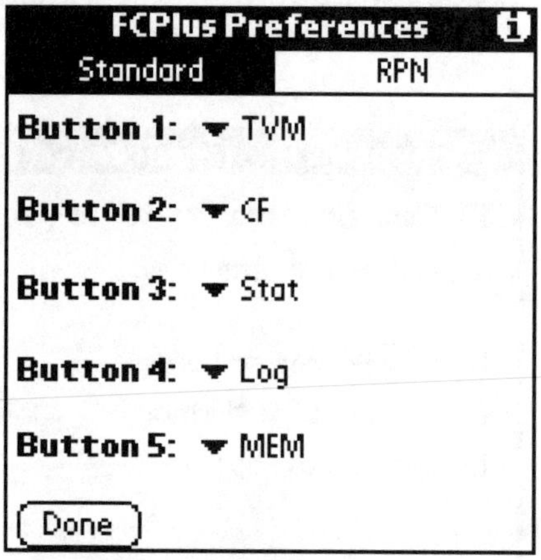

Figure 13-5: FCPlus Preferences

FCPlus Professional's manual is exceptional. In approximately 72 pages, it takes you through the entire power of the application and illustrates what you should see onscreen.

The preferences setup in this application is used to designate certain button preferences for the Main Screen. You can also switch between Standard and RPN by selecting the appropriate button. For each of the five buttons you can choose a different type of worksheet. These choices then appear on the main screen on the buttons running from top to bottom on the right-hand side and result in shortcuts to your favorite worksheets. Naturally, you can also access the worksheets from the drop-down menu.

The choices for the worksheets are Breakeven, Calculation Log, Calendar, Cash Flow, Depreciation, Interest Conversion, Memory, Statistics, and Time Value of Money. Each screen has a tips section to step you through the data entry and general use of the worksheet.

FinCalc (Financial Consultant)

Developer: LandWare
Cost: $29.95
Footprint: 51K

This problem solver (see Figure 13-6) for our favorite connected organizers is designed specifically for real estate, retailing, and business professionals who need to make fundamental financial decisions quickly and accurately.

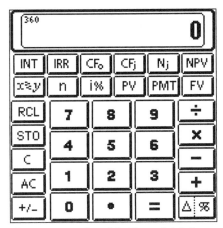

Figure 13-6: FinCalc's Financial Solver

Solver, a new feature, enables you to perform a range of different calculations with point-and-tap ease. Solver's forms enable you to enter the known variables and use a single tap to solve for the unknown quantity. The use of pop-up menus provides single-tap access to over 90 functions, while maintaining an uncluttered interface.

Financial and business solutions covered are:

✦ Solution of savings, loans, mortgages, and lease problems using the time and money functions

✦ Generation of onscreen amortization schedules using a single tap to calculate loan balances, interest, and principal portions

✦ Conversion between nominal and effective interest rates using periodic or continuous compounding

✦ Calculation of future or past dates and the number of days between dates using the choice of two different date formats.

The Financial Consultant also provides a number of additional scientific functions via the SCI or FIN drop-down menus, investment, statistics, and a myriad of other financial and data analysis functions.

RPN

Developer: Russel Y. Webb
Cost: $15 (shareware)
Footprint: 37.8K

This program is a powerful shareware application and is a great addition for the professional who requires stack notation on the job. The instructions for its use, however, are somewhat sparse and assume your knowledge of reverse Polish notation and stack operations. To give it justice, I've included the text instructions, slightly modified to give you some idea of the program's power. This instruction set is designed to walk you through an actual step-by-step process to use the application.

Once you have loaded the application into your Palm handheld, you can:

✦ Press the scroll keys on your Palm Organizer to scroll through the installed function sets.

✦ Press the Navigate button (see Figure 13-7, above the EEX button) in RPN to display a list of installed function sets.

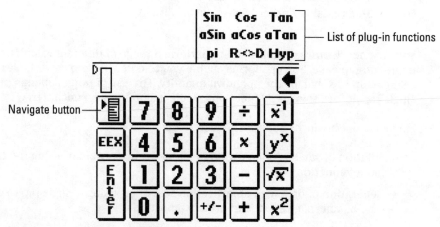

Figure 13-7: RPN Navigate button

✦ Enter several numbers using the keypad and the Enter button.

✦ Drag numbers from the stack or the 0 to 9 storage variables. Drop them wherever they seem to be able to go (the stack, storage variables, some buttons, and some functions).

✦ Tap the mode display (to the left of the input line) to access the mode menu.

✦ Put the number 3 on the stack and select "places(n)" from the mode menu.

✦ Select "scientific" from the mode menu.

✦ Select Extra ➪ Help from the menu; now tapping functions in the upper right displays help for the function (some function do not have a help string). Select Extra ➪ Help to turn help off.

Some basic notes to remember:

✦ The stack is 40 elements deep and wraps around (that is, items are dropped from the bottom, as room is needed).

✦ If the maximum exponential value is exceeded or a computational error occurs, the stack displays Numerical Error.

✦ Enter makes a copy of the current number if there is no input.

✦ The delete button deletes the current number if there is no input.

✦ Tapping a number on the stack moves it to the top of the stack.

The basic idea of a postfix calculator such as RPN (see Figure 13-8), is that all operations take their arguments from a stack, which means that all numbers required by an operation are entered before the operation is selected. Rather than debate the benefits of this calculator style, I'll show a few examples. Note that operations "enter" the current input (see the first example).

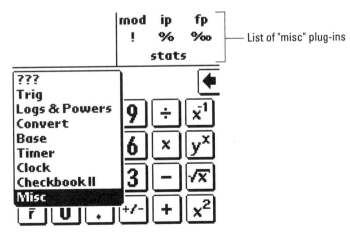

Figure 13-8: RPN calculations

Math Function	*Data Entry Sequence*
1. 4+2	4 enter 2 enter + —> 4 enter 2 +
2. 12*(4+3)	12 enter 4 enter 3 + * —> 4 enter 3 + 12 *
3. (12+sin(7))/(11*3.1415)	7 sin 12 + 11 enter 3.1415 * /

Try it, keeping in mind that operations affect the numbers that are already displayed.

In a different vein, I mentioned that calculators are not just designed to add and subtract and do other specific numerical calculations. There are "calculators" with specific purposes in mind, such as date and time calculators. The one that gives me the best functionality for my business travels is a metric converter. The capability to convert gallons to liters, yards to meters, and so on is a definite asset. The one I use is MetriCalc.

MetriCalc

Developer: StingerSoft
Cost: Freeware
Footprint: 13.7K

This small but effective conversion calculator (see Figure 13-9) is designed for one thing — which it does well — conversions. If you consider some mathematical calculations as conversions, such as the function "square root of," then that's exactly what happens here. For true conversions from one weight method to another or length expressed in metric versus yards or from gallons to liters, MetriCalc does it all.

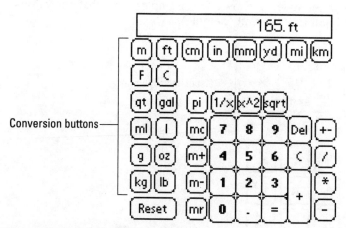

Figure 13-9: MetriCalc

There is no manual to be found for this application, so for those of you who like to use a program before reading its documentation, here's one for you. The program is as it shows on launch. It looks and acts just like a calculator. There are no drop-down menu items for information screens or, for that matter, help. In fact, there is almost no need for instruction. To get a conversion of anything, just enter the value on the calculator screen and indicate what that value represents (such as gal) by tapping the appropriate button. Then tap the button of the unit of measure that you want your value converted to. It's as simple as that. After entering a value and unit of measure, you can press M+ to save that value in memory and then use it to do repetitions of conversions.

This program is great if you travel, and it would be a good addition to any expense-tracking software that you may use. It happens that most expense managers have currency converters built in, but not metric or other system converters. This one fills that gap quite well. It fails, however, to provide any method for saving results to memos or other text applications, and there is no way to save those results to your desktop. Nonetheless, MetriCalc is a good tool.

Spreadsheets

Okay, so where do you go from here? What is the next logical step? What answers the question of layout and presentation, imbedded formulas, and, portability? Well, here's your answer: spreadsheets. Most people these days own a computer of some kind and Microsoft Excel or Lotus 1-2-3 is usually loaded on that computer.

Why use a spreadsheet on a handheld? It has been said that the spreadsheet is the most useful application program ever developed for the personal computer. With a spreadsheet, you can not only compute the answer to a complicated formula, you can play "what-if" with that value. You can visually drill down into the component parts of the formula to enable easy modification of one or more variables and immediately see how it affects the results. Not only are spreadsheets useful for mathematical computing, they have a place in our day-to-day information-process-ing needs. The column/row representation of data is a common style used every day. Even if you do not have any need to calculate, a spreadsheet can still be useful. You can use a spreadsheet to display any data that can be organized in rows and columns. Many people use spreadsheets as a small database, integrating table lookups with raw data.

The combination of a spreadsheet with the organizer enables you to create specific solutions for everyday tasks. Unfortunately, no *built-in* applications represent spread-sheets for the Palm Organizer. However, if you consider the Expense application as a means to an end, you can collect data for use in a spreadsheet in the Expense pro-gram and export that data (tab delimited) to your desktop for further processing.

As in the Calculator section, there are a number of spreadsheet applications that are similar in form and function. Rather than repeating the obvious for each appli-cation, Table 13-2 identifies the spreadsheets and their most common attributes. Following the table are several short descriptions of spreadsheet programs and any additional notable information.

Table 13-2
Spreadsheet Features

Spreadsheet Name	Author	Size	Cost	Characteristics													Sync		
				Built-in Functions	Cell formatting	# of Col/Rows	Formula Capable	Undo	Cut/Paste	Adj. Column Width	Database functions	Table functions	WorkBook Capable	Freeze Row/Col	Protect	Relative Reference	To/From Excel	To/From File	Other
Tinysheet 2.0	StarFort Software	36K	$10	x	x	255	x	x	x	x				x				x	x
MiniCalc	Solutions in Hand	54K	$24	x	x				x	x				x	x	x		x	
Quicksheet 4	Cutting Edge Software	160K	$50	x	x	n/a	x	x	x	x	x	x	x	x	x	x	x		

TinySheet

Developer: Iambic Software
Cost: $19.95
Footprint: 36K

The original spreadsheet for the Palm Organizer (see Figure 13-10) is back, with an all-new Version 3.0 update. You get larger sheet sizes, horizontal/vertical scroll bars, and versatile cell formatting among other enhancements to the original product. Palm IIIc users even get color support!

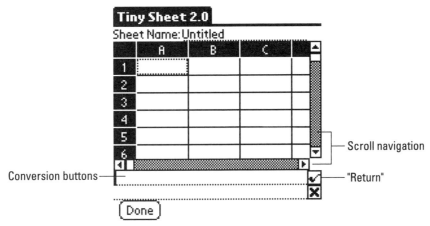

Figure 13-10: TinySheet

Spreadsheets are imported and exported via tab-delimited data files through the built-in Memo Pad application. These files are automatically HotSynced to and from your desktop. Just remember that the memo file should have the first line as a title name because this is the line that TinySheet will use as its sheet title when you import the file.

This application represents great functionality for the price and does not require you to purchase additional desktop software. It is best used, however, as a database (column/row) application. You can construct excellent files via Word or Excel and import them (as tab-delimited files) into the application for your reference needs.

MiniCalc

Developer: Solutions in Hand
Cost: $24.95 (shareware)
Footprint: 54K

MiniCalc (see Figure 13-11) enables you to work with MS Excel 97. It's also the only spreadsheet program for the Palm Organizer that supports a precision to

15 significant digits. MiniCalc combines small viewing size and speed with large spreadsheets. Its features include 55 built-in math, financial, statistics, date/time, and other functions, as well as column or range cell formatting.

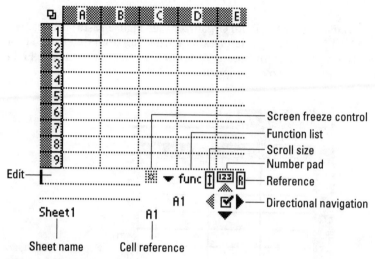

Figure 13-11: MiniCalc

There is a special keyboard with 25 keys, and screen cell references enable "tap" formula editing with WYSIWYG (What You See Is What You Get) column and row resizing. MiniCalc supports absolute and relative cell referencing, multicell copy/paste functionality, and CSV (comma-separated values) conversion for non-Excel 97 users. Finally, it has category support, the ability to freeze columns/rows, and password protection for sheets.

The manual is well written and gives you the salient details of the program's functioning, but it does not go into the functioning of a spreadsheet as such. A sample of the manual follows.

Main screen detail

To select a cell, tap it. The selected cell data will show up in the edit area. To select a column or row, you have to tap its header. To select a range, you drag the stylus across the cells you would like to select. The selected area will have a solid frame. Various buttons, indicators, and texts show you the sheet's current state, position, and selection.

The installation of the program, the Excel add-in, and the conversion package are different between a PC and a Mac. The PC version has a full setup program, whereas the Mac version requires the user to install the appropriate pieces by hand. In addition, you have to download the appropriate programs from Apple (in this case Java's SDK package) in order to compile the conversion program for CVS conversion.

MiniCalc can be synced with a PC workstation and has a special conversion application that comes with it. For the Macintosh environment, you need to use the Java CSV converter to accomplish the same thing.

Quicksheet

Developer: Cutting Edge Software
Cost: $49.95
Footprint: 160K

Quicksheet (Figure 13-12) is a fully functional application that enables you to work with spreadsheets on your Palm Organizer. Bidirectional connectivity with Microsoft Excel enables you to take existing spreadsheets and synchronize them with your handheld, and vice versa. It works just like your desktop spreadsheet, but in a more compact manner.

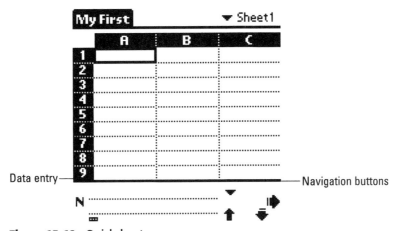

Data entry ⎯⎯⎯ Navigation buttons

Figure 13-12: Quicksheet

Note   For those who need to be able to attach spreadsheets to e-mail, Cutting Edge now offers a plug-in for Actual Software's MultiMail. A graphing product, QuickChart, will be available by the time this book is published. For more information, see their Web site at www.cesinc.com.

Summary of features

I'm not getting into the mechanics of spreadsheets, as you can find volumes (no pun intended) on the subject at your favorite bookstore. In addition, if you own Excel or Lotus 1-2-3, the manuals do a far better job of enlightening you on the subject than I can. Instead, to show some of the power of Quicksheet, here are its major functions.

Quicksheet has 45 built-in scientific, financial, statistical, date and time, and aggregate functions. It supports up to 15 named sheets per workbook, enables you to link the sheets, and has a comprehensive set of cell-editing features that enable to you create and modify spreadsheets easily on the Palm Organizer. Formulas with relative cell references are kept intact when copied and moved around. The program also enables you to format cells in a number of different ways and to name styles throughout the open spreadsheet for easy use.

Quicksheet supports row and column freezing, column resizing, and cell locking with sheet protection to guard against accidental changes to critical formulas. It enables you to search an open spreadsheet for a value or formula, and then replace that value with another; it also supports beaming spreadsheets between devices with infrared (IR) compatibility and supports Palm's Find feature.

Quicksheet has a Microsoft Excel Add-In that enables to you work in Excel to open and save spreadsheets for synchronization with Quicksheet on your Palm handheld. It also supports multiple users synchronizing with a single PC, a single user synchronizing with multiple PCs, and multiple users synchronizing with a single PC on a common set of spreadsheets. (Now that's a mouthful!) Using Quicksheet on the Palm Organizer and Microsoft Excel with the Quicksheet add-in on your desktop, you can synchronize your spreadsheets for mathematical computing, information retrieval, and data collection on the go.

The manual is a professionally written document that covers the entire application in 59 pages. Read it — it's more than just a little bit useful. It helps you obtain all the benefits of the program! Installation of the Quicksheet environment is a two-step process and is generally comparable between the two desktop platforms (Windows and Mac). One application is loaded in your Palm Organizer and one application resides on your desktop. The desktop is actually an Excel add-in that gives cross-application functionality by converting formats between an actual Excel spreadsheet and Quicksheet itself.

Expense Managers

From the calculators and the spreadsheet, we proceed to the next level of complexity and functionality: Expense Managers. A lot of programs are disguised as expense managers. However, many are designed for a very specialized purpose, such as a checkbook manager or an expense recorder (database). The distinction between the categories is blurred even more when you consider hours worked or project management from the expense aspect for billing to clients. Finally, you have the line between expense and finance managers to contend with. If the functionality is similar from one to the other, or if they can be made to function the same, are they not the same? To get some idea of the true expense managers (both financial and expense definitions), read on.

One question you need to answer is why do you need a personal expense manager — what makes it so important? You also have to answer a second question, which is one that most people do not think of until they are on a business trip: Does this application respond to your questions while you are away or only when you return to your home or office? What I am getting at here is this: Do you want something that records things for you, or do you want it to do more? Functions such as running balances, accounts, categories of expenses, projects, hours worked, checking limits, and reporting might be some of your prerequisites. So, once more, do you want these functions to happen only when you return home, or are they important while you are on the road?

The businessperson or professional who is away from the office more often than not generally needs as much functionality as can be crammed into their Palm Organizer. You must, of course, also consider the impact on the handheld from a memory standpoint and cost of purchase of the application. In the final analysis, you also look at what you need on the desktop and its capability to synchronize with your handheld. Do you already own the right application or do you need to buy it?

Pretend for a minute that you're a consultant with a home business. You have a home computer with Microsoft Office, Intuit's Quicken, Palm Desktop, and not too much else. Your business is a fledgling enterprise that just keeps the bills paid. You own a Palm III with 2MB of memory. You travel to your customers who are generally an air flight away. You usually complete a project within 2 weeks. What do you think you would look for in an application(s) that you would describe as *the* all-around package?

If you fit my description, you need an inexpensive package that does not use much of your handheld's memory and that gives you both details and summary information while you are on the road. You need the information by client or project (maybe hours worked), by account (business or personal are some that come to mind), by bank or credit card balance, with the addition of applying notes to expenses. This application should be HotSyncable to your desktop to import the appropriate information to either a special Excel spreadsheet, or to Quicken, or, as a last resort, to an application that would be purchased with the Palm Organizer. This way, you can bill your clients quickly and accurately and have the appropriate information available for your company accounts.

What I have described is an application suite — one for the Palm Organizer and one for your desktop. It would only use between 100 and 200K of memory in the organizer, would synchronize with Quicken on your desktop, and would cost less than, say, $75.00. Now, that's one tall bill to fill; so do we have any winners? Let's find out.

Remember that before you buy, you try! Many companies have demo or trial versions available, and it's far better to try one for nothing, making sure it meets all your needs in the sequence that is important to you. You might also check to see that it does not oblige you to purchase additional support applications.

Table 13-3 summarizes the main functions of the applications that I reviewed in answering my business needs. The chart also demonstrates the differences between very specific expense applications, such as checkbook loggers versus expense managers, as well as applications that synchronize with the desktop and those that do not. Following Table 13-3, I identify a number of alternative products in brief detail. We step through the built-in application in a little more detail, so that you can see what the basic package includes, and then we review each of the other product's differences or specialties.

Table 13-3
Finance/Expense Manager Comparison

Product	Maker	Memory Footprint	Cost	Modular (single app)	Integrated Suite	Accounts	Categories	Currencies	Types/Classes	Hours	Security	Trips	Clients	Projects	Split Transactions	Reporting	Balances (Totals)	Sync-able (note)	Finance Manager	Expense Manager	Integrated (Fin/Exp)
Expense (built-in)	Palm		nil	×		×	×	×	×									×	×		
MicoMoney	Landware	38.9	unknown	×		×	×										×	×	×		
Money Minder	Infinity Softworks	22	unknown	×		×			×										×		
AllMoney	iambic Software	83.7	19.95	×		×	×		×								×		×		
UltraSoft Money	Infinity Softworks	177.6	34.95	×		×			×						×		×	×	×		
Pocket Money	Catamount Software	105	beta	×			×	×					×			×	×		×		
Informed Exp. Creator	Shana Corp		free(basic)																		
Expense Plus	Walletware	294	69.95		×	×	×	×	×			×	×	×	×	×	×	×			
MamPro.Easy	Edelman/Choukhman	89	29.95		×	×	×	×	×		×					×		×		×	
Pocket Quicken	Landware	70.7	39.95	×		×	×		×						×	×	×	×			×
Qmate	Steve Dakin	75	20	×		×					×				×	×	×	×			
QuickBudget	QuickSense Software	126.5	19.95	×							×						×	×	×		
ExpenzPro/Hourz	Zoskware	64.4	79.95			×	×	×	×	×			×	×				×		×	
Expense Director	iambic Software	164	79.95	×		×	×	×	×	×	×		×	×	×			×		×	×

Built-in (PALM OS) Expense

The built-in Expense application is surprisingly effective if all you want is an expense *recorder*.

Using the information is rather simple as well. Whenever you synchronize with your desktop, the Expense conduit downloads a tab-delimited text file to your Palm directory. You can then import this data into your favorite spreadsheet. Simple, but effective.

The Expense application (see Figure 13-13) is more of a categorized database-handling tool than a real expense manager. It records according to categories (types) of expenditures, has the capability to append notes (such as who you purchased lunch for that day), and maintains mileage if so desired.

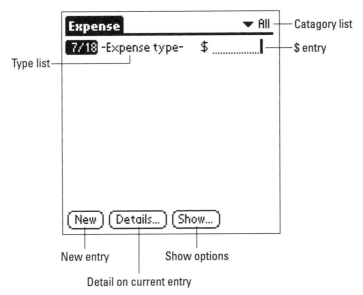

Figure 13-13: Expense application

Now you can walk though this application from data entry to synchronization, and then import the data into an Excel spreadsheet. This process enables you to assess this program's functionality and compare it to other shareware/commercial packages to determine your needs accordingly.

Using the Expense application

In all cases, the best place to start is with Preferences. Tap Menu⟹ Options ⟹ Preferences to access the setup area. In Palm's Expense application, you can set and edit the currency type and, if you like, select an automatic fill function. Automatic Fill is efficient from the standpoint that after you have entered a number of different types of payments, categories, and so on, the application remembers those entries. When you start to enter information that is the same, Expense fills in the balance of the data after the first two or three characters. Some people may find this annoying or distracting, but it is a great time saver.

This being done, you can now start to enter expense data (see Figure 13-14). Tap New on the main screen to be presented with a template line for data entry. Tap the expense-type marker and a pop-up list of 28 expense types appears. Pick the one that best suits your expense situation (for this example, choose Car Rental). Then tap the amount line to the right of the expense type and enter $37.50 as the value of the expense.

Figure 13-14: Adding an expense entry

You are not finished yet! Tap Details to bring up an additional screen to identify the Category, Payment method, Vendor (who you paid), City, and Attendees. From this screen, you can also tap Note to add any pertinent comments about the expense.

Tap the Category down arrow for a list of preset city names, as well as the choice to edit the categories. For this example select the option to edit. You will see another screen that shows all currently defined category fields. Tap New and create a new category called Project Alpha. If you do not want to have the preset categories in the data, you can also delete them. I suggest that you delete the inappropriate ones.

Now pick a payment method from the pop-up list by tapping the down marker next to Payment. Most business expenses (if you work for someone other than yourself) are usually paid through a credit card and reimbursed through an expense claim.

Follow this by tapping the Currency down marker. Note that by choosing Edit currencies you can change this pop-up list to display up to five currencies from a number of countries.

Next comes the name of the vendor and the city. To complete this expense, enter "Norton Rentals" as the vendor and "New York" as the city. Now, assume that you also had a passenger, and you want to identify that fact for future reference. Tap Attendees and up comes a lined screen where you can list names (or anything else you desire). Put in the name "Jonathan Slight," and then tap OK. You can also use the Lookup button to find the person's name in Palm's built-in Address Book. (This assumes, of course, that the person in question is already noted in your address book.)

In my case, my boss may ask why I rented a vehicle if the location of the hotel where I stayed was close to the client office. I want to be able to note the reason, so I now tap Note and put in my note ("sprained ankle and had to carry demonstration materials"). Who said I didn't have a good imagination!

Guess what? You have completed an entire expense record. There's one more button called Show; tap to see what it's all about. Seems like a pseudo-preference. This option screen enables you to show your expense records by date or type, by mileage or kilometers (if applicable), and to show — or not — the currency symbol.

Now you are done. You've seen how you can enter a considerable amount of useful expense information if you plan your data entry in advance (categories, notes, and so on).

On the main entry screen, at the top right, is a category name — you'll most likely see "All" with a down arrow next to it. This enables you to choose the category, in this case Project Alpha, and see only the records relating to that category. As you might guess, you can record personal expenses, as well as business expenses, by creating a Personal expense category.

What this application lacks however, is the ability to show split transactions or transfers. You can simulate these by entering individual records per split for a total combined result of the one original expense. Needless to say, you can do a lot with this program.

Moving the data to your PC or Mac

Now, how do you get the information out of the Palm Organizer and into something that you can use for further processing?

There are two different methods: One deals with PC desktops and one with Macs. The PC platform has an expense application that the data is synchronized to, whereas on the Mac, the data is synchronized to an expense.txt, tab-delimited file.

On the PC (provided you have Excel 5.0 or greater) call up the Palm Desktop and click the Expense icon. You will first be asked if you want to disable macros — don't — and then you will see the Expense Report Open dialog box. Select the categories and, if you want, the dates range, for the data that you want to import. If you've used multiple currencies, the first time you open the spreadsheet you will also see the Expense Exchange dialog box; if you want to set rates, you can. Clicking Options enables you to enter personal information and select which of the five templates you want to use. After you have finished, your data will appear in Excel in a specifically designed expense format.

The Mac requires you to design your own spreadsheet. That design is left up to you. However, to show how to get the basic data into Excel, choose Open in the Excel File menu and navigate to your expense.txt data file (located in your Palm\USER\<your name> directory). Excel will identify the file as text and will come up with a text import wizard. The first wizard screen asks for information related to the file, such as type (Tab Delimited, Fixed Width), and which row you want the data to start at in the new sheet. It then shows the preview of the data contained within the text file. The next screen asks for the type of delimiter (just leave it as is because Excel autodetects the format). The next screen enables you to highlight a column and tell the wizard what type of data is in that column (date, general, text, and so on). It also enables you to tell Excel to skip rows of nonessential data. When done, click Finish and the data is imported into an unformatted spreadsheet. All you have to do at this point is format it the way you want.

Now you may not want to be bothered with the design and import of the data into an Excel spreadsheet. In that case, there is a great form application called Informed Expense Creator (basic version is free) that takes the expense data and places it into one of five possible formats. WalletWare also offers an application, called Expense Reporter, that gives Mac users the same functionality as PC users for the desktop. Read on to learn about this and other products.

Palm Expense's shortcomings

The greatest failing with the Palm Expense application is that you cannot, on the Palm Organizer itself, maintain a running total of accounts, which in my particular case is important because I have frequently overdrawn a number of accounts. It isn't until you synchronize to your desktop and import the tab-delimited file into Excel or another spreadsheet that you can manipulate, total, and cross-tabulate your expense information.

Naturally, you could do a fast calculation of the total of the expenses by listing them, calculating the total, and then maintaining a note of the total expenses, as well as the date and time that you last did that function. However, this is not very efficient.

To me, and probably to many business-oriented persons, an alternative solution to expense management is a necessity. In this particular field, quite a few very good shareware and commercial applications are available for both the Palm Organizer and the desktop. The following programs range from good to best and from inexpensive to more expensive.

A major point to remember: After you have chosen and purchased your application, read the documentation! And, finally, do not forget to fill in or construct the accounts, categories, and other base information. It makes for less difficulty at less appropriate times, such as when you are on your trip. Put in your account balances and every piece of information you can think of, so that you can derive the most power and utility from the application.

Other programs

The following pages offer a sampling of the programs that have been identified as expense managers. Some of these are more like the built-in Expense application and others attempt to fill all the needs of the traveling businessperson. To give you some idea of their power, how and what they do are described in some depth.

First, however, I have listed (with a brief description) a number of programs that are meant to reside on the Palm, and are not designed to be synchronized to the desktop. For Mac users, a number of these programs can export the data via Memo Pad data in tab-delimited files. After these program descriptions, you will find a particular program designed to take the built-in Expense application data and put it in fancy forms with some power behind the forms for data management. Finally, you will find the high-end products that compete for your attention.

To keep you on track, you should assess any application in light of your needs. My comments appear at the end of the chapter. "To meet or not to meet," that is the question.

AllMoney

Developer: Iambic Software
Cost: $19.95
Footprint: 83.7K

AllMoney is a standalone program that enables you to identify accounts, types of expenses, and transaction categories. It also maintains running balances. It has a rather nice feature in that you can actually edit the transaction type icons. This program does not synchronize to the desktop.

Another nice feature is the capability to record standard expenditures by the use of memorized commands that you subsequently point to. The program then asks whether you wish to post the item. This means that all my monthly standard expenditures related to my car, insurance, electricity, food, and so on can be preestablished, and I only have to choose the one I want and click Post! That is definitely a time and effort saver.

Money Minder

Developer: Infinity Softworks
Cost: $15.00
Footprint: 22K

Money minder is an expense recorder, plain and simple. It enables you to identify expenses by type and description and also gives you the option of appending a memo note to each transaction. That's where the functionality stops. Syncing to the desktop is unavailable.

PocketMoney

Developer: Catamount Software
Cost: $20.00
Footprint: 105K

PocketMoney is an expense recorder that enables you to identify expenses by Account, Category, and Payee. It has the transaction functions of Withdrawal, Deposit, and Transfer. Running balances are kept by class of business. This program provides a good reporting feature by filtering how to show your transactions. Again, this is a program that does not synchronize to the desktop.

By now, you should have some idea of what these programs are like. In general, none sync to the desktop and each has one or two peculiar attributes that differentiate it. Evaluating their business functionality, and considering lowest cost, you might want to stick with the built-in Expense application. So then, what takes the Expense application one step further? Read on.

Informed Palm Expense Creator

Developer: Shana Corporation
Cost: Freeware (the advanced version is $39.95)

The Informed Palm Expense Creator (see Figure 13-15) is a form application. A form application is a special kind of electronic form designed to function like a standalone application. The Informed Palm Expense Creator form application is used to select and transfer expense data from your Palm-connected organizer to an expense form on your desktop.

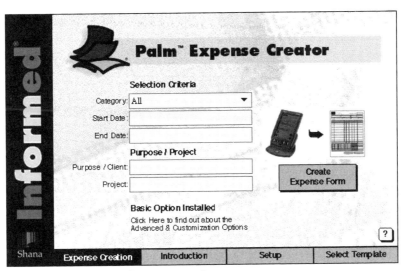

Figure 13-15: Informed Expense Desktop

With the Informed Palm Expense Creator, you can transfer expense information from your Palm Organizer to professionally designed, highly functional electronic forms on your Windows or Mac OS computer. You can select among many different expense form styles, and you can use Informed Filler's powerful database to store all your expense forms, manage those that have been submitted and those that have been paid, produce simple reports, and more.

The Informed Palm Expense Creator is based on Shana Corporation's Informed electronic forms software. The Informed product line consists of two primary products: Informed Designer and Informed Filler. You design forms using Informed Designer and fill out forms using Informed Filler. You can route your forms using e-mail, sign them electronically with digital signatures, and submit them directly to your database, thereby avoiding the need to print them at all.

The Informed Palm Expense Creator (basic/free) comes with five predesigned expense forms and a copy of Informed Filler that works with these forms. The manual is in Acrobat's PDF format and steps you through a basic setup to establish an expense template. The program is designed to reside on the desktop and take HotSynced Palm Expense information to fill in the blanks on an expense template that you choose.

Although this is a very elegant and powerful application on the desktop, it doesn't meet the needs of the traveler or businessperson on the road. On the desktop, the application shines. It certainly fits the bill as an alternative to creating your own spreadsheets.

I recommend that you obtain this product to dump your built-in Expense data into, particularly if you choose not to purchase a specific expense manager. Remember that it's free for the basic version.

QuikBudget

Developer: QuikSense Software
Cost: $19.95
Footprint: 126.5K

QuikBudget (see Figure 13-16) uses the term "wallets" instead of the term "account." Rather novel indeed! QuikBudget enables you to create up to 16 virtual wallets in your Palm Organizer. Just tell the wallet how much to add and it will do it for you every week, two weeks, half-month, or month. The wallets can overflow into Savings if you were particularly frugal during one pay period. QuikBudget gets you started with Dining, Entertainment, Groceries, and Household wallets.

Wallets		▼ All
Name	**Budget**	**Remain**
*Savings	0.00	0.00
Dining	150.00	150.00
Entertainment	25.00	25.00
Groceries	250.00	250.00
Household	50.00	50.00
List **Total:**	475.00	475.00
(Expenses)(Payday)	(New)	

Figure 13-16: QuikBudget

Spending money from wallets is easy. Just click the name of the wallet and add a new transaction. Enter the amount and a comment about the purchase. If you enter the same comment again later, QuikBudget will autofill for you. QuikBudget also includes a tax, tip, and currency calculator. After you hit OK, QuikBudget will deduct the money from the wallet and add the transaction to the list.

If you were to categorize each wallet and name each one to the account or category of the expenses you will incur, you could use this program quite effectively as an advanced version of Expense. You could designate one wallet as a master and all others as subwallets. That way you also get running balances.

The program includes a conduit for Windows users. Mac users will discover the data file is backed up to the desktop on each HotSync, and the file is tab delimited. You can import this information into Excel or other ODBC-intelligent software. ODBC means Open Database Connectivity and is a standard that is often used to transfer data between differing applications. In many cases, the applications have a specific "driver" that is used to access and import the data from one application to another. Some of the programs that use this standard are Excel, Word, Microsoft Project, and FileMaker.

The next two products are both designed to work with Intuit Software's Quicken. The major difference between the two is that QMate HotSyncs to a Quicken file (qif format) or a tab-delimited file for importing into a spreadsheet, whereas Pocket Quicken HotSyncs directly to the desktop Quicken 98 (or newer) application. Naturally, there is also a cost difference. QMate is described in some depth to provide you with the basics and particularly to walk you through a HotSync to a data file rather than to an application. The applications that follow are described in brief; just enough to give you a sense of their particular functions/attributes. These applications are comparable to QMate in that the information gathered is generally the same.

QMate

Developer: Steve Dakin
Cost: $20.00
Footprint: 75K

QMate (see Figure 13-17) is essentially a (Q)uicken companion for the Palm in that it synchronizes to a Quicken file format (not directly to Quicken as does Pocket Quicken, described later in this chapter) and relies on category information that is imported from Quicken into the Palm application.

There are two primary forms in QMate: one for accounts and the other for transactions. After you enter your account information, you will spend most of your time in the Transactions form. Before you can enter any transactions, you must create one or more accounts.

QMate supports QuickFill for fast category entry. To take advantage of this feature, you must import your list of Quicken categories into QMate.

QMate - Transactions

▼ Chequing		$ 2982.12
6/20	Budget	-$ 199.89
6/20	Cash	-$ 20.00

(New) (Show...) (Accounts)

New transaction │ Go to accounts screen

Show transition preferences

Figure 13-17: QMate

To make entering repeated transactions easier, QMate supports memorized transactions. After a transaction is memorized, QMate uses QuickFill in the Payee field to match the desired transaction. After exiting the Payee field when a match is found, QMate fills in the rest of the transaction fields with the values used in the previous entry of that memorized transaction. There is one difference between the way QMate and Quicken fill out fields after a memorized transaction has been matched. In QMate, if your memorized transaction contains a number field value (nonspecial value), and the account into which you are entering the new transaction is not a credit card account type, it will automatically enter the next number in sequence for that account.

To see the list of transactions that are presently memorized, press the Payee button on the New/Edit Transaction dialog box. This displays the Select Payee dialog box, which enables you to view, delete, and use items from your memorized transactions list (see Figure 13-18).

Split transactions are a way of breaking down a transaction into parts, each part of which can have a separate amount, category, and memo. The main category (what is used as the category in a nonsplit transaction) is not used in the split case because split has its own category, but the main memo field may be used (in addition to any memos used for the splits). This is a nice feature—you can split costs between business/personal and other categories (see Figure 13-19).

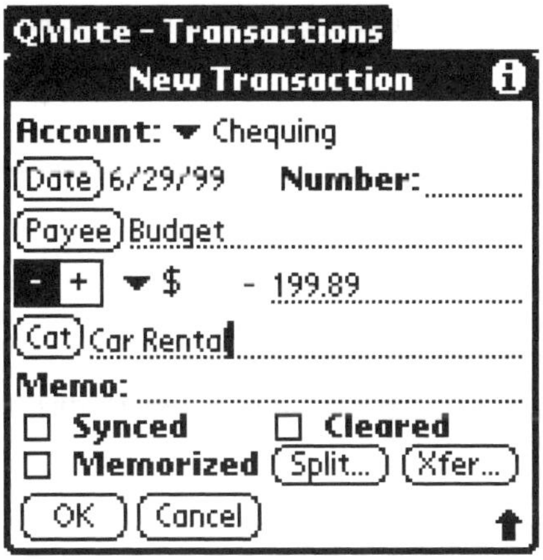

Figure 13-18: QMate transaction screen

Figure 13-19: A split transaction in QMate

To move a transaction from one account to another, select the transaction on the Transactions form. This displays the Edit Transaction dialog box for that transaction. Change the selection in the account pop-up list and select OK. The account balances for the two affected accounts will be updated according to the transaction amount, taking into account the currencies of the two accounts.

QMate also supports account transfer transactions (see Figure 13-20). An important note about transfer categories: In QMate, only one of the accounts will contain an entry for the transaction, but both balances will be updated as per the rules of transfers. The reason only one account contains an entry for each transaction is that some versions Quicken will automatically add a corresponding entry for the account which does not contain the actual transfer transaction.

Figure 13-20: QMate transfer screen

QMate supports multiple currencies, up to 32, including conversion rates. Each account in QMate can use a different currency symbol. Similarly, each transaction can have a different currency used for the amounts it contains. By default, transactions inherit the currency specified for the account in which they are created.

You may not want to store transactions on your Palm device indefinitely. Again, remember RAM. The database kept on the Palm increases in size with the number of records maintained. Once you've synced your QMate transactions, you can quickly delete them by selecting the Options ➪ Purge menu item. In the purge dialog box, you can specify the criteria that QMate should use to determine the transactions that should be purged. The criteria include account (Individual or All), Cleared Status, Synced Status, and Number of days old.

Setting the Synced and Cleared Status for all transactions

If you want to resynchronize transactions for any reason, you can quickly clear the synchronized status of all transactions by selecting the Options ➪ Synced/Cleared Status menu item and selecting the No option next to the Synced label. Similarly, if you want to prevent all transactions from being synced, set the synced status by selecting the Yes option next to the Synced label. Selecting No Change will leave the Synced status unchanged for all transactions. The cleared status can be updated in the same way. The synced and cleared status can also be set or cleared for individual transactions via the Transactions Details dialog box.

QuickFill (see Figure 13-21) can be an irritant when an automatically offered name or other information is similar to, but not the same as, the entry you're trying to make. However, QMate offers an alternative. I just elect not to access the feature by not checking the memorized box on any of my transactions. Others who use Quicken and QMate love it. Go figure!

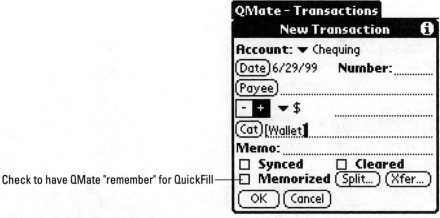

Check to have QMate "remember" for QuickFill

Figure 13-21: QMate QuickFill

HotSyncing to the desktop

Before we get to the next very similar product, let's step through a synchronization and import of the QMate data file into Quicken, as well as a transfer of information from Quicken to your Palm. As this is the only really significant difference from the Pocket Quicken product, you should know how to use this facility and be able to assess whether you are able to perform these easy functions, or wish to even bother with it.

Using QSync for Windows

QSync saves the .QIF files it generates in the QMate output directory you specify in the QSetup program. If you're using Quicken 6, 98, or 99 and have selected the Single QIF File Format setting, then QSync will save all transactions to a single file called QMate.QIF.

To ensure that this feature operates correctly, your QMate and Quicken account names must match exactly. If you're not using the Single QIF File Format setting, then the file names QSync uses for the .QIF files match your QMate account names. For example, if you have accounts called "Checking" and "VISA" entered in QMate, then you will end up with two .QIF files after a HotSync: Checking.QIF and VISA.QIF. Depending on the settings you specify in QSetup, QSync will either append transaction information to any existing .QIF file or overwrite the .QIF file with any new information (see Figure 13-22).

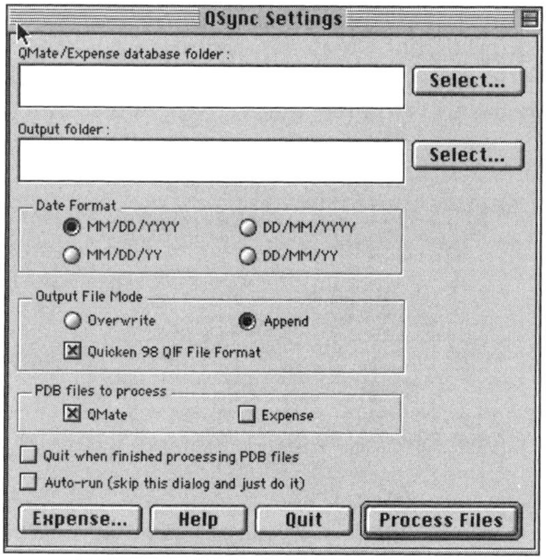

Figure 13-22: QSync settings

To import the transactions in these QIF files into Quicken, use Quicken's import command (File ➪ File Operations ➪ Import menu command) and select the QIF file(s) that QSync generated.

Important: When importing the single QMate.qif file into Quicken (Version 6 or later) you should check the Transactions and Account List checkboxes on Quicken's QIF Import dialog box and leave all others unchecked.

To import transactions from Quicken into QMate, use Quicken's export command to create a QIF file containing the transactions you wish to import into QMate (your Quicken manual and online help will have more information on how to perform this step).

Caution

The filenames you use for the data exported from Quicken must match your QMate account names exactly (not including the .qif extension). For example, if you have a QMate account called "Checking" then the QIF file to import into that account must be called checking.qif (case doesn't matter). Also, the import files must be located in the input directory you specified in QSetup when you installed QSync (rerun QSetup as often as you like to change this or any other setting).

After each QIF file is imported, it is moved to a subdirectory of your input directory called "Imported" (QSync creates it automatically, if necessary). This prevents the files from being imported more than once, and alleviates the need for you to move or delete them manually. Files already stored in the Imported directory (for example, those that have already been imported) are overwritten with newer imported files.

QSync looks for a file called CatList.qif in your QMate input directory during a HotSync operation. It understands the file format that Quicken uses for importing and exporting categories. To create a CatList.qif file, follow these steps:

1. Choose the export menu command (in Quicken 6 choose File ➪ File Operations ➪ Export; in Quicken 99 choose File ➪ Export).

2. In the ensuing dialog box, type a path and file name in the "QIF File to Export to:" field. The path must match your QMate input directory; enter **CatList.qif** as the file name.

3. Pick an account (checking, savings, and so on) in the "Quicken Account to Export from:" list.

4. In the Export Items section, uncheck all boxes except the Category List box. Select OK.

After following the preceding steps, you will have a properly formatted file that QSync will use to import categories into QMate during the next HotSync operation.

If you have problems importing categories after you have created the CatList.qif file, please check your HotSync log for messages. Note: QSync will only import category information into QMate if the category list on your Palm device is empty. This is the case after you install QMate and run it for the first time, or when you select the Delete Categories command from the Lists menu in QMate.

To import memorized transactions, follow the instructions in the previous section for creating a category export file from Quicken. Call the file **memorized.qif** and place it in your QMate input directory. Also, instead of checking the Category List checkbox, select only the Memorized Transactions checkbox. Perform a HotSync operation and the transactions in that file will be available in QMate as memorized transactions.

Using QSync for Mac

In Quicken for the Mac, use these steps to create a CatList.qif file:

1. Using Quicken, display your category list window.

2. Choose the File ➪ Export Categories menu command.

3. You will be presented with a save dialog box. Navigate to the QMate database (input) folder, enter **CatList.qif** as the file name and click Save.

After creating the CatList.qif file, use the following steps to import the categories into QMate:

1. Run QSync Mac and press Process Files. Provided you have specified the input folder and CatList.qif filename correctly, QSync Mac will create a QMateCategoriesDB.pdb file in your output folder.

2. Use the Install App program to install the QMateCategoriesDB.pdb file onto your organizer.

3. Perform a HotSync operation and you will have your categories imported into QMate.

Note

QSync will translate the CatList.qif file to a QMateCategoriesDB.pdb file each time you tell it to process the files in your input folder. Your QMate categories will only be installed or updated, however, when you use Install App and HotSync to install the QMateCategoriesDB.pdb file on your Palm device. To accelerate the processing time of QSync, you can move your CatList.qif to a location other than your QMate database folder after you successfully import your categories.

Each time you run QSync it outputs to a file how many accounts were processed and how many transactions were transferred (and skipped) for each of those accounts. The output file is called QSyncLog and can be found in the folder you specified as your Output folder.

Simple isn't it? Even though you might not own Quicken (desktop), the combination of QMate, QSync, and a spreadsheet application can also be used, is still an effective process, and certainly comes at the right price. QMate has a number of very good features that appeal to me as a businessperson. These features (among others) are split transactions, purging synced data (remember my comment on RAM!), the ability to synchronize to a file format for a program that I own on the desktop, and running totals. On the Palm Organizer, the report display is basic but functional.

Now let's take a brief look at a product that is designed to be the companion to Quicken 98 (or better) and HotSyncs directly into Quicken.

Pocket Quicken

Developer: Landware
Cost: $39.95
Footprint: 177K (includes categories)

Pocket Quicken is stated to be the standard in mobile financial tracking software, in that it transforms your organizer into a mobile money manager. There is no double entry and you can always keep your accounts current.

Pocket Quicken enables you to keep your Quicken 98 (or newer) information current when you are away from your desk.

Included are two of Quicken's shortcuts: QuickFill and Memorized transactions. Combined, these features enable you to record day-to-day transactions with only two strokes of the stylus. Just start writing the payee's name and a new transaction is automatically created with all the details filled out. This presupposes that you have already HotSynced to the desktop application to obtain all the historical data.

Your financial information can also be made to be safe and secure. You can assign your own private PIN number to Pocket Quicken (see Figure 13-23) to ensure that only you have access to your financial activity. Pocket Quicken also maintains a backup of your transactions each time you HotSync your organizer.

Figure 13-23: Pocket Quicken security PIN

When you HotSync your Palm Organizer, the Pocket Quicken conduit immediately runs the Quicken application and imports that information without any intervention from the user. You do not have to create files, import them, or provide any additional information for this seamless process to work. You do, however, still have to set up the desktop application correctly and import the categories and accounts to your Palm Organizer.

Comments

You should consider the QMate product in terms of price and very similar functionality. The major difference between this application and QMate is that Pocket Quicken HotSyncs directly to a desktop application of a similar function (Quicken 98 or newer), whereas QMate synchronizes to a Quicken-compatible import file, which results in one more step and a greater likelihood of errors in information transmission.

Note   Both QMate and Pocket Quicken can get their account and category information from the desktop Quicken product. However, the data (expenses) transfer is one way only, from the Palm Organizer to the desktop. Updating your Palm application with current expense transaction information from the desktop requires double keying! A full synchronization between both platforms would make these products just short of fantastic.

Now let's review several other packages that have comparable functionality.

UltraSoft Money Pocket Edition

Developer: Infinity Softworks
Cost: $34.95
Footprint: 177.6K

UltraSoft Money enables you to record transactions, identify accounts, types, and categories, and append memos to each transaction. You can also indicate whether the transaction has been reconciled to your bank or other account and maintain a running total. A nice feature is that you can also record split transactions. This program also has a reasonable amount of help provided online. This program is a mirror of Pocket Quicken, but synchronizes to Microsoft Money on the PC through its own conduit.

MAM Pro (Report Pro)

Developers: Max Edelman and Alex Choukhman
Cost: $29.95 for MAM Pro ($9.95 for MAM Report, $19.95 for Easy version)
Footprint: 89K (full suite)

MAM Suite is a collection of Palm OS applications for managing your finances. It is easy to use and at the same time very powerful. The applications included are:

✦ **MAM Pro**—The professional version of MultiCurrency Account Manager

✦ **MAM Easy**—A simpler version of MultiCurrency Account Manager

✦ **MAM Report**—The reporting module to be used in combination with MAM Pro/Easy

✦ **MAM Now**—A fast transaction entry module for use with MAM Pro/Easy

✦ **MAM Viewer**—MacOS program that enables viewing and exporting of transactions to desktop programs

MAM Now enables quick entry of transactions using your fingertip. It also does currency calculations. It can be very useful when you need to note the amount of a transaction on the spot, before you forget it, such as when you are in a shop or a restaurant. You can later use MAM Easy or MAM Pro to review the transactions entered and add all the necessary details. MAM Now features large buttons that facilitate easy fingertip operation and a big display with large characters that is readable from a distance. MAM Now was made as a separate program to let you start it from the application launcher using your finger. Sounds almost like the Palm built-in calculator, doesn't it?

MAM Pro (see Figure 13-24) enables you to track transactions in both domestic and foreign currencies. It supports multiple accounts and currencies complete with the exchange rates, so it's great for recording everyday payments as well as the ones that occur while traveling abroad.

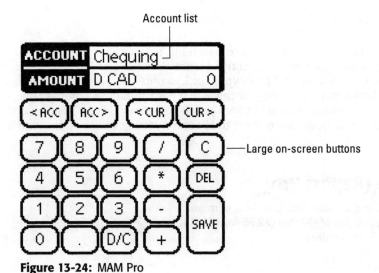

Figure 13-24: MAM Pro

You can classify each transaction using different criteria such as categories, trips, or projects. This makes MAM Pro a good choice for tracking all your business expenses. You can make transfers from one account to another. Balances for each account, as well as the total balance, show precisely how much money you have. A warning function will alert you when you overdraw an account. You can record future transactions before they occur so you won't need to remember to enter them later. Customizable transaction views and multiple preference settings let you set up MAM Pro to suit your needs. A Purge function lets you delete old transactions while maintaining your running balance. Using MAM Pro Conduit (Windows only), you can transfer the transactions to spreadsheets.

There are two versions of MAM Pro, the Pro and Easy versions. The Easy version has the same functionality but less capacity — that is, fewer number of accounts and so on. Oh, and the Easy version is also $10.00 cheaper.

MAM Report is a part of MAM Suite package and is complementary to MAM Easy or MAM Pro. It's a very powerful tool that lets you summarize your transactions as one total amount. Alternatively, you can get the amount split by accounts, currencies, categories, and so on. This way, it's simple to know how much you spent (for instance, in U.S. dollars [USD] compared with German deutsche marks [DM]), or to see your account balances in one screen. But MAM Report is really special in its filtering capabilities. MAM Report enables you to create customized sets of conditions that will perform the exact calculation and summarization that you need. Some examples of its use are "Calculate amount of all Cleared transactions in your Checking account" and "Get the total of all the Billable transactions in USD." MAM Report also supports budgets and income plans, as well as many other advanced functions.

MAM Viewer is a PC- and Mac OS-compatible application for reviewing and exporting transactions into desktop programs such as Excel.

The manuals are written in a consistent and clear manner and are well documented by drawings at all of the important points.

The Preferences menu item is short and sweet with just a few items, such as password protect, whether or not to show cents, and how the export of data material should be handled (Tab Delimited or Comma). The real setup is in a drop-down menu called Setup. Who would have thought? Again, it is recommended that you set up your accounts, currencies used, clients, categories, trips, and projects prior to starting off and entering raw data. Planning your approach in these packages makes for less work in the end. That is not to say that you cannot add new categories, clients, or the like later on; it's just more efficient if you do it early in the process.

You can synchronize to your desktop via the MAM Pro Conduit for Windows. This enables you to import the data into your favorite spreadsheet. For Mac, there is the Viewer desktop program that can be used to access the MAM-backed up data and then to export that data to a spreadsheet.

ExpensePlus

Developer: WalletWare
Cost: $69.95
Footprint: 294K

ExpensePlus (see Figure 13-25) provides a comprehensive way to report, categorize, and store the expenses you incur for events, projects, and trips. ExpensePlus was designed specifically for people that travel or spend money on behalf of an employer. The application comes with a number of expense templates to use, or you can link directly to custom reports created by your employer, to Microsoft Excel, Access, FileMaker, or another ODBC-savvy application. This does not mean that it is only for the business-oriented. You can use this program quite effectively to track your personal expenses as well.

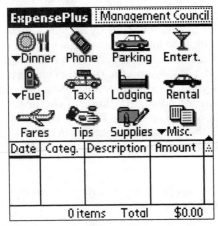

Figure 13-25: ExpensePlus main screen

The manual (which is in Acrobat PDF format) that comes with the application is very well laid out, comprehensive, and written in a language and sequence that anyone can follow. The installation instructions cover Windows and Macintosh environments, as well as the HotSync install process to get it on your Palm Organizer. All relevant sections of the manual are fully documented, with screen drawings that help you navigate through the setup and running of the program.

The Preferences section of this program (see Figure 13-26) is necessary to complete. I know that many people do not like to follow a structured approach to running a new program; it's so much more fun to jump right in and start entry. However, because this application is so good, completing the Preferences section highlights rather quickly the power and scope of the program. It establishes the front end of almost everything that you do in the application, from classification of expenses to mileage-rate-reimbursement values, international currencies, accounts, payment sources, clients, and so on.

Detail preferences buttons —

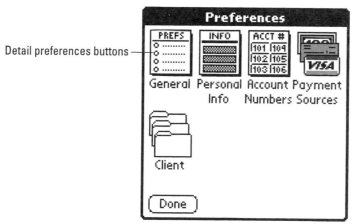

Figure 13-26: ExpensePlus Preferences

When you start this program, you see the quality work that went into the design of the front-end display, from the well-designed and laid-out icons (see Figure 13-27) that represent the different categories to the expense list area at the bottom of the screen. Tapping at the far right can expand the expense list. This hides the icons and stretches out the list.

Figure 13-27: ExpensePlus icons

You can even modify or add to the list of icons/expense categories (see Figure 13-28). Other icons, such as Meal, Fuel, and Misc, have drop-down menus that enable you to choose from types within those categories.

Design or assign your own icon

Figure 13-28: Changing icons in ExpensePlus

ExpensePlus data is exported to the desktop through the ExpensePlus conduit and this data can be viewed through the ExpensePlus Receiver and/or Excel spreadsheet applications. There are even a number of expense templates that can be used as-is to import the expense data.

The ExpensePlus program is a dream, but you have to consider the cost in terms of your handheld's precious memory as well as the cost of the application.

ExpenzPro

Developer: Zoskware
Cost: $39.95 ($79.95 for full suite)
Footprint: 64.4 (basic), 203K (full suite)

ExpenzPro and Reportz are two parts of a reporting process that enables you to capture the expenses you incur on business trips or your projects and transfer the information to your accounting system, invoices, or company expense reports. Again, this suite of programs is geared more to the traveler or business professional and is designed around the information required by these people. However, these applications also lend themselves to the private individual. For owners of stock

Palm devices, the cost in terms of memory space required may be the deciding factor. At a shade over 203K, the full suite is a hefty premium to pay for those Palm Organizers that have only 2MB of Ram.

Time reporting with HourzPro

HourzPro is a reporting process that enables you to capture the time you incur on your projects and transfer the information to your accounting system, invoices, or timecards.

You use HourzPro as your time-gathering tool. HourzPro provides a user interface that is easily customized to your unique situation. The easiest way to capture your time is to enter it in HourzPro as you work (see Figure 13-29).

Figure 13-29: HourzPro Step 1

When it's time to transfer your accumulated time to your accounting system, you use Reportz to generate a report of your HourzPro time entries. You select criteria, such as last month's work on a specific project, and Reportz creates a text report in one of several formats. You select and customize the format to best match your accounting system and billing needs (see Figure 13-30).

After you have generated one or more reports, you simply perform a HotSync operation (see Figure 13-31). The ZoskSync conduit transfers the reports to your PC and stores them in a folder of your choosing. For the Mac, the file generated through Reportz is a tab-delimited file output into the Memo Pad. You can import this file directly into Excel.

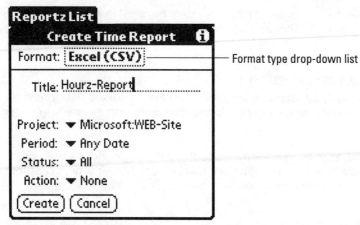

Figure 13-30: HourzPro Step 2

Figure 13-31: HourzPro Step 3

The final step depends on your accounting system (see Figure 13-32). You can simply open the file if you created a tab- or comma-delimited report. Also, you can import your data into a custom database, such as Microsoft Access or Claris's FileMaker Pro. If you use QuickBooks Pro, you can import the time report into your QuickBooks Pro company file. Once your data is in QuickBooks Pro, you can easily assign the time and expenses to invoices, print time reports, and transfer the time to payroll.

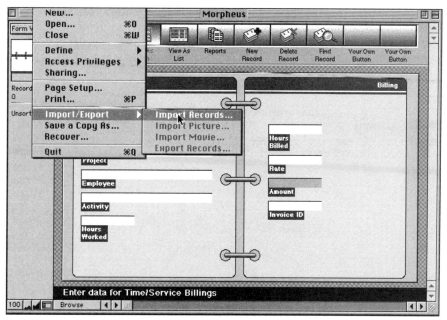

Figure 13-32: HourzPro Step 4

Expense reporting with ExpenzPro

You use ExpenzPro as your expense gathering tool. ExpenzPro is also easily customized to your unique situation. Again, the easiest way to capture your expenses is to enter them as they are incurred (see Figure 13-33).

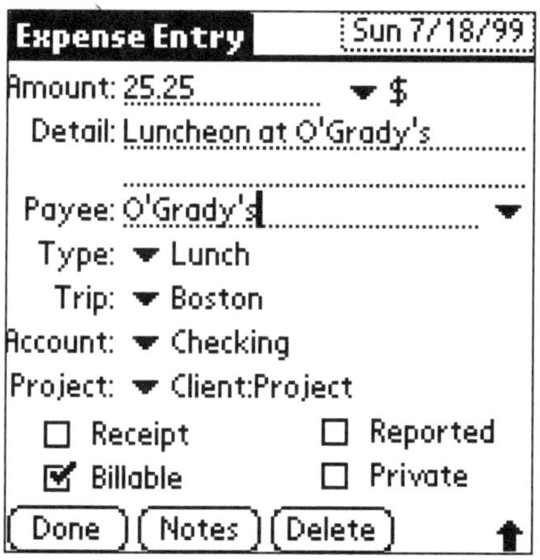

Figure 13-33: ExpenzPro Step 1

When it's time to transfer your expenses to your accounting system or company expense report, you use Reportz to generate a report of your ExpenzPro Time Entries. You select criteria, such as "the business trip to MacWorld" or "last month's expenses for Alpha Centuri Inc.," and Reportz creates a text report in one of several formats. You select and customize the format to best match your accounting system or expense report format (see Figure 13-34).

Figure 13-34: ExpenzPro Step 2

After you have generated one or more reports, simply HotSync your Palm Organizer. The ZoskSync conduit transfers the reports to your PC and stores them in a folder of your choosing (see Figure 13-35). For the Mac, the file generated through Reportz is a tab-delimited file output into the Memo Pad. You can take this file and import it directly into Excel.

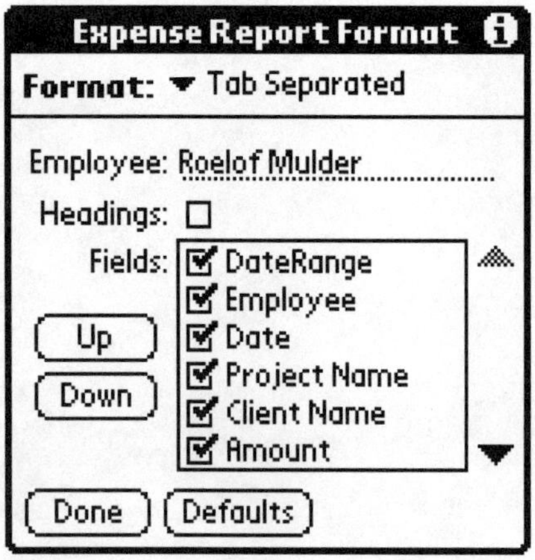

Figure 13-35: ExpenzPro Step 3

The final step depends on your expense reporting system (see Figure 13-36). You can simply open the file if you created a tab- or comma-delimited report. Also, you can import your data into a custom database such as Microsoft Access, Claris's FileMaker Pro, or Excel.

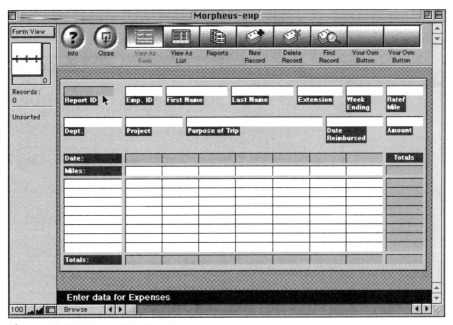

Figure 13-36: ExpenzPro Step 4

If you use QuickBooks, you can import the expense report into your QuickBooks company file. After your data is in QuickBooks, you can assign the expenses to projects and invoices.

The manual comes with the distribution of the application, is very well laid out, and describes a basic modus operandi towards use and data entry. ExpenzPro is built in a modular fashion in that each component can stand on its own (and can be loaded separately) but the components can be accessed from one another through the appropriate icon on the initial front screen.

TimeReporter 2000

Developer: Iambic Software
Cost: $149.95
Footprint: 164K

As of this writing, this version of TimeReporter is in beta format. It's another integrated package similar to Zoskware's Expenz/Reportz combination. You can do all the basic things in the expense portion that you can in others, but—strangely enough—the Palm application does not provide running balances. You can do the usual identification of types, accounts, clients, and projects, filter by dates, and link to datebook information. A real difference here is that you can also use an e-mail process (if you have the appropriate modem and e-mail account) to send and receive data.

Expense entry screen

Another linked feature is an auto log where you can identify type of record (such as mileage), the client, project, and purpose (see Figure 13-37).

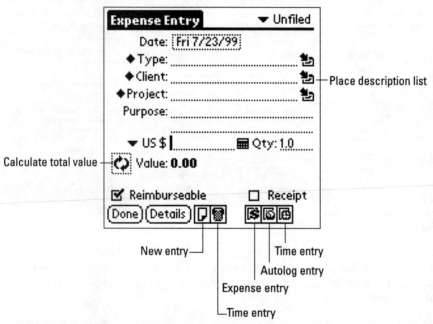

Figure 13-37: TimeReporter 2000 expense entry

AutoLog screen

The application as a whole also has a memory feature similar to QuickFill or Autofill that memorizes, in a list form, all of the entries previously entered in the particular field you are in (see Figure 13-38).

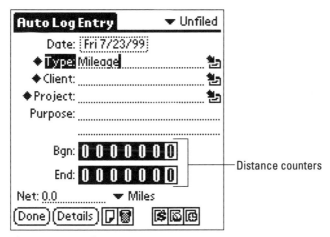

Figure 13-38: TimeReporter 2000 AutoLog screen

For time and project functions, TimeReporter also has an extensive entry screen to track and maintain time spent by client, project, and activity. The clock function is a nifty rotating hourglass. To put in standard start/stop times from 5 minutes to 55 minutes and hours just tap the time bar and a new screen comes up for you to identify exact times. You can also just capture the time spent as a direct figure by tapping the word Duration to set between 5 minutes to 90 minutes.

Time entry screen

In most cases, you can add selections such as client, project activity, payee, and so on, to an ongoing list for future selection by tapping the arrow-to-list icon (see Figure 13-39). The next time you tap the type or other identifier, a pop-up menu gives you the choice of that list.

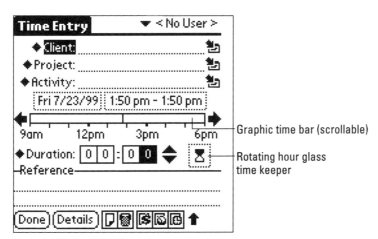

Figure 13-39: TimeReporter 2000 entry screen

After your data entry, be it time, expense, or AutoLog, and after you press Done, you get a summary page that can be filtered to show the types or other grouping that you may want. This more or less mirrors what the desktop application displays.

Expense summary page

TimeReporter synchronizes to a desktop application, but only on the PC. This application is very versatile; it can use information from your address book for the contacts and also can dump information to Quicken, Microsoft Money, and directly into an Excel spreadsheet through an export function (see Figure 13-40).

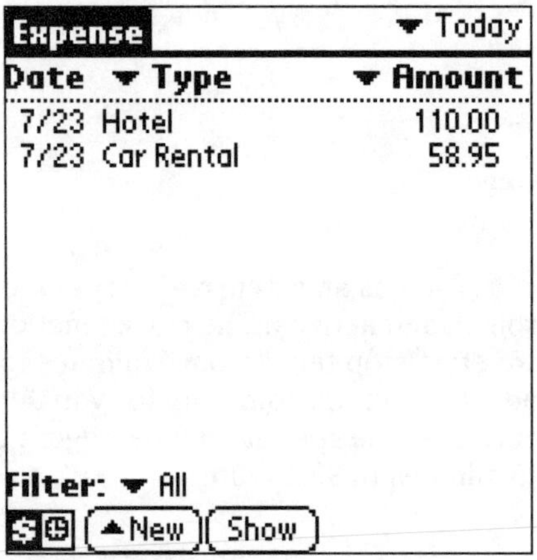

Figure 13-40: TimeReporter 2000 expense summary

The desktop application is very good. It has what I like to see in a desktop application: versatility. Figures 13-41 through 13-45 highlight — but do not attempt to describe — the main areas within the desktop application that mirror the data information from the Palm Organizer.

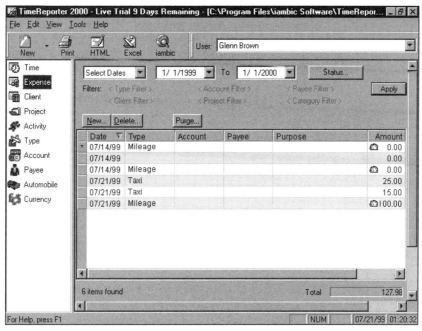

Figure 13-41: Expense report screen

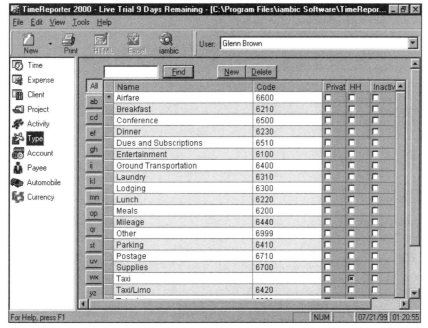

Figure 13-42: Type screen

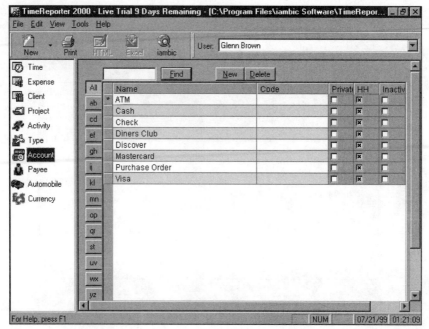

Figure 13-43: Account screen

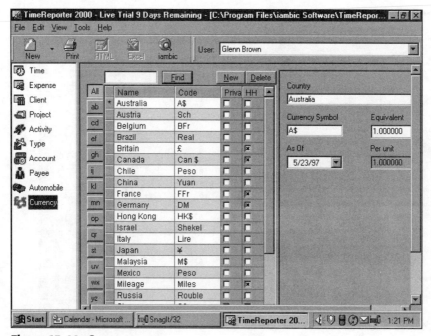

Figure 13-44: Currency screen

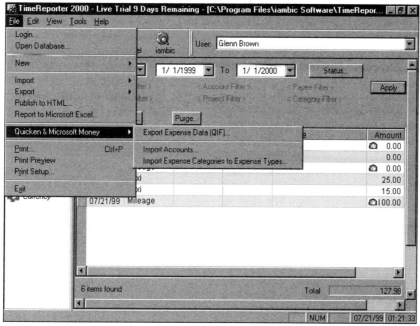

Figure 13-45: Export drop-down menu item

As in any decent Windows application, you can highlight rows and columns and move them around to modify your view for that screen. There are many filters that can also be applied to show only the information you want shown or exported.

From any of the preceding figures, you can also access other available screens related to an auto log or to clients, activities, and payees. Again, versatility is the key: Anything at a reasonable price that goes to this length to ensure that you have multiple solutions for your business needs is the one to take.

My Choices

Now you've gone through the entire chapter, avidly read each section, and hung onto all the words, but you still cannot put it together, right? Too much information? Not enough? Well, in light of my fictitious scenario that I stated at the start, here's how I see the answer to the problem.

You always need a calculator, so there is not an option of going without one. The built-in Calculator application is a tad too basic, even if the price is right. I have a real problem with memory in that I cannot remember my college math formulas, so "canned" formulas are a must. For all else, you also do not need anything more than a calculator that can do basic math, some functionality related to present value, loan amortization, and not too much else. So, for a calculator, the choice is SynCalc. The reasons are price and functionality. But you also might have a need for a metric calculator, so MetriCalc is also included in this choice.

Now for spreadsheets, the question is why do I need one when I am away from the office? I could maintain a database concerning sales in a spreadsheet or something of the like, but not in my case. So, I think under the circumstances described in the scenario, I don't need one. Again, match your needs to the application!

Now comes the hard part: Expense Managers. Do I need a finance manager rather than an expense manager, or do I need something that does both? The answer is the latter, something that does both.

The options as I see them are QMate, Pocket Quicken, MAM Pro suite, ExpensePlus, and finally, the ExpenzPro suite. Choices and more choices. In the analysis, you have a few things to consider. QMate and Pocket Quicken are virtually the same, and both synchronize (either by file or directly) to the desktop Quicken product (which I own). The other three do virtually everything I want, and in one case, hours as well, but synchronize to nonspecific applications or files only on the desktop. What's more, with the exception of the first two choices, the RAM requirements are huge. My choice then, based on my scenario, is Pocket Quicken. I did waffle a little bit here in that I personally like the functionality and interface of ExpensePlus; however, when you are in business, you cannot always go with the nicest. You must go with the best.

The only thing missing from this is a project-tracking facility for hours. Zoskware has it in HourzPro, but there may be cheaper ones out there. Overall, I chose the best for my business. You now have the same task. Identify your needs and match up the programs.

Summary

✦ In the calculator field, pick one that is not too complex unless your work requires it. Choose one that is expandable so that you can derive the greatest facility from it.

✦ If you're traveling abroad, make sure to take along a metric calculator, either standalone or built in a calculator.

✦ Spreadsheets are great tools; however, unless you need to capture or transport database information, such as stock items, costing, and availability, the spreadsheet's functionality on the road is somewhat suspect. If you have experience and knowledge in spreadsheets, you could build an expense tracker and use it effectively.

✦ If you really have no option but to buy an additional expense package, you can stick with the Palm Expense application and still get the information to your desktop. I recommend that you obtain either the free Informed Expense Creator or develop your own spreadsheet on the desktop to capture and format your expense data. Remember that using this method you do not have an indication of total expenses on the Palm.

✦ If you have little money to spend and want a good expense/finance manager, there are only a few things to consider: Do you need to have this information only while you travel? Do you need to subsequently dump the information to your desktop? Do you need both Palm and desktop options?

✦ Watch your Palm memory; some of these expense managers can take up a chunk of memory. Remember that it's not only the program size, but also the databases it creates and supports that add up to the total size.

✦ Suit your program requirements directly to your business (or personal) needs. Functionality is the name of the game and presentation should take a back seat.

✦   ✦   ✦

Reading with PalmBook

In This Chapter

Reading documents

Using document tools

Making your own
documents

Finding and loading
documents

One of Jeff Hawkin's original concepts for the Palm Handheld was as a viewer for information created elsewhere. The Memo Pad offers great capabilities, but it does have limitations, including a dearth of advanced features and a 4K limit. Rick Bram was the first to create a utility to overcome these limitations, with his appropriately named shareware application Doc. The application has been upgraded and is now available commercially as AportisDoc. The Doc file format is the de facto standard on the Palm platform.

NuvoMedia's Rocket eBook and the SoftBook Reader are two examples of expensive electronic book readers available. Why not do the same by adding a Doc reading utility to your Palm Organizer? You'll have to put up with a smaller screen and a less extensive library of new titles, but the savings are significant.

This chapter looks at AportisDoc and its competition, focusing on how to read documents on your Palm Organizer. The chapter also looks at how to find and load documents, and how to make your own Palm-readable documents. There is also a quick look at several utilities that may make reading documents on your Palm Organizer easier.

Reading Documents

Because this software category started with Rick Bram's Doc, I begin by looking at the common capabilities of some of the programs designed to read the Palm Doc format: AportisDoc Mobile Edition, SmartDoc, and TealDoc. Details on each of the programs follow this overview.

Opening documents

After loading the application and at least one document, tap the application icon to launch it. If this is the first time you've opened the document on your Palm Organizer, the application will take a few seconds to prescan the document for bookmarks (this delay only occurs once for each loaded document). After the application is open, a list of the documents loaded on your Palm Organizer displays. Tap the document you want to open.

 On your return to this screen after reading a document, the most recently opened document is indicated in the listing, either with a bullet, a darkened icon, or a dotted outline (depending on the reader you are using).

Navigating documents

Finding your way around a document on your Palm Organizer is easy—tap the top or bottom of the screen or use the hardware scroll buttons to scroll the view of your document up and down. If you want to zoom to a part of the document, tap on the percentage, and then enter the number that represents which part of the document you want to jump to; for example, use 75 to jump to three-quarters of the way through the document.

 The Zoom feature in the document readers for the Palm Organizer represents how far you have read through the document as a percentage, rather than the magnification that computer users may expect.

Bookmarks

Document reader Bookmarks, like Post-It Notes that you might have used to mark your place in a novel or textbook, enable you to jump to a predetermined location in a document just by making a menu selection.

All but the most rudimentary document readers have bookmarks; some of these document readers can also create multiple bookmarks in a document. To set a bookmark, scroll to the view you want, tap the BookMark icon in the lower right-hand corner, and select the Add BookMark menu choice.

Find

The capability to search for something specific is a big advantage of reading an electronic document. These applications deliver that advantage with a Find command that enables you to look for a word in the loaded document. Some document readers also offer a global find that enables you to search all of your document files at one time, and others offer more advanced search and replace capabilities.

Display

One of the great features added with the Palm III was support for multiple font sizes, and most of these applications enable you to read your documents in the three standard Palm font sizes. Some go further by adding more font sizes or the capability to change the line spacing. Another feature is the capability of rotating the screen. Although the active screen is a square measuring 160 × 160 pixels, some users still find it advantageous to be able to move page-up and page-down by operating the scroll button positioned to the right of the screen rather than below it.

AutoScroll

When politicians or media personalities give a speech, they often use a device known as a teleprompter that automatically scrolls the text of their speech in front of them. This enables them to read their speech without requiring any other interaction from them. Some of these document readers give you the same capability, by integrating a hands-free AutoScroll feature.

Document Tools

Let's have a look at some of the document readers available for your Palm Organizer. We'll start with the document readers I mentioned above—AportisDoc, SmartDoc, and TealDoc—and add a pretty good freeware alternative, CSpotRun. Next, I look at a few products that approach documents in different ways: RichReader, OnTap, iSilo, and Documents To Go. I've included a features comparison table at the end of this section (see Table 14-1), but you will probably want to try these document readers for yourself before you decide which tool is right for you.

AportisDoc comes in three versions: the freeware Reader, the shareware Mobile Edition, and the commercial Professional Edition. The Professional Edition is slated for release soon.

AportisDoc Reader

Developer: Aportis
Cost: Freeware
Footprint: 55K

The Reader is just that, a tool for reading large documents on your Palm Organizer. It has limited functionality: for example, it only offers two fonts. The Reader's Find button, shown in Figure 14-1, isn't full feature; it actually opens a dialog box advertising the Find capability of the shareware versions. You'll find similar ads in the menu commands. Still, this reader provides a good freeware alternative that gives you a decent experience of document reading while introducing you to many of the features you can get by upgrading to a more advanced shareware version from Aportis.

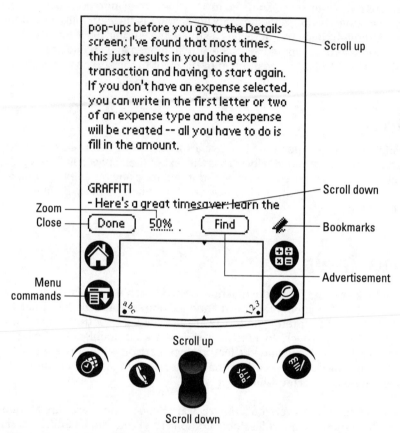

Figure 14-1: AportisDoc Reader

AportisDoc Mobile Edition

Developer: Aportis
Cost: $30.00 (shareware)
Footprint: 61K

The AportisDoc Mobile Edition adds considerable functionality: it enables you to find and copy text, create categories, control preferences, add Bookmarks, and use four fonts instead of the two choices offered in the freeware Reader. Sophisticated preferences enable you to tailor the Mobile Edition, including the capability to select text (by default, tapping onscreen scrolls the document), strip extra linefeeds to compress the document onscreen, configure the way scrolling works, and more.

Display options enable you to set a "virtual" screen that is wider than the 160 pixels of your Palm Organizer. This can be especially handy if you're trying to read tables of data.

I particularly like the teleprompter function, which must be accessed through the Display menu or by using a Graffiti command stroke. This enables you to read a document hands-free. If you want to use the hardware commands shown in Figure 14-2, tap the menu icon, select Set Up Prompter from the Display menu, and then tap to select Use Hardware Buttons.

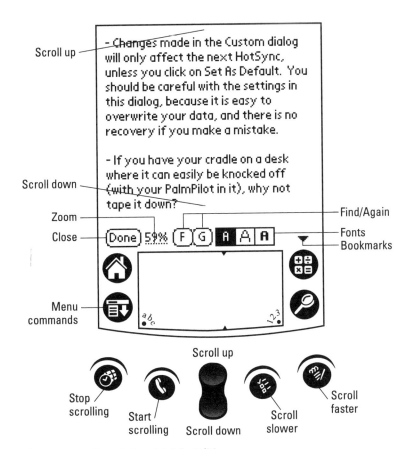

Figure 14-2: AportisDoc Mobile Edition

The $39.95 Professional Edition adds computer software that enables you to create AportisDoc documents from Microsoft Word, text, and HTML. This edition also has the capability to preset bookmarks. In addition to the document conversion utilities that follow in this chapter, there are document conversion services available on the Internet at http://pilot.screwdriver.net.

SmartDoc

Developer: TapWorks
Cost: $19.95 (shareware)
Footprint: 114K

SmartDoc is an impressive newcomer to the field, whose developers paid great attention to detail. The interface, shown in Figure 14-3, does a good job of integrating Palm standards, using standard categories and an onscreen scroll bar that can be used along with the hardware buttons to scroll up and down in a document. The scroll bar can even be toggled to the left-hand side.

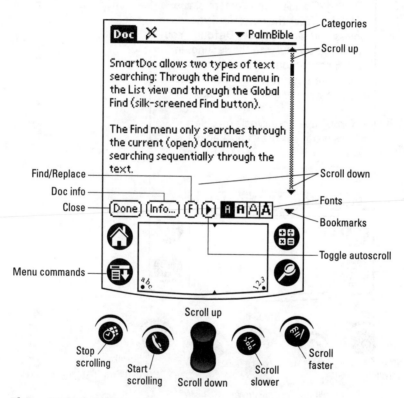

Figure 14-3: SmartDoc

 Tip   If you're left-handed, you may want to have all of your scroll bars on the left. If so, check out Neal Bridges' LeftHack in Chapter 22.

Tap the pencil icon in the upper left-hand corner to toggle the edit status of the document. With editing turned off (the pencil will have a line through it), you can scroll through the document by tapping the screen. Tap the top half to scroll up, and tap the bottom to scroll down. The closer you are to the edge of the screen, the faster

SmartDoc will scroll. With editing turned on, text selection is enabled. Double-tap a word to select it, triple tap to select the paragraph, or quadruple tap to select the entire document.

The file-listing screen also has a lot of depth. Clicking the icon to the left of the file name pops up the menu shown in Figure 14-4, which gives you access to a number of file manipulation options, including adding a memo, beaming, or even compressing documents. Tap the icons to the right of the document icon to determine their statuses: whether or not they are backed up on HotSync, included in global find, or designated as private records. Noncompressed files are shown bold, and you can specify whether you want to display the date the document was created or viewed.

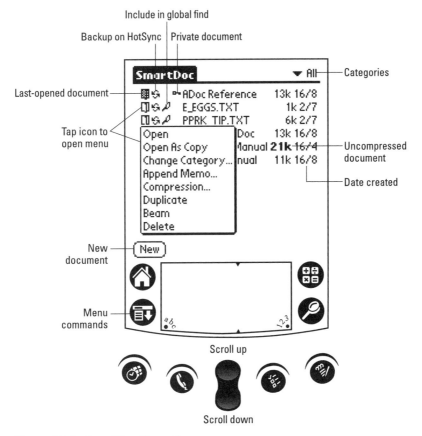

Figure 14-4: SmartDoc file options

 Note If you find that a document disappears when you are tapping on this screen, it just means that you have changed it to a private record. Tap on the Applications button, and then on Palm's Security application. Then change Private Records from "Hide" to "Show." The document will be visible again.

TealDoc

Developer: TealPoint Software
Cost: $16.95 (shareware)
Footprint: 44K

TealPoint expanded the capabilities of the Doc format when it introduced TealDoc, which was the first document reader with the capability to embed graphics and links within documents. These are supported by preparing a text document with special HTML-style tags, which TealDoc converts appropriately (see Figure 14-5). Also included are support for multiple display fonts, bookmarks, and a find command. One unique feature is the capability to encrypt documents, with a password required either the first time or every time a document is opened on your Palm Organizer.

Figure 14-5: TealDoc

Tapping the Zoom (at 0 percent in Figure 14-6) will replace the find/fonts display with one that shows your scroll and AutoScroll status. The top bar shows where you are in the document, and you can drag the bar around to quickly jump to another location. The bottom bar is the AutoScroll bar. The bar in the center turns solid black when AutoScroll is turned on, and the four buttons correspond to the hardware buttons on your Palm Organizer.

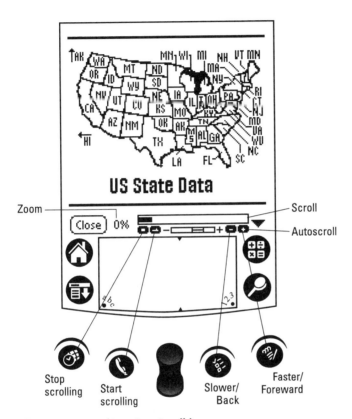

Figure 14-6: TealDoc AutoScroll bar

CSpotRun

Developer: Bill Clagett
Cost: Freeware
Footprint: 16K

There have been numerous freeware document readers created for the Palm Organizer since Rick Bram released Doc. Yamada Tatsushi's shareware J-Doc was the first to enable you to rotate the screen, and CSpotRun (see Figure 14-7) is the only other that I know of that offers the same functionality. One useful feature is that the text can be scrolled up or down by tapping the top or bottom of the document, regardless of orientation. Other features include a Zoom function (limited to increments of 10 percent) and support for multiple fonts and line spacing.

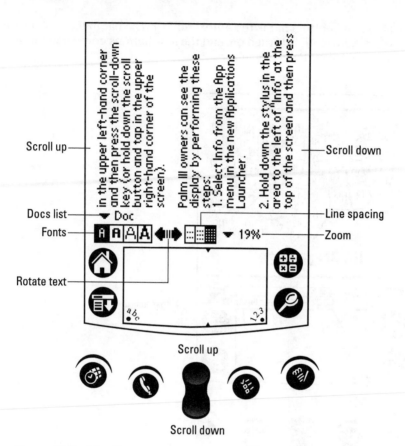

Scroll up

Scroll down

Figure 14-7: CSpotRun

RichReader

Developer: Michael Arena
Cost: $14.95 (Shareware)
Footprint: 115K

Michael Arena obviously wanted more when he set out to create RichReader (see Figure 14-8). This application can render Rich Text Format (RTF) files on your Palm Organizer's screen. This means that your document can include italicized, bolded, or underlined text in various sizes. For the most part, the font support in the document readers covered so far in this chapter is limited to global changes: you can make all of the text bigger or bolder, but not individual characters. Other features of RichReader include support for paragraph justification, centering for titles, bullets, and bookmarks, and the capability to read standard AportisDoc format files. Included with the program are utilities for Windows users to convert RTF or HTML files into Palm-readable documents.

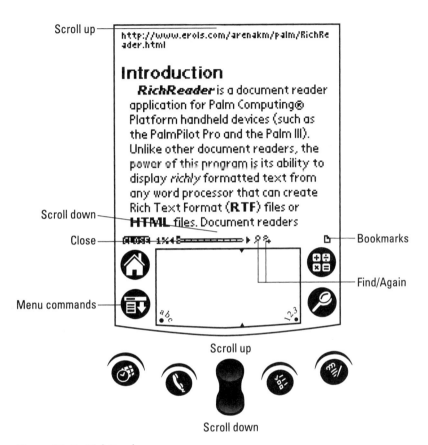

Figure 14-8: RichReader

OnTap

Developer: Aegean Associates, Inc.
Cost: $39.95 (commercial)
Footprint: 78K

Aegean Associates has taken a completely different route with OnTap (see Figure 14-9). The biggest difference between its reader and the other readers is that Aegean uses a proprietary format, and does not include the tools to make your own documents, although registered users can upload files to Aegean's Web site for conversion.

The upside? The documents are as close to HTML as you will see on your Palm Organizer, with support for multiple fonts, styles, sizes, and graphics. What gives these documents their punch is the support for hyperlinks in the document. This enables Palm Organizer users from any computing platform to create easy to use, professional-looking, quick reference guides for Palm Organizers within hours.

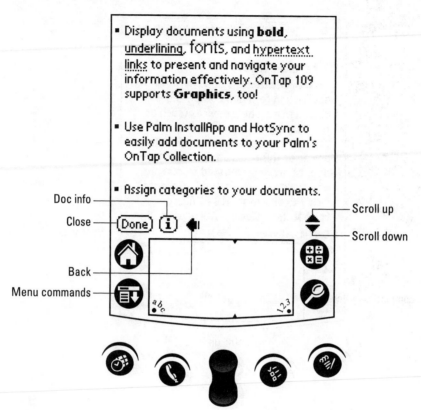

- Display documents using **bold**, underlining, fonts, and hypertext links to present and navigate your information effectively. OnTap 109 supports **Graphics**, too!

- Use Palm InstallApp and HotSync to easily add documents to your Palm's OnTap Collection.

- Assign categories to your documents.

Doc info

Close — (Done) (i)

Back

Menu commands

Scroll up

Scroll down

Figure 14-9: OnTap

iSilo

Developer: DC & Co.
Cost: $12.50 (shareware)
Footprint: 60K

If you like the idea of fully formatted HTML documents with formatted text and active links, but would rather convert your own documents, take look at iSilo (see Figure 14-10). This full-featured reader uses its own format, which offers compression 20 percent better than the Doc format. The elegant interface is well thought out. For example, the scroll bars can be set for each document or globally, and you can decide whether you want them to appear on the right side, left side, or not at all.

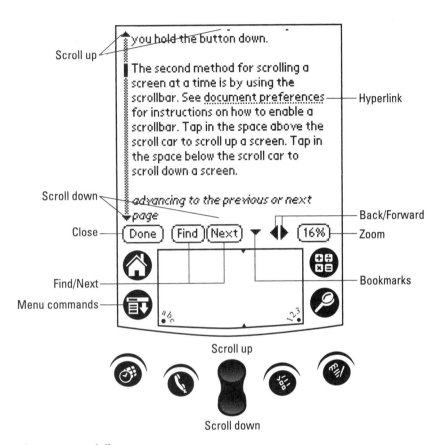

Figure 14-10: iSilo

iSilo ships with its own document-conversion utility (see Figure 14-11), which enables you to convert HTML and text documents to iSilo format. Currently there are Windows and Macintosh versions, along with command-line versions for DOS, Linux Intel, Solaris Sparc, and Windows. The only limitation with this utility is that it doesn't read standard Doc files, but these can easily be converted to the iSilo format.

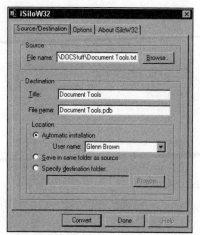

Figure 14-11: iSilo document conversion

Documents To Go

Developer: DataViz
Cost: $39.95 (Commercial)
Footprint: 101K

DataViz's approach is simplicity itself: once you've installed Documents To Go on your computer (Windows or Macintosh), all you need to do is drag a word processing or spreadsheet document to the desktop application (or icon), and it will be converted, compressed, and loaded on your Palm Organizer with your next HotSync (see Figure 14-12). Even better, if you change the original document on your computer, Documents To Go will update the handheld version with the next HotSync. This truly fulfills Jeff Hawkins' vision of the Palm Organizer as a viewer of documents created elsewhere.

After you've installed Documents To Go on your Palm Organizer, you'll find that you have three new applications for your Palm Organizer: Documents To Go, SheetView, and WordView. The Documents To Go application serves as a launcher for either type of document, while the other two, as their names suggest, launch text documents and spreadsheets.The interface for WordView (see Figure 14-13) is somewhat spartan, but it does offer multiple fonts in which to view your documents.

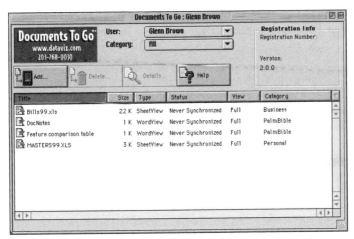

Figure 14-12: Documents To Go

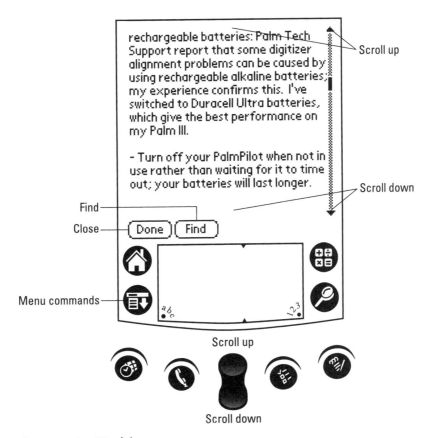

Figure 14-13: WordView

The gem of this application is SheetView (see Figure 14-14), which lets you view spreadsheets on your Palm Organizer.

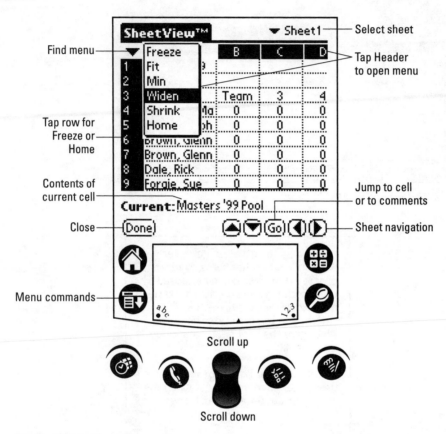

Figure 14-14: SheetView

Tip

After opening a spreadsheet in SheetView, tap the triangle in the upper left-hand corner (labeled Find in Figure 14-14), and select Fit. SheetView adjusts the column widths for you, making the sheet easier to read.

Feature Comparisons

Table 14-1 compares features of the various document readers. You will probably want to try these for yourself before you decide which tool is right for you.

Caution

If you decide to delete one of these document readers from your Palm Organizer to install another, you may need to reinstall your documents because they are deleted along with the old application. TealDoc offers the capability to convert your documents to a public format, which avoids the problem.

Table 14-1
Document Reader Feature Comparison Table

Product	Add Bookmarks	Find	Auto Scroll	Graphics	Creator	Fonts
AportisDoc Reader	No	No	No	No	No	2
AportisDoc Mobile Edition	Yes	Global	Yes	No	No	4
CSpotRun	No	No	No	No	No	4
Docs to Go	No	Yes	No	No	Yes	Yes
iSilo	Yes	Yes	No	No	Yes	Yes
OnTap	No	Yes	Yes	Yes	Yes	Yes
RichReader	Yes	Yes	No	No	Yes	Yes
SmartDoc	Yes	Global	Yes	No	Yes	4
TealDoc	Yes	Global	No	Yes	No	3

Making Your Own Documents

Now that you've loaded one of these utilities, how do you convert your own documents to a format that you can read on your Palm Organizer? If you have OnTap, go to its Web site (www.ontaptech.com/ontap/), and if you're using Documents To Go, just drag your documents to its desktop icon. If you're using one of the other applications, read on.

Preparing a document for conversion

First, prepare your document for conversion. Figure 14-15 is an excerpt from this chapter in Microsoft Word 98 format. Use your word processor's Save As command to save your document in text format (with or without line breaks). Take a look at the document, and note that all the formatting and graphics have disappeared. If there are figure references (for example, "see Figure A"), you may as well delete them because the figures themselves are gone. (If you must have graphics, take a look at TealDoc.) Remove the extra line spaces and reformat your main headings using ALL CAPS if you want them to stand out. If you want, you can also add underlining by using a short row of dashes underneath your main headings.

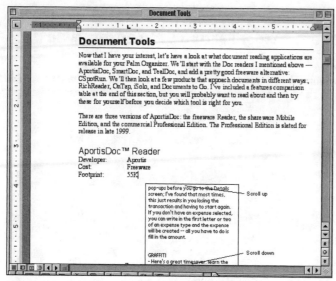

Figure 14-15: A document before conversion

Figure 14-16 shows the same passage after preparation for use on your Palm Organizer.

Figure 14-16: A document after conversion

Figure 14-17 shows what it looks like loaded in AportisDoc.

```
* DOCUMENT TOOLS
--------------
Now that I have your interest, let's
have a look at what document reading
applications are available for your
Palm Organizer. We'll start with the
Doc readers I mentioned above --
AportisDoc, SmartDoc, and TealDoc,
and add a pretty good freeware
alternative: CSpotRun. We'll then look
at a few products th┌ DOCUMENT TOOL┐
documents in differ│ AportisDoc(tm) │
RichReader, OnTap, │ Add A Bookmark │
```
(Done) .0% (F)(G) [A][A][A]   ▼

Figure 14-17: Document viewed in AportisDoc

Creating automatic bookmarks

You can format your documents so that your headings are automatically converted to bookmarks when they are opened in your document reader. This is currently supported in SmartDoc and TealDocIt is planned for future releases of AportisDoc Professional and RichReader.

Select a unique bookmark character (any symbol will do, as long as it isn't used elsewhere in your document. Aportis suggests "–," but I prefer to use *). Tag each of your headings with this symbol, for example, –HEADING. You'll also need to let the application know which character you've used by putting it at the end of the document in angle brackets, for example, <*>.

Note The symbol used for bookmarks cannot be more than 4 characters long, and bookmarks themselves cannot exceed 15 characters in length.

Caution If you do decide to use the "--" recommended by Aportis, just remember that you won't be able to use dashed underlines or double dashes to replace em dashes, because they will be misinterpreted as bookmarks.

In TealDoc you can also create a tag for each bookmark you want to add, by inserting <BOOKMARK>. If you want the name of the bookmark to be included, use the format <BOOKMARK NAME="Contents">. Consult the TealDoc manual for more on using tags to customize your documents for TealDoc.

Conversion utilities

There is no shortage of good utilities to convert your text files to .pdb files that you can read on your Palm Organizer. All do about the same job as far as the conversion is concerned; the big differences between them are the user interface and the available options.

MakeDoc

Developer: Pat Beirne
Cost: Freeware

Pat Beirne's MakeDoc (see Figure 14-18) was the original Doc conversion utility for the Palm platform. The command-line interface was designed for DOS users; others have since added their own interface for Windows and other platforms. There are now versions available for Amiga, DOS, Macintosh, and Unix users.

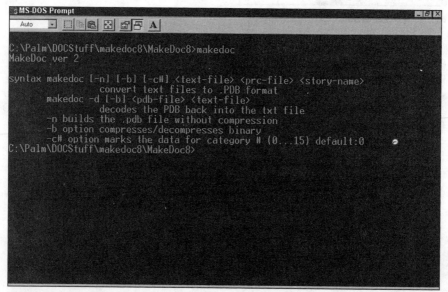

Figure 14-18: MakeDoc

To run the program, switch to DOS mode (Start ➪ Run ➪ Command), and then type in the name of the source file, the name of the Palm-readable file, and the name of the document. For example:

```
makedoc doctools.txt doctools.pdb "Document Tools"
```

MakeDocW

Developer: Mark Pierce
Cost: Freeware

If the help file for MakeDoc's command-line interface in Figure 14-18 confused you, use this utility instead of MakeDoc. Mark Pierce took the back-end conversion utility of MakeDoc and wrote an easy-to-use Windows interface for it (see Figure 14-19). After opening the application, all you need to do is to click Browse to select the file to convert, and then click Convert. If you want, MakeDocW will even auto-install your document, so that it is available for reading on your Palm Organizer after the next HotSync.

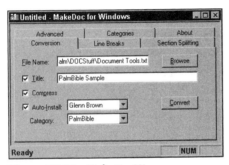

Figure 14-19: MakeDocW

DocInOut

Developer: Skip Bremner
Cost: Freeware

Skip Bremner's freeware DocInOut goes that extra mile, adding the capability to convert HanDBase files to JFile format. The application acts as a Windows 9*x* shell for the conversion utilities, which reside in the same directory as DocInOut. First, make a few simple selections from among the options shown in Figure 14-20.

Next, right-click a text document to get the contextual menu, which includes the option to Make Pilot Doc (see Figure 14-21).

If you make that selection, you'll get the dialog box shown in Figure 14-22. From there, making a Palm-readable document is as simple as clicking Make Doc.

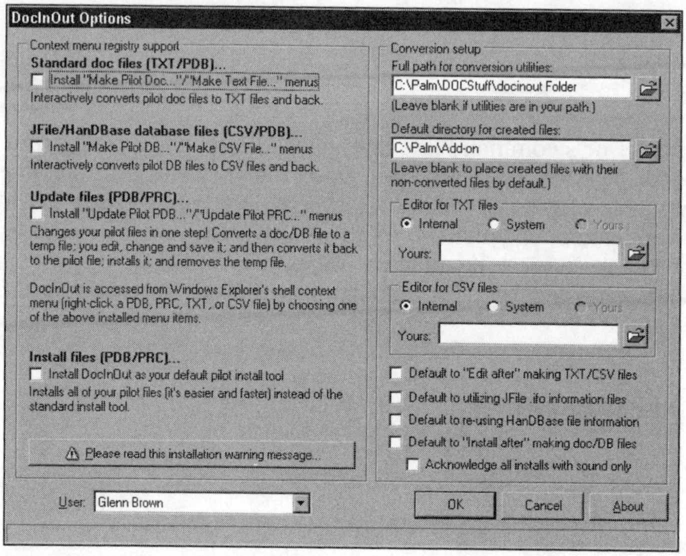

Figure 14-20: DocInOut options

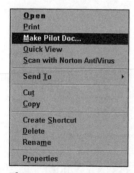

Figure 14-21: DocInOut contextual menu

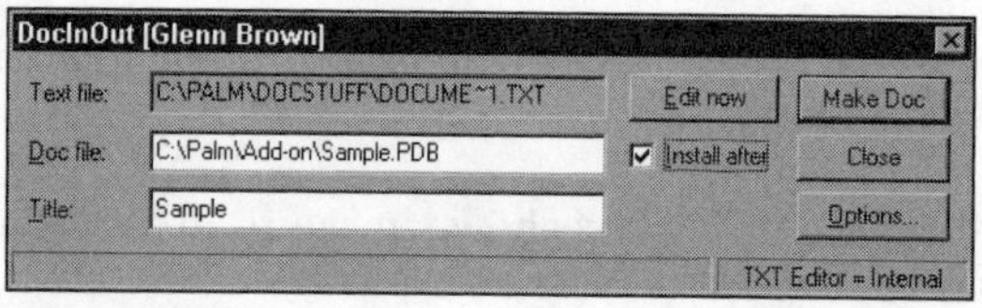

Figure 14-22: Making a Palm-readable document

MakeDocDD

Developer: Masatoshi Yoshizawa
Cost: Freeware

Macintosh users shouldn't feel left out—Masatoshi Yoshizawa (Yoz) has written a Macintosh front-end called MakeDocDD. You can click the program icon to make a few simple settings (see Figure 14-23), and then all you have to do is to drag and drop files to the program icon, and it will make a Palm-readable copy for you.

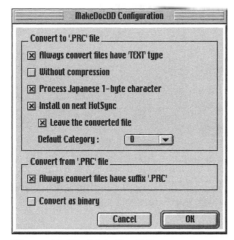

Figure 14-23: MakeDocDD

Note For MakeDocDD to work correctly, you will need to rebuild your desktop after you install the program. Restart your Macintosh and press Ô and Option while starting up. You will see a dialog box asking if you want to rebuild the desktop; click Yes.

Mac Palm Doc

Developer: Software from Plum Island
Cost: $10.00

Mac Palm Doc offers two-way conversion: it can convert documents into Palm-readable Doc format, and it can convert Palm .pdb document files back into text (see Figure 14-24). This utility also enables you to preconfigure which characters should be recognized as bookmarks.

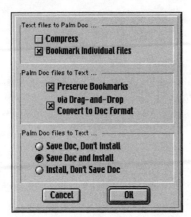

Figure 14-24: Mac Palm Doc settings

Finding and Loading Docs

Loading documents on your Palm Organizer is easy: Just install the .pdb file in the same fashion as you would install an application and then HotSync. The document you've loaded is now available from within your document-reading application. For more on loading files on your Palm Organizer, see Chapter 11.

On the Internet

Three types of free documents are available on the Internet. There are collections of works on which copyright has expired, e-zines that bring news and views, and reference material. Commercial sites will also sell you new works in electronic format. Here are a few examples to start your exploration.

MemoWare

www.MemoWare.com

This is arguably the most complete archive of documents for the Palm Organizer. There are over 2,500 documents here, listed under Reference and Literature groups, and subdivided into 33 categories. Reference material includes Business, Computers, Entertainment, Medicine, Palm-Related, Sports, and more. The Literature grouping includes Adventure, Biography, Children's, Humor, Mystery, Novels, Science Fiction, Shakespeare, and e-zines. If you're looking for something to read on your Palm Organizer, this is probably the best place to start.

Mary Jo's E-Texts
www.dogpatch.org/etext.html

This page has a good collection of children's classics — the Oz books, the Tom Swift books, *The Adventures of Pinocchio*, *Selected Fairy Tales* by the Brothers Grimm, Rudyard Kipling's *The Jungle Book*, *Robin Hood*, *Black Beauty*, and more for you to download and enjoy with your children.

The Pilot Newspaper Daily
www.i2iuk.com/welcome.htm

This free service enables you to custom tailor news that you would like e-mailed to your computer in Doc format, for reading on your Palm Organizer. You can select U.S., U.K., German, Australian, or Canadian news to be delivered when you want. Mine specifies U.S. Business and Technology updates, along with Canadian Top Stories, and Entertainment News. This service alone makes having a document reader on your Palm Organizer worthwhile!

HandJive Magazine
www.handjivemag.com/index.shtml

This bimonthly newsletter covers music, movies, news, and technology, focusing on both the Apple Newton and the Palm Organizer.

Mind's Eye Fiction
http://tale.com/

This site takes an approach similar to shareware with the works it offers: You can read the first chapter of any book online, and then decide whether you want to buy and read the rest. Categories include Fantasy, Horror, Humor, Mystery, Romance, Science Fiction, and Western. All works are available in Palm-readable Doc format.

Online Originals
www.onlineoriginals.com

Online Originals is a London-based publisher of all-new, book-length works that can be purchased in Palm-readable format. Samples are available at the Web site.

Peanut Press
www.peanutpress.com

This site offers contemporary works that can be read on your Palm Organizer using the Peanut Reader, which is included with every purchase. Categories include Action/ Adventure, History, Horror, Nonfiction, Romance, Science Fiction and Fantasy, Travel, and more. Two notable inclusions are electronic versions of the Star Trek books and Tap Magazine (my favorite Palm-specific magazine, which can also be found at www.tapmagazine.com).

überchix
www.uberchix.com

This is the home of Kristen Brennan's full-length e-book, *Buffalo Girls*. Very professional and done with a real sense of humor — be sure to check out this site.

Summary

Your Palm Organizer can serve you well as a reader of documents created elsewhere, especially if you use one of the available document-reading applications.

Consider one of the more advanced readers if you need graphics or hyperlinked text in your documents.

Take some time to learn the features of the application that you choose to use; you'll be surprised at how easy and powerful these tools are. Pay special attention to the different settings you can make to fine-tune scrolling.

Be careful when using the AutoScroll settings in these applications — some can disable your Palm Organizer's auto-shutoff feature, which means that they may drain your battery completely if left unattended.

Spending a little time preparing your text documents before converting them can make a big difference to the final product on your Palm Organizer.

✦　　✦　　✦

Traveling with Your Palm Handheld

✦ ✦ ✦ ✦

In This Chapter

Using what you have

Conversions

Time travel

Finding your way

Travelogue

✦ ✦ ✦ ✦

This chapter looks at what you have and what you may need to help you when traveling with the Palm Handheld. The handheld format makes it an ideal companion when traveling. Here I look at currency conversion utilities, travel clocks, mapping programs, and general-purpose travel software. If you travel, I'm sure you'll find something here that will pique your interest; and even if you stay at home, I'm sure you'll find a few useful tools.

Using What You Have

There is a lot that is already available on your Palm Handheld that can help you when traveling. Here are a few ideas to get you started:

✦ Enter your travel itinerary in the Date Book application.

✦ Enter destination contact information—hotels, motels, and even campsites have telephones—in your Address Book.

✦ Create a trip category, and then use the To Do list to create packing and other lists for yourself.

✦ Use the Memo Pad to store travel notes and foreign language phrases.

✦ Use the Expense application to record your travel expenses (see Chapter 13 for more on the Expense application).

✦ Use the built-in calculator to do currency rate conversions.

Tip

If you're traveling, just tap in the exchange rate and load it in the calculator's memory by tapping M+. Now conversions are quick and easy: tap the number in foreign currency, tap times, and then tap MR to recall your saved exchange rate.

✦ Set up for a remote HotSync operation. If you have a modem, you may want to set up your handheld for remote synchronizing with your base computer. If you work on a WAN (wide area network), you may be able to set up for a Network HotSync operation (see Chapter 6 for details).

✦ Set up the command stroke to shut off and lock.

✦ Enter your personal information, making sure to offer a reward for the return of your handheld.

TravelWare

Don't forget when you're traveling that you need power for your Palm Handheld—pack extra batteries and a HotSync cable. Palm V owners will need to pack a cradle for anything beyond an overnight trip. If you travel regularly, consider Palm's great travel kit. It includes a HotSync cable, a power cable with international charger, adapters for the United Kingdom, Europe, and Australia, and a nylon carrying bag. I recommend it highly.

Conversions

One of the first tools that you will want when traveling is something to help with conversions: temperature, distance, and especially money. This section focuses on tools that can help you sort out your money while traveling in a foreign land. Table 15-1 compares some of the available conversion utilities. For metric conversions, consider one of the multipurpose tools, or try MetriCalc (see Chapter 13 for more on this freeware utility).

Table 15-1 Conversion Utilities							
Model	**Price**	**Size**	**Rates**	**Tips**	**Taxes**	**Totals**	**Metric**
Advanced Traveler	$10.00	39K	Manual	Yes	Yes	Yes	
CurrCalc	$12.95	72K	Manual				Yes
Currency	Free	70K	Online		Yes		
CurrencyX	$8.00	27K	Online				
Foreign	$7.00	15K	Manual				

Advanced Traveler

Advanced Traveler, developed by Bill Ezell, does currency and time conversions, computes taxes and tips, and saves as many different locations as you wish (see Figure 15-1). Conversions can be posted to a memo so that you can track what you spend. The entry screen looks like a small invoice, and when you enter an amount, it computes any taxes or tips and shows a grand total. This is of limited value in Europe where tax and tips are usually included in the prices. However, travelers to the U.S. and Canada can use it. Canadians may find it particularly useful because there are usually two taxes applied to purchases, and tips are not included. Registration gives you the ability to save multiple locales, each with its own currency and tax rates.

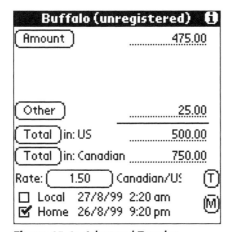

Figure 15-1: Advanced Traveler

CurrCalc

Bozidar Benc's CurrCalc currency calculator is a combination of unit converter and standard calculator (see Figure 15-2). Up to 15 conversion categories can be defined with 200 items in each category, making it a universal conversion engine. Currency conversion is specified in a "cross-rates" list in which your home currency is defined as 1.00 units and all other currencies are specified in relation to it — the same way that exchange information appears in the newspaper. The digit display is large and easy to read, even in a dim restaurant. Simply tap the large calculator-style buttons to make entries. The units being converted can be switched by tapping them to reveal a drop-down menu of choices.

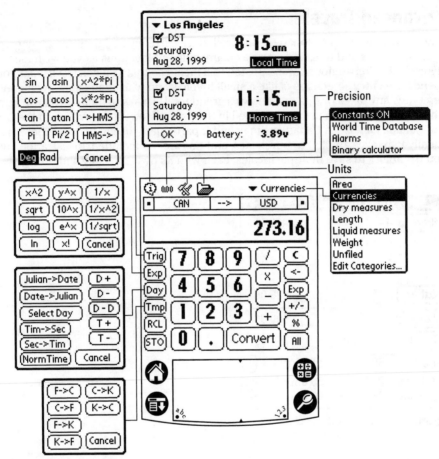

Figure 15-2: CurrCalc

Currency

Currency (see Figure 15-3), developed by Henrique Martins, is impressive. With it, you can select up to eight rates to be displayed, configure a single tax, and have use of a simple calculator. Even better, this freeware application offers free daily rate updates on the Internet (at www.members.xoom.com/HM_martins/currex.htm). Two versions are available: One version supports 174 currencies, and the second supports 66 currencies.

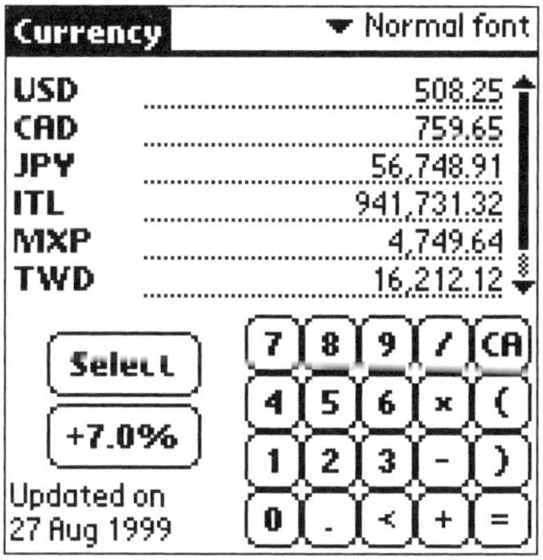

Figure 15-3: Currency

CurrencyX

This shareware product was developed by Armando Neves and offers a configurable list of currencies (see Figure 15-4). Enter a figure in one, and it performs the exchange to all displayed currencies. A RateSync feature enables you to download daily exchange rate updates from the Internet. Unless you live in Europe or the United States, you'll find this to be of limited value — rates can only be Euro- or dollar-based.

Figure 15-4: CurrencyX

Foreign

Edmund Seto's Foreign (see Figure 15-5) has over 150 different foreign rates built in with a very readable, large-digit display and one-touch conversion back-and-forth between two currencies. The program works well but selecting a new currency pair from two lists that are both 150 entries long is less than optimal.

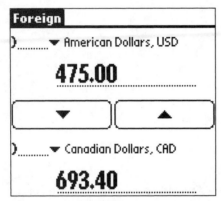

Figure 15-5: Foreign

Time Travel

Your Palm Handheld may have a wimpy speaker, but you can set it to ring long enough and loud enough to wake you up. Most of the clocks covered here also include support for multiple time zones, making them ideal travel clocks. If you travel regularly, you may want to consider one of the Date Book replacements that offer support for multiple time zones — see Chapter 20 for more on DateBk3 and TZDateBook. Table 15-2 compares some of the available clocks.

Table 15-2 PalmClocks								
Product	**Price**	**Size**	**Alarms**	**Snooze**	**Zones**	**Timer**	**Stopwatch**	**Battery**
Big Clock	Free	32K	4	Yes	3	Yes	No	No
CClock	$19.95	30K	No	No	4	No	No	No
Cesium	$7.00	41K	3	Yes	2	Yes	Yes	Yes
Clock III	$19.95	66K	9	Yes	2	Yes	Yes	Yes
Clock Pro	$12.00	43K	1	Yes	3	Yes	Yes	Yes

Product	Price	Size	Alarms	Snooze	Zones	Timer	Stopwatch	Battery
FPS Clock	$9.95	20K	1	Yes	No	No	No	No
Multi Clock	$10.00	26K	3	Yes	2	No	No	Yes
Time Zone	$15.00	98K	3	No	15	No	No	No

Big Clock

As shown in Figure 15-6, Jens Rupp's BigClock is aptly named — this is one *big* clock! It is also a full-featured clock, especially when you consider the price. BigClock includes multiple alarms with snooze, multiple time zones (including the capability to change what time alarms should be based on — home or travel), and support for the TaleLight. If you really like BigClock, send Jens a $10.00 shareware fee, and he will send a Windows utility that enables you to change the display font used by BigClock.

CClock

SMC Innovations' CClock offers a unique linear view of multiple time zones, which can be useful if your business or travel involves different locations. The demo version (see Figure 15-7) is limited to a sample database of four cities; the release version includes an editable database of over 700 cities.

Figure 15-6: Big Clock

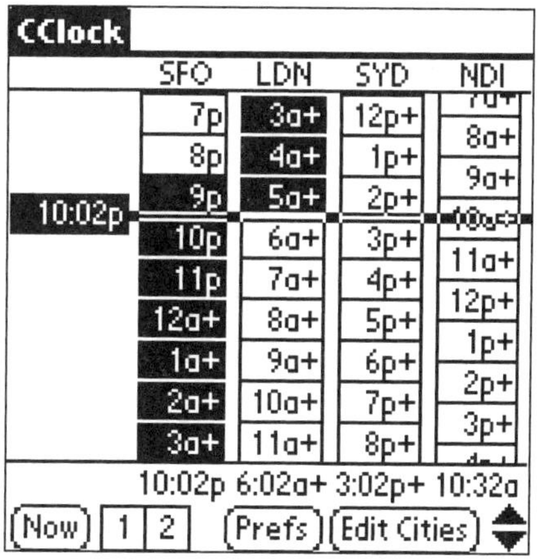

Figure 15-7: CClock

Cesium

Andrew Ball's Chronos was one of the first clocks available for the Palm Handheld; it was renamed ClockWorks for a short period, and it is now known as Cesium (see Figure 15-8). Don't let the low price fool you—this is one of the best clocks available for the Palm OS. Cesium features three display modes. Cesium's clock display mode shows the time, date, battery level, and preset time zones selected from a pop-up menu. The timer and stopwatch display modes each show date and time. Large numbers and text are used in all display modes, and the digits in all display modes can be set by touching them. Even better, start and stop work by touching anywhere on the screen. I highly recommend this one.

Clock III

Clock III from Little Wing Software Development was originally called Pilot Clock. It offers four screens: a clock (showing date, time, battery, and time zone), a timer (showing time, date, alarm controls, loudness, and duration), a stopwatch (showing date, time, and separate lap/split timers), and alarms (with a separate screen for setting multiple alarms). Clock III (see Figure 15-9) is definitely the most complete product here—you get what you pay for.

Clock III is also the only program that uses your Palm Handheld's hardware buttons to turn it into a sophisticated stopwatch/timer (see Figure 15-10); all of the others require a screen tap to start or stop.

Figure 15-8: Cesium   **Figure 15-9:** Clock III

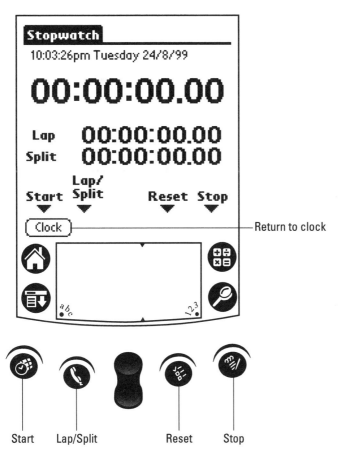

Figure 15-10: Use the Palm's hardware buttons to control Clock III's stopwatch.

ClockPro

Maple Top Software's ClockPro offers a unique, customizable interface (see Figure 15-11)—you can change many of the screen elements to suit your needs, with icons appearing onscreen as features are activated. ClockPro also has the distinction of having the largest time display of any of the products in this section.

FPS Clock

As Figure 15-12 shows, FPS Clock (from Fighter Pilot Software) offers a simple, easy-to-use interface, with a large clock display. All parameters are clearly displayed on one screen, including continuous display of date, time (analog clock), and battery voltage. Sleep time can be configured from one to five minutes or never.

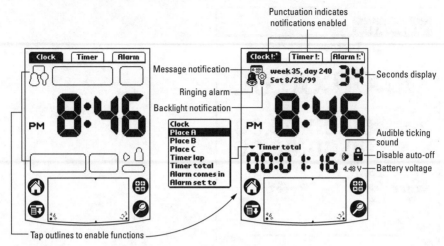

Figure 15-11: Tap the outlines to enable ClockPro's functions.

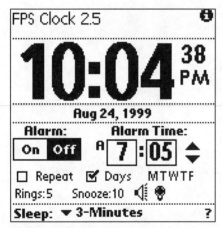

Figure 15-12: FPS Clock

multiClock

PalmAdd Software's multiClock is particularly suited to the millennium—it includes all of the expected features (multiple time zones, alarms, and a moon display), and offers a configurable countdown timer (see Figure 15-13). If you'd rather, the same space can be configured to display battery voltage.

Caution   The Palm OS only allows your handheld to "wake" for an alarm or other action at whole-minute intervals (for example, 12:00:00). If you need an alarm or action to be triggered at a precise time (for example, 12:00:25), disable your handheld's auto-off feature—just be cautious, because this setting can quickly drain your batteries.

Figure 15-13: multiClock

TimeZone

TimeZone from Cromerica Technologies, LLC, is for the world traveler, It includes data on more than 900 sites, cities, countries, and regions, and calculates the date and time for each of them relative to a home location. Data about locations is displayed in a form of scrolling list located in the lower portion of the screen (see Figure 15-14). Additional features include an enhanced find function, location filtering, and the capability to set up to three alarms.

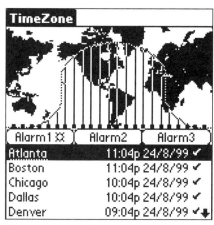

Figure 15-14: TimeZone

Finding your way

One of the first things you'll need when traveling is maps — of city, country, and region. Wouldn't it be great if someone could shrink them to pocket size? Map utilities have one huge advantage over the paper variety: You never have to fold them. Mapping information is available freely in the United States, but because most of the rest of the world charges, the end result is that these applications are currently limited to U.S. maps. This means that those of us who live elsewhere still suffer trying to fold paper maps.

HandMap

Developer: Evolutionary Systems
Cost: Freeware (basic version; they sell the Deluxe and Pro versions)
Footprint: 175K

Evolutionary Systems markets three versions of their HandMap application: the freeware basic version, a $16.00 Deluxe version which adds a layered map format, and a $35 Pro version which adds plug-ins with GPS support and an export capability. HandMap (see Figure 15-15) enables you to search for streets or landmarks, plan routes, and create custom markers to identify landmarks.

StreetSigns

Developer: Trekware Corporation
Cost: $49.95
Footprint: 62K (depends on maps loaded)

StreetSigns (see Figure 15-16) takes a different approach; all of Trekware's maps are available to registered users on its Web site at `www.trekware.com`.

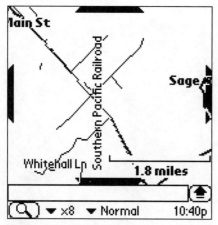

Figure 15-15: HandMap

Figure 15-16: StreetSigns Manhattan

The StreetSigns application combines detailed maps with travel information, which enables the application to tell you where you are and direct you to the nearest restaurant (see Figure 15-17).

Figure 15-17: Looking for dinner . . .

Travelogue

Whenever we travel, many of us keep statistics including mileage covered and money spent. Sometimes this is for tax purposes, but often we just want to *know*. The Palm Handheld does a great job of helping us track information; these programs make it even easier!

AirMiles

Developer: Hands High Software
Cost: $29.95
Footprint: 60K

Most who travel frequently will end up joining one of more of the various plans that the airlines have to encourage travelers to use their services, incentives that enable you to accumulate points toward free travel or seating upgrades. The trick is that you need to keep track of your points to make sure the airlines record them correctly, and most people want to know when they qualify for that free trip to Hawaii. AirMiles (Figure 15-18) makes it easier to track this information.

Figure 15-18: AirMiles

Vehicle logs

For years, I have kept a little book of all of the maintenance, gas, oil, and other service on my car so that I can track performance. The Palm Handheld makes a great substitute for that little book, and it can also calculate my mileage! Two of these programs (Palm Miles and Trip) are strictly intended to record trip and vehicle usage information — primarily for tax purposes; they do not track gas mileage or other maintenance costs.

AutoLog

Developer: Mobile Generation Software
Cost: $12.95
Footprint: 38K

AutoLog (see Figure 15-19) enables you to capture all of your vehicle expenses — gas, service, repairs, and payments — along with billable miles. The application includes support for up to 15 vehicles, and has the capability to report on different date ranges. The program makes it easy to enter data by automatically incrementing your mileage. A companion program, AutoLog Extractor, enables PC users to export their AutoLog information to Microsoft Excel.

Fill Up

Developer: Marc Schneider
Cost: $5.00
Footprint: 27K

Fill Up (Figure 15-20) tracks your fuel consumption, with support for both American (miles per gallon) and European (liters per 100 kilometers) formats. The program allows up to 20 different vehicle lists, each with up to 100 vehicles. Unique graphing capabilities enable you to graph your fuel consumption, routes, and fill-ups.

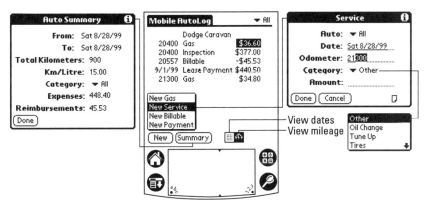

Figure 15-19: AutoLog

```
Fill Up V1.3
The average consumption is
49.05 KM per 10.00 LITERS

VEHICLE-NAME: Caravan          ▼
DATE          KM      LITERS    CO.
21. Aug 1999  298.00   60.00   49.66
25. Aug 1999  280.00   61.00   45.90
7. Aug 1999   300.00   58.00   51.72
28. Aug 1999  .............  ............  -------
no date!      .............  ............  -------
no date!      .............  ............  -------
no date!      .............  ............  -------
no date!      .............  ............  -------
```

Figure 15-20: Fill Up

Highway Manager

Developer: Zorglub Software
Cost: $10.00
Footprint: 51K

Highway Manager is a complete gas mileage application with full support for metric and English measurements. Features include support for both absolute and relative distances, tracking up to ten vehicles and up to ten currencies, trip statistics, and notes. One unique feature is the capability to switch on the fly between metric and English measurements (the dotted line in Figure 15-21), with automatic conversion of data: miles to kilometers and gallons to liters. This makes the program an essential for those like me who calculate using both measurement systems. The program includes a conduit that enables you to export your data to .csv (comma-separated values) files on your PC and very professional-looking documentation in Adobe Acrobat format. I stopped writing this chapter long enough to register my copy!

Palm Miles

Developer: Maple Ware Technologies, Ltd.
Cost: $10.00
Footprint: 12K

If you don't need to track your gas mileage or service information, but you do want to track your trip mileage and places visited, then consider Palm Miles. Features include the capability to store dates, starting location and destination, and the distance traveled either in miles or kilometers. VCR-like controls at the bottom of the screen (see Figure 15-22) enable you to review your trip data.

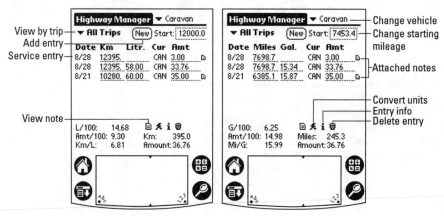

Figure 15-21: Highway Manager

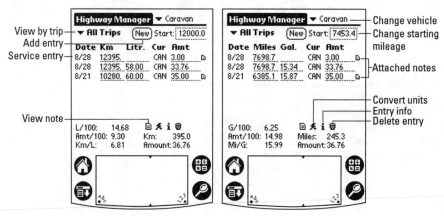

Figure 15-22: Palm Miles

Trip

Developer: Hands High Software
Cost: $19.95
Footprint. 56K

Trip (see Figure 15-23) is a full-featured application that enables you to record trip information other than fuel and other costs. Features include full integration with your built-in Address Book, Memo PLUS template notes capability, support for up to 15 vehicles, and the capability to export data to either your built-in Memo Pad or Expense application.

Figure 15-23: Trip

VehicleLog

Developer: Little Wing Software Development
Cost: $19.95
Footprint: 36K

VehicleLog is the program in this section with which I am most familiar; as you can see from Figure 15-24 I have been using it for the past two years to store information about my Dodge Caravan. Straightforward entry screens make it easy to maintain trip, fuel, and service data, and a flexible calculation screen makes it easy to gauge performance. Features include support for English and metric measurements, records for up to seven vehicles, and the capability to export data to a file that can be imported into a spreadsheet on your computer.

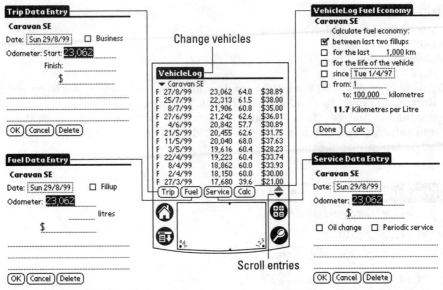

Figure 15-24: VehicleLog's screens

Vehicle Tracker

Developer: Stand Alone Software
Cost: $19.95
Footprint: 41K

Vehicle Tracker (see Figure 15-25) includes support for up to 15 vehicles, detailed maintenance records, support for English and metric measurements, and support for multiple currencies. Detailed viewing options enable you to select whether or not to view business or completed items, gas or maintenance records, and which date ranges to view.

Travel data

Information is critical when you travel. You need the answers to these questions: What is the language? What should you eat? Where should you go? These three utilities all provide important information in the handheld.

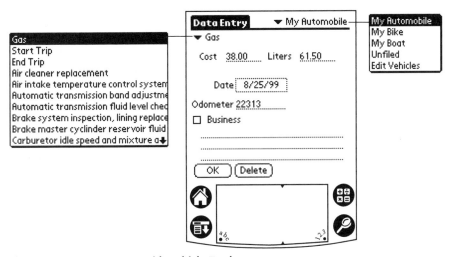

Figure 15-25: Data entry with Vehicle Tracker

Small Talk

Developer: Concept Kitchens
Cost: $79.99
Footprint: 131K (minimum, 194K complete)

Small Talk is the only program of its type: a two-way graphical translator for the Palm OS. Using a familiar flash card metaphor (see Figure 15-26), it is easy to navigate your way through common phrases and their translations. The program also includes a means for the other person to respond, complete with translations. Language modules in English, French, Italian, Spanish, German, and Japanese can be loaded as needed.

TealMeal

Developer: TealPoint Software
Cost: $13.95
Footprint: 35K

TealMeal helps with the universal question: Where are we going to eat? As Figure 15-27 shows, the decision has never been easier, with filtering by type or category. Even better, you can tap the Wheel of Food and have TealMeal select for you. This great little shareware program has become a standard on the Palm OS. TealPoint has more than 60 city databases available on its Web site (www.tealpoint.com), and the program includes utilities so that you can create your own database, either on your Palm Handheld or on your Windows or Macintosh computer.

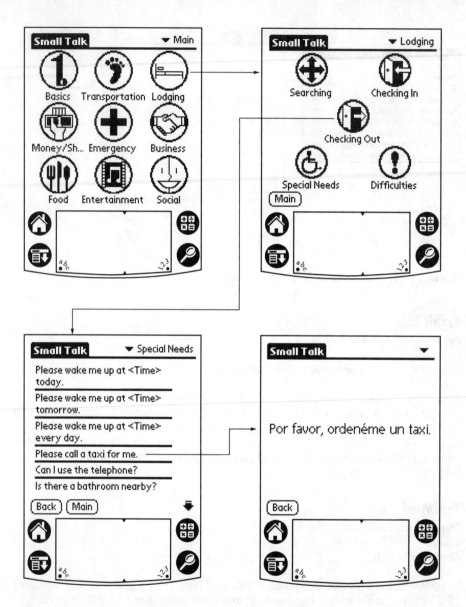

Figure 15-26: Using Small Talk to order a taxi in Spanish

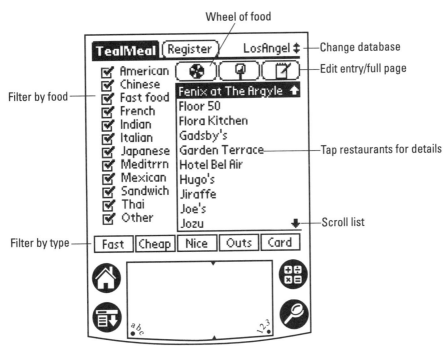

Figure 15-27: TealMeal

WorldFAQ

Developer: Creative Digital Publishing Inc.
Cost: $39.95
Footprint: 60K

FAQ is the common Internet abbreviation for "frequently asked questions"; WorldFAQ (see Figure 15-28) is just that; a collection of useful information about 720 world cities, countries, currency regions, and time zones. Information includes daylight savings time, dates and times, latitudes and longitudes, telephone codes, airport names and codes, currency exchange rates, and populations. You can calculate absolute and relative dates and times around the world, find currency conversion rates, sunrise and sunset times, and distances. If you want, you can add and delete cities and store your own information in location Notes. Different versions of WorldFAQ and WorldFAQ Lite were bundled with some Palm III models and can be upgraded to the current version for a reduced price—check Creative Digital Publishing's Web site www.cdpubs.com for details.

Figure 15-28: WorldFAQ

Travel tools

These utilities provide the equivalent of a Palm-sized version of the Swiss Army knife — each offering a variety of functionality.

Abroad

Developer: Yoshimitsu Kanai
Cost: $10.00 (shareware)
Footprint: 120K

Abroad is a suite of three applications: Currency Exchange, Unit Conversion, and World Clock, with a Country Information Database (Figure 15-29). Abroad does a one-to-many conversion: Enter an amount in the local currency, and it converts it to nine other currencies. Other than seeing how much your Wienerschnitzel would cost in nine other countries, I can't see much use for the multiple display; I just want to see 200 Shillings converted to Canadian dollars. The world clock feature keeps you from phoning home at unusual hours. The unit conversion also has a one-to-many display, and it is a more useful feature here. Abroad comes with very good HTML documentation.

Gulliver

Developer: Landware
Cost: $39.95
Footprint: 150K (complete)

For those who do any amount of airline travel, Gulliver (or TravelTracker, which is covered next) is a must. This application stores everything you need to know — keeping your flight information handy, hotel and rental reservations, and even your frequent flyer number (see Figure 15-30). Data entry is a breeze; the program makes good use of pop-up lists and auto-fill fields. Start tapping your entry, and Gulliver will usually complete it for you. Even better, flight information is automatically copied to your built-in Date Book. If you need to conserve space on your Palm Handheld, databases for airlines, cities, hotels, and car rental agencies can be loaded separately.

Figure 15-29: Abroad

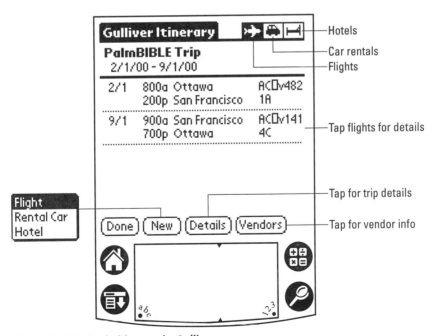

Figure 15-30: A trip itinerary in Gulliver

TravelTracker

Developer: SilverWARE
Cost: $29.95
Footprint: 219K (+31K for TravelSetup)

TravelTracker and Gulliver (listed previously) are virtually identical applications. They both enable you to track flight, hotel, and rental reservations, but TravelTracker offers just a bit more—slightly better and more configurable interaction with your built-in applications, the capability to track frequent flyer miles, and an integrated view of your trips (see Figure 15-31). On the other hand, I think that Gulliver may have a slight edge in its supporting information, and it has a footprint of almost 70K less. I suggest you try the demo versions of each and make your own decision.

WorldMate

Developer: Common Sense
Cost: $15.00
Footprint: 53K

WorldMate (see Figure 15-32) is a unique application that enables you to compare three things: clocks, clothes, and currencies. Up to four clocks can be displayed on the main screen. The clothing screen compares the different U.S., European, and U.K. sizes. And the currencies converter enables you to have shopping lists in three currencies.

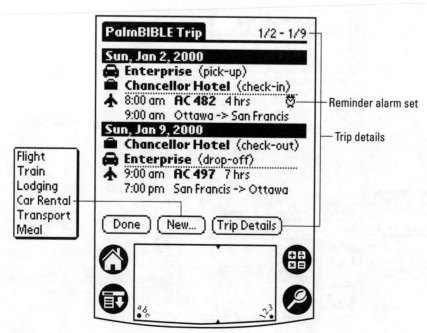

Figure 15-31: TravelTracker

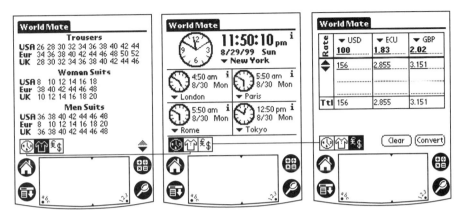

Figure 15-32: WorldMate

Summary

✦ Don't overlook your Palm Handheld's built-in applications that offer plenty of added functionality that can be useful when traveling.

✦ Remember to take spare power with you when you travel — batteries for PalmPilot and Palm III/VII users, and a cradle or travel kit for Palm V users.

✦ Those on a budget can't go wrong with the freeware combination of Currency and MetriCalc for conversions. CurrCalc is the best of the shareware offerings, while Advanced Traveler a good choice if you need running totals.

✦ My recommendation for a Palm clock is easy. Cesium easily tops its more expensive competitors, with one exception: Clock III's use of hardware buttons makes it a must-have if you use the stopwatch or timer functions.

✦ The utilities that replace the worn notebook in the glove compartment of your car are all good, but I think Highway Manager is the best of the current lot.

✦ Of the all-around tools, both Gulliver and TravelTracker are essentials for jet-setters; on the basis of price, the nod goes to TravelTracker.

✦   ✦   ✦

Communicating via Your Palm OS Handheld

In This Chapter

Built-in e-mail

Telecommunications

Required settings

How to connect

Telecommunications using the Palm OS is an exciting area that has been undergoing unbelievable growth in the past two years. There have been new products, new ways of connecting, and even a new Palm device that truly deserves the "connected" name: the Palm VII. This chapter begins with the built-in e-mail capabilities, and then looks at how to set up your handheld for telecommunications, along with the available software and hardware choices.

This chapter would not have been possible without the help of a lot of people. I'd particularly like to thank:

+ **Sean Costello** of Online Technical Systems for the dial-up connection, and his advice and help with cellular technologies

+ **Karl Joseph** of Bell Mobility for his sidebar on CDMA connections

+ **Angela Power** of JP Systems for her sidebar on Troubleshooting Palm Telecommunications

+ **John Powers** of MyPilot.com for his table on Wireless Digital Connections

+ **Alan Urban** of Palm, Inc. for providing me with a Palm V modem and a GSM connection kit (amongst other things)

+ **Lorraine Wheeler** of Actual Software for her sidebar on using the Ericsson 888/Ir cellular telephone

Built-in E-mail

The Palm OS comes with built-in e-mail capability, albeit one with two significant caveats:

✦ You can read and respond to e-mail on your handheld, but no e-mail is actually received or sent until you perform a HotSync. Your Palm Organizer acts as a remote input tool, enabling you to review and reply to your e-mail while away from your Windows computer.

✦ You must HotSync to a Windows computer—this feature is not available to users of Macintosh or other operating systems.

Setup

The majority of those working in office environments will find that they can use this feature. Here's how you set it up:

✦ Select Custom from the HotSync pop-up list (click the small HotSync icon in the Process Tray at the bottom right-hand corner of your Windows 95/98/NT4 screen)

✦ You'll see a listing of the conduits installed on your computer, double-click Mail (or select it and click Change)

✦ If you haven't set up mail before, you'll get a dialog box asking if you'd like to set up mail; click Yes to get the dialog box shown in Figure 16-1

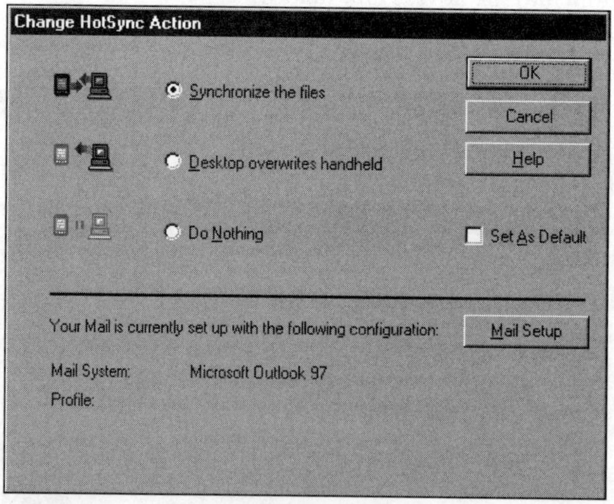

Figure 16-1: Mail conduit setup

✦ Click Mail Setup to get the dialog box shown in Figure 16-2; the only step left is to select your e-mail type, and then you're done!

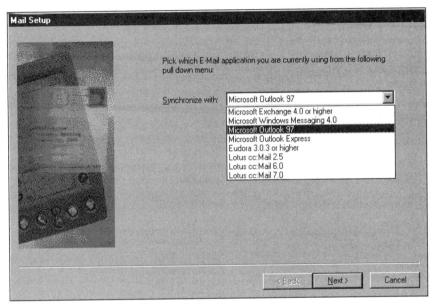

Figure 16-2: Selecting your e-mail client

Using e-mail

After you've set up e-mail to HotSync with your handheld, the first synchronization transfers mail to your Palm Organizer. Tapping on Palm's Mail icon opens an inbox display like that shown in Figure 16-3.

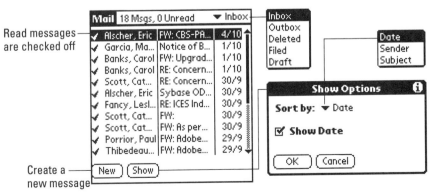

Figure 16-3: You've got mail.

Five views are available from the picklist in the upper right-hand corner:

✦ **Inbox** displays messages HotSynced from your computer; tapping on any one opens it for viewing. Once closed, a checkmark appears to let you know that you've read the message.

✦ **Outbox** displays a list of your responses that will be sent with your next HotSync.

✦ **Deleted** shows a list of messages you have deleted; you can clear this out by selecting Purge Deleted from the Message menu.

✦ **Filed** shows a list of messages you have filed.

✦ **Draft** shows a list of responses that you have yet to complete.

Tapping on any of your messages enables you to read and respond to your mail, as shown in Figure 16-4. You can use your Palm Organizer's hardware scroll buttons to scroll up and down in each message—when you reach the end of one message, it beeps to let you know that it has opened the next. Tapping New enables you to create a new message.

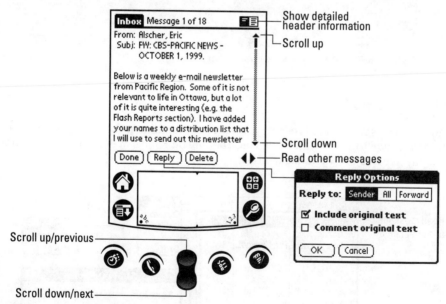

Figure 16-4: Reading your mail

If you tap Reply in any of your messages, you'll first set your Reply Options (as shown in Figure 16-4), and then you'll be able to draft a response (see Figure 16-5). Tapping Details in this screen enables you to set the priority of your message (low/normal/high), make it a blind carbon copy, add your signature block, and have your e-mail software confirm reading or delivery of your message.

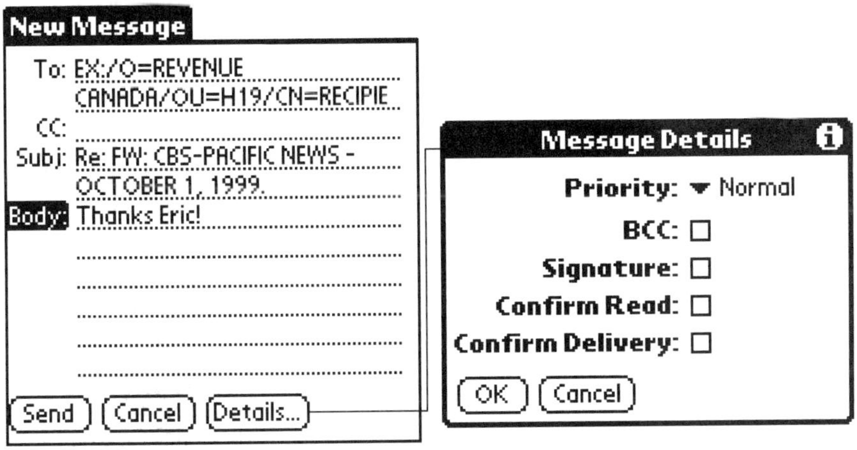

Figure 16-5: Answering your mail

Settings

The Options menu offers four menu items:

✦ **Font** enables you to change the display size of the viewing font.

✦ **Preferences** (see Figure 16-6) enables you to toggle the confirmation of deleted messages and to create a signature block that can be appended to your messages.

Figure 16-6: E-mail preferences

✦ **HotSync Options** (see Figure 16-7) enables you to specify how your e-mail should be transferred when you perform a HotSync and how long a message you will accept before it should be shortened (with the complete version left on your computer). My personal preference is to use the Unread setting, which enables me to quickly read new messages but enables me to do most e-mail management on my desktop computer.

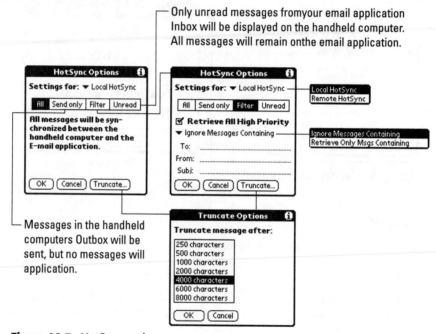

Only unread messages fromyour email application Inbox will be displayed on the handheld computer. All messages will remain onthe email application.

Messages in the handheld computers Outbox will be sent, but no messages will application.

Figure 16-7: HotSync options

✦ **About Mail** shows version and author information.

Telecommunications

Now we come to the fun stuff — here's where we truly make your Palm Organizer "connected." The biggest limitation to Palm's built-in e-mail capabilities is that you don't have a direct connection using your handheld. This section looks at some products that extend the reach of your Palm Organizer, enabling you to connect using a modem attached to a telephone line or wireless cellular communications. There are several basic categories that we'll look at: e-mail, browsing the Internet, faxing, and paging. Each category gives you handheld capabilities that were impossible until recently.

All of these options require setup and some means of connection; see "Setup" and "How to Connect" later in this chapter for details.

E-mail

In my experience, perhaps the most asked-for addition to the Palm Organizer is, can I get e-mail on it? For many, this is the reason to carry an eight-pound laptop—I think six ounces, plus a few more for a cable or modem, is much more reasonable. The difference between this and your handheld's built-in capabilities is huge: Instead of sending and receiving only when you HotSync, these applications enable you to send and receive wirelessly, *now*.

HandMail

Developer: SmartCode Software
Cost: $49.95
Footprint: 201K

HandMail was the first commercial e-mail application for the Palm OS; it is still the one I rely on. AOL users in particular will appreciate HandMail's capability to interface with the world's largest online service. Features include the ability to integrate with Palm Organizer's built-in applications, look up e-mail addresses in your Address Book, and attach Memo Pad documents to your outgoing messages.

Those using the Palm Vx (and those who have updated to OS 3.3) will need to upgrade to HandMail Version 2.1 or newer; Version 2.0 does not run under Palm OS 3.3.

MultiMail

Developer: Actual Software
Cost: $39.95
Footprint: 174K

MultiMail (see Figure 16-8) comes in two flavors: a shareware Discovery version, which can be registered for $10.00, and a full-blown Pro version for $39.95. Don't let the price fool you. This is probably the best e-mail package available for the Palm OS. Both versions offer support for IMAP4, which, if supported by your ISP, is a far superior method of e-mail access for Palm users than POP3. The Pro version adds a wealth of features, including available conduits for both Windows and Macintosh users and support for a wide variety of attachments, including Palm pdb/prc, Quicksheet, .wav, Microsoft Word, vCard, HTML, CSV, and Zip files. A Setup Wizard (see Figure 16-9) makes MultiMail the easiest of these packages to set up and configure.

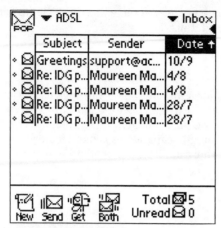

Figure 16-8: MultiMail Pro

Figure 16-9: MultiMail setup wizard

One-Touch Mail

Developer: JP Systems
Cost: $39.95
Footprint: 171K

One-Touch Mail offers great integration with your Palm Organizer's Address Book. As you can see in Figure 16-10, the main screen enables you to toggle between your mail and Address Book views (Figure 16-11). The program includes support for text or Memo Pad attachments, along with vCard and vCalendar formats, which enable the recipient to drop information directly into their Address Book or Calendar without having to reformat. Other features include advanced filing and filtering options, and the capability to create and use custom canned messages.

Figure 16-10: One-Touch Mail

Figure 16-11: One-Touch addresses listing

JP Systems' Top Five Technical Support Questions

Angela Powers, who does technical support for JP Systems, the makers of One-Touch Mail, provided these questions and answers.

1. Can I connect my Palm Organizer to my cellular telephone?

You need to make sure that your cell uses one of the digital technologies that support wireless data transfer (GSM, TDMA, or CDMA), and you need to contact your cellular provider to make sure that you have data transfer enabled on your phone.

2. I have a Brand X cellular telephone. Which technology does it use?

The easiest way to determine this is to check with your cellular provider or the manufacturer's Web site.

3. Where do I find all the information I need to configure One-Touch Mail?

You can look in the preferences of the Internet browser you use on your computer (most likely Microsoft Internet Explorer or Netscape Communicator), but the easiest way is to use the setup information provided by your Internet provider.

One-Touch Mail does not work with AOL or MSN.

Also, WorldNet (ATT) is an exception; you'll need to contact them directly to configure remote access.

4. How do I attach a Word document to my e-mail?

One-Touch Mail enables text-only attachments to be added to your e-mail.

5. How do I synchronize my handheld e-mail with Microsoft Outlook?

Upgrade to version 2.0 of One-Touch Mail.

pdQSuite

Developer: Qualcomm
Cost: $44.95
Footprint: 377K to 211K (Eudora), 105K (pdQbrowser), 61K (scratchpad)

As this book goes to press, Qualcomm has made available a great alternative for connected Palm owners: the pdQsuite of applications (see Figure 16-12), previously only available with Qualcomm's pdQ Smartphone. A 30-day trial version is available on the CD-ROM, with the current pricing of the complete package set at $44.95. pdQsuite includes support for both e-mail and Internet browsing by including pdQbrowser, a text-only Internet browser, and pdQsuite Eudora, an e-mail application that includes a conduit to enable Windows 95/98 users to HotSync with a MAPI-compliant e-mail program.

Figure 16-12: pdQsuite

 As of this writing, PdQsuite does not work with TCP/IP network connections via infrared.

ProxiMail

Developer: ProxiNet
Cost: Free (beta)
Footprint: 42K (plus 23K of plug-ins)

This simple application (see Figure 16-13) is based on Top Gun Postman (discussed next). The biggest difference between the two is that ProxiMail enables you to configure up to five e-mail accounts.

Figure 16-13: ProxiMail

Top Gun Postman

Developer: Ian Goldberg and Steve Gribble
Cost: Free (beta)
Footprint: 34K

Top Gun Postman (see Figure 16-14) is a simple freeware application that enables you to send and receive e-mail but not attachments.

Figure 16-14: Top Gun Postman

Browsing

As with e-mail, there are two ways to surf the Internet with your Palm Organizer: offline and connected. AvantGo enables you to preselect text versions of Web pages for downloading to your handheld, HandWeb and ProxiWeb enable you to connect directly, and pdQsuite (discussed earlier) enables you to do both offline and connected browsing.

AvantGo

Developer: AvantGo, Inc.
Cost: Free
Footprint: 241K (plus 100K or more of downloads)

AvantGo (see Figure 16-15) is free client software that enables you to specify information that should be updated and downloaded to your handheld when you HotSync. The conduit is slick! Once you've specified what information you want, it does a quick update with each HotSync. The interface is simple—underlined links work as you would expect them to, and a home icon jumps you back to your home page. There is only one limitation to this wonderful tool: The more you download, the more memory this application requires (AvantGo currently occupies 799K on my Palm Vx).

Figure 16-15: AvantGo

HandWeb

Developer: SmartCode Software
Cost: $49.95
Footprint: 174K (including 40K cache)

AvantGo is a great tool, but it isn't *live*. HandWeb (see Figure 16-16) enables you to connect your Palm Organizer directly to the Web, giving you a 160×160 portal to the Internet. Preferences enable you to view graphics, but my recommendation (which is also the default setting) is to leave them turned off. A simple interface enables you quick access to your favorite sites (see Figure 16-17), with support for offline browsing (like AvantGo), bookmarks, configurable cache, and history. I find this application the handiest for quick news fixes and for accessing Internet e-mail (like Microsoft's HotMail). I prefer a large color monitor and high-speed access for most surfing.

Figure 16-16: HandWeb

Figure 16-17: HandWeb sites

Note Version 2.1 of HandWeb (current as of this writing) does not include support for America Online (all other Internet Service Providers are covered), frames, or SSL (secure sockets layers for online purchasing). Users with Palm OS 3.3 (or newer) installed will need to update to at least HandWeb Version 2.1; Version 2.0 is not compatible.

ProxiWeb

Developer: ProxiNet
Cost: Free (beta)
Footprint: 114K

ProxiWeb offers a surprisingly complete solution, especially considering its current (free) price. A simple interface (see Figure 16-18) provides quick access to those settings that matter when making a quick foray for information on the Internet.

Figure 16-18: ProxiWeb

Faxing

Faxing may be the reason to buy a modem for your Palm Organizer. Think of it: not only can you send a fax directly from your handheld, but the addition of fax software also gives you a printer in every fax-equipped office in the world!

HandFax

Developer: SmartCode Software
Cost: $49.95
Footprint: 79K

HandFax (see Figure 16-19) is an elegant solution that enables you to use your Palm Organizer to send faxes whenever and wherever you'd like, complete with custom cover pages. The program offers good integration with the Palm OS, with the capability to look up fax numbers from within your Address Book and the capability to quickly fax notes and Memos.

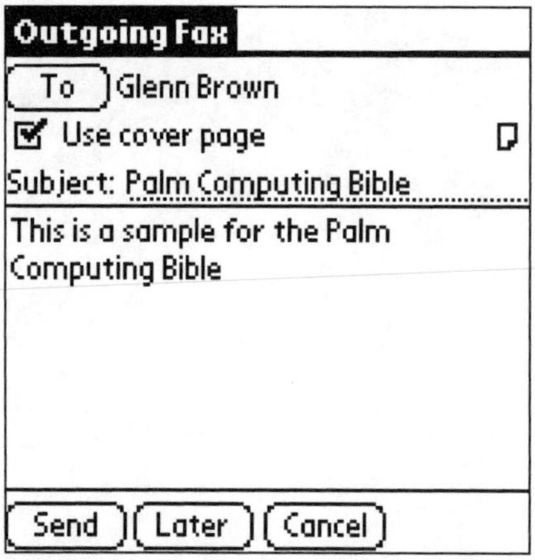

Outgoing Fax

(To) Glenn Brown
☑ Use cover page
Subject: Palm Computing Bible
This is a sample for the Palm
Computing Bible

(Send)(Later)(Cancel)

Figure 16-19: HandFax

Caution HandFax 2.0 does not work over IrDA and does not work with all models of cellular telephone.

Note If you are using Option's SnapOn GSM adapter, you need to set the baud rate to 38400 when using HandFax.

Mobile WinFax

Developer: Symantec Software
Cost: $44.99
Footprint: 270K

If you use a fax modem attached to your computer, you'll want to consider Mobile WinFax (see Figure 16-20). This program enables you to send and receive faxes directly on your modem-equipped handheld, and it also enables you to create faxes that will be sent using your computer's fax modem after your next HotSync.

Figure 16-20: Mobile WinFax

Paging

Paging enables others to contact you without the high cost or intrusiveness of a cellular telephone. There are three basic classes of paging devices: one-way pagers that broadcast information to your pager; two-way pagers that enable you to respond to pages; and pagers that send back an acknowledgement, so that you know whether you have missed a page.

Synapse Pager

Developer: Synapse
Cost: $129.95

The release of the Motorola Pager by Synapse (see Figure 16-21) offered the first wireless means of connecting the Palm Organizer with the outside world. Available for the original PalmPilots and Palm III devices, the Synapse paging upgrade includes 2MB of memory upgrade and the paging device itself.

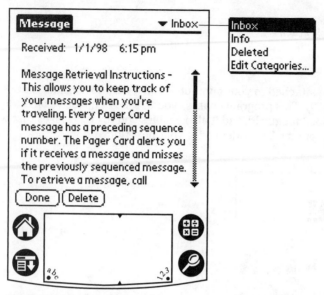

Figure 16-21: Synapse Pager

PageNOW!

Developer: Mark/Space
Cost: $39.95
Footprint: 87K

PageNOW! (see Figure 16-22) offers something completely different: the capability to *send* messages to text pagers and to PCS/GSM digital telephones. PageNOW includes support for all paging services (using the TAPI protocol) and all SMS (Short Messaging Service) devices using ETSI/GSM standard protocols. It works with Palm's modems as well as external Hayes-compatible modems.

Figure 16-22: PageNOW!

Other tools

The following are two other communications tools that you may find useful.

HandPHONE

Developer: Smartcode Software
Cost: $49.95
Footprint: 83K

On most cellular telephones, it is a real pain to enter all of your phone contact information, especially when most, if not all, of the information is already in your Palm Organizer's Address Book. HandPHONE enables you to share information between your handheld and your cellular. Opening the application presents you with a list derived from your Address Book, with each phone number shown as a separate listing (see Figure 16-23). HandPHONE also lets you edit and receive SMS (Short Message System) messages (providing that your telephone supports them) and dial your phone using your handheld. It also displays battery, signal, and other information from your cell phone.

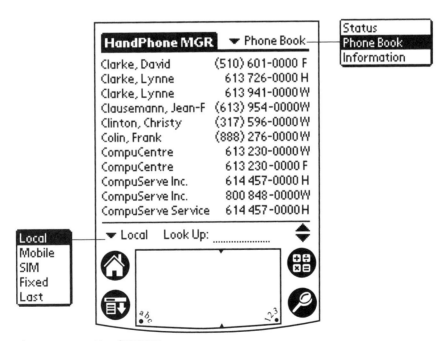

Figure 16-23: HandPHONE

Note HandPHONE does not support all cellular telephones; consult the compatibility list posted at www.smartcodesoft.com/products/handhelds/hh_handphone. html before purchasing. The current version (1.2.1) supports the Siemens S25 and the Ericsson 888 via infrared without the need for a cable.

iKnapsack

Developer: Foundation Systems
Cost: $19.95 (shareware)
Footprint: 31K

Those who regularly connect using their Palm Organizer should check out iKnapsack (see Figure 16-24). This unique application uses plug-ins to enable you to move Internet content such as addresses and dates directly to your handheld. Palm VII owners will also find that the application includes support for Web clippings.

Figure 16-24: IKnapsack

Setup

The hardest part of telecommunications with the Palm (or any other OS for that matter) is set up. This section looks at the settings you need to configure to connect your Palm Organizer/modem combination to the Internet for both e-mail and browsing purposes.

Palm modem preferences

This is where you tell your handheld what type of modem you are using to connect with. Figure 16-25 shows the settings for my Palm V modem.

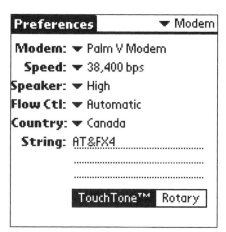

Figure 16-25: Modem preferences

✦ **Modem:** Select (or add) your modem type.

✦ **Speed:** This number should be set to a number at or higher than the actual rated speed of your modem. If you are not sure, don't worry; just select the highest speed, and the modem will "kick down," matching the correct speed when a connection is made.

✦ **Speaker:** This is where you can specify whether or not you want to hear your modem connecting—I leave mine set to "high" (which really isn't that loud). The sound gives an audible clue about your connection, and it ends once the connection is made.

✦ **Flow Ctr:** Flow control is the means by which your modem "talks" to the connection at the other end.

✦ **Country:** Select your country from the pop-up list.

✦ **String:** This line of text is an initialization string that configures your modem; consult your manual for details on the correction string for your device.

This screen also enables you to select TouchTone or Rotary dialing; this depends on your phone service (almost all use TouchTone).

New Feature

Palm OS 3.3 replaced the Modem Preferences screen with a new Connection screen (see Figure 16-26). To add a new device, tap New to open the Edit screen. Name your device (probably a modem), select Connection, Dialing, and Volume, and then tap Details to set the Speed, Flow Control, and Initialization String.

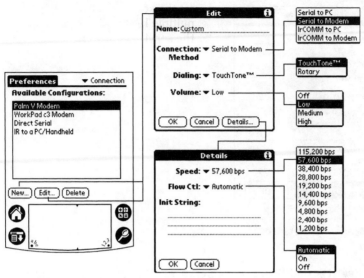

Figure 16-26: Adding a new modem under OS 3.3

Connection settings

Setup is the hardest part of connecting any computer, including Palm Organizers. This section runs through the setup process step by step. The first thing you'll need is a means of connecting your handheld to the outside world, which is usually a modem, although some cellular telephones can act as a modem (see the "How to Connect" section later in this chapter for details). The next requirement is a dial-up connection of some kind — this will usually be an ISP.

Note Those of us lucky enough to have a high-speed connection, either via cable modem or DSL connection, will discover that the fast connection may come with a caveat: there may be no means of connecting via telephone line. Those with a xDSL (Digital Subscriber Line) connection through their telephone company may find they have a dial-up line for remote connections. If not, the solution is to pay a service provider for a dial-up connection. The good news is that you shouldn't need a lot of connection time: The most effective use of your Palm's modem is a quick connect and get (information).

Network preferences

The first thing to do for both e-mail and Web browsing is to tell your Palm Organizer how to connect by configuring TCP/IP (Transmission Control Protocol/Internet Protocol). Let's start by opening your Palm Organizer's Preferences screen and selecting Network from the menu in the upper right-hand corner.

1. Tap the Menu icon, and select New to get the screen shown in Figure 16-27. You can use this method to configure multiple Internet access accounts. Overwrite "Untitled" with the name of the service you wish to configure.

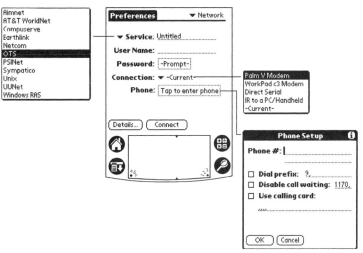

Figure 16-27: Network preferences

Note   The menu shown in Figure 16-27 includes two additions I have made for dial-up accounts: Online Technical Systems (OTS) and Bell Sympatico.

2. Enter your username as provided by your service provider.

3. Tap the Prompt box to enter your password as provided by your service provider. If you don't enter your password here, you'll need to do so manually every time you connect.

4. Select your connection type from the pop-up list (see the "Palm Modem Preferences" section earlier in this chapter if your connection method isn't listed).

5. Tap to open the Phone Setup dialog box, and then enter the telephone number you will be using to access your dial-up account. This dialog box also lets you specify a dial prefix (common in many offices and hotels; I use 8 to reach an outside line at my office), disable call waiting (many services use 1170; if this doesn't work for you, check with your telephone company), and enter calling card information.

Tip   When setting up numbers for your modem, commas are used to indicate a brief pause. If your telephone system needs more time to connect, just add another comma or two.

6. After you've finished here, tap Details (see Figure 16-28) to set up your TCP/IP connection.

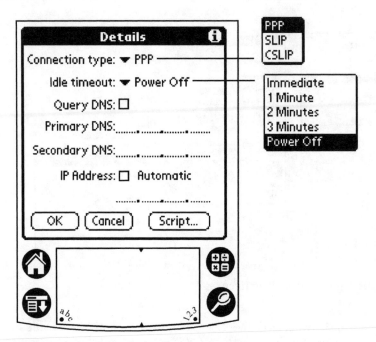

Figure 16-28: Network details

7. Select your provider's TCP/IP protocol (most use **PPP** — Point-to-Point Protocol).

8. The **Idle timeout** is the time before your handheld will disconnect from the host. Unless you are advised otherwise, select Power Off.

9. In most cases, you'll be able to check off **Query DNS**, but if you must enter Domain Named Server addresses, this is the place to do so.

10. Unless your provider provides a fixed IP address (most assign IP addresses on connection), place a check next to **Automatic**.

11. Most Internet service providers provide autologin, but there may still be some that require you to manually enter your information. If so, tap the Script button to prepare a login script.

If you do need to write a login script, you'll either need to contact your service provider for an example, or log on manually with your computer using a terminal package so that you can determine the exact steps required. Once you know what you need, the process is simple. In the example shown in the following steps, I've built a sample script to respond with your username and password—in each case the left-hand selection is made from the pop-up list provided:

1. Select Wait For Prompt, and then type the last four or five characters of the login query. In the example, I've used the last four characters of "username."

2. Select Send User ID—the software sends your user ID as entered in the main Network preferences screen (Figure 16-29).

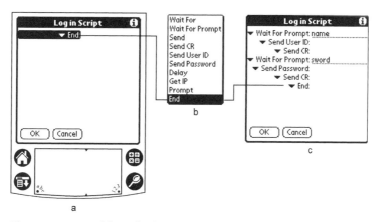

Figure 16-29: Writing a login script

3. Select Send CR to tell the software to send a carriage return.

4. Select Wait For Prompt, and then type the last four or five characters of the login query. In the example, I've used the last five characters of "password."

5. Select Send Password—the software sends your password as entered in the main Network preferences screen (Figure 16-29).

6. Select Send CR to tell the software to send a carriage return.

7. Select End to tell the software you've finished.

Mail setup

If you want to set up your Palm Organizer to send and receive e-mail, you'll also have to set up your mailbox (in most cases POP3) and your outgoing mail (SMTP) preferences. You'll find definitions of these and other terms in the Glossary found in Appendix B; your ISP should provide you with the information that you need to complete these fields.

POP3 preferences

This is where you tell the software about your incoming (POP3) mailbox. The terminology used and the means to get there are slightly different for each application, but the information itself remains the same:

1. The electronic address of your POP3 server—this can be a numeric IP address (111.222.333.4) or a name such as pop3.hostname.com.

2. The name of your POP3 account—this is usually your_name or your.name (without the @ sign).

3. The password for your e-mail account.

4. Some of these applications give you the option to "Leave mail on server"; this enables you to select whether or not e-mail you have read and deleted will be available on your computer when you connect.

Tip   No matter which of your e-mail accounts you use to connect with, you should be able to enter mailbox information for your other (Internet) e-mail accounts. This enables you to check your regular home and other e-mails using a dialup account.

HandMail

Select POP3 from the Setup Menu, and then enter your information:

1. Server

2. Mailbox

3. Password

4. Leave mail on server (checkbox)

The More button enables you to tell the software to use authentication (APOP) and to specify a TCP Port (the default is 110). Normally, these can remain at the default settings. HandMail enables you to configure up to five e-mail accounts.

MultiMail

The first time you configure MultiMail, a Wizard steps you through the process. You can rerun this Wizard at any time by selecting Setup Wizard from the Options Menu. If you just need to set up an e-mail account, select Server from the Options Menu.

1. Server

2. Username

3. Password

4. Tap More to access Advanced Settings, and then check off Leave mail on server

MultiMail enables you to configure up to eight separate e-mail accounts; each can be titled as you like, and each can be POP, IMAP, or NNTP accounts.

One-Touch Mail
Select SMTP/POP3 from the Setup menu, and then tap the POP3 button (at the top of the screen) to flip to that screen.

1. POP3 Server

2. Mail server user name

3. Password

4. Leave mail on server (checkbox)

One-Touch Mail enables you to configure up to six mailboxes.

pdQ Eudora
The first time you run Eudora, select Getting Started from the Options menu to perform the essential setup. To configure additional accounts, select Mail Checking from the Options menu, and then add your information:

1. Incoming Server (POP)

2. Username

3. Once you have done the preceding two steps, select Change Password from the Mail menu to set your e-mail password.

4. Eudora leaves mail on the server by default; tapping More Prefs enables you to specify the circumstances under which messages should be deleted from the server.

ProxiMail
On the main screen, tap Preferences, and then tap the POP Prefs button.

1. POP Server

2. Username

3. Password

4. Select Delete from server if you want e-mail to be deleted from the server after you have downloaded it to your handheld.

ProxiMail enables you to configure up to five e-mail accounts, each of which can be uniquely named. The POP Preferences screen also enables you to specify authentication (APOP) if required.

Top Gun Postman

Select POP Prefs from the Options menu, and then enter your information:

1. POP Server

2. Username

3. Password

4. Select Delete from server if you want e-mail to be deleted from the server after you have downloaded it to your handheld.

Top Gun Postman enables you to configure one e-mail account. The POP Preferences screen also enables you to specify authentication (APOP) if required.

SMTP preferences

This is where you tell the software about your outgoing (SMTP) mailbox. The terminology used and the means to get there are slightly different for each application, but the information itself remains the same:

1. The electronic address of your SMTP server—this can be a numeric IP address (111.222.333.4) or a name such as smtp.hostname.com.

2. Your e-mail address, such as your.name@hostname.com.

3. Some applications enable you to include your real name (for example, Your Name).

Tip   While you can pick up most e-mail using a dialup account, most ISPs do not let you send e-mail from another dialup account. This means that if you are responding to e-mail picked up remotely, you'll need to remember to respond to it using your dialup account.

HandMail

Select SMTP from the Setup menu, and then enter your information:

1. Server

2. E-mail

3. Name

Tapping More enables you to specify the signature information to be added to your responses, and which TCP Port to use (the default is 25). You can set up your signature block information by selecting Signatures from the Setup menu. Select the Default account checkbox if this is the account you wish to normally send e-mail from.

MultiMail

The first time you configure MultiMail, a Wizard steps you through the process. You can rerun this Wizard at any time by selecting Setup Wizard from the Options Menu. If you just need to set up an e-mail account, select Server from the Options Menu and tap the SMTP button.

1. Server

2. E-mail

3. Name

Tapping the Signature button enables you to set up your signature block.

One-Touch Mail

Select SMTP/POP3 from the Setup menu; SMTP should be selected at the top of the screen.

1. SMTP Server Address

2. E-mail Address

3. Your name

Select the Default account checkbox if this is the account you wish to normally send e-mail from.

pdQ Eudora

The first time you run Eudora, select Getting Started from the Options menu to perform the essential setup. To configure additional accounts, select Mail Sending from the Options menu and then add your information:

1. Outgoing Server (SMTP)

2. Return Address (optional)

3. Real Name

Tapping More Prefs enables you to set up your signature block and to specify an automatic blind carbon copy, which you can use to copy e-mails to your home account.

ProxiMail

On the main screen, tap Preferences and then tap the SMTP Prefs button:

1. SMTP server

2. Your e-mail address

3. Your name

Top Gun Postman

Select SMTP Prefs from the Options menu and then enter your information:

1. SMTP server

2. Your e-mail address

3. Your name

How to Connect

So far, we've discussed the types of communication that you can do with your Palm Organizer (e-mail, browsing, faxing, and paging), and how to set up and configure your handheld to communicate. The only thing left to discuss is the means of connecting to the outside world. Your connection will usually involve a modem of some kind, which can be connected to the Internet either by telephone line or by wireless.

Devices

A modem of some kind can be an invaluable tool for Palm users who travel. In addition to the connectivity options covered in this chapter, Palm provides the required software to HotSync your handheld using a modem. As this book goes to press, Novatel has started testing its OmniSky Minstrel V Modem. For more information, check out its Web site at www.omnisky.com.

Global Pulse

Developer: MyPilot
Cost: $129.00 ($169.00 bundled with HandMail and HandWeb)

If you have a Nokia 5000 or 6000 series GSM cellular telephone, there is an alternative to attaching a modem—the Global Pulse. This is basically a cable that attaches your Palm III or Palm V series Organizer to your cell phone, which can act as a 9600bps modem, providing you have data-enabled service.

Option SnapOn modem adapter

Developer: Option International
Cost: $119.00

The Option SnapOn modem (see Figure 16-30) looks identical to the standard Palm modem (as well it should; they share the same case). There is, however, one significant difference: the SnapOn Modem enables you to connect your Palm Organizer directly to a GSM cellular telephone. The SnapOn modem is available for a number of popular cellular telephones, including models from Ericsson, Nokia, and Panasonic—see www.option.com/handsets.htm for a complete listing. For those who need landline modem capabilities as well, Option also sells a line of PCMCIA 9600bps GSM/33.6bps standard modem cards that can be used with the Parachute add-on device.

Figure 16-30: SnapOn modem

Palm III modem

Developer: Palm
Cost: $129.00

The Palm III modem is a 9600-baud modem that comes in a standard case that Palm has used since PalmPilot days; it clips to the bottom of the PalmPilot, Palm III, and Palm VII series of organizers. An available A/C adapter is a worthwhile addition for those who plan to connect on a regular basis.

Palm V modem

Developer: Palm
Cost: $169.00

The Palm V Modem (see Figure 16-31) comes in a sleek case to fit under the Palm V and Vx organizers. Palm also makes a GSM adapter kit for this 33.6-baud modem. The kit (see Figure 16-32) costs $89.00, and is available for certain models of Nokia and Ericsson cellular telephones.

Figure 16-31: Palm V Modem

Figure 16-32: Palm V
Modem with GSM kit

Palm VII

Developer: Palm
Cost: $499.00

The Palm VII connects wirelessly using CDPD packets; coverage is currently limited
to the United States. See Chapter 7 for more on the Palm VII.

Synapse Pager card

Developer: Synapse
Cost: $129.95

The Synapse Pager card is an upgrade that upgrades the PalmPilot to all of the specifications (except IR support) of the Palm III: 2MB of memory and OS 3.0. A slight bulge in the back is all that indicates that this upgrade also puts a Motorola Pager in your handheld, complete with Address Book integration to identify incoming pages. A new version (see Figure 16-33) is now available for the Palm III.

Figure 16-33: Synapse Pager in a Palm III

Wireless connections

Note GSM, in general, has the most connectivity options for wireless networking. Palm.net and SkyTel have wireless networking, although connection to the Internet is always through a proxy. The TDMA network has a network upgrade projected for 2000 that will enable wireless data transmission.

Wireless connections with a Palm Organizer can be fairly straightforward if you buy a Palm VII. Some people will want to push the envelope with other devices, especially cellular connections. The first things you need to determine are availability, coverage, and costs. Does your cellular provider offer data, and does its coverage extend to where you need to connect? Equally important are the costs involved — is there a flat monthly fee or do they charge by the amount of data transmitted? These are questions you should resolve before committing to a solution.

The technologies you are most likely to run into are:

✦ **CDMA** (Code Division Multiple Access) is a wireless cellular technology that enables the carrier to split up available bandwidth and offers up to 28,800bps data transfer rates. CDMA PCS cellular telephones can act as modems, which means that a cable connection may be all that you need to communicate with your Palm Organizer.

✦ **CDPD** (Cellular Digital Packet Data) is the means of cellular communication used by the Palm VII.

✦ **GSM** (Global System for Mobile Communications) is the most widely implemented wireless protocol worldwide; it offers transfer rates up to 9600bps. This happens to be how I connect (using a Palm V modem attached to my Palm Vx with a GSM kit attached to a Nokia 5190 cellular telephone).

✦ **iDEN** (Integrated Data Enhanced Network) is a cellular technology offered by ClearNet Mike and Nextel that offers data transfer rates up to 19,200bps. There is a Palm cabling kit that enables you to connect the Motorola i1000 Plus (the cellular phone used by ClearNet Mike) directly to your handheld.

✦ **TDMA** (Time Division Multiple Access) is wireless protocol that offers up to 19,200bps access.

IR with Ericsson 888

Thanks to Lorraine Wheeler of Actual Software for providing this sidebar on her experience connecting her Palm Organizer to her Ericsson 888 cellular telephone via infrared.

Do you need to be connected with your voice mail and e-mail when you are out of the office? I just connect wirelessly using two devices that each only weigh a few ounces. All I carry is my Palm device and my cellular phone. I get lots of jealous looks at airports, especially during delays.

Here are the basic tools I need to send and receive e-mail through my cellular phone. I have an Ericsson i888 World phone, service through Omnipoint, a Palm IIIx, and Actual Software's MultiMail Pro software loaded on my Palm IIIx. With all these pieces in place, I can send and receive e-mail from anywhere. My only requirement is a flat surface because I don't have enough hands to hold the Palm device and the phone, and to tap the Receive button at the same time!

Overall, this setup is amazing. I can send and receive e-mail from anywhere. It works flawlessly in the United States and throughout Europe. The coverage in the United States is a little spotty. When using it on the train between Boston and New York City, I sporadically lose my signal. I have no problems in big cities and at airports. In Europe, it worked everywhere I went. The cost is reasonable. I pay approximately $50 for 300 minutes per month. These minutes can be voice or data. It also comes with voice mail and news services.

CDMA

Thanks to Karl Joseph of Bell Mobility for writing this sidebar on connecting his Palm Organizer to his CDMA cellular telephone.

The Palm Organizer can now be connected to CDMA digital PCS cellular phones for data connections. This is comparable to the GSM service because no modem is necessary. However, unlike the GSM offering, CDMA data services are slightly faster at 14.4kbps. The data transfer is accomplished by connecting the Pilot to the CDMA cellular phone via a serial cable and a CDMA cellular provider that offers data services over their CDMA network (you'll also need the palm HotSync cable for this; more on that later). Also, data over CDMA, like the GSM data services, cannot function unless you are in your cellular provider's digital coverage area. Please note there may be additional charges for data connections over your cellular network as well. My cellular carrier charges a flat 15 cents a minute for data connections.

With that in mind, here's what's needed: a Palm OS Handheld device using Palm OS 2.0 or higher; a CDMA cell phone such as the Nokia 6185, the Qualcomm QCP-2700, or the Qualcomm QCP-2700F (the Nokia 6185 was used in my tests); a compatible cellular provider (Bell Mobility in Ontario, Canada); the cellular-to-serial cable; and your Pilot HotSync cable. The HotSync cradle does work for this, but I feel safe in assuming that for most traveling users the HotSync cable is more convenient.

Getting started is quite simple. The cellular data cable connects to my Nokia 6185 cell phone; at the other end there is a DB9F connector. The data cable also comes with a DB9M–DB9M adapter to use when connecting the Palm HotSync cable to the data cable. Once everything is connected, the Pilot configuration is straightforward. The modem section of Preferences needs to be set to standard modem with a speed setting of 19,200bps. (Although the Pilot is being configured for 19,200bps, the actual data rate is 14,400bps.) My initialization string is set to AT&FX4; however, this setting may vary between cellular providers. The modem volume setting is irrelevant; it can be set to anything. Because this is a digital connection, the analog squelching normally associated with regular modems doesn't apply. I tested Internet access, e-mail, and faxing, and all my connections were established silently.

Continued

Continued

The Net

First, I updated the Network section of Preferences with my ISP's (Sympatico) settings and dial-up number. Logging in for the first time was somewhat tricky. My PalmPilot kept getting no response from the "modem." I had to turn my phone off and on a few times before my Pilot would recognize the modem. After the initial login, subsequent logins worked without a hitch. Now logging in is as simple as pressing Connect. My Nokia 6185 dialed into my ISP and connected.

I was able to surf with Smartcode's HandWeb after I was connected. The data rate was a cool 14.4kbps, so pages appeared within a reasonable time frame. Keeping in mind that there are both airtime charges and ISP charges when connected, casual surfing is not something I do or recommend. E-mail, on the other hand, with its connect-send-receive-disconnect usage is much more economical and feasible for this type of connection.

Smartcode's HandMail and Actual Software's MultiMail Pro sent and received mail without a hitch. (MultiMail 3.0 requires Palm OS 3.*x* or higher.)

A few logistical problems to consider when accessing the Internet for e-mail or surfing with your Pilot and CDMA phone. My ISP assigns me a "local" dialup number to use for connecting. Local calling areas for cell phones differ from that of landlines, so it may be necessary to add area codes, get new access numbers and, in some cases, even dial long distance. Fortunately, my cellular carrier and ISP already thought of a solution to this problem. Instead of using a seven-digit access number to dial for Internet access, I have been assigned a five-digit access number (pound symbol plus four digits), which is only available from my cell phone. The result is local calling into my ISP regardless of where I am. This type of service requires your ISP and cellular carrier to work together.

Just the fax

For faxing, I tested Smartcode's HandFax and the newer entrant, Symantec's Mobile Winfax. I did have some problems with Mobile Winfax. It failed to send faxes because it could not initialize the "modem" properly. Mobile Winfax has its own modem configuration that apparently is incompatible with my CDMA phone. (Any Pilot program that doesn't use the built-in modem section of preferences to dial in may not work with the CDMA connection.) Smartcode's Handfax does use the built-in modem properties, and it worked without a hitch.

Sending and receiving faxes does have a few considerations though. I wouldn't recommend sending or receiving more than a five-page fax at a time. As with Internet access, sending faxes also incurs airtime charges. Even worse, although the maximum data rate for CDMA faxes is 14.4kbps, the actual transmission/reception speed of the fax is determined by the capabilities of the fax machine on the other end. There are lots of 9600bps fax machines out there and even a few 2400bps.

Overall

After a connection is established, most Pilot programs operate as if you were connected to a landline using a regular modem. I did determine during my tests that prolonged CDMA data use for either faxing or Internet access did run down the battery on both my Pilot and my cell phone. The battery life was reduced by approximately one quarter on both devices. However, the capability to get e-mail anywhere is most useful and outweighs the slight battery drain.

Summary

✦ Your Palm Organizer has the capability to HotSync your office e-mail to your handheld, which can be a powerful tool when you're away from your network machine.

✦ The e-mail programs available for the Palm platform offer a range of features and prices — choose MultiMail Discovery, ProxiMail, or Top Gun Postman for the basics; look to the commercial packages for additional features and functionality.

✦ Most users will find that connectivity costs and speeds make most Internet browsing impractical on their Palm Organizer; I chose AvantGo to grab the news I need.

✦ Road warriors with a Palm modem should not overlook the print functionality offered by fax software.

✦ Wireless connectivity is a reality for the Palm platform, but you first need to ensure that your cellular provider has enabled data. This is one area where careful comparison shopping is worthwhile to ensure that your chosen solution works best for you.

✦   ✦   ✦

Drawing and Listening with Your Palm

◆ ◆ ◆ ◆

In This Chapter

Art in your Palm

Graphics utilities

Making music

Palm instruments

◆ ◆ ◆ ◆

The Palm Organizer as a multimedia machine? You've got to be kidding—I need my speakers, my big screen, and my fast connection. Then again, there are tools that let you create artwork and music on your handheld. In this chapter, I take a quick look at a few of these tools, along with utilities that support them.

Graphics

You'd think there was an attachment to add a Wacom tablet to the Palm, given the number of drawing programs available for our favorite handheld. I'll end the suspense right now: If you need a paint program for your Palm Organizer, TealPaint remains the best of its class. Still, there are freeware alternatives and shareware programs with specialized functions you may need or want, so read on.

Art in your Palm

I have to admit I didn't buy my Palm Organizer to use it as a drawing tablet, but don't tell these programmers that you can't draw on a six-ounce pad. Table 17-1 compares several of the available drawing programs.

	Table 17-1 **Palm Art**						
Application	**Price**	**Size**	**Format**	**Shapes**	**Fills**	**Pens**	**Viewer**
DiddleBug	free	41K	paint	4	8	7	n/a
DinkyPad	$5.00	20K	paint	2	n/a	5	Win
PalmDraw	$10.00	40K	draw	4	n/a	1	Win
PenDraw	$15.00	11K	draw	4	8	7	n/a
Q Draw	free	27K	draw	4	7	3	Mac
Q Paint	free	17K	paint	4	7	3	Mac
Simple Sketch	beta	37K	paint	4	2	7	n/a
TealPaint	$17.95	45K	paint	5	15	12	Win/Mac

Note   Most of these programs are pixel-based (on the computer sometimes referred to as bitmapped) painting programs — images are created and edited by turning on and off individual pixels. A few of these programs are vector-based drawing programs, which enable resizing or moving of elements after they have been placed.

None of these programs includes a true two-way conduit, but some do offer viewers that enable you to export your artwork to your desktop computer.

DiddleBug

DiddleBug (see Figure 17-1) is a paint program developed by Mitch Blevins. It includes a countdown timer with alarm, smoothing capabilities, and the capability to export to your Palm Organizer's built-in applications or a variety of third-party applications.

Figure 17-1: DiddleBug

Dinky Pad

I believe Dinky Pad from Daggerware was the first paint program for the Palm Organizer. It offers multiple width pens, an eraser, simple rectangle and square shapes, and a virtual canvas up to 2040 pixels high that can be accessed using your handheld's scroll buttons (see Figure 17-2).

PalmDraw

Brad Goodman's PalmDraw (see Figure 17-3) is a sophisticated drawing program for the Palm Organizer. It supports text, basic shapes, lines, and Bézier curves; it includes grid and zoom capabilities; and it can export PostScript files and print to a serial printer!

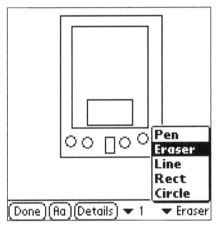

Figure 17-2: Dinky Pad   **Figure 17-3:** PalmDraw

PenDraw

Patrick Dublanchet developed PenDraw (see Figure 17-4). It is a fairly complete drawing application for your Palm Organizer and, like TealPaint, it includes an undo feature.

Q Draw and Q Paint

This pair of freeware applications from Quantom World offers both drawing and paint functionality, complete with the capability to cut and paste between the two. You can also export your work to your Mac. Figure 17-5 shows the drawing program, and Figure 17-6 shows the painting program.

Figure 17-4: PenDraw

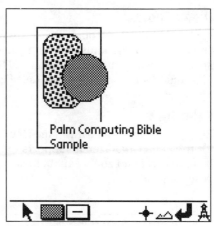

Figure 17-5: Q Draw

Figure 17-6: Q Paint

SimpleSketch

Synergy Solutions' SimpleSketch (Figure 17-7) is a tool for creating and storing quick pictures on your handheld. In addition to the usual tools, it supports text in three sizes and has the capability to beam your masterpieces.

TealPaint

TealPoint Software doesn't do anything halfway, and TealPaint (Figure 17-8) is no exception. This solid paint program offers a full slate of tools, including fills and patterns, support for animation, an undo feature, and more. It is easily the best of the field, and I certainly recommend it.

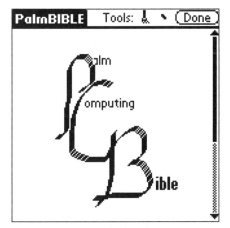

Figure 17-7: SimpleSketch

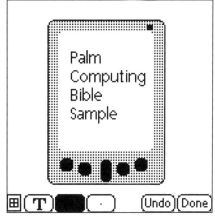

Figure 17-8: TealPaint

Graphics viewers

These programs provide the capability to view grayscale images on your handheld, which means that you can display some fairly good images. This opens up a whole new world, especially if you have a scanner. With a graphic viewer, you can load in your organizer route maps, family and other photos, logos, hint sheets, and all sorts of information that can be better presented graphically. Surprisingly, even graphics with 16 shades of gray can be as small as 16K when converted into Palm's .pdb format, so space is not the issue you might expect it to be.

AlbumToGo

Developer: ClubPhoto
Cost: Freeware
Footprint: 48K (plus images loaded)

AlbumToGo is an impressive utility, and it is freeware! AlbumToGo is available in both Windows and Macintosh flavors. Both offer the capability to convert JPG images into Palm-loadable format (see Figure 17-9). These files can be opened, annotated, beamed, or deleted within the Palm application.

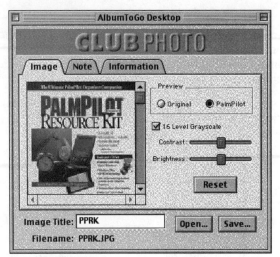

Figure 17-9: Convert your JPG file using the desktop application . . .

The real gem is the viewer shown in Figure 17-10. It is a slideshow application, complete with screen transition effects.

 New Feature   A new color version of AlbumToGo is bundled with the Palm IIIc.

Figure 17-10: . . . and then view it on your Palm Organizer.

Image Viewer III

Developer: Art Dahm
Cost: $12.95 (shareware)
Footprint: 49K (plus loaded images)

Image Viewer III (Figure 17-11) enables you to view grayscale images on your Pilot. An Image Converter utility enables Windows users to convert images from a variety of formats into HotSyncable .pdb files. What do you get for your money? A polished application with a virtual scrolling screen that enables you to store images larger than your handheld's 160 × 160 pixel screen.

You also get support for beaming and the capability to view 16 shades of gray (see Figure 17-12) on every Palm Organizer since the Palm III.

Figure 17-11: Manhattan subways viewed using Image Viewer III

Figure 17-12: Image Viewer III showing 16 shades of gray

Note

I know it is not a word, but let's add *HotSyncable* to the Palm users' jargon — and define it as a file that can be loaded on your handheld with a HotSync.

PhotoAlbum

Developer: OBE Systems
Cost: Freeware
Footprint: 34K (plus images loaded)

Like AlbumToGo, PhotoAlbum is a viewer that enables you to display grayscale images on your Palm Organizer. A Windows application enables you to convert .bmp images into "albums" that can be read on your Palm Organizer (see Figure 17-13).

Spec

Developer: Joseph Strout
Cost: Freeware
Footprint: 10K (plus images loaded)

Spec (Figure 17-14) is a freeware grayscale viewer for your Palm Organizer. It enables you to view a single Image Viewer graphic (maximum of eight shades of gray) on your handheld.

Figure 17-13: OBE Systems' PhotoAlbum

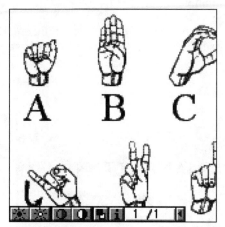

Figure 17-14: Using Spec to view an Image Viewer document

Converting images

Now that you're convinced that you want to load pictures in your handheld, where do you start?

✦ **AlbumToGo:** This one is easy, just open your JPG images in AlbumToGo's desktop application and save them as .pdb files. If your files are in another format, use a paint program or conversion utility to save copies in JPG format.

✦ **Image Converter III:** This utility, the companion to Image Viewer III (above), can convert GIF, JPG, PCX, DIB, RLE, and TGA graphics files to Image Viewer format.

✦ **Graphics Converter:** Macintosh users have it easy. Graphics Converter (at $35, one of the great buys in shareware) can open almost every graphic format known, and it can save files in .pdb format. Check out LemkeSoft's Web site at www.lemkesoft.de for more information.

Graphics utilities

These utilities, more than anything else, show off the graphics capabilities of the Palm Organizer.

BackDropEZ

Developer: Twilight Edge Software
Cost: $18.00
Footprint: 56K (varies with images loaded)

Do you have a green background on your computer or a picture loaded on your desktop? BackDropEZ is perfect for those who live to customize. BackDropEZ (Figure 17-15) enables you to have a 4-bit (eight shades of gray) grayscale image as a backdrop on every screen. To do its magic, BackDropEZ requires that you install and use its $5.00 shareware utility, TrapWeaver.

Figure 17-15: BackDropEZ

Tip Remember to save your images at sizes equal to or greater than your Palm Organizer's 160 × 160 pixel screen. Otherwise, they won't display or load in BackDropEZ.

EtchASketch

Developer: Glenn Abisia
Cost: $1
Footprint: 3K

Remember the Etch-A-Sketch drawing pad that had two knobs to control your pen while drawing? The Palm version is virtually identical (see Figure 17-16), with one minor flaw: The Erase command (in the menu) should be named Shake.

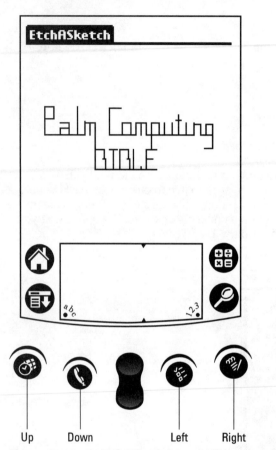

Up   Down   Left   Right

Figure 17-16: An EtchASketch for your Palm Organizer

IcoEdit

Developer: MapleTop Software
Cost: $10.00
Footprint: 28K

Bored by the icons on your handheld? Wish you could create your own custom
icons? This powerful icon editor (Figure 17-17) runs on your Palm Organizer,
enabling you to customize your applications' icons (don't worry, the defaults can
easily be restored), create icons for DateBk3, create small icons for applications
that don't have them, and rearrange the display of icons in the Application
Launcher. IcoEdit also has a number of utility functions, including the capability
to export a list of all of your installed applications to your Memo Pad.

PalmFractals

Developer: Rainer Persicke
Cost: Freeware
Footprint: 66K (requires MathLib, which has 54K footprint)

Fractals are complex mathematical creations that can result in very psychedelic-looking (1960s flashback) graphics. Given how long these types of calculations took on high-end computers just a few years ago it's amazing that this freeware application duplicates the feat on the Palm OS (see Figure 17-18).

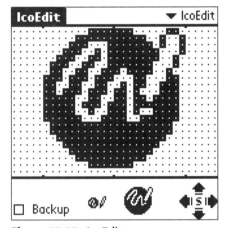

Figure 17-17: IcoEdit   **Figure 17-18:** PalmFract

PalmSmear

Developer: Mark Chao-Kuang Yang
Cost: Freeware
Footprint: 175K (with one image loaded)

Kai Krause's Goo was an amazing application — a consumer-level graphics program that let you contort your friend's faces on a computer with a simple click and drag, and then create animations using your creations. I see from an old e-mail address that Mark worked for MetaCreations at one time. I'm sure that's what inspired PalmSmear — this amazing application does the same thing on the Palm OS (see Figure 17-19). Mark also includes PalmSmearDroplet, a program that lets you create PalmSmear images of your friends' faces. If this doesn't show off the graphic capabilities of our favorite toy, nothing does!

Figure 17-19: PalmSmear

Music

Palm devices don't have speakers — they use a tiny crystal to make sound. But this hasn't stopped determined programmers from adding capabilties we didn't know we needed.

Palm instruments

These applications turn your Palm Organizer into a miniature musical instrument when the real thing isn't available. Table 17-2 compares several of these programs.

Table 17-2 Palm Instruments					
Program	*Price*	*Size*	*Notation*	*Range*	*Recording*
EbonyIvory	free	4K	no	1.5 octaves	yes
MiniMusic	$29.95	19K	no	5 octaves	no
PalmPiano	$5.00	7K	yes	4 octaves	no
PocketPiano	free	51K	yes	4 octaves	no
PocketSynth	$10.00	16K	yes	4 octaves	no

EbonyIvory

EbonyIvory, developed by Tony Leung (Figure 17-20), is a simple freeware program that enables you to play tunes by tapping a piano keyboard. The corresponding notes are displayed in music notation.

miniMusic NotePad

miniMusic NotePad (Figure 17-21) is the most useful of the Palm musical instruments and has the largest range. It is comprised of three applications: miniGrid, which can be used to write melodies using a grid for those uncomfortable with written music; miniPiano, which transcribes notes into music notation; and miniScore, a music-scoring application that lets you write music using your Palm Organizer. Features include support for bass and treble clefs (although with a single voice, only one can be used at a time), key signatures, and tempo. The release version adds support for up to four voices, a song database, enhanced editing, and a desktop conduit.

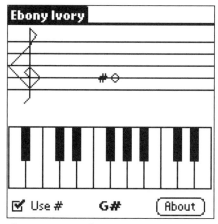

Figure 17-20: EbonyIvory

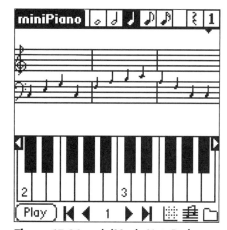

Figure 17-21: miniMusic NotePad

Palm Piano

Palm Piano (Figure 17-22), developed by Thomas Jawer, is a simple recording tool for keyboard players; just tap the notes to create a song.

Pocket Piano

Barry Christian's freeware Pocket Piano—soon to be renamed PalmAria—is a piano-based music recorder that runs under PocketC (Figure 17-23). To use it, first tap the PocketC icon in the Launcher, and then tap Pocket Piano in the list that displays.

Figure 17-22: PalmPiano

Figure 17-23: Pocket Piano

PocketSynth

Eric Cheng developed PocketSynth (Figure 17-24). It was one of the first music recorders available for the Palm Organizer. It features a pocket keyboard and metronome, and allows notes from different octaves, with varying duration and tempo.

Figure 17-24: PocketSynth

Musical tools

This section groups musical tools and teaching tools. I begin with Busker, which is a lot of fun.

Busker

Developer: Iain Barclay
Cost: $7.95
Footprint: 16K

Busker (Figure 17-25) enables you to use your handheld as a controller for WinAmp, which plays music on your PC. It utilizes your Palm Organizer's serial connection to pass data to your computer, effectively giving you a connected remote control for WinAmp. Even better, Busker supports infrared, which can turn your Busker-equipped handheld into a true remote!

FretBoard

Developer: Dave MacLeod
Cost: Freeware
Footprint: 13K

As a guitar player, here's one I can appreciate. FretBoard (Figure 17-26) displays chords and scales for a wide variety of stringed instruments in both standard and open tunings.

Figure 17-25: Busker

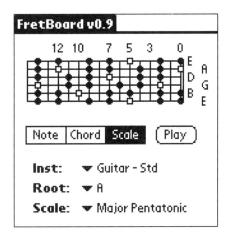

Figure 17-26: FretBoard

McChords

Developer: Michael McCollister
Cost: Freeware
Footprint: 6K

Keyboard players need not feel left out — McChords (Figure 17-27) displays chords and scales in different keys. Just tap the interval you need and your Palm Organizer turns into a musical cheat sheet.

PalmChord

Developer: Rick Eesley
Cost: $12.00
Footprint: 23K

PalmChord (Figure 17-28) is a powerful utility for displaying guitar chords, and it supports multiple tunings. Tap in the chord that you want, and PalmChord calculates the possible fingerings using factors such as finger span, root as bass note, and number of open strings. After PalmChord has calculated your chord variants, tap one in the listing to see it displayed on the FretBoard, or tap Play to hear it.

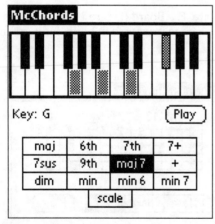

Figure 17-27: McChords

Figure 17-28: PalmChord

Pocket Beat

Developer: Gary Duke
Cost: $12.00
Footprint: 108K (includes PocketC Runtime and MathLib)

Pocket Beat (Figure 17-29) offers a limited version of a beat machine in your handheld, with synthesized snare, kick, and hi-hat sounds. To be honest, I could only distinguish two sounds on my Palm V, neither of which sounded anything like a drum. Still, the application may be worthwhile as a practice aid, to help with timing.

Responsive Metronome

Developer: Responsive Software
Cost: $8.00 (shareware)
Footprint: 5K

A decent metronome is expensive, so why not turn your Palm Organizer into one? This is exactly what Responsive Metronome (Figure 17-30) does for you. The authors have a sense of humor: Tempo can be set using the scroll buttons anywhere from MuchaTooSlowsimo (25 beats per minute) to MuchaTooFasto (300 beats per minute), with normal tempos between the two. Responsive Metronome requires Palm OS 2 or better.

Figure 17-29: Pocket Beat

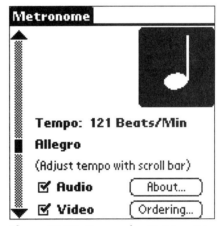

Figure 17-30: Responsive Metronome

Tempo

Developer: Storm Comunicazione & Tecnologia
Cost: $10.00
Footprint: 9K

Tempo (Figure 17-31) is another digital metronome — it uses a familiar graphic to display tempos anywhere from Largo (40 beats per minute) to Prestissimo (240 beats per minute). Unique features include the capability to have accents and to measure tempo real-time by pressing a button.

Tuning Fork

Developer: Arcosoft Inc.
Cost: $10.00 (shareware)
Footprint: 6K

Here's another great tool for musicians: Tuning Fork (Figure 17-32) turns your Palm Organizer into a configurable tone generator, enabling you to simulate a real tuning fork. I've always used a tuning fork on the top of my guitar (a 1972 Guild D40, if anyone is curious) so that the guitar can amplify the sound. Somehow, it just isn't the same with my Palm V.

Figure 17-31: Tempo   Figure 17-32: Tuning Fork

Summary

✦ If you want to draw on your Palm Organizer, the best tool currently available is TealPaint.

✦ All sorts of practical applications for tools enable you to view graphics on your handheld — the two best available are the freeware AlbumToGo, and Art Dahm's shareware Image Viewer.

✦ Customizing your Palm? With BackDropEZ and IcoEdit you can create your own unique look.

✦ If you can spare 175K, nothing does a better job of showing off the power of your Palm Organizer than Mark Chao-Kuang Yang's PalmSmear.

✦ Only one music-plating tool stands out as one that a musician may want to use on his or her handheld: miniMusic NotePad.

✦ FretBoard, McChord, and PalmChord all offer musicians a chance to brush up on their scales and chords.

✦ Responsive Metronome and Tempo both provide good alternatives to the traditional metronome.

✦   ✦   ✦

Adding Toys to Your Palm

C H A P T E R

18

◆ ◆ ◆ ◆

In This Chapter

Palm's games

Adventure games

Arcade games

Board games

Card games

Diversions

Word games

Game utilities

◆ ◆ ◆ ◆

The *Palm OS Bible*'s purpose is to provide solutions and to inspire advanced users to build and use the tools that are available for their Palm Organizers. This chapter is a bit different in that it doesn't offer any solutions, but it is a lot of fun. This chapter looks at games for the Palm Organizer.

Game programmers tend to push the envelope more than others do. If there is a programming trick or call that a game programmer can use to tweak an extra ounce of performance for their game, you can bet it will be used. Some of these programming tricks are not recommended by Palm, Inc., and some result in software that may not work on newer versions of the Palm OS. Good examples are the games up first in this chapter — they don't run on Organizers running OS 3.1 or newer. Many of these games have been updated with color versions for the new Palm IIIc.

Palm's Games

When Palm first started shipping the PalmPilot, a few games were included that are based on old favorites. These are all still available at Palm's Web site: www.palm.com/downloads/gameslic.html.

Caution   These games do not work on Palm Organizers that use OS 3.1 or newer (Palm IIIx, V, or VII).

Hardball

Developer: Palm
URL: www.palm.com
Footprint: 18K

Hardball is a simple arcade game based on the arcade game Bricks. In this version (shown in Figure 18-1), you play against your Palm Organizer to clear a wall of bricks using the scroll up button to start a ball moving, and then using the hardware buttons to move a paddle left and right to keep the ball in play.

Mine Hunt

Developer: Palm
URL: www.palm.com
Footprint: 9K

Figure 18-2 is a view of a Palm-sized version of the classic Minesweeper game. You tap to uncover squares to discover where the mines are hidden. Tapping a clear box displays that box and all adjacent boxes, but if you tap a mine, the game is over. After you've cleared a box, it displays how many mines are hidden in all directions from that box. This enables you to deduce where the mines should be hidden; you tag them by pressing the scroll up or down key while tapping the box. There are four difficulty levels, with each level increasing the number of mines hidden on the screen.

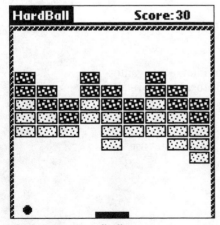

Figure 18-1: Hardball   **Figure 18-2:** Mine Hunt

Puzzle

Developer: Palm
URL: www.palm.com
Footprint: 4K

Remember the little plastic puzzles where you shifted blocks around until you had them arranged in order? Well, this game enables you to turn your expensive Organizer into the electronic equivalent of a 50-cent toy (see Figure 18-3). Tap a square to move it to the empty space; repeat until you're finished or bored.

SubHunt

Developer: Palm
URL: www.palm.com
Footprint: 18K

In this simple arcade game (shown in Figure 18-4), you use the Date Book and Memo Pad buttons to move your ship left and right, and the Address Book and To Do List buttons to drop depth charges to hit submarines that pass underneath you. But watch out — on the higher levels some submarines fire back.

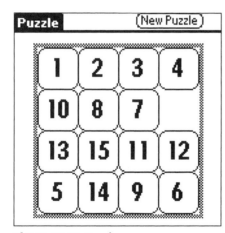

Figure 18-3: Puzzle

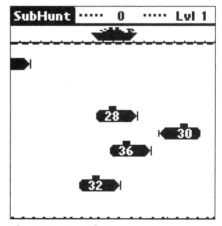

Figure 18-4: SubHunt

Adventure Games

To be perfectly honest, this is a game genre I never thought I'd see on the Palm platform. These developers have stretched the bounds of what you would think the Palm Organizer can do, some tapping the grayscale capabilities and creating their own rules. Not all of these games run on the latest operating system (3.5), but they are, nevertheless, amazing.

Dark Haven

Developer: Gasdorf Software
Cost: $24.95
Footprint: 370K

Don't let the first glance fool you — the simple overhead graphics shown in Figure 18-5 sit atop a serious adventure game. You start by creating your character, which you train and mold into a hero that can conquer this huge game. Play as good or evil, as warrior, sorcerer, cleric, or thief — the choice is yours. The unregistered version enables you access to the Arena area to try your hand at training a hero; registration unlocks the rest of the game.

Dragon Bane

Developer: Palm Creations
Cost: $24.95
Footprint: 211K

Dragon Bane does something others have not done on the Palm Organizer: It provides a first-person view — you play the game as though you are looking through your hero's eyes. As Figure 18-6 shows, the game accomplishes this by using grayscale images. Dragon Bane features 20 levels of traps and puzzles, over 30 spells, and 40 different monsters to vanquish. Auto-mapping and multiple game saves help make the game more manageable. The unregistered demo enables you to play the first three levels; registering lets you continue your quest.

Dungeoneers

Developer: Andrew Brault
Cost: $15.00 (shareware)
Footprint: 94K

Dungeoneers is another unique adventure game for the Palm Organizer: it takes the top-down view, adds great grayscale graphics (see Figure 18-7), and uses spaceships in a randomly generated dungeon. This well-crafted game is a lot of fun; I plan to spend a bit more time with it after I've finished writing the *Palm OS Bible*. Registration enables you to progress past the third level of the dungeon.

Kyle's Quest

Developer: Kyle Poole
Cost: $15.00 (shareware)
Footprint: 137K (with Bone's Quest loaded)

Kyle's Quest is the original adventure game for the Palm platform. This game offers the top-down black and white view of the world pictured in Figure 18-8 for your hero to explore. A Level Editor permits additional quests; 20 are available as of this writing, with more on the way.

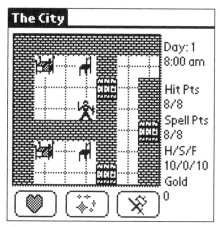

Figure 18-5: Dark Haven's opening screen

Figure 18-6: Dragon Bane

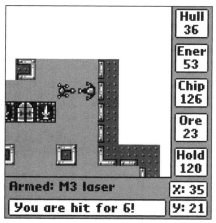

Figure 18-7: Dungeoneers

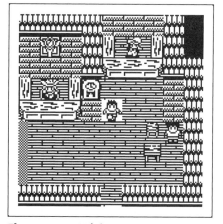

Figure 18-8: Kyle's Quest

Arcade Games

My definition of a good arcade game is simple: it requires as much dexterity as thought. These games will appeal to the action fans out there. Be forewarned: Many are addictive enough to cause serious drain of your batteries!

Anakin

Developer: Jaler Group
Cost: $5.00 (shareware)
Footprint: 36K

This game, which is based on the watch-based game Helmut, is one where you must move your character across the screen, avoiding missiles and other flying objects (see Figure 18-9). The first of the seven levels is free; to access the rest you must register the program.

Figure 18-9: Anakin

Bubblet

Developer: Frank Fejes
Cost: $10.00 (shareware)
Footprint: 21K

You can play a quick game of this simple, yet addictive, shareware game in under a minute. The object is simple: you tap to burst groups of bubbles, and the remaining bubbles drop down the screen to fill in the newly cleared spaces. The more bubbles you clear with one tap, the more points you get (see Figure 18-10). You start with two points for two bubbles; three gives that number incremented by two and added to the previous number (resulting in six), and so on. Clearing 25 bubbles at once nets 600 points! There are four modes of play: Standard, Continuous, Shifter, and Megashifter. In Continuous mode, rows are added to the left-hand side of the screen as columns are cleared. Shifter mode shifts bubbles to the right and down as others are popped. Megashifter mode combines Shifter and Continuous. Registration brings one important feature: the capability to undo moves. I registered the program the day I tried it.

Caution Let me make this perfectly clear: I have wasted more time on this game than on all the rest of the games in this chapter put together. For the record, I have played well over 13,000 games, with an average score of 215. Don't say you haven't been forewarned.

Cue*pert

Developer: Alexander Hinds
Cost: $14.95 (shareware)
Footprint: 39K

Cue*pert is a Palm-sized clone of the 1980s arcade game Q*Bert. The object is simple: tap to move your character diagonally one square at a time. As you move, the squares change color (see Figure 18-11); after all have changed, you move to the next level. You need to avoid the bad guys and grab the bonus characters to make it through 30 levels and five worlds.

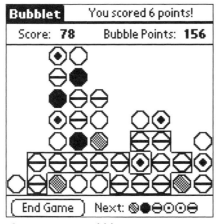

Figure 18-10: Bubblet

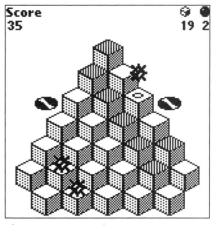

Figure 18-11: Cue*pert

Dakota

Developer: Virtual Overload
Cost: $15.00 (shareware)
Footprint: 19K

I don't remember which was the first side-scrolling platform game in the arcades, but I do know they have become popular on game boxes — Sonic for the Sega Genesis is probably the best known. Dakota, shown in Figure 18-12, brings the excitement of these great games to the 160 × 160 screen of your PalmPilot.

> **Note**   Version 1.06 of Dakota is required to run under Palm OS 3.1 or greater.

Froggy

Developer: Tim Smith
Cost: $10.00 (shareware)
Footprint: 43K

This one is impressive: It's a clone of the classic arcade game Frogger (see Figure 18-13), complete with four-color graphics and animation. The object of this game is to navigate your frog across a busy stream by jumping from log to log while avoiding your enemies. Sounds simple? Try it. Registration brings new levels and enemies.

Figure 18-12: The adventures of Dakota

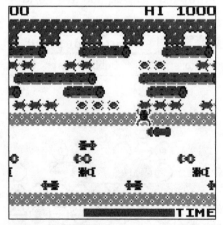

Figure 18-13: Froggy

Galax

Developer: Tim Smith
Cost: Freeware
Footprint: 33K

Tim's rendition of the classic arcade game Galaxian is pictured in Figure 18-14. Use the hardware keys to move your ship left and right, firing at wave after wave of incoming aliens. It's every bit as addictive as its big brother.

Impactor

Developer: Julian Scott
Cost: $10.00 (shareware)
Footprint: 37K

Impactor (shown in Figure 18-15) is a clone of Arkanoid, one of my favorite arcade games. In this updated version of Bricks, you move your paddle left and right to keep bouncing a ball to the top of the screen where it destroys a row of bricks. The catch? Some bricks release power-up items, which give you additional powers. Chasing the power-ups can be dangerous; it is easy to lose your character trying to catch them. The demo version lets you try the first of 32 levels. I have only three games loaded right now, and this is one of them.

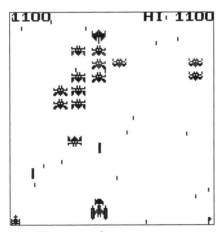

Figure 18-14: Galax

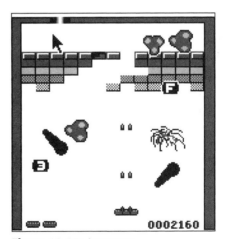

Figure 18-15: Impactor

PAC

Developer: Philip Jaquenoud
Cost: Freeware
Footprint: 12K

Figure 18-16 shows Philip's version of the classic Atari arcade game Pac-Man. Use the hardware keys to navigate your character through the maze, eating all the pellets. The power-ups in each corner give you a few seconds of superstrength, during which you can chase the bad guys.

Mulg II

Developer: Till Harbaum
Cost: Freeware
Footprint: 51K

This is an amazing piece of original freeware. Great 3D grayscale graphics (see Figure 18-17) and an original plot! The idea here is to guide your marble out of the maze, which you do by tapping onscreen. The classic game includes 16 levels, and Tom Smallwood has written a Windows 95 Level Editor which is available at www. cyberramp.net/~swamper/jedi/mulg.htm. If you really like the game, you can even add a tilt sensor (see www.ibr.cs.tu-bs.de/~harbaum/pilot/adxl202. html), and play the game just by tilting your Palm Organizer!

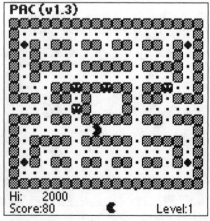

Figure 18-16: PAC

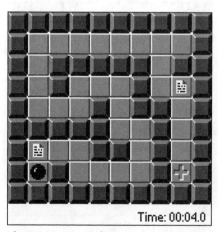

Figure 18-17: Mulg II

Reptoids

Developer: Synergy Systems
Cost: Freeware
Footprint: 29K

Reptoids is a freeware version of the classic Atari arcade game Asteroids. Use the hardware buttons to navigate through space, blasting asteroids and avoiding the shots from enemy ships (see Figure 18-18).

Tetrin

Developer: Hide
Cost: $8.00 (shareware)
Footprint: 21K

Tetrin (see Figure 18-19) is a Palm-sized version of the classic Russian game Tetris. Different shaped blocks descend from the top of the screen; use the Date Book and Address Book buttons to move them left and right on the screen, and the To Do List and Memo Pad buttons to rotate them. If you fill in a line completely, it is removed from the screen. The blocks come faster and faster on each level.

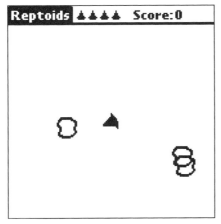

Figure 18-18: Reptoids

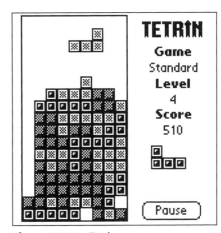

Figure 18-19: Tetrin

Board Games

In the *PalmPilot Organizer Resource Kit*, I defined parlor games as those that one might play in a parlor (if one had a parlor): card, board, and word games. Since that book was published, an unbelievable flood of games and other applications have appeared for the Palm platform. I have separated these into their original categories, so that I can focus on some of the best of each type. This first section covers games that are based on those originally played as board games; the type of game that you may have enjoyed on a rainy Sunday afternoon. Just because these games require more thought than manual dexterity doesn't make them any less addictive than the arcade-style games.

BattleShip

Developer: Hans-Rudolph Graf
Cost: PostCardWare (send him a postcard)
Footprint: 16K

This one should be familiar: the classic battleship game, but written for your Palm Organizer (see Figure 18-20). Options enable you to set the size of the board and the level of the game; place your ships and see if you can beat the computer!

Blackout

Developer: Jeff Jetton
Cost: $7.00 (shareware)
Footprint: 15K

The object of Blackout is to change all of the white squares to black (see Figure 18-21). To change a square, tap it—this also changes the colors of adjacent squares, so it isn't as easy as it sounds! Jeff maintains a Blackout Hall of Fame on his Web site at www.mindspring.com/~jetton/pilot/bhof.html where he lists registered users who have completed all 35 levels.

Chinese Checkers

Developer: AK Analytics
Cost: $7.00 (shareware)
Footprint: 16K

Remember playing Chinese Checkers on the six-sided metal board, with marbles as pieces? This version of Chinese Checkers for your PalmPilot (see Figure 18-22) has everything but the board and marbles, including a decent electronic opponent.

Desdemona

Developer: Mindgear
Cost: $12.00 (shareware)
Footprint: 23K

Desdemona (shown in Figure 18-23) is the Palm-sized version of the tile-flipping game Othello (or Reversi). The idea is simple: you and your electronic opponent take turns adding tiles to the board. Any tiles that your tiles surround change to your color, and vice-versa. Simple concept, but it is difficult to beat the computer at higher levels. Registration brings a number of features, including the capability to play at difficulty levels above easy, high scores, hints, and more.

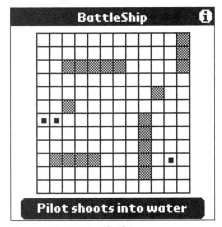

Figure 18-20: BattleShip

Figure 18-21: Blackout

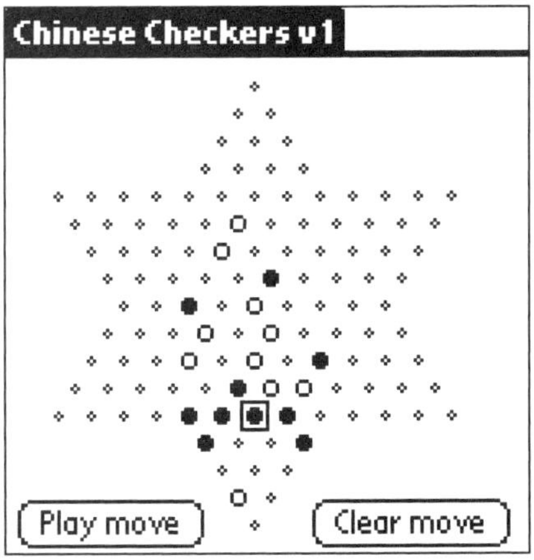

Figure 18-22: Chinese Checkers

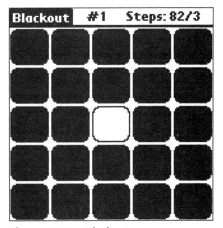

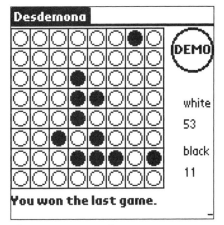

Figure 18-23: Desdemona

JStones

Developer: Land-J Technologies
Cost: $12.00 (shareware)
Footprint: 13K

The clever tile placement game seen in Figure 18-24 is reminiscent of the Japanese game Ishido. The object is to place 72 stones in a 12 × 8 grid, each matching it's neighbor by color, pattern, or both.

Mind Master

Developer: David Harcombe
Cost: $7.50 (shareware)
Footprint: 14K

Mind Master (see Figure 18-25) is David's Palm Organizer version of the classic peg game MasterMind. The idea is to guess the order of four to six shapes. The game provides clues after each guess, which help you deduce the answer.

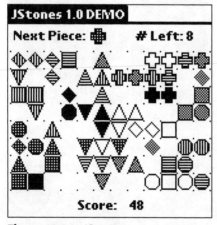

Figure 18-24: JStones

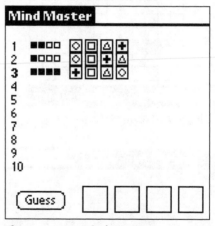

Figure 18-25: Mind Master

Overload

Developer: David Graham
Cost: $10.00 (shareware)
Footprint: 10K

In this tile-placement game, the object is to take over the board (see Figure 18-26). The twist is that you can pile pieces on top of each other — these eventually become unstable and take over the surrounding squares (hence the name Overload).

PalmJongg

Developer: Tan Kok Mun
Cost: $12.00 (shareware)
Footprint: 40K

This Palm Organizer-sized version of the mahjong tile-removing game has a few nice touches: the board resizes as you remove pieces, and double-tapping a tile searches for a match (see Figure 18-27).

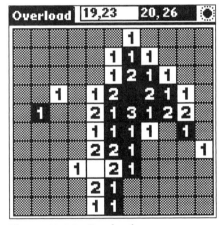

Figure 18-26: Overload

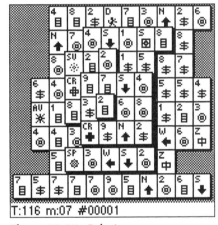

Figure 18-27: PalmJongg

Pegged!

Developer: Tan Kok Mun
Cost: $12.00 (shareware)
Footprint: 15K

The object of Pegged! (see Figure 18-28) is to remove pegs by jumping — each jump removes the piece jumped over, you can only jump one piece at a time, and jumps can only be horizontal or vertical. Tan has added some nice touches: you can play a series of puzzles of increasing difficulty, the board can be in different shapes, and you can undo your last move.

Perplex

Developer: DovCom
Cost: $6.00 (shareware)
Footprint: 8K

Perplex is much like the sliding number or alphabet puzzles: the object is to move
the large square block at the top center of the puzzle to the bottom center by sliding the blocks into adjacent empty areas (see Figure 18-29).

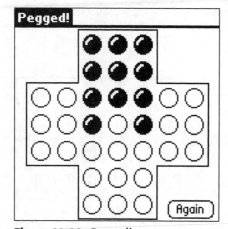

Figure 18-28: Pegged!   **Figure 18-29:** Perplex

PilotSenso

Developer: Hans-Rudolph Graf
Cost: PostCardWare (send him a postcard)
Footprint: 7K

Remember the plastic electronic game in which you had to remember a sequence of
beeps? PilotSenso (shown in Figure 18-30) gives you the Palm Organizer version of
this memory game—see how long a sequence you can duplicate.

Sokoban

Developer: Bill Kirby
Cost: $12.00
Footprint: 17K

Sokoban is a maze game; on each level you must figure out how to push the blocks
to their intended destinations. This well-done version includes the 3D display shown
in Figure 18-31.

PilotSenso
A
D
B
C
player move

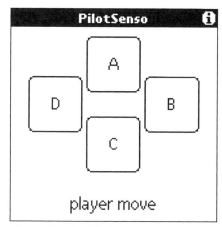

Figure 18-30: PilotSenso

Moves: 0
Pushes: 0
Level
01

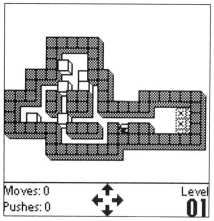

Figure 18-31: Sokoban

yahtChallenge

Developer: Tan Kok Mun
Cost: $12.00
Footprint: 24K

Figure 18-32 shows yahtChallenge, a nice Palm Organizer rendition of Yahtzee, the classic dice-rolling game, with options for challenge series and three or four dice rolls.

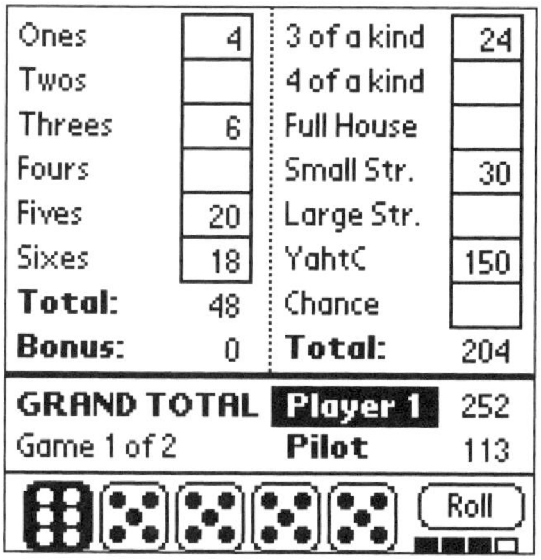

Ones 4
Twos
Threes 6
Fours
Fives 20
Sixes 18
Total: 48
Bonus: 0
3 of a kind 24
4 of a kind
Full House
Small Str. 30
Large Str.
YahtC 150
Chance
Total: 204
GRAND TOTAL
Player 1 252
Game 1 of 2
Pilot 113
Roll

Figure 18-32: yahtChallenge

Card Games

Card games seem to me to be a natural on the Palm Organizer. You can play several variations of solitaire and several multiplayer games against electronic opponents. These games enable you to take a minute for a quiet diversion.

4Corners Solitaire

Developer: Seahorse Software
Cost: $5.00
Footprint: 22K

Seahorse Software specializes in card games, such as solitaire and some of your old favorites. Be sure to check out the rest of their software on the CD-ROM. The object of 4Corners Solitaire (see Figure 18-33) is to move all of the cards to the four corners in increasing order, while following suit.

BlackJack Simulator

Developer: John M. Stoneham
Cost: $24.00 (shareware)
Footprint: 34K

This shareware application (see Figure 18-34) teaches you to refine your Blackjack strategy. The shareware version shows you how the trainer works; you need to register in order to use the Blackjack Tutor, Counting Tracker, or the Editor functionality.

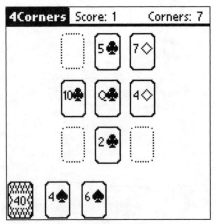

Figure 18-33: 4Corners Solitaire

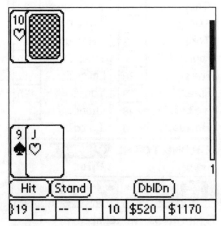

Figure 18-34: BlackJack Simulator

BlackJack Solitaire

Developer: Seahorse Software
Cost: $5.00 (shareware)
Footprint: 26K

This original is very addictive. You have 30 seconds to place cards in one of five trays (shown in Figure 18-35), each tray building a Blackjack hand, and you can only skip one card. Two more rounds follow, with your score based on your point totals and time left. This one will keep you coming back for another try at the high score.

Crazy 8's

Developer: Seahorse Software
Cost: $5.00 (shareware)
Footprint: 34K

See Figure 18-36 for a Palm-sized version of a childhood favorite—Crazy 8's. The object of this game is to get rid of your cards before your opponents do.

Figure 18-35: BlackJack Solitaire

Figure 18-36: Crazy 8's

Cribbage

Developer: Dave Mayes
Cost: Freeware
Footprint: 22K

Cribbage (see Figure 18-37) is a good example of why I find it hard to believe Dave Mayes releases his software as freeware. He's recently upgraded Cribbage with better graphics and the capability to play Muggins (taking points your opponent misses). This is a game I learned from my late grandfather, who used to say to me, when I missed a point: "How much is that? Not when *I* went to school." This is a great version of one of the best card games!

Golf Solitaire

Developer: Jeff Jetton
Cost: $8.00
Footprint: 28K

The objective of this solitaire card game is to reduce your score by moving the 35 upper cards, one at a time, to the pile at the bottom of the screen (see Figure 18-38). Jeff tells me that there is an Easter Egg hidden in this game, but no one has found it yet!

Figure 18-37: Cribbage

Figure 18-38: Golf Solitaire

Hearts

Developer: Dave Mayes
Cost: Freeware
Footprint: 28K

This card game has been a favorite of mine for years, and Dave's faithful rendition enables you to play without having to find three other players! The hearts are one point each, and the Queen of Spades is worth 13 points. The object is to take all or none in a series of tricks where you must follow suit if you can (see Figure 18-39).

Klondike

Developer: Bill Kirby
Cost: $12.00 (shareware)
Footprint: 18K

The shareware game shown in Figure 18-40 brings perhaps the most famous of card solitaire games to the Palm Organizer. You remember this one: you deal seven rows of cards, skip the first row and deal six, and so on, until you have dealt 28 cards. The object is to build each of the suits from ace up. I'd go on, but I suspect you've already started a game without me.

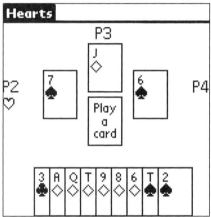

Figure 18-39: Hearts

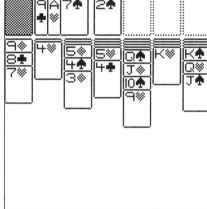

Figure 18-40: Klondike

Pyramid Solitaire

Developer: Seahorse Software
Cost: Freeware
Footprint: 28K

Pyramid Solitaire (shown in Figure 18-41) is another of my favorite solitaire card games. The object is to remove all of the cards in pairs that total 13: 5 and 8, 2 and Jack, and so on (Kings are free).

Rally 1000

Developer: Dave Mayes
Cost: Freeware
Footprint: 20K

Rally is Dave's Palm Organizer version of the card game Mille Bornes (1000 Milestones), and one of my favorite diversions on the Palm Organizer. In this game, your object is to play traffic cards (green light, mileage) to complete a trip, all the while preventing your opponent from winning by giving them red lights or traffic hazards (see Figure 18-42). Don't worry if you don't know the game; a complete description is built into the game's help.

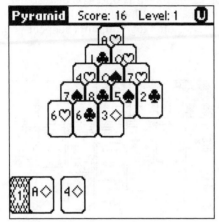

Figure 18-41: Pyramid Solitaire

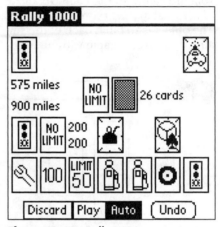

Figure 18-42: Rally 1000

Rummy

Developer: Seahorse Software
Cost: $8.00 (shareware)
Footprint: 30K

This is one of my favorite two-player card games, Rummy 500. The object of the game is to lay down all of your cards in matched sets or in sequence before your opponent. The settings for this game enable you to configure how your hand should be sorted, and how long the game should last (see Figure 18-43).

Texas Hold'Em

Developer: Yoshiharu Kiyono
Cost: $12.00 (shareware)
Footprint: 37K

This game is the most recent entry on my Palm Organizer. How he's done it, I don't know, but Yoshiharu has managed to squeeze an eight-player game of Texas Hold'Em (see Figure 18-44), complete with card animations, into the Palm Organizer. If you like poker, you owe it to yourself to give this one a look.

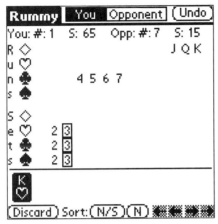

Figure 18-43: Rummy

Figure 18-44: Texas Hold'Em

Diversions

These entertaining applications aren't necessarily games, but they are certainly entertaining.

Biorhythms

Developer: Jeff Jetton
Cost: $5.00 (shareware)
Footprint: 11K

Biorhythms (see Figure 18-45) tracks the cycles of your physical, emotional, and mental health, and graphs them so that you know when it is better to stay in bed. It enables you to record up to five birthdays for easy access.

Buzzword Generator

Developer: David MacLeod
Cost: Freeware
Footprint: 11K

If you're looking for a new TLA (three-letter acronym), this cute application may do the trick: it generates buzzwords — you can even create your own word files! Figure 18-46 shows the Buzzword Generator.

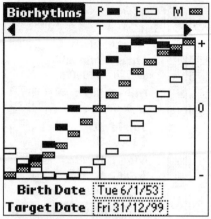

Figure 18-45: Biorhythms

Figure 18-46: Buzzword Generator

Caution

Buzzword Generator does not work on the Palm III, but it will run on the earlier Palm Organizers and on the Palm V.

PilotCE

Developer: Art Dahm
Cost: Freeware
Footprint: 36K

Here's a great one: the Pilot version of Windows CE (see Figure 18-47). Just remember you get what you've paid for.

TrekSounds

Developer: Glen Aspeslagh
Cost: $8.00
Footprint: 36K

If you're a Trekkie, your Palm Organizer won't be complete without these last two items. Glen has written a Hack that enables you to replace your system sounds with those from the Star Trek series (see Figure 18-48).

Cross-Reference

TrekSounds is a HackMaster Hack. For more on Hacks, what they are, and how to load and unload them, see Chapter 22.

Figure 18-47: PilotCE

Figure 18-48: TrekSounds

Tricorder II

Developer: Jeff Jetton
Cost: Freeware
Footprint: 16K

Want to turn your Palm Organizer into a fully functional Tricorder, one every bit as useful as the ones used in the Star Trek series? This freeware application shown in Figure 18-49, is a hoot—it even has support for Gary Mayhak's TaleLight (see Chapter 23). If you really want to send money, Jeff suggests you donate to the St. Jude Children's Research Hospital (www.stjude.org).

Figure 18-49: Tricorder II

Word Games

For those with an intellectual bent, there are a plethora of word games available to twist your mind while riding on the train.

Jookerie!

Developer: Land-J
Cost: $12.00
Footprint: 20K

In this original word game, you and your opponent each make up a bogus word definition and then compete to pick the correct definition (see Figure 18-50).

Scramblet

Developer: Frank Fejes
Cost: $15.00
Footprint: 85K

In Scramblet (see Figure 18-51), the object is to find as many words as you can from seven jumbled letters. Frank has written Scramblet and Wordlet (Wordlet is listed next) to share a common dictionary; if you want more of a challenge, he has other word files available on his Web site at www.oopdreams.com/wordlet.

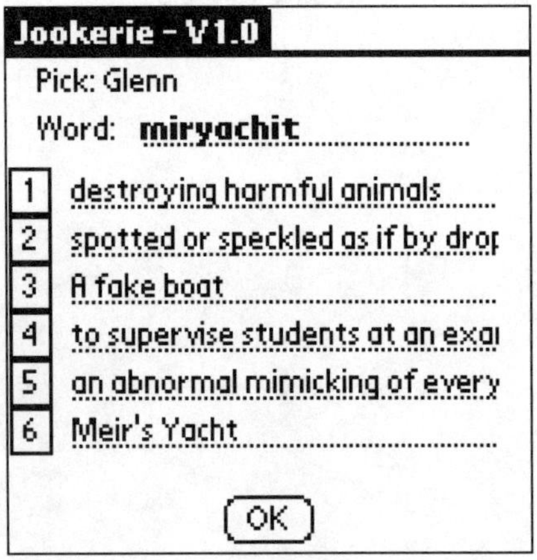

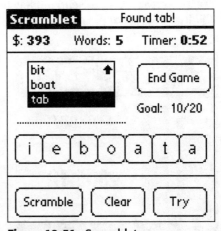

Figure 18-50: Jookerie!

Figure 18-51: Scramblet

Wordlet

Developer: Frank Fejes
Cost: $15.00
Footprint: 106K

In Wordlet, you try to make as many word as you can from adjacent tiles in a jumbled 4×4 grid of letters (see Figure 18-52).

XWord

Developer: Penguin Software
Cost: $10.00
Footprint: 23K

If you're a crossword puzzle fan, this nicely done implementation may be the answer (see Figure 18-53). Penguin also makes available its freeware DOS-based utility Puz2Pil, which enables you to import crossword puzzles into your Palm Organizer. Puz2Pil currently supports these formats: Crossword Express Professional (www.puzzledepot.com/cwe/down1.shtml), USA Today (www.usatoday.com/life/puzzles/puzzle.htm), New York Times (www.nytimes.com), and the London Times (www.sunday-times.co.uk).

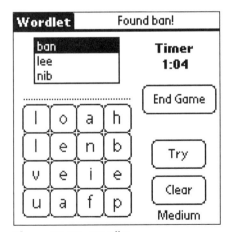
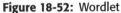

Figure 18-52: Wordlet

Figure 18-53: XWord

Game Utilities

This last section covers something completely different: game utilities. These tools help you score or play your favorite sports and games. Coaches and athletes should also check out Steven's Creek Software at www.stevenscreek.com/pilot.

DicePro

Developer: Rival Game Labs
Cost: Freeware
Footprint: 33K

If you play dice games, particularly role-playing games, then you need this freeware utility (see Figure 18-54) for your Palm Organizer. If you're into Live Action Role-Playing, be sure to check out Rival Game Labs' VPARP dice-rolling utility for Vampire (or any of the White Wolf Storyteller-based) LARPs.

Gamer's Die Roller

Developer: Art Dahm
Cost: $7.00 (shareware)
Footprint: 15K

Here's another dice-rolling utility for your Palm Organizer (see Figure 18-55). Features include the capability of rolling up to 20 three-, four-, six-, eight-, ten-, twelve-, twenty-, or hundred-sided dice at a time; the capability of assigning up to 24 custom die rolls; custom die rolls that can test for success or failure against a value or that can compute AD&D "To Hit" armor class; and large buttons for finger-touch or stylus control.

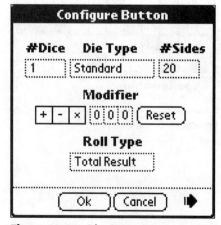

Figure 18-54: DicePro

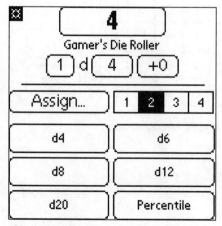

Figure 18-55: Gamer's Die Roller

GolfTrac

Developer: FPS Software
Cost: $29.95
Footprint: 136K

GolfTrac (shown in Figure 18-56) is a sophisticated scoring utility for the Palm-carrying golf nut. Features include the capability to keep scores, putts, and penalty strokes for up to four players, record on-course statistics as you play, compare averages from your favorite courses while on the course, and track drives, bunkers, sand saves, greens, and free throws. FPS has a Windows conduit that enables you to download your game statistics to your personal computer.

IntelliGolf

Developer: Karrier Communications
Cost: $29.95/$39.95 (with Windows conduit)
Footprint: 73K

IntelliGolf (see Figure 18-57) is a complete Palm-based golf tool, with on-course golf scoring and wagering, Internet course downloads, uploads, round archival, score card printing, and performance statistics. IntelliGolf includes more than 60 performance statistics to help you improve your game. The $29.95 Par edition gives you complete scoring, statistics, and wagering for your Palm Organizer, and the $39.95 Birdie edition adds a Windows conduit for downloading information to your personal computer, Internet-based download access to thousands of courses worldwide, and handicap approximation.

Figure 18-56: GolfTrac

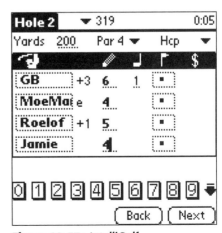

Figure 18-57: IntelliGolf

Pilot-Frotz

Developer: Alien Hunter
Cost: Freeware
Footprint: 49K

My first introduction to adventure gaming was Infocom's text adventure games. These were so good, you'd swear there was someone in your computer calling you names. Figure 18-58 shows Pilot-Frotz, a utility that brings Infocom's Z-interpreter to the Palm Organizer, enabling you to play some of these great games. The best place to start looking for games is at Interactive Fiction (www.geocities.com/Heartland/9590/interactive.htm). You might also want to check out Activision's site; Activision has made the original Zork series available at www.activision.com/games/demos.asp.

What's the Score?

Developer: Steve Tattersall
Cost: PostCardWare
Footprint: 22K

What's the Score (see Figure 18-59) enables you to track scores for almost any game — Scrabble, Cribbage, Magic the Gathering, and many more — as long as the scores remain in the range –99,999 to 99,999.

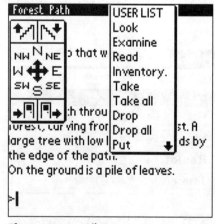

Figure 18-58: Pilot-Frotz

Figure 18-59: What's the Score?

Summary

You can find an abundance of games for your Palm Organizer. My only warning: Make sure you have lots of batteries in stock!

When Palm shipped the first Pilot, their games were amongst the very few available. That has changed dramatically in the past few years.

There is now something for everyone: great adventures; classic arcade games; thought-provoking board, card, and word games; interesting diversions; and utilities that help you with other games.

Many of these games fall into two broad categories: Palm-sized updates of old classics, and new, original games — both are fun to try. Good luck!

✦   ✦   ✦

Downloading and Accessing Applications

◆ ◆ ◆ ◆

In This Chapter

Downloading
software

Accessing
company sites

Accessing
author sites

Accessing software
collections

Accessing
online stores

Palm hardware sites

Finding news
and information

◆ ◆ ◆ ◆

Want to find the latest hardware or software for your Palm Organizer, get news, or just chat with someone with the same interests (the Palm Organizer, of course!)? Try the Web. It was hard to limit this list — there are hundreds and hundreds of great Palm Organizer sites on the Web, including one dedicated to the *Palm OS Bible*. More are added every day. This chapter provides a few tips for downloading software from the Internet, and lists some of the best places to start looking. Remember that the World Wide Web changes daily, so the addresses and content may have changed by the time this book is published.

This book is full of Internet addresses, covering almost all developers mentioned in the *Palm OS Bible*. This chapter helps you get started exploring the Internet for more information about your Palm Organizer and third-party software. See Chapter 16 if you want to surf the Internet *using* your Palm Organizer.

Downloading Software

The Web is an endless source for new applications and updates for your Palm Organizer, and their relatively small file size makes downloading a breeze. The first thing you'll discover is that most files on the Internet are compressed. Compression uses sophisticated software to strip out blank spaces and redundant information from files, creating a much smaller file that takes less time to transmit and requires less storage space. It also enables software authors to combine a number of files, ensuring that you get the necessary components and documentation. The downside? You need a utility on your computer to expand these files. If you have a PC, then you should look for PKZip or WinZip (typically included with Windows software) to expand your files. Macintosh owners need a tool such as StuffIt Expander. The good news is that expand-only utilities are freely available from most download sites. You can also find them at:

✦ www.pkware.com (PKZip)

✦ www.asizip.com (PKZip, MacZip)

✦ www.winzip.com (WinZip)

✦ www.aladdinsys.com (StuffIt Expander)

Tip   None of the files on the CD-ROM that accompanies the *Palm OS Bible* are compressed, so you don't need to figure out how to expand them, or which utility to use. You should, however, copy files to your computer's hard drive before loading them. If not, you may have problems upgrading in the future.

Filename extensions

How do you know what tool to use? Your first indicator is the filename extension used; even though the DOS 8.3 file-naming convention isn't required by modern operating systems, it is still the standard on the Internet. Some of the extensions that are used and the tool that created them (and, therefore, to use to expand them) are as follows.

For compressed files:

.zip	Used by PKZip and WinZip (PC)
.sit	Used by Stuffit (Macintosh)
.sea	Self-extracting archive, a file that will automatically expand without requiring you to have a decoder utility (Macintosh). These files can also be created as self-expanding .exe files for Windows users.

For other files:

.doc	A document file, meant for reading with your word processor
.gif	CompuServe's Graphics Interchange Format, for images
.htm (or **.html**)	Hypertext Markup Language is the language of the Web. Some developers distribute their documentation in HTML format. You can open and read these documents in your Internet Browser (probably Netscape or Microsoft Explorer).

.pdf	Adobe Acrobat's Portable Document Format, the platform-independent format some developers use for their documentation. You'll find the Acrobat Reader on the CD-ROM.
.pdb	A Palm database file
.prc	A Palm program (Palm Resource Code)
.txt	A text file that is meant to be read using your word processor

File organization

My recommendation is to make a separate directory on your PC or Mac for your Palm Organizer downloads. That way you can find the file if you need it later for reloading. The easiest method is to expand each compressed file in a new directory or folder, which you've titled with the program's name. In the folder, you're likely to find documentation, update information, and the program (.prc) itself. I recommend that you read the README or other documentation files — authors often put critical information in them, including requirements, instructions, and useful tips. Some Palm Organizer applications have special requirements — for example, they might need HackMaster or a run-time application in order to run — and the README is where you learn about these requirements.

After you've downloaded a program, do an install and a HotSync to have a new application on your Palm Organizer. See Chapter 6 for more on loading software and on removing applications to free up space for new ones.

 Tip This one is important: On your computer, make another, separate, directory for the files that you loaded on your Palm Organizer. In it put duplicates of all of the .prc and .pdb files that you loaded so that you have a mirror of the contents of your Palm Organizer. These files are small, so they won't take up much memory. This backup directory will save untold grief the first time you have to reload all of your applications after a hard reset or crash.

 New Feature Version 3.3 of the Palm OS that shipped with the Palm Vx automatically backs up all of your files for you, so that you can easily recover in the case of a hard reset or crash.

 Tip Users of Palm OS 3.2 or earlier should look at Alexander Hind's Backup Buddy. This essential utility automatically backs up all of the files on your Palm Organizer, including files loaded in flash memory. For more on Backup Buddy, see Chapters 11 and 21.

Shareware

Shareware is software that lets you try the program before buying. Some shareware programs are crippled or limited in some fashion to encourage you to register, some are not. In all cases, if you find yourself using a shareware application, you are obligated to pay the fee.

Now that there are safe means to use your credit card on the Internet, there is no excuse for not registering the shareware you use. You'll be pleasantly surprised by the benefits — I've received more updates, bug fixes, and support from Palm Organizer shareware authors than from the some of the computer applications that I paid hundreds of dollars more for!

Accessing Company Sites

The first two here are pretty obvious: Palm and IBM. The rest comprise some of the best of a growing number of companies producing products for the Palm Organizer. All have demos on the CD-ROM.

3Com/Palm

www.Palm.com

This one should be pretty obvious: the mothership. The content-rich Web pages that start at www.palm.com offer the first stop on the Internet for most new Palm users (see Figure 19-1). Here you'll find system and desktop updates, games, and products for sale. The graphics and offers change often; return regularly to check out the latest. Don't forget to sign up for the InSync Online news service.

IBM WorkPad

www.pc.ibm.com/us/workpad

Owners of IBM's version of the Palm Organizer should check out their home base.

Concept Kitchen

www.conceptkitchen.com

This is the place to go if you want screen cleaning or protecting accessories for your Palm Organizer. Concept Kitchen has also released a multilingual translation application for the Palm Organizer called Small Talk and the new ruggedized Bumper case.

DovCom

www.dovcom.com

DovCom is the home of one of the first and most prolific Palm Organizer developers; coverage of DovCom's software is found throughout this book.

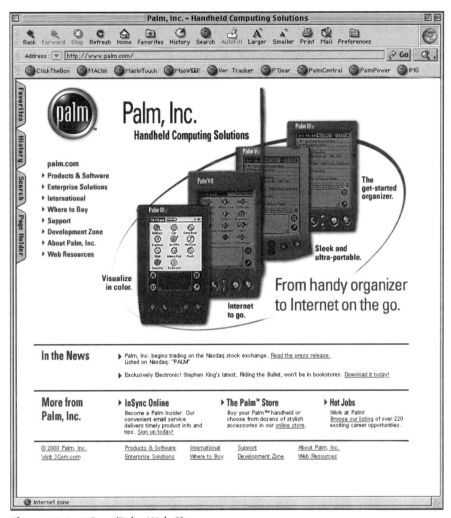

Figure 19-1: 3Com/Palm Web Site

LandWare

www.landware.com

LandWare develops commercial software for the Palm Organizer, the Newton, and Windows CE devices — its products are covered throughout the book.

TealPoint

www.tealpoint.com

TealPoint makes great software for the Palm Organizer — TealPaint, TealDoc, TealScript, and more. These shareware programs are covered throughout the book and are found on the CD-ROM. Figure 19-2 shows the TealPoint Web site.

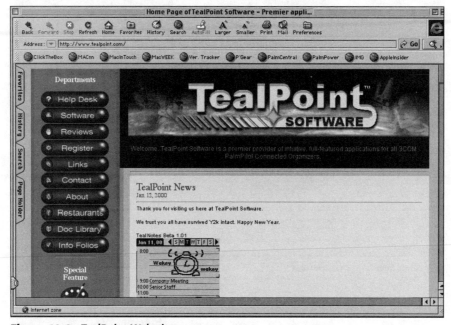

Figure 19-2: TealPoint Web site

Accessing Author Sites

Quite a few Palm Organizer software authors have put up their own home pages with updates and news about their products. Software from all of the following authors is found on the CD-ROM.

Daggerware

www.daggerware.com

This is the home of Edward Keyes' HackMaster, an essential utility for extending your Palm Organizer's operating system. See Chapters 11 and 22 for more on HackMaster.

Firepad

http://www.firepad.com

Firepad makes FireViewer, a program that enables you to view large images using your handheld. Figure 19-3 shows the Firepad Web site.

PalmGlyph Software

www.palmglyph.com

This is Rick Bram's site, featuring Doc, MED, and ZIP. Doc became AportisDoc, MED is his Multiuser Editable Database, and ZIP is a utility that enables you to play interactive games such as Zork on your Palm Organizer.

Peter's Pilot Pages

www.pstec.de/ppp

Peter Strobel's is a great site if you want to know more about batteries and power for your Palm Organizer. Peter has also written some pretty good software to track the performance of the batteries in your Palm Organizer.

pilotBASIC

http://home.pacific.net.sg/~kokmun

Tan Kok Mun's site is devoted to Palm apps written in Basic.

Ron's Palm Information Page

www.nicholson.com/rhn/pilot.html

This is the home of Ronald H. Nicholson, Jr.'s cBaspad Tiny Basic.

überchix

www.uberchix.com

It is obvious (to me, anyway) that the authors of this well-designed site have a sense of humor (see Figure 19-4).

Figure 19-3: The Firepad Web site

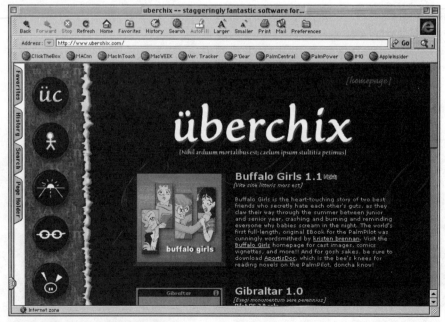

Figure 19-4: überchix Web site

Accessing Software Collections

Software junkie? Need a fix of new software? You've come to the right place. This section includes some great Web sites that feature the best available Palm software.

Eurocool

`www.eurocool.com/palm`

This site has 700 Palm Organizer titles, which can be sorted and viewed any way you'd like — by category, type, author, and more. It is definitely worth a look.

The PilotZone

`www.pdacentral.com/pilotzone`

Scott Swedorski runs this Tucows site (see Figure 19-5). It is no surprise that it features lots of software and great graphics.

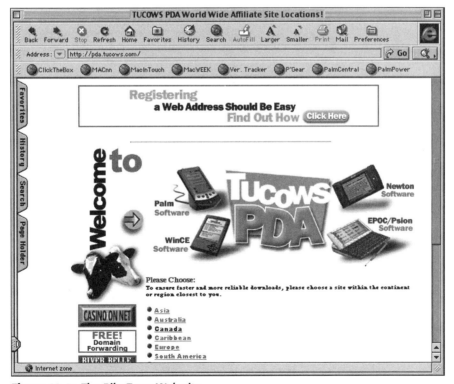

Figure 19-5: The PilotZone Web site

Accessing Online Stores

The advent of e-commerce has made online buying a reality. Advances in encryption and browser technology make it safe to use your credit card to buy online, and it sure is a lot easier than before!

Computer Concepts

www.compcon.com

My long-time personal friend David Melamed runs an Ottawa-based site. He offers computer software and hardware, including Palm Organizers and accessories, and has consistently offered the best prices in Ottawa for Palm accessories (see Figure 19-6).

Figure 19-6: Computer Concepts Web site

Handago

`http://new.palmcentral.com/home.shtml`

This site started out as a hobby site developed by Raymond Lau, the author of the Macintosh compression utility StuffIt. Handago (previously PalmCentral) offers similar features to PalmGear HQ. I check both sites daily, because each seems able to find some updates and information before the other.

PalmGear HQ

`www.palmgear.com`

PalmGear started out as PilotGear HQ, which became PalmPilotGear HQ and, finally, PalmGear, as they complied with Palm's wishes to conform to the Palm brand identity. It is arguably the best Palm Organizer site up today (see Figure 19-7), featuring a great mix of freeware, shareware, and commercial applications. I've bought from them several times and I don't know how I could have finished this book without their mailing list. Kenny West and J. D. Crouch run a great site, offering shareware and the means to register it, sales of commercial software and hardware, news, and information.

Figure 19-7: PalmGear HQ Web site

Note   Thanks to Rodney Capron and the staff at PalmGear for producing the great CD-ROM that accompanies the *Palm OS Bible*.

PDA Mart

www.pdamart.com

This site offers PDA-related news and products, including news about and products for the Palm Organizer.

Palm Hardware Sites

Hardware buffs aren't left out of the wealth of products available for the Palm Organizer — there are lots of products available. The following sites are among my favorite Palm-related Web destinations. They have news, reviews, new shareware, and commercial software and updates — all of which can be purchased online.

20-20Consumer

http://20-20consumer.com

Want the best price on a new Palm Organizer? This independent site updates and maintains price comparisons on a number of products, including our favorite — the Palm Organizer.

Bike Brain

www.bikebrain.com

This site covers Velotrend's Bike Brain, which can turn your Palm Organizer into an onboard computer for your bicycle. Too cool!

efigV8

www.efig.com

The Palm V is a wonderful device, but power users will find 2MB of memory limiting — I know I do. The cure? Send your Palm V and $250 off to efig, and they'll upgrade it to 8MB of memory. (Or pass on your Palm V to a friend, relative, or coworker and buy the new, 8MB Palm Vx with its 20MHz processor.)

MidWest PCB Designs

www.midwestpcbdesigns.com

These people make The Bridge, a device that enables you to synchronize your Palm Organizer without taking it out of its case. An updated version enables you to synchronize your Palm V in an older PalmPilot or Palm III cradle.

Option International

www.option.com/snapon.htm

Palm V users can connect their modems to a GSM phone. Option International has a device called the Snap that connects to your PalmPilot or Palm III and to your GSM cellular phone, which enables you to surf wireless. See Chapter 16 for more on the Snap device.

PageMart

www.pagemart.com/index.html

This is the home of the Synapse pager card for the Palm Organizer. See Chapter 16 for more on the Synapse card.

PalmColors

www.palmcolors.com

The Palm Organizer is just like the original Ford—you can have it in any color you'd like as long as it's gray. IBM WorkPads, of course, get the original Ford color: black. This site offers color cases in eight colors plus clear for the PalmPilot and Palm III models.

Palm Keyboards

www.jimthompson.net/pilot/keyboard.htm

This interesting site shows some of the keyboards available to attach to your Palm Organizer.

PDA Panache

www.pdapanache.com

If you want to upgrade your stylus to a high-quality metal one, here's the only place you need to look. See Chapter 23 for more about replacement styli for your Palm Organizer.

Revolv Design

www.revolvdesign.com

This is the home of Revolv's UniMount for your car or van and UniMount for Golf. See Chapter 23 for more on the UniMount.

Rhinoskin

www.rhinoskin.com

This is home of the Rhinoskin Titanium case for your Palm Organizer. See Chapter 23 for more on Rhinoskin's products.

Steve's Pilot Tech Page

www.twinbrothers.com/steve/pilot

Here's a site for the hardware techies; it features images of Palm Organizer upgrade cards.

TaleLight

http://members.aol.com/gmayhak/tcl/light.htm

This is the home of Gary Mayhak's TaleLight, a neat light that attaches to the serial port on your Palm Organizer. Gary also manufactures HotLink Connector, a miniconnector for data transfer between two Palm Organizers, and TaleVibes, a device that vibrates to let you know that an alarm has gone off in your pocket. You'll also find instructions for making an IrDA device for those who want to add the capability of infrared communications.

Technology Resources Group

www.trgnet.com

The hardware section of this chapter wouldn't be complete without TRG. I suspect that no one outside Palm knows the insides of the Palm Organizer better than these guys, who specialize in memory upgrades.

Finding News and Information

Want to know more about the Palm Organizer or the new Palm III? Want to find the answer to a problem, or get the latest news? These sites feature news and information of interest to Palm Organizer owners.

Calvin's PalmPilot FAQ

www.pilotfaq.com

Calvin Parker wrote the *Complete Palm Organizer Guide*, one of the first books on the Palm Organizer. His site features frequently asked questions (FAQs) about the Palm Organizer.

Canada's Premiere Palm User Group

www.CanadaPUG.com

This Web site provides a news, meeting, and discussion area for Canadian and other Palm Organizer users.

The Gadgeteer

www.the-gadgeteer.com

Julie Strietelmeier has put together a great site for those of us who like PDAs and other gadgets.

Interactive fiction

www.geocities.com/Heartland/9590/interactive.htm

Want to play Zork and more on your Palm Organizer? First, go to PalmGlyph (www.palmglyph.com) and download ZIP, and then come back here for Infocom classics and other interactive games for your Palm Organizer.

John's Palm Organizer page

http://web.cgocable.net/~seco/pilot/index.htm

John Cosentini's great tips page, featuring FAQ, tips and tricks, and Palm Organizer modifications. My only problem is that it is best viewed at 1024 × 768 resolution, and my Palm Organizer doesn't go past 640 × 480!

MemoWare.com

www.memoware.com

This unique site features over 2,500 documents (novels, reports, text books, lists, tables, short stories, jokes, and so on) formatted for the Palm Organizer. See Chapter 14 for more Web sites featuring Web-readable documents.

The PalmGuru

www.palmguru.com

This site provides reviews of Palm-related products. There is also a pretty good new user FAQ section, which provides answers to frequently asked questions for new Palm users.

PalmOS.com

www.palmos.com

This site has a nice clean design, with information, reviews, software, and chat sections (see Figure 19-8).

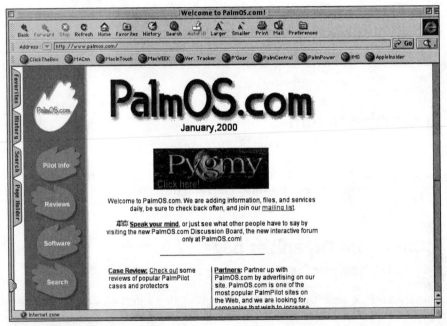

Figure 19-8: PalmOS.com Web site

PalmPilot World

www2.southwind.net/~miked/pilot/pilot.html

This site has some really interesting information and links. I particularly like the hardware and future links sections.

PalmPower Magazine

www.palmpower.com

This is perhaps the best Palm Organizer news site—they seem to be the first with news on new products and developments in the Palm world. *PalmPower Magazine* is an online, electronic-only publication that brings a fair bit of professionalism from the traditional publishing world.

PalmStation

www.palmstation.com

This is a very good news and information site with reviews, a question area, and more. Check it out!

The Palm Tree

www.thepalmtree.com

This is an interesting site with lots of news, tips, and links to all sorts of useful information.

Pen Computing Magazine

www.pencomputing.com

This is the Web site of the premiere magazine for those of us interested in all types of pen computing, including the Palm Organizer. (You might also want to consider subscribing to the paper version of this worthy magazine.)

Pilot Tips 'n' Tricks

www.novadesign.com/kermit/index.htm

A good tips site that also lists some of the PDA newsgroups (see Figure 19-9). Kermit coauthored PilotCE with Art Dahm.

Pilot Internet File Converter

http://pilot.screwdriver.net

This site provides a service by converting HTML and other files into Palm Organizer-readable versions.

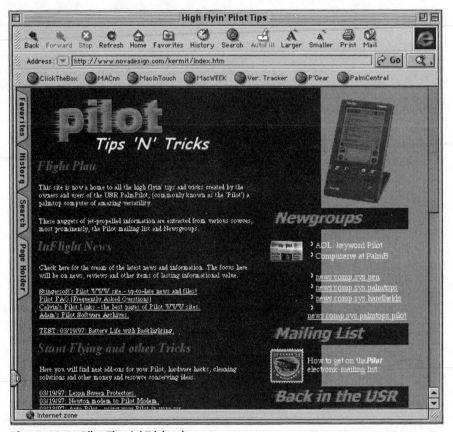

Figure 19-9: Pilot Tips 'n' Tricks site

The Starfleet Pilot

www.geocities.com/SiliconValley/Peaks/1161

This Palm Organizer site is for Star Trek fans.

Tap Magazine

www.tapmagazine.com

This is the online site of *Tap Magazine*, the best (and I think only) printed Palm Organizer magazine. I've subscribed since I first learned about it a year ago.

Finding More . . .

Want more? These sites will lead you to hundreds of Palm Organizer sites around the world.

Calvin's Web Links

www.pilotfaq.com/linksoft.htm

Calvin Parker's is perhaps the most complete set of Palm-related links on the Internet.

MagiMac Publishing

www.magimac.com

This is my Web site, which has, amongst other things, an online, updated version of the links in this chapter.

New England Palm Users Group

www.ne-palm.org/links.htm

This site provides all sorts of interesting Palm-related links, along with information on the New England Users' Group.

Palm Organizer Web Ring

www.geocities.com/SiliconValley/Lakes/9600

Many of the sites listed here belong to the Palm Organizer Web Ring. After you've entered one site, you can jump to the next, previous, or a random site. It's a great way to find new Palm Organizer sites!

PalmStock

www.palmstock.com

This news site has a nostalgic, 1970s look. It currently has 228 groovy Palm-related links.

Summary

✦ The Internet offers a lot for those with Palm Organizers. Start with Palm's Web site to check out the latest news and operating system updates.

✦ The Palm Store, PalmGear, PalmCentral, and Tucows offer one-stop news, reviews, updates, and software, with the capability to buy or register software — both commercial and shareware — online.

✦ Don't forget to check out the online version of this listing at MagiMac.com!

✦   ✦   ✦

Making Your
Palm Even Better

✦ ✦ ✦ ✦

In This Part

Chapter 20
Maintaining and
Enhancing Your Palm

Chapter 21
Customizing Your
Palm with Utilities

Chapter 22
Extending
Functionality with
HackMaster

Chapter 23
Accessorizing
Your Palm

Chapter 24
Troubleshooting
Your Palm

✦ ✦ ✦ ✦

Maintaining and Enhancing Your Palm

In This Chapter

Core application replacements

Application helpers

Supercharging your Palm Organizer

◆   ◆   ◆   ◆

The basic functionality that is included with your Palm Organizer is all many users need. There are, however, those of us who cannot resist tweaking, who'd rather have a version that they can customize to their liking. This chapter looks at how to supercharge your Palm Organizer by replacing the basic applications with third-party versions.

The applications in the chapter are acknowledged by many as some of the best — the most powerful and useful programs available for your Palm Organizer. Each takes the basic functionality that Palm ships in its organizers and adds capabilities that can make them even more useful.

Core Application Replacements

Palm, Inc. has done a number of things right. One was to make available to developers the source code for its core applications. This has enabled programmers to write some pretty spectacular software that extends the basic functionality far beyond the originals. All of these applications add features to your core applications, as well as work with the original databases. This means that there are no compromises: You don't have to give up HotSyncing to your favorite desktop application, and you can revert to the stock software at any time.

DateBook replacements

We start this chapter with some of the best third-party applications available for the Palm Organizer. A basic function of our favorite handheld is as a personal information manager (PIM). These applications extend that functionality in different ways. My choice? I use both Action Names and Datebk3. If had to choose between the two, I'd choose Action Names. Its icon support (including an editor) is better, and I like the contact integration. Try them yourself to see which you like the best. Table 20-1 identifies four DateBook replacements and compares their attributes to those of the standard DateBook.

Table 20-1						
DateBook Replacements						
Program	Size	Cost	Views	Icons	Integrates Contacts	Time Zones
Standard DateBook	n/a	Free	3	No	No	No
Action Names	183K	$19.95	10	Yes	Yes	No
Actioneer	89K	$19.95	n/a	No	Yes	No
DateBk3	260K	$20.00	7	Yes	No	Yes
TZDateBook	141K	$15.00	3	No	No	Yes

Action Names

Developer: Iambic Software
Cost: $19.95
Footprint: 183K

Action Names ties together the three basic PIM functions of the Palm Organizer — Address Book, DateBook, and To Do List — in one application. Each of the four main views — Agenda (see Figure 20-1), Week (Figure 20-2), Month (Figure 20-3), and Quarter (Figure 20-4) — offers variations totaling ten different views of your calendar. I rely mainly on the Agenda view, which can display both appointments and to-do items. Both can also be displayed in advance of their due date.

Figure 20-1: Action Names Agenda

Figure 20-2: Action Names Week View

Figure 20-3: Action Names Month View

Figure 20-4: Action Names Quarterly View

The real strength of this powerhouse is contact integration (see Figure 20-5). When you add a new meeting, call, or to-do item, you can add contact information, which it draws from your Address Book. Then, when you decide to act on a call or to-do item, the contact information is at your fingertips. This is an improvement on Palm's Phone Lookup feature because the complete contact information (not just the name and phone number) is linked to your task.

Figure 20-5: Adding a Contact in
Action Names

Tip

One limitation of Action Names is its lack of support for IR. The workaround is simple, however; just launch Palm's DateBook or To Do List when you need to beam an item.

Actioneer

Developer: Actioneer, Inc.
Cost: $19.95
Footprint: 88K

Actioneer provides an interface that enables quick entry of data into any or all of your standard applications. It does this by reversing the order in which you do things. Instead of selecting an application first and then entering data, you enter data first and Actioneer selects the application into which that data will be entered.

When you first load Actioneer, it scans your Palm Organizer for keywords. This enables the program to act as an interpreter for you, assigning items to the appropriate Palm applications. The program also reassigns itself to the Memo Pad hardware button for easy access. (Don't worry, you can still easily call up the Memo Pad application by pressing the Memo button for a second.)

Figure 20-6 shows an example of how the program works: If I enter the words, "Call Alex tomorrow," Actioneer recognizes the keywords "call" and "tomorrow" and creates a DateBook item to "Call Alex" on the following day.

Tip

In the preceding example, Actioneer will show "Call Alex tomorrow" on your calendar, which is not exactly what you meant. Use Actioneer's preferences to select Strip Date/Time Keywords (see Figure 20-7), and the reference will change to "Call Alex."

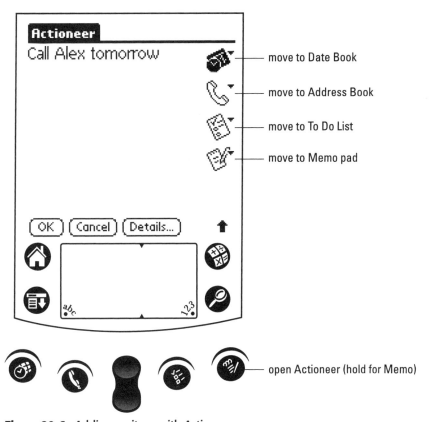

move to Date Book

move to Address Book

move to To Do List

move to Memo pad

open Actioneer (hold for Memo)

Figure 20-6: Adding an item with Actioneer

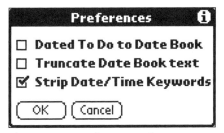

Figure 20-7: Actioneer Preferences

Actioneer can be configured to use keywords to recognize your contacts, categories, whatever you want, speeding entry dramatically. Actioneer also makes Windows versions of its software for Microsoft Outlook and Lotus Notes users.

Datebk3

Developer: Pimlico Software
Cost: $20.00
Footprint: 260K

DateBk3 combines the DateBook and To Do List functions of the Palm Organizer in one of the biggest (and most complete) applications available for the Palm Organizer. Figure 20-8 shows a little of the attention to detail that this program has throughout — support for floating appointments, the capability to move appointments forward or back by days, and configurable views.

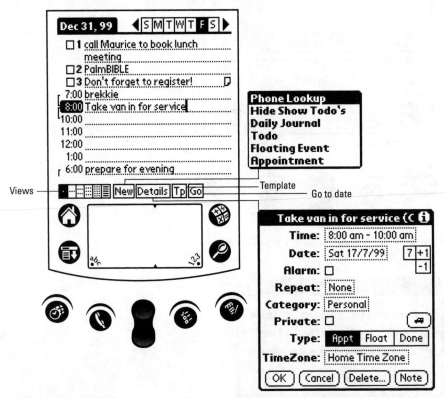

Figure 20-8: DateBk3

Start by adding handy one-week (see Figure 20-9) and two-week views, and then add year (Figure 20-10) and list views, support for icons, and multiple time zones. I particularly like the flexibility that DateBk3 provides to enable you to configure the display of To Do items. As you can see in Figure 20-11, you can specify which categories (and levels) should be displayed on your calendar, and whether they should be displayed in advance of their due dates.

Figure 20-9: DateBk3 Week View

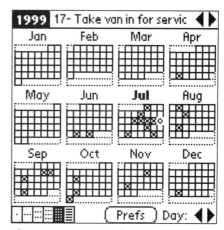

Figure 20-10: DateBk3 Year View

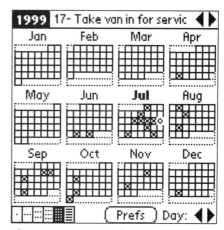

Figure 20-11: DateBk3 To Do Preferences

Note

All of the profits from the sale of Pimlico's shareware products go to the Dewar Wildlife Trust, Inc., a nonprofit corporation which funds various wildlife conservation projects — including its own project to build a sanctuary for Western Lowland Gorillas in the North Georgia Mountains in the year 2000. A simplified version of DateBk3 called DateBook+ is bundled with the Handspring Visor.

TZDateBook

Developer: Cromerica Technologies LLC
Cost: $15.00
Footprint: 141K

TZDateBook is Cromerica's companion to its TimeZone application. As you can
see from Figure 20-12, this DateBook replacement gives you support for dual time
zones, which is great if you're travelling. A utility called TZInit gives you access to
an editable database of over 900 locations.

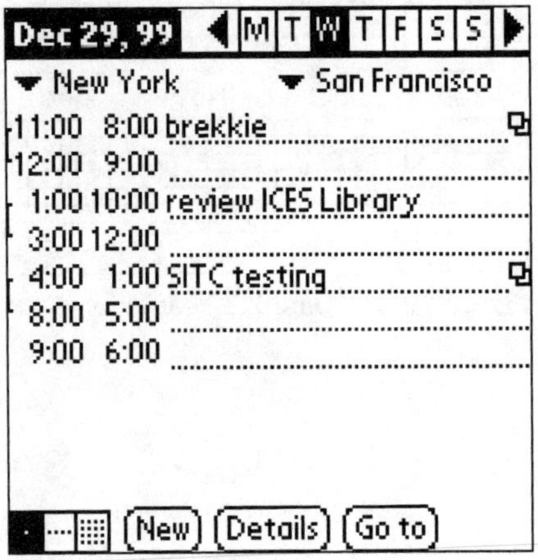

Figure 20-12: TZDateBook's Dual Time
Zone Display

Address Book replacements

Your Palm Organizer's Address Book application is pretty good, but there is always
room for improvement. Each of these applications adds features and functionality.
I'll end the suspense by telling you now that my favorite is SuperNames. For those
on a RAM diet, you can't go wrong with TealPhones. Table 20-2 identifies five
Address Book replacements, and lists various attributes in comparison with the
standard Address Book.

Address+

Developer: Paul Taylor
Cost: Freeware
Footprint: 47K

Address+ (see Figure 20-13) adds two useful features to the Address Book: the capability to copy information when creating a new record (to simplify adding multiple
people from one company) and two new sort orders. The new sort routine has the
added bonus of being faster than the standard application.

Table 20-2
Address Book Replacements

Program	Size	Cost	Sorts	Copy to New	AlphaBar	Links
Standard Address Book	n/a	Free	2	No	No	No
Address+	47K	Free	4	Yes	No	No
AddressPro	68K	$19.95	Unlimited	Yes	Yes	No
PalmPad	55K	$15.00	3	No	No	No
SuperNames	152K	$19.95	4	Yes	No	Yes
TealPhone	53K	$17.95	3	Yes	Yes	No

Figure 20-13: Address+

Address Pro

Developer: Jacob Zinger
Cost: $19.95 (shareware)
Footprint: 68K

Address Pro adds a new interface (see Figure 20-14) that enables you to select the first and second fields to sort on without limiting you to the standard "Last Name, First Name" and "Company, Last Name" sorts. This means that you can sort by city, state, area code, or whatever makes sense to you. Address Pro also adds an alphabetical bar so that you can jump to a section of your Address Book without having to use Graffiti.

Note   Address Pro requires Palm OS 3.0 or newer to run.

PalmPad

Developer: Ursini Dante
Cost: $15.00
Footprint: 55K

PalmPad enables you to filter your address book entries by country, state, or city just by selecting from pop-up lists from the top of the screen (see Figure 20-15).

Figure 20-14: Address Pro

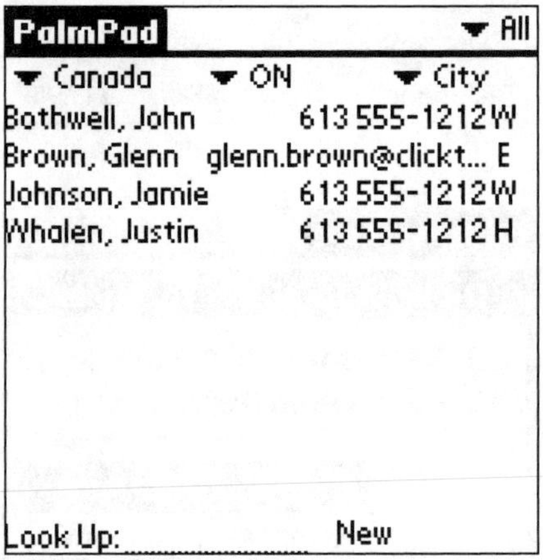

Figure 20-15: PalmPad

SuperNames

Developer: Stand Alone Software
Cost: $19.95
Footprint: 152K

SuperNames (see Figure 20-16) does one thing that its competition doesn't: It enables you to link Address Book items to each other, to appointments, and to To Do items (see Figure 20-17). This powerful feature enables you to use your Address Book as a contact manager, tracking the connections between people and recording your appointments. The redesigned tabbed interface works well, especially when adding new records. A configurable pop-up display shows the last 15 addresses you've looked up. All of this power does come with a price—the application is large. Fortunately, Stand Alone Software provides a fully functional 30-day demo that enables you to check it out for yourself.

Figure 20-16: SuperNames

Figure 20-17: Links in SuperNames

TealPhone

Developer: TealPoint Software
Cost: $17.95
Footprint: 52K

Imagine the standard Address Book application on steroids and you have an idea of what TealPhone is like. It stores multiple sorts (first/last/company), so switching the sort order is instant. The display (see Figure 20-18) features an oversized data display area with quick access to all of your contact's information. The program shows an attention to detail that is typical of TealPoint's applications, including a powerful search capability and new pop-up lists to aid with entering new records.

Figure 20-18: TealPhone

To Do List replacements

There are actually two products in this category: ToDo+, discussed here, is a replacement for your handheld's built-in To Do List, and Action Names, discussed earlier in this chapter, which combines DateBook and To Do List functionality.

ToDo+

Developer: Hands High Software
Cost: $19.95
Footprint: 85K

Another powerhouse application—ToDo+ (see Figure 20-19) enables you to add drawings or alarms to your To Do items and to create repeating tasks. Powerful viewing options also let you span categories to see what you need to do now. Attached drawings and notes can use Memo PLUS templates (covered next).

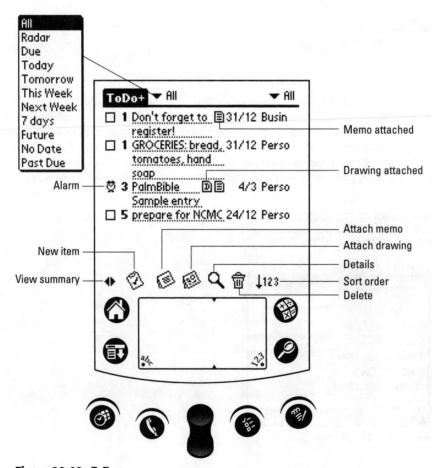

Figure 20-19: ToDo+

Memo Pad replacements

The built-in Memo Pad is overlooked by many users, yet it offers capabilities unequaled by the other built-in applications for easily moving data between your handheld and PC. These two replacements supplement the built-in application — one with templates and graphics, the other with spell checking.

Memo PLUS

Developer: Hands High Software
Cost: $14.95
Footprint: 65K

Memo PLUS (see Figure 20-20) adds two features to your Memo Pad: the capability to create and view drawings in graphics mode, and the capability to create and use text and graphics templates. The only shortcoming — and I know this is a lot to ask — is that I'd like to have graphics *and* text in the same memo.

NoteTaker

Developer: Evolutionary Systems
Cost: $18.00
Footprint: 114–146K (depends on the dictionary loaded)

NoteTaker takes a different approach; it adds a spell checker (see Figure 20-21) to your Memo Pad. Three different dictionaries are provided, so that you can install based on the memory available on your Palm Organizer.

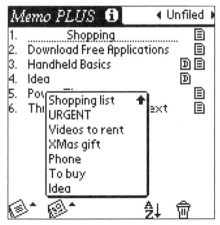

Figure 20-20: Memo PLUS

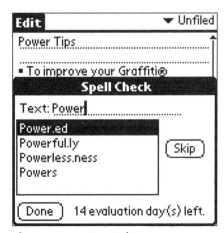

Figure 20-21: NoteTaker

Application launchers

One of the applications you use the most is Palm's built-in Application Launcher. Early renditions were somewhat limited (the first had no category views), so third-party developers jumped in, delivering tabbed views, pop-up lists, and other methods for easy access to your software.

Most of these applications add similar improvements, which leads to the comparison in Table 20-3. Some, such as CoLaunch, Commander, GoBar, and TealLaunch, offer completely new or different functionality. You need to read the text to see what these products offer.

			Table 20-3			
			Application Launcher Replacements			
Program	Size	Cost	Icon View	List View	Mini-Icons	Tabs
Standard Application Launcher	n/a	Free	Yes	Yes	No	No
CoLaunch	20K	$8.00	n/a	n/a	n/a	n/a
Commander	45K	$14.95	Yes	Yes	No	No
GoBar	49K	$14.00	Yes	No	No	No
LaunchPad	23K	Free	Yes	No	3	Yes
Launcher III	30K	Free	Yes	Yes	4	Yes
Launch'Em	97K	$10.00	Yes	Yes	12	Yes
PAL	21K	$12.00	Yes	No	4	No
QuickLaunch	26K	$39.95	Yes	Yes	6	Yes
TealLaunch	18K	$11.95	No	Yes	n/a	n/a

CoLaunch

Developer: Maple
Cost: $8.00
Footprint: 20K

CoLaunch (see Figure 20-22) takes a completely different approach, entirely bypassing icon or list displays. Instead, this utility enables you to configure the hardware buttons and Graffiti to launch applications. You do this by specifying combinations—press this button, and then scroll up, or press To Do followed by a Graffiti stroke. This enables powerusers to configure their handheld to do what looks like magic, launching apps with their own custom settings.

Commander

Developer: Palmation
Cost: $14.95
Footprint: 45K

Commander (Figure 20-23) combines replacements for your built-in Launcher Application and the Security Application. This combination enables Commander to give you more complete and configurable control over access to your Palm Organizer—you can set automatic locking, hiding of private records, and other options, including new ShortCut commands.

Figure 20-22: CoLaunch

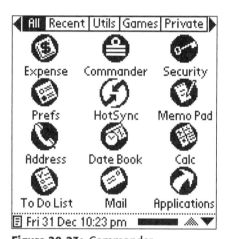

Figure 20-23: Commander

GoBar

Developer: Digivello
Cost: $14.00
Footprint: 49K

If you like the Start Menu on your PC (or Action GoMac, if you're a Mac user), you'll love GoBar. This utility gives you completely configurable icon screens, plus a pop-up menu (see Figure 20-24) that provides access to settings and utilities as well as to all of your applications.

LaunchPad

Developer: Eric Kenslow
Cost: Freeware
Footprint: 23K

LaunchPad was one of the first Application Launchers available, providing a tabbed interface (see Figure 20-25) that makes accessing your applications easy. The bottom of the screen includes day/date and battery display, along with mini-icons that provide quick access to your Palm Organizer's Preferences screen, power off, and lock functions.

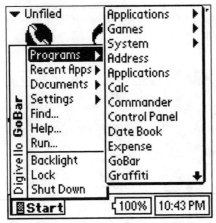

Figure 20-24: The GoBar pop-up menu

Figure 20-25: LaunchPad

Tip   Even if you install one of these replacements for Palm's built-in Launcher, you'll still need access to the original when you want to get info or delete applications. Fortunately, as soon as you install a third-party launcher, the Palm OS automatically adds an Applications icon, as shown in Figure 20-25.

Launcher III

Developer: Bozidar Benc
Cost: Freeware
Footprint: 30K

Launcher III takes the tabbed interface of LaunchPad, and runs with it, adding the capability to configure how icons are displayed onscreen (see Figure 20-26), including a list view and more mini-icons for additional utility.

Tip   Figure 20-25 and Figure 20-26 illustrate one of my favorite techniques when configuring a Launcher: I create a "Palm" tab or category, so that I have quick and easy access to Palm's built-in applications.

Figure 20-26: Icons displayed onscreen with Launcher III

Launch'Em

Developer: Synergy Solutions, Inc.
Cost: $10.00
Footprint: 97K

This one is the bomb. With Version 2.0 Launch'Em (see Figure 20-27) added features never seen before on a Palm Organizer. Tabs can be left, right, top, or bottom, and customized with themes (see Figure 20-28). Each tab can have its own view and sort. Want to create a favorites page? Launch'Em supports drag and drop, so you can create a screen with duplicates of icons from other pages. This app includes full support for Palm data types, including docs and Hacks, as well as a collapsible display at the bottom of the screen. A built-in Hack enables you to jump back to your previous application with a stroke, or to call up a popup a list of your most recent or most commonly used applications. Can you guess which launcher I use?

PAL

Developer: DovCom
Cost: $12.00 (shareware)
Footprint: 21K

PAL (Pilot Application Launcher) is another of the original launch utilities for the Palm Organizer, including a Category feature (see Figure 20-29) that enables you to quickly switch between screens of application categories. A Hack (PALHack.prc) enables older Pilot 1000/5000 users to run PAL by tapping the Applications button (not required for newer handhelds).

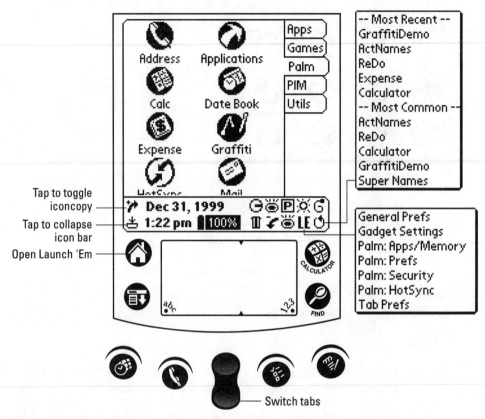

Figure 20-27: Launch'Em

Figure 20-28: Launch'Em Customized

Figure 20-29: PAL

QuickLaunch

Developer: Landware
Cost: $39.95 (as part of QuickPac)
Footprint: 26K

QuickLaunch lets you "have it your way." You can choose between a pop-up list of categories and a tabbed interface (see Figure 20-30), or between icons and text. You can also select up to six of ten mini-icons, including a handy favorites pop-up list. QuickLaunch is sold by Landware as part of its QuickPac software collection, which also includes QuickAgenda (discussed later in this chapter), QuickPad (a drawing program), and QuickText (a text-editing enhancement).

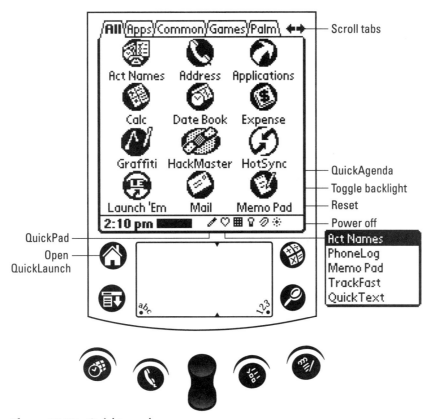

Figure 20-30: QuickLaunch

TealLaunch

Developer: TealPoint Software
Cost: $11.95
Footprint: 18K

TealLaunch runs as a system extension using HackMaster (see Chapter 22 for more on HackMaster). Once you've set up TealLaunch's Preferences (see Figure 20-31), you can make your Palm Organizer dance. The popup window in Figure 20-32 gives you instant access to a predefined list of applications, plus buttons with commonly used functions. Your handheld's buttons can be configured to act in different ways, depending on whether the TealLaunch window is open, or whether you tap the button or hold it down for a second. Once learned, this can be a real timesaver for the Palm poweruser.

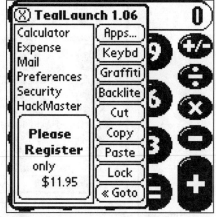

Figure 20-31: TealLaunch Preferences

Figure 20-32: The TealLaunch pop-up window

Application Helpers

You don't have to completely replace your core applications — a number of programs add to what is already built into your Palm Organizer.

DateBook helpers

These helper applications will work with your built-in DateBook, or with the DateBook replacements discussed earlier in the chapter. Each adds its own unique functionality.

DateMate

Developer: PalmMate
Cost: $19.95
Footprint: 53K

If you can't remember important dates — especially birthdays and anniversaries — check out DateMate. This application has a simple interface (see Figure 20-33) that lets you quickly add important dates, to which you can also add alarms and memos. Even better, you can configure it to automatically extract important dates based on the custom fields in your Address Book.

DatePlan

Developer: Denis Faivre
Cost: $12.00
Footprint: 19K

If you like the idea of being able to have icons displayed on your monthly calendar, similar to Action Names and DateBk3 (discussed earlier in this chapter) but don't have enough room for the larger applications, have a look at DatePlan (Figure 20-34). This application replaces your DateBook's monthly view with a configurable graphics view, which can include icons, shading, and tagging of weeks based on a fiscal calendar. If you want the additional features, it can also work in conjunction with DateBk3, giving you more control over your calendar display than you ever thought possible!

Figure 20-33: DateMate   **Figure 20-34:** DatePlan

Date Wheel

Developer: DeftSoft
Cost: Freeware
Footprint: 10K

Date Wheel (see Figure 20-35) is the electronic handheld version of the plastic wheel calendar used by businesses to calculate lead times. Set two of three parameters, and Date Wheel will calculate the third; lock down a figure and you can adjust to set optimum dates.

Palm Planner

Developer: Thomas Jawer
Cost: $10.00
Footprint: 23K

Here's another supplement that gives you a graphic view of your calendar without the RAM overhead of the DateBook replacements. Palm Planner (see Figure 20-36) gives you graphical month and yearly overview, while retaining direct access to your built-in DateBook application.

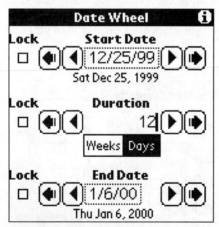

Figure 20-35: Date Wheel

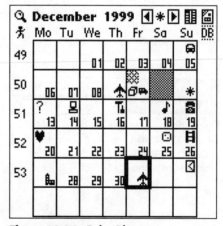

Figure 20-36: Palm Planner

Startup displays

These four applications all share a similar goal: to show you a quick overview (your "day at glance"), so that you can quickly deal with what is most important.

Agenda

Developer: DovCom
Cost: $12.00
Footprint: 24K

Agenda (see Figure 20-37) provides a simple overview of your appointments and to do items, with tabs that enable you to view items for today, tomorrow, or this week. The bottom of the screen shows date, time, and battery information, and buttons enable you to perform a soft reset, a shut down and lock, or a simple power off.

QuickAgenda

Developer: Landware
Cost: $39.95 (as part of QuickPac)
Footprint: 31K

QuickAgenda uses an interface similar to Agenda, with some significant additions: it displays to do items and appointments on the same tabs (see Figure 20-38), and you can select up to 6 tools (out of 10) for instant onscreen access. QuickAgenda is sold by Landware as part of their QuickPac software collection, which also includes QuickLaunch (discussed earlier in this chapter), QuickPad (a drawing program), and QuickText (a text-editing enhancement).

Figure 20-37: Agenda

Figure 20-38: QuickAgenda

TealGlance

Developer: TealPoint Software
Cost: $11.95
Footprint: 24K

TealGlance (see Figure 20-39) combines a digital or analog clock with day, date, appointment, and To Do List items. TealGlance's Settings are called via HackMaster (see Figure 20-40). For more on HackMaster, see Chapter 22.

Figure 20-39: TealGlance

Figure 20-40: TealGlance Settings

Today

Developer: Synergy Solutions, Inc.
Cost: $17.95
Footprint: 29K

Today (see Figure 20-41) offers a familiar tabbed interface that combines appointment and to do items to give you a quick overview. Today is available separately or as part of Synergy's PDActivate (formerly Hi-Five) collection of utilities.

Logging tools

Want to track the things you track on your Palm Organizer? Have I confused you yet? These tools add project management functionality to your handheld.

PalmJournal

Developer: Intrepid Software
Cost: $14.00
Footprint: 14K

PalmJournal (see Figure 20-42) is basically an electronic version of a diary program; it enables you to record information and export it to your Memo Pad, To Do List, or a Windows companion application.

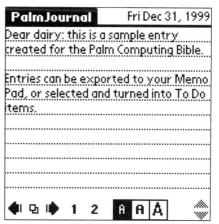

Figure 20-41: Today's tabbed interface   **Figure 20-42:** PalmJournal

PocketJournal

Developer: Chapura Software
Cost: $39.95
Footprint: 56K

The journaling function in Microsoft Outlook is one many users overlook. It's a shame, because this powerful tracking tool exponentially adds to the program's capabilities. Journaling enables you to automatically track data entered in Outlook — e-mail, to do items, phone calls, you name it. The key is that this data is tracked by project, category, or person, so you can keep a diary of activities. Once you've used it, you'll be hooked. For anything that you want to track, just create a new item in PocketJournal (see Figure 20-43). Whenever you want, you can review your activities, either in PocketJournal (see Figure 20-44) or in Microsoft Outlook.

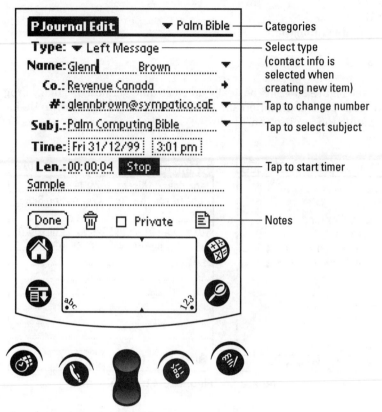

Figure 20-43: PocketJournal entry

PhoneLog

Developer: Hands High Software
Cost: $19.95
Footprint: 58K

One of the things I find myself doing a lot with PocketJournal (just described) is tracking telephone calls — did I leave a message, did we talk, and so on. PhoneLog (see Figure 20-45) does a good job of tracking phone calls, and if that's all you need, it sells for half the price. Not surprisingly, the interface is similar to PocketJournal, which Hands High authored for Chapura.

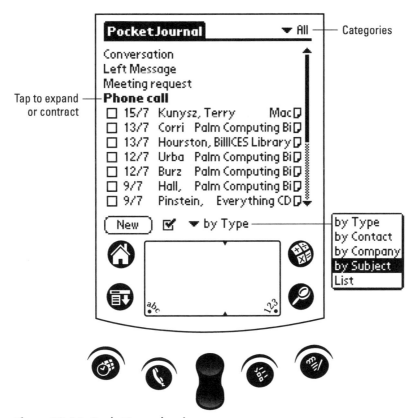

Figure 20-44: PocketJournal review

Figure 20-45: PhoneLog

TrackFast

Developer: Vision 7 Software
Cost: $30.00
Footprint: 81K

This one may be the ultimate solution if you want to link the data on your Palm Organizer. TrackFast (see Figure 20-46) is the only Palm application I know of that can integrate data from all four of your primary applications. It uses two main components: *Tracks* can be projects, people, events, or anything you want to keep track of. Each Track consists of a series of *Entries*. You can create links in your entries to any of the four primary applications by selecting the appropriate icon (see Figure 20-47). A 30-day evaluation is available. My suggestion is to run through the tutorial in the user guide and try it yourself.

Figure 20-46: TrackFast   **Figure 20-47:** TrackFast Links

More essentials

Here are a couple of utilities that fill a few gaps in your To Do List functionality.

Plonk!

Developer: Brad Goodman
Cost: $5.00
Footprint: 6K

This is one of my favorites. Plonk! (see Figure 20-48) enables you to automate procrastination by automatically forwarding uncompleted To Do items to today's date.

ReDo

Developer: Rick Huebner
Cost: $10.00
Footprint: 38K

One of the shortcomings of Palm's built-in To Do List is that it's incapable of scheduling recurring items. ReDo (see Figure 20-49) enables you to set reminders that will automatically appear on your To Do List at whatever time you schedule them for.

Figure 20-48: Plonk!

Figure 20-49: Scheduling items with ReDo

Supercharging Your Palm Handheld

Okay, you've replaced all of the applications in your Palm—so, where do you go from here? The first thing to do is to create easy access to the new applications.

Mapping the buttons

Open your Palm Organizer's Preferences and select Buttons from the pop-up list in the upper right-hand corner. As Figure 20-50 shows, this screen enables you to remap the hardware buttons to any application you installed on your handheld. Figure 20-51 shows how the buttons are mapped on my Palm V. I use Alan Pinstein's Contrast Button Hack to remap the contrast button to Cesium (see Chapter 15 for more on Cesium). You'll learn more about MenuHack and FindHack, along with HackMaster, in Chapter 22.

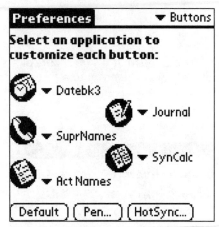

Figure 20-50: Remapping the buttons

Tip   If you reassign your buttons, you can still launch the original applications—you just have to use the Applications Launcher.

Utilities

As you add applications to your Palm Organizer, you'll find that you start running out of memory and will have to make some tough decisions. Here are two easy ones: check out TRG's FlashPro, which gives any Palm III or newer an additional 800K of memory, and Alexander Hind's BackupBuddy, which backs up your new software with every HotSync. You'll learn more about these utilities in Chapter 21.

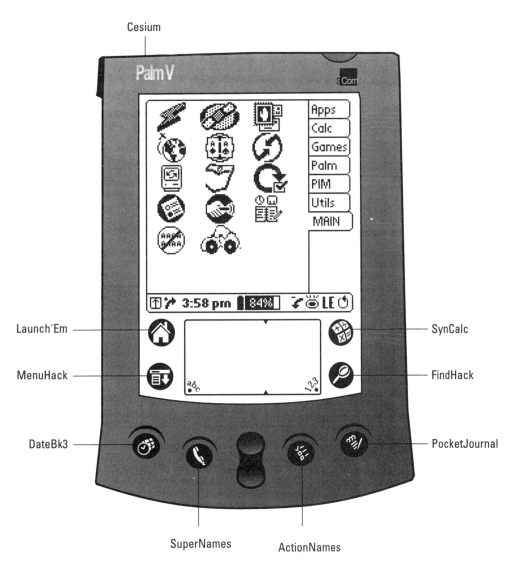

Figure 20-51: How the buttons are mapped on Glenn's Palm V

Summary

✦ If you have room on your Palm Organizer, either DateBk3 or Action Names make a great choice for PIM integration — DateBk3 if you need support for multiple time zones, and Action Names if you need contact integration.

✦ For my money, the best choices for Address Book replacements are SuperNames and TealPhone, with the nod going to SuperNames if you can spare the room.

✦ The third-party utilities offer much more than your built-in Application Launcher. In this category, I use Launch'Em, with TealLaunch being a close second if a transparent utility is the goal.

✦ The journaling capabilities of PalmJournal are so convenient that I've also started using the mirror functionality in Microsoft Outlook. I find this to be a great addition if you need to track people and projects.

✦ Don't forget to remap your handheld's buttons to access your new applications after you've installed them — it will make using them a much better experience.

✦   ✦   ✦

Customizing Your Palm with Utilities

In This Chapter

Backup

Batteries

Beaming

Memory

Security

Speedups

System Tools

More Tools

What kind of toy would the Palm Organizer be without utilities? It ships with the basics and third-party developers have stepped in, and created many more. This chapter deals with backup, both manual and automated; batteries and battery utilities; and beaming, out of the box and with some interesting applications. We also look at memory, how to manage it and how to squeeze out more; security to keep your private records private; and system tools that let you tweak your Palm's operating system. I make no attempt to discuss all of the tools that are available for your handheld — only the very best available tools.

Backup

I'm always surprised when I talk to computer users and discover how many run without backups. In my view, there are two types of users: Those who have already lost data to a crash and those who *will*. This applies equally to Palm users — the more you add to your handheld, the more likely you are to experience a crash. You can recover from most crashes with a soft or warm reset, but there will come a time when only a hard reset will restart your handheld — and that means that your precious data will be gone.

Palm Resets

You can reset your Palm device in three ways:

> ✦ **Soft Reset:** Gently insert the end of a paperclip or your stylus' reset pin (Palm III and newer) in the reset hole on the back of your handheld: Your Palm Organizer should restart with all data intact.

✦ **Warm Reset:** Hold down the Scroll Up button while performing a soft reset; your handheld will restart without loading third-party extensions and Hacks.

✦ **Hard Reset:** Hold down the Power button while performing a soft reset, pause until you see the Palm logo, and then release the Power button. Your Palm Organizer will display a message asking you to confirm that you want to delete all data from your handheld. If you confirm, it will revert to its original condition without any of your data or programs.

See Chapter 24 for more on troubleshooting Palm Organizer problems.

Restoring your data

A hard reset doesn't have to be a disaster—a HotSync should recover your data, at least back to the state of your previous HotSync. The only problem is that most of your third-party applications do not reinstall automatically, which means you'll have some work to do.

Manual backups

With a little preparation and work, you can make a complete restore easy. The first thing to do is to create two directories—one for installed applications, and one for those you have removed (I call mine PalmLOAD and PalmOFF). When you install a new or updated application on your Palm Organizer, just drag a copy of the .prc and .pdb files to the PalmLOAD directory. Whenever you delete an application from your handheld, remember to move the corresponding .prc and .pdb files from the PalmLOAD to the PalmOFF directory. What is the payoff for all this work? When you need to reload your third-party applications, all you have to do is drag the contents of your PalmLOAD directory to open the Install Tool and perform a HotSync. This *was* the process I used until I discovered BackupBuddy.

New Feature

If you're using Palm OS 3.3 (which shipped with the Palm Vx organizer), you can safely ignore this manual backup strategy; backup of installed applications is one of the new features built into the upgrade. All users with flash memory (all Palm Organizers since the Palm III except the Palm IIIe) can download and install the update.

BackupBuddy

Developer: Alexander Hinds
Cost: $19.95

If you install third-party applications on your Palm Organizer, and you haven't or can't upgrade to OS 3.3, this one is a must—see Chapter 6 for more details (or use the preceding manual alternative). The bonus is a much more powerful utility than that built into even OS 3.3, complete with support for TRG's FlashPro (more on this one later in this chapter), and both Windows and Macintosh versions are available.

FlashPack

Developer: Technology Resource Group (TRG)
Cost: Included with FlashPro
Footprint: 17K

This essential utility was originally distributed by Sam Denton as freeware and is now included with TRG's excellent FlashPro utility. This is one utility I highly recommend to those who travel, and to computer support staffs that must support those who do. Imagine that you're out of town (or even in a meeting) without a HotSync cradle, and your Palm Organizer crashes, taking with it critical information, and requiring a hard reset. FlashPack (see Figure 21-1) enables you to restore your handheld's databases without having to perform a HotSync. Can you say *miracle*?

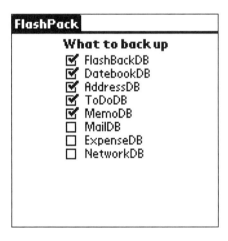

Figure 21-1: FlashPack can back up your essential data

Palm Buddy

Developer: Florent Pillet
Cost: $20.00 (shareware)
Footprint: 14K

Florent takes a different approach to backup and install with his Macintosh application Palm Buddy. Turn off HotSyncing, and Palm Buddy will create a direct, *live* link to your Palm Organizer. See Chapter 6 for complete coverage.

Batteries

I'd like to thank Peter Strobel for his help with this section. Not only has he written some of the best battery software available for the Palm platform, he is one of the experts, if not the expert, on batteries used in our favorite handheld. See Appendix D for Peter's technical analysis of batteries and the Palm Organizer.

Unless you have a Palm V, Vx, or a new IIIc, batteries are an important topic. Your Palm Organizer's Launcher includes a display (see Figure 21-2) that gives you an indication of how much juice you have left, and the operating system will warn you when your batteries get low; but many users want a more precise idea of how long they have left. Those who use third-party application launchers (see Chapter 20) are, in most cases, able to see more detail about their batteries' condition. At minimum, I recommend carrying a spare set of batteries, and using any of these utilities to give you a better estimate of when you'll have to use them.

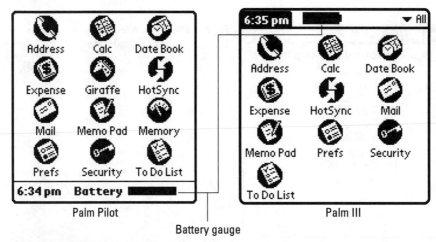

Palm Pilot

Battery gauge

Palm III

Figure 21-2: The Standard Battery Gauge

Extending battery life

Long battery life is one of the benefits of using a Palm Organizer; with average use, you can expect three to five weeks of life from a set of AAA batteries. There are a few things that you can do to reduce the frequency of battery changes:

✦ Change the Auto-off setting in Preferences ➪ General to one minute.

✦ Limit your use of the backlight (it quickly uses batteries).

✦ Remove your handheld from the cradle immediately after a HotSync (unless you have a Palm IIIc, V or Vx organizer, which recharge in the cradle)—the serial port places a very small drain on your handheld's batteries).

✦ Turn off Beaming in Preferences ➪ General (this will result in a very small power saving).

Tip

The new Duracell Ultra batteries are great for high-current, high-draining devices (such as cameras), but they have no higher capacity, just a higher peak current. This means that there is no greater benefit to using them instead of regular Duracell batteries in your Palm Organizer.

Caution

Battery manufacturers don't like to talk about it, but *all* replaceable batteries (including the so-called leak-proof ones) start to leak when totally empty and still under load—even if the load is small. 3Com recommends that you take out the batteries if the device is not used for a long period of time. A good estimate for fully recharged NiMHs (550mAh) is eight weeks; fully charged alkalines should be good for three to four months.

BatteryInfo

Developer: Tammy Cravit
Cost: $5.00 (shareware)
Footprint: 11K

This shareware application (see Figure 21-3) displays voltage information, lets you select your battery type (including support for the Palm V's lithium battery), and lets you edit your handheld's warning and critical voltage thresholds.

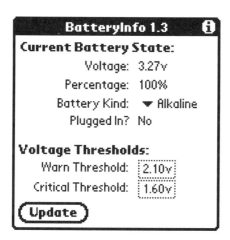

Figure 21-3: BatteryInfo

Caution

Palm warns against changing the voltage thresholds. Changing these settings can allow your battery to drain completely, without notice. Unless you really know what you are doing and are prepared to risk the consequences, these settings are best left at their defaults.

Battery Monitor

Developer: Peter Strobel
Cost: $8.00 (shareware)
Footprint: 11K

I suspect few people know more about battery performance than Peter; check out
his Web site (www.pstec.de/ppp) or Appendix D if you'd like to learn more yourself. Peter's software exemplifies the quality level I have found in much of what is
available for the Palm Organizer — the very best. Battery Monitor (see Figure 21-4)
tracks the performance of your Palm Organizer's batteries to give you an accurate
guess of just how much longer you can expect your batteries to last.

Voltage Control

Developer: Peter Strobel
Cost: $8.00 (shareware)
Footprint: 4K

On the surface, VoltageControl (see Figure 21-5) is a simple display of the voltage
left in your PalmPilot's batteries. Look a little more closely though, and you'll see
more: configurable low-battery warning levels and the capability to hide the display
until your first warning. This is an essential tool for those who use rechargeable
batteries. The program ships with a utility that enables Windows users to configure
their settings, and Max Edelman (see Chapter 13 for coverage of his MAM Suite
application) has written VCPatch, which enables Mac users to customize their
Voltage Control settings.

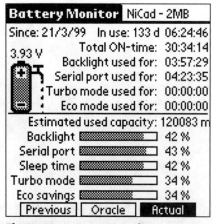

Figure 21-4: Battery Monitor

Figure 21-5: Address Book showing Voltage
Control in the lower right-hand corner

Voltage Display

Developer: Peter Strobel
Cost: Freeware
Footprint: 2K

This freeware utility (see Figure 21-6) gives those who use Palm's Application Launcher a numeric display of their remaining battery power.

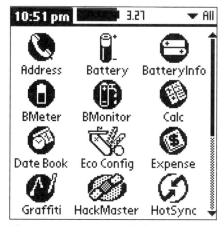

Figure 21-6: Voltage Display

Beaming

The Palm III brought with it a wonderful new feature: the capability to beam data using a built-in infrared port. This enables users to quickly pass electronic business cards, shareware applications, and other data through thin air.

Built-in applications

All of the built-in applications support beaming. As an example, if you want to beam contact information, tap the menu icon and select Beam Address from the Record menu. You should make sure your handheld is within 4 to 36 inches of the device you want to beam to and you'll see a dialog box like "a" in Figure 21-7. If your handhelds aren't correctly aligned, you may see a Searching dialog box ("b" in Figure 21-7). Once aligned, the owners of receiving devices will see a dialog box ("c" in Figure 21-7) asking whether they want to accept the beam. If they tap Yes, they'll receive your information.

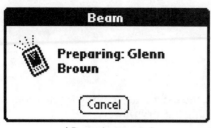

a) Preparing to send

b) Searching for target

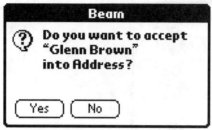

c) Receiving beam confirmation

Figure 21-7: Beaming an address

Tip   If your intended recipient doesn't receive your beam, the first thing to check is that he or she has Beam Receive: On in Preferences ⇨ General.

Date Book

Select an event by tapping it, and then tap the Menu icon and select Beam Event from the Record menu. As with all of the built-in applications, Command+B is the Graffiti stroke for beaming a selected item.

Address Book

The first thing you should do here is to select your own contact information, and then tap on the Menu icon and choose Select Business Card from the Record menu — an icon will appear in the top center (see Figure 21-8). This lets your Palm Organizer know which record to beam when you choose Beam Business Card from the same menu later.

Tip   Once you've completed the Select Business Card process, you can instantly beam your business card to any other IR (infrared)-enabled Palm Organizer by simply pressing the Address button. You may want to create a limited copy of your personal information for beaming purposes, especially if you use notes to store private reminders.

You can also beam a category from the list view, or open a contact and select Beam Address.

To Do List, Memo Pad

From the list view, you can tap the Menu icon and chose Beam Category from the Record menu, or you can open an individual item and choose Beam Item or Memo.

Application Launcher

You can also beam applications and data from the Applications Launcher. Just select Beam from the App menu to get the dialog box shown in Figure 21-9. Built-in and other locked files will display in the listing with a lock icon. Beaming other files is as simple is tapping to select, and then tapping Beam. Remember to beam only demo versions of your applications, not commercial products or registered shareware.

Figure 21-8: Business card selected

Figure 21-9: Applications to beam

New Feature Palm OS 3.3 includes beaming enhancements, including infrared HotSync (see Chapter 6) and support for the IrCOMM implementation of IrDA standards. This means that your Palm Organizer can communicate with any device that supports the IrCOMM standard, such as an Ericsson cell phone.

IR applications

Third-party support for Palm's IR (infrared) capabilities has come a long way since the Palm III was first introduced. IS/Complete even markets a series of IR Games (great for that boring meeting) on its Web site at www.iscomplete.org. The following are a few of the more interesting infrared products available for your handheld.

Beam Box

Developer: Jeremy Radlow
Cost: $5.00 (shareware)
Footprint: 14K

Beam Box (see Figure 21-10) provides a quick and easy way to filter files for beaming, so you can quickly find and send what you want. Beam Box will let you beam more than .prc applications. In fact, it's the only way I know of to beam HackMaster Hacks, application databases, and text documents (like novels, reports, and reference documents) that require readers such as AportisDoc. Beam Box also provides a mechanism that enables you to beam a demo version of your registered shareware.

Note   For Beam Box to work it has to be on both handhelds. If it isn't installed on the other device, you first have to beam over the application.

BeamLink

Developer: JP Systems, Inc.
Cost: $49.95
Footprint: 130K

If you have a two-way pager (specifically a GlenAyre AccessLink II with two-way service from Skytel or MCI), you can use the IR port on your III- or V-series Organizer to send and receive messages (see Figure 21-11). The software also enables you to upload up to 1500 address book entries to your pager.

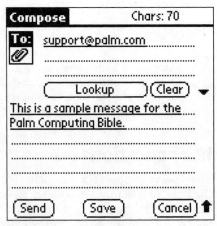

Figure 21-10: Using Beam Box to beam applications

Figure 21-11: BeamLink

IRP2PChat

Developer: IS/Complete
Cost: $15.00
Footprint: 47K

IS/Complete specializes in infrared applications, with IR games, applications, and utilities, including IrPrint and IrLink (for infrared HotSyncing). IRP2PChat offers real-time whiteboard communication using IR-equipped Palm Organizers. While connected, you can chat or share a graphics tablet (see Figure 21-12).

PageNOW!

Developer: Mark/Space Softworks, Inc.
Cost: $79.95
Footprint: 61K

PageNOW! (see Figure 21-13) enables you to send messages to your pager or cellular phone.

PageNOW! sends messages using one of three protocols:

1. A modem phone call to any paging/phone service that supports the TAP protocol

2. A SMS (short messaging service) message using a PCS phone/modem (data-enabled GSM cellular phone attached to an Option International Snap On modem, or via IR using an Ericsson 888)

3. Using a modem to make a TCP connection to a paging server that supports the SNPP protocol

For more on PageNOW! and telecommunications using your Palm Organizer, see Chapter 16.

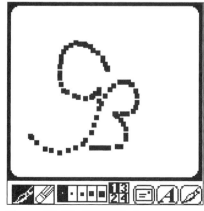

Figure 21-12: IRP2PChat

Figure 21-13: PageNOW!

PalmPrint

Developer: Stevens Creek Software
Cost: $19.95
Footprint: 25K

PalmPrint (see Figure 21-14) lets you print directly from your Palm Organizer either via serial cable or through infared. PalmPrint supports the three most common printer languages: PCL, Epson-compatible, and Postscript, so the chances are good that your printer is included. Supported infared printers include the Canon BJC-50 and BJC-80, Citizen PN60I, and Hewlett-Packard DeskJet 340, LaserJet 6P, and LaserJet 6MP. Third-party support for PalmPrint includes MultiMail Pro, HanDBase, and Satellite Forms.

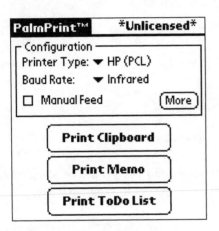

Figure 21-14: PalmPrint

Remote controls

The addition of an infrared port meant that it was inevitable that third-party developers would figure out how to turn your handheld into a learning remote, and they did — with products such as OmniRemote, PalmRemote, and WedgeTV. There was considerable press about the new capabilities: Wouldn't it mean that thieves could use a Palm Organizer to steal your car? Not likely. If this were a possibility, then why not use a $10.00 learning remote control device? The reality is that most car security systems use radio frequencies, not IR. In any case, if a thief has your keys long enough to train a learning remote, why not just use the keys? A much more practical application (after your television) is to teach your handheld to mimic an X-10 controller, so that it can run your *house*.

Note   The strength of the infrared signal from your handheld is dependent on the model. Palm III devices seem to have the shortest range, with the Palm V outdoing them somewhat; the real surprise is that the best signal is obtained from Palm's 2MB upgrade kit for the PalmPilot. IR signal can be very directional; I find with careful aiming that I can easily get 15 feet or better with my Palm V. If you find you want better range, check out Gary Mayhak's IR Blaster at http://members.aol.com/gmayhak/tcl/blaster.htm.

OmniRemote

Developer: Pacific NeoTek
Cost: $19.95
Footprint: 18K

As soon as I saw this one, I had to have it. OmniRemote (see Figure 21-15) turns your IR-equipped Palm Organizer into a remote control that you can use replace all of the remotes in your house. The demo version enables you to configure one television; registration enables you to build and configure your own remotes. All you need do to create a new remote is to decide which buttons you want to display, and then place them onscreen. The next step is to "train" your handheld — tap the button you want to configure, and then align your remote with your Palm Organizer and press the corresponding button. In a few seconds, you'll hear a beep, and the button will change from a dotted to a solid outline. Redo this process for all of your buttons, and you're done. Buttons can call macros or other screens; you can even configure your hardware buttons.

Figure 21-15: The remote control for my bedroom TV

PalmRemote

Developer: Hiromu Okada
Cost: $20.00
Footprint: 48K

PalmRemote (see Figure 21-16) is another powerhouse utility that turns your Palm Organizer into a learning remote. The difference is that it also has built-in codes for a number of common brands of televisions and VCRs, so you may not have to program it to use it (it works "out of the box" on my Sony television). With multiple views for each device, and full support for Graffiti, this program does everything you'd ever want your remote to do.

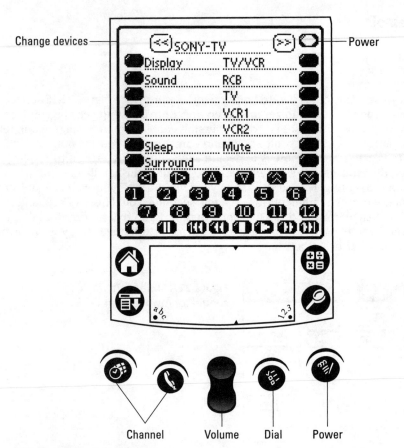

Change devices ——— SONY-TV   Power

Display   TV/VCR
Sound   RCB
           TV
           VCR1
           VCR2
Sleep   Mute
Surround

Channel   Volume   Dial   Power

Figure 21-16: PalmRemote

Wedge TV

Developer: PalmVision Software
Cost: $30.00
Footprint: 77K

Wedge TV (see Figure 21-17) offers learning remote capability for The Wedge, an infrared device that fits in the Palm III cradle. Check out Gary Mayhak's Web site at http://members.aol.com/~gmayhak/tcl/wedge.htm for more on The Wedge.

Figure 21-17: Wedge TV

Memory

The Palm Organizer ships with limited tools to handle memory. Prior to OS 3.0, the Memory application (see Figure 21-18) enabled users to view their applications, both by size and by number of records, and to delete applications. Palm OS 3.0 rolled the Memory application's functionality into the Application Launcher, where you can delete applications or view by version, size, or number of records (see Figure 21-19).

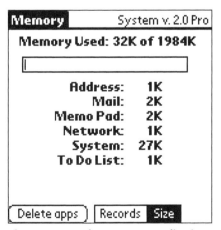

Figure 21-18: The Memory application (OS 2.0)

Figure 21-19: Application Info (OS 3.0)

Recovering space

What do you do when you start to run out of room on your handheld? The first thing to do is to take a good look at your installed applications — there may be a few that you no longer use that can be deleted. You may be able to free up a bit more space by using the Purge command in your Date Book and To Do List applications to archive completed appointments and items. If you can't live with memory limitations, you may want to consider one of the memory upgrades covered in Chapter 23.

Note   You will find that you can't delete Palm's built-in applications to save space, even if you are using a third-party replacement application. The reason is simple: These applications are loaded (along with the operating system) into the ROM of your handheld — so deleting them (even if you could) won't save any space.

Memory fragmentation

All versions of the Palm OS prior to version 3.0 were subject to memory fragmentation problems. This is where pieces of an application's data are stored in different places in your handheld's memory, rather than in one block. The free space shown by the Memory application may actually be smaller blocks of memory. How does this affect you? If you only have small blocks of free space, some Palm applications may not load. The cure is to use either Deskfree's Recycle or TRG's Defragger to defragment the memory in your PalmPilot. These applications defragment your PalmPilot's memory, moving all of the data and free space together into contiguous blocks, freeing up space to load applications.

FlashPro

Developer: Technology Resource Group (TRG)
Cost: $29.95
Footprint: 43K

Starting with the Palm III, all Palm Organizers, except the Palm IIIe, have shipped with 2MB of flash memory in addition to their RAM allotment. The intent of Flash memory is to enable Palm to upgrade the version of the OS in your handheld. The current OS takes a little over 1.1MB of your Flash memory, leaving a little over 800K free. No one outside of 3Com understands Palm memory better than do the wizards at TRG; they figured out how to load programs into the unused Flash memory in your handheld.

TRG's original program, FlashBuilder III, required a Windows 9*x*/NT application to load applications. Their latest and greatest is FlashPro, which doesn't require a desktop component to work (see Figure 21-20). This essential utility enables you to move programs back and forth between RAM and Flash memory. Not only do you get almost a megabyte for your $30.00, but there are advantages to loading applications into Flash memory: it frees up your regular memory, programs cannot be lost due to crashes or power failures, and memory access is faster.

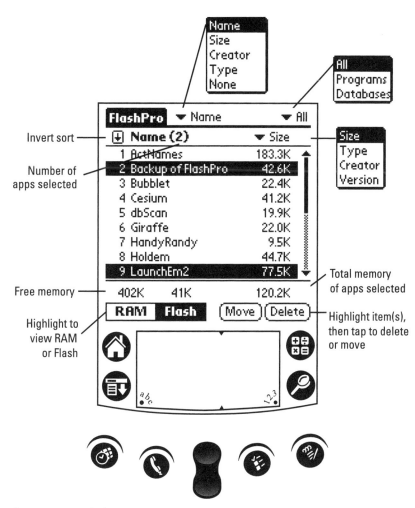

Figure 21-20: FlashPro

Moving an application to Flash

Moving an application into Flash memory is easy:

1. Open FlashPro. If HackMaster is installed, you'll see a message warning you not to move, copy, or delete enabled Hacks (the warning can be turned off in Preferences).

2. You'll see a listing of all files loaded in RAM—tap the file or files you want to move into Flash memory, and then tap the Move button to display a dialog box like that shown in Figure 21-21. In a few seconds, your application will be loaded into Flash memory, and you'll have freed up the corresponding amount of memory in your handheld.

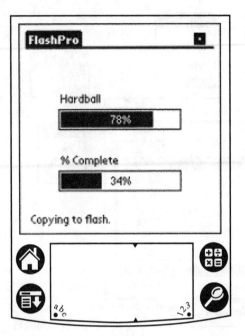

Figure 21-21: Moving a file into Flash memory

Note If you have difficulty running an application from Flash memory, reverse the process (tap on the file in the Flash listing to select it, and then select Move) to move it back to regular memory.

What doesn't run?

Most applications run fine from Flash memory, but there are some that don't work properly. such as most HackMaster Hacks, read/write databases (which need to update themselves), some applications or their data files. You'll find an updated compatibility listing at `www.asynccomputing.com/cgi-bin/ displayTRGCompatListing.pl`.

Note Unlike regular RAM in the newer Palm devices, Flash memory can fragment. Fortunately, FlashPro includes a tool (see Figure 21-22) that you can use to defragment after changing your Flash configuration. You will need to have 64K of memory free in order to defragment your Flash.

Third-party support

FlashPack (discussed earlier in this chapter) is a great companion, enabling you to automatically backup your essential data files to nonvolatile Flash memory. FlashPack is now supported by TRG, and is included with FlashPro. Users of Synergy's Launch'Em 2.0 (see Chapter 20) may want to try Andrew Penner's Flash'Em, a $5.00 shareware plug-in that enables you to drag applications to Flash memory using Launch'Em.

Aside from its memory capabilities, FlashPro is a powerful application that enables you to filter and view file types and to delete files (both from regular and Flash memory). This is a true essential for the Palm poweruser; I can't recommend it highly enough.

Security

Your Palm Organizer comes with pretty decent security software (see Figure 21-23).

The password you assign on the Palm Security settings screen is used for the following tasks:

✦ Hiding and showing private records, which you can create in any of the primary applications.

✦ Hiding and showing private records in the Palm desktop software on your computer.

✦ Accessing your handheld when the Turn Off & Lock Device command is used.

If you are concerned about someone snooping on your handheld, set the Preferences ➪ Buttons ➪ Pen command to Turn Off & Lock; then a stroke up from the Graffiti area will turn off your handheld, locking it so that your password is required access your information.

✦ Changing the password.

If you forget your password, you can assign a new one, but all private records will be deleted.

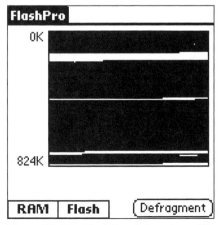

Figure 21-22: FlashPro defragging utility

Figure 21-23: Palm Security settings

Caution   If you use FlashPro, remember that data stored in Flash memory is not erased with a hard reset, which means that it can be easily recovered. For this reason, you should not backup to Flash memory data that you want to secure.

Third-party security applications

There are two types of security applications available for the Palm Organizer: those that lock your handheld from unwanted access, and those that encrypt specified records to protect them. Table 21-1 highlights the features of the security applications covered in this section. One thing to bear in mind with security applications is that the more secure you make your data, the bigger a pain it can be to get at; you should try the demo versions of those applications you are interested in before purchase. Greater security also comes with greater risk: if you forget your password, your information may be gone forever.

Table 21-1
Palm Security Applications

Name	Version	Price	Size	Type	Conduit	Security
Commander	1.32	$14.95	45K	Lock	n/a	Medium
OnlyMe	1.5	$9.95	36K	Lock	n/a	Low
Padlock Plus	1.1	$4.95	10K	Lock	n/a	Medium
TealLock	1.87	$11.95	34K	Lock	n/a	Medium
JAWS Memo	1.03	$19.95	42K	Encryption	Memo	4096 bit
Mobile Account Manager	2.02	$19.95	38K	Encryption	Memo	Proprietary
Password Store	1.7	$15.00	45K	Encryption	Memo	Blowfish
Secret!	2.3	$35.00	31K	Encryption	Yes	Proprietary
TopSecret Desktop	1.2	$27.50	27K	Encryption	Yes	TEA

Lock utilities

These utilities strengthen your handheld's built-in Turn Off & Lock capability, enabling you to fine-tune when and how your Palm Organizer is locked. Commander (see Chapter 20) extends the concept by integrating security into their application-launching utility.

OnlyMe

Developer: Tranzoa Co.
Cost: $9.95 (shareware)
Footprint: 36K (plus 4K for background image)

This simple utility (see Figure 21-24) locks your handheld every time you turn it off. The first thing you see when it is turned on, is a display showing the time, owner information (which it draws from Preferences ➪ Owner), an optional background picture, and a graphic representation of your Palm Organizer's main buttons — press the right key combination and you're in. You can enter the combination using Graffiti, tapping the onscreen buttons, or by pressing the hardware keys. OnlyMe is convenient and easy to use.

Padlock Plus

Developer: Daniel McCarty
Cost: $4.95 (shareware)
Footprint: 10K

Padlock Plus (see Figure 21-25) is another utility that will lock your handheld when you turn it off. The AutoLock feature is nice; the "Smart" setting will only lock when you turn off your handheld with the Power button; "Always" also locks when your handheld times out.

Caution This program runs as a HackMaster Hack, which means that it will only prevent a novice from viewing your data — a simple warm boot enables anyone to bypass Hacks (see Chapter 21 for more on HackMaster), and thus your security.

Figure 21-24: OnlyMe settings

Figure 21-25: Configuring Padlock Plus

TealLock

Developer: TealPoint Software|
Cost: $11.95 (shareware)
Footprint: 34K

TealLock is a solid replacement for the Palm's security application. I recommend that you use TealLock's settings to change the message to one that offers a reward for your Palm Organizer (see Figure 21-26). Flexible activation settings enable you to fine-tune locking and hiding of private records.

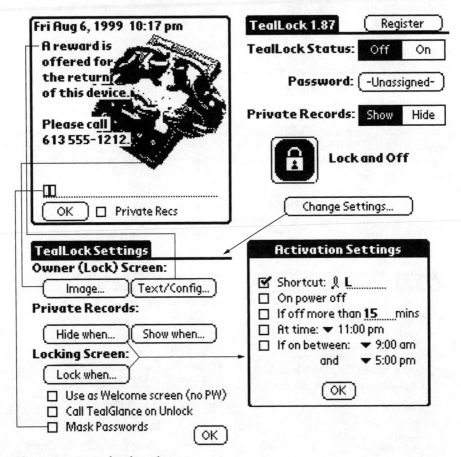

Figure 21-26: TealLock settings

 Caution Don't use the "Use as Welcome screen (no PW)" unless you want to disable TealLock's security features — "no PW" means no password.

Encryption utilities

The following utilities should prove useful for a variety of encryption and security needs.

JAWS Memo

Developer: JAWS Technology, Inc.
Cost: $19.95
Footprint: 42K

Want security? JAWS Memo (Figure 21-27) gives you a new version of your Memo Pad with one significant addition: the capability to encrypt a memo or category. JAWS Memo uses a 4096-bit encryption key, which makes it the leader in this class. Once a memo has been encrypted, a lock icon is displayed in the memo list. Opening it in Palm's Memo Pad or in your computer's desktop software will give you gibberish, as shown to the right in Figure 21-27. The demo version enables you to encrypt up to three memos.

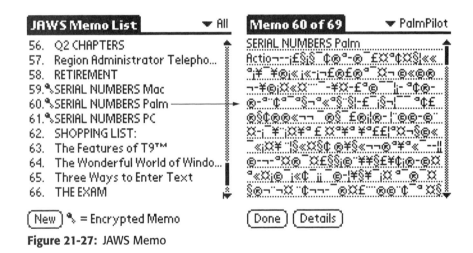

Figure 21-27: JAWS Memo

Tip   Want to keep a backup of your credit card information on your Palm Organizer? The demo version of JAWS Memo enables you to encrypt up to three memos, which means that you can store important information without worrying. This is the utility I use to lock my information.

Mobile Account Manager

Developer: Mobile Generation Software
Cost: $19.95
Footprint: 38K

Mobile Account Manager (see Figure 21-28) uses an interface much like Palm's built-in Address Book and includes a find command. The program supports importing and exporting via the Memo Pad, but the authors acknowledge that this means your data could be compromised on the desktop, and enables you to turn off backup of the data during HotSync. Mobile Generation uses its own encryption scheme, which is not strong enough to trigger U.S. export laws but should be enough to discourage all but the most experienced and determined of hackers.

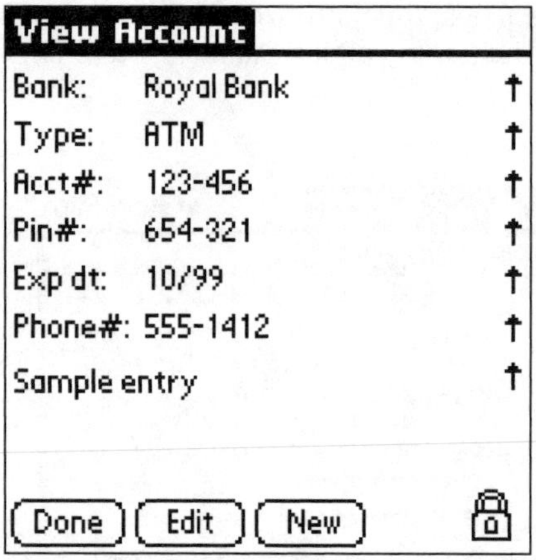

View Account		
Bank:	Royal Bank	↑
Type:	ATM	↑
Acct#:	123-456	↑
Pin#:	654-321	↑
Exp dt:	10/99	↑
Phone#:	555-1412	↑
Sample entry		↑

(Done) (Edit) (New)   🔒

Figure 21-28: Mobile Account Manager

 Caution

If you use the Export to Memo Pad (from the Options menu), the record you export will be available for viewing in the Memo Pad application. This enables you to export data to your desktop computer—just remember that this data is *not* secure.

Password Store

Developer: Stand Alone Software
Cost: $19.95
Footprint: 38K

The Password Store uses the Blowfish encryption method to secure your data using an interface, not unlike your Address Book. As you can see in Figure 21-29, tapping on either a new or an existing record brings you to a details screen where you can add or review information or attach notes. You can use either the system password or set a unique password to open Password Store.

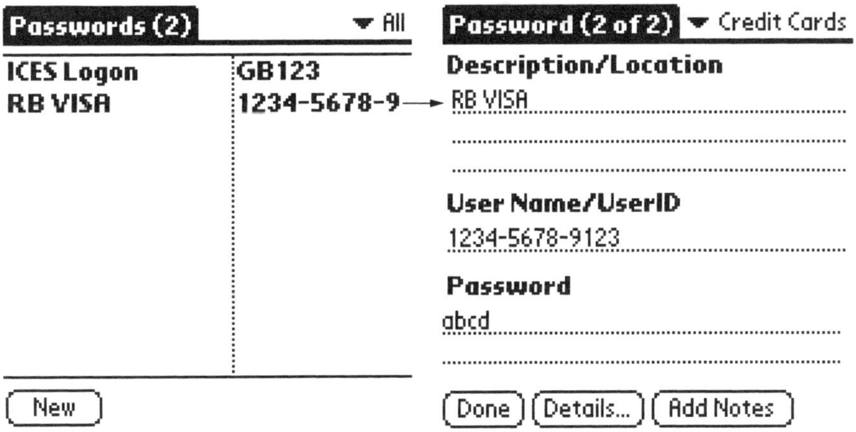

Figure 21-29: Password Store

Secret!

Developer: Andreas Linke
Cost: $19.00 ($35 with desktop software)
Footprint: 31K

Secret! provides a mechanism for locking up passwords and PIN numbers that you want to store on your PalmPilot, but couldn't before because of lack of security. It uses a reasonably strong encryption algorithm to keep amateur hackers from your valuable data (see Figure 21-30). One feature that makes it stand out from its competition is a Windows desktop version and a conduit that enables you to view your data on your computer after entering your password (see Figure 21-31).

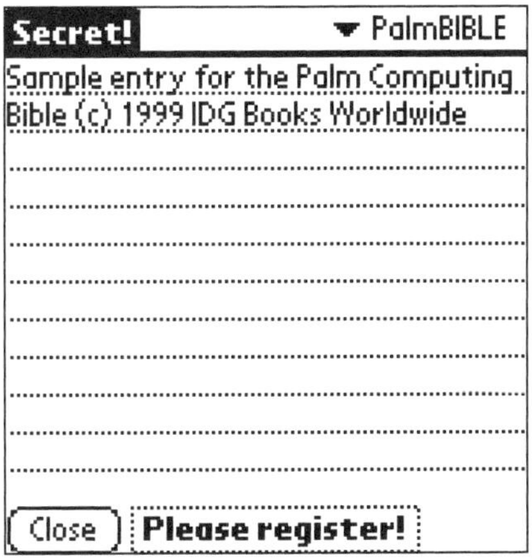

Figure 21-30: Secret!

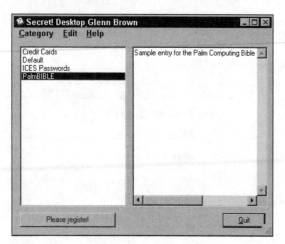

Figure 21-31: Secret! Desktop

The program also supports transaction numbers (TANS), so that you can record and use one-time passwords for secure transactions. The application has two minor flaws: The handheld application requires that you create a new category for each new record, and text display in the Windows component does not word wrap.

TopSecret Desktop

Developer: ClickLite
Cost: $27.50 (shareware)
Footprint: 27K

TopSecret Desktop provides Windows users with an elegant handheld/computer solution. The program uses the Tiny Encryption Algorithm (TEA), using 128-byte encryption keys. The program provides a simple Memo Pad-like interface on your Palm Organizer (see Figure 21-32), with a mirror application that runs on your Windows computer (see Figure 21-33).

Figure 21-32: TopSecret

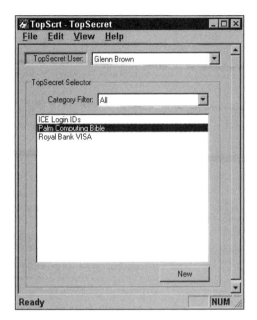

Figure 21-33: TopSecret Desktop

Speedups

If you want to speed up your computer one trick is to overclock the processor, forcing it to run faster. There are side effects: added heat, reduced stability, and software incompatibilities. The good news with the Palm Organizer is that heat doesn't seem to be an issue, although compatibility can be — beaming and HotSyncing in particular may be affected, especially at higher speeds. Table 21-2 lists four utilities that you can use to overclock your Palm Organizer.

<table>
<tr><td colspan="9" align="center">Table 21-2
Overclocking Your Palm Organizer *</td></tr>
<tr><td>*Name*</td><td>*Version*</td><td>*Price*</td><td>*Size*</td><td>*Underclock*</td><td>*Overclock*</td><td>*Test*</td><td>*HotSync*</td><td>*IR*</td></tr>
<tr><td>AfterBurner][</td><td>2.2</td><td>Free</td><td>13K</td><td>3</td><td>6</td><td>267%</td><td>Yes</td><td>No</td></tr>
<tr><td>CruiseControl</td><td>1.01</td><td>Free</td><td>3K</td><td>No</td><td>1</td><td>149%</td><td>Yes</td><td>Yes</td></tr>
<tr><td>EcoHack</td><td>2.2</td><td>$8.00</td><td>10K</td><td>1</td><td>3</td><td>138%</td><td>—</td><td>—</td></tr>
<tr><td>Tornado V</td><td>1.1</td><td>$10.00</td><td>10K</td><td>3</td><td>6</td><td>198%</td><td>Yes</td><td>Yes</td></tr>
</table>

*These tests were done using a Palm V and Neal Bridges Quartus Forth Benchmark version 1.4 (you'll see it later in the bottom right-hand corner of Figure 21-35), a utility that can measure the performance of your Palm Organizer. All tests were done with Hacks disabled, except those required by the application itself. The Underclock and Overclock columns indicate how many speeds are available to either save batteries or speed up your handheld.

Note   My experience has been that there is very little noticeable speed improvement
with any of the overclocking utilities listed in Table 21-2. The Palm OS is optimized
in a fashion that makes it very efficient — and how do you get faster than "instant"?

EcoHack

Developer: Peter Strobel
Cost: $8.00 (shareware)
Footprint: 10K

A little over a year ago, Peter Strobel introduced EcoHack. This HackMaster Hack
(see Chapter 22 for more on HackMaster and Hacks) was designed to slow down
your Palm Organizer from 16MHz to 10MHz to extend your battery life. My favorite
feature of this software, however, wasn't saving battery life — it was the capability
to speed up the clock to 19, 21, or 23MHz. The program ships with a utility called
EConfig that enables you to tailor the individual speed settings of your applications.
Figure 21-34 shows EConfig, along with the strokes that enable you to change your
handheld's clock speed on the fly.

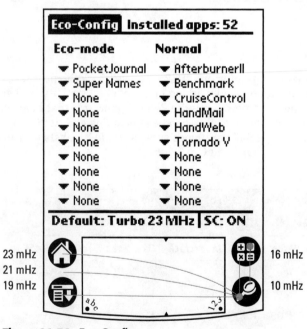

Figure 21-34: Eco-Config

Caution

The current version of EcoHack (2.2) does not run properly on devices that use the DragonBall EZ processor (Palm IIIc/IIIe/IIIx, and Palm V/Vx).

Afterburner][

Developer: Jean-Paul Gavini
Cost: Freeware
Footprint: 13K

As Table 21-2 illustrates, this utility (Figure 21-35) is the speed demon of the group, almost tripling the speed of your handheld. The downside is that beaming does not work at the higher speeds. This is not a big problem; you can specify normal speed of those applications that you regularly beam (for example, Address Book), and it will work fine.

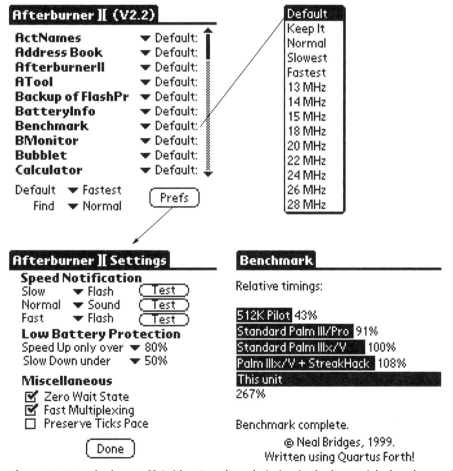

Figure 21-35: Afterburner][(with a Benchmark timing in the lower right-hand corner)

CruiseControl

Developer: Alexander Hinds
Cost: Freeware
Footprint: 3K

CruiseControl takes a much simpler approach (see Figure 21-36): This freeware utility bumps the speed of your handheld by 50 percent. There are no individual application settings (it's either on or off), but I have yet to encounter an application that doesn't run with it on.

Figure 21-36: CruiseControl

Tornado V

Developer: IS/Complete
Cost: $10.00
Footprint: 10K

IS/Complete wrote Tornado (see Figure 21-37) to be fast *and* compatible. It offers global and individual settings for your applications, and does not interfere with either HotSyncing or infrared operations.

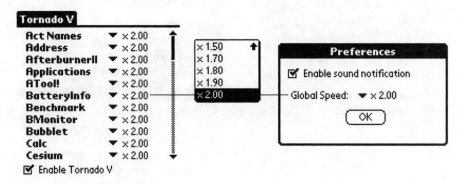

Figure 21-37: Tornado V

System Tools

These utilities are the universal tools, offering functionality for all users from the novice to the poweruser.

ATool!

Developer: Marty Wilber
Cost: Freeware
Footprint: 16K

ATool! (Figure 21-38) is for the basic Palm Organizer user. Several handy tools are displayed on one screen, including a calendar calculator (it tells the number of hours and days between the current and another date), battery graph and battery date functions, a reset function for those needed soft resets, access to Graffiti help, and a random coin toss.

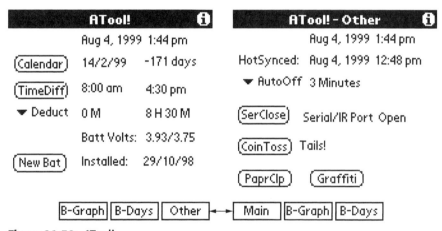

Figure 21-38: ATool!

Pilot Explorer

Developer: Scott Powell
Cost: $14.00 (shareware)
Footprint: 46K (60K with plug-ins)

Pilot Explorer is a GUI (graphical user interface) utility for browsing the contents of your Palm Organizer. This utility is meant for intermediate or expert PalmPilot users. The interface (Figure 21-39) takes getting used to. Databases appear in a "treelike" fashion on the left two-thirds of the display, while the remaining one-third displays either the number or items stored in the particular database or the default data for the entry (for example, telephone records show a phone number). To view contents of databases, plug-ins are required. The main PalmPilot database plug-ins (battery, calculator, clock, PIM, and trash) are provided; third-party plug-ins for other application databases are not provided. Entries in the main PalmPilot databases can be created, edited, or deleted.

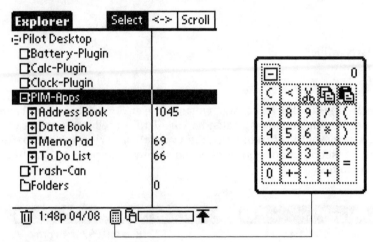

Figure 21-39: Pilot Explorer

FPS Utility Pro

Developer: Fighter Pilot Software
Cost: $15.00 (shareware)
Footprint: 38K

FPS Utility Pro features a clean simple interface (see Figure 21-40) that gives easy access to the program's core functionality: memory and HotSync information, battery warning levels, access to soft reset and debug modes, and the capability to change the auto-off (sleep) timing on your Palm Organizer.

This powerful application gives you the ability to change battery-warning levels or to extend the auto-sleep capability to the point where you can completely run down your handheld without warning.

If you tap the Debug icon, you'll be warned that FPS Utility Pro will open the serial port and invoke the debugger, which can be of use to programmers. Once you do so, you'll find that you can't use the serial port for other things, such as HotSyncing. A simple reset is all that is needed to restore your serial port's setting to normal.

The Database view is where FPS Utility Pro shows its horsepower: You can sort, view, and edit all of the databases in your Palm Organizer. After you tap a Database to select it (see Figure 21-41), tapping the icons at the bottom of the screen (from left to right) do the following:

✦ Give you detailed information on the database.

✦ Enable you to delete the database.

✦ Beam the database.

✦ Copy the database information to your Memo Pad.

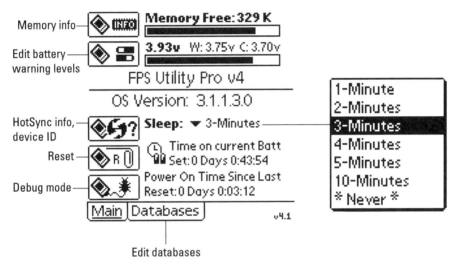

Figure 21-40: FPS Utility Pro

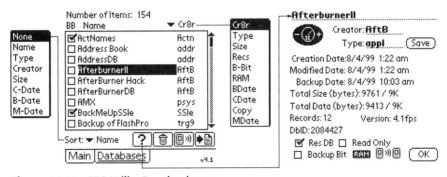

Figure 21-41: FPS Utility Pro databases

All this power comes with a caveat: You can *really* mess up your handheld if you're not careful. That said, this is clearly the best general-purpose utility tool available for your Palm Organizer.

More Tools

This chapter ends with three unique, inexpensive utilities that can help keep your Palm Organizer running smoothly.

dbScan

Developer: Pimlico Software
Cost: Freeware (included with DateBk3)
Footprint: 20K

Version 3 of the Palm OS brings with it a small flaw: Every reset causes three ShortCuts to be duplicated in your handheld. Pimlico Software makes available as freeware its utility, dbScan (see Figure 21-42), that deletes these duplicates for you. See Chapter 20 for more on Pimlico's flagship application, DateBk3.

TrapWeaver

Developer: Twilight Edge Software
Cost: $5.00 (shareware)
Footprint: 14K

One risk of running third-party applications is the possibility of conflicts. This can be especially true of HackMaster Hacks, which should not be removed before you disable them. TrapWeaver (see Figure 21-43) is a utility that prevents conflicts resulting from patch removal. This application provides memory protection for the patches installed by the HackMaster Hacks you have installed. The simple recap: My Palm Vx crashes less often with TrapWeaver installed.

Figure 21-42: dbScan

Figure 21-43: TrapWeaver

UnDupe

Developer: Stevens Creek Software
Cost: $4.95
Footprint: 10K

Every once in a while during a HotSync you'll get duplicate entries — sometimes hundreds, and they can be a real pain to get rid of manually. Immediately after the first time I tried this utility (see Figure 21-44), I logged on to PalmGear and registered it. It is that good. (The demo version *finds* but does not delete duplicates.) Take my word for it: $4.95 is cheap for what this great utility does.

Figure 21-44: UnDupe

Summary

✦ Backup Buddy is an essential tool for those who install third-party applications on their Palm Organizers, particularly those who have not yet upgraded to OS 3.3 or better.

✦ You can fine-tune your settings to minimize battery use, but the biggest savings will come from limiting your use of backlighting.

✦ If you use beaming on your Palm Organizer, you're likely to be labeled a Palm geek (not that that's a bad thing . . .).

✦ FlashPro is another essential utility for those able to use it, adding 800K and a memory tool for under $30.00.

✦ If you need more security than what is built into your handheld, take a look at the applications in this chapter to see which fits your needs.

✦ If you want your Palm Organizer to go faster, Afterburner is my choice for both speed and price.

✦ FPS Utility Pro remains at the top of the heap for advanced system utilities for the Palm Organizer.

✦ UnDupe will pay for itself the first time you use it.

✦   ✦   ✦

Extending Functionality with HackMaster

✦ ✦ ✦ ✦

In This Chapter

What is HackMaster?

The care and feeding of HackMaster

Daggerware Hacks

Third-party Hacks

Registered Hacks

✦ ✦ ✦ ✦

One of the limitations of the Palm OS, as far as programmers were concerned, was the lack of a mechanism that enabled them to patch into the operating system at a low level to create global changes. Edward Keyes, a graduate student at MIT, changed this when he released HackMaster in October 1996. This $5.00 shareware application has had a significant impact on the Palm platform, enabling programmers to create all sorts of magic for our favorite handheld. Windows has TSRs (terminate and stay resident applications), the Macintosh has extensions and control panels, and the Palm OS has HackMaster.

What Is HackMaster?

Developer: Daggerware
Cost: $5.00 (shareware)
Footprint: 10K

HackMaster (see Figure 22-1) is the key piece of software required for all Hacks (or extensions) to your Palm Organizer's operating system.

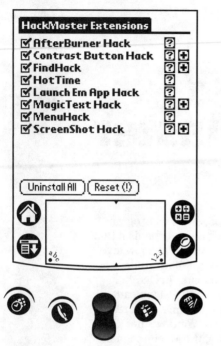

Figure 22-1: Activating HackMaster Hacks

Care and feeding

The power that HackMaster offers comes with a price. Your Palm Organizer will be slightly more complicated to use, but the payoff can be big. Here is what's involved.

Loading and unloading Hacks

Okay, you've downloaded a new Hack or copied it from the CD-ROM that accompanies this book. Now what? The first step is to make sure that both HackMaster and your new Hack are installed on your handheld (see Chapter 11 for more on loading files on your Palm Organizer). Tap the HackMaster icon to get a screen like that shown in Figure 22-1. You'll see a list of the Hacks installed on your Palm Organizer. Activating a Hack is simple—just tap the box to the left of the Hack's name. Tap again to remove the checkmark and deactivate the Hack.

Note

The sort order for HackMaster's listing is not alphabetical; items are sorted in the order you load them. If you want them to sort alphabetically, you need to activate them in reverse order. Other than appearance, I have yet to see any significant difference made by changing the load order of Hacks.

Caution You *must* use HackMaster to disable any installed Hack before you can safely delete it from your PalmPilot's memory. I find it best to be overcautious — whenever I'm going to delete Hacks, I use HackMaster's Uninstall All command (which should really be called Deactivate All because the Hacks are still on your handheld), and then reactivate when I'm finished.

When things go wrong

A risk of using software as powerful as HackMaster is that your handheld might crash after installation. This can be due to poorly written software or conflicts with another Hack or application, and it can even prevent your Palm Organizer from starting. The cure? Just perform a *warm reset*: Hold the Scroll button in the up position while using a paperclip or your stylus' pin to reset your handheld (see Chapter 24 for more on resetting your Palm Organizer). A warm reset will restart your handheld with all of your Hacks disabled, much like booting Windows in safe mode, or the Macintosh with extensions off. After your handheld restarts, you can delete the errant Hack. The good news is that this happens rarely, but it sure is nice to know the cure when you need it.

Utility software

Two utility applications covered in Chapter 21 deserve special mention here: FlashPro and TrapWeaver. FlashPro will warn you that you must disable Hacks before deleting or moving them. TrapWeaver's patching mechanism claims to offer some protection from the affects of deleting an active Hack. I can't guarantee your satisfaction, but I have yet to experience a crash since I registered and installed TrapWeaver.

Daggerware Hacks

HackMaster's author, Edward Keyes, has released a number of shareware utilities, including a couple of Hacks: AppHack and MenuHack.

AppHack

Developer: Daggerware
Cost: $5.00 (shareware)
Footprint: 9K

AppHack (see Figure 22-2) enables you to configure the silk-screened icons at the bottom of your PalmPilot's screen, so that each icon can give access to multiple applications.

Figure 22-2: Fast access with AppHack

MenuHack

Developer: Daggerware
Cost: Freeware
Footprint: 2K

Ever tried to tap in the menu bar to get a menu to drop down, like you do on your computer? MenuHack is a freeware utility from the author of HackMaster that gives you functionality that should have been built into the operating system.

Third-Party Hacks

The capability to patch into the Palm OS has made HackMaster very popular with programmers — as of this writing there are 179 Hacks listed at PalmGear HQ, and the number keeps growing. This is a testament to the stability of HackMaster itself. This section gives a sampling of just a few of the many Hacks available for the Palm Organizer. You may also want to look for these additional Hacks discussed elsewhere in the book: Afterburner (Chapter 21), FitalyHack (Chapter 3), and TealGlance (Chapter 20).

AltCtrlHack Pro

Developer: IS/Complete
Cost: $10.00 (shareware)
Footprint: 19K

AltCtrlHack Pro (see Figure 22-3) enables you to map your hardware buttons any way you want, including settings for double-taps — the first tap launches one application, the second tap, when made within a second after the first tap, launches a different one. You can also configure menu commands to hardware buttons, enabling quick use without your stylus. This Hack also includes integration with IS/Complete's IrLink, IrPrint, and IrSync products.

Figure 22-3: Configuring your buttons with AltCtrlHack Pro

CatHack

Developer: Iain Barclay
Cost: $4.95 (shareware)
Footprint: 7K

This simple HackMaster Hack makes your category selections in your Palm Organizer's built-in applications "sticky," so if you make a category selection in one application, the next application will default to the same category. This can make life simpler, especially if your categories revolve around home and office life.

ClockHack

Developer: Iain Barclay
Cost: Freeware
Footprint: 3K

This hack gives you a configurable onscreen clock. Figure 22-4 shows the clock overlaying ClockHack's settings screen (thanks to a bit of Photoshop magic).

Figure 22-4: ClockHack preferences

Contrast Button Hack

Developer: Synergy Solutions
Cost: Freeware
Footprint: 4K

The Palm V has an additional hardware button that the other Palm devices don't have: the Contrast Button. This elegant little freeware Hack (see Figure 22-5) enables you to specify the application that should be launched when you press the Contrast button; a second tap still opens Palm's Contrast dialog box. The only shortcoming is that the Contrast button can't be used to power on your handheld like the main application buttons. I have mine set to open Cesium, so I can have an admittedly expensive desk clock at the office.

Figure 22-5: Contrast Button Hack

Daylight Savings Hack

Developer: Bozidar Benc
Cost: Freeware
Footprint: 5K

This freeware Hack (see Figure 22-6) can automatically adjust your PalmPilot's internal clock for daylight savings time.

EVEdit

Developer: EVSoft Co., Ltd.
Cost: $16.00 (shareware)
Footprint: 55K

EVEdit (see Figure 22-7) has become a jack of all trades, combining all sorts of functionality, including Graffiti echo (see your Graffiti strokes mirrored onscreen), multiple clipboards and undos, MenuHack functionality (tap the menu bar to access menus), and drag-and-drop text functions.

Figure 22-6: Daylight Savings Hack settings

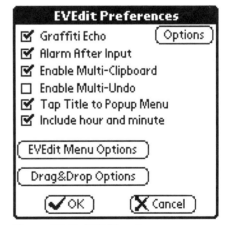

Figure 22-7: EVEdit preferences

FlashHack

Developer: Iain Barclay
Cost: Freeware

This freeware hack is written to support Gary Mayhak's TaleLight (see Chapter 23 or `http://members.aol.com:/gmayhak/tcl/light.htm`). If you have a TaleLight installed, FlashHack flashes its light whenever an alarm goes off, providing you with the option of a silent alarm.

GadgetHack

Developer: Daniel McCarty
Cost: $4.95 (shareware)
Footprint: 12K

Daniel has found a clever place to hide his GadgetHack: in the menu bar of your applications. One tap displays time, a second tap displays battery information, and a third tap gives you utility functionality—all completely configurable (see Figure 22-8).

Glowhack

Developer: DovCom
Cost: Freeware
Footprint: 3K

This clever hack (see Figure 22-9) enables you to configure your PalmPilot's back-light to default to on whenever you turn it on during specified hours.

Figure 22-8: GadgetHack settings

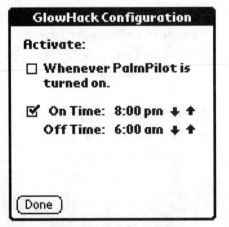

Figure 22-9: GlowHack settings

HushHack

Developer: Jeff Jetton
Cost: Freeware
Footprint: 3K

If you need a silent alarm but don't yet have a TaleLight (see Chapter 23), then HushHack is the answer—it flashes your screen to let you know that an alarm has gone off.

LeftHack

Developer: Neal Bridges
Cost: $10.00 (shareware)
Footprint: 3K

The Palm V enables those who are left-handed to switch their stylus and cover, but the scroll bars in every application are on the right-hand side. If you find this inconvenient, try Neal Bridge's LeftHack (see Figure 22-10), which moves your scroll bars to the left side of the screen.

Figure 22-10: LeftHack offers left-handed scroll bars

LightHack

Developer: Neal Bridges
Cost: $5.00 (shareware)
Footprint: 1K

Some users prefer the standard backlighting used in the PalmPilot and Palm III, while others prefer the inverted look of the Palm V. LightHack keeps everyone happy: It can reverse the process regardless of which model you own.

PhoneLookUp Hack

Developer: Denis Faivre
Cost: $5.00 (shareware)
Footprint: 6K

The Phone Lookup feature is great: a simple stroke and you can select a contact's information to add to a Date Book appointment or a To Do item. The only limitation is the amount of information you get: First Name, Last Name, and Phone Number. What if you want more, such as an address or other information? PhoneLookUp Hack (see Figure 22-11) offers an elegant solution: You can configure exactly what information from your Address Book should be pasted with a Phone Lookup.

Figure 22-11: Configuring PhoneLookUp Hack

StreakHack

Developer: Neal Bridges
Cost: $5.00 (shareware)
Footprint: 2K

Some models of the new Palm IIIx exhibit streaking of the screen, which can be noticeable at startup and in the Date Book. StreakHack fixes the problem, with the added benefit of speeding up your Palm IIIx by 8 percent.

SpellCheck

Developer: Scott Powell
Cost: $18.00 (shareware)
Footprint: 111K

I think spelling errors are worse on your handheld than on your computer, mainly because errors are easier to fix on your PC. SpellCheck (see Figure 22-12) closes the gap, giving you a spell checker for your Palm Organizer.

SymbolHack

Developer: Florent Pillet
Cost: $6.00 (shareware)
Footprint: 8K

SymbolHack (see Figure 22-13) helps you access hard-to-write symbols by popping up a small symbols table when you access the keyboard, which remains accessible via a button at the bottom of the table.

Figure 22-12: Configuring SpellCheck   **Figure 22-13:** SymbolHack

TealMagnify

Developer: TealPoint Software
Cost: $11.95 (shareware)
Footprint: 7K

This Hack (see Figure 22-14) enables you to magnify a part of your handheld's screen. Activation is clever: It uses the silk-screened Find button, which remains active with a double tap.

TrekSounds

Developer: Glen Aspeslagh
Cost: $8.00 (shareware)
Footprint: 37K

Here's one no true Trekkie can live without: TrekSounds (see Figure 22-15) gives your Palm Organizer configurable sounds, straight from the TV series. Additional settings enable you to configure the volume and a Graffiti stroke to quickly disable during a board meeting.

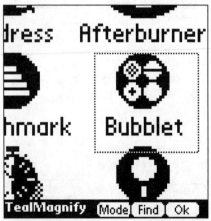

Figure 22-14: Zoom in with TealMagnify

Figure 22-15: TrekSounds

Registered Hacks

Some of the functionality offered by the following Hacks is so elegant you'll wonder why it wasn't built into the Palm OS in the first place. I have paid my shareware fees for all of the products in this section, including (of course) HackMaster. Also look for these Hacks, covered elsewhere in the book: Afterburner, BatteryMonitor, and EcoHack (all in Chapter 21), Launch'Em Hack (Chapter 20), and TealScript (Chapter 3).

Paying for What You Use

Some of the biggest advantages of writing a book about the Palm Organizer are freebies—
I have more Palm software than most can imagine. With this book, I made it my policy not
to ask for free copies of shareware programs that I use—I have paid my shareware fees for
all of the programs in this section.

FindHack

Developer: Florent Pillet
Cost: $6.00 (shareware)
Footprint: 11K

The Palm OS's built-in Find command has a number of limitations: It searches all of
the databases on your handheld (which may cause a crash), it can't remember multiple search criteria, and it doesn't allow the use of wildcards. All of these are fixed
with FindHack (see Figure 22-16), an well-designed utility from the author of Aportis
BrainForest.

Figure 22-16: FindHack

HotTime

Developer: AVStor
Cost: $5.00 (shareware)
Footprint: 6K

This pleasing little Hack does one thing: It synchronizes your handheld's clock
with your computer every time you HotSync — two quick beeps, and you're done. A
number of shareware utilities enable Windows and Macintosh users to synchronize
their system clocks to an atomic signal, so with HotTime you'll have no more
excuses for being late!

MagicText

Developer: Synergy Solutions
Cost: $39.95 (part of PDActivate)
Footprint: 37K

MagicText is a powerhouse application that provides two functionalities: drag-and-drop text editing (double-tap a word to select it, and then *drag* it to where you want it) and a context-sensitive, configurable, pop-up menu (that's a mouthful!), which provides quick access to data and utilities (see Figure 22-17). Try this one for a few days and you'll be hooked!

ScreenShot Hack

Developer: Andreas Linke
Cost: $5.00 (shareware)
Footprint: 9K

A number of applications have screens that can't be captured using Palm's developer emulator POSE (Palm OS Emulator); some crash, some make calls the emulator doesn't like, and some are difficult to set up in emulation. ScreenShot Hack (see Figure 22-18) is an essential utility for anyone who needs to capture Palm screens for printing or documentation—a quick Graffiti stroke or tap captures the screen. After your next HotSync, you run a Windows application that is included with ScreenShot Hack to convert the data into bitmap format. I couldn't have done this book without it!

Figure 22-17: MagicText

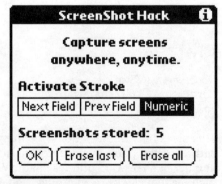

Figure 22-18: ScreenShot Hack

Tip   As you can see from Figure 22-18, you can use ScreenShot Hack's settings to assign a Graffiti stroke or a tap where you would normally tap to bring up the numeric keyboard. I find the last option (Numeric) the most convenient, but you'll find that you'll have to restore the setting after HotSyncing; the program often restores the default setting (Next Field).

Snoozer

Developer: Iain Barclay
Cost: $5.00 (shareware)
Footprint: 13K

If you're like me, you need something or someone to nag you to get up in the morning. The Palm alarm can be set so that most will wake to it, but it could use a snooze feature, which is exactly what Snoozer offers. Snoozer (see Figure 22-19) combines a HackMaster Hack with an application to configure your settings.

Figure 22-19: Snoozer

SwitchHack

Developer: Murray Dowling
Cost: $5.00 (shareware)
Footprint: 4K

Why should Windows users be the only ones to be able to switch between applications? SwitchHack brings Alt+Tab functionality to the Palm OS. A simple tap and drag from the Applications icon to the Graffiti area is all it takes to switch between your two most recent applications. Even better, a stroke from the silk-screened Applications icon down to the Menu icon pops up a menu of your ten most recently used applications (see Figure 22-20).

Figure 22-20: SwitchHack

Summary

✦ HackMaster provides a mechanism for extending the Palm OS.

✦ Remember to deactivate Hacks before deleting them.

✦ If you find your Palm in an unstable state and need to delete a Hack, a warm reset (scroll up + reset) will restart your handheld without loading any Hacks.

✦ ✦ ✦

Accessorizing Your Palm

✦ ✦ ✦ ✦

In This Chapter

Cases

Styli

Keyboards

Memory upgrades

More goodies

Springboard modules

✦ ✦ ✦ ✦

The world is divided into two types of computer users: those who live for software, and those who live for hardware. This chapter is for the hardware fans out there: things to buy to accessorize your Palm Organizer — cases, pens, memory upgrades, and other assorted goodies.

Cases

The sleeve cases that came with the PalmPilot, the plastic flip cover that comes with the Palm III series, and the Palm V series leather cover are good, but each could offer more functionality and protection. The Palm V offers a new means of attaching cases — instead of Velcro or other attachments, there are rails on both sides that can be used to attach a cover. The Palm V's leather cover looks nice, but the buttons can be accidentally pressed when covered — a problem that many Palm V users overcome with a new case. Let's have a look at some of the replacement cases available, including those marketed by Palm.

Tip

Want to find a budget case for your Palm Organizer? Try looking in a photography supply store. The small cases made for cameras are ideally suited for the Palm Organizer — look for those made by Europa, Lowepro, and Zing (the Zing Medium is a perfect fit for a Palm III).

Bumper case

Developer: Concept Kitchen
Cost: $39.95

If you lead an active life, you may want to carry your Palm Organizer with you places where you'll risk breaking it (ask me—I've broken two). Concept Kitchen has a solution: its Bumper case (see Figure 23-1) surrounds your handheld in a protective shell, while an IR window enables you to beam from within. You'll find a number of nice touches here: an insert enables the case to be used with Palm V series organizers, grooves in the sides enable stylus storage, and a well-designed cover swivels from front to back. Although I doubt that the Bumper is waterproof, it certainly is water-resistant. The Bumper case is available in yellow or gray for all Palm models except for the Palm VII. I recommend it.

Figure 23-1: The Bumper case

BurroPak

Developer: LandWare
Cost: $39.95

The BurroPak (see Figure 23-2) is great: a shoulder holster with a velcro closure that allows for easy access, no matter what you're wearing. This unique case also works well as a carrying case for Rhino's titanium case. The only downside is a fairly high geek factor.

Deluxe leather carrying case

Developer: 3Com
Cost: $64.95

Palm's deluxe leather carrying case (see Figure 23-3) is an expensive, beautiful wallet that is available for both the Palm III and Palm V series organizers. The size (about three times the size of the Palm Organizer) is its biggest downfall. However, it doubles as a wallet and checkbook holder, so if you like everything in one place it could be right for you.

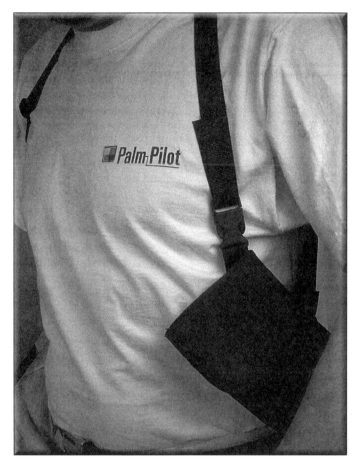

Figure 23-2: The author modeling the BurroPak

Figure 23-3: Deluxe leather carrying case

Dooney & Bourke cases

Developer: Dooney & Bourke (sold by Palm)
Cost: $49.95

The Dooney & Bourke cases (see Figure 23-4) are elegant leather cases that are available for both the Palm III and Palm V series. I find myself using one when I wear a suit, because they offer a little more resistance (the hardshell can fall out of your pocket a little more easily), and they look more refined.

Figure 23-4: Dooney & Bourke slim cases

FlipCase

Developer: Synergy Solutions, Inc
Cost: $22.95/$29.95 (with belt clip)

Synergy's FlipCase (see Figures 23-5 and 23-6) has a completely different design: a wrap-around attached with three Velcro strips. It has a number of things going for it: It works equally well for left- and right-handed users, you can HotSync without removing the case, and you can order it with a detachable belt clip. This is my favorite case for the Palm III series.

Figure 23-5: FlipCase closed

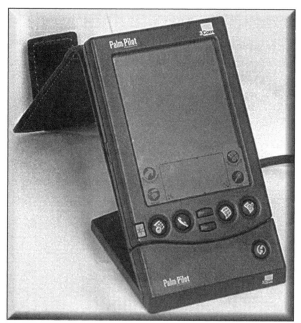

Figure 23-6: FlipCase in HotSync cradle

Hardshell case

Developer: Palm
Cost: $39.95

The Palm hardshell case (see Figure 23-7) is the one I use for my Palm Vx; it offers great protection and a stylish look. The catalog illustration shows a black version that did not make it to production; all cases are black plastic with brushed aluminum front and back inserts. They are surprisingly rugged—I've been using mine for over a year without a problem. The only design flaw is that they are made for right-handers only; subtle differences between the top and bottom mean that this case will not work when mounted on the Palm V's right-side rail.

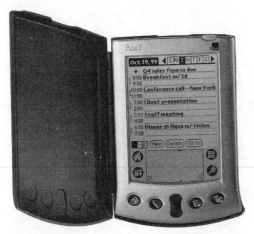

Figure 23-7: The Palm V hardshell case

Leather belt clip case

Developer: Palm Inc.
Cost: $24.95

The leather belt clip case (see Figure 23-8) is basically a slipcover with a Velcro top and a clip to attach it to your belt. I don't find this design particularly convenient because you have to take your Palm Organizer out of the case to use it.

PalmGlove

Developer: Palm Inc.
Cost: $29.95

The PalmGlove (see Figure 23-9) is marketed by Palm for the Palm III and Palm VII series and wraps your handheld in protective neoprene (wetsuit material) with an incredibly tactile feel. The result is a very nice sports case. It is available in multiple colors, and, if you can live without a belt loop, this case is one of the best available.

Figure 23-8: Leather belt clip case

Figure 23-9: PalmGlove

RhinoPak 1000 Sport Case

Developer: Rhinoskin
Cost: $26.95

Rhinoskin has a unique collection of cases. All its cases are designed for rugged protection of your Palm Organizer. The RhinoPak 1000 Sport Case (see Figure 23-10) is a small case that is made from water-resistant Cordura. Features include a reinforced plastic insert to protect your screen, a belt loop, and an interior mesh card pocket.

Figure 23-10: Rhinoskin cases (from left to right: RhinoPak 1000, 2000, and Titanium)

RhinoPak 2000 Sport Ute case

Developer: Rhinoskin
Cost: $49.95

The RhinoPak 2000 Sport Ute case (see Figure 23-11) is a larger case that is one of the very few that make room for a Palm Organizer modem. It is also designed with the active user in mind. This case is also made of Cordura, and has belt loops and two exterior pockets (with four zipper pulls). Inside is a mesh pocket for your modem, elastic loops for a stylus and a set of batteries, and straps to secure your Palm Organizer. Of all the cases I tested, this one made those who saw it the most jealous.

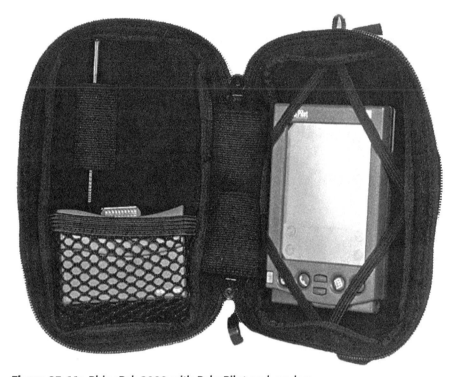

Figure 23-11: RhinoPak 2000 with PalmPilot and modem

Rhinoskin Palm V molded hardcase

Developer: Rhinoskin
Cost: $79.95

Many users were disappointed to discover that Palm's hardshell case for the Palm V was in fact a plastic case with thin aluminum inserts. Those users finally have a solution: the Rhinoskin Palm V molded hardcase (see Figure 23-12), an aircraft-grade aluminum case with a padded interior. This case provides protection from drops and collisions and offers an IR port for use when the case is open (see Figure 23-13).

Figure 23-12: Rhinoskin molded hardcase

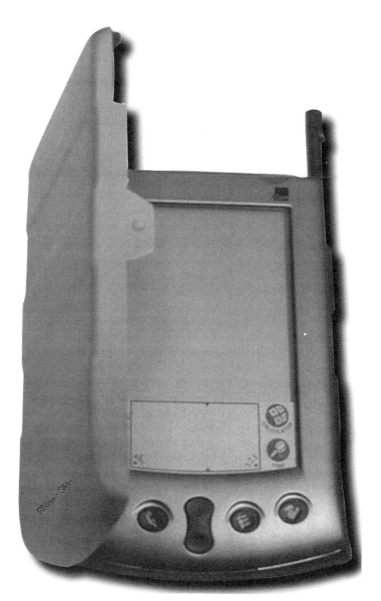

Figure 23-13: The hardcase open

Rhinoskin ShockSuits

Developer: Rhinoskin
Cost: $34.95

Rhinoskin has its own lightweight drop-resistant case: the ShockSuit SportCase (see Figure 23-14). The ShockSuit is made from polyethylene foam with molded reinforced corners that help protect your handheld from inadvertent drops. A lined interior with rigid inserts protects your handheld inside the case. Other features include a stylus and belt clips and a HotSync cable port. It is available in black, blue, or gray for PalmPilots and the Palm III series Organizers.

Figure 23-14: Rhinoskin ShockSuits

Slim leather carrying case

Developer: Palm Inc.
Cost: $24.95

Palm's slim leather carrying case (see Figure 23-15) is one of my favorite cases: a high-quality black leather case that adds little to the size of your Palm Organizer. The Palm III version attaches to your handheld with a single piece of Velcro, the Palm V version attaches using the side rail. A Premiere version in higher quality leather is also available for the Palm III and VII series ($39.95) and Palm V series ($49.95).

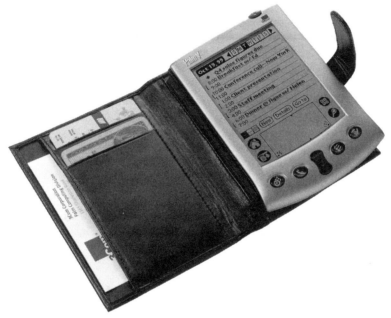

Figure 23-15: The slim leather case

Slipper

Developer: E&B Company
Cost: $29.95 ($36.95 for Palm VII)

The Slipper is a form-fitting leather case that fits like a glove, with a flip-back screen cover. A clever design lets you HotSync without removing the case. A belt clip is available, and Palm V owners can also choose a wallet version for $39.95. By the time you read this, E&B will have a version of the Slipper case available for Handspring's Visor.

SportSuit

Developer: MarWare
Cost: $22.95

The SportSuit (see Figure 23-16) is a little neoprene case that has become the one I use most. You can attach your Palm III or Palm V series Organizer using Velcro, or use the SportSuit as a slipcase, which is what I do with my Palm Vx and hardshell case. An external flap is convenient for a card (or, in my case, sunglasses), and a belt loop makes it easy to carry. A SportSuit II is available for Palm VII owners at $24.95, and the SportSuit III at $19.95 is strictly a slipcase design.

Figure 23-16: SportSuit

Targus case

Developer: Targus
Cost: $19.95

Targus is known for its computer and other cases, so it should come as no surprise that Targus makes a case specially designed for Palm Organizers. Available in nylon or leather, the Targus Palm case (see Figure 23-17) attaches without Velcro and includes room for spare batteries and two pockets for credit cards or other cards. At $19.95, it is certainly worth considering.

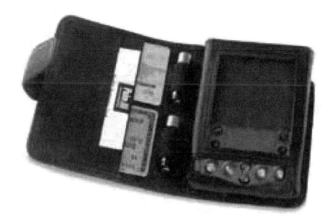

Figure 23-17: Targus' Palm case

Titanium hardcase/TI Slider

Developer: Rhinoskin
Cost: $59.95/$99.95

This is the ultimate protection for your Palm Organizer: a titanium hardcase. It is the ideal solution if you work in active or rugged environments — the only caveat is that it does not waterproof your Palm Organizer. The original design works well for all PalmPilot and Palm III models, although Palm III owners need to lift the right side slightly when removing their stylus. A new and improved design, the TI Slider (see Figure 23-18), enables the cover to slide to the back and is available for Palm III and Palm V series owners. Inside, your Palm Organizer is cushioned with a neoprene liner featuring a cutout for an ID card and a business card clip cushioned on top of the screen. Rhinoskin also make a ClipPak Cordova case for the hardcase that includes a belt clip, which I find works well with Rhinoskin's RhinoPak 2000 Sport Ute case. It also fits perfectly in LandWare's BurroPak, and I have no reason to believe it wouldn't stop a bullet! The hardcase adds to your Palm Organizer's weight and bulk, but if you need protection, this is the ideal solution.

Figure 23-18: The Rhinoskin TI Slider

Visionary 2000 case

Developer: Visionary 2000
Cost: $29.95

The Visonary 2000 (see Figure 23-19) is a clear Plexiglas screen cover that attaches with a textured vinyl strip on the left side of your Palm Organizer and a Velcro closure on the right side. Attaching the cover leaves your Palm Organizer's contrast wheel and front buttons exposed, making it ideal for checking your schedule or reading a document. The added $\frac{1}{16}$th of an inch is enough to prevent use of most of the leather cases covered here, but it works well with both the BurroPak and RhinoPak cases. The Visionary 2000 comes bundled with software and Concept Kitchen's WriteRight screen protectors and Brain Wash screen-cleaning kit.

Figure 23-19: The Visionary 2000 screen cover

Styli

Palm has shipped three different types and sizes of styli: the original plastic stylus that came with the Pilot and PalmPilot, the three-piece stylus of the Palm III and Palm VII series, and the all-black three-piece stylus of the Palm V series. The newer three-piece metal styli include a great feature: a built-in reset pin, which is available by unscrewing the plastic top. This section discusses some of the replacement styli you can buy for your Palm Organizer, as shown in Figure 23-20 (from left to right): E&B styli in gold, titanium, and silver; Concept Kitchen's Desktop Stylus; PDA Panache DUO; and Palm Organizer styli in black chrome, gold plate, and silver chrome.

Figure 23-20: Replacement styli for the Palm Organizer

Concept Kitchen

Concept Kitchen's aptly named Desktop Stylus is a stand and stylus combination (it's the centerpiece in Figure 23-20) for your office — or wherever you use your Palm Organizer the most. It has a nice heft, a good nib, and the rubber grip is very comfortable to write with. It is available for $27.95 or as part of Concept Kitchen's $69.95 PDA Starter Kit, which also includes two of their Karma Cloths, a dozen each of their Brain Wash cleaning system kits and WriteRight screen overlays (all are discussed later in this chapter).

iPoint 5

E&B and PalmGear HQ comarket the iPoint Stylus. This brass "nail" is designed as a replacement for the Palm V stylus. One end unscrews to reveal a reset pin, and the other end unscrews to give you a built-in pen. It is available in titanium with blue highlights for $18.95.

PalmPoint Dual Action stylus

The PalmPoint Dual Action stylus (see Figure 23-21) is an unusual looking stylus that is designed specifically for the Palm V — it fits perfectly in either side rail, even with the hardshell case. It can be used as a regular stylus, and a twist reveals a ballpoint pen. It is available from Palm's site for $39.95.

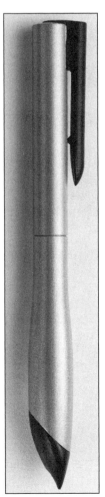

Figure 23-21: PalmPoint Dual Action stylus

PDA Panache

PDA Panache specializes in stylus replacement, so it should come as no surprise that its styli are the best. PDA's first PalmPilot product was nicknamed the "Black Nail"; the latest version of this stylus ($13.95) is the best you can get for a PalmPilot (see Figure 23-22). Subtle improvements make this one a classic: a fine nib, tapered design, and a hex cap (so it won't roll off the table). The P33 ($15.95) is designed as a replacement for the Palm III stylus, and includes a screw-off cap with a built-in reset pin. At $17.95, the P55 is similarly designed for the Palm V. PDA Panache makes a number of specialized pens, including the DUO, a $19.95 combination pen and stylus, and the Beacon LED, a lighted stylus for $29.95. PDA also makes stylus inserts for Cross, MontBlanc, and Rotring Multi pens.

Figure 23-22: The PDA Panache "Black Nail" showing the hex head design

Keyboards

There is no Palm accessory with a higher wow factor than a keyboard—when people see it, they begin to recognize some of the "hidden" potential of the Palm Organizer. It is quite something to see it dawn on people that this tiny handheld might actually function as a true laptop replacement. The advent of Palm keyboards leaves room for an enterprising shareware author to write a Palm text editor to extend the Memo Pad's functionality.

FreeKey

Developer: Nick Harvey
Cost: Freeware
Footprint: 6K

LandWare made a commercial product called PiloKey that enabled you to connect an Apple Newton keyboard and use it with your Palm Organizer. There was only one problem: Apple no longer makes the Newton, and keyboards are scarcer than hen's teeth. Still, if you can find one, Nick Harvey's aptly named FreeKey will help you connect.

GoType Pro

Developer: LandWare
Cost: $89.95

Of all the Palm toys I've received (and there have been quite a few) none has elicited more positive comment than the GoType Pro (see Figure 23-23). Designed and manufactured by Innogear for LandWare, this three-quarter-size keyboard offers amazing functionality. Want to HotSync? No problem, a cable is included to attach to your computer, effectively turning the GoType Pro into a second cradle. There is even a power plug, although you'll need to use a power adapter from your Palm V cradle (this is not sold separately). Nice touches abound: user-configurable function keys, which give access to your handheld's applications; left and right-side stylus holders; even a macro for quick HotSyncing. To initiate the macro press Shift+F3 for a dialog box that gives you five seconds to flip the switch (in the same place as the HotSync button on your cradle—centered beneath your handheld) to initiate the HotSync process. Palm III series owners should check out the GoType.

Figure 23-23: The GoType Pro keyboard

Note   After HotSyncing with the GoType Pro, you'll need to flip the switch back to keyboard mode ("abc"), and tap your Palm V off and on for it to re-recognize the keyboard.

Drawbacks? Not many—the keys are a bit small for touch-typing (although still much faster than Graffiti for taking notes), and I'd like to see some enterprising shareware developer write a Palm text editor (this is something LandWare tells me it is working on).

KeySync

Developer: iBiz Technology Corp.
Cost: $89.00

The KeySync keyboard (see Figure 23-24) is about the same size as the GoType, but its makers made different choices. Connection to your handheld is via your cradle, which means one size fits all Palm Organizers. The keyboard itself is a bit larger, and the keys have more travel than the GoType. The drawback to this design is that you need to carry a cradle with you—there is no pass-through HotSync. The KeySync requires three AAA batteries, which means that it doesn't draw any power from your handheld.

Figure 23-24: KeySync keyboard

Palm Portable Keyboard

Developer: Think Outside
Cost: $99.00

This keyboard (see Figures 23-25 and 23-26) is straight from a James Bond movie: Barely larger than a Palm III, it opens out to a full-sized keyboard. It so impressed the folks at Palm that it is now marketed as a Palm accessory. This keyboard draws the small power it needs from your handheld. The only limitation is that you can't use it on your lap; it needs a hard surface to keep it level.

Figure 23-25: Palm Portable keyboard

Figure 23-26: Stowed Palm Portable keyboard

Memory Upgrades

From the beginning, Palm powerusers have wanted more RAM for more applications and more data. It doesn't really matter how much memory is available, there is always something that will need even more. Technology Resource Group (TRG) stepped up and started manufacturing memory expansion boards that outperformed the originals, and it hasn't looked back. I have used almost all of these boards; all have been great. When others were using a 2MB Palm III, mine had 12MB (8MB RAM/4MB Flash); I now have a TRGpro with 30MB (8MB RAM, 2MB Flash, and a 20MB Compact Flash card).

SuperPilot, Xtra Xtra Pro

Developer: Technology Resource Group
Cost: See Table 23-1 for current configurations

Table 23-1
TRG Memory Upgrades

Upgrade	Price	Memory	Flash	Model	Software
SuperPilot II XL	$149.95	8MB	2MB	Palm III	FlashbuilderIII
Xtra Xtra	$99.95	8MB	2MB*	Palm IIIx	none
Xtra Xtra Pro	$169.95	8MB	4MB*	Palm IIIx	FlashPro

* The Xtra Xtra boards' Flash numbers include 2MB of Flash that is used from the Palm IIIx's motherboard.

This one is heaven for software and hardware junkies: the TRG SuperPilot or Xtra Xtra memory upgrade for your Palm III series organizer. The board replaces your memory board with a new one and includes software to download your original PalmPilot ROM image to the new chip.

The SuperPilot was the first introduction to Flash memory for Palm users. This is memory that can be "flashed" or loaded with new software. The advantage is that Flash memory is nonvolatile — it will store its information, even without power, whereas standard RAM loses its contents when it loses power. This means that information stored in Flash memory can survive a power outage and even a hard reset.

With the exception of the Palm IIIe and Palm VII, all Palm Organizers since the Palm III (Palm III, Palm IIIx, Palm V, and Palm Vx, and their IBM equivalents) have used 2MB of Flash memory in addition to their regular RAM.

Note The Palm VII includes 2MB of Flash memory, but the device's extended OS fills it entirely.

This Flash memory is used to store the Palm OS. Palm recently made Version 3.3 of its OS available on its Web site for downloading; owners of these devices can use the software provided to upgrade their handhelds to the new OS.

 Note Handspring's Visors do not have Flash memory.

TRG's software enables users of these handhelds — and of those equipped with their memory upgrade boards — to access the unused portion of the Flash memory. The Palm OS leaves about 800K of the 2MB free (the 3.3 upgrade takes about 64K more than Version 3.0, leaving about 750K free). FlashBuilder is TRG's Windows-based Flash loading software. FlashPro is the successor to FlashBuilder and is far superior: It enables you to load programs and data into Flash memory without using your computer. For more on FlashPro, see Chapter 21. See Chapter 1 for more on TRG's new TRGpro handheld.

Technology Resource Group

This sidebar is based on an interview with Mike Walter (TRG's lead software engineer) and Doug Devries (TRG's lead hardware engineer). They are two of the five original cofounders of TRG.

Technology Resource Group (TRG) was formed in 1992 by five engineers who were laid off from a Grid competitor called DFM. With few technology prospects in Iowa, the five formed TRG, doing contract engineering from 1992 until 1996. Doug Devries was looking for a means of recording project hours and decided to try a PalmPilot. He liked it, but wanted more memory, which he soon figured out how to add. TRG did a small production run that sold out the first day, and then a second, larger run, that also sold out, putting TRG in the Palm memory upgrade business.

TRG's first device, the SuperPilot, had 3MB of static RAM, which was more expensive, but used less power than the pseudostatic RAM that Palm was using at the time. The result was a big memory boost and longer battery life. Another problem to overcome was the Palm OS, which TRG could not distribute. The solution was an application that enabled the user to transfer the OS from their original memory chips to TRG's upgrade. Even better, users could use another utility, called FlashBuilder, to load applications into the unused portion of Flash RAM — about 800K of memory.

TRG's next major accomplishment was the DRAM controller designed for the SuperPilot II XL, which had 8MB of RAM and 2MB of Flash memory. This controller enabled the Palm Organizer to use much less expensive DRAM — the design was so good that Palm licensed the technology, and more than half of the Palm III's shipped use TRG's technology.

Continued

Continued

FlashBuilder III enabled users to move applications into nonvolatile Flash memory, but it had limitations: the biggest was that it required a Windows computer to load applications. TRG's next product, FlashPro, provided a great solution: on-unit loading, which eliminated the need for computer loading of Flash memory.

The Xtra Xtra board was designed in conjunction with Palm at the same time that Palm was working on the Palm IIIx. This board doubled the Palm IIIx's memory to 8MB. A Pro version with 2MB of Flash memory was designed for the Japanese market, where the entire 2MB of onboard Flash memory is taken up by the OS. FlashPro proved to be so popular that Xtra Xtra Pro became a worldwide best seller, overtaking Xtra Xtra.

TRG's memory upgrade products have long been popular with both powerusers and vertical markets, where large databases require more memory than is available on Palm's devices. Two things that both groups have been asking of TRG are for the capability to load even larger databases and for improved audio capabilities for louder alarms and telephone dialing. TRG looked at a number of expansion options — proprietary, SmartMedia, PCMCIA, and Compact Flash — and they chose Compact Flash. Proprietary cards have cost issues and require third-party support, SmartMedia is storage only, and most PCMCIA cards require 5-volt power instead of the Palm's 3 volts. Compact Flash offers a variety of expansion options, which are already available at reasonable prices. It is ironic that TRG started doing Palm memory upgrades because of a propriety slot in the Palm Organizer and has now come full circle, releasing a Palm device with a standard expansion slot.

efigV8 upgrade

Developer: efig.com, Inc.
Cost: $249.00

Until the release of the Palm Vx, there was only one way to get 8MB in a Palm V: the efigV8 upgrade. efig (Electronic Fast Integration Group) has figured out the daunting task of opening a Palm V, replacing the 2MB DRAM with an 8MB version, and resealing the unit — with a warranty. efig also sells new, upgraded units for $635, although I am at a loss to understand why anyone would buy one instead of Palm's Vx model.

Assorted Goodies

I still can't believe all the great stuff that is available for the Palm Organizer. This section details some of the essential (and not-so-essential) accessories that are available.

Brain Wash

Developer: Concept Kitchen
Cost: $14.95

Brain Wash is a two-stage wet-and-dry cleaning kit for your Palm Organizer. I was skeptical until I tried it — it was able to take off six months of crud (I'm sure that's the technically correct word) from my Palm Organizer that regular cleaning couldn't touch. In the middle of writing this, I stopped and used a Brain Wash to clean my Palm V; now it looks like new again! It is available in a box of 12 for $14.95 or as part of Concept Kitchen's PDA Starter Kit.

BikeBrain

Developer: Velotrend
Cost: $89.95 ($99.95 for Palm V series)

Velotrend's BikeBrain (see Figure 23-27) turns your Palm III or V series Organizer into a complete bicycle computer. A companion application for your computer (Windows or Macintosh) enables you to download route information into your handheld, which is shock-mounted onto your bicycle's handlebars. In addition to cyclometer functionality with speed and distance readings, BikeBrain enables you to HotSync information back to your computer for post-ride analysis.

Figure 23-27: BikeBrain

CardScan

Developer: Corex Technologies Corp.
Cost: $299.00

Ever come back from a business trip with a pile of business cards that you want entered into your handheld? You have two choices: key the information (or have someone enter it for you) or use the Corex CardScan (see Figure 23-28). This amazing card scanner comes with Windows software (see Figure 23-29) that enables it to synchronize with almost every Personal Information Manager made. Even better, CardScan includes a conduit that enables it to synchronize with the Palm Organizer. How well does it work? I found that standard business cards were a breeze — the OCR (optical character recognition) software included is great. In a stack of a dozen cards, I typically had to make two or three minor corrections. Not surprisingly, the software does have some problems handling unusual designs (it automatically does rotations, but some cards are, well, strange) and accented characters in foreign languages, but these accounted for less than 5 percent of the cards I tried.

Figure 23-28: The Corex CardScan attached to an IBM WorkPad and ThinkPad

goVox digital voice recorder

Developer: LandWare
Cost: $49.95

The goVox (see Figure 23-30) replaces the flipcover on your Palm III series Organizer with a stand-alone digital voice recorder. The recorder is entirely self-contained and records up to 99 messages or a total of eight minutes. A Palm V-series version should be available by the time this book is published. No need to be jealous of the voice capabilities of the Windows CE devices any more!

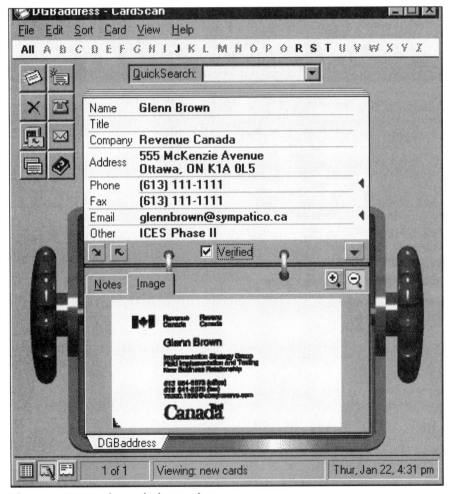

Figure 23-29: CardScan desktop software

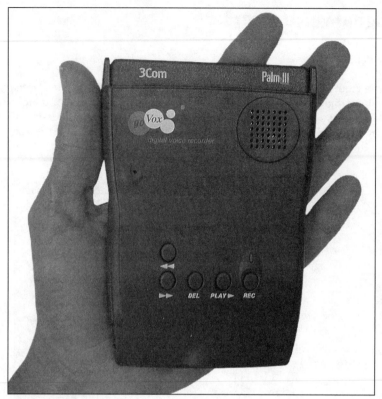

Figure 23-30: goVox

GSM upgrade kit

Developer: Palm Inc.
Cost: $89.00

If you travel with your Palm V and you're using a Nokia or Ericsson GSM cell phone, you need this one. The GSM upgrade enables you to connect many Nokia or Ericsson GSM cell phones directly to your Palm V modem, giving you wireless connectivity for e-mail or Web browsing. The kit includes a connection cable and a CD-ROM with software that upgrades your modem with GSM capabilities. See Chapter 16 for more on telecommunications with your Palm Organizer.

ImagiProbe

Developer: ImagiWorks
Cost: $499.00

The ImagiProbe is an amazing product that combines hardware and software to turn a Palm III or VII series Organizer into a portable data-acquisition tool (see Figure 23-31). Applications include educational, scientific, commercial, and personal.

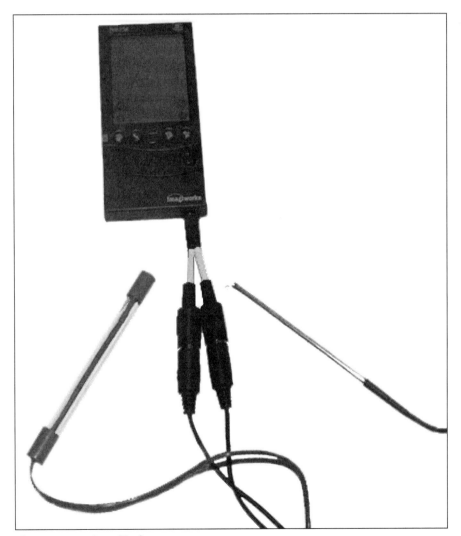

Figure 23-31: ImagiProbe

A module clips to the bottom of the handheld, enabling you to attach sensors to gather information. Palm-based software enables you to configure how, when, and what to gather, and a conduit moves your data to your Windows or Macintosh computer for analysis, manipulation, and reporting. Included connectors enable you to attach one or two DIN-5 sensors; the hardware supports sensors that measure in the range of 0 to 5 volts with power requirements not exceeding 200mA. Commonly available sensors enable you to measure:

- ✦ Acceleration
- ✦ Barometric pressure
- ✦ CO_2
- ✦ Conductivity
- ✦ Current
- ✦ Dissolved oxygen
- ✦ EKG
- ✦ Flow
- ✦ Heart rate

- ✦ Light
- ✦ Magnetic fields
- ✦ pH
- ✦ Pressure (psi)
- ✦ Relative humidity
- ✦ Respiration
- ✦ Force (newtons)
- ✦ Temperature (thermistor, thermocouple)
- ✦ Voltage

ImagiWorks also has Springboard modules designed for the Handspring Visor: SensorScience is a version designed for family, and TechCoach provides a portable means to track physiologic information and to manage your personal health using a wireless heart rate monitor.

Karma Cloth

Developer: Concept Kitchen
Cost: $9.95

This ultrasoft leather-cleaning cloth does a great job of keeping your Palm Organizer's screen clean. Available separately or as part of Concept Kitchen's PDA Starter Kit.

Tip   Want an inexpensive alternative for cleaning your handheld? Try buying an eyeglass cleaning cloth at an optician's—these are great for daily cleaning of your Palm Organizer's screen. I reserve the Karma Cloth for those occasions when extrastrength cleaning is required.

PalmConnect USB kit

Developer: Palm Inc.
Cost: $39.95

Palm's PalmConnect kit is an essential for Macintosh users: it enables those with USB, but without serial ports (like the iMacs and newer G3s and G4s), to HotSync to their Macs. PalmConnect includes a CD-ROM with Version 2.5 of the Palm

Desktop for Macintosh. This USB-serial connector (see Figure 23-32) can also be used by Windows users who have a free USB port on their PC.

Figure 23-32: PalmConnect USB connector

Palm Navigator

Developer: Precision Navigation
Cost: $39.95

The Palm Navigator (see Figure 23-33) is one of the more creative uses made of the modem casing that Palm makes available for hardware developers. A compass sensor in the clip-on attachment overlays a live, draggable compass rose on top of map images that you HotSync from your Windows PC to your handheld. Precision Navigation has another use for the casing — to house its $79.95 Weather Station, which includes temperature and barometric sensors and software to help you predict the weather from your handheld.

Figure 23-33: Palm Navigator's map compass

TaleLight, TaleVibes

Developer: Tech Center Labs
Cost: $12.00/$39.95

Nothing is worse than sitting in a meeting and having an alarm go off at the wrong time. Gary Mayhak has two silent alarm solutions. The TaleLight (see Figure 23-34) is a light that fits in the bottom of your Palm Organizer, and TaleVibes is a vibrating device that also attaches to your Palm Organizer's serial port. Several software packages now support the TaleLight — my favorites are Snoozer and Tricorder II. Hardware fans should check out Gary's site: He is working on some cool stuff including RedHotLink, an IrDA module, and The Wedge, a remote control/tone dialer.

Figure 23-34: Three TaleLights in action

Travel kit

Developer: Palm Inc.
Cost: $49.95

If you have a Palm V series Organizer and you travel, you'll need to find a way to recharge your handheld, and you'll probably want to HotSync, either remotely or to a laptop. This means that you need to schlep your cradle around with you. If you're traveling overseas, you'll also need to carry a voltage converter and adapters. Palm thought of all of this and came up with the idea of a second cradle for the traveler: their Palm V Travel Kit (see Figure 23-35). It includes a HotSync cable, power cable, AC adapter, and international adapters, all in a compact nylon case.

UniMount

Developer: Revolve Design
Cost: $69.95

Remember the old telephone address books with the sliding tabs that you moved up and down to select a page? Revolve Design includes this concept in a cleverly designed mounting system called UniMount (see Figure 23-36). The tab on the right side enables you to find information on your Palm Organizer with one hand. The UniMount has a number of mounting options, including a universal kit that works in your car or on your desk, and a flex mount designed for your vehicle, which is available with an optional cellular phone holder. One version is also designed for attachment to a golf cart, and new version is designed for Handspring's Visor.

Figure 23-35: Palm Travel Kit

Figure 23-36: The UniMount universal kit

WriteRight

Developer: Concept Kitchen
Cost: $27.95 for 12

If you're worried that your stylus will scratch your Palm Organizer's screen, you may want to look at a means to protect the screen. There are lots of homegrown solutions: clear adhesive tape and clear sticky notes are the two I read about most often. The problem is, they don't look as good as they should. The solution is Concept Kitchen's WriteRights, which are available in a 12-pack, or as part of their PDA Starter Kit. These are not easy to apply; the trick is to carefully apply them using a credit card to keep out air bubbles. A complete set of illustrated instructions is available on Concept Kitchen's Web site.

Tip I prefer to cut the WriteRight into three pieces and apply it only on the high-traffic Graffiti part of my Palm Organizer's screen. That way, a package lasts three times longer!

Springboard Cards

Some of the most interesting Palm add-ons are Springboard modules for Handspring's new Visor. This section takes a quick look at three new Springboard modules from Innogear, the makers of LandWare's GoType keyboards. See Chapter 8 for more on the Visor and other Springboard modules.

InfoMitt

Developer: Innogear
Cost: $49.95

Innogear doesn't do anything half way, as you will see from reading about their first Springboard modules. The InfoMitt (see Figure 23-37) is a pager as a Springboard module, with a paging service plan from Global Access. Features include voicemail, caller ID, nationwide service (United States only), and more. Included is Mark/Space's PageNOW! for the Palm OS, which gives you an "InBox" for pages and messages, a means of responding to messages via modem, and integration with the Visors Address Book and Calendar applications.

Figure 23-37: InfoMitt

MiniJam

Developer: Innogear
Cost: TBA

MP3s are highly compressed sound files that you can download from the Internet, retaining a high-quality digital sound. The MiniJam Springboard module (see Figure 23-38) turns your Visor into an MP3 Player and Voice Recorder. Available in four models with memory up to 32MB, it is the only Springboard module to date that offers its own expansion slot — an external MMC (Multimedia Card) memory expansion slot. MMC cards are about the size of a postage stamp, and are available in 32 and 64MB sizes. The MiniJam is a good example of the advantages of the Springboard open-face design, with its own controls, optional external power, and standard 3.5mm headphone jack. MiniJam includes a Visor application called MiniJukeBox that mirrors the hardware controls, while displaying file quality, playlist information, an equalizer screen, and track information.

Figure 23-38: MiniJam

6Pack

Developer: Innogear
Cost: TBA

The working name for what may be the ultimate Springboard card is "6Pack" (see Figure 23-39). The name may change by the time this is printed, but the effect it will have on users won't. Imagine a card with a flashing alarm light, a vibrating alarm, a cellular modem, a standard 33.6kbps modem, a voice recorder, and 8MB of Flash memory! This design overcomes one of the only drawbacks to the Springboard design: You can only have one card installed at a time. I want one.

Figure 23-39: 6Pack

Summary

✦ There is an almost overwhelming set of choices when it comes to cases for your handheld. I use Synergy's FlipCase for PalmPilot; for the Palm III series I use Palm's hardshell case with the MarWare SportSuit as a slipcase. There are some great alternatives for those who lead active lives, starting with neoprene cases such as the SportSuit and PalmGlove, protective cases such as the Bumper and ShockSuit, and for those who need the ultimate, Rhinoskin's TI Slider.

✦ For those who demand the very best, third-party styli add feel, heft, and finish that the originals may lack. My personal favorites are the replacement styli from PDA Panache.

✦ Graffiti is great, but for note taking it is hard to beat a keyboard. If you need to use the device on your lap, LandWare's GoType is the choice; if you work on a hard surface, the Stowaway is the way to go.

✦ TRG's memory upgrades can breathe new life into your Palm III series Organizer, especially for the poweruser.

✦ Expect to see some interesting and creative upgrades for the Handspring Visor over the next year in the form of new Springboard modules.

✦ If you want read more reviews on Palm hardware, with in-depth product comparisons, I highly recommend TAP Magazine (www.tapmagazine.com). This is the first (and to my knowledge only) print magazine exclusive to the Palm, offering bimonthly coverage on all things of interest to Palm users.

✦   ✦   ✦

Troubleshooting Your Palm

Palms Organizers come as close as any computing devices have ever come to the ideal appliance—one that never has problems—because it just *works*. I've found that most problems occur when you connect your Palm Organizer to your computer. There are, however, a few things you might run into, and this chapter should cover most of them.

General Troubleshooting Tips

Let's start with a few general precautions, before we jump to specific problems and solutions.

Backup loaded files

The wonderful third-party software you load into your Palm Organizer comes with a penalty: the more you load, the likelier you are to have a problem that requires a hard reset. Even though your next HotSync will restore your data, you will have to reload all of your third-party applications. I maintain a folder on my computer that contains copies of the current version of all of the .prc and .pdb files I have loaded into my Palm Organizer. If I remove a file from my handheld, I delete it from the folder; if I add a new app, I copy the .prc. and drag it in. Is it worth the effort? You bet. The first time your Palm Organizer crashes, all you have to do to restore is load all of the files from the folder, and then HotSync. I also maintain a Flashload folder, for a quick reload of all of the applications I have loaded into the Flash using TRG's FlashPro application. For more on the FlashPro, see Chapter 21.

Tip There is a far easier and better solution to back up your applications. Florent Pillet's shareware utility Backup Buddy will back up all of your applications, including those loaded in Flash memory. See Chapter 21 for more on this essential utility.

In This Chapter

General troubleshooting tips

Hardware problems

HotSync problems

Software problems

Telecommunications

More help

Those who are using Palm OS 3.3 no longer need to back up their applications; the operating system now does that automatically, performing a complete restore after a hard reset.

A bulletproof Palm Organizer

Want to make your Palm Organizer bulletproof? The combination of TRG's utilities FlashPro and FlashPack enables you to back up your essential data into Flash memory. Why would you want to do this? Flash memory is *nonvolatile* — information stored there will survive dead batteries and even a hard reset. This means that you can recover your essentials, even when you can't HotSync. Here's what to do if you're on the road, you've lost all of your data (probably due to a hard reset), and you can't do a HotSync:

✦ Tap FlashPro (it will have a "BU" on the icon), it will tell you it is a backup copy running out of Flash memory. Then tap the Restore button to move a copy back into RAM.

✦ Tap the Applications icon, and then tap FlashRestor; it will ask what you want to restore. Make sure all the items you want are checked and then tap the Restore button.

 See Chapter 21 for more on FlashPro and FlashPack.

CD-ROM software

Problem: I've registered an application, but I can't install the new .prc.

There is a problem in the 3Com install program when installing any .prc file from a CD-ROM. If you have previously installed the demo version of any software from a CD-ROM, you must delete all traces of that software from your PC before installing the release version. Use the Find selection from your Windows Start menu to hunt down any copies of the .prc that may be hiding, and delete them. Then try the installation procedure again. To avoid this problem, I recommend that you copy files from the CD-ROM to your computer's hard drive before installation.

Deinstalling third-party launchers on a Palm III

Problem: I removed a third-party application launcher from my Palm III, and now the built-in launcher doesn't work correctly.

If you install and then remove a third-party launch utility on a Palm III, you'll find that you need to tap two application icons to get to the new launcher — the silk-screened one and the one that was added — to enable you to delete applications when using another launcher. A hard reset alone will not revert your Palm III to the built-in launcher. What you need to do is to delete from your Backup folder (mine is Palm Desktop/BrownG/Backup) all traces of the third-party launcher, and then perform a hard reset and HotSync.

Graffiti notes

Problem: My Palm Organizer can't read the Graffiti characters I create.

If you're having problems with Graffiti, try the alternate strokes (see Chapter 3), they often work more reliably, especially if drawn as large as possible. I had the privilege of interviewing Jeff Hawkins (one of Palm's founders) for the PalmPilot Resource Kit, and he stressed this point, mentioning that the alternate V and Y strokes are more reliable.

Here's a few to get you started:

✦ Make a loop, like the shortcut stroke, except backwards, going from the lower right, looping around, and finishing at the lower left.

✦ Make it sharp-edged, like a sideways M.

✦ Make a 6 on the alpha side.

✦ Make a backward V instead of the regular V with a tail.

✦ Make a diagonal line from the upper right to the lower left and back on the number side of the Graffiti area.

Memory

Problem: My Palm Organizer has run out of room to load new applications.

The solution is simple: delete programs or data if you need more space. Deleting applications is easy: tap the Application icon and then tap the Menu icon and select Delete from the App menu (see Figure 24-1). As described previously, highlight the application you want to delete, and tap the Delete button (see Figure 24-2).

Figure 24-1: Delete menu item

Figure 24-2: Deleting an application

Note   When you delete an application, remember to delete the associated databases as well; it is usually not too hard to figure out which ones they are.

With 1.x and 2.x versions of the Palm Organizer OS, the Memory application is used to delete unwanted applications from your Palm Organizer's memory. The process is simple: Tap the Application icon and then tap the Memory icon to open the application (see Figure 24-3). Highlight the application you want to delete and tap the Delete button (see Figure 24-4).

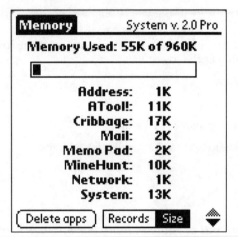

Figure 24-3: The Memory application

Figure 24-4: Deleting an application

Memory fragmentation

Problem: My Palm Organizer says it has enough room to load new applications, but when I try, I get a "not enough memory" message.

Prior to version 3 of the Palm OS, memory tended to fragment. Some applications, notably HackMaster Hacks, can tie up blocks of memory, making it impossible to load applications, even though there is enough free RAM. Say, for example you have 200K of memory free and you try to load a 105K application, only to get a "not enough memory" message—one of your Hacks could be sitting in the middle of your 200K, leaving you with two 100K blocks of noncontiguous free space. One simple solution is to turn off all HackMaster Hacks before loading new applications.

There are a number of utilities that you can use to defragment your Palm Organizer, including:

✦ Recycle (available from www.deskfree.com)

✦ TRG Defragger

Under the Palm 3.0 OS, memory is one big block that doesn't fragment, so there is no benefit to defragmenting a Palm using version 3.0 (or better) of the OS.

Resetting your Palm

Problem: My Palm Organizer has crashed with a "fatal error" message. How do I restart?

The Palm Organizer comes with a built-in escape valve: the reset. The first thing to try when things go wrong with your Palm Organizer — it freezes up, you get a fatal error message, or a reset dialog box locks the screen — is to find a paper clip and gently press it into the reset hole on the back of your Palm Organizer. This is called a "soft" reset; it reboots your Palm Organizer, leaving all of your information intact. Your Palm Organizer should restart with this sequence:

1. You'll see the "Palm Platform" screen (those using older devices will see "Welcome to Palm III" or a similar message, depending on their device).

2. If you have HackMaster installed, you'll be offered a chance to reinstall your Hacks.

3. The main Preferences screen will display.

 Those with older Palm devices should carry a paper clip. You can cut a plastic-covered one and fit it in the battery compartment; even better, keep a business card with a paper clip on it in your Palm Organizer case. It will help get the Palm Organizer back to you if a nontechnical person finds it, and the paper clip helps if the Palm Organizer ever freezes up.

 Palm III (and newer) owners no longer need to carry a paper clip — the top of the new stylus unscrews, giving you a built-in reset pin. Be careful when screwing the top back on; it is easy to strip the threads because the cap is hard plastic and the barrel is metal.

 Want to know more about the sometimes cryptic error messages you may get on your Palm Organizer? Check out Appendix D for Alan Pinstein's article on error messages.

Warm reset

Problem: My Palm Organizer keeps flashing the "Welcome to Palm III" screen when I perform a soft reset, but it won't reboot. Do I have to do a hard reset?

At some point, many Palm Organizer users end up doing a hard reset of their Palm Organizers when they find that a soft reset does not work. A typical symptom is the "looping reset" when the Palm Organizer Splash screen keeps on flashing after pressing Reset, or a small box appears in the top-left corner (indicating that the Palm's Debug monitor is active).

What causes this problem? The most common cause is a partially loaded application—often from a failed HotSync. The HotSync application may hang if it runs into a problem and that can leave an incomplete program fragment on the Palm Organizer. The problem is that when a normal reset is done, the Palm Organizer sends a message to each application on the Palm Organizer to tell it that a reset was done. The partially loaded application tries to run and, of course, crashes the Palm Organizer because it was never loaded properly.

What many users do not know is that you can recover from this problem *without* doing a hard reset. Once you know this trick, you will hardly ever find a need to do a hard reset. This "lukewarm" reset is done by holding the Up button while pressing the Reset button. The Palm Organizer performs a normal reset but does not send the message to each application. It will also not load any Hacks and it will not load any Palm OS update (the equivalent of Windows safe mode or Macintosh extensions off). You can now launch the Memory application and delete the offending application, at which point a normal reset can be performed.

Hard reset

Problem: Okay, I've tried a soft reset and a "warm" reset, but my Palm Organizer still won't reboot. What do I do now?

At times, neither a soft nor a warm reset will do the trick, and desperate measures are called for. A hard reset erases all of the information on your Palm Organizer, restoring it to "factory" condition. You should be able to get back most of your data; a HotSync will restore the data saved when you did your previous synchronization, and you can reload your third-party applications.

1. While holding the power key on, gently push a paper clip into the reset hole on the back of your Palm Organizer.

2. The screen will display the message: "Erase all data? YES—'up' button, NO—any other button." Press the Up button. Your Palm Organizer will revert to factory condition (empty).

3. Open the Palm Organizer Desktop software and select Custom from the HotSync menu.

4. One at a time, select each of the conduits (Date Book and so forth), click the Change button, and then select Desktop Overwrites Palm Organizer.

5. Perform a HotSync to restore the data on your Palm Organizer.

Note   You'll need to reinstall any third-party software you had loaded before doing a hard reset. This is why you should keep a backup copy of all of your loaded applications (see "Backup Loaded Files" at the beginning of this Chapter).

The great news for those who use either Backup Buddy or Palm OS 3.3 is that a HotSync will automatically restore all of their backed up data, including their applications.

Don't worry about your HotSync settings, they will revert back to the defaults after you HotSync.

Hardware

You're more likely to run into problems with hardware than with software when using your Palm Organizer. This section covers the main hardware issues you might encounter.

Handheld

If you take good care, there are few things that can go wrong with your Palm Organizer. I have learned that keeping it in a pocket and then accidentally smashing it into a table (breaking the screen) is *not* a good idea. This section looks at batteries, care of the case (and what's inside it), and your screen.

Batteries

Problem: My Palm Organizer's batteries have run out, and I'm worried that I will lose data when I change the batteries. Is there anything I can do to reduce the risk?

Contrary to popular belief, changing the batteries one at a time will make no difference. Your handheld should retain data for about a week after it powers down; my advice is to put in fresh batteries as soon as possible.

To increase your battery life, use the backlighting sparingly, set the auto-off to one minute, or even turn it off before waiting for it to time out, and, unless you have a Palm V (or Vx or IIIc), don't leave your handheld in the cradle — it places a small drain on your batteries.

There is no measurable benefit to using Duracell's new Ultra batteries in your Palm Organizer — these are designed for high-current, high-draining devices such as cameras, and have no higher capacity (just a higher current peak) than regular Duracell batteries.

Rechargeable batteries

Problem: I'm a Palm Organizer fanatic, and my battery bills are starting to add up. Can I use rechargeable batteries?

I was using up batteries in a week so I tried the "Pure Energy" Alkaline Rechargeables. These batteries maintain a higher charge than most other rechargeables, but there are still precautions that you must take.

The voltage from rechargeable batteries tends to drop off suddenly when they are low on power, whereas regular batteries offer a more gradual drop in power. This quick drop off can be a disaster, especially if you have a database crash that leaves your Palm Organizer on all night. If your handheld loses power completely, you will not only have to resynchronize, but you'll also have to reload. Even worse, some add-on databases are not restored with a synchronization, which means you may lose data. Here's what I recommend if you're going to use rechargeable batteries:

✦ Watch the battery level and switch batteries at about 40 to 50 percent.

✦ Carry a spare set of regular batteries for emergencies.

✦ Backup to your computer regularly (especially before changing batteries).

✦ As suggested previously, change the batteries one at a time — this can help when you're changing batteries that are close to dead.

✦ I recommend Peter Strobel's shareware utility Battery Monitor, which enables you to closely track your batteries' performance (see Chapter 21). For more technical information about batteries, read his article in Appendix E or check out his Web site (www.pstec.de/ppp/).

Problem: I'm constantly having problems with my Palm Organizer recognizing taps. I fix the problem by realigning the digitizer, but the problem returns in a few days.

This is the negative side of using rechargeable batteries: Palm Tech Support reports that using rechargeable alkaline batteries can cause some digitizer alignment problems, and my experience confirms this. There are those who dispute this (though I *have* experienced it), so you may want to take this advice with a grain of salt.

Loose memory board

Problem: I'm having difficulty turning on my Palm Organizer. Sometimes it won't respond.

Note   This advice applies only to older devices (Pilot, PalmPilot, and Palm III), not to newer devices (Palm IIIc/IIIx/IIIxe/IIIe, Palm V/Vx, and Palm VII), which do not have an accessible memory board. Palm IIIx owners may get a shock — there is an empty bracket where the memory card was in older units, which allows for later expansion.

If you are experiencing intermittent problems with turning on your Palm Organizer, and you have tried the other techniques described in this chapter (new batteries, resets, and so on), you might want to try reseating the memory board. This is especially true for those who have performed a memory upgrade.

Caution   The memory boards used in the Palm Organizer are susceptible to static charges. Make sure you are grounded: The easiest way is to use a grounding strap (available for a few dollars at Radio Shack). At a bare minimum, make sure you are touching grounded metal (your computer case may suffice) before proceeding.

Here are the steps for reseating your memory board. (Instructions for reseating the memory board for the Palm III follow immediately after.)

Pilot and Palm Organizers

1. Do a HotSync to make sure you have a current backup.

2. Remove the batteries from your Palm Organizer.

3. Gently stick a small paper clip in the hole directly under the memory door to unlatch it, and then remove the memory door on the back of your Palm Organizer.

4. After the door is removed, the memory board will be exposed.

5. On either side of the board are vertical, cream-colored arms that are holding it down. At the top of those arms are retaining clips that you need to push out in order for them to release the board (see Figure 24-5). I find the easiest approach is to spread the retaining clips apart with my thumbnails, while using my forefingers to gently pull the memory card up about half an inch.

6. Gently pull the card out. If it sticks, gently pull from one side, and then the other.

7. Inspect the contacts inside your Palm Organizer to ensure that none are bent or damaged.

8. The best way to put the memory card back into your Palm Organizer is to carefully reinsert the contact end first, placing the board at the same half inch out angle as in Step 5.

9. Push the board down and in until the retaining clips snap over the board. I give it a push down at this point, to make sure the contacts are seated correctly.

10. Put the memory door back on, put the batteries back in, and then press the reset button on the back of your Palm Organizer.

11. Open the Desktop software and select Custom from the HotSync menu.

12. Select "Desktop Overwrites Palm Organizer" for Date Book, Address Book, Memo Pad, and To Do.

13. Run HotSync again to restore your data.

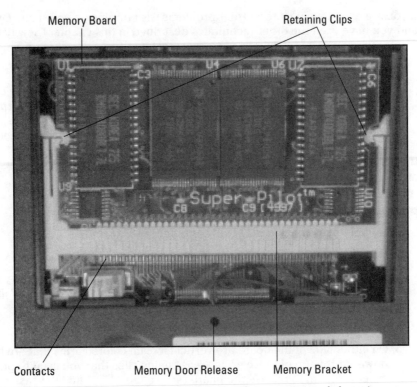

Memory Board   Retaining Clips

Contacts   Memory Door Release   Memory Bracket

Figure 24-5: Memory close-up (TRG SuperPilot memory card shown)

Note   The retaining clips on the IBM WorkPad are metal, rather than plastic, but they work the same way.

HotSync will restore the default settings after syncing.

Palm III

Removing the back from a Palm III is a little more challenging. Before you start, you'll need a #0 screwdriver (I bought mine in a set of five from Radio Shack for $4.00).

1. Do a HotSync to make sure you have a current backup.

2. Remove and set aside the batteries and battery door.

3. Carefully unscrew the four screws that hold the back on your Palm III (see Figure 24-6).

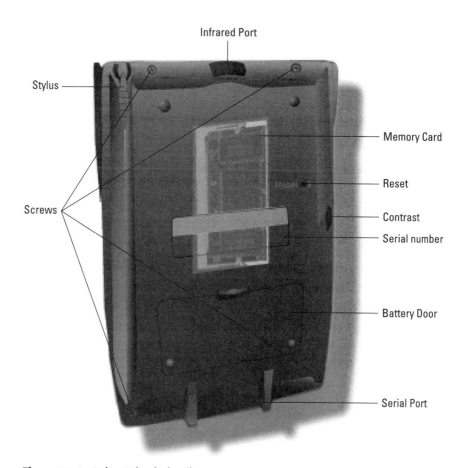

Infrared Port

Stylus

Memory Card

Reset

Screws

Contrast

Serial number

Battery Door

Serial Port

Figure 24-6: Palm III back details

4. The first time you separate the two halves it may be stiff. Use a fingernail or the head of a small screwdriver to gently pry the two halves apart. As you can see in Figure 24-6, the memory card is oriented horizontally, rather than vertically.

5. Proceed through Steps 5 to 13 as described previously in "Pilot and Palm Organizers."

Caution

Use special care when reassembling your Palm III — the threads on #0 screws are easy to strip, especially when going into plastic.

If this doesn't fix the problem, you may need to have your Palm Organizer repaired.

Repairs

Problem: I dropped my Palm Organizer and broke the screen. My life is in ruin. What do I do?

Drop or break your Palm Organizer and you are likely to experience Palm Organizer withdrawal. It happened to me; I bought a new Palm Organizer within 24 hours of accidentally smashing the screen on my first Pilot.

According to Palm Tech Support, the only time there is a charge for repair within the warranty period is when

✦ The screen is damaged.

✦ The unit was physically damaged (for example, water damage, the unit was dropped and the board was cracked, the unit was partially eaten by a family pet).

Palm now offers what it calls the Palm Protection Plan, which enables you to obtain a one-time screen replacement for your new handheld. Under this plan, a first-year screen replacement for the IIIc/VII models is $44.99; for all other models the price is $29.99. A one-year extension program with one-time screen replacement for the IIIc/VII models is $54.99; for all other models the price is $39.99. Given my experience with accidentally broken screens (I've paid $100 each to replace both of the screens I broke), I'd say the plan is a bargain.

The housing itself is covered under the warranty and requires no charge for repair (providing you are still within the warranty period). To get your Palm Organizer repaired you can either

✦ Call the Palm Organizer Tech Support line at (847) 676-1441; or

✦ E-mail your name, telephone number, shipping address (not a P.O. Box), Palm Organizer model (PalmPilot Professional, Palm III, Palm V, and so on), serial number, and a description of the problem to: support@palm.usr.com (use "SRO" in the subject header).

After Palm receives your information, it will arrange to have a box sent to you so that you can overnight the Palm Organizer back to them (assuming that you reside in the continental United States or Canada). Make sure that you have HotSynced your information because your Palm Organizer's memory will be erased during repair. Palm will repair your Palm Organizer within two business days from the time it is received, and will overnight it back to you.

Screen issues

The screen is the most delicate (and expensive) part of your Palm Organizer; it pays to take care of it. This section looks at how to protect and maintain your screen, and how to handle screen-related problems.

Protecting the screen

Problem: I'm worried that excessive use may scratch the screen of my Palm Organizer. Is there anything I can do to protect the screen?

One of the best solutions for clear screen protectors is Concept Kitchen's. They come in a pack of 12 and you change them once every month or two. Other solutions for just the Graffiti area include Post-It Notes on the Graffiti area, the clear Post-It tabs, and cellophane tape.

Another good solution is the adhesiveless GlassRites. They are very simple: a rectangle of the same plastic that is used on the Palm's screen is cut a little bigger than the screen. The edges slide between the display and the bezel, and once in place, you can hardly tell it's there. It is tricky to install, but the directions are good. The price is insanely inexpensive: $14.95 for 12 of them, at least a year's supply. They also have a nonglossy version, the PilotRite, that is said to feel more like paper. For more information, try `http://members.aol.com/PilotRite/index.html`.

Note In my experience, all of the screen protection solutions make it harder to read your Palm Organizer's screen. I use Concept Kitchen's WriteRight screen protectors, cut down to the size of the Graffiti screen. This way I get the best of both worlds: protection where it's needed most, and high visibility for the display area. As a bonus, I can easily cover the Graffiti area three times with a single sheet. Check out Concept Kitchen's Web site at `www.conceptkitchen.com` for WriteRight application techniques.

Tip If you want to protect the Graffiti area on your Palm Organizer, and add functionality to Graffiti, check out TapPad (see Chapter 3 for more on TapPad).

Cleaning the screen

Problem: The screen on my Palm Organizer has become grungy and hard to read. What can I do to clean it?

A lot of people are worried about scratches on their screen. As with a lot of optic devices, most scratches probably result from improper cleaning. Cleaning the screen "dry" causes scratches by grinding dirt into the plastic. If you don't clean often enough, scratches are formed by dirt being embedded in the tip of the stylus (which, by itself, cannot scratch the screen). The solution is simple: get a microfiber cleaning cloth. This is a superdense nylon cloth that is safe to clean optics with. It is often found in the camera section of a department store (Wal-Mart, in particular, sells a large package for about $4). You only need a hand-sized piece for cleaning the Palm Organizer, which compresses nicely in the pocket. As an added bonus, you can also safely clean eyeglasses, CD-ROMs, and any other scratchable optic device that you encounter.

For daily cleaning, I use Concept Kitchen's Karma cloth, an incredibly soft piece of optical-grade cleaning cloth. To be honest, I've also had success with a good-quality lens cleaning cloth (I have one by Kanebo called Hitecloth; it cost me about $4.95, it's washable, and it works). To restore the luster to your screen, the best I've seen so far is Concept Kitchen's BrainWash, a wet-and-dry cleaning system. Check out Concept Kitchen's products at www.conceptkitchen.com. To remove scratches, I use Tim Warner's Screen Clean, which is touted as being able to remove 99 percent of all scratches. This mildly abrasive product needs to be used cautiously, but it does seem to work. For more information, check out Tim's site at www.timwarner.com.

Screen problems

Problem: I've broken the screen on my Palm Organizer can it be replaced?

As of this writing, nonwarranty repair for the screen costs $100 and is payable by Visa or MasterCard only. This includes overnight shipping both ways, within the continental United States and Canada. The normal turnaround time is under a week. See the preceding "Repairs" section for more information on fixing a broken screen.

Problem: I can't read the screen on my Palm Organizer because the letters are too faint.

If you can't read the screen, try adjusting the contrast wheel. If you've recently upgraded your memory, try reseating the chip (see "Loose Memory Board" earlier in this chapter).

Problem: My Palm Organizer has developed a dark spot in the center of the screen that stays there even when I turn it off.

If your Palm Organizer has a small, hazy, dark spot in the center of the screen (whether or not it is turned on), this may be a problem caused by pressure combined with a component that was too tall in some PalmPilot Professional units. Contact 3Com/Palm to see if it can be repaired or replaced under warranty.

Problem: My Palm Organizer no longer responds correctly when I tap it.

Here's one that will drive you crazy: Your Palm Organizer no longer responds to taps, or they register above or below your stylus. What you need to do is to redigitize your screen:

1. Tap the Applications icon.

2. Select Preferences.

3. Select Digitizer from the pull-down menu in the upper right-hand corner of the screen.

4. To reset your Digitizer, tap the three targets that appear.

If this doesn't work, try a hard reset. Be aware that this is a known symptom if you are using rechargeable alkaline batteries. Try switching to regular alkaline batteries. I did, and I've abandoned rechargeables as a result.

Palm VII Diagnostics application

The Diagnostics application is designed specifically for the Palm VII and is listed in the Application Launcher screen. To launch the application, tap the Diagnostics icon. You can use this application to find information in these areas:

✦ Wireless signal strength in your area

✦ Status of the Palm VII activation

✦ Details about the charging status of the internal transmitter

✦ Wireless base station to which the Palm VII is connected

The signal strength is weak

To improve the signal strength, make sure the antenna is pointing straight up. If you hold your Palm VII in your hand, raise the antenna to 135 degrees. If you put it on a flat surface, raise the antenna to 90 degrees.

Internal transmitter is always charging

If you consistently receive a message that the transmitter is being charged when you attempt to initiate a wireless transaction, contact Customer Care for possible hardware problems.

Lost network connection

If you lose network connection during a wireless transaction, try the transaction again. If it fails repeatedly, move to a different location with stronger signal strength and try again.

Long wait for response

If your query response is taking longer than usual, stop the transaction. Move to a different location with stronger signal strength and try again.

HotSync Problems

As I said at the beginning of this chapter, the biggest single source of problems for Palm Organizer users is the computer interface. When HotSyncing doesn't work, it can be frustrating to track down the problem.

HotSync Log

The first place your should look if you are having problems with a HotSync (other than connecting) is in the HotSync Log, which will usually pinpoint the problem for you. If you need or want more detailed information, you can turn on verbose logging using Backup Buddy (Mac users can do the same thing by checking "Show more detail in HotSync Log" in the HotSync Software Setup dialog box).

Overwritten data

Problem: Help! I've accidentally selected "Handheld overwrites Desktop," and now all my data is gone.

Don't panic — there are backup copies of your main data files within the user-named folder on your computer. Here's how you fix the problem (this example uses Address Book data):

1. Navigate to your user-named folder; mine is C:\Palm\BrownG.

2. Open the Address folder.

3. Rename the Address.dat file as Address.old (or whatever you'd like).

4. Rename the Address.bak file as Address.dat.

5. Confirm that your conduit setting is "Synchronize."

6. HotSync to recover your data.

Caution   According to Phil Purpura of Chapura Software (the makers of PocketMirror), those of us who HotSync to multiple machines have a greater risk of accidentally overwriting our data; I suspect that the extra backup gives us a false sense of security. I have several times tried to correct a problem on one of my backup machines, only to discover I've duplicated my folly on both. The lesson? Be careful when selecting the overwrite options.

Rebound data

Problem: Every time I HotSync, data that I deleted from my handheld keeps coming back. How do I get rid of it?

It is likely that there is still a copy of the program or data archived in the backup folder on your computer, and HotSyncing is reinstalling it. To permanently delete the file, you should

✦ Open your user-named folder (in the Palm or Pilot folder)

✦ Open the backup folder

✦ Delete the backup copy of the program your are trying to remove

✦ Confirm that the program is no longer on your handheld; if it is, tap the Menu icon, select Delete, and delete it

✦ After the next HotSync, the recurring program should no longer appear

Windows

If you're having problems HotSyncing, there are a few tricks to try to kick-start the HotSync process:

✦ Is HotSync running? Windows 9*x* and NT users will see a HotSync icon in the System Tray; if not, relaunch HotSync Manager.

✦ Try closing HotSync Manager and restarting it (this fixes 90 percent of all HotSync connection problems).

✦ Try changing the speed of the synchronization to 9600 baud under HotSync/ Setup/Local.

✦ If HotSyncing quits immediately, try deleting the serial ports from Windows 95 (they will automatically reinstall).

✦ If you find that HotSync dies when trying to load an application, there may not be enough contiguous free memory left in your Palm Organizer to load the application. The solution is to run a defragmentation utility (see "Memory Fragmentation" earlier in this chapter) or delete applications to free up memory.

✦ Check the contacts in your cradle; you may need to use a toothpick to pull them out a hair more to make contact.

Disabling the automatic timeout

Problem: My Palm Organizer turns itself off before it finishes HotSyncing.

Sometimes, especially if you have a lot of data to synchronize, the HotSync process will time out. If this happens to you, there is a developer's tool that will disable your Palm Organizer's automatic timeout. From the HotSync screen, press the Up and Down buttons at the same time, and tap in the upper right-hand corner of the screen. You'll see the message "Developer's Backdoor, DLServer Wait Forever is ON." Tap OK, and you should be able to HotSync without problems. Don't worry; this state only lasts until you change applications or turn off your Palm Organizer.

If you happen to tap on the lower right-hand corner of the screen, you'll see a bunch of code written on your screen—this is the debugger, which is useless to you without special hardware. Switch applications, and things will return to normal.

Fatal errors when reinstalling ListMaker

Problem: I'm trying to reinstall ListMaker 1.0, and HotSync keeps failing.

If you have to reinstall ListMaker 1.0 (part of Synergy Software's Hi-Five), you must install the ListMakerDB.pdb file on one HotSync, and the ListMaker.prc on the next HotSync. Your HotSync will crash with a fatal error if your reverse the order or try to synchronize both at the same time. This problem is cured with Version 1.5 of ListMaker.

Laptop IRQ conflicts

Problem: I'm getting IRQ errors when I try to set up the Palm Organizer software on my Dell laptop.

If you're having IRQ problems with a Dell laptop, consider disabling the laptop's IR functionality using the SETUP function key—the IR on the laptop uses the same IRQ as the serial port.

Registry Problems

Windows 9*x* and NT users have their own special set of problems, which can only be solved by editing the Windows Registry. The Registry is a database that stores all of the settings for your computer, including installed software. Imagine an INI file on steroids.

Conduit problems

Problem: My Palm Organizer applications no longer synchronize with a HotSync, and when I view the settings under the HotSync/Custom menu, they display as "component," instead of their proper names.

A conduit is the software that communicates between your Palm Organizer and your computer. Your Palm Organizer comes with conduits for the Date and Address Books, To Do List, Mail, and so on. You can experience problems with some third-party conduits, especially if you add and then uninstall them. The first symptom will be that some of your Palm Organizer applications are no longer being synchronized. If you look under HotSync/Custom, some or all of your Palm Organizer's applications have been renamed "component," and you can't change the settings for them.

I have seen reports of problems with a number of programs that may have been incorrectly uninstalled, including Ascend 97, Lotus Organizer 97, and SideKick 98. These problems do not necessarily mean that there is a problem with the Palm Organizer software you have installed on your computer; just that it may have been incorrectly uninstalled. The first time I encountered the problem, I called Ivan Phillips of Pendragon Software, who graciously solved the problem for me. My problem turned out to be the installation (actually the de-installation) of the demo version of Palmetta Mail.

Here's the process you'll need to follow to fix the problem.

Backing up the Registry

Editing the Windows Registry (see Figure 24-7) is not for the faint of heart; deleting the wrong file can do serious damage.

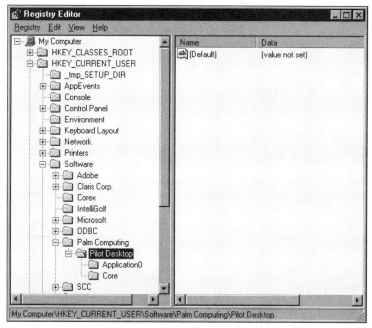

Figure 24-7: Windows Registry

The first step before editing registry entries (which must be done live), is to make a backup copy:

1. Select Run from the Start menu and type **regedit** (Figure 24-8)

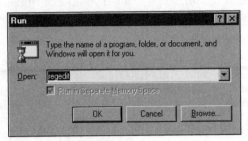

Figure 24-8: Running Regedit

2. Select Export Registry file from the Registry menu

3. Type **backup.reg** and save the file to your C:\Windows folder

Delete the entry
Click the HKEY_CURRENT_USER folder, and delete the entries that pertain to your conduit software (Application 0, AscAppAddress, and so on). Do *not* delete ApplicationMail, ApplicationExpense, or any of the Components. The following is a sample (this is what the Palm Organizer desktop places in your Registry):

> ✦ HKEY_CURRENT_USER
>> ✦ Software
>>> ✦ US Robotics (or Palm)
>>>> ✦ Pilot Desktop

HotSync problems with Windows 3.11

Problem: I've deinstalled a third-party application from my Windows 3.11 computer and HotSync no longer works.

If you're experiencing HotSync problems under Windows 3.11 after deinstalling third-party conduits, try this:

1. Close the Palm Organizer Desktop software and the HotSync Manager.

2. Delete the PILOT.INI file from C:\Windows.

3. Select Run from the File menu and type **c:\pilot\hotsync –r**.

Your HotSync Manager should restart and you should be able to synchronize with the Palm Organizer Desktop software. If you are running the 2.0 Desktop, you will no longer be able to use the mail or expense applications; you need to reinstall the Palm Desktop software.

Mac HotSync problems

Problem: I'm having problems initiating or completing a HotSync on my Macintosh. Is there anything I can do to fix the problem?

The advent of MacPac 2 brought faster and more reliable HotSyncing to the Macintosh platform; Windows users finally caught up in speed with the Palm OS 3.3 upgrade. Still, problems can occur. Here are a few tricks that should help you:

- ✦ Open your Control Panels and make sure HotSync is running.

- ✦ If you find that the HotSync button just turns your handheld on or that the HotSync process doesn't start within approximately 15 seconds, try turning HotSync off and on (as with Windows, this seems to cure 90 percent of all HotSync connection problems).

- ✦ Sometimes, a second HotSync will fail, and the cure is to reboot your Mac.

- ✦ Run without extensions (make sure AppleTalk is off).

- ✦ Set your serial port speed to 9600 baud.

- ✦ Turn off HotSync, press the HotSync button on your Palm Organizer's cradle, and then reactivate HotSync.

Problem: I've just HotSynced my Macintosh, but the HotSync log does not display information about the just-performed HotSync.

If you leave the HotSync Log dialog box open when you perform a HotSync, it will not correctly update; the cure is to close and then reopen the HotSync Log.

Corrupted resources

Problem: When I try to HotSync, I get the message: "An unknown device error has occurred. HotSync is terminating." How do I get HotSync working again?

I had this problem on my Mac, coincidentally, while writing this chapter. I used Casady & Greene's Conflict Catcher 4.0.1 to diagnose the conflict, which it identified as Shared Library Manager 2.01. The problem didn't occur with the same resource running under OS 8.1; my conclusion is that the resource was corrupt — a clean reinstall fixed the problem.

G3 HotSync problems

Problem: I have a new Macintosh G3 computer, and I'm having difficulty HotSyncing. How do I fix this problem?

With the G3 Macintosh machines, there are two different ways to get your Palm Organizer to HotSync:

✦ If the Macintosh is running, make sure the option to run HotSync Monitor at startup is not selected. Restart your Mac and then go to the HotSync Control Panel and turn the HotSync Monitor on. Immediately after turning on HotSync Monitor, press the HotSync button on the Palm Organizer cradle. After the synchronization is complete, you can turn off the HotSync Monitor.

✦ If the Macintosh is running, make sure the option to run HotSync Monitor at startup is not selected. Shut down your Mac and then unplug the cradle. Restart with extensions off (hold down the Shift key during bootup). Go to Control Panel, set the port to access Printer Port, set the speed to 9600, and turn on HotSync Monitor. Finally, plug the Palm Organizer cradle into the Printer Port and try a HotSync.

Memory leaks

Problem: The connection between my Palm Organizer and my Macintosh is dropped during the HotSync process. How can I force all of my data to be synchronized?

Version 1.0x of the Palm Organizer Desktop software for the Macintosh tended to have memory "leaks" which could be made worse if you had a lot of data to HotSync. If HotSync is timing out, the cure may be to select Custom from the HotSync menu, and synchronize each component (Address Book, Date Book, and so on) individually. I use this technique whenever I have a lot of new applications to install (or when reinstalling after a hard reset). I first HotSync the Pilot applications with Install set to "Do Nothing," then reverse the process for the second HotSync by turning off all of the application conduits and enabling install.

New Feature

I can think of no reason for Macintosh users not to upgrade to the latest version of MacPac (Palm Desktop 2.5 as of this writing) — the application is enormously improved, eliminating this and other problems, and providing Mac users with a Desktop application far superior to the Windows equivalent.

PilotMoney

Problem: After performing a hard reset, I can no longer do a HotSync. How do I restore the connection?

According to Palm's documentation, the PilotMoney conduit is not compatible with the Macintosh Pilot Desktop software (Version 1.01). With PilotMoney installed, when you attempt to restore after a hard reset, the Pilot Desktop application will quit and HotSync will be disabled. To prevent this from happening, you must delete the MoneyDB.pdb file from your Backup folder before HotSyncing after a hard reset.

Wacom tablets

Problem: I've just connected a Wacom drawing tablet to my Macintosh, and now I can no longer HotSync.

A conflict existed between the Palm software and the extensions used by Wacom drawing tablets. The fix was to turn off the Wacom extensions using Extensions Manager, and then restart before doing a HotSync. You may want to create an extensions set that excludes the Wacom extensions and includes HotSync Monitor to automate the process. A better solution is to upgrade to the current version of Wacom's drivers, which fixes the problem.

Visor HotSync

Problem: When I attempt to HotSync my Handspring Visor to my Macintosh, I get the message "The HotSync Preferences file was damaged and has been replaced. Please check your settings in the Serial Port Settings tab of the HotSync Software Setup window."

This is a known issue with some configurations when using third-party USB cards. The fix is to open HotSync Manager, reset your USB settings, and then toggle HotSyncing on and off. There is a fix for Mac OS 9.0.4 users, available from Handspring's web site (www.handspring.com).

Software

Software problems are few and far between under the Palm OS; this is one of the reasons we all love it. In a few instances simple precautions will eliminate or reduce the few problems that exist.

Handheld

The more third-party software you install on your handheld, the greater the risk that something will go wrong. Here are a few notes that may help.

Flash memory

Technology Resource Group (TRG) first introduced the idea of loading applications into unused Flash memory with its FlashBuilder product. The latest incarnation of the product is FlashPro, which enables loading of data and applications into flash memory without the use of a computer. See Chapter 21 for more on FlashPro.

Problem: I've just moved a new application into Flash memory, and now the program crashes when I run it.

The fix here is simple: move the application back to regular RAM. For a listing of applications that can be loaded into Flash memory, see www.asynccomputing. com/cgi-bin/displayTRGCompatListing.pl.

Problem: I've just loaded an updated program on my Palm Organizer, but the old version still displays when I tap the icon.

If you install a program update on your handheld while an older version is still loaded in Flash memory, your Palm Organizer will only "see" the version in Flash memory. The cure is to delete the older version, which you can do by deleting it from Flash memory or by copying the newer version into Flash memory to overwrite the outdated one.

Problem: I want to upgrade to Palm OS 3.3. How will that affect the applications I have installed in Flash memory using FlashPro?

The new Palm OS is 64K larger than the previous version, so installing it will wipe out your Flash memory. The first thing to do is to create a complete backup of the applications installed in Flash memory. The easiest way to do this is with Backup Buddy, although you can simply note which applications are in Flash memory and simply reload them later. You also need Version 1.06 or newer of FlashPro. After you've installed the OS update, rerun FlashPro Setup, and then reinstall your Flash memory applications, bearing in mind that you have slightly less space than before.

HackMaster

Hacks must be disabled before you delete them; otherwise, you risk a crash (which can normally be cured by a HotSync). TRG's FlashPro includes a screen warning you against moving or deleting enabled HackMaster Hacks. See Chapter 22 for more on HackMaster and HackMaster Hacks.

PocketQuicken

Problem: When I HotSync my handheld, I get the following message in PocketQuicken Sync: "Unable to extract account and/or category information (err 13 — 'Generic Quicken file error')."

You will get this error message if you attempt to HotSync PocketQuicken when your Quicken file is open on your computer. The cure is to close the file before HotSyncing.

Problem: When I HotSync my handheld, I get the following message in PocketQuicken Sync: "Unable to extract account and/or category information (err 8 — 'Invalid Quicken password')."

You only get this message if you are running Quicken on two machines. Change the access password on one, but do not make a corresponding change on the other computer.

Caution   I recommend against trying to run the Quicken/PocketQuicken conduit combination on more than one computer; it is too easy for the conduit to create duplicate entries in this configuration.

Computer

As I said at the beginning of this chapter, most of your Palm Organizer problems (if any) will involve your computer.

Loading Expense macro
Problem: I get the message "Compile Error in hidden module: mExpenseDialogCode" when I try to load the Expense Macro on my PC.

The solution to this problem is to upgrade to Version 2.1 (or newer) of the Palm Desktop software.

Install tool with IntelliSync
Problem: I've just loaded IntelliSync and now I can't load applications onto my Palm Organizer.

If you find that the Palm Organizer Install Application no longer works after you install IntelliSync, the solution is to reinstall the Palm Organizer Desktop software. The reinstallation won't disrupt IntelliSync, and you'll be able to install again.

Macintosh
Problem: I want to use a program that does not offer a Macintosh conduit.

Users who want to use some of the Windows-only third-party conduits may want to try Connectix Software's Virtual PC 3.0.

Tip   If you're trying to HotSync using Virtual PC on a Macintosh, make sure that the HotSync Monitor is not running on the Mac side before you boot Windows. Otherwise, the faster Mac side will intercept the HotSync request.

Corrupted Palm Desktop Preferences

Problem: When I attempt to launch Palm's Macintosh desktop software, I get the message "Invalid Configuration. Terminating Palm Desktop" or "Can't find Palm Desktop Preferences," and the software does not load.

If you get one of these messages, your Palm Organizer Desktop Preferences file is corrupt. The solution is to delete the file Palm Desktop Preferences from Preferences folder (which is in your System folder) and restart the Palm Desktop application. You may have to reset your preferences in the desktop application, but at least it will run.

Telecommunications

Those lucky enough to have a modem for their Palm Organizer have some special problems to deal with.

Long-distance calling cards

Problem: I want to use my long-distance credit card number when connecting using my Palm Organizer modem, but I need to enter more characters than allowed.

To get around the 36-character-and-comma limitation of the modem dial-up string to connect using a long-distance calling card, try using one of the storable dial strings. Under Preferences ➪ Modem set the string to something similar to this: **AT&FX4S7=90&Z0=1234567890**.

This sets the dial timeout to 90 seconds and stores the string 1234567890 (which is the calling card number) in register zero (0). Then do the following:

✦ Under Preferences ➪ Network, tap the phone string.

✦ Set Phone # to the regular seven digits of your local ISP or RAS # (for example, 5551212).

✦ Set Dial prefix to the long distance carrier # (in this case AT&T) plus the area code of the preceding phone number (for example, 9,18002255288,,,,1617). Note that the "9," (including the comma) is usually necessary in hotels.

✦ Set Use calling card to stored register at: ,S=0.

The final dial string to the modem will be something similar to ATDT9,18002255288,,,,16175551212,S=0, which is 36 digits. You can experiment with the number of commas necessary to achieve the correct delay. When I am on the road (in a hotel or office) I simply check the Dial prefix and Use calling card check-boxes. When I am home (where the number is a local call) I simply uncheck both boxes and only the seven-digit number is dialed.

DTR problems

Problem: I'm using PalmTelnet, a Palm Organizer modem cable, and a US Robotics modem. When going "offline," the modem doesn't hang up. I have the modem set to hang up when DTR is dropped. What's wrong?

The Palm Organizer modem cable doesn't drop DTR (pin 20) properly. The modem hangs up when DTR drops. Wire a DB25-DB25 adapter with pins 2, 3, and 7 straight through, and pin 4 on the Palm Organizer side to pin 20 on the Cabletron side.

Problem: I'm using PalmTelnet, a Palm Organizer modem cable, and vendor-supplied adapters connected to a Cabletron Hub's Console port. For some reason, this doesn't work. No menu appears. What could be wrong?

The Palm Organizer modem cable doesn't drop DTR (pin 20) properly. The Cabletron hubs need to see DTR go from low to high in order to initialize its menus. Wire a DB25-DB25 adapter with pins 2, 3, and 7 straight through, and pin 4 on the Palm Organizer side to pin 20 on the Cabletron side. Hardware handshaking is disabled in this configuration, but the Palm Organizer seems to do well without it.

More Help

The Palm Web site (www.palm.com) has a great section (www.palm.com/cust-supp/helpnotes/indexhn.html) devoted to troubleshooting FAQ (frequently asked questions). Another good place to get troubleshooting tips and information on the Palm Organizer is on CompuServe (GO PALM ORGANIZER); the technical support offered there is the best. Also, don't forget to check out Calvin's FAQ on PalmGearHQ (www.palmgear.com/).

Summary

✦ Backup Buddy is an essential backup tool, especially for those who use TRG's FlashPro and for those who have not yet upgraded to Palm OS 3.3.

✦ A soft reset will cure most crashes on your Palm Organizer, and a warm reset will help you recover from most other crashes. A hard reset should *only* be used as a last resort.

✦ PalmPilot and Palm III owners can cure some bootup problems by carefully reseating the memory card in their handhelds.

✦ If you are concerned about scratches on your handheld's screen, consider one of the third-party screen protection products. Get more mileage from them by cutting them down to the size of your handheld's Graffiti area.

✦ The number one HotSync problem on both Windows and the Macintosh is the circumstance in which your handheld cannot connect with your desktop computer: nine times out of ten, the fix is to close and reopen HotSync Manager.

✦ The HotSync Log often provides good information as to what might be a problem with one of your conduits.

✦ The first place to look for troubleshooting information is Palm's Web site at `www.palm.com/custsupp/helpnotes/indexhn.html`.

✦   ✦   ✦

Easter Eggs

E aster Eggs are secret tricks built into programs by programmers, often as a hidden "signature." There are quite
a few built into the Palm OS — in fact, it is the only device I
know of with an Easter Eggs–enabled mode!

Note I've just tested all of these with the new versions of the
Palm OS, and they still work! This just goes to show that
our favorite company still has a sense of humor.

Team Credits

To get a display of the authors of the Pilot on a Pilot or
PalmPilot:

1. Tap Applications, and then tap the Memory application.

2. Hold the stylus on the Memory block in the upper left-
   hand corner, and then press the Scroll Down key (or
   hold down the Scroll button and tap in the upper right-
   hand corner of the screen).

For Palm III and Palm V owners to see the display:

1. Select Info from the App menu in the new Applications
   Launcher.

2. Hold down the stylus in the area to the left of "Info" at
   the top of the screen, and then press the Scroll Down
   key.

For Palm VII owners to get a listing of the Palm VII team:

1. Turn on the Easter Egg mode (see the "Taxi" section
   later in this Appendix).

2. Open the Palm.Net PQA.

3. Tap just above the lower left-hand corner (some of the names also have a picture, which you can open by tapping just above and to the right of the name).

Not to be left out, the designers of Handspring's version of the Palm OS have their own listing:

1. Tap on the Launcher.

2. While pressing the Scroll Up button, tap the time block in the upper left-hand corner, and you'll get an animated logo (which they call "Flip") with a listing of the Visor team.

DOS Message

Here's one for computer geeks:

1. In the Giraffe game, hold your stylus in the area above the Giraffe title line and then press the Scroll Down key.

2. You'll see the message:

```
Not ready reading drive C
Abort, Retry, Fail?
```

3. Tapping anywhere on the screen brings you back to Giraffe.

Giraffe Author

Chris Raff, the author of Giraffe, managed to get his picture into the Pilot. Here's how to view it:

1. In the Giraffe game, hold the stylus in the lower right-hand area of the display (to the right of Help), and then press the Scroll Up button. A picture of Chris (he's on the left) and Rob Haitani, taken at one of Palm's early Christmas parties, will show sideways onscreen.

Note   Rob Haitani was Palm's product manager for the original Pilot. Interestingly, he is now the product manager for the Visor at Handspring. In addition to helping me with Chapter 8, Rob gave me the details of the Easter Egg built into Handspring's version of the Palm OS.

2. Tapping anywhere on the screen brings you back to Giraffe.

Sheldon

The original Palm logo was an abstract palm tree, and Sheldon the dancing palm tree (see Figure A-1) has been the Palm mascot since those early days.

 Figure A-1: Sheldon

Here's how to see Sheldon:

1. In the Giraffe game, tap the Help button.

2. Draw the # character. If you can't remember the Graffiti stroke for the pound sign, tap down to the next screen (dot and then the N in reverse). Sheldon will briefly appear somewhere onscreen.

Taxi

Taxi was one of the first code names for the Pilot, and the authors left one for you to find. Instructions follow for both OS 1.0 and OS 2/3.

Pilot (OS 1.0)

To see the Taxi with a Pilot 1000 or 5000 running Palm OS 1.0:

1. Tap the Find icon.

2. Press the Scroll Down button and draw a horizontal line left from the center of the Graffiti area to the left side of the screen. A Taxi will drive across the screen.

The only problem with this Easter Egg is that it was written to go off occasionally, which could be a problem if you were showing the Pilot to your boss. The first patch to the Palm OS removed the random appearance of the Taxi and replaced it with the only Easter Egg mode that I know of.

The Easter Egg enabler is easy to invoke. Open General Preferences, and then draw a small clockwise circle (starting from 12 o'clock) above the calculator; an Easter Egg will appear onscreen (see Figure A-2).

Figure A-2: Easter Eggs enabled

Taxi (OS 2/3)

PalmPilot and Palm Organizer owners can see the Taxi, too:

1. Enable the Easter Egg mode (described previously), and then open the Memo Pad.

2. Press the Scroll Down button and draw a horizontal line left from the center of the Graffiti area to the left side of the screen. A Taxi will bounce across the screen.

TRGpro

The wizards at Technology Resource Group have built an Easter Egg into their new TRGpro:

1. Open the application launcher.

2. Tap the Menu icon, and then select System Info from the App menu.

3. Write an **a** in the Graffiti area; system information will appear onscreen.

More Easter Eggs

Want more? Tim Warner maintains a list of Easter Eggs on his Web site at www.timwarner.com/palmos/egg.phtml.

✦   ✦   ✦

Dot Commands

When I wrote the *PalmPilot Resource Kit*, the original draft included Palm's Dot Commands. Glenn Rotte, the technical editor, convinced me that these commands should not be published because of the risk that they pose to inexperienced users. I still agree with that sentiment, but this book is called the *Palm OS Bible*, which is meant to be a more comprehensive sort of book; thus, I think they need to be included for completeness' sake.

Caution   The Dot commands are ones that Palm has built into its operating system for programmers and developers. I have used all varieties of Palm Organizers, from the original Pilot to the latest, and I have never had need for these. I recommend that you take the same approach. Those who are curious should try these with extreme caution; they have the capability to wipe out your handheld. You've been warned!

These are all ShortCuts formed by the Shortcut Graffiti stroke (it looks like a lowercase cursive letter "l," followed by a dot, and then the character indicated in the table. The easiest way to do this is to open a new memo, and then do the ShortCut.

1	This opens debug mode and opens the serial port. If left in this condition, your batteries will be completely drained. A soft reset reverts your handheld.
2	Another debug mode that opens the serial port. If left in this condition, your batteries will be completely drained. A soft reset reverts your handheld.
3	Disables your Palm Organizer's capability to shut itself off automatically. A soft reset reverts your handheld.
4	Flashes your user name and number. The Palm Organizer has a unique number; some developers use the combination of the user name/ID number when generating serial numbers.

5   Removes the user configuration and HotSync log. This is a guaranteed way to create duplicate entries and screw up your data.

6   Displays the ROM date, which can be of assistance to Palm's technical support.

7   Toggles between NiCad and alkaline batteries; this shortcut corrects the battery display if you are using NiCads.

The following Dot Commands were added with OS 3.1:

8   Toggles the inverse backlighting on OS 3.1 or newer devices (Palm IIIx, V, and VII). See Chapter 22 for a HackMaster Hack that provides the same functionality.

i   Enables beam receive for a short time, for those who prefer to leave beaming turned off in the General Prefs screen.

s   Toggles back and forth between serial and IR modes (for those who are doing IR HotSyncs).

t   Toggles the loopback mode for the IR Exchange Manager, which enables you to test beaming software by simulating the process without another device.

Tip   A minor bug affects those able to use these new commands: every time you do a soft reset, the three alpha Dot commands are re-added to your Palm Organizer's Graffiti ShortCuts database. The downside is that this occupies space on your handheld, albeit a small amount, which can become significant if you reset regularly. The fix is simple: use Pimlico Software's dbScan (it is on the CD-ROM) to clean up duplicate ShortCut entries.

✦   ✦   ✦

Palm Errors

Crash. Freeze. Bomb. Sad Mac. Blue Screen of Death. Segmentation Fault. Illegal Operation. 0x0010A59F.

If you've used a computer for more than a few hours, you are undoubtedly familiar with one of these phrases. They are just a few of the ominous, feared, heart-stopping messages displayed by your computer for no apparent reason.

If you take a trip down memory lane, I'm sure that you can recall the first time it happened to you. I remember my first time. It was a Thursday. I was typing in my report "When Dinosaurs Ruled the Earth" for a fifth-grade project. Almost done, I thought, and then it would be time for milk and cookies! But, alas, my Mac had a different plan. Apparently, it wasn't time for milk and cookies; instead, it was the perfect moment for an error of Type 10, which the Mac gleefully informed me via a dialog box that said "An error of Type 10" has occurred. When things like this pop up on screen, there's only one thing you're sure of — that it's not a good sign. "What have I done?" I wondered. Let's see . . . I pressed the little print icon, and then I think I pressed Enter . . . hmmm. . . . What did I do wrong?

I was 10, and using my parents' computer. I recall noticing that my heart had stopped beating. I looked past the computer to make sure no one had noticed what was going on, the exact same response as when you knock over a vase or launch a baseball through a window. When I was 8 and I broke a vase, I knew exactly what to do. I got out the tape and glue and put it back together. No problem. But with a computer, I saw no ideal place to put either the glue or the tape. So I clicked, typed, and pushed every key combination I could think of for a good five minutes, and nothing changed. There was only one thing left to try. The power button. I looked at it, and it looked right back at me. It was like a staredown between Indiana Jones and a big, big snake. I inched my finger closer and closer, and I quickly turned off the power. The screen went dark. Well, I guessed that I should turn it back on to make sure it still worked. . . . The familiar chime greeted me as I turned

This appendix was written exclusively for Glenn Brown/IDG Books Worldwide by Alan Pinstein. Copyright © 2000 Synergy Solutions, Inc. All rights reserved.

the power switch back on, and the Mac came back to life. Victory! As a kid, you must realize how important it is to have something that you can get away with breaking.

I am now a programmer. I know all about computers. I no longer worry when things crash. But most of you reading this book are not programmers. I share this story with you so that you realize that even us computer geeks understand how helpless and frustrated one feels when your computer crashes on you.

So, what on earth is this story doing in a book on the Palm Organizer? Well, as great as the Palm Organizer is, it's still just a computer. It has a processor, RAM, serial port, and a monitor, just like the one sitting on your desktop. And, just like the computer sitting on your desk, it can crash. And when it crashes, the Palm OS has its very own error dialog box. I'll explain what some of the more common errors mean, and tell you how to deal with them.

First, it's very important to realize that crashes are *never* your fault. They are invariably the result of a bug in a program. You should never feel as if you've done something wrong when an error dialog box comes on screen. The error occurs because the program encounters a situation it wasn't set up to deal with, or possibly because it simply deals with a situation incorrectly. All bugs can be fixed, and it's possible (and in fact, desired) for a programmer to create a program that just won't crash. Ever!

To help programmers out with creating bug-free programs, Palm created many programs and help venues for developers. One is the Platinum Certification program. This is a software testing service performed by an independent company, Quality Partners, Inc. A variety of tests are performed to make sure that the program being tested works in a variety of situations that are likely to cause a program to crash. Quality Partners makes sure that the software performs gracefully. For instance, Quality Partners makes sure that your program correctly handles itself when there is little or no memory left on your Palm. It also uses a technique called "Gremlins" that basically pretends to use your program by pushing buttons, choosing menu items, and entering text in your program. Each Gremlin event does one of the things just mentioned. To pass the Gremlins portion of the Platinum Certification test, your application needs to survive 1,000,000 of these Gremlins. If an application passes the Platinum Certification test, you've got pretty good reassurance that it won't crash when you're using it. I say pretty good because Platinum Certification isn't a guarantee against crashing. But a certified application has a very high probability of not causing you any problems.

Palm OS Errors

General unresponsiveness/freezes

If your Palm simply seems frozen or unresponsive, it may have crashed. However, it may just be doing something that takes a *long* time. If you ever think that your Palm is frozen, you should wait three to five minutes before resetting it; it may just be "thinking."

An example: When a program requests memory to save your data, the OS tries to find enough memory and then it tells the program that it either succeeded or failed in finding this memory. If you have a Palm OS 1.*x* or 2.*x* device and have very little memory left on the device, the OS can spend a long time figuring out whether there is enough memory for the program.

However, if the Palm stays frozen for more than three to five minutes, you can be pretty sure that it's frozen. This can happen when a situation called an "infinite loop" occurs. For example, this code:

```
while (true) {
counter = counter + 1;
}
```

is an infinite loop because it will *never* finish. If a program ever ran this code, it would be frozen, and the only way around it would be to reset. Infinite loop conditions are the result of faulty logic in a program.

Fatal exception

The fatal exception dialog box is a general-purpose dialog box that appears when a program does something that the processor can't do. It gets quite complicated to explain, but all processors have a set of instructions and requirements for each instruction. If an error occurs in executing one of these instructions, the processor generates an "exception." Exception is synonymous with "error." There are hundreds, if not thousands, of reasons why a processor will generate an exception. If the error seems vague, that's because it is.

An example: Assume that you're standing at the base of a 1000-foot vertical cliff with a friend, and he says to you, "climb to the top of this cliff." You'd give him a funny look, right? Well, a "fatal exception" is your Palm Organizer's way of giving a funny look to a program that asks it to do something it can't.

Explicitly generated errors

The preceding errors occur when something unexpected happens in a program and, thus, it either freezes or causes the processor to generate an exception. There is another type of error that is generated on purpose, as the result of what's called an "assert" in the programming world. An assert, from the word "assertion," is a program's way of verifying that certain conditions are met. For example, assume that your friend (the same one who told you to climb the cliff) asks you to go to the store and buy a gallon of milk. He hands you 25 cents to pay for it. Well, you know for sure that 25 cents won't pay for a gallon of milk, so you say to him "That's not enough money!" You've just performed an "assert." You have checked the current situation (you have 25 cents to buy a gallon of milk) and found that there is a problem, so you say something about the problematic conditions. In programming, an assert looks something like this:

```
ErrFatalDisplayIf( myNum > largestAllowedNum, "myNumber is too
big" );
```

If this line of code is in a program, and myNum is greater than largestAllowedNum, an error dialog box will pop up that has the name of the source file that this assert is in, along with the line number of the source file that the error occurred on:

```
"MySourceFile.c, line 25, myNumber is too big"
```

Because this error appears onscreen, you now have an exact idea of where the error occurred in your program! Asserts such as this make it easier to catch errors when programming.

Memory manager errors

There are a variety asserts performed by the memory manager. If you have a Palm OS 1.x or 2.x device, the source code file that contains the memory manager is called "MemoryMgr.c"; on Palm OS 3.x and greater, the source file is called "MemoryMgrNew.c."

Here is a list of some of the more common errors and what they mean:

✦ **"Invalid chunk ptr," "Invalid handle."** All memory is tracked via *pointers* and *handles*, which are basically addresses, very similar to street addresses. The OS has a list of *all* valid addresses, and each time a program uses a memory manager routine, the OS performs an assert on the address it's given to make sure that it is a valid address. If the address isn't valid, the assert displays one of these messages. Think of this as a "return to sender" on a piece of mail with a bad address.

✦ **"Chunk over-locked," "Chunk under-locked."** Each movable memory chunk needs to be locked to be used. The OS has routines that enable you to lock and unlock memory chunks. You can lock a chunk up to 15 times. The OS keeps track of the lock count of each chunk. If you try to lock a chunk the sixteenth time, it generates a "chunk over-locked" error; if you try to unlock a chunk that isn't locked at all, the OS generates a "chunk under-locked" error.

Data manager errors

The are also many asserts performed by the data manager (DataMgr.c). The data manager is the OS source code that deals with saving data permanently on your Palm Organizer, and is what programmers use to create, edit, and delete databases within their programs.

Here is a list of some of the more common errors and what they mean:

✦ **"Error getting rec."** To safely *save* data to a record, a program must tell the OS that it is about to write data to that record. Only one thing can be writing to a record at a time. When a program is done writing to a record, it tells the OS that it's done. If one part of a program asks to *write* to a record before another part of the program tells the OS that it's *done* writing to the record, an "Error getting rec" occurs.

✦ **"Index out of range."** Each database on the Palm Organizer has records in it. The records are numbered, starting at 0. The number of each record is called the "record index." Thus, if a database has five records, the last index that is valid is 4. If a program asks for a record index that does not exist, the OS generates an "Index out of range" error.

Programmers Need Your Help

I hope that you've enjoyed, or at least understood, my explanations of some of the more common causes of crashes on the Palm Organizer. Please remember that it is not your fault when one of these errors occurs — bugs in a program always cause them. However, programmers like to fix all of the bugs in their programs, and they need your help. So, anytime your Palm Organizer crashes while using a program, you should write down the exact error that is displayed. You should also try to remember what you did that resulted in the error. Pass all this information along to the developer of the program. This information is extremely valuable in tracking down and fixing bugs. If a programmer can reproduce the bug on demand, it is usually very easy to go in and fix the bug. And that means that you can get a new version of the program with one less bug!

✦　　✦　　✦

Palm Batteries

I "met" Peter over the Internet while writing the PalmPilot Resource Kit. *Peter has written some of the best battery software for Palm devices, including Battery Monitor, EcoHack, and Voltage Control (see Chapter 21 for more on Peter's software). As a registered user, I would e-mail asking whether he had patches for new or custom memory cards from TRG; invariably he would send me a patch within hours. It turned out that we were among the very few lucky users with 12MB SuperPilot cards in our Palm IIIs!*

*Peter is definitely a hardware fanatic; one look at his Web site (*www.pstec.de/ppp/*) makes that clear. When I started work on the* Palm OS Bible, *I wanted to include a definitive piece on batteries — what works and why — so I turned to Peter to write this appendix (thanks!).*

Before we discuss the various battery types that Palm devices can be powered with, it is important to know a bit about the internal power supply concept and how it works. From the first Pilot 1000 to the Palm VII, all Palm devices are equipped with switched-power stabilizers, which supply the 3.3V that all Palm units need internally for their electronics. A switched-power stabilizer is a kind of high frequency transformer, which is able to convert an input voltage to any lower or higher output voltage with an efficiency of 80 to 90 percent. That's why there are some little coils in every Palm unit. Except for the Palm V, all Palm devices take advantage of the "step-up" feature (higher output voltage than input voltage), because they are supplied with a battery voltage of 2 to 3V, the typical range of a pair of alkaline AAAs. The stabilizer works even with an input voltage as little as 1.5V and still keeps the 3.3V on its output stable. So, Palm units are best suited to be supplied by batteries that deliver most of their energy at a lower voltage, like rechargeable NiCads or NiMHs. These batteries have a typical voltage of 2.4V for two AAA cells.

Returning to battery management for a moment, you should know that the hardware for measuring the battery voltage is no high-precision matter. In fact, the A/D converter circuit in all Palms can easily be off by up to +/– 0.2V, which means the discussion about whether the first low battery warning is happening at 2.0V or 2.1V is academic. The same goes for the absolute minimum voltage at which a Palm device is still working. A battery reading of 1.7V or 1.5V doesn't make a bit difference if the meter is off by 0.2V. And in case you ever heard about the "legendary" 0.79V shut-off voltage, forget it. I have no idea where that came from, but no Palm unit can work at that voltage. My best explanation is that this number came up as a "per cell" voltage, which would make a true minimum of 1.58V for two cells, which sounds reasonable.

So, now that we know that the Palm doesn't really care about the exact input voltage and that all sources between roughly 2V and 3V work equally well, we should learn a bit more about the consumption of a Palm device. As with all modern, battery-operated units, the Palm device has a power management system that prevents waste of power when it's not needed. That's why it's not possible to predict a battery lifetime; it depends on what you're using your Palm for. For example, a Palm III organizer with backlight on, running an action game, needs approximately five times the current as the same Palm III organizer just sitting there, showing an address book entry. And there is an additional consumption for using the serial port or the infrared port. Every tap on the screen and press on a button consumes a bit of current. The Palm OS checks the power requirements 100 times each second and sets the CPU state accordingly. So, it's really hard to say a Palm device can run a given number of hours on a standard battery.

But to give you a brief impression of what to expect from the different battery capacities, here are a few typical consumption numbers. In the off state, a Palm Organizer consumes typically between 0.2 and 0.3mA (milliamperes), which is needed for data retention and the real-time clock that works all the time. When switched on and just sitting there, about 16mA are needed. When the CPU is fully working, the current increases to 50 to 60mA. The backlight consumes about 30 to 35mA.

When this current flows for one hour it consumes that number of mAh (milliampere hours). A typical calculation assumes a fully running CPU 50 percent of the time, which would result in an average current of about 35mA (16mA idle + 54mA busy = 70mA/2 = 35mA). Now you add a percentage for backlight, plus the 0.2mA minimum that the Palm always needs to retain its data, which adds up to approximately 5mAh each day.

Finally, which batteries can be used with the Palm Organizer? The standard AAAs, preferably the alkaline type, NiCads, NiMHs, and the so-called renewables, which are basically alkalines that are made rechargeable with a slightly different chemistry, are usable with the Palm Organizer.

Alkaline Batteries

Originally, the Palm device was designed to use ordinary alkaline cells. Of all battery types, alkaline cells have two major advantages. First, they offer the highest capacity, approximately 1100 to 1200mAh, which gives the average user a continuous operating time of approximately 25 to 30 hours. Second, they have a linear, flat discharge curve; that is, at a given load, the voltage decreases constantly over time from an initial 3V (two cells) to 1.8V, at which point the batteries are basically empty. So, it's very easy to predict the end of the battery life by just checking the voltage. You will learn later that most rechargeable batteries don't have that nice, linear discharge curve. And, finally, alkaline batteries are very convenient. They can be stored for years without losing much energy, and the next pair is just as far away as the next convenience store.

Because that all sounds quite good, why not use alkaline cells all the time? Well, if you're a poweruser or you happen to use the backlight a lot, you might want to look for less expensive power generators than to go through several sets of alkaline cells every month.

Nickel Cadmium (NiCad) Batteries

There's not much to say about NiCad batteries, except that you shouldn't use them, because AAA Nickel Metal Hydrate (NiMH) batteries are commonly available on the market. For use with the Palm devices, NiCads have only disadvantages compared to NiMHs. They have half the capacity, typically 250mAh, and they show a strong "memory effect." That is, if you don't empty them completely but often only recharge them, they quickly lose a good portion of their already limited capacity. Additionally, NiCads have the steepest discharge curve at the end of the charge, so you get the shortest warning time of all batteries. NiCad cells are still the first choice for real high-current devices, but for low-current Palms, they are a bad choice.

Nickel Metal Hydrate (NiMH) Batteries

Probably the best choice at the moment is the NiMH rechargeable battery. The best of these (I recommend the Panasonic) have a capacity of 650mAh, which lasts for approximately 12 to 15 hours of continuous work. They can be recharged easily within one to two hours and, if treated right, they have a lifetime of about 500 cycles. NiMHs have nearly no memory effect, which means you can also recharge them when they are not completely empty. Unless someone comes up with a really clever modification of the cradle and of the Palm units, the best recommendation is to get two sets of NiMHs, one always waiting in an external charger while the other set is in use.

Using rechargeable batteries in your Palm device feels basically the same as using ordinary alkaline batteries. The switched power supply makes sure that the lower input voltage of the NiMH cells is also converted to the required 3.3V supply for the logic. The only drawback is that during discharge the voltage curve of a NiMH battery is not as linear as that of an alkaline battery. NiMHs show a typical voltage of 2.7V to 2.8V right after taking them out of the charger. That voltage quickly drops to 2.4V to 2.5V and remains there for approximately 80 percent of the time. During that "2.4V-phase" it is very hard to tell, whether there is 70 percent or 30 percent of the power left. Then, toward the end of the charge, from about 2.2V to 2.3V on, the voltage again drops quite quickly. You can assume that NiMHs at about 2.3V will give you no more than about 40 to 60 minutes of continuous operation time (without backlight!) until they completely die; that is, until they drop below 1.8V. There are several shareware applications that enable you to change the warning levels for the use of rechargeable batteries. The OS's default first warning at 2.1V is definitely too low for NiMHs. A good value for a first warning is between 2.30 and 2.35V, and the last warning should occur at 2.0V.

Another absolute no-no for NiMHs is to deep discharge them; that is, discharge them further below 1.8V (or 0.9V per cell). With a good charger, they can be partly "revitalized" after such a deep discharge, but it doesn't do them any good and doing so shortens their life. So, even if you don't use your Pilot, empty NiMHs should always be changed for charged ones, because the Palm unit draws current even when it is off. And the empty ones should be recharged as soon as possible, because storing empty NiMHs is bad for them. That doesn't mean you have to panic if you are on the road, storing them a few days empty until you come home is not a problem.

Now, which charger is recommended for NiMHs? Well, of course, the best — but the best can be quite expensive. In general, all NiMH-approved chargers use more or less intelligent ways to determine when charging is complete and to keep the inserted batteries fresh. Whether a NiCad charger is usable or not depends on the method it uses to determine the end-of-charge condition.

The better NiCad chargers are the most problematic ones because they use the so-called "negative slope" detection. Each type of rechargeable shows a typical voltage curve during charge. Basically, the voltage increases constantly over a certain time. Then when the battery becomes full, the voltage slope increases slightly. After reaching a top value, NiCad cells show a decrease again, while the voltage of NiMH cells remain more or less at that top value. The negative slope detection now waits for that decrease and terminates charge then. This is bad for NiMHs because they don't have that negative slope. For them the "zero slope" detection is used. That is, the charger terminates the charge when the voltage doesn't increase anymore for a certain time. So older, intelligent NiCad chargers are likely to overcharge NiMHs while waiting for the negative slope that either doesn't come or is too small to be detected.

The next problem is the trickle charge rate of NiCad chargers. That's the current used after the actual charge to compensate for the self-discharge of all rechargeable batteries. While NiCads can take up to one-twentieth of their nominal capacity (so called "1/20C"), NiMHs are more sensitive for too-high trickle rates. Manufacturers generally recommend a very little trickle charge only, possibly less then 1/40C. There are chargers on the market in the $5 to $10 range, that just fill up the batteries with a low constant current within 8 to 12 hours; then you have to remove the batteries. Such a low-cost charger paired with some manual work is still better than a NiCad charger with the wrong intelligence. Having two battery sets that you swap once a week so that each set is charged about 25 times per year makes academic whether you need a charger that ensures a 500-cycle cell life.

A last hint for the use of rechargeable batteries: use the undocumented shortcut ".7." With that, you can switch the battery gauge's calibration. Just go to an empty notepad (or any other text input field) and enter the shortcut symbol (see Appendix B for a description of the undocumented ShortCuts in the Palm OS.) You will get feedback about the current calibration. For OS versions prior to 3.1, that shortcut is a toggle function between alkaline and NiCad. In OS 3.1, you get three different possibilities: alkaline, NiCad, or rechargeable alkalines. For NiMH, use the NiCad calibration; both types have a very similar discharge characteristic. The advantage of switching to NiCad is that the battery gauge shows a full battery at 2.5V and follows more accurately the discharge characteristic of rechargeable batteries.

New Feature For OS 3.3, 3Com implemented a very accurate lookup table for the unlinear discharge curve of rechargeable batteries. It's especially optimized for NiMHs.

Rechargeable Alkalines or Renewables

Renewable batteries are basically ordinary alkaline batteries with a slightly changed chemistry and an additional safety valve. Their only advantage is the higher cell voltage of 1.5V per cell, so that they are 100 percent "voltage compatible" with normal batteries. Because all Palm devices work as well at a lower input voltage, that advantage is meaningless for Palm devices, and renewables are not recommended for use with the Palm. The chemistry of alkaline batteries is not designed for recharging, making their performance as poor as that of rechargeables. Renewables barely reach more than 50 cycles. Often their reach is far less, and then only if you treat them very carefully. For example, a renewable doesn't like to be discharged completely, because then it's either not possible or hard to recharge, decreasing the battery's life span even further. It is best to recharge them when they are still 30 to 50 percent full. It's not only inconvenient to constantly watch battery usage so as not to exceed that discharge limit, but recharging them while they are still 30 to 50 percent full also reduces their truly usable capacity. And there is another serious problem with renewable batteries: If mistreated, they can leak and damage or destroy the Palm unit.

 Caution   Remember, we're talking about *rechargeable* alkalines. Never ever try to recharge an ordinary alkaline battery!

Lithium Batteries

There is some confusion about the two different types of Lithium batteries. Most users think of the rechargeable Li-ion battery which is used in the Palm V organizer when referring to "Lithium batteries." But that battery has a cell voltage of 3.4V to 3.6V (depending on the manufacturer), so you would have to find a Li-ion pack with the form factor of two AAA cells to use it in a Palm III organizer. Even if there were AAA-sized Li-ion cells on the market, two of them would result in a voltage of 6.8V to 7.2V, which is obviously too high for the Palm device. Additionally, Li-ion cells need a charger that is exactly (accurate to 0.1V!) matched to their nominal voltage. Finally, Li-ion cells incorporate a little security electronic that prevents voltages from becoming too high or too low. Too high or too low voltage instantly destroys a Li-ion cell. In other words, if a device is not made for Li-ion batteries, it's hard to use it with them.

The only available Lithium cell with a voltage of 1.5V is a special primary cell (not rechargeable), and it offers about 30 percent more capacity at 30 percent less weight than good alkaline batteries do. That sounds very promising, but they are only available as AA cells and cost approximately four times the price of alkaline batteries, so they are not a serious alternative.

Special Devices — the Palm V and the Palm VII

The Palm V and the Palm VII organizers are special when it comes to their power supplies.

The Palm V organizer is the first Palm device that uses a fixed installed rechargeable battery. It's a prismatic (rectangular) single Li-ion cell with a capacity of about 350mAh at 3.8V. Because the stored energy in a battery also depends on the voltage (energy = voltage × mAh), the Li-ion in the Palm V organizer is comparable to two 500 to 600mAh NiMHs at 2.4V. Thus, the Palm V organizer gives you about the same continuous operation time as a Palm IIIx organizer with rechargeable NiMHs, approximately 21 hours for the average user. If you have the chance to drop your Palm V organizer into its cradle at least once a week for about two hours, you can truly forget about the battery. No overcharging, no danger of recharging it too early, no deep discharge — the supplied AC adapter/charger and the little security circuit in the Palm V Organizer takes care of these problems. If batteries are a concern for you, then buy the Palm V Organizer; it is the most convenient.

At first glance, the Palm VII Organizer looks as if two ordinary AAA cells power it, but that's only half of the story. The transceiver electronics for the wireless connection gets power from a separate NiCad battery pack. Why? Because the high-frequency transmitter in the Palm VII Organizer needs very high, short power bursts that would overload a switched power converter small enough to fit in the Palm. So, the NiCad pack acts as a buffer by supplying the high-current bursts for a short time when needed and recharging at a much lower current during idle times. The NiCad pack consists of four cells with a capacity of about 30mAh, which is very little power. The cells are recharged on a predetermined schedule using a separate 8.4V power converter that draws about 100mA from the main AAA batteries during charge. The NiCad pack is normally held at 6V to 7V. Because the 100mA are quite high for ordinary AAA alkaline batteries, the OS prevents the use of the Palm VII Organizer as a PDA during these recharge cycles. If you use your Palm VII Organizer a lot, I recommend that you use rechargeable NiMH batteries.

Choose Your Batteries

You have basically two reasonable ways to power a Palm Organizer. If you use ordinary alkaline batteries and you don't go through more than a pair each month, stay with them. It isn't worthwhile to invest in rechargeable batteries and a charger. If you're using your Palm a lot, use NiMH batteries; there is no reason to waste your money and to pollute our environment with empty batteries.

✦   ✦   ✦

Using Pendragon Forms

This appendix is excerpted from *The Official Pendragon Forms for Palm OS Starter Kit* and is reprinted with permission. Copyright © 1999 Pendragon Software Corporation/IDG Books Worldwide. All rights reserved.

Pendragon Forms is a software package for building database applications for Palm organizers, the family of personal digital assistants which includes the best-selling 3Com PalmPilot and Palm III devices.

This appendix looks at why the Palm platform is a good choice for deploying an application to a mobile workforce, and why Pendragon Forms is a good choice for rapid development of your own custom Palm application.

The Palm Platform

The Palm Platform is a collective name for the Palm operating system (OS) and the hardware devices on which it runs.

The Palm platform is the most successful handheld platform ever. It has succeeded for several reasons: size and battery life, the Graffiti handwriting recognition system, and HotSync technology.

Size and battery life

The 3Com Palm Organizer is a pocket-sized device with excellent battery life. It is not unusual for Palm devices that run on AAA batteries to last a month compared with a battery life of less than a week on competing handheld platforms.

Interestingly, the electronics technology used in the first few generations of the platform was not revolutionary. The central processing unit (CPU) was a low-power, integrated variant of the Motorola 68000, the same chip that powered the original Macintosh more than ten years earlier. In fact, it was the slow speed of the CPU that made the long battery life possible, because the faster a CPU runs, the more power is required.

What makes Palm devices revolutionary is the software. The Palm OS software that runs on the handheld is designed to be "lightweight" so that applications are very responsive, even without a high-performance CPU. Even today, although the newer Palm devices such as the Palm V and Palm VII, run on a different CPU (the Motorola DragonBall EZ), the clock speed is still 16MHz — the same as the original Palm organizer. Competing handheld platforms that run the Windows CE operating system run on CPUs with clock speeds of 75–133MHz, but to the handheld user, these devices do not appear to be faster than a Palm device because of the responsiveness of the Palm OS.

Graffiti handwriting recognition

The Palm OS features a handwriting recognition system called *Graffiti*. Graffiti is an easy-to-learn writing system similar to normal block lettering. Its success is due to the fact that it places the burden of writing on the user instead of on the handheld, and also requires less computing power than devices that interpret the user's natural writing style.

HotSync technology

The other key component of the Palm platform is the HotSync technology. The HotSync mechanism enables a Palm device to synchronize with a desktop PC at the touch of a button. Palm handhelds include a cradle that plugs into a PC. The cradle has a single button for initiating the HotSync data transfer.

The HotSync Manager software that runs on the PC is an extensible system, enabling third-party applications to "plug in" to the system. Once plugged in, applications participate in the HotSync data transfer when the HotSync button is pressed.

As a personal organizer, a Palm device combines small size, long battery life, ease of use, and the ability to synchronize with a desktop PC. This has proven to be a winning combination; over four million Palm devices have been sold. The popularity and low cost of the device has also made it an attractive platform for third-party developers, who have created a wide range of programs that expand the original functionality of the Palm Organizer.

Types of Palm devices

Several Palm devices are on the market today — most are manufactured by the Palm division of 3Com Corporation. 3Com has also licensed the right to develop Palm devices to several other key partners, who have created their own handheld devices that run on the Palm OS. These devices include the IBM WorkPad, the Symbol Technologies SPT 1500 bar code scanning solution, the Qualcomm pdQ Smart Phone, and the HandSpring Visor.

Table E-1 shows a comparison of the Palm devices.

Table E-1
Palm OS Devices

Product Name	Description	Standard Memory
3Com Palm III	The current base model has an infrared port, a serial port, and 160 × 160 pixel display.	2MB
3Com Palm IIIx	This model has the same dimensions as a Palm III, but has an internal slot for memory expansion and a high-contrast display.	4MB
3Com Palm IIIe	The entry-level version of the Palm IIIx ships with 2MB of memory.	2MB
3Com Palm V	The smallest Palm OS device to date, this model incorporates a high-contrast LCD display in an anodized aluminum case. The Palm V has a built-in rechargeable battery.	2MB
3Com Palm VII	Slightly larger than the Palm III, this model incorporates wireless connectivity for executing Web transactions and lookups.	2MB
IBM WorkPad	IBM offers its own branded versions of the Palm V and the Palm IIIx.	2MB/4MB
Qualcomm pdQ Smart Phone	A CDMA cellular phone with a built-in Palm III, enabling wireless access for Palm applications.	2MB
Symbol Technologies SPT-1500	Based on the Palm III, this model incorporates a laser barcode scanner into the top of the handheld.	2MB
Symbol Technologies SPT-1700 and SPT1740	The SPT 1700 is a rugged version of the SPT 1500. The SPT 1740 has wireless local area networking.	2MB (expandable to 8MB)
Handspring Visor and Visor Deluxe	Palm OS computer with Springboard expansion slot for adding hardware and software modules.	2MB (Visor); 8MB (Visor Deluxe)

What Is Pendragon Forms?

Pendragon Forms is a database application that enables you to create your own custom forms for your Palm Organizer.

The capability of customizing a form — a template that collects fields of information — extends the functionality of your Palm Organizer. In addition to using the built-in Palm applications such as the Address Book, Date Book, and Memo Pad, you can customize forms for surveys, inspections, patient tracking, work orders — the list is endless.

Originally launched by Pendragon Software in November 1996, Pendragon Forms was one of the first commercial products for the Palm platform to use a conduit and the HotSync technology. The conduit gives the handheld the capability to send data to the PC, and once the data has been uploaded to the PC, it is then possible to generate reports and analyze data collected by mobile workers.

How Does Pendragon Forms Work?

Pendragon Forms consists of three main components:

✦ **The Pendragon Forms Manager.** This is a database that runs on your PC. The Pendragon Forms Manager is used to create forms, manage which forms are sent to the handheld, and view data that is sent from the handheld to the PC. All forms that you create are stored in this database, which is stored in Microsoft Access format. For each form that you send to the Palm Organizer, Pendragon Forms creates a separate database table within the Pendragon Forms Manager for storing data associated with the form.

✦ **The Pendragon Forms program for Palm OS.** This is an application that you install on your Palm Organizer. The Pendragon Forms program interprets form designs that are sent from the PC and displays the forms so that you can fill in the fields.

✦ **The Pendragon Forms conduit.** This is a plug-in to the HotSync Manager that enables forms, and data associated with those forms, to be synchronized during the HotSync data transfer. During a HotSync data transfer, the HotSync Manager synchronizes the built-in applications and then gives control to the Pendragon Forms conduit to synchronize forms and data.

Creating a working form starts in the Form Designer in the Pendragon Forms Manager. The Form Designer presents you with simple screens for entering the fields on your form and setting their attributes.

Before a form design can be sent to the Palm device, you must freeze the form. Freezing a form creates the associated database table in the Pendragon Forms Manager database for storing the records that are created on the handheld. The form can then be selected for distribution to the handheld.

During a HotSync data transfer, the Pendragon Forms conduit sends the form design to the Palm Organizer. After the HotSync data transfer is complete, the Pendragon Forms program on the handheld displays a list of forms that were sent to the Palm device. Filling in a form creates a record on the handheld. You can create new records or view and modify existing records for each form on the handheld. Whenever you perform a HotSync data transfer, new and changed records are sent to the PC.

Tip   Pendragon Forms Version 3 supports bidirectional synchronization, meaning that if records are entered on the PC they are sent to the handheld during the HotSync data transfer. Many applications use this capability to send reference data or work orders from the PC to the Palm device.

Figure E-1 shows the relationship between the Pendragon Forms Manager on the PC, the Pendragon Forms conduit, and the Pendragon Forms program on the Palm device.

Deciding if Pendragon Forms Is the Right Development Tool

Users of Pendragon Forms don't need programming skills to create their own custom forms. This makes the product ideal for those who want to create and deploy a Palm application with a minimal development cycle. A form with ten fields can take as little as ten minutes to create with Pendragon Forms.

However, in making a product that is as easy to use as Pendragon Forms, some flexibility and performance had to be sacrificed. It is not possible to access all the features of the Palm Organizer or to build the fastest applications with Pendragon Forms.

The best way to create a software solution for any given application is to write a custom program in a low-level language such as C or C++. These languages produce the smallest and fastest programs. Unfortunately, C and C++ are hard to learn and use. Learning to develop for the Palm OS can take a couple of months even for skilled developers. Even after the low-level programming tools are mastered, it can still take many hours just to produce a single screen to display on the handheld, and writing conduit software for synchronizing an application with a desktop or server can be more complex than building the program for the handheld. A typical handheld application consisting of a Palm OS program and a conduit takes months of development time by skilled developers and is, therefore, very expensive.

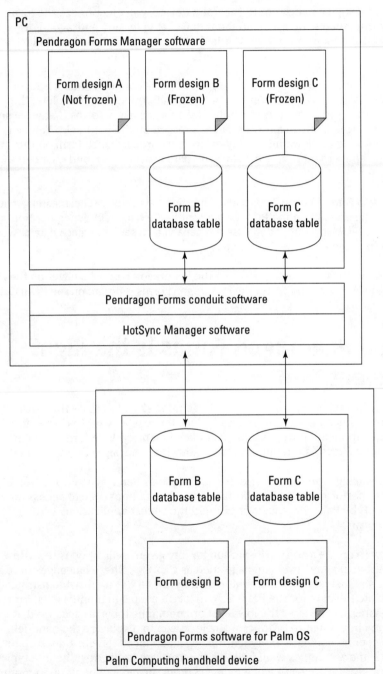

Figure E-1: Relationship between the Pendragon Forms components

Pendragon Forms is designed to provide the answer to a wide range of development needs with little or no programming, and may be the only option for nonprogrammers on a tight budget. For example, a field service work order application that might take three months of development in C++ can be built in just a couple of hours with Pendragon Forms.

So when should you use the low-level programming tools instead of Pendragon Forms? The easiest way to answer this question is to try creating a form with Pendragon Forms to see if it meets your data collection needs. If after a few hours of experimentation you are unable to get the functionality you need or the performance you require, then you probably need to look at other development tools. Some factors affecting this decision are listed as follows:

✦ Large databases that maintain thousands of records on the handheld may not be appropriate for Pendragon Forms. Managing this volume of data may require special programming techniques with low-level tools and may require a custom conduit to reduce synchronization time.

✦ Pendragon Forms automatically handles the layout of the handheld screens for you. Custom screen layouts require the use of other development tools.

✦ Pendragon Forms can synchronize with various databases and enables you to extend its capabilities by writing your own programs on the PC with popular tools such as Visual Basic. However, if you want to synchronize with non-database formats such as HTML, you will likely need to work with other tools.

Note that even when the final application must be written with another development tool, it may still be helpful to build a prototype application with Pendragon Forms. Prototypes built with Pendragon Forms are excellent tools for testing the feasibility and usability of handheld applications.

Getting Started: Installing Pendragon Forms

To install the evaluation version of Pendragon Forms that comes with this book, do the following (see the sidebar for your system requirements):

1. Close any applications not in use, especially the HotSync Manager and the Microsoft Office toolbar. (To close the HotSync Manager, right-click the icon with the red and blue arrows in the system tray at the right side of your Windows Taskbar, and choose Exit.)

2. Insert the CD-ROM into the CD-ROM drive. If the CD-ROM does not automatically start, click the Windows Start button, and then choose Run. Type ***D:\SETUP***, where *D* is the drive letter referring to your CD-ROM drive. Press Enter.

3. Click Install Pendragon Forms.

4. A Pendragon Forms Installation dialog box prompts you to choose which version of Microsoft Access you have, if any. If you have the default option, click OK. If not, click the correct option, and then click OK.

5. Follow the onscreen prompts to complete the installation.

6. After installing the software, you may need to restart your PC.

7. To open the Pendragon Forms Manager on the PC, click Start ⇨ Programs ⇨ Pendragon Forms 3.0 ⇨ Pendragon Forms Manager. You will be prompted to enter your Palm username. (If you do not know your Palm username, tap the HotSync icon on the handheld, and the username will appear in the upper-right corner of the handheld screen.)

8. To install Pendragon Forms on the Palm device, click Start ⇨ Programs ⇨ Pendragon Forms 3.0 ⇨ Install Forms 3.0 on Handheld.

9. The Palm Install Tool will run. Verify that your handheld username is selected, and click OK. Verify that the FORMS3.PRC program is selected. The FORMS3.PRC program is typically in the C:\Program Files\Forms3 folder.

10. Click Done on the Palm Install Tool, and then perform a HotSync data transfer. After synchronizing, tap Applications on the handheld to verify that the Forms icon is present (see Figure E-2).

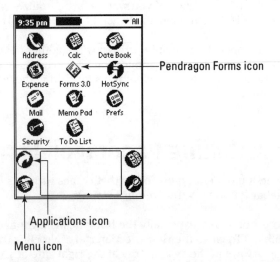

Figure E-2: Pendragon Forms on the Palm Organizer

System Requirements for Pendragon Forms

On the PC, Pendragon Forms requires Windows 9x or Windows NT4.0 (with Service Pack 3 or higher). A minimum of 32MB RAM and 25MB free hard disk space are required for installation. Microsoft Access 97 or later is not required, but is recommended. If you do not have Microsoft Access, note that a run-time version of Access 97 is installed when Pendragon Forms installs.

On the handheld, Pendragon Forms requires Palm OS 3.0 or higher, 2MB RAM (Total Memory), HotSync Manager 3.0 or higher. Pendragon Forms works with all handheld devices referenced in Table E-1. The FORMS3.PRC program on the Palm takes up 165K of memory on the handheld before any form designs or data is added.

Designing a Form

In Pendragon Forms, all forms are designed in the Pendragon Forms Manager on the PC before being sent to the handheld. The design process has three steps:

1. Designing (creating) a form

2. Freezing the form design

3. Distributing the form to the handheld

Once you have sent a form to the handheld, you can enter data on the handheld and upload data to the PC.

In the Pendragon Forms Manager on the PC, you use the Form Designer window to create a form. Every form that you create has a name, and for each item of data that you want to collect on the form, you need to create a separate field. A field has a name and a field type. The field name prompts the handheld user for the input that is needed in a field. (For example, a field name called Customer Name is asking the user to enter the name of a customer in that field.) The field type determines the type of data that you can enter in that particular field.

To access the Form Designer window, click the New button in the Pendragon Forms Manager, as shown in Figure E-3.

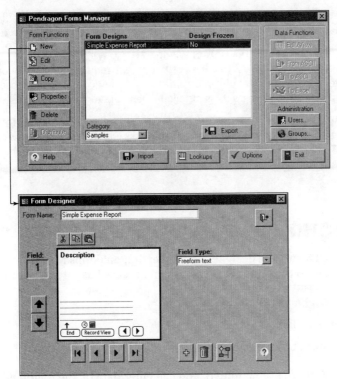

Figure E-3: Clicking the New button brings up the
Form Designer window.

The Form Designer window includes a Form Name field for you to type a name for
the form. For each field that you want to add to your form:

1. Type a name for the field in the Field area of the Form Designer window. The
   field name tells the handheld user what type of information is expected in
   the field.

2. Select a field type for the field. The field type determines what type of data
   the handheld user can enter. You can choose from 21 field types.

3. Depending on the field type that you select, you need to enter additional
   information. For example, a pop-up list is a field type that displays a list of
   items on the handheld. When you select a pop-up list as the field type, a
   Popup Options box appears for you to enter the items that you want the
   handheld user to see in the list.

4. Click the + button to add another field on the form. A form can have up to
   250 fields.

Tip If you are viewing the last field of a form, you can also click the right arrow button in the Form Designer window to add a new field to the end of the form.

Note If you have a form with 250 fields, you will not be able to store as many records on the handheld as, say, with a form that has ten fields. Moving from one field to the next will also be slower, but not enough to make the form unusable.

5. Click the Close button to close the Forms Designer and save your form design. (You will not be prompted to provide a file name. All form designs are stored internally within one database file, the forms3.mdb file in the C:\Program Files\Forms3 folder. If you are using Microsoft Access 2000, the file name is forms32k.mdb) Your form design is not saved until you click the Close button.

To illustrate the rationale behind selecting different field types for different fields, let's look at the four fields that make up a Simple Expense Report form. Each field name tells the handheld user what type of data is expected to be entered in the field, and a field type is selected to make data entry as quick and accurate as possible. For example, if you want the handheld user to enter a date, use a date field type, which forces the handheld user to enter a date — the field will accept no other type of input. This speeds up data entry because the handheld user uses fewer Graffiti strokes and more stylus-tapping selections.

The first field on the expense report is a Description field, shown in the bottom part of Figure E-3. A freeform Text field is used as the field type, because you need to be able to enter anything. The description might be "Business Trip to See XYZ Company," or "Annual Company Conference." A Text field, as it is usually referred to, enables you to enter up to 255 characters on the handheld.

The next item that you may need to record on the expense report is the date on which the expense was incurred. Figure E-4 illustrates a Date of Expense field. To ensure that only a date can be entered in this field, select a Date Only field type.

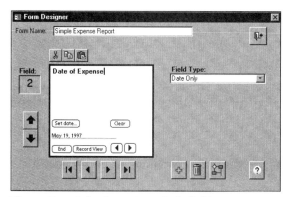

Figure E-4: Selecting a Date Only field

Because travel expenses generally fall into fixed categories, a pop-up list is used in the next field, shown in Figure E-5. On the handheld, a pop-up list lets the user select an item from the list with one tap of the stylus, thus avoiding the need to enter whole words. In this example, the pop-up list has options Air, Car, Meal, Hotel, Taxi, Tips, Other.

A pop-up list can store up to 512 characters for the entire list. Each item in the list must appear on a separate line in order to make it possible to select an individual item with one tap of the stylus on the handheld. Pressing Enter to add a new line counts as 2 characters. In Figure E-5, the pop-up list containing the options Air, Car, Meal, Hotel, Taxi, Tips, Other takes up a total of 40 characters — 28 characters for all the letters in the list, and pressing Enter six times adds 12 characters.

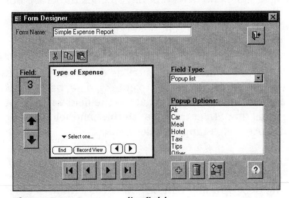

Figure E-5: A pop-up list field

Create an Amount field to record the dollar amount of the expense. Figure E-6 shows that a Currency field is used as the field type to ensure that numbers are entered as dollars and cents.

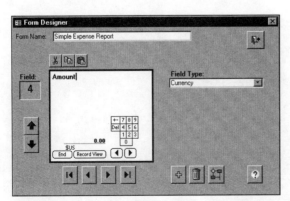

Figure E-6: A Currency field

What's Important about the First Field on a Form?

By default, the first field on a form is used as a Display Key field. This means that when you are reviewing records on the handheld, you will see the first field of each record displayed. In order to distinguish between different records, you should make the first field on a form a field that is generally unique across records.

As the following figure illustrates, a pop-up list and a Yes/No checkbox are not recommended as the Display Key, because many records can have the same value.

A Yes/No field or a pop-up list is not a good choice for the first field on a form.

Text fields, Numeric fields, and Date fields are more likely to be unique across records. The following figure shows a better choice for the Display Key, which makes it easier to tell records apart.

A Text field is a good choice as the first field on a form, because records are easy to distinguish.

If you cannot make the first field on your form a unique field, you can choose to change which field is the Display Key, by setting the Display Key property of a field.

Editing a form design

You can edit form designs in the Form Designer window. Note that changes are not saved until you close the Form Designer window.

To edit a form design, click the name of the form, and then click the Edit button.

The editing tools available in the Form Designer window are shown in Table E-2.

Table E-2
Editing Buttons in the Form Designer Window

Button	Description
✚	Add a new field. The new field is added after the currently displayed field.
🗑	Delete the currently displayed field.
⬆	Move a field earlier in the sequence on the form. For example, move field 10 into position 9.
⬇	Move a field later in the sequence on the form. For example, move field 16 into position 17.
◀|	Display the First field on the form.
◀	Display the Previous field on the form.
▶	Display the Next field on the form. If you are on the last field of the form, this button creates a new field at the end of the form.
|▶	Display the Last field on the form.
✂	Cut the current field out of the form and place it on the Pendragon Forms clipboard (not the Windows clipboard).
📋	Copy the current field to a clipboard.
📋	Paste the contents of the clipboard into the field after the currently displayed field.
🔲	Save the form design and close the Form Designer window.
🔲	The Advanced Field Properties button is used to set advanced field properties and create scripts.

Freezing a Form Design

Once you have created a form design, you need to freeze the form design before you can send the form to the handheld. The Form Properties window is where you freeze the form design, and where you specify how long you want records to remain on the handheld.

When you freeze a form, you make certain aspects of it read-only. A database table has to be created to store the records associated with the form, and three aspects of the form become fixed ("read-only") when you freeze a form — the number of database columns, the names of the database columns, and the data types used in each column (such as Text or Numeric). Other aspects of a form can be changed — the form name and the names of the fields, for example.

Freezing a form design creates a database table in the Pendragon Forms Manager database on your PC for storing records associated with the form. Each column in the database table corresponds to a field on your form. Column names are derived from the first 60 characters of your field names, minus spaces and punctuation.

Once a form is frozen, you cannot add or delete fields, but you can change Data Persistence options. If you freeze a form and then realize that you need to add or delete fields, you can make a copy of the form. A copy is not frozen and can be modified in any way.

Note

Copying a form is similar to doing a Save As, except that the copy contains the form design only, not any data that has been collected in the original form.

To access the Form Properties window, click the Properties button in the Pendragon Forms Manager, as shown in Figure E-7.

The Form Properties window includes a Data Persistence section that is used to determine how long records will remain on the handheld. Because the memory on the handheld is much smaller than the storage space on a PC, setting an appropriate Data Persistence option is an important part of managing data on the handheld. To use this feature, select one of the following options:

✦ **Default option — No Data Persistence checkboxes checked.** After a HotSync data transfer, records are removed from the handheld. This option is useful if you are entering large amounts of data on the handheld that you do not need once the records have been sent to the PC.

✦ **Keep a Copy of Records on Handheld.** If you check this box, then records will be uploaded to the PC during synchronization, but a copy of the records will remain on the handheld after the HotSync process. This option is recommended if you want to back up information to the PC but you also need to keep records with you in the mobile handheld environment. This option is also useful if you are testing form designs, and you need to compare data on the handheld with data on the PC.

✦ **Keep New Records on Handheld for X Days.** If you enter a number of days from 0 to 999, then after a HotSync data transfer, records will continue to be stored on the handheld for the specified number of days. This is useful if you need to refer to records on the handheld for a limited time, such as a week or a month, and beyond that time you no longer need the outdated records on the handheld.

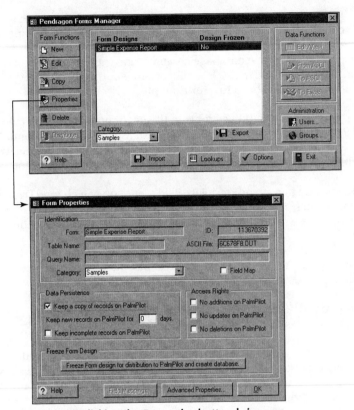

Figure E-7: Clicking the Properties button brings up the Form Properties window.

♦ **Keep Incomplete Records on Handheld.** This option requires a Completion Checkbox field on your form in order to work. (If you know you will need this option, add a Completion Checkbox field to your form when you design the form.) If you check the Keep Incomplete Records on Handheld option, then only those records with the Completion Checkbox checked will be removed from the handheld. This option is useful if you cannot predict the exact number of days that you will need records on the handheld and so you want to control when individual records are removed.

Tip

You can change Data Persistence options at any time. For example, if you want to change from keeping all records on the handheld to keeping records for five days only, uncheck the Keep a Copy of Records on Handheld checkbox, and instead enter the number **5** in the option Keep New Records on Handheld for X Days. If the form is already on the Palm Organizer and you change a Data Persistence option, you will need to redistribute the form to the handheld for the change to take effect. To redistribute a form design, close the Properties window, click the name of the form in the Forms Manager, and then click the Distribute button.

Click the Freeze Form Design button to freeze the form design. You will be prompted to confirm this action. Freezing a form design creates a database table in the Pendragon Forms Manager database for storing the records that are created when you fill out the form on the handheld. The database table includes one database column for each field on your form, plus four columns that are used internally by Pendragon Forms. You can freeze a form only once. After the form design has been frozen, you can close the Form Properties window.

After you freeze a form design, you will notice that fields in the Identification section of the Form Properties window are automatically filled in (see Figure E-8). The Table Name corresponds to the name of the database table that has been created for storing records associated with the form.

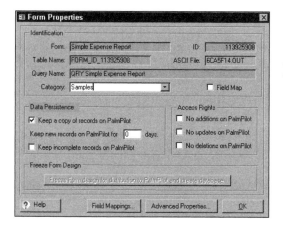

Figure E-8: Fields in the Identification section of the Form Properties window are automatically filled in after you freeze a form design.

Sending a Form to the Handheld

Once a form design has been frozen, you can send the form to the handheld. In the Pendragon Forms Manager, you use the Distribute button (see Figure E-9) to mark a form for distribution to the handheld during the next HotSync data transfer.

For a form to be sent to the handheld, the form must be assigned to a group in which the handheld is a member. In the single-user case, this is taken care of automatically.

When you first install Pendragon Forms on your PC, you are prompted to enter a handheld username. This handheld username is automatically added as an active user in the Default User Group. When you distribute a form, the form design is marked for distribution to all users in the Default User Group. In a single-user scenario, this means that when you click the Distribute button, your handheld device will receive the form design during the next HotSync data transfer.

Organizing Form Designs into Categories

The Form Properties window contains a Category field that you can use to organize your form designs. A category is like a folder used for storing form designs. For example, if you are designing several forms for one data collection project, you may want to place all the forms related to that project in a category of their own.

When you create a new form, the default category is Unfiled. If you type a category name in the Properties window, a new category will be created, and the form design will be assigned to that category. Once a category has been created, other forms can be placed into that category by clicking the name of the form, clicking the Properties button, and selecting the category to which you want to assign the form.

You can choose to display the form designs in a given category by clicking the Category field in the Pendragon Forms Manager window. The All category shows all form designs that you have created. The Samples category is a special category used for sample forms that are mentioned in this book. Because you are not likely to need the sample forms once you are familiar with using Pendragon Forms, the forms in the Samples category do not appear when you select the All category.

If you are using Pendragon Forms in a multiuser environment, you will need to add users to the active User List and set up User Groups to determine which forms are sent to which handheld devices. When you click the Distribute button, the selected form will be sent to all the handheld users belonging to the User Group that contains the form.

Figure E-9 shows that you must select a frozen form in order for the Distribute button to be active. Click the name of a form to select the form, and then click the Distribute button. A dialog box informs you that the form has been updated for distribution.

Figure E-9: The Distribute button in the Pendragon Forms Manager

Tip You can distribute more than one form at a time by repeating the process of selecting a form and then clicking the Distribute button.

Perform a HotSync data transfer. During the synchronization process, you will see the message *Synchronizing Pendragon Forms*. This indicates that the Pendragon Forms conduit is active and is sending form designs to the handheld.

After the HotSync process is complete, tap the Forms icon on the handheld. The form you designed will appear in the list of forms.

Entering Records on the Handheld

Once you have sent a form to the handheld, you can begin entering records. Tap the Forms icon, and a Forms List screen shows the form designs that have been sent to the handheld.

As shown in Figure E-10, the Forms List screen contains a New button for creating new records and a Review button for reviewing records that have previously been entered on the handheld or that have been downloaded from the PC.

Figure E-10: The Forms List screen on the handheld

To create a new record on the handheld, tap the name of a form, and then tap the New button to create a new record for the selected form.

By default, the form is displayed in Field View. As shown in Figure E-11, Field View displays one field on the handheld screen at a time. Enter the required information for the field, and then tap the right arrow button to move to the next field on the form.

When you have stepped through all the fields on the form, you will return to the Forms List screen. You can also choose to exit a record at any time by tapping the End button.

Figure E-11: Field View on the handheld

 Note   You may exit without completing all fields, unless the form was created with all fields set to Required. If you leave the Pendragon Forms application without tapping the End button (for example, by tapping the Applications button on the handheld and then tapping the Address Book application), when you return to the Pendragon Forms application you will be in the same form and same field that was being displayed when you left the Pendragon Forms application.

Using Field View and Record View

Pendragon Forms can show you two views of a form on the handheld. Field View, seen in Figure E-11, displays one field at a time. Record View, shown in Figure E-12, displays several fields at a time in a two-column format — field names in the left-hand column, and responses in the right-hand column. Record View can display up to 11 fields at once.

Figure E-12: Record View on the handheld

Field View is useful if you want to step through a form in sequence. Because only one field is displayed at a time on the handheld screen, you can use the field name to display detailed instructions to the handheld user. Field View is also used when writing branching scripts. Because the handheld user sees only one field at a time, branching scripts can be used to select which field is displayed next, depending on the input in the current field.

Naming Fields for Use in Both Field View and Record View

A field name can contain up to 255 characters. However, if the field name extends past five lines in the Form Designer window, the portion that scrolls out of view will not be visible on the handheld.

As the following figure illustrates, a long field name can be useful in Field View to display instructions to the handheld user. However, the same field name shown in Record View, as in the second figure, can be unclear to the handheld user.

A long field name, as displayed in Field View.

The same field name truncates poorly in Record View.

The first line of a field name is significant—when you view a form on the handheld in Record View, only characters on the first line (or up to a colon on the first line) of a field name are displayed. By entering an abbreviated field name on the first line of the field name, with additional instructions on the second line, you can create a field whose name is readable in both Field View and Record View. (Note that pressing Enter counts as two characters in the field name.)

The following figure demonstrates a long field name that looks good in Field View and has been formatted so that the same field is also readable in Record View.

A long field name that has been formatted for use in Record View is still readable in Field View.

In Record View, field names that have been formatted appropriately are readable.

Record View is useful if the information that you are recording is primarily in Yes/No checkboxes or pop-up lists. By displaying eleven fields onscreen at once, you can easily enter information with a minimum of stylus taps. Record View is also useful if you use the same form repeatedly and you do not need to see the full names of the fields because you are familiar with the form.

You can switch between Field View and Record View at any time.

✦ If you are in Field View, tap the Record View button to switch to Record View.

✦ If you are in Record View, tap the name of a field in the left-hand column to switch to Field View for that field.

Uploading and Viewing Data on the PC

After you have entered new records on the handheld, you can perform a HotSync data transfer to upload the data to the desktop PC.

To view the data that has been uploaded to the PC:

1. Click Start ➪ Programs ➪ Pendragon Forms ➪ Pendragon Forms Manager.

2. Click the name of a form.

3. Click the Edit/View button (see Figure E-13).

Figure E-13: The Edit/View button in the Pendragon Forms Manager

As Figure E-14 illustrates, an Access form is displayed in Datasheet view to enable you to view and modify your data. (The entire Pendragon Forms program on the PC is a Microsoft Access database.) Datasheet View displays your fields in database columns, and your records in rows.

RecordID	UnitID	UserName	TimeStamp	Description	DateOfExpens	TypeOfExpens	Amount
0	0	Sarah Jane	999 6:37:31 PM	Trip to Washing	09/27/1999	Hotel	$150.00
0	0	Sarah Jane	39 10:36:25 AM	Trip to Washing	09/27/1999	Meal	$24.36
0	0	Sarah Jane	39 10:37:26 AM	Trip to Washing	09/27/1999	Taxi	$15.00
0	0	Sarah Jane	39 11:38:20 AM	Lunch with #1 c	09/30/1999	Meal	$55.75
0	0	Sarah Jane	39 11:39:14 AM	Lunch with #1 c	09/30/1999	Tips	$8.00
0	0	Sarah Jane	399 5:24:22 PM	Conference in C	10/06/1999	Air	$249.00
0	0	Sarah Jane	399 5:25:04 PM	Conference in C	10/06/1999	Meal	$22.50
0	0	No one	39 10:50:19 AM				

Figure E-14: Viewing records that have been uploaded to the PC

In addition to the fields on your form, note four additional database columns: RecordID, UnitID, UserName, and TimeStamp. These four fields are generated every time you create a new record. Pendragon Forms uses the UnitID, UserName, and TimeStamp to uniquely identify individual records. The UserName is your Palm username. By default, only records with your UserName will be sent to your hand-held device. The TimeStamp is the creation date and time of the record. If you are keeping records on the handheld for a specific number of days, the TimeStamp is used to determine when a record should be removed.

Bidirectional Synchronization

Pendragon Forms supports bidirectional synchronization, meaning that during the HotSync process, records from the handheld will be uploaded to the PC, and records on the PC will be downloaded to the handheld.

When you are viewing data on the PC, you can therefore choose to enter new records or modify existing records.

If you create a new record on the PC, you need to select your UserName for the record to be sent to your handheld device on the next HotSync data transfer.

Caution   Note that when you modify existing records, the synchronization rule is that if both the handheld and the PC modify the same record, the changes on the handheld will overwrite the changes on the PC.

Making Changes to a Frozen Form

While you are in the process of designing and testing a form, you are likely to want to make changes to your form design. Once a form design has been frozen, you can change some aspects of the form design , but not others.

Items that can be changed on a frozen form are

- ✦ Form Properties, such as Data Persistence options for determining which records are removed from the handheld
- ✦ Advanced Form Properties
- ✦ Advanced Field Properties and Scripts
- ✦ Field names
- ✦ Selection of which Lookup List is referenced in a Lookup List field
- ✦ Selection of which form will be used as a subform

If you make a change to a frozen form, you need to click the name of the form and click the Distribute button to send the changes to the handheld during the next HotSync data transfer.

Items that cannot be changed on a frozen form are

- ✦ Addition or deletion of fields
- ✦ Items in a pop-up list or multiselection list field
- ✦ The field type used in a given field
- ✦ Database column names

If you need to change one of these, you can copy the form design and modify the copy.

Copying a Form Design

You may want to copy a form design if you want to use one form as the starting point for the design of a different form, or if you want to make changes to a form that has been frozen.

When you copy a form, the copy is not frozen. Also, any data in the original form is not transferred into the copy.

To copy a form:

1. In the Pendragon Forms Manager, click the name of a form, and then click the Copy button.

2. The copied form will have the same name as the original, plus an asterisk (*) at the end. You can edit the form to change its name, and then edit fields.

3. When the copy is created, the database column names will remain the same as in the original form design. This is to facilitate importing data from the original form into the copy.

Printing a Form Design

While you are designing a form, it may be useful to print the form design so that you can see the order of the fields on the form.

Pendragon Forms has three report options for printing form designs:

✦ The Form Design Report displays nine fields per page.

✦ The Detailed Form Design Report displays two fields per page and includes scripts. This option is very paper-intensive, and you may want to set your printer properties to print two pages per physical page to reduce the amount of paper that you use.

✦ The Screen Preview Report displays four fields per page and shows a sample of what the handheld looks like in Field View for each field.

To print a form design, click the name of a form. Click the File menu and then select a report option. Press Ctrl+P to print the report.

Summary

✦ This appendix outlined the Palm platform and how Pendragon Forms works to enable you to create custom applications for Palm Organizers. It also gave you an overview of how Pendragon Forms works. Forms are created on the PC and sent to the Palm Organizer, where you can fill in the forms. When you perform a HotSync data transfer, your data is sent back to the PC, where it can be viewed.

✦　　✦　　✦

Contacts

This appendix lists the current contact information for the products mentioned in the *Palm OS Bible*, and is current as of the date of writing. Wherever possible, addresses are shown for companies. In most cases, only electronic addresses are listed for shareware authors. These products are not necessarily on the CD-ROM that accompanies this book.

Glenn Abisia
glenn.abisia@kla-tencor.com
Application: EtchASketch

Actioneer, Inc.
539 Bryant Street
San Francisco, CA 94107
sales@actioneer.com
www.actioneer.com
Application: Actioneer

Arcosoft Inc.
35B-10520 Yonge Street, Suite 111
Richmond Hill, Ontario
Canada L4C 3C7
support@arcosoft.com
www.arcosoft.com
Applications: EbonyIvory, SketchPad, TuningFork

Actual Software Corporation
195 Andover Street
Andover, MA 01810
actual@actualsoft.com
www.actualsoft.com
Application: MultiMail Pro

Aegean Associates, Inc.
1046 Murray Hill Avenue
Pittsburgh, PA 15217
support@ontaptech.com
www.ontaptech.com/ontap
Application: OnTap

AHo Interactive Software
checklist@aho.ch
www.aho.ch
Application: CheckList

AK Analytics Ltd.
info@akuk.demon.co.uk
www.akuk.demon.co.uk/pilot.htm
Application: Chinese Checkers

Charles Aldarondo
Virtual Overload
Aldarondo@uiuc.edu
www.virtualoverload.com
Application: Dakota

Aportis
P.O. Box 86336
Portland, OR 97286-0336
custcare@aportis.com
www.aportis.com
Applications: AportisDoc, BrainForest

Apple Computer, Inc.
1 Infinite Loop
Cupertino, CA 95014-2084
www.apple.com
Application: OS 9.0

Michael Arena
arenamj@erols.com
http://users.erols.com/are-
nakm/palm
Application: RichReader

Glen Aspenslagh
gaspesla@wheatonma.edu
http://welcome.to/glenspace
Applications: FastApp, TrekSounds

Asycs
support@asycs.com
www.asycs.com
Application: FastPhrase

AvantGo, Inc.
1700 S. Amphlett Boulevard, Suite 300
San Mateo, CA 94402
http://corp.avantgo.com/contact/
sales.html
www.avantgo.com
Application: AvantGo

AVStor
support@avstor.com
www.avstor.com
Application: HotTime

Andrew Ball
cesium@interaccess.com
http://homepage.interaccess.com/
~aball
Application: Cesium

Iain Barclay
House of Maus
iain@hausofmaus.com
www.hausofmaus.com
Applications: BugMe!, Busker, CatHack,
CurrEx, ClockHack, FlashHack, FoundMe?,
Maus, Online VT100, SimpleTerm, Snoozer,
WristRest

Pat Beirne
pat.beirne@sympatico.ca
Application: MakeDoc

Bell*2 Labo
palm@ewoks.net
www.ewoks.net/palm/indexe.html
Application: Hi View

Bozidar Benc
benc@benc.hr
www.benc.hr
Applications: CurrCalc, Country Codes,
Daylight Savings Hack, Launcher III, Pilot's
Wind Computer, Pop-up Suite, Weight &
Balance

Mitch Blevins
mitch@debian.org
Application: Diddlebug

Rick Bram
rickb@aportis.com
www.palmglyph.com
Applications: Doc (now AportisDoc),
Pop!, ZIP

Skip Bremer
skip.bremer@tasb.org
www.geocities.com/SiliconValley/
Foothills/1307
Application: DocInOut

Neal Bridges
nbridges@interlog.com
www.quartus.net
Applications: LeftHack, LightHack,
StreakHack

Brochu Software
jbrochu@sitelink.net
www.TapPad.com
Application: TapPad

Catamount Software
P.O. Box 8276
Essex, VT 05451
info@catamount.com
www.catamount.com
Application: PocketMoney

Chapura
P.O. Box 191029
Mobile, AL 36619
(888) 898-2310
(334) 660-7970
www.chapura.com
Applications: PocketJournal,
PocketMirror

Eric Cheng
echeng@cs.stanford.edu
Application: PocketSynth

Barry Christian
barrychristian@usa.net
www.csraonline.com/pilot
Applications: PalmAria, PalmRule

Chronos LC
1305 Elm Avenue
Provo, UT 84604
(801) 957-1774
info@chronosnet.com
www.chronosnet.com
Application: Consultant

Bill Clagett
wtc@pobox.com
www.mindspring.com/~clagett/bill/
palmos/cspotrun/index.html
Application: CSpotRun

Class Action P/L
contact@classactionpl.com
www.classactionpl.com
Application: Time Traveler

ClickLite
clicklite@clicklite.com
www.clicklite.com
Application: Top Secret

ClubPhoto
albumtogo@clubphoto.com
www.clubphoto.com
Application: Album To Go

Code City
enquiries@codecity.com.au
www.codecity.com.au
Application: CityTime

Common Sense
WorldMate@PalmMate.com
www.PalmMate.com
Application: WorldMate

Communications Intelligence Corp.
275 Shoreline Drive, Suite 500
Redwood Shores, CA 94065
support@cic.com
www.cic.com
Application: Jot

Concept Kitchens
326 Fell Street
San Francisco, CA 94102
info@conceptkitchen.com
www.conceptkitchen.com
Applications: Brain Wash, Bumper
Case, Karma Cloth, Small Talk

Corex Technologies Corp.
130 Prospect Street
Cambridge, MA 02139
sales@corex.com
www.corex.com
Application: CardScan

Tammy Cravit
tammy@warmfuzzy.com
Application: BatteryInfo

Creative Digital Publishing, Inc.
wtime@cdpubs.com
www.cdpubs.com
Application: WorldFAQ

Cromerica Technologies LLC
444 Castro Street, Suite 421
Mountain View, CA 94041
(650) 943-1300
info@cromerica.com
www.cromerica.com
Applications: Time Zone, TZDateBook

Cutting Edge Software, Inc.
5960 West Parker Road, Suite 278
Plano, TX 75093
support@cesinc.com
www.cesinc.com
Application: QuickSheet

Cyclos
support@cyclos.com
www.cyclos.com
Application: Hi-Note

Daggerware
higuys@daggerware.com
www.daggerware.com
Applications: AppHack, HackMaster,
MenuHack

Art Dahm
palm@dahm.com
http://palm.dahm.com
Applications: Gamer's Die Roller, Image
Viewer III, PilotCE

Ursini Dante
ursini.sebastien@pmintl.ch
www.ubiteck.com/Palmpilot
Application: PalmPad

DataViz
55 Corporate Drive
Trumbull, CT 06611
(203) 268-0030
info@dataviz.com
www.dataviz.com
Applications: Desktop to Go, Documents
to Go

Day-Timers, Inc.
One Day-Timer Plaza
Allentown, PA 18195-1551
(800) 225-5005
www.daytimer.com
Application: Day-Timer for Windows

DC & Co.
email@iSilo.com
www.iSilo.com
Application: iSolo

DDH Software
P.O. Box 970971
Boca Raton, FL 33497-0971
sales@ddhsoftware.com
www.ddhsoftware.com
Application: HanDBase

DeftSoft
DeftSoft@mailcity.com
www.members.tripod.com/
~DeftSoft/index.html
Application: Date Wheel

Sam Denton
sam.denton@maryville.com
www2.crosswinds.net/~samwyse/
FlashPack.html
Application: FlashPack

Deskfree
murray@deskfree.com
www.deskfree.com
Application: Recycle

Digivello
support@digivello.com
www.digivello.com
Application: GoBar

DovCom
P.O. Box 580
Provo, UT 84603-0580
support@dovcom.com
www.dovcom.com
Applications: FlipIt, PAL, Perplex

DS International, Inc.
5286 W. Karen Drive
Glendale, AZ 85308
(602) 548-7003
sales@dsi-usa.com
www.dsi-usa.com
Application: KeySync keyboard

Patrick Dublanchet
100575.3651@compuserv.com
Application: PenDraw

Gary Duke
garyduke@idirect.com
http://web.idirect.com/
~garyduke/pbeat
Application: Pocket Beat

E&B Company
12265 World Trade Drive, Suite B
San Diego, CA 92128
julie_g@ebcases.com
Products: Slipper and other cases

Max Edelman and Alex Choukhman
info@mamsuite.com
www.mamsuite.com
Applications: MAM Pro, VC Patch

Rick Eesley
reesley@eclipse.net
Application: PalmChrod

eFig.com, Inc.
support@efig.com
www.efig.com
Application: V8 memory upgrade

Ericsson
www.ericsson.com
Product: Model 888 cellular telephone

Evolutionary Systems
scottpowell@kagi.com
www.evolutionary.net
Applications: EarthTime, Emerald Hunt,
HandMap, MakeDict, Pilot Explorer,
SpellCheck, Translation Dictionary

EVsoft
zouyang@evscl.com
www.evscl.com/en/en_home.html
Application: EVedit

Bill Ezell
wje@sii-nh.com
www.mv.com/users/wje/pilot.html
Application: Advanced Traveler

Denis Faivre
dfaivre@ablivio.com
www.ablivio.com
Applications: DatePlan, Euro, PhoneLookup
Hack

Fighter Pilot Software
2876 Kimberly Drive
Maineville, OH 45039
(513) 583-0707
fps@dishernet.com
www.fps.com/pilot
Applications: FPS Clock, FPSUtil Pro,
GolfTrac, HandyCap

Foundation Systems
P.O. Box 2330
Stanford, CA 94309-2330
info@tow.com
www.tow.com
Application: iKnapsack

Franklin Covey
2200 West Parkway Boulevard
Salt Lake City, UT 84119
(800) 975-9995
www.tech.franklincovey.com
Applications: Franklin Ascend,
Franklin Planner

Shuji Fukumoto
fukumoto@wakuwaku.ne.jp
www.umap.net
Applications: FlipFive,
PocketGammon, Pocket Paint

Jean-Paul Gavini
ThePilotMan2000@hotmail.com
www.gavini.com/Public/index.htm
Applications: FlipFive,
PocketGammon

Gregg Geschke
geschke@itronic.com
www.geocities.com/Silicon
Valley/Haven/1559/shoplist.htm
Application: ShopList

Ian Goldberg and Steve Gribble
iang@cs.berkeley.edu;gribble@cs.
berkeley.edu
www.isaac.cs.berkeley.edu/pilot
Application: Top Gun Postman

Brad Goodman
goodman@oai.com
www.alcita.com/palmpilot
Applications: PalmDraw, PalmFactory,
Plonk!, SoftGPS

Hans-Rudolph Graf
grafh@kapsch.net
http://members.tripod.com/~hrgraf
Applications: BattleShip, PilotSenso

David Graham
davidg@kagi.com
www.pcug.org.au/~davidg/pilot.html
Application: Overload

Hands High Software
1290 Cypress Street
East Palo Alto, CA 94303
info@HandsHigh.com
www.HandsHigh.com
Applications: AirMiles, Memo PLUS,
PhoneLog,ThoughtMill, ToDo PLUS, Trip

Handspring Inc.
189 Bernardo Avenue
Mountain View, CA 94043-5203
(650) 230-5000
info@handspring.com
www.handspring.com
Product: Visor

David Harcombe
David.Harcombe@bigfoot.com
www.gramercy.demon.co.uk/
PilotCentral.html
Application: Mind Master

Nick Harvey
njaharve@uwaterloo.ca
www.undergrad.math.uwaterloo.ca/
~njaharve/freekey.html
Application: FreeKey

David Haupert
dhaupert@ddhsoftware.com
www.ddhsoftware.com
Applications: Hangman, WPM

Alexander Hinds
sales@backupbuddy.com
www.backupbuddy.com
Application: BackupBuddy

Rick Huebner
rhuebner@probe.net
Applications: MathPad, Parens, ReDo

Iambic Software
2 North First Street, Suite 212
San Francisco, CA 95113
sales@iambic.com
www.iambic.com
Application: Action Names

iBiz Technology Corporation
1919 West Lone Cactus
Phoenix, AZ 85027
(623) 492-9200
sales@ibizcorp.com
www.ibizcorp.com
Product: KeySync

ImagiWorks, Inc.
60 East 3rd Street, Suite 230
San Mateo, CA 94401
info@imagiworks.com
www.imagiworks.com
Applications: ImagiProbe,
SensorScience

Infinity Softworks
1315 NW 185th Avenue, Suite 180
Beaverton, OR 97006
elia@infinitysw.com
www.infinitysw.com
Application: FCPlus Professional

Intrepid Software Solutions, Inc.
cscullion@intrepidsoft.com
www.intrepidsoft.com
Applications: Area Codes,
PalmJournal, PeriodicTable

Isbister International
1111 Belt Line Road, Suite 204
Garland, TX 75040
(972) 495-6724
www.isbister.com
Application: ChaosSync for PalmPilot

I/S Complete
info@ISComplete.com
www.iscomplete.org
Applications: AltCtrlHack Pro, IrBattleship,
IrSync, IrPrint, Tornado V

Jaeger Technologies
1000 Royal Heights Road, Apt. 9
Belleville, IL 62226-5491
scott@jaegertech.com
www.jaegertech.com
Application: JT WOF

Phillip Jaquenoud
philj@cre.canon.co.uk
www.cre.canon.co.uk/~philj/pilot.
html
Application: PAC

Thomas Jawer
tjawer@bigfoot.com
www.snafu.de/~tjawer/tjhome.htm
Applications: Alarm, Palm Angle, Palm
Planner, Palm Searcher, Piano,
Sun Compass, Timer

JAWS Technology, Inc.
1013-17th Street
Calgary, Alberta
Canada T2T 0A7
info@jawstech.com
www.jawstech.com
Application: JAWS Memo

Jeff Jetton
jeffjetton@aol.com
www.mindspring.com/~jetton/pilot
Applications: Biorhythms, Blackout, Golf
Solitaire, HuchHack,Tricorder II

JP Systems, Inc.
2695 Villa Creek, Suite 240
Dallas, TX 75234
support@jpsystems.com
www.jpsystems.com
Applications: BeamLink, One-Touch Mail

Yoshimitsu Kanai
ykanai@kagi.com
Application: Abroad!

Karrier Communications
3450 Palmer Drive #4162
Cameron Park, CA 95682
info@intelligolf.com
www.intelligolf.com
Application: IntelliGolf

Eric Kenslow
erick@metainfo.com
Application: Launch Pad

Bill Kirby
bkirby@wwg.com
www.electronhut.com/pilot
Applications: Blocks, Graffiti Help,
Klondike

Derek Kwan
e_lib@hotmail.com
Application: Pilot Info Manager

Land-J Technologies
c/o J. J. Lehett, P.O. Box 677461
Orlando, FL 32867-7461
JLEHETT@IAG.NET
www.land-j.com
Applications: Jookerie!, J-File, J-Pack,
J-Shopper, J-Stones, J-Tutor

Landware
P.O. Box 25
Oradell, NJ 07649
info@landware.com
www.landware.com
Applications: Financial Consultant,
GoType, Gulliver, PiloKey, Pocket
Quicken, QuickPac

Lemke Software
LemkeSoft@aol.com
www.lemkesoft.de
Application: Graphic Converter

Andreas Linke
a.linke@sap-ag.de
www.tphys.uni-
heidelberg.de/~linke/pilot
Applications: ScreenShot Hack, Secret

Little Wing Software Development
1265 Larch Avenue
Moraga, CA 94556-2625
James@LWSD.com
www.lwsd.com
Applications: Clock III, Vehicle Log

Lotus Development Corporation
55 Cambridge Parkway
Cambridge, MA 02142
(800) 872-3387 xD669
www.lotus.com
Applications: Easy Sync, Lotus Organizer

Dave MacLeod
davmac@bigfoot.com
www.davmac.co.uk
Applications: Buzzword Generator,
FretBoard

Macmillan Digital Publishing
www.macmillansoftware.com
Application: TigerWoods PGA Golf Tour

MapleTop Software
info@mapletop.com
www.mapletop.com
Applications: ClockPro, CoLaunch, IcoEdit

Maple Ware Technologies, Ltd.
sales@mapleware.com
www.mapleware.com
Application: Palm Miles

Mark/Space Softworks, Inc.
111 West St. John, Suite 333
San Jose, CA 95113
(408) 293-7299
info@markspace.com
www.markspace.com
Application: PageNOW!

Henrique Martins
hm_martins@xoommail.com
http://members.xoom.com/
HM_Martins/currex.htm
Application: Currency

MarWare
info@marware.com
www.marware.com
Application: SportSuit

Maximizer Technologies
1090 West Pender Street, 9th Floor
Vancouver, BC
Canada V6E 2N7
(604) 601-8000
www.maximizer.com
Application: Maximizer Link

Scott Maxwell
Author@QuikBudget.com
www.quikbudget.com
Application: Quik Budget

Dave Mayes
mayes@cts.com
Applications: Cribbage, Hearts, Rally 1000

Gary Mayhak
gmayhak@aol.com
http://members.aol.com/
gmayhak/tcl
Applications: IR Blaster, TaleLight,
TaleVibes, The Wedge

Daniel McCarty
mcdan@csi.com
http://ourworld.compuserve.com/h
omepages/mcdan/palm/index.html
Applications: Graspeedy, Padlock Plus

Michael McCollister
Mike_McCollister@msn.com
http://members.xoom.com/mjmdlm/
palm
Application: McChords

Microsoft Corporation
feedback@microsoft.com
www.microsoft.com
Applications: Excel, Outlook, Windows,
Word

Midwest PCB Designs Inc.
damiani@midwestpcbdesigns.com
www.midwestpcbdesigns.com
Application: The Bridge

Mindgear
R.Kose@mindgear.com
www.mindgear.com
Application: Desdemona

miniMusic
support@5thwall.com
www.5thwall.com/minimusic
Application: miniMusic NotePad

Mobile Generation Software
info@mobilegeneration.com
www.mobilegeneration.com
Applications: Mobile Account Manager,
Mobile AutoLog

Tan Kok Mun
kokmun@pacific.net.sg
http://home.pacific.net.sg/~kokmun
Applications: InComing, PalmJongg,
Pegged!, YahtChallenge

MyPilot
info@mypilot.com
www.mypilot.com
Application: Global Pulse

Armando Neves
armando@thinkingbytes.com
www.thinkingbytes.com
Application: CurrencyX

Nokia
Keilalahdentie 4, FIN-02150 Espoo
P.O. Box 226, FIN-0045 Nokia Group
Finland
Phone: 358-9-180-71
www.nokia.com/main.html
Application: 5190 cellular telephone

NuvoMedia, Inc.
310 Villa Street
Mountain View, CA 94041
info@rocket-ebook.com
www.nuvomedia.com
Product: Rocket eBook

OBE Systems
PilotPhoto@aol.com
http://members.aol.com/
PilotPhoto
Application: PhotoAlbum

Harry Ohlsen
harryo@ise.com.au
http://wr.com.au/harryo
Applications: CharHack, Crossbow

Rui Oliveira
rco@di.uminho.pt
http://shiva.di.uminho.pt/~rco
/pilot.html
Applications: CaseToggle Hack,
MiddleCaps

Hiromu Okada
okada.hiromu@nifty.nifty.ne.jp
http://hp.vector.co.jp/authors
/VA005810/indexe.htm
Application: PalmRemote

Okna Corporation
P.O. Box 788
Lyndhurst, New Jersey 07071-0788
(201) 909-8600
www.okna.com
Application: Desktop Set

ON Technology
One Cambridge Center
Cambridge, MA 02142
(617) 374-1400
info@on.com
www.meetingmaker6.com
Application: Meeting Maker

oopdreams
5 Warwick Court
South Elgin, IL 60177
feedback@oopdreams.com
www.oopdreams.com
Applications: Bubblet, MoneyMinder,
Scramblet, Wordlet

Option International, NV
Kolonel Begaultlaan 45
B-3012 Leuven
Belgium
+32 (0) 16 31 74 11
(800) 394-8641 (North America)
www.option.com
support@option.com
support.usa@option.com (North America)
Application: Snap-on Modem

Pacific Neo-Tek
sales@pacificneotek.com
www.pacificneotek.com/
linkProducts.htm
Application: OmniRemote

PalmAdd Softwaresupport@palmadd.com
www.palmadd.com
Application: multi*Clock*

Palmation
sales@palmation.com
www.palmation.com
Application: Commander

PalmMate
DateMate@PalmMate.com
www.PalmMate.com
Application: DateMate

PalmVision
http://home.att.net/~ah-man
Application: Wedge TV

PDA Panache
P.O. Box 49
Lake Grove, NY 11755
(800) 270-7196
info@pdapanache.com
www.pdapanache.com
Products: The Black Nail and other
custom styli

David A. Pearson
davep@hagbard.demon.co.uk
www.acemake.com/hagbard
Application: 5X5

Penguin Software
dpgerdes@roadkill.com
www.roadkill.com/penguin
Applications: Puz2Pil, XWord

Andrew Penner
apenner@andrew.cmu.edu
www.coed.org/~apenner/computers
Application: Flash'Em

Rainer Persicke
rps@persicke.de
www.persicke.de
Application: PalmFract

Mark Pierce
Mark_Pierce@compuserve.com
http://ourworld.compuserve.com
/homepages/Mark_Pierce
Application: MakeDocW

Florent Pillet
Florent.Pillet@wanadoo.fr
http://perso.wanadoo.fr/fpillet
Applications: FindHack, Palm Buddy,
SymbolHack (also Aportis BrainForest)

Pimlico Software
cesd@gorilla-haven.org
www.gorilla-haven.org/pimlico
Applications: DateBk3, dbScan

Kyle Poole
nebula@golden.net
www.kpoole.com
Application: Kyle's Quest

Scott Powell
scottpowell@kagi.com
www.evolutionary.net
Applications: Emerald Hunt, Pilot Explorer,
SpellCheck

Precision Navigation, Inc
5464 Skylane Boulevard
Santa Rosa, CA 95403
(707) 566-2260
sales@precisionnav.com
www.precisionnav.com
Applications: Palm Navigator, Weatherguide

Jeff Pritchard
jeffp@home.com
Application: TimeHack

Proxinet
5801 Christie Avenue, Suite 300
Emeryville, CA 94608
(510) 923-9160
info@proxinet.com
www.proxinet.com
Applications: ProxiMail, ProxiWeb

Puma Technologies
2550 North First Street, Suite 500
San Jose, CA 95131
(800) 248-2795
(408) 321-7650
www.pumatech.com
Applications: IntelliSync, IntelliSync
Anywhere, Satellite Forms

Ophir Prusak
ophir@netvision.net.il
www.prusak.com/pilot.html
Application: ERacer

Thomas Pundt
pundt@rp-online.de
wwwmath.uni-muenster.de/u/hol-
ger/pilot
*(Note that there should be no period
after* www *in the Web site address.)*
Application: Pilot Mines

Qualcomm Incorporated
5775 Morehouse Drive
San Diego, CA 92121
(858) 587-1121
www.qualcomm.com
Product: pdQ smartphone

Quantum World
quanta@t3.rim.or.jp
www.t3.rim.or.jp/~quanta/English
Applications: Q Draw, Q Paint

Jeremy Radlow
radlow@inkverse.com
www.inkverse.com
Applications: Beam Box, ScreenWrite

Responsive Software
support@responsivesoftware.com
www.responsivesoftware.com
Application: Responsive Metronome

Revolve Design
6600 Silacci Way
Gilroy, CA 95020
(408) 848-1695
info@revolvedesign.com
www.revolvedesign.com
Application: UniMount

Rhinoskin
info@rhinoskin.com
www.rhinoskin.com
Products: RhinoPak, ShockSuite,
Titanium Case

Rival Game Labsrivalgamelabs@geoci-
ties.com
www.geocities.com/TimesSquare/
Realm/9565
Applications: DicePro, VLARP

Jens Rupp
jens@gacel.de
http://come.to/pilot
Application: BigClock

Marc Schneider
M_S_E@bigfoot.com
http://ourworld.compuserve.com/
homepages/M_S_E/pilot.htm
Application: Fillup

Seahorse Software
scubajl@umd.umich.edu
www.prismnet.com/~jlee/ss/ss.html
Applications: 4 Corners Solitaire, Euchre,
Pyramid Solitaire

Edmund Seto
edmund@sparky.berkeley.edu
http://sparky.berkeley.edu/~edmund
/palmpilot.htm
Application: Foreign

Shana Corporation
9744-45 Avenue
Edmonton, Alberta
Canada T6E 5C5
info@shana.com
www.shana.com
Product: Informed Expense Creator

SilverWARE
sales@silverware.com
www.silverware.com
Application: TravelTracker

Smartcode Software
sales@smartcodesoft.com
www.smartcodesoft.com
Applications: HandFAX, HandMAIL,
HandPHONE, , HandWEB

SMC Innovations
techsupport@smcinnovations.com
www.smcinnovations.com
Application: CClock

Tim Smith
tim@pilotfan.com
www.pilotfan.com/galax
Application: Galax

SoftBook Press
1075 Curtis Street
Menlo Park, CA 94025
info@softbook.com
www.softbook.com
Product: SoftBook Reader

Softcare Clinical Informatics
11832 Sunrise Drive
Bainbridge Island, WA 98110
staff@softclin.com
www.dietlog.com
Products: DietLog, ExerLog

SoftEssence
daustin@kagi.com
www.cyclos.com/se
Product: PCHi-Note

Software from Plum Island
glenn@softplum.com
www.softplum.com
Application: Mac Palm Doc

Solutions in Hand
solutions@hand.org
http://home.att.net/~a.
bootman/SolutionsInHand.html
Application: MiniCalc

Stand Alone Software (SAS)
erik@standalone.com
www.standalone.com
Applications: Dragon Pinball, Super
Names, Vehicle Tracker

Stevens Creek Software
21346 Rumford Drive
Cupertino, CA 95014
sales@stevenscreek.com
www.stevenscreek.com/pilot
Applications: Athlete's Calculator, Athlete's
Diary, PalmPrint, Undupe

StingerSoft
stinger@laurenson.com
Applications: Memo Sort, MetriCalc

Storm Communizione & Tecnologia
Via B. De Rolandi 1
20156 Milan, Italy
info@storm.it
www.storm.it/index.sql?section=
software&lang=eng
Application: Tempo

Joseph Strout
jstrout@ucsd.edu
www.strout.net/pilotsoft/spec/inde
x.html
Applications: SnapShot, Spec

Peter Strobel
PSPilot@pstec.de
www.pstec.de/ppp
Applications: Battery Monitor, EcoHack,
Voltage Control, Voltage Display

Yukinari Suzuki
ysuzuki@gix.or.jp
www.gix.or.jp/~ysuzuki/download_
page.html
Applications: HotSyncCSM, SimpleInst

Symantec Corporation
10201 Torre Avenue
Cupertino, CA 95014
(800) 868-9974
www.symantec.com
Applications: ACT PalmPilot Link, Mobile
WinFax

Symbol Technologies
www.symbol.com
Products: SPT 1500, SPT 1700 handhelds

Synergy Solutions, Inc.
info@synsolutions.com
www.synsolutions.com
Applications: Reptoids, PDActivate
(Launch'Em, Listmaker, SynCalc, Today)

Tap Magazine
c/o GoPilot Publishing
P.O. Box 62805
Colorado Springs, CO 80962
(888) 406-4048
subscribe@tapmagazine.com
www.tapmagazine.com
Product: Tap Magazine

Tapnsee Software
tapnsee@xoommail.com
www.tapnsee.com
Application: SuperList

TapWorks
info@tapworks.com
www.tapworks.com
Application: SmartDoc

Yamada Tatsuchi
1405-1-203 Yanokuchi,
Inagi, Tokyo 206 Japan
Application: J-Doc

Steve Tattersall
tatts@adam.com.au
Application: What's the Score?

Paul Taylor
ptaylor@mediaone.net
Application: Address+

TealPoint Software
454 Las Gallinas Avenue, Suite 318
San Rafael, CA 94903-3618
contact@tealpoint.com
www.tealpoint.com
Applications: TealDoc, TealEcho,
TealGlance, TealLaunch, TealPhone,
TealScript

Tech Center Labs
gmayhak@aol.com
http://members.aol.com/gmayhak/
tcl/light.htm
Applications: TaleLight, TaleVibes

Technology Resource Group
2851 104th Street, Suite H
Des Moines, IA 50322-7522
info@trgnet.com
www.trgnet.com
Applications: FlashBuilder, FlashPro,
SuperPilot and Xtra Xtra boards, TRGpro

TechSmith Corporation
P.O. Box 4758
East Lansing, MI 48826-4758
(517) 333-2100
snagit@techsmith.com
www.techsmith.com
Application: SnagIt

Tegic Communications, Inc.
2001 Western Avenue, Suite 250
Seattle, WA 98121
info@tegic.com
www.tegic.com
Application: T9

Tele-Support Software
97829 Shopping Center Ave. Suite G1
Brookings, OR 97415
(800) 386-1623
www.tssw.com
Application: Companion Link

Think Outside
337 S. Cedros Avenue, Suite G
Solana Beach, CA 92075
(858) 793-2900
info@thinkoutside.com
www.thinkoutside.com
Product: Stowaway Portable Keyboard

Tintagel Software
pm172@columbia.edu
www.geocities.com/SiliconValle
y/Horizon/9316
Application: WorldClock

Tranzoa, Co.
info@tranzoa.com
www.tranzoa.com
Application: OnlyMe

TrekWare Corporation
info@trekware.com
www.trekware.com
Application: StreetSigns

Rob Tsuk
support@fmsync.com
www.fmsync.com
Application: FMSync

Twilight Edge Software
twilight_edge@hotmail.com
Applications: Backdrop, Trapweaver

Ultra Software Systems Ltd.
sales@ultrasoft.com
www.ultrasoft.com
Application: Ultrasoft Money Pocket
Edition

Velotrend
sales@velotrend.com
www.bikebrain.com
Application: BikeBrain

Vision 7 Software
3404 East Calle Alarcon
Tucson, AZ 85716
TrackFast@vision7.com
www.vision7.com
Application: TrackFast

Visionary 2000
andrew@visionary2000.com
www.visionary2000.com
Application: Visionary2000 Clear Cover

Stephen T. Wangner
swangner@earthling.net
www.arkwin.com/flip/flip.html
Application: Babel

Walletware
14978 Sand Canyon, Suite B
Irvine, CA 92618-2112
WalletWare@smtp27.bellglobal.com
www.walletware.com
Application: ExpensePlus

Russ Webb
rw20@cornell.edu
http://kale.ee.cornell.edu/pilot
Application: RPN

Bill Westerman
wwester@ibm.net
www.lsds.com/westerman/pilot.html
Application: Tronic

Marty Wilber
mwilber@mcs.com
www.enteract.com/~mwilber
Application: ATool

Masatoshi Yoshizawa
yoz@pobox.com
www.pluto.dti.ne.jp/~yoz/
PilotSoft-e.html
Application: MakeDocDD

Jacob Zinger
sjzinger@geocities.com
www.geocities.com/SiliconValley/
Campus/7631/index.html
Application: AddressPro

Zorblub Software
cvandend@zorglub.com
www.zorglub.com
Application: Highway Manager

Zoskware
support@zoskware.com
www.zoskware.com
Applications: ExpensePro, HourzPro,
Reportz

✦　　✦　　✦

On Our Palms

Here's where we put our money where our mouths are. This appendix lists the applications we have on our Palm Organizers. I say "we" because I've asked the three people who contributed the most to the writing of this book — Roelof Mulder, who wrote Chapter 13 and did most of the tip research; May Tsoi, who wrote Chapter 7; and my technical editor, Michael Lunsford, who has done far more work than is normal for a tech editor — to help me list the applications they have on their Palms.

Glenn's Palm Vx

I'm lucky to have a number of devices — a TRGpro with 30MB of memory, a Handspring Visor with 16MB of RAM, and a Qualcomm pdQ, but my daily device is the 8MB Palm Vx.

One advantage of writing a book such as the *Palm OS Bible* is the toys — hardware and software. With this book, I made a conscious decision to support the shareware community by buying those shareware programs that I use, rather than asking for freebies. I can't say enough good things about the PalmPilot developer community. It provides software, prices, and support that are the best. The shareware authors, in particular, provide outstanding value and support. I highly recommend all of these products.

Applications
- ◆ Action Names (registered shareware)
- ◆ BrainForest (commercial software)
- ◆ Cesium (registered shareware)
- ◆ DateBk3 (registered shareware)
- ◆ Documents To Go (commercial software)
- ◆ HandMail (commercial software)

+ HandWeb (commercial software)

+ Handy Randy (commercial software)

+ Highway Manager (registered shareware)

+ iKnapsack (registered shareware)

+ Launch'Em (registered shareware)

+ ListMaker (registered shareware)

+ MetriCalc (freeware)

+ MultiMail (commercial software)

+ OmniRemote (registered shareware)

+ One-Touch Mail (commercial software)

+ Parens Lite (freeware)

+ Pendragon Forms (commercial software)

+ Pocket Journal (commercial software)

+ PocketQuicken (commercial software)

+ QuickSheet (commercial software)

+ SuperNames (registered shareware)

+ SynCalc (registered shareware)

+ TealDoc (registered shareware)

+ Travel Tracker (registered shareware)

Games

+ Bubblet (registered shareware)

+ Hold'Em (registered shareware)

+ Impactor (registered shareware)

+ Omaha (registered shareware)

+ SFCave (freeware)

+ SimCity (commercial software)

+ Wordlet (registered shareware)

Utilities

- ✦ dbScan (registered shareware)
- ✦ FlashPack (commercial software)
- ✦ FlashPro (commercial software)
- ✦ HackMaster (registered shareware)
- ✦ HotTime (registered shareware)
- ✦ Palm Buddy (registered shareware)
- ✦ Palm Portable Keyboard (driver for Stowaway)
- ✦ TrapWeaver (registered shareware)
- ✦ UnDupe (registered shareware)

Hacks

- ✦ ContrastButton Hack (freeware)
- ✦ FindHack (registered shareware)
- ✦ HotTime (disabled) (registered shareware)
- ✦ Launch'Em App Hack (registered shareware)
- ✦ ScreenShotHack (registered shareware)
- ✦ TapPad (registered shareware)

Note   HotTime is currently disabled because Version 1.01 is not compatible with Version 3.3 of the Palm OS, which is on the Palm Vx. This will undoubtedly be fixed with an upgrade long before you read this.

Roelof Mulder

Roelof's Palm Organizer is a Palm IIIx with a TRG Xtra Xtra Pro, giving it 8MB of RAM and 3MB of Flash memory.

Applications

- ✦ Action Names
- ✦ AutoLog
- ✦ BrainForest

- ✦ Cesium
- ✦ DateBk3
- ✦ Documents To Go
- ✦ HandFax
- ✦ HandMail
- ✦ HandWeb
- ✦ Outliner
- ✦ Pocket Journal
- ✦ RichReader

Financial

- ✦ ExpensePlus
- ✦ FCPlus
- ✦ FinCalc
- ✦ MetricCalc
- ✦ PocketQuicken
- ✦ Qmate
- ✦ Quicksheet

Games

- ✦ Bubblet
- ✦ Hearts
- ✦ Klondike
- ✦ PalmJong
- ✦ PacMac

Utilities

- ✦ Atool!
- ✦ dbScan
- ✦ FlashPro
- ✦ FPS Utility
- ✦ HackMaster
- ✦ OmniRemote

May Tsoi

May is a product manager at Palm in the Palm VII area, which makes her uniquely qualified to write the chapter on the Palm VII. On her Palm VII, May installed the standard 23 Web clipping applications, plus the following:

- ✦ Amazon.com
- ✦ Excite
- ✦ Go Translator (translates text into French, Spanish, German, Italian, and Portuguese)
- ✦ Horoscope
- ✦ Quickadd
- ✦ Thinairmail (for Hotmail)

Michael Lunsford

Michael is the Palm V manager at Palm, and the technical editor for the *Palm OS Bible*. Michael has the following software loaded on his Palm Vx:

Applications

- ✦ Album to Go (family pictures)
- ✦ Aportis Doc (book six of *War and Peace*)
- ✦ AvantGo
- ✦ BeamBox
- ✦ BeamLink (use to connect with SkyTel Pager)
- ✦ CityTime
- ✦ Compass
- ✦ ImageViewer (maps and photo)
- ✦ InfoBeam (similar to Web clipping)
- ✦ MMPlayer (animated cartoon of Grommet with music)
- ✦ Parens
- ✦ Secret
- ✦ TealPaint

HackMaster Hacks

- ◆ LightHack
- ◆ SelectHack
- ◆ SwitchHack
- ◆ TealEcho
- ◆ VClockHack

Games

- ◆ Block Party
- ◆ FreeCell
- ◆ Hardball
- ◆ Hearts
- ◆ IRPong (realtime IR game)
- ◆ Klondike
- ◆ Maze Race
- ◆ Minehunt
- ◆ Palm SFCave (addictive game)
- ◆ Pocket Chess
- ◆ Puzzle
- ◆ SoftGPS
- ◆ Subhunt

◆   ◆   ◆

What's on the CD-ROM

The CD-ROM that comes with this book was produced by the wonderful staff at PalmGear (www.palmgear.com), *the* premiere Web site for Palm users. I'm sure you'll enjoy the demos and shareware on this CD-ROM and how easy it is to find, install, and run the sample programs from PalmGear's FileMaker interface.

The CD-ROM contains programs from all of PalmGear's software groups, as summarized by the following categories:

- ✦ Astronomy
- ✦ Basic
- ✦ Business
- ✦ Calculators
- ✦ Clock/Calendar
- ✦ Communications
- ✦ DALauncher
- ✦ Data Input Alternatives
- ✦ Database
- ✦ Desktop
- ✦ Development
- ✦ Diet/Fitness
- ✦ Doc
- ✦ Doc Legal
- ✦ Doc/E-book
- ✦ Document Reader
- ✦ Download Tools

- ✦ Educational
- ✦ Enhancements
- ✦ Financial
- ✦ Games
- ✦ Graphics
- ✦ HackMaster
- ✦ HanDBase Applets
- ✦ HandScape Views
- ✦ Hobbies
- ✦ Infrared Apps
- ✦ Internet
- ✦ Internet Palm PQA
- ✦ JFile Databases
- ✦ Language/Reference
- ✦ Medical
- ✦ Memo Plus Templates
- ✦ Misc/Fun
- ✦ MobileDB Databases
- ✦ MultiMail
- ✦ Music
- ✦ Navigation
- ✦ Network/E-mail
- ✦ OS Patches
- ✦ Palm PQA: Misc.
- ✦ Palm PQA: News
- ✦ Palm PQA: Search Engines
- ✦ Palm PQA: Travel/Entertainment
- ✦ PIM's/Synchronize
- ✦ PocketC Applets
- ✦ Religion
- ✦ ROM Replacements

✦ Science

✦ Security

✦ Shopping

✦ Sound

✦ Sports

✦ Spreadsheet

✦ TealInfo Module

✦ ThinkDB Database

✦ Time Management

✦ Travel

✦ Travel/Navigation

✦ Utilities

Using the CD-ROM

Using the CD-ROM couldn't be easier. Just remove the CD-ROM from its protective holder in the back of the book. Then follow these simple steps:

1. Insert the CD-ROM into your CD-ROM drive.

2. Wait a few seconds as the FileMaker program loads.

If, for whatever reason, your PC isn't set up to autostart CD-ROMs, follow these steps instead:

1. Insert the CD-ROM into your CD-ROM drive.

2. Open My Computer (double-click the My Computer icon on your Windows desktop).

3. Right-click the icon for your CD-ROM drive and choose Explore from the shortcut menu that appears.

4. Scroll down to and double-click the icon for the program named Palm_Computing_Bible.exe.

Macintosh users have it easy: just click the CD-ROM icon after it spins up. Then, double-click the Palm OS Bible icon.

About PalmGear

PalmGear H.Q., a privately owned company, is the leading Internet source for Palm OS software, hardware, accessories, news, and information. An award-winning e-commerce site, PalmGear H.Q. provides the Internet's most successful portal for bringing shareware developers and users together to promote the Palm OS community. PalmGear H.Q. is also a development partner of Palm and Handspring and markets its own line of accessories and software for the Palm OS platform

Programs on the CD-ROM

Rodney Capron of Synthenet and the folks at PalmGear have produced what is, in my opinion, the best collection of Palm software currently available. I am sure that all Palm users will find many interesting applications here. A complete list of applications and utilities is provided on the included CD-ROM in PDF format.

✦   ✦   ✦

Glossary

*Thanks to Sean Costello of Online Technical Systems
(*www.ots.ca*) for his help with these definitions.*

10BaseT Twisted Pairs Ethernet Standard; a wiring standard used for Ethernet networks. 10BaseT networks operate at 10 megabits per second, now supplanted by faster 100BaseT networks.

ADB Apple Desktop Bus; the means Apple used to connect keyboards, mice, and other peripherals prior to their adoption of USB.

Adobe Type Manager (ATM) A computer font-management utility made by Adobe Systems, Inc.

ADSL Asymmetrical Digital Subscriber Loop; a high-speed means of connecting to the Internet (asymmetrical because upload speeds are typically one-third of download rates).

AIFF Audio Interchange File Format, a Windows sound format.

API Application Programming Interface; a standard for programming in a particular environment, such as the Palm OS.

APOP Authenticated POP; basically encryption added to the Post Office Protocol (*see* POP3).

application launcher A PalmPilot utility for loading applications. Tapping the silk-screened arrow icon (a house icon on newer Palm Organizers) by default starts the application launcher.

ASCII American Standard Code Information Interchange; a file transfer protocol that assigns binary code to approximately 256 characters, including the alphabet. Often used to describe raw text files.

auto-off The Palm Organizer preference setting that specifies how long the Palm Organizer should stay on before turning off to preserve battery life.

BASIC Beginner's All-purpose Symbolic Instruction Code; a programming language.

beaming Sending data or a file using the Palm Organizer's infrared port.

Bézier curve An adjustable curve, usually with handles, made popular with PostScript drawing packages such as Adobe Illustrator and Macromedia Freehand.

BIOS Basic Input Output System; firmware that stores your computer's configuration information, and is responsible for testing hardware, starting the OS, and so on.

Bluetooth An industry specification for short-range, high-frequency wireless communications between computers, cell phones, pagers, and handheld devices within a 30-foot range.

.bmp A file extension that identifies a bitmap graphic, the standard file format for pixel-based Windows graphics.

bps Bits per second; a measure of the speed of data transfer.

cache High-speed memory that a computer uses to store frequently used instructions.

cdev Control Panel Device; a Macintosh system extension that can be adjusted via a Control Panel.

CDPD Cellular Digital Packet Data; a means of cellular communication (see Chapter 16).

CDMA *See* Code Division Multiple Access.

CDRAM Cached DRAM; a type of memory. *See* Dynamic Random Access Memory.

CHRP Common Hardware Reference Platform; a standard set by Apple when it supported clone manufacturers.

CISC Complex Instruction Set Computing; this is the type of processor currently produced by Intel.

Code Division Multiple Access Code Division Multiple Access (CDMA) is a wireless protocol supplied in the United States by carriers like AirTouch Communications, Bell Atlantic Mobile, PCS PrimeCo, and Sprint PCS, and in Canada by Bell Mobility. This technology enables a carrier to split up bandwidth, and offers up to 28800-bps data transfer rates.

compact flash A new smaller card standard for computers and digital cameras; the new TRGpro is the first Palm handheld device to incorporate a compact flash slot. The most common devices are memory cards, although network, modem, and other devices are available.

conduit Software that enables you to synchronize data between your Palm Organizer and your computer.

contrast button The button on the top of the Palm V (and Palm Vx) that gives you access to screen contrast settings.

contrast wheel The wheel on the left side of every Palm device (except the Palm V series) used to adjust screen contrast.

CPU Central Processing Unit; the brain of your computer.

cradle The stand for your Palm Organizer that, when connected to your computer, enables you to HotSync information back and forth.

CRC Cyclic redundancy check; a means to confirm that compressed files expand correctly.

CSLIP Compressed Serial Line Internet Protocol; a standard for connecting to the Internet. The compression is used on the headers on the packets, which increases throughput.

CSM Control Strip Module; the plug-in module for the Macintosh Control Strip.

.csv Comma-separated values; table-based data, usually exported from spreadsheets, in which commas are used to indicate new records. (*See also* tab-delimited data.)

data enabled For you to use your digital cellular phone to transmit data, your cellular provider must enable data transmission for your service.

DBMS DataBase Management System; a database, which is a program for storing and organizing data.

digitizer The software in your Palm Organizer that interprets what you do with your stylus (taps and Graffiti). You can recalibrate your digitizer by selecting Preferences ⇨ Digitizer.

DLL Dynamic Link Library; a Windows resource file.

DNS Domain Name Server; a lookup table on a computer that resolves (points to) Internet Protocol (IP) addresses.

.doc In the Windows world, this is the file extension for documents created by Microsoft Word; in the Palm world, this is the standard document format started by Rick Bram's Doc (now AportisDoc).

DOS Disk Operating System; technically, this is any computer operating system booted from a disk when a computer is booted. The term usually refers to MS-DOS, the underpinnings of Microsoft Windows.

dpi Dots per inch; a measure of the quality of a printer. The more dots per inch produced by a printer, the sharper the image it produces.

DRAM Dynamic RAM; less expensive but offers the same power consumption and slightly better performance than PSRAM; the memory now used in all Palm devices. (*See* PSRAM.)

DSL Digital Subscriber Loop; a high-speed means of connecting to the Internet using telephone lines.

encryption The process of scrambling a file for security purposes so that it can only be unscrambled (decrypted) with an appropriate key.

FAQ Frequently Asked Questions; files that explain the solutions to common problems or highlight the features of a new product.

FAT File Allocation Table; the main directory of your computer's hard drive.

fatal exception A crash on your Palm Organizer. (Performing a reset should restart your handheld device.)

file linking The process of linking a text file on your Windows computer to a Memo Pad entry on your Palm Organizer. If changes are made to the document on your computer, they are reflected on your handheld after the next HotSync.

firewall An electronic "moat" around a company's computer system, designed to prevent unauthorized access.

firmware Software that is loaded into a chip, usually to prevent corruption of critical data; examples include a computer's BIOS, the Palm OS, and software loaded into the SpringBoard modules available for the HandSpring Visor. (*See also* freeware *and* shareware.)

flash RAM The nonvolatile random access memory in the Palm III and most of the newer Palm devices — with the exception of the Palm IIIe — that is used to load the Palm OS. The unused portion of this memory is used by TRG's FlashPro.

flow control This is a setting that tells your modem how to talk to other devices (xon/xoff/none).

freeware Software that is distributed without cost to the user, while the author retains the copyright. (*See also* firmware *and* shareware.)

FTP File Transfer Protocol; a means of transferring Internet data without the overhead of a browser.

GIF (.gif) Graphics Interchange Format; proprietary graphics compression standard of CompuServe (now of UniSys).

GPS Global Positioning System; a satellite-based system that enables wireless devices to precisely determine their location in three dimensions.

Graffiti Palm's built-in handwriting recognition system (see Chapter 3).

Gremlins Gremlins are the deliberate bugs or problems thrown at a Palm Application during Platinum Certification to ensure that the application will run under all conditions.

GSM Global System for Mobile Communications; the most widely implemented wireless protocol, available from Omnipoint Communications, Pacific Bell Mobile Systems, Western Wireless, and FIDO in Canada. Offers transfer rates up to 9600 bps.

Hack The tiny operating system patches written to run under HackMaster.

HackMaster A shareware program that enables programmers to extend the Palm OS by applying patches (small snippets of code that change the way the Palm OS works).

hard reset Performing a reset while holding the power button and then confirming that you want to erase all information in your handheld. Do this only as a last resort (see Chapter 24). (*See also* soft reset *and* warm reset.)

hardware buttons The buttons across the bottom of your Palm Organizer: Date Book, Address Book, Scroll, To Do List, and Memo Pad. Palm V owners also have a Contrast button on the top of their handheld devices.

HDSL High-speed Digital Subscriber Loop; a high-speed method of connecting to the Internet using telephone lines.

HotSync The process of synchronizing the data in your Palm Organizer and on your computer (desktop or laptop).

HTML HyperText Markup Language; the language used to create Web pages.

HTTP HyperText Transfer Protocol; used as the start of an Internet address (as in `http://`).

IDE Integrated Drive Electronics; a type of hard drive controller. This is the device that connects your computer's CPU to the hard drive.

IDEN Integrated Data Enhanced Network is a cellular technology offered by Clearnet Mike and Nextel that offers data transfer rates up to 19200 bps.

IMAP4 Internet Mail Access Protocol Version 4; this protocol enables you to access e-mail from multiple locations (home, office, a laptop, and your handheld) without having to transfer files. In contrast, the POP3 protocol expects you to download messages to your local machine and delete them from the server.

IP Internet Protocol; the means by which devices communicate over the Internet.

IrDA A standard for infrared communications maintained by the Infrared Data Association.

ISDN Integrated Services Digital Network; a means of connecting to the Internet using telephone lines. Typically this involves two 64K bands that can be bonded together, providing a 128K connection, or used separately to enable use of one of the lines for voice or fax communication.

ISP Internet Service Provider; your on-ramp to the Internet. An Internet Service Provider is a company that provides access to the Internet, either directly, or via a dial-up connection.

Jot The handwriting recognition system used on Windows CE devices, also available for the Palm OS.

JPEG (.jpg) Joint Photographic Experts Group; a lossy (meaning some image degradation) picture compression standard.

KB Kilobyte; a measure of data equal to 1,024 bytes.

kbps Kilobits per second; a measure of data transfer rate equal to 1,024 bytes per second.

LAN Local Area Network; a means of connecting computers together for communications and sharing of printers and other devices, typically restricted to a floor or building. (*See also* WAN.)

Li-Ion Lithium-ion is the type of high-capacity batteries used in the Palm V and Palm Vx.

MB Megabyte; a measure of data equal to 1,024 kilobytes.

memory fragmentation When data is stored by a computer, the hard drive may not always have room to store large files in one contiguous location. As a result, the file may be split into smaller pieces. Devices that use versions of the Palm OS prior to 3.0 were subject to memory fragmentation, as is the flash RAM in all Palm devices.

MHz MegaHertz; a measure of the speed of a computer processor.

MO Magneto Optical; a standard for recordable optical disks.

Motorola Dragonball The processors used in Palm devices; the Palm IIIx and newer devices use the EZ version.

MPEG Motion Picture Experts Group; a standard for video compression.

NiCd Nickel Cadmium battery (pronounced "nicad"); a type of rechargeable battery.

Ni-MH Nickle Metal-Hydrate; a type of battery.

OEM Original Equipment Manufacturer; support is not necessarily provided by the device manufacturer.

OS Operating System; the software that runs a computer.

PC card *See* PCMCIA card.

PCMCIA card Personal Computer Memory Card International Association cards, now more widely know as *PC cards*; cards that add functionality to laptops and other portable devices, including modems, network cards, and hard drives.

.pcx A file extension that identifies a Paintbrush bitmap graphics file format.

PDA Personal Digital Assistant; the acronym attributed to then Apple CEO John Scully, who used it to describe the Apple Newton handheld device.

.pdb The file extension for Palm data files.

.pdf The file extension for the Portable Document Format created by Adobe Acrobat.

phone lookup A means of quickly adding contact information to a Calendar or To Do List entry on your Palm Organizer.

PIM Personal Information Manager; software that lets you manage aspects of your life, such as contacts, your calendar, and your to do list.

pixel-based Graphics software that is based on screen dots (pixels) as opposed to the lines and shapes used by vector-based drawing applications that are created by mathematical instructions. (*See also* vector-based.)

Platinum Certification A testing process whereby Palm Computing establishes a quality level for third-party software for the Palm OS.

plug-in Some software is written to enable other programmers to write extensions to the original code that add functionality; these are often referred to as plug-ins.

POP3 Post Office Protocol Version 3; a standard for receiving e-mail messages over the Internet.

POSE Palm OS Emulator, a tool that enables developers to emulate the Palm OS on their computers.

PPC PowerPC; the Apple/IBM/Motorola processor family used in Macintosh and other computers.

PPP Point-to-Point Protocol; a dial-up standard for modems.

.prc The file extension for Palm OS applications.

private records Records on your handheld that have been marked as "private" can be hidden from those who do not know your password.

proxy A known, controlled hole in a firewall; a security feature designed to restrict access to a computer or a network. (*See also* firewall.)

PSRAM Pseudostatic RAM; low power (but higher than SRAM), high-performance, high-cost memory. This was used in older Palm devices; new devices use DRAM.

public domain software A type of freeware application where the author has given up all rights to a program, enabling others to change or use it as they wish.

RAID Redundant Array of Inexpensive Disks; a means of connecting hard drives together to increase performance.

RAM Random Access Memory; the chips in your computer that store data—active programs and other data files—once the computer has booted up. This information must be saved (usually to a hard drive) for it to be retained between startups.

README file A text file used by developers to let you know of last-minute updates or instructions that may not be in their other documentation.

reset A reset of your handheld is performed by gently pushing a paper clip or the pin in your stylus into the reset hole on the back of your Palm Organizer. Often this will fix crash-related problems with no loss of data. Also known as a *soft reset*. (*See also* hard reset, soft reset, *and* warm reset.)

RISC Reduced Instruction Set Computer; the type of processor used in the Apple Macintosh computer.

ROM Read Only Memory; typically on a chip in your computer that stores operating system information.

runtime application Some software development languages require a "runtime" version of the development language, which is an extremely limited version that enables programs written in that language to run.

SCSI Small Computer System Interface; a relatively high-speed method of connecting peripheral devices such as hard drives, CD-ROMs, and scanners.

SDK Software Developer's Kit; tools that help programmers create software.

.sea Self-Extracting Archive; a Macintosh compressed file that does not require utility software to decompress.

serial port The connection at the bottom of your Palm Organizer that makes contact in the cradle to transfer data during HotSyncing.

shareware Software that enables you to try out the program before buying. Unless you register, some shareware programs stop working after a limited trial period. In all cases, if you find yourself using a shareware application, you are obligated to pay the usually nominal fee. (*See also* firmware *and* freeware.)

ShortCut Glossary entries on your Palm Organizer that can be expanded with a definable stroke; for example, ShortCut-DTS expands to the current date and time. The ShortCut Graffiti stroke is written like a lowercase cursive letter "l."

silk-screened icons The four icons painted to the left and right of the Graffiti area on your Palm Organizer's screen, used for the Application Launcher, Menu, Calculator, and Find.

.sit The file extension used for files compressed using the Macintosh utility StuffIt.

SLIP Serial Line Interface Protocol; a modem connection standard similar to PPP (*see also* PPP).

SMS Short Messaging Service, used by cell phones to transmit alphanumeric data.

SMTP Simple Mail Transfer Protocol; a standard for sending (outgoing) e-mail messages over the Internet.

SNAFU Situation Normal, All Fouled Up.

soft reset A reset of your handheld performed by gently pushing a paper clip or the pin in your stylus into the reset hole on the back of your Palm Organizer. Often, this will fix crash-related problems with no loss of data. (*See also* hard reset *and* warm reset.)

SRAM Static Random Access Memory; very low power, expensive memory used in older TRG memory upgrades.

SSL Secure Sockets Layer; a means of providing encryption in Internet browser software.

stylus The inkless pen used to write on your Palm Organizer.

tab-delimited data Table-based data, usually exported from spreadsheets, in which tabs are used to indicate new records. (*See also* .csv.)

TDMA Time Division Multiple Access. A wireless protocol available from AT&T, BellSouth, and Southwestern Bell, and from AT&T and Cantel in Canada. TDMA offers up to 19200 bps access.

Telnet Internet client/server protocol for terminal sessions.

TIFF (.tif) Tagged Image File Format; a cross-platform format for graphics files.

TLA Three Letter Acronym.

TSR Terminate-and-Stay-Resident; Windows applications that load at startup and run in the background.

TT TrueType; Apple's scalable font technology.

URL Uniform Resource Locator; an address protocol used to identify resources on the Internet, such as Web sites, FTP sites, and e-mail addresses.

USB Universal Serial Bus; a means of connecting keyboards, mice, and other peripherals to computers.

vector-based Graphics packages that are based on lines and shapes that can be resized without degradation; the most popular examples are PostScript drawing packages such as Adobe Illustrator and Macromedia Freehand. (*See also* pixel-based.)

verbose logging A setting for the HotSync Log that records every process; Windows users can enable this setting using the shareware program, BackupBuddy. Mac users can do so by selecting "Show more detail in HotSync Log" in the HotSync Software Setup dialog box.

wait state A term used to describe how computers handle processes; the time for all processes to synchronize. The newer Palm devices have fewer wait states, which has resulted in a performance boost.

WAN Wide Area Network; a means of connecting computers together for communications and sharing of printers and other devices; a WAN differs from a LAN in that it connects computers in different buildings. (*See also* LAN.)

WAP Wireless Application Protocol; a standard for connecting cellular phones, PDAs, and other wireless handheld devices.

warm reset A reset performed while holding the scroll up button; restarts your Palm Organizer bypassing any installed system patches and HackMaster Hacks. (*See also* reset, hard reset, *and* soft reset.)

.wav A file extension that identifies waveform audio files — a Windows standard that stores sound in a waveform audio format.

Web clipping Palm Computing's standard for snippets of information downloaded from the Internet in Palm-sized chunks.

Windows CE An operating system developed by Microsoft to run on handheld devices; the OS is somewhat like a stripped-down version of Windows and has not been as popular as the Palm OS.

WWW World Wide Web; a component of the Internet.

.zip The file extension used for files compressed by PKZip or WinZip.

Index

A

ABCNEWS.com, 164
Abroad, 400
accent acute (´), 56
accent grave (`), 54, 56
ACT Palm Organizer Link, 144
Action Names, 267, 516–518
Actioneer, 518–519
acute accent (´), 56
adding contacts, Address Book, 84–85
adding items, To Do List, 92–93
Address+, 522–523
Address Book
    adding contacts, 84–85
    Address+, 522–523
    Address Card icon, 85
    Address Pro, 523–524
    assigning categories, 87–88
    Beam Business Card, 85, 94
    Beam Category, 90
    categories, 87–88
    Category Filter, 90
    editing contacts, 86–87
    fax phone number, 84
    fields, 90–91
    finding contacts, 85–86
    Font menu, 91
    Handspring Visor, 176
    home phone number, 84
    importing contacts, 88–90
    introduction, 33, 86
    main phone number, 84
    mobile phone number, 84
    opening, 83
    Options menu, 90
    other phone number, 84
    pager phone number, 84
    Palm Desktop, Windows, 199–201
    PalmPad, 524
    phone number categories, 84
    Preferences menu, 91
    Record menu, 90
    Rename Custom Fields option, 94
    replacements, 522–525
    Select Business Card, 85
    SuperNames, 524–525
    TealPhone, 525
    work phone number, 84
Address Card icon, Address Book, 85
Address field, Address Book, 90
Address folder, 214
Address Pro, 523–524
address.bak file, 214
address.dat file, 214
Advance Traveler, 381
Advanced Calculator, 180–182
adventure games
    Dark Haven, 464
    Dragon Bane, 464
    Dungeoneers, 464
    Kyle's Quest, 465
Afterburner][, 575
Agenda, 537
Agenda View, Date Book, 76
AirMiles, 391–392
alarm set icon, Date Book, 72
Alarm Sound, Date Book, 79
AlbumToGo, 445–446
aligning the digitizer, 25
alladinsys.com, 494
AllMoney, 321–322
AltCtrlHack Pro, 586–587
ampersand, 54
Anakin, 466
AportisDoc Mobile Edition, 356–357
AportisDoc Reader, 355–356
apostrophe, 54
AppHack, 585

Apple Newton, 3
application helpers
    DateBook, 534–536
    DateMate, 535
    DatePlan, 535
    DateWheel, 536
    Palm Planner, 536
Application Launcher
    App menu, 103
    Beam, 103
    Category, 104
    CoLaunch, 528–529
    Commander, 529
    GoBar, 529
    Info screen, 105
    Launch'Em, 531
    Launcher III, 530–531
    LaunchPad, 530
    Options menu, 106
    overview, 102–103
    PAL, 531–532
    QuickLaunch, 533
    replacements, 528–534
    TealLaunch, 534
applications, 35
arcade games
    Anakin, 466
    Bubblet, 466–467
    Cue*pert, 467
    Dakota, 468
    Froggy, 468
    Galax, 469
    Impactor, 469
    Mulg II, 470
    PAC, 470
    Reptoids, 471
    Tetrin, 471
Archived_Files folder, 214
Arranger, 289–290
asizip.com, 494
assigning categories
    Address Book, 87–88
    To Do List, 94

asterisk, 54
at sign, 54
Athlete's Diary, 147, 287
ATool!, 577
Attach Note, Date Book, 77
AutoLog, 392
autoscroll, documents, 355
AvantGo, 415–416

B
BackDropEZ, 449
backslash, 54
backspace character, 48
backup
    BackupBuddy, 548–549
    FlashPack, 549
    hard reset, 548
    loaded files, 640
    manual, 548
    Palm Buddy, 549
    soft reset, 547
    warm reset, 548
Backup folder, 214
BackupBuddy, 148–149, 278–279, 548–549
Bank of America, 164
bar code reader, 12, 179
basic alphabet, Graffiti, 46–47
Basic Application Command Keys, 98
batteries
    Battery Monitor, 552
    BatteryInfo, 551
    compartment, Handspring Visor, 177
    installation, 24
    life, extending, 550–551
    troubleshooting, 645–646
    Voltage Control, 552
    Voltage Display, 553
Battery Monitor, 552
BatteryInfo, 551
BattleShip, 472
BB.prf file, 215
Beam Box, 556

beaming
    applications, built-in, 553–555
    Beam Box, 556
    Beam Business Card, 85, 90
    Beam Category, 90
    Beam Event, 77
    BeamLink, 556
    infrared applications, 555–558
    IRP2Chat, 557
    OmniRemote, 559
    PageNOW!, 557
    PalmPrint, 558
    PalmRemote, 559–560
    remote controls, 558–561
    Wedge TV, 560–561
BeamLink, 556
beginning em, 55
beginning qm, 55
beta, 55
Big Clock, 385
BikeBrain, 504, 625
Biorhythms, 483
black triangles, 39
BlackJack Simulator, 478
BlackJack Solitaire, 479
Blackout, 472
Bluetooth Communications, 179
board games
    BattleShip, 472
    Blackout, 472
    Chinese Checkers, 472
    Desdemona, 473
    JStones, 474
    Mind Master, 474
    Overload, 474–475
    PalmJongg, 475
    Pegged!, 475
    Perplex, 476
    PilotSenso, 476
    Sokoban, 476–477
    yahtChallenge, 477
bookmarks, documents, 354
boxed text, 39

BrainForest, 290–292
BrainForest Professional, 146
BrainWash, 624
breakfast ShortCut, 52
The Bridge, 133
browsing
    AvantGo, 415–416
    HandWeb, 416–417
    overview, 415
    ProxiWeb, 417
Bubblet, 466–467
bullet, 55
Bumper case, 600
BurroPak, 600
Busker, 455
buttons, 39, 544
Buttons Preferences, 107
Buzzword Generator, 483–484

C

Calculator
    application comparison, 302
    built-in, 300–301
    FCPlus Professional, 304–305
    FinCalc, 305–306
    Handspring Visor, 176
    MetriCalc, 308
    overview, 35, 110, 299
    RPN, 306–308
    shareware, 301
    SynCalc, 303
calculator icon, 49
Calendar, 227–228
Call History, pdQ, 14
Calvin's PalmPilot FAQ, 507
Calvin's Web Links, 511
Canada's Premier Palm User Group, 507
caps lock, 48
card games
    BlackJack Simulator, 478
    BlackJack Solitaire, 479
    Crazy 8's, 479

Continued

card games *(continued)*
  Cribbage, 479–480
  4Corners Solitaire, 478
  Golf Solitaire, 480
  Hearts, 480
  Klondike, 481
  Pyramid Solitaire, 481
  Rally 1000, 481–482
  Rummy, 482
  Texas Hold'Em, 482–483
CardScan, 626
carriage return, 48
carrot sign, 54
cases
  Bumper case, 600
  BurroPak, 600
  Deluxe leather carrying case, 600
  Dooney & Bourke cases, 602
  FlipCase, 602
  Hardshell case, 604
  Leather belt clip case, 604
  overview, 599
  PalmGlove, 604–605
  RhinoPak 1000 Sport Case, 606
  RhinoPak 2000 Sport Ute case, 606–607
  Rhinoskin Palm V molded hardcase, 607
  Rhinoskin ShockSuits, 610
  Slim leather carrying case, 610–611
  Slipper, 611
  SportSuit, 612
  Targus case, 612–613
  TI Slider, 613
  Titanium hardcase, 613
  Visionary 2000 case, 615
CaseToggle, 60
categories, Address Book, 87–88
Category Filter, Address Book, 90
CatHack, 587
CClock, 385
CD-ROM software, 640
CDMA, 13. *See* Code Division Multiple
    Access
CDPD. *See* Cellular Digital Packet Data

cedilla, 56
Cellular Digital Packet Data (CDPD), 18,
    436–438
cellular phone, 179
cents, 55
Cesium, 268, 386
Change Repeat dialog box, Date Book, 72
ChaosSync for Palm Organizers, 144
Chapura PocketMirror, 30
CharHack, 60
checkboxes, 40
CheckList, 282–283
Chinese Checkers, 472
Chronos Consultant, 249–254
circumflex, 56
City field, Address Book, 90
CityTime, 182–184
clear, 54
Clock III, 269, 386–387
clock software, 384–385
ClockHack, 587
ClockPro, 387
Code Division Multiple Access (CDMA), 436
CoLaunch, 528–529
colon, 54
color, 20
color device, 8
comma, 54
command strokes, high-efficiency, 98
Commander, 529
commercial demos, 258
Compact Flash Slot, 16
Company field, Address Book, 89
compression, 493–495
computer, troubleshooting, 663–664
Computer Concepts, 502
Concept Kitchen, 178, 496, 616
conduits, 125–127, 246–249
connection, modem
  Global Pulse, 432
  Option SnapOn modem adapter, 432
  overview, 432
  Palm III modem, 433

Palm V modem, 433
Palm VII modem, 434
Synapse Pager card, 435
connection, wireless
Cellular Digital Packet Data (CDPD),
436–438
Code Division Multiple Access (CDMA),
436
Ericcsson 888, 436–437
Global System for Mobile
Communications (GSM), 436
Integrated Data Enhance Network
(iDEN), 436
overview, 435–436
Time Division Multiple Access (TDMA),
436
Consultant, 146
contacts, Address Book
adding, 84–85
assigning categories, 87–88
editing, 86–87
finding, 85–86
importing, 88–90
Contacts List, 228–231
Contrast, 176
Contrast Button, 36
Contrast Button Hack, 271, 588
conversion, documents, 369–372
conversion software, travel, 380
Copy command, 196
Copy, Date Book, 78
Copyright, 55
country, 26, 110
Country field, Address Book, 90
Covey Reference Library, 178
cradle, 8, 30
Cradle Guides, 36
Crazy 8's, 479
Create menu, 238
Cribbage, 479–480
CruiseControl, 576
CSpotRun, 361–362
Cue*pert, 467

CurrCalc, 381–382
Currency, 382–383
CurrencyX, 383
Cursor, 198
Custom fields, Address Book, 90
Cut command, 196
Cut, Date Book, 78

D

Daggerware, 498
Dakota, 468
Dark Haven, 464
dash, 54
Datastick Systems, 178
date, 26–27
date and time stamp ShortCut, 52
Date Book
accessing, 34, 68
Action Names, 516–518
Actioneer, 518–519
Agenda View, 76–77
alarm set icon, 75
Alarm Sound, 79
application helpers, 534–536
Change Repeat dialog box, 72
Datebk3, 520–521
Day View screen, 73–76
Display Options menu, 80–81
Edit menu, 78
editing appointments, 70–73
entering data, 69–73
Event Details dialog box, 70
Font menu, 78
Handspring Visor, 176
introduction, 33, 71–72
Month View, 76
note attached, 75
Options menu, 78
Palm Desktop, Windows, 194–197
Phone Lookup, 81–83
Play Every feature, 79
Preferences menu, 79

Continued

Date Book *(continued)*
  Record menu, 77
  recurring event icon, 75
  Remind Me, 79
  replacements, 516–522
  Set Time dialog box, 73–74
  setting appointment time, 73–74
  Show Daily Repeating Events, 81
  Show Timed Events, 81
  Show Untimed Events, 81
  TZDateBook, 522
  Week View, 75–76
Date Book+, 179–180
date stamp ShortCut, 52
DateBk3, 70, 268520–521
datebook.bak file, 214
datebook.dat file, 214
Datebook folder, 214
DateMate, 535
DatePlan, 535
DateWheel, 536
Day-Timer Organizer for Windows, 145
Day View screen, Date Book, 73–76
Daylight Savings Hack, 589
dbScan, 580
default setting, 110
degree, 55–56
Delete Event, Date Book, 77
Delete Note, Date Book, 77
deleting files, 265–266
Deluxe leather carrying case, 600
Desdemona, 473
Desktop Set, 145
Desktop To Go, 142–143
Devices Team, 19
Diagnostics application, 653
Dialer, pdQ, 14
DicePro, 488
DiddleBug, 442
DietLog, 287–288
Digital Audio Player, 179
digital camera, 179
Digitizer Preferences, 109
Dinky Pad, 443

dinner ShortCut, 52
display, documents, 355
Display Options menu, Date Book, 80–81
division sign, 55
DocInOut, 373–374
.doc file, 494
documents
  AportisDoc Mobile Edition, 356–357
  AportisDoc Reader, 355–356
  autoscroll, 355
  bookmarks, 354
  conversion, 369–372
  CSpotRun, 361–362
  display, 355
  DocInOut, 373–374
  Documents to Go, 366–368
  features, readers, 368–369
  find, 354
  HandJive Magazine, 377
  Internet, 376
  iSilo, 364–365
  MacPalm Doc, 375–376
  MakeDoc, 372
  MakeDocDD, 375
  MakeDocW, 373
  Mary Jo's E-Texts, 377
  MemoWare, 377
  Mind's Eye Fiction, 377
  navigating, 354
  OnTap, 363–364
  overview, 353
  Peanut Press, 377–378
  The Pilot Newspaper Daily, 377
  reading, 354
  RichReader, 362–363
  SmartDoc, 358–359
  TealDoc, 360–361
  überchix, 377–378
Documents to Go, 147, 366–368
dollar sign, 54
Dooney & Bourke cases, 602
dotted boxes, 38
DovCom, 406
Dragon Bane, 464

DragonBall EZ processor, 8
Dual Action stylus, 617
Dungeoneers, 464

E

e-mail
    confirmation, 117–118
    deleted, 408
    draft, 408
    filed, 408
    folder, 214
    font, 409
    HandMail, 411
    HotSync, 410
    inbox, 408
    mail.bak, 214
    mail.dat, 214
    menus, 118–119
    MultiMail, 411–412
    One-Touch Mail, 412–413
    outbox, 408
    overview, 116–117
    pdQSuite, 413–414
    preferences, 409
    ProxiMail, 414
    sending, 407–409
    setting up, 117
    settings, 409–410
    setup, 406–407
    Top Gun Postman, 415
E-mail field, Address Book, 90
EA Sports Tiger Woods PGA Golf Tour, 178
Easter Eggs, 56, 667–670
Easy Sync, 145
ebonyivory, 453
EcoHack, 574
Edit menu
    basic application command keys, 98
    Date Book, 78
    Palm Desktop, Macintosh, 236–237
    Palm Desktop, Windows, 208
    To Do List, 95
editing appointments, Date Book, 70–73
editing contacts, Address Book, 86–87
editing items, To Do List, 92–93

eFig V8, 504, 624
Electronic Arts, 178
Electronic Books, 179
encryption utilities, 569–573
entering data, 27, 72–77
equal sign, 54, 55
Ericsson 888, 436–437
ESPN.com, 164
Etak, 17, 165
EtchASketch, 449–450
E*Trade, 165
Eurocool, 501
EVEdit, 57–58, 589
Event Details dialog box, Date Book, 70
exclamation mark, 54
Expense Application
    accessing, 114–115
    Microsoft Excel, 115–116
    moving to PC, 115–116
Expense folder, 214
expense manager
    AllMoney, 321–322
    built-in, 317–321
    ExpensePlus, 336–338
    ExpenzPro, 338–343
    Informed Palm Expense Creator, 322–324
    MAM Pro, 333–335
    MoneyMinder, 322
    overview, 147, 314–316
    Pocket Money, 322
    PocketQuicken, 332–333
    QMate, 325–332
    Quikbudget, 324–325
    recommendations, author, 349–350
    Report Pro, 333–335
    TimeReporter 2000, 343–349
    UltraSoft Money Pocket Edition, 333
Expense Plus, 147
expense.bak, 214
expense.db, 214
ExpensePlus, 336–338
expense.txt, 214
ExpenzPro, 338–343
Extended Shift characters, 53–55

F

FastPhrase, 62
fax
    Address Book, 84, 89
    Handfax, 418
    Mobile WinFax, 419
    overview, 418
FCPlus Professional, 304–305
features, back
    Cradle Guides, 36
    Modem Latch, 36
    pins, 38
    Reset button, 37
    Serial Number, 36
    Serial Port, 36
    Stylus/Cover Tracks, 36
features, front
    Address Book, 33
    applications, 35
    Calculator, 35
    Contrast Button, 34
    Date Book, 33
    To Do List, 33
    Find, 35
    front view, 32
    infrared port, 34
    Memo Pad, 33
    menus, 35
    power button, 33–34
    Scroll Button, 33
    silk-screen area, 34–35
feedback, 57–57
Fidelity Investments, 164
fields, Address Book, 89–90
file linking, HotSync, 130–132
File menu
    Palm Desktop, Macintosh, 235–236
    Palm Desktop, Windows, 207
FileMover, 185–187
files, organizing, 495
Fill Up, 392–393
FinCalc, 305–306
Find, 35, 107, 176, 196

find, documents, 354
FindHack, 271, 595
finding contacts, Address Book, 89
First Name field, Address Book, 89
Fitaly, 63
flag, HotSync, 139–140
Flash memory, 7, 661–662
FlashHack, 589
FlashPack, 549
FlashPro, 16, 277–278, 562–565
FlipCase, 602
flow control default setting, 110
FM Sync, 148
Fodor's, 165
Font menu
    Address Book, 91
    Date Book, 78
Foreign, 384
Format Preferences, 109
4Coners Solitaire, 478
FPS Clock, 387–388
FPS Utility Pro, 578–579
fragmentation, memory, 562
Franklin Ascend, 145
Franklin-Covey, 12, 178
Franklin Planner, 12
FreeKey, 618–619
freeware, 258
FretBoard, 455
Froggy, 468
Frommer's, 165
front view, 32

G

The Gadgeteer, 507
GadgetHack, 590
Galax, 469
Gamer's Die Roller, 488
games
    adventure, 464–465
    arcade, 466–471
    board, 472–477
    card, 478–483

DicePro, 488
Gamer's Die Roller, 488
GolfTrac, 489
IntelliGolf, 489
overview, 461
Palm, 461–463
Pilot-Frotz, 490
utilities, 488–490
What's the Score?, 490
word, 486–487
GEOS Zoomer, 4
getting started
    aligning the digitizer, 25
    battery installation, 24
    country, 26
    date, 26–27
    entering data, 26–27
    Graffiti, 26–28
    HotSync, 29–31
    Palm III, 28–29
    Preferences application, 26
    stylus, 25
    time, 26
    turning on, 24
    Users' Manuals, 23
    Welcome application, 24
.gif file, 494
Giraffe Game, 56–57
Glenayre, 178
Global System for Mobile Communications
        (GSM), 436, 628
Glowhack, 590
goals, Palm Computing, 5
GoBar, 529
Golf Solitaire, 480
GolfTrac, 489
GoType Pro, 619–620
goVox digital voice recorder, 627
GPS Radio, 179
Graffiti
    alternatives, 63–65
    basic alphabet, 46–47
    Caps Lock, 51

Caps Shift, 51
characters, 59–60
Command, 51
Extended Shift, 51, 56–58
feedback, 57–59
Handspring Visor, 176
help, 56
hint sheet, 48
movement, 49
numbers, 48
overview, 4, 18, 27–28
punctuation, 48–49
Punctuation Shift, 51, 55–56
shift strokes, 50–51
ShortCut, 51–56
troubleshooting, 641
Graffiti Tips application, 101–102
graphics
    AlbumToGo, 445–446
    BackDropEZ, 449
    DiddleBug, 442
    Dinky Pad, 443
    EtchASketch, 449–450
    Graphics Converter, 448
    IcoEdit, 450
    Image Converter III, 448
    Image Viewer III, 447
    overview, 441–442
    PalmDraw, 443
    PalmFractals, 451
    PalmSmear, 451
    Pen Draw, 443
    PhotoAlbum, 447
    Q Draw, 443–444
    Q Paint, 443–444
    SimpleSketch, 444
    Spec, 448
    TealPaint, 445
Graphics Converter, 448
Graspeedy, 59
grave accent (`), 56
greater than, 54
GRiDPad, 4

GSM. *See* Global System for Mobile Communications

Gulliver, 400–401

H

HackMaster
  AltCtrlHack Pro, 586–587
  AppHack, 585
  CatHack, 587
  ClockHack, 587
  Contrast Button Hack, 588
  Daylight Savings Hack, 589
  EVEdit, 57–58, 589
  FindHack, 595
  FlashHack, 589
  GadgetHack, 590
  Glowhack, 590
  Graspeedy, 59
  HotTime, 595
  HushHack, 590
  LeftHack, 591
  LightHack, 591
  loading, 584–585
  MagicText, 596
  MenuHack, 586
  MiddleCaps, 59
  overview, 264, 269–270, 583
  PhoneLookUp Hack, 592
  ScreenShot Hack, 596
  Screenwrite, 58
  Snoozer, 597
  SpellCheck, 593
  StreakHack, 592
  SwitchHack, 597–598
  SymbolHack, 593
  TealMagnify, 594
  TrekSounds, 594
  troubleshooting, 662
Handago, 503
Handfax, 418
HandJive Magazine, 377
HandMail, 411, 428, 430
HandMap, 390

HandPHONE, 421–422
Handspring Visor
  Address Book, 176
  Advanced Calculator, 180–182
  appearance, 175–177
  backup card, 185
  Battery compartment, 177
  Calculator, 176
  CityTime, 182–184
  Contrast, 176
  DateBook, 176
  Date Book+, 179–170, 179–180
  To Do List, 176
  FileMover, 185–187
  Find, 176
  Graffiti area, 176
  Infrared port, 177
  Launcher, 176
  MacPac, 187–188
  Memo Pad, 176
  Menu, 176
  Microphone, 176
  models, 174–175
  overview, 15, 17, 179–180
  Power, 176
  Reset, 177
  Scroll Up/Down, 176
  Stylus, 177
  Tiger Woods golf module, 187
  USB port, 177
HandWeb, 416–417
hard reset, 37, 548
Hardball, 462
Hardshell case, 604
Hawkins, Jeff, 3–4
Hearts, 480
Help, Date Book, 78
Help command, 196
helpers, startup displays, 536–537
Hi-Note, 292–294
Highway Manager, 393
hint sheet, Graffiti, 48
history, Palm, 3–6

history list, Web clipping, 169
Home field, Address Book, 89
home phone number, Address Book, 84
HotSync
    accessing manager, 122–124
    configuring conduits, 125–128
    CSM, 150–151, 261
    e-mail, 410
    file linking, 131–132
    flag, 138–139
    infrared (IR), 137–138
    log, 139–141
    Macintosh conduit, 127–128
    modem, 133–136
    multiple devices, 151–152
    network, 136–137
    Palm Desktop, Macintosh, 239–244
    Palm Desktop, Windows, 209–212
    sync utilities, 148–151
    third-party products (Macintosh),
        146–150
    third-party products (Windows),
        141–145
    troubleshooting, 654–661
    usernames, 152–153
HotSync.log, 215
HotTime, 595
.htm file, 494
HushHack, 590

I

IBM
    C3, 17
    ThinkPad, 12
    WorkPad, 3, 11–12, 496
IcoEdit, 450
iDEN. See Integrated Data Enhance
        Network
iKnapsack, 422
Image Converter III, 448
Image Viewer III, 447
images, converting, 448
ImagiProbe, 629–630

Imagiworks, 178
iMessenger
    attachments, 168
    checking, 168
    creating messages, 167
    Deleted, 167, 169
    Draft, 167
    e-mail list, 166
    editing, 168
    Filed, 167, 169
    hard reset, 171
    Inbox, 167
    mailbox, 170–171
    Outbox, 167
    overview, 164–165
    preferences, 169–170
    reading, 168
    reroute, 169–170
    retention time, 170
    sending, 168
    signature, 169–170
    sorting, 169–170
Impactor, 469
import.csv, 298
importing contacts, Address Book, 88–90
inbox, e-mail, 408
inches, 54
InfoMitt, 634
Informed Palm Expense Creator, 322–324
infrared (IR)
    applications, 555–558
    connectivity, 7
    HotSync, 137–138
    port, 36, 177
Innogear, 178
Install folder, 214
installation, batteries, 24
Instant Palm Desktop, 244–245
INSTAPP.EXE, 259
Integral, 55
Integrated Data Enhance Network (iDEN),
        436
IntelliGolf, 489

IntelliSync, 143–144
IntelliSync Anywhere, 144
Interactive fiction, 507
Interface, 222–227
Internet documents, 376
iPoint 5, 617
IRP2Chat, 557
iSilo, 364–365

J

Japan, 11
JAWS Memo, 569
John's Palm Organizer page, 507
Jookerie!, 486
Jot, 64
Journal folder, 214
journal.dat, 214
JP Systems, 178
JShopper, 283–284
JStones, 474

K

Karma Cloth, 63
keyboard
    Date Book, 78
    FreeKey, 618–619
    GoType Pro, 619–620
    KeySync, 620
    Palm Portable Keyboard, 620–621
keyboard shortcuts. *See* command strokes,
        high-efficiency
KeySync, 620
Klondike, 481
Kyle's Quest, 465

L

Landware, 178, 497
Last Name field, Address Book, 89
Launch'Em, 273–274, 531
Launcher, 176
Launcher III, 530–531
launching, Web clipping, 167
LaunchPad, 530
Leather belt clip case, 604

left braces, 54
left bracket, 54
left parentheses, 54
left quotations, 55
left single quotation, 55
LeftHack, 591
less than, 54
licensees, 10
ligature, 56
LightHack, 591
List applications
    CheckList, 282–283
    JShopper, 283–284
    ListMaker, 274, 284–285, 294
    overview, 281–282
    ShopList, 285–286
ListMaker, 274, 284–285, 294
lithium-ion battery, 8
loading documents, 264
loading programs, 258–259
Locate menu, 238–239
lock utilities, 566–568
log, HotSync, 139–141
Logging applications
    Athlete's Diary, 287
    DietLog, 287–288
    overview, 286–287
    PalmJournal, 539
    PhoneLog, 540–541
    PocketJournal, 539–540
    TrackFast, 542
Lonely Planet CitySync PDA Travel Guides,
        178
Lotus, 7
Lotus Organizer, 145
lunch ShortCut, 52
Lunsford, Michael, 3, 17–18

M

Mace, Michael, 3, 19
Macintosh conduit, HotSync, 127–127
MacPalm Doc, 375–376
Macropac International, 17
MacZip, 494

MagicText, 271–272, 596
MagiMac Publishing, 511
mail.bak, 214
mail.dat, 214
main phone number, Address Book, 84
MakeDoc, 372
MakeDocDD, 375
MakeDocW, 373
MAM Pro, 333–335
manual backup, 548
MAPI, 7
MapQuest ToGo, 164
MarcoSoft, 178
Mary Jo's E-Texts, 377
MasterCard, 165
Maximizer Link, 145
McChords, 456
Meeting Maker, 148
meeting ShortCut, 52
Memo Pad
    assigning categories, 97
    editing memos, 97
    entering new memos, 96
    Handspring Visor, 176
    Memo PLUS, 527
    menus, 97
    NoteTaker, 527
    opening, 34, 96
    overview, 33, 99–100
    Palm Desktop, Windows, 204–206
    replacements, 527
Memo PLUS, 527
Memopad folder, 214
memopad.bak, 214
memory
    add, 54
    board, 646–650
    clear, 54
    eFig V8 upgrade, 624
    FlashPro, 562–565
    fragmentation, 562
    overview, 561
    recall, 54
    space, recovering, 562

SuperPilot, 622–623
    troubleshooting, 641–643
    upgrades, 622–624
    Xtra Xtra Pro, 622–623
MemoWare, 377
Memoware.com, 507
Menu, Handspring Visor, 176
Menu, Palm Desktop, 206
MenuHack, 273, 586
menus, 35
Merriam Webster Dictionary, 165, 178
MetriCalc, 308
Microphone, 176
Microsoft
    Excel, 115–116
    Outlook, 12, 215–216
    Project, 296–299
    Windows CE devices, 3
MiddleCaps, 59
MidWest PCB Designs, 505
milestones, Palm Computing, 5–6
Mind Master, 474
Mind's Eye Fiction, 377
Mine Hunt, 462
MiniCalc, 311–313
MiniJam, 636
miniMusic NotePad, 453
minus sign, 55
Mobile Account Manager, 570
mobile phone number, Address Book, 84
Mobile WinFax, 419
models, Handspring Visor, 174–175
modem
    default setting, 110
    Global Pulse, 432
    HotSync, 133–136
    Option SnapOn modem adapter, 432
    overview, 432
    Palm III modem, 433
    Palm V modem, 433
    Palm VII modem, 434
    preferences, 110, 422–424
    Synapse Pager card, 435
Modem Latch, 36

MoneyMinder, 322
Month View, Date Book, 76
Motorola, 7–8
Moviephone.com, 165
MP3 Player, 178
Mulg II, 470
multiClock, 388–389
MultiMail, 411–412, 428–429, 431
MultiMail Pro, 148
multiple devices, HotSync, 151–153
multiplication, 55
music
    Busker, 455
    ebonyivory, 453
    FretBoard, 455
    McChords, 456
    miniMusic NotePad, 453
    overview, 452
    Palm Piano, 453
    PalmChord, 456
    Pocket Beat, 456–457
    Pocket Piano, 453
    PocketSynth, 454
    Responsive Metronome, 457
    Tempo, 457
    Tuning Fork, 457
My Little Buddy, 259–260
MyCorder Analog Data Acquisitions
        System, 178

N

Navicom, 179
navigating documents, 354
network, HotSync, 136–137
Network HotSync kit, 7
network preferences, 111–112, 424–427
New England Palm Users Group, 511
New Event, Date Book, 77
New Item command, 196
Newton, 18
Nokia, 19
note attached, Date Book, 75
Note field, Address Book, 90

Notes, Palm Desktop, 233–235
NoteTaker, 527
null, 55
numbers, Graffiti, 48

O

Official Airline Guide, 165
omega, 55
OmniRemote, 179, 275, 559
One-Touch Mail, 412–413, 429, 431
One-Touch Messaging, 178
OnlyMe, 567
OnTap, 363–364
open
    Address Book, 83
    To Do List, 92
Option International, 505
Options menu
    Address Book, 90
    basic application command keys, 98
    Date Book, 78
    To Do List, 95
Other field, Address Book, 89
other phone number, Address Book, 84
outbox, e-mail, 408
outline software
    Arranger, 289–290
    BrainForest, 290–292
    overview, 288–289
over-the-air icon, Web clipping, 169
Overload, 474–475
Owner Preferences, 112

P

PAC, 470
Pacific Neo-Tek, 179
Padlock Plus, 567
PageMart, 505
PageNOW!, 420, 557
pager, 179
pager phone number, Address Book, 84
paging
    integrated card, 7
    overview, 419

PageNOW!, 420
Synapse Pager, 419–420
PAL, 531–532
Palm
  product overview, 16–17
  Web site, 496
Palm Buddy, 150, 262, 549
Palm Desktop, Macintosh
  attached notes, 224
  Calendar, 227–228
  Chronos Consultant, 249–254
  compared to handheld version, 221–222
  compared to Windows, 220
  conduits, 246–249
  Contacts List, 228–231
  Create menu, 238
  dividers, 224–225
  Edit menu, 236–237
  File menu, 235–236
  Help, 244
  HotSync menu, 239–244
  Instant Palm Desktop, 244–245
  interface, 222–227
  Locate menu, 238–239
  multiple views, 222–224
  new features, 219–220
  Notes, 233–235
  overview, 219
  sorting, 225–227
  Task List, 231–233
  View menu, 237–238
Palm Desktop, Windows
  accessing, 194
  Address Book, 199–201
  cursor, 198
  Date Book, 194–197
  To Do List, 201–204
  Edit menu, 208
  File menu, 207
  HotSync, 209–212
  Memo Pad, 204–206
  menu bar, 196
  menus, 206
  Microsoft Outlook, 215–216

printing, 207
private records, 208
profiles, 209
Tools menu, 209
user-named folder, 213–215
View menu, 208–209
Palm games
  Hardball, 462
  Mine Hunt, 462
  Puzzle, 463
  SubHunt, 463
Palm III, 7, 28–29
Palm IIIc, 16
Palm IIIc/IIIxe, 8–9
Palm IIIe, 17
Palm IIIx, 17
Palm IIIx/IIIe, 7–8
Palm IIIxe, 17
Palm Keyboards, 505
Palm Miles, 394
Palm Navigator, 631
Palm Organizer Web Ring, 511
Palm OS interface
  black triangles, 39–40
  boxed text, 40
  buttons, 39
  checkboxes, 40
  dotted boxes, 38
  overview, 8, 18
  pick lists, 39
  scrolling windows, 40–41
  text cursor, 40
Palm Piano, 453
Palm Planner, 536
Palm Portable Keyboard, 620–621
The Palm Tree, 509
Palm V, 17
Palm V/Vx, 9
Palm VII
  antenna, 156–157
  batteries, 157
  Certicom, 159
  compatibility, 157

Continued

Palm VII (continued)
  encryption, 159
  iMessenger, 158–159
  internal transmitter, 157
  overview, 10, 16, 161–162
  Palm.Net, 159
  service costs, 159
  setting up, 160–161
Palm Vx, 17
PalmChord, 456
PalmColors, 505
PalmConnect USB kit, 630–631
PalmDraw, 443
PalmFractals, 451
PalmGear HQ, 503
PalmGlove, 604–605
PalmGlyph Software, 499
The PalmGuru, 508
PalmJongg, 475
PalmJournal, 539
PalmMac, 261
Palm.Net
  coverage maps, 171
  downloading, 172
  My Account, 171
  overview, 19, 165, 171
  support, 171
  Web resources, 172
PalmOS.com, 508
PalmPad, 524
PalmPilot, 7
PalmPilot World, 508
PalmPower Magazine, 509
PalmPrint, 558
PalmProject, 297–298
PalmRemote, 559–560
PalmSmear, 451
PalmStation, 509
PalmStock, 511
Password Store, 570–571
Paste command, 196
Paste, Date Book, 78
PDA. See personal digital assistant

PDA Mart, 504
PDA Panache, 505, 618
.pdb file, 214, 495
.pdf file, 495
pdQ Eudora, 429, 431
pdQalert, 14
pdQbrowser, 14
pdQmail, 14
pdQSuite, 413–414
Peanut Press, 179, 377–378
Pegged!, 475
Pen Computing Magazine, 509
Pen Draw, 443
percent sign, 54
period, 48, 54
Perplex, 476
personal digital assistant (PDA), 3
personal information
  manager (PIM), 7, 32, 94
Personal TechCoach, 178
Peter's Pilot Pages, 499
Phone Lookup, Date Book, 81
phone number categories,
  Address Book, 84
PhoneLog, 540–541
PhoneLookUp Hack, 592
PhotoAlbum, 447
pick lists, 39
Pilot, 7
Pilot Explorer, 577–578
Pilot-Frotz, 490
Pilot Internet File Converter, 509
The Pilot Newspaper Daily, 377
pilotBASIC, 499
PilotCE, 484
Pilot's Tips 'n Tricks, 509
PilotSenso, 476
The PilotZone, 500
PIM. See personal information manager
Pimlico Software, 70
pins, 37
pkware.com, 494
PKZip, 494

Platform Business Unit, 19
Play Every feature, Date Book, 79
Plonk!, 543
plus sign, 54, 55
PMSettings.dat file, 214
Pocket Beat, 456–457
PocketJournal, 141, 539–540
PocketMirror, 141
Pocket Money, 322
Pocket Piano, 453
Pocket Quicken, 148, 275, 332–333, 662–663
PocketSynth, 454
POP3 preferences, 428
postcardware, 258
pound sign, 54
Pounds, 55
power, Handspring Visor, 176
power button, 33
PQuicken folder, 214
.prc file, 214, 495
preferences, e-mail, 409
Preferences application, 26
Preferences menu
    Address Book, 91
    Date Book, 79
Print command, 196
Printing, Palm Desktop, 207
Private field, Address Book, 90
Private records, 208
products
    Palm III, 7
    Palm IIIc/IIIxe, 8
    Palm IIIx/IIIe, 7–8
    Palm V/Vx, 9
    Palm VII, 10
    PalmPilot, 7
    Pilot, 7
Profiles, Palm Desktop, 209
Project@Hand, 296–297
ProxiMail, 414, 429, 431
ProxiWeb, 417
public domain software, 258
punctuation, Graffiti, 48–49

Punctuation Shift characters, 53–54
Purge, Date Book, 77
Puzzle, 463
Pyramid Solitaire, 481

Q
Q Draw, 443–444
Q Paint, 443–444
QMate, 325–332
Qualcomm, 13–16
query form, Web clipping, 167–168
question mark, 54
Quick Backup, 178
QuickAgenda, 537
QuickLaunch, 533
Quicksheet, 313–314
Quikbudget, 324–325

R
Rally 1000, 481–482
reading documents, 354
rechargeable batteries, 646
Record menu
    Address Book, 90
    basic application command keys, 98
    Date Book, 77
    To Do List, 94–95
recurring event icon, Date Book, 73
ReDo, 543
Registered, 55
Remind Me, Date Book, 79
remote control, 558–561
Rename Custom Fields option,
       Address Book, 91
repairs, hardware, 650
replacements
    Address Book, 522–525
    Application Launcher, 528–534
    Date Book, 516–522
    To Do List, 526
    Memo Pad, 527
Report Pro, 333–335
Reptoids, 471
reset

button, 36
Handspring Visor, 177
hard, 548
soft, 547
troubleshooting, 643–645
warm, 548
Responsive Metronome, 457
Revolv Design, 506
RhinoPak 1000 Sport Case, 606
RhinoPak 2000 Sport Ute case, 606–607
Rhinoskin, 506
Rhinoskin Palm V molded hardcase, 607
Rhinoskin ShockSuits, 610
RichReader, 362–363
right braces, 54
right bracket, 54
right parentheses, 56
right quotations, 55
right single quotation, 55
RioPort, 179
ROM_Files folder, 214
Ron's Palm Information Page, 499
RPN, 306–308
Rummy, 482
run-time files, 264
running new applications, 262–264

S

Save command, 196
Scramblet, 486
screen
    cleaning, 651
    protecting, 651
    troubleshooting, 652–653
ScreenShot Hack, 596
ScreenWrite, 58
Scroll Button, 33
Scroll Up/Down, Handspring Visor, 176
scrolling windows, 40–41
.sea file, 484
Secret!, 571–572
Section Mark, 55
security
    encryption utilities, 569–573

JAWS Memo, 569
lock utilities, 566–568
Mobile Account Manager, 570
OnlyMe, 567
overview, 565
Padlock Plus, 567
Password Store, 570–571
Preferences, 113–114
Secret!, 571–572
TealLock, 568
TopSecret Desktop, 572–573
Select All, Date Book, 78
Select Business Card, Address Book, 85
semicolon, 54
Sensor Science, 178
Serial Number, 36–37
Serial Port, 37–38
Set Time dialog box, Date Book, 69–70
setting appointment time, Date Book,
    69–70
settings, e-mail, 409–410
setup, e-mail, 406–407
Setup dialog box, Palm Desktop, 240–241
shareware, 257–258, 495–496
shift, 48
ShopList, 285–286
ShortCuts, 52, 113
Show Daily Repeating Events, Date Book,
    81
Show Timed Events, Date Book, 81
Show Untimed Events, Date Book, 81
signal strength, Web clipping, 168
silk-screen area, 34–35
SimpleSketch, 444
.sit file, 494
6Pack, 636
slash, 54
Slim leather carrying case, 610–611
Slipper, 611
Small Talk, 397
Smart Card reader, 179
smart phone, 19
SmartDoc, 358–359
SMTP preferences, 430

Snoozer, 597
soft reset, 547
software, downloading, 493–494
Software Development Kit (SDK), 5
Sokoban, 476–477
Sony Walkman, 3
sorting, Palm Desktop, 225–227
source code, 5
space, recovering, 562
space character, 48
speaker default setting, 110
Spec, 448
speed default setting, 110
speedups
    Afterburner][, 575
    CruiseControl, 576
    EcoHack, 574
    overview, 575–574
    Tornado V, 576
SpellCheck, 593
SportSuit, 612
spreadsheet
    MiniCalc, 311–313
    overview, 309–310
    Quicksheet, 313–314
    TinySheet, 311
SPT 1500, 12, 16
The Starfleet Pilot, 510
startup displays
    Agenda, 537
    helpers, 536–537
    QuickAgenda, 537
    TealGlance, 538
    Today, 538
State field, Address Book, 90
Steve's Pilot Tech Page, 506
StreakHack, 592
Streetrak Integrated GPS & Street-Level
        Mapping, 178
StreetSigns, 390–391
string default setting, 110
StuffIt Expander, 494
stylus

Concept Kitchen, 616
Dual Action stylus, 617
Handspring Visor, 177
iPoint 5, 617
overview, 25, 615
PDA Panache, 618
Stylus/Cover Tracks, 36
SubHunt, 463
SuperNames, 524–525
SuperPilot, 622–623
SwitchHack, 597–598
Sycom Recorder Digital Recorder and
        Playback, 179
Symbol, 12, 16
SymbolHack, 61, 593
Synapse Pager, 9, 419–420
sync utilities, HotSync, 148–151
SynCalc, 303
sync.ini, 215
system tools
    ATool!, 577
    FPS Utility Pro, 578–579
    Pilot Explorer, 577–578

T

T9, 64
tab, 54
TaleLight, 506, 632
TaleVibes, 632
Tap Magazine, 510
Tap This!, 499
TapPad, 64
Targus case, 612–613
Task List, Palm Desktop, 231–233
TDMA. *See* Time Division Multiple Access
TealDoc, 276, 360–361
TealEcho, 58–59
TealGlance, 538
TealLaunch, 534
TealLock, 568
TealMagnify, 594
TealMeal, 397–399
TealPaint, 445

TealPhone, 525
TealPoint, 498
TealScript, 61
Technology Resources Group (TRG), 16, 506
telecommunications
    HandMail, 428, 430
    mail setup, 427–432
    modem preferences, 422–424
    MultiMail, 428–429, 431
    network preferences, 424–427
    One-Touch Mail, 429, 431
    overview, 405
    pdQ Eudora, 429, 431
    POP3 preferences, 428
    ProxiMail, 429, 431
    setup, 422
    SMTP preferences, 430
    Top Gun Postman, 415, 430, 432
    troubleshooting, 664–665
Tempo, 457
Tetrin, 471
Texas Hold'Em, 482–483
text cursor, 41
TheStreet.com, 165
third-party launchers, deinstalling, 640
third-party products, HotSync
    Macintosh, 146–148
    Windows, 141–145
ThoughtMill, 294–295
3Com PalmPilot Professional, 3
TI Slider, 613
Ticketmaster, 165
Tiger Woods golf module, 187
tilde, 54, 56
time, 26
Time Division Multiple Access (TDMA), 436
time stamp ShortCut, 52
TimeReporter 2000, 343–349
TimeZone, 389
TinySheet, 311
Titanium hardcase, 613
Title field, Address Book, 89

To Do List
    adding items, 92–93
    assigning categories, 94
    Edit menu, 95
    editing items, 93–93
    Handspring Visor, 176
    introduction, 33, 95
    opening, 92
    Options menu, 95
    Palm Desktop, Windows, 201–204
    Record menu, 94–95
    replacements, 526
    ToDo PLUS, 526
Today, 538
Todo folder, 215
ToDo PLUS, 286, 526
todo.bak, 215
todo.dat, 215
Tools menu, Palm Desktop, 209
Top Gun Postman, 415, 430, 432
TopSecret Desktop, 572–573
Tornado V, 576
TrackFast, 542
trademark, 55
TrapWeaver, 580
travel
    Abroad, 400
    Advance Traveler, 381
    AirMiles, 391–392
    AutoLog, 392
    Big Clock, 385
    CClock, 385
    Cesium, 386
    Clock III, 386–387
    clock software, 384–385
    ClockPro, 387
    conversion software, 380
    CurrCalc, 381–382
    Currency, 382–383
    CurrencyX, 383
    Fill Up, 392–393
    Foreign, 384

FPS Clock, 387–388
Gulliver, 400–401
HandMap, 390
Highway Manager, 393
multiClock, 388–389
overview, 379–380
Palm Miles, 394
Small Talk, 397
StreetSigns, 390–391
TealMeal, 397–399
TimeZone, 389
TravelTracker, 402
travelware, 380
Trip, 395
Vehicle Tracker, 396
VehicleLog, 395–396
WorldMate, 402–403
WorldFAQ, 399
Travel Kit, 632
Travelocity.com, 164
TravelTracker, 402
travelware, 380
TrekSounds, 484, 594
TRGpro, 9, 16, 17
Tricorder II, 485
Trip, 395
Tuning Fork, 457
turning on, 24
20-20 Consumer, 504
.txt file, 495
TZDateBook, 522

U

überchix, 377–378, 499
UltraSoft Money Pocket Edition, 333
umlaut, 56
underscore, 54
Undo command, 196
Undo, Date Book, 78
UnDupe, 151, 277, 581
UniMount, 633
upgrades, memory, 622–624
UPS, 165

US Robotics, 7
US WEST Dex, 164
USB port, 177
User menu, 240–241
User-named folder, 213–215
usernames, HotSync, 152–153
Users' Manuals, 23
utilities, 544
    Application Launcher, 102–106
    Button Preferences, 107–109
    Calculator, 106
    Digitizer Preferences, 109
    Expense Application, 114–116
    Find, 107
    Format Preferences, 109
    Graffiti Tips, 101–102
    HotSync, 107
    Mail, 116–119
    Modem Preferences, 110–111
    Network Preferences, 111–112
    Owner Preferences, 112
    Security Preferences, 113–114
    ShortCuts, 113

V

various.dba, 214
Vehicle Tracker, 396
VehicleLog, 276, 395–396
vertical divider, 54
video game, 179
video out module, 179
View menu
    Palm Desktop, Macintosh, 237–238
    Palm Desktop, Windows, 208–209
VIM, 7
Visa, 165
Visionary 2000 case, 615
Visor Deluxe, 9, 17
Visor models, 175
Visor Solo, 17
Voice Recorder, 178
Voltage Control, 552
Voltage Display, 553

W

warm reset, 548
Weather Channel, 164
Web clipping
  ABCNEWS.com, 164
  Bank of America, 165
  developing applications, 166
  ESPN.com, 164
  Etak, 165
  E*Trade, 165
  Fidelity Investments, 164
  Fodor's, 165
  Frommer's, 165
  history list, 163–164
  launching, 161
  MapQuest ToGo, 164
  MasterCard, 165
  Merriam-Webster, 165
  Moviephone.com, 165
  Official Airline Guide, 165
  over-the-air icon, 163
  overview, 158
  query form, 161–163
  signal strength, 162
  size, 163
  TheStreet.com, 165
  Ticketmaster, 165
  Travelocity.com, 164
  UPS, 165
  US WEST Dex, 164
  Visa, 165
  Weather Channel, 164
  WSJ.com, 164
  Yahoo! People Search, 164
Wedge TV, 560–561
Week View, Date Book, 75–76

Welcome application, 24
What's the Score?, 490
WinZip, 494
wireless
  cellular integration, 20
  LAN, 12
  modem, 179
  technology, 13
Wireless Communications Solutions, 178
word games
  Jookerie!, 486
  Scramblet, 486
  Wordlet, 487
  XWord, 487
Wordlet, 487
Work field, Address Book, 89
work phone number, Address Book, 84
WorkPad PC, 11–12
WorldFAQ, 399
WorldMate, 402–403
WriteRight, 634
WSJ.com, 164

X

Xtra Xtra, 16, 622–623
XWord, 487

Y

Yahoo! People Search, 164
yahtChallenge, 477
Yen, 55

Z

Zip field, Address Book, 90
.zip file, 494
Zoomer, 18

IDG Books Worldwide, Inc.
End-User License Agreement

READ THIS. You should carefully read these terms and conditions before opening the software packet(s) included with this book ("Book"). This is a license agreement ("Agreement") between you and IDG Books Worldwide, Inc. ("IDGB"). By opening the accompanying software packet(s), you acknowledge that you have read and accept the following terms and conditions. If you do not agree and do not want to be bound by such terms and conditions, promptly return the Book and the unopened software packet(s) to the place you obtained them for a full refund.

1. **License Grant.** IDGB grants to you (either an individual or entity) a nonexclusive license to use one copy of the enclosed software program(s) (collectively, the "Software") solely for your own personal or business purposes on a single computer (whether a standard computer or a workstation component of a multiuser network). The Software is in use on a computer when it is loaded into temporary memory (RAM) or installed into permanent memory (hard disk, CD-ROM, or other storage device). IDGB reserves all rights not expressly granted herein.

2. **Ownership.** IDGB is the owner of all right, title, and interest, including copyright, in and to the compilation of the Software recorded on the disk(s) or CD-ROM ("Software Media"). Copyright to the individual programs recorded on the Software Media is owned by the author or other authorized copyright owner of each program. Ownership of the Software and all proprietary rights relating thereto remain with IDGB and its licensers.

3. **Restrictions On Use and Transfer.**

    (a) You may only (i) make one copy of the Software for backup or archival purposes, or (ii) transfer the Software to a single hard disk, provided that you keep the original for backup or archival purposes. You may not (i) rent or lease the Software, (ii) copy or reproduce the Software through a LAN or other network system or through any computer subscriber system or bulletin-board system, or (iii) modify, adapt, or create derivative works based on the Software.

    (b) You may not reverse engineer, decompile, or disassemble the Software. You may transfer the Software and user documentation on a permanent basis, provided that the transferee agrees to accept the terms and conditions of this Agreement and you retain no copies. If the Software is an update or has been updated, any transfer must include the most recent update and all prior versions.

4. **Restrictions on Use of Individual Programs.** You must follow the individual requirements and restrictions detailed for each individual program in Appendix H of this Book. These limitations are also contained in the individual license

agreements recorded on the Software Media. These limitations may include a requirement that after using the program for a specified period of time, the user must pay a registration fee or discontinue use. By opening the Software packet(s), you will be agreeing to abide by the licenses and restrictions for these individual programs that are detailed in Appendix H and on the Software Media. None of the material on this Software Media or listed in this Book may ever be redistributed, in original or modified form, for commercial purposes.

5. Limited Warranty.

    (a) IDGB warrants that the Software and Software Media are free from defects in materials and workmanship under normal use for a period of sixty (60) days from the date of purchase of this Book. If IDGB receives notification within the warranty period of defects in materials or workmanship, IDGB will replace the defective Software Media.

    (b) **IDGB AND THE AUTHORS OF THE BOOK DISCLAIM ALL OTHER WARRANTIES, EXPRESS OR IMPLIED, INCLUDING WITHOUT LIMITATION IMPLIED WARRANTIES OF MERCHANTABILITY AND FITNESS FOR A PARTICULAR PURPOSE, WITH RESPECT TO THE SOFTWARE, THE PROGRAMS, THE SOURCE CODE CONTAINED THEREIN, AND/OR THE TECHNIQUES DESCRIBED IN THIS BOOK. IDGB DOES NOT WARRANT THAT THE FUNCTIONS CONTAINED IN THE SOFTWARE WILL MEET YOUR REQUIREMENTS OR THAT THE OPERATION OF THE SOFTWARE WILL BE ERROR FREE.**

    (c) This limited warranty gives you specific legal rights, and you may have other rights that vary from jurisdiction to jurisdiction.

6. Remedies.

    (a) IDGB's entire liability and your exclusive remedy for defects in materials and workmanship shall be limited to replacement of the Software Media, which may be returned to IDGB with a copy of your receipt at the following address: Software Media Fulfillment Department, Attn.: *Palm OS Bible*, IDG Books Worldwide, Inc., 10475 Crosspoint Blvd., Indianapolis, IN 46256, or call 1-800-762-2974. Please allow three to four weeks for delivery. This Limited Warranty is void if failure of the Software Media has resulted from accident, abuse, or misapplication. Any replacement Software Media will be warranted for the remainder of the original warranty period or thirty (30) days, whichever is longer.

    (b) In no event shall IDGB or the authors be liable for any damages whatsoever (including without limitation damages for loss of business profits, business interruption, loss of business information, or any other pecuniary loss) arising from the use of or inability to use the Book or the Software, even if IDGB has been advised of the possibility of such damages.

(c) Because some jurisdictions do not allow the exclusion or limitation of liability for consequential or incidental damages, the above limitation or exclusion may not apply to you.

7. **U.S. Government Restricted Rights.** Use, duplication, or disclosure of the Software by the U.S. Government is subject to restrictions stated in paragraph (c)(1)(ii) of the Rights in Technical Data and Computer Software clause of DFARS 252.227-7013, and in subparagraphs (a) through (d) of the Commercial Computer — Restricted Rights clause at FAR 52.227-19, and in similar clauses in the NASA FAR supplement, when applicable.

8. **General.** This Agreement constitutes the entire understanding of the parties and revokes and supersedes all prior agreements, oral or written, between them and may not be modified or amended except in a writing signed by both parties hereto that specifically refers to this Agreement. This Agreement shall take precedence over any other documents that may be in conflict herewith. If any one or more provisions contained in this Agreement are held by any court or tribunal to be invalid, illegal, or otherwise unenforceable, each and every other provision shall remain in full force and effect.

Special Offer!

Buy *The Official Pendragon™ Forms for Palm OS® Starter Kit* and upgrade your evaluation copy of Pendragon Forms to the full version for only $99.95 (regularly $149).*

Pendragon Forms 3.0 evaluation version and more on CD-ROM!

SPECIAL OFFER
Upgrade your evaluation copy for only $99.95 (regularly $149)
See inside for details

Transform Palm OS devices into mobile data-collection tools

Streamline data collection with customized Pendragon forms

Synchronize Pendragon Forms with your existing databases

Debra Sancho and Ivan Phillips
Pendragon Software Corporation

The Official Pendragon Forms for Palm OS Starter Kit.

Pendragon Forms software lets you transform a Palm OS organizer into a powerful mobile data collection device. This complete guide gives you all the inside tips and tricks you need to create robust forms and scripts that are tailored to your specific needs — from expense reports to merchandise inventories. You'll discover how to automate with bar code readers, link Pendragon forms to external databases, and more — all with no programming skill required.

0-7645-4651-1 $39.99 US/$59.99CAN/36.99UK

The companion CD-ROM includes Pendragon Forms 3.0 evaluation version. Upgrade from the Pendragon Forms Evaluation Edition to the full version for only $99.95.

* See *The Official Pendragon Forms for Palm OS Starter Kit* for full details. Offer expires December 31, 2000. Void where prohibited.

The Official Pendragon Forms for Palm OS Starter Kit
is available wherever books are sold, or call
1-800-762-2974

For more information about IDG Books Worldwide's book series, visit our web site at www.idgbooks.com

IDG
BOOKS
WORLDWIDE

Pendragon Forms is a trademark of Pendragon Software Corporation. Palm OS is a registered trademark of Palm Computing, Inc., 3Com Corporation, or its subsidiaries. The IDG Books Worldwide logo is a registered trademark under exclusive license to IDG Books Worldwide, Inc., from International Data Group, Inc. M&T Books and the M&T Books logo are trademarks of IDG Books Worldwide, Inc.

my2cents.idgbooks.com

Register This Book — And Win!

Visit **http://my2cents.idgbooks.com** to register this book and we'll automatically enter you in our fantastic monthly prize giveaway. It's also your opportunity to give us feedback: let us know what you thought of this book and how you would like to see other topics covered.

Discover IDG Books Online!

The IDG Books Online Web site is your online resource for tackling technology — at home and at the office. Frequently updated, the IDG Books Online Web site features exclusive software, insider information, online books, and live events!

10 Productive & Career-Enhancing Things You Can Do at www.idgbooks.com

- Nab source code for your own programming projects.

- Download software.

- Read Web exclusives: special articles and book excerpts by IDG Books Worldwide authors.

- Take advantage of resources to help you advance your career as a Novell or Microsoft professional.

- Buy IDG Books Worldwide titles or find a convenient bookstore that carries them.

- Register your book and win a prize.

- Chat live online with authors.

- Sign up for regular e-mail updates about our latest books.

- Suggest a book you'd like to read or write.

- Give us your 2¢ about our books and about our Web site.

You say you're not on the Web yet? It's easy to get started with IDG Books' *Discover the Internet*, available at local retailers everywhere.

CD-ROM Installation Instructions

Using the CD-ROM couldn't be easier. Just remove the CD-ROM from its protective holder in the back of the book. Then follow these simple steps:

1. Insert the CD-ROM into your CD-ROM drive.

2. Wait a few seconds as the FileMaker program loads.

If, for whatever reason, your PC isn't set up to autostart CD-ROMs, follow these steps instead:

1. Insert the CD-ROM into your CD-ROM drive.

2. Open My Computer (double-click the My Computer icon on your Windows desktop).

3. Right-click the icon for your CD-ROM drive and choose Explore from the shortcut menu that appears.

4. Scroll down to and double-click the icon for the program named Palm_Computing_Bible.exe.

Macintosh users have it easy: just click the CD-ROM icon after it spins up.

For more information on the *Palm OS Bible* CD-ROM and its contents, please see Appendix H.